TRIBES
WITH
FLAGS

TRIBES

WITH

FLAGS

A Dangerous Passage Through the Chaos of the Middle East

CHARLES GLASS

THE ATLANTIC MONTHLY PRESS
NEW YORK

First published in Great Britain in 1990 by Martin Secker & Warburg Limited
First Atlantic Monthly Press edition, April 1990

Printed in the United States of America

Library of Congress Cataloging-in-Publication Data

Glass, Charles, 1951–
   Tribes with flags: a dangerous passage through the chaos of the Middle East /
by Charles Glass.
   Includes index.
   ISBN 0-87113-267-2
   1. Middle East—Description and travel. 2. Glass, Charles, 1951–
—Journeys—Middle East. 3. Middle East—Politics and
government—1945– I. Title.
DS49.7.G53   1989   915.6′044—dc19   89-157

The Atlantic Monthly Press
19 Union Square West
New York, NY 10003

FIRST PRINTING

For Julia, Edward, George, Hester,
Beatrix and Fiona
and to the memory of Mouna Bustros

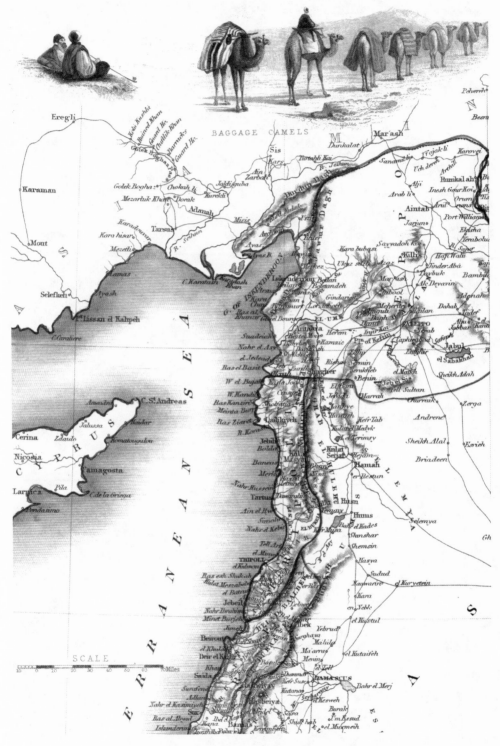

Detail from "Syria", Tallis' *Atlas*, 1841

CONTENTS

PART FIVE

"A man may find Naples or Palermo merely pretty;
but the deeper violet, the splendour
and desolation of the Levant waters
is something that drives into the soul."

James Elroy Flecker
Beirut, October 1914

INTRODUCTION

FROM ALEXANDRETTA TO AQABA

Tribes with Flags sets out to tell a simple story of a journey by land from Alexandretta, the last corner of the Arab world still a part of Turkey, to Aqaba, the first Turkish citadel liberated during the Arab revolt in 1917. The intended itinerary crossed an area known as the Levant or as Greater Syria – the southern Turkish coast around Alexandretta port and the modern statelets known in our day as Syria, Lebanon, Israel and Jordan. The region from the Bay of Alexandretta in the north to the Gulf of Aqaba in the south, bordered in the east by the great Syrian Desert and the west by the Mediterranean Sea, has served as a theatre in which a repertory company of players learn the words, occasionally the languages, of ever-changing plays. Backstage, they pursue age-old dramas of tribal rivalry and the quest for dominance in a land of scarce resources. My purpose was to convey to other souls the "splendour and desolation" of the Levant's waters, its land and these people.

I began the journey in March 1987 and planned to reach the Turkish fortress at Aqaba four months later, the trip providing a framework for a literary and spiritual ramble through the history of a tormented land. My objective was twofold: first, to explore the former Arab portion of the Ottoman Empire, the territory ostensibly liberated by the British and the Arabs in 1918, when the Lawrence of Arabia legend was born; and second, to tell the story, not of one journey, but of many, drawing on the works of earlier travellers, like the Spanish Arab Ibn Jubayr and the Jewish Rabbi Benjamin of Tudela in the twelfth century, the North African world traveller Ibn Batuta a century and a half later, and the many Europeans and Americans who followed, like the Abbé Mariti, John Lewis Burckhardt, Lady Hester Stanhope, Alexander Kinglake, Alfonse de Lamartine, Sir Richard Burton, Edward Montagu, Gerard de Nerval, Benjamin Disraeli, Mark Twain, James Elroy Flecker, T. E. Lawrence, Marmaduke Pickthall, Freya Stark, James Morris and even Noël Coward, who wrote of Lebanon in 1943, "I shall come back to this country later on. I should like to see what it is like when there *really* isn't a war on."

There was another war on when my trip came abruptly to an end. I was half of the distance to Aqaba when some of the many participants in the war kidnapped me. By miraculous good fortune, I managed to escape two months later. My achievement – leaving an apartment in the dead of night while my young guards slept, and finding my way through the streets of a city I had known for fifteen years – was neither courageous nor heroic, especially when compared to the many escapes by prisoners of war, who were far younger than me, from more efficient organisations like the Gestapo, the British Army and the Israeli Defence Forces. The fact that I was kidnapped at all illustrated how dangerous the region, still suffering from enforced division into states its people did not want, had become for visitors and residents alike. It is likely to remain unsafe until the tribes reach a *modus vivendi* or until the outside world, which exports its modern weapons to the Levant and incautiously meddles in its conflicts, imposes a settlement.

The idea for the book came to me in Beirut in 1983, while I was living there as a journalist and observing the American navy offshore. I was reading Sir Steven Runciman's classic A *History of the Crusades*, and I realised that the US Navy would soon abandon the Levantine coast just as the Genoan and Pisan fleets had left the Crusader cities eight centuries earlier. Runciman and other historians of the Levant proved far more reliable guides to events unfolding along the eastern Mediterranean coast than any modern political analysts, diplomats or soldiers. I went to Scotland to see Runciman, who lived in a house built around a peel tower in which Scots border farmers used to take refuge from English sheep raiders. By then in his eighties, the historian advised me to follow the traditional invasion route through Greater Syria. This was from north to south, the route the Crusaders and, before them, Alexander the Great had used. A few invaders had come from the south, like the Arabs in the seventh century and the British in the twentieth, and the Persians had come from the east, but the northern route was more common. In preparing his classic study, Runciman had been over the terrain, studying all the castles left by the Crusaders and their Muslim opponents. I knew the land already, having lived in Lebanon for six years, but I asked Runciman what I was likely to find by following the invasion path. He said, "The history of the region is almost a history of war. I found in writing about the Crusades that one could write about wars the whole time. It has always been a battleground, even now." The Israeli general Yigal Yadin said much the same thing, and had modelled his tactics against the Arabs in the 1948 war on his understanding of Roman campaigns on the same hills and valleys two thousand years earlier. He concluded, "The topography of war doesn't change very much." Along every step of the way, I found monuments to fallen armies, ancient and modern battlefields and cemeteries holding the remains of long-dead warriors.

The chronic reality of war in the Levant has changed as little as its topography. "Phoenician fleets once covered these silent waters," Eliot Warburton wrote of the Levant coast in 1845 in *The Crescent and the Cross*, "wealthy cities once fringed those lonely shores; and, during three thousand years, war has led all the nations of the earth in terrible procession along those plains." The procession has not ended. In the century and a half since Warburton wrote, Britain, France, Italy, Russia, Austria-Hungary, Germany, Egypt, the United States of America and Iran have sent their warships or their soldiers to the same coast. The English poet James Elroy Flecker had watched the Italian fleet bombard Lebanon in 1912 from nearly the spot where I had seen the American navy shell the same coast in 1983 – in both instances to no effect whatsoever. It was as though great empires had to prove themselves above all in the Levant, to the dismay or more often the profit of the tribes who dwelled there.

In the years since the First World War and the break-up of the Ottoman Empire, the people of the region have pursued their own objectives through warfare. From the end of the war that closed four centuries of Turkish rule, the people of the Levant rose against the French and British who had occupied them. The French shelled Damascus and bombed the Druze mountains in the 1920s. The British hanged and shot thousands of Palestinian Arabs in the 1930s. The Arab population of Palestine and the Jewish settlers who had come to displace them fought one another in the 1940s. With the independence of Lebanon and Syria in 1946 and of Israel in 1948, the colonial borders proved useful only as initial lines of battle and, later, as demilitarised zones. The Lebanese reverted to the most primitive tribalism and, with the help of half a dozen outside powers, destroyed their land and cities and drew borders within borders.

"Egypt is the only nation-state in the Middle East. The rest are tribes with flags," said an old friend and retired Egyptian diplomat, Tahseen Basheer. The Levant tribes have always asserted their independence from the empires that nominally controlled them, often to their cost. They dwell in a poor land, a field of battle for the greater, richer lands on all sides of them – the lands of Anatolia, of Persia and of Egypt. The Turks were nominal suzerains for four centuries, but they exerted control through local tribal leaders, usually playing them off against one another to assure ultimate Turkish dominance. The Sublime Porte, as the government in Constantinople was known, adjusted to the fact that the tribes did not want to be governed. William Eton wrote in 1798 in *A Survey of the Turkish Empire*: "All the inhabitants of the mountains, from Smyrna to Palestine, are perfectly independent, and are considered by the Porte as enemies, whom they attack whenever there is an opportunity. They are composed of different nations, who have their own sovereigns or lords, and are even of different religions." The fact they were all Ottoman subjects, in a vast empire of religious, ethnic and linguistic minorities, meant as little as the passports in this century that describe them as Lebanese, Syrian, Israeli, Jordanian or, in the case of most Palestinian Arabs, "stateless".

Tribal conflicts animate Levantine culture and form the Levantines' view of the world. The tribes – really communities with language, sect and locality in common – have survived Rome, Byzantium, the Arab empire, the Crusader states, the Mamelukes, the Ottomans, the Zionists and, more recently, local nationalists and religious zealots. The bearded young men preaching the doctrines of Karl Marx or Ayatollah Khomeini come and go, but the great majority of the Levant's people still look to traditional community and sectarian leaders for protection, favours, money and jobs. Loyalty to family, village, tribe and sect has always been stronger than ideology. Ideology comes and goes out of fashion. Loyalty does not.

Travel in this region of wars and tribes has always had its dangers and its pleasures. Noël Coward did not realise it at the time, but there really wasn't a war on in Lebanon during his visit, save for a series of brief skirmishes between the Vichy French and the invading British army from Palestine. The Lebanese were content to stand idly by, making what money they could selling souvenirs to troops on both sides. Lebanon's real war came later. It was a function, I believe, of the break-up of the Ottoman Empire and the Anglo-French division of the empire into little states whose populations were doomed to years of war and misery.

The battlefields were also vineyards, and fruit trees sprouted from ancient graves. Where men had drawn swords, hurled spears and fired automatic rifles, children played. Rivers that armies had forded in the night to surround an enemy provided family picnic sites. The sea in which navies displayed their cannon was beautiful to look at and cool to swim in. With what little there was from the land and sea, the people made their lives rich and lavish. The divisions that were a source of conflict also gave wealth: in any market-place in the Levant, there are the costumes of the desert bedouin, the Kurdish mountaineer, the Druze peasant and the Armenian businessman. Arabic, Armenian, Hebrew and Kurdish, as well as the imported colonial Turkish, French and English, are languages of the Levant. In a small area, there seem to be the sights, sounds and smells of all the world.

Throughout the book, I use the term Levant to refer to the eastern Mediterranean coast. The word has gone out of fashion, perhaps because of its identification with the imperial era. Yet I find it useful, less politically charged then the geographers' "Greater Syria", more bearable and romantic than the aid agencies' "Southwestern Asia". Eliot Warburton wrote in 1845:

The "Levant" of the Italians, the "Orient" of the French, and the "Morgenland" of the Germans, are pretty paraphrases of the "East". The former term is applied, not only to the shores, but to the seas, over which the sun *rises* to the morningward of Malta. Bright and blue as it is, and fringed by the brightest and most memorial shores, it is yet a very lonely sea: wild winds, that are almost Typhoons, sweep over it; iron coasts wrap it round, and to the south of Cerigo there is not a safe harbour in all its wide expanse, save that of Alexandria.

When the term Levant was still in popular use, *Nuttall's Standard Dictionary of the English Language* (Frederick Warne & Co., Ltd., London and New York) defined the word in 1926 as

1.1 **Levant**, le-vant', *a.* eastern or at the point where the sun rises: *s.* a country to the east; the eastern coasts of the Mediterranean Sea (L. *levo*, to raise).

1.2 **Levant**, le-vant', *v.n.* to decamp

1.3 **Levanter**, le-van'-tur, *s.* a strong easterly wind in the Mediterranean; one who bets at a horse-race, and runs away without paying the wager lost.

My own circumstances differed somewhat from those of the earlier travellers. Unlike my predecessors in Levantine travel, I was only half an outsider – part native, part imperial actor. My maternal grandparents had been born in the last century in what became Lebanon, Christian subjects of the Ottoman Sultan, and emigrated to California as young children. They met as adults and dared to marry across the sectarian divide – my grandmother was a Maronite Catholic and my grandfather a Greek Catholic – to the shock of both their families. Yet I am really an American, born and raised on the Pacific coast, whose paternal ancestors came to North America from Ireland in the late seventeenth century. "If you're half Irish and half Lebanese," an Irish-American Jesuit who once taught me said, "you're at least half crazy." Sometimes, I suppose I was crazy to undertake the journey I did, especially to visit Beirut at a time when one tribe had adopted the tactic of kidnapping Americans and Europeans. Like a Levanter, if not a Levantine, I was lucky to be able to run away without paying the wager lost. Others have not been so lucky, having been murdered or kept, at this writing, in cruel solitary confinement.

At times, I looked on the region from the point of view of the outsider, the American whose advanced technology, education and wealth gave him a special vantage-point from which to view the people of the Levant. At other times, I looked through Levantine eyes at a world both threatening

5

and hostile. I could feel as one with the people of Beirut, on both the Christian and Muslim sides, when I hid with them underground to stay alive during artillery bombardments. Most of the time, they saw me as the outsider, but I am grateful to those who on occasion treated me as one of their own, a member of their tribe.

Most of the people who helped me in the preparation of this book are mentioned in my account of the journey. Others have asked me not to use their names, out of fear of governments or armed gangs. Others deserve special mention here for all their kindness and help. Most of all, I must thank Professor Albert Hourani of St Anthony's College, Oxford, whose capable hand guided me every step of my way. He advised me before the journey on places to visit, books to read and people to see. He read and corrected the manuscript, saving me from many embarrassing errors and omissions. I should also like to express my gratitude to Hany Salaam, who offered me the use of a room in his house in France in which I finished writing the book while I lived in a small rented shack nearby. Not only he, but his family and staff, were most helpful. Without his offer, it is unlikely I would have found the solitude I needed to finish the book. Among my colleagues at ABC News, I have to thank Roone Arledge, David Burke, Peter Jennings, Paul Friedman, Irwin Weiner and the staff of the news desks in London and New York for their unqualified support to me and my family during and after my kidnapping in Beirut. At the ABC News Inter-Active Video office in New York, Bill Lord, David Boorman, Robin Levene and Thomasina Nitas gave me hours of coaching and support in the use of a word-processor and helped me to retrieve days of work that would otherwise have been lost in the ether of high-technology computing. Lucia Butt of ABC kindly typed part of the manuscript. I am grateful to the staff of the Travellers' Club in London for allowing me to use the library in off hours and helping me to find the books I needed. I have also to say thank you to my agents, Gillon Aitken and Andrew Wylie, and my publishers, Dan Franklin at Secker and Warburg and Ann Godoff at Atlantic Monthly Press, for their advice and their patience in awaiting a manuscript that took twice as long to write as I had intended. The first version of the book was twice as long as it should have been, and I am most grateful to John Blackwell of Secker and Warburg for improving the book by paring it down significantly. In the pages that were discarded are the names of many people who helped me on my way through the region. Among them are Umberto and Samia Draghi, Anthony Akras, Sadeq al-Azzem, Ali and Eda Ersoy, Mr and Mrs Abdallah Tanzi, Intisar Adhami, Assad Kamal Elias, Sabbagh Kabbani, Jihad Zuheiri, Akram Shuhaib and Father John Donohue, S.J.

Some of the people to whom I am indebted for their help on my way are at war with the others. Had I finished the journey, and managed to include Israel and Jordan, I would undoubtedly have met more people who were sworn enemies of those who had offered me hospitality. I met and had meals with the Druze leader Walid Jumblatt, whose forces have killed many Christians; with Palestinian commandos who have fought against Israelis and Lebanese; with Christians who have murdered Palestinians. Had I continued, I would have shared time with the Israelis who have dispossessed the Palestinians and bombed the Lebanese. Ultimately, they – Muslims, Christians and Jews, Kurds, Armenians, Circassians, Arabs and Israelis, all the tribes and communities – have to live with one another, and it is not my place to take sides. I sympathise with them all, and, in my defence, I refer to the tale told by one of my favourite Levantine travellers, Marmaduke Pickthall. He toured the Levant in 1894 and published *Oriental Encounters* in 1918. In the book, he recounts how he and his servant, Rashid, sought refuge from a storm in the house of a Circassian warrior named Huseyn Agha. After dinner, Agha's grown son tells the English traveller,

> "I like thee, O khawajah [sir]. I had once a son about thy age. Say, O my father, is there not a strong resemblance?"
>
> Thereafter he talked quite as much as the old man, giving me the history of their emigration from the Caucasus to escape the yoke of the accursed Muscovite, and enumerating all the troubles which attended their first coming into Syria.
>
> "We are not subjects of the Government," he told me, "but allies; and we have special privileges. But the dishonoured dogs round here forget old compacts, and want us to pay taxes like mere fellahin [peasants]."
>
> We sat up talking far into the night, while the storm raged without, and the rain and the sea-spray pounded on the shutters; and never have I met with kinder treatment. It was the custom for chance comers to have food at evening only and leave betimes next morning. But our host, when I awoke in splendid sunlight, had breakfast ready – sour milk and Arab bread and fragrant coffee – and when I went out to my horse he followed me, and thrust two roasted fowls into my saddle-bags, exclaiming "Zad!" – which means "food for the road." And much to my abashment he and the old man fell upon my neck and kissed me on both cheeks.

Pickthall and Rashid rode on to a caravanserai, where they saw Ottoman soldiers. One of the soldiers told them an Englishman had been recently wounded and was dying.

> "He had a large company, with several camels. But near the village of —— he was attacked by the Circassians, and was so

foolish as to make resistance. They took everything he had of worth – his arms, his money – and killed a camel-driver, besides wounding him. It happened yesterday before the storm. They say I should take vengeance for him. What am I – a corporal with six men – to strive with Huseyn Agha and his cavalry! It needs a regiment."

He went grumbling off. Rashid and I were staring hard at one another; for the village named was that where we had spent the night, and Huseyn Agha's roasted fowls were in our saddle-bags.

Rashid, as I could see, was troubled upon my account. He kept silence a good while. At last he said:

"It's like this, my lord. Each man must see with his own eyes and not another's. People are as one finds them, good or bad. They change with each man's vision, yet remain the same. For us those highway robbers are good people; we must bless them; having cause to do so. This other man is free to curse them, if he will. Good to their friends, bad to their enemies. What creature of the sons of Adam can condemn them quite?"

Pickthall converted to Islam, and he later produced one of the best English translations of the Koran. A devout Muslim in Tripoli, Libya – himself a refugee from Levantime wars, a native of Jerusalem and a graduate of Balliol College, Oxford – gave me his own copy of the Pickthall translation. He inscribed the frontispiece to me a day after warplanes from my country bombed his family house and killed his seventeen-year-old granddaughter. I treasure it to this day.

Charles Glass
Roquebrune Cap Martin, France

PART ONE

CHAPTER ONE

THE LEGACY OF ALEXANDER

Three dogs pulled and tore the flesh from the corpse. The lamb's rib-cage was already bare, and still they clawed at the body and snatched lumps of meat with their jaws. They had opened the animal up from its soft stomach, and the wool was stretched aside to expose the food within. The entrails were mostly eaten, but the lamb's head was untouched. Its eyes were open and blank. The dogs' paws, their jowls and the hair around their eyes were stained, like the ground, dark red. One dog growled for a moment to warn another not to tread on its portion of the dead prey. Then it silently rejoined the feast, the grim work of devouring what each could of the lamb before they abandoned its carcass to the flies.

The black and white mongrels and the lamb were the only signs of life or death in the barren limestone hills. We were on the highway to Alexandretta, and the driver had stopped the bus and gone into a solitary hut just off the road. No one asked why. This was not, I would learn, unusual. Buses did not keep schedules here, and drivers made their money from more than the transport of passengers. They delivered food and parcels, they carried letters, they smuggled gold, cigarettes, coffee, refugees, drugs and weapons across borders. "A bus like this," one man explained, "can support a whole family."

Several passengers including myself had used the unscheduled stop to get out and stretch our legs. The sun was going down. I walked several yards from the bus to be alone. I was watching the dogs when another passenger approached me. "Do you have a degree?" he asked me in English. His accent was slight. He seemed to be in his mid-forties. He wore a grey zip jacket, khaki trousers and old, unpolished shoes. On his lip was a thin moustache.

"I'm sorry . . ?" I said.

"A degree in something, from a university?"

"Yes, in philosophy."

"*Falsafi*," he said in Arabic. Then in English, "That's very good."

"And you?"

"Mechanical engineering."

"Something practical, not like philosophy . . ."

"I have a textile factory in Damascus," he said. "I'm here to buy materials."

"Are they better here in Turkey than in Syria?"

"Ha," he laughed. "You cannot find them in Syria. Anyway, this is Syria."

"*Surie al-Kubra?*" Greater Syria, I asked in Arabic.

He laughed again, patting my back. "You speak Arabic?"

"Only a little."

"Smoke?" He held out an open pack of Marlboro. "You have a family?"

I nodded.

"I have three children," he said proudly.

The Syrian textile manufacturer had established that, for the duration of the bus journey, we belonged to the same tribe. We were both non-Turks, both had university degrees and both had children. It was bond enough to keep loneliness and the dogs at bay on the dark, perilous road, in a bus crowded with forty strangers, in a land that was not ours. The driver came out of the hut, carrying a small package. We followed him onto the bus. Without discussion, the Syrian took the empty seat next to mine. The bus coughed and bumped its way towards Alexandretta, while the Syrian and I talked into the night.

It was nearly midnight when we reached the edge of Alexandretta, a port town whose form it was impossible to distinguish beyond the glare of the highway and car lights. When we passed a sign which said in Turkish and English, "Iskenderun, pop. 173,700", I asked the driver to stop. Handing me down my bags and typewriter, the Syrian told me to call him when I reached Damascus. I agreed, knowing it was unlikely. We would not need each other there, where he would be home among his people, where I had friends, where our common levels of education and fatherhood counted for nothing. Alliances here lasted only as long as the need for them, a truth we implicitly shared as he reached his hand out the window to shake mine in farewell. Now alone at the side of the road, I watched the red lights of the bus disappear into the warm Levantine night.

The first strains of the music woke me early. The only sound which should have disturbed the peace of Friday, the Muslim sabbath, was the muezzin's call to prayer. The sound coming through my window was from a brass band, whose music sounded like a cross between a Handel anthem and a John Philip Sousa march. I went downstairs to the lobby of the Hatayli Oteli and looked out the front door towards the seafront. A parade of what looked like half the population of Alexandretta was marching along the corniche like irregulars at the end of a long campaign. Women carried

12

wreaths and men wore ribbons, and all walked out of step with the triumphal music.

Was this, I wondered, Turkey's national day? Had democracy been restored? Perhaps war had been declared? I asked the porter what was happening. Discovering we had no common language, I pointed at the parade and tried to look puzzled.

"Polis Bayram," he said. *"Bayram"* was Arabic, and apparently also Turkish, for "feast" or "holy day". *"Polis"* was Turkish for "police", and pronounced the same way. I learned later in the day that Turkey was celebrating the anniversary of the founding in 1845 of the Ottoman Police. Everyone in Iskenderun seemed to be wearing a small green and red paper badge, with the Turkish crescent and star in its centre, saying, "10 Nisan Polis Günü". Despite the obvious enthusiasm of the crowd for the festivities, there was something strange about it. Turkey was the first country I'd known to celebrate the creation of a police force. It seemed to me that the establishment of the police was an admission of failure, an acknowledgement that man was inherently evil and had to be controlled, a cause for regret rather than joy.

No one in the hotel spoke anything other than Turkish, but a young man and young woman behind the reception desk struggled to recall a few words of English. I wanted to telephone the tourist office to see whether I could obtain a car and guide to show me around Alexandretta. I telephoned the number listed in the *Fodor Guide*, which turned out to be the house of an irate woman speaking only Turkish. The receptionists found another number. It was the tourist office, but the man at the other end spoke no English. The receptionists suggested I walk to the tourist office and assured me someone there would speak English. In a way, they were right.

The hotel porter led me along the wide seafront drive, where drab concrete offices and shops faced the port, to the tourist office on the ground floor of an old building. Inside, a man in a tweed jacket and necktie introduced himself as Mehmet Udimir. He spoke a few, very few, words of English. He said Udimir meant Iron, and made a fist to show it. He was the only person in the tiny, cavern-like room. I explained I needed a guide. He handed me a pamphlet.

Iskenderun is situades atthe foot of the Amanos mountains. It's about 5 km. wide. The elimate is temperate, and during the winter it is like spring . . . The raining season is winter. The surrounding mountains are covered with fir forests. Iskenderun is one of the most important port-towns of Turkey. Iskenderun was founded (Alexandrietta) by Alexander the Great after his victory at Issos, The town, in order to distinguish it from Iskendiriye (Alexandria) in Egypt, was given the name of Alexandria Minor in the 17 the century . . .

"No, no," I said. "Not this sort of guide. I need a man who speaks English, to show me the historic buildings."

"Okay," he said, standing up, walking outside and locking the door behind us. I had acquired a guide.

"You see church first," he said, turning left and leading us away from the seafront into the town. "Church is very old."

"How old?"

He thought for a minute, but could not give me the date in English. He took a pen and paper out of his pocket and wrote. He handed me the paper. It said, "1901."

"Very old," I said.

"Then you see library," he promised.

"How old is that?"

He wrote again on the paper and handed it to me. "1868."

We had not reached the relics of Alexander's invasion, but we were headed, as far as time goes, in the right direction. We walked past the Roman Catholic Church of the Annunciation, but he did not stop there. He merely pointed at it, saying, "Church very old," and continued across a small, leafy side road to the library. Mehmet Udimir took me into a shaded courtyard behind a stone wall and into a building which looked as though it had once been a large private house on two floors. We walked upstairs, passing reading rooms where schoolchildren were studying. On the walls of each room were portraits – some of them photographs, others prints of oil paintings – of the father of modern Turkey, Moustafa Kemal Atatürk. An Islamic historian in Beirut had once told me, "Atatürk was a man of contradictions, even in his name: Moustafa means 'chosen one', Kemal means 'perfection', Atatürk means 'Father of the Turks'. Yet he was neither chosen nor perfect nor even a Turk."

We walked into an office, and I sat down on one of three wooden chairs facing a large desk. Mehmet sat behind the desk and under another portrait of Atatürk. This painting was almost life-size, in full colour, and showed Atatürk in white tie and tails, his arms casually folded, looking handsome and rather like Noël Coward. His red hair, blue eyes and reddish lips looked anything but Turkish, and it was little wonder his enemies had accused him of having a Greek father and a Jewish mother.

An ancient man, wearing an old, baggy suit, shuffled slowly into the office carrying a tray with glasses of tea on it. His facial features were like a Mongolian's. He said nothing to either of us, but put the glasses on the desk. It was clear that Mehmet Udimir was not merely the director of

14

The restaurant was filling up with working men, businessmen and a few families with children. The waiter brought me an Efes beer, a Turkish lager apparently from Ephesus, which was cold and tasted good. Between bits of food and drink, we talked about Turkey, religion, politics and the Arab world which Turkey had once ruled and had since forgotten.

"Today in Turkey," Kavak said, "there are some conservative people who dream of the return of the Ottoman Empire, but the military wants democracy. Meanwhile, Russia is working underground here. It wants to take advantage of Turkey."

A minute later, he said, "Atatürk was from Thessaloniki. He was very keen on Europe and on democracy. It was very hard for Turks to accept a democratic way of life. Eighty per cent of the people think this country should be European."

Eating my eastern food, I found it hard to think of this country as a part of Europe. All the food was good, similar in substance to that in the rest of the eastern Mediterranean, but spicier and prepared slightly differently. The hommous, a familiar paste of mashed chick-peas and tahina, was made in a Turkish way, covered not only with olive oil, as in Lebanon and Syria, but with ground red and black pepper, whole green chilli peppers and slices of tomato. As in Syria, we scooped it up with warm, flat bread, but the bread was thicker than Arabic bread and had seeds on top. Delicious as the food was, in Europe it would always be "ethnic".

Turkey nonetheless had applied to join the European Community. Kavak said the prejudice against Turkish membership was unfair, particularly when it was based on history. "There were problems in 1914. There was persecution of the Armenians and Assyrian Christians, but it is wrong to blame Turkey for the actions of the Ottoman Empire. We do not blame West Germany today for Hitler."

I asked him about the city. "Iskenderun," he said, using its proper name in both Turkish and Arabic, "has changed. It was a famous seaport, very deep, for big ships. It is close to Iraq. It has been very important in supplying Iraq in the war against Iran. Many people came from eastern Turkey to settle here. We have the biggest iron and steel factory in Turkey, ISDEMIR." ISDEMIR was the acronym of the state-owned Iskenderun Demir Celik. "The factory has 16,000 employees and 2,000 managers. This is 18,000 people plus their families. All were brought from outside."

"Has this shifted the population balance here in favour of Turks?"

"Until 1964, perhaps sixty per cent of the people here were Arabs and forty per cent Turkish. The Arabs were mainly in agriculture and fishing. Today, the population of Iskenderun is approximately 175,000. Twenty-five per cent maximum are Arabs. The other seventy-five per cent are Turkish, with some Kurds."

18

tourism in Alexandretta, he was also the chief librarian. I felt as though I'd strayed into one of those small American towns in which the same man, simply by changing hats, served as policeman, judge, fire chief, mayor and coroner. I was certain that if I asked Mehmet to take me to the head of the chamber of commerce, we would walk into another office, where he would sit down behind another desk and another old man would bring us tea. That way, I could confirm the answers to my questions to the tourism director with quotes from the chief librarian and the head of the chamber of commerce. It was an old journalistic trick, but one Mehmet inadvertently prevented me from playing by never telling me anything.

Another old man, better dressed and more distinguished, came into the office. He must have been in his late sixties, and he had a trim moustache. After shaking my hand, he sat down. "I was his teacher," he said in English, indicating Mehmet. "I am free now."

"Retired?"

"Yes," he said. "I come to see Mehmet one day each month."

Mehmet smiled and appeared to ask him what he had said. They then spoke for a minute in Turkish.

"And you?" the retired teacher asked. "You are tourist?"

"Sort of," I explained. "I am writing a book."

"You are going to Antakya?"

"Yes." Antakya was Turkish and Arabic for Antioch, the city in which the disciples of Christ were first given the name "Christians".

"In Antakya, you are to look at two places famous, the church and the museum."

The first old man returned with more tea, served as everywhere else in the Levant hot in clear glasses with no milk and much sugar.

We were talking when a thin young man with black hair, a short black beard and a hawk's nose, came in and sat down. The retired teacher told me the young man had recently returned to Alexandretta from Istanbul after the death of his father. The father's restaurant had closed, and he had come to arrange his family's affairs before returning to Istanbul. The young man, in his mid-twenties, spoke a few words of English, rather like Mehmet. He offered to help me find my way around Alexandretta. His name was Munir. He told me he was half Turkish and half Iranian.

Friends in Beirut and Damascus, I said, had given me the names of people to see in Alexandretta, traders named Makzoumé and Tanzi. Mehmet tried to telephone Tanzi for me, but there was no reply. He could not find a number for Makzoumé, so he asked Munir to take me to the Makzoumé Shipping Company nearby. We finished our tea, and I thanked the director of tourism and chief librarian for his help. He and his former teacher said they would see me again.

15

It was a short distance to Makzoumé's offices, back in the direction of the sea. The offices of the Makzoumé Shipping Company were more European than Oriental, with fitted carpets, modern furniture and paintings. There was no old man with tea, but there was an attractive secretary at a desk in an outer office. She showed us into Makzoumé's inner office, where we sat in silence while he finished making telephone calls. He was an old man, a little overweight and well dressed in woollen trousers and a cardigan. He looked more European than Turkish or Arab, and, as it turned out, behaved more like a European than a Levantine.

While we sat waiting, he spoke on the telephone in Turkish, French and Arabic. When he finished, he asked me why I was there. He was the first person I met in Alexandretta who spoke fluent English. I was hopeful that he could guide me through my first day in his city. I explained that mutual friends, who had been his neighbours when he lived in Beirut, had given me his name as a man who would help me in Alexandretta.

"I don't think so," he said. He could do nothing, because he was leaving for Europe the next day. "Perhaps this young man can help you."

"He is trying," I said. "But he has been away from here for years, and he does not speak English."

"I am sorry," Makzoumé said, the resignation in his voice betraying more relief than regret.

As we left his offices, he called out, "You could try the British Consul."

Munir and I walked to the Catoni Maritime Agencies, an Ottoman stone building which backed onto the sea and had for years served a secondary purpose as British Consulate in Alexandretta. The front room was a shipping company and travel agency, in which a woman was preparing airline tickets for a customer seated by her desk. I asked where we could find the British Consul.

She indicated a door to another office, and Munir and I went in. The first sights to greet us on entering were three large portraits: in the centre, of course, was Atatürk, to his right was Queen Elizabeth and on his left was Prince Philip, who in Turkey, if nowhere else, was never referred to as "Phil the Greek". The portraits of the British queen and her husband, bedecked in medals and ribbons, were nearly as dated as that of Atatürk, obviously made many years and many chins ago. Beneath the portraits sat a soberly dressed middle-aged woman, who looked as unassuming as the luminaries behind her were grand. When she saw us, she looked up from her desk with its small British and Turkish flags and smiled. "May I help you?" she asked.

She understood immediately when I explained the purpose of my journey and why I had begun in Alexandretta. She was just old enough to remember that the province had been part of Syria until 1939, although

too young to have been born when the whole region was u Ottomans. Hind Koba, MBE, had been Her Majes Alexandretta for nearly thirty years. I told her that I had only two people in Alexandretta, Makzoumé, who had n and Abdallah Tanzi, whose telephone did not answer.

"Abdallah Tanzi," she said, "is my brother-in-law. We building." She thought it would not be difficult to find hir to make appointments with a variety of people who woul idea what Alexandretta was like and how its life had change was to a lawyer named Kavak, who said he could see me

Walking through the streets, which were becoming more morning grew late, Munir used his few words of English, g gift of an expressive face to tell me that his life was unha Shiite in a Sunni Muslim country. He was half-Iranian i distrusted Iran. His father was dead. He owed taxes restaurant, which had closed as a result. He had to care fo family in Alexandretta, and he yearned for the cosmo Istanbul. "Maybe one year," he said. "Maybe two." Then Alexandretta again for the pleasures of the north.

We found Kavak's office in a modern, if run-down bu flights of stairs, past various shops selling women's clothe supplies. A dark-haired man in his mid-thirties opened th "avukat", introducing himself as Yalçin Kavak. We follow room filled with law books and a large desk covered in seemed to be no picture of Atatürk, but a small staff displa flag. We had been squeezed into the little office for a few Kavak invited us to lunch. Munir had to leave for an appoint he would see me later at Mehmet Udimir's library.

Kavak took me to what was called a "popular" restaura Ekspres Lokantasi, for "typical" Turkish food. We found large rectangular room, with simple wooden tables and cha were bare except for the mandatory portrait of Atatürk. Neitl the lights overhead were on. We sat at a table near the front w was no menu. A waiter asked us what we wanted. When we a available, he told us to come into the kitchen. The kitche from the dining-room by nothing more than a glass-fronte and a food warmer, both chest-high. In the refrigerator were of raw meat, lying in trays of blood, chops, beef, spiced minco *kofta*, all ready for grilling, and salads and cold vegetables. Th full of stews, cooked vegetables, meat pies and *dolma*, stuf like vine leaves and courgettes. Kavak advised me to have a and aubergines, with yogurt, hommous and cold artichokes waiter looked pleased with the choice.

"Did they all come here for work?"

"The eastern cities in Turkey do not offer enough. People have to come to the western cities to progress. Even me, I was a lawyer in the east, in Merdin. I was doing well there, but I had to come to Iskenderun."

"Is there any Syrian influence here?"

"If you study Hatay," he said, using the Turkish name for the province, "you must look at Syria. In Syria, I think twenty-five per cent of the people are Alawi, forty-five per cent are Sunni and thirty per cent are Christian, including Armenians and Assyrians. The man who became president of Syria is Alawi. He didn't come to power democratically. He wants to remain president. He puts Alawis in important positions, as military commanders and security police. He is afraid. Of what? Who is against him? The Muslim Brothers, the Iraqi Baath Party. Because of this opposition, twenty-five per cent of the population is not enough for him. This is why, I heard, clever young Alawis from Samandag, in the far south, are being taken to study at the university in Damascus. They study medicine or go into the military and don't come back." The Alawis are a dissident sect of Shiite Muslims, who live mainly in the hills along the sea between northern Lebanon and Alexandretta.

Kavak said he had been active in politics. "Before 1980, I belonged to the Social Democratic Party, the democratic left. In Turkey, the Communist Party is forbidden. This is why some people who are not social democrats, but Marxists, work in the Social Democratic Party. They work together and support each other. If you want to succeed, you have to cooperate with the communists. I did not want to. Also, with my work, I don't have enough time."

When the waiter brought us the main course, I reflected that Kavak was an unusual man, though just how unusual I had yet to discover. He looked like a conventional lawyer in his dark three-piece suit, his hair combed neatly back, his face shaved. Yet he had mentioned things that were banned in Turkey: 1914, Armenians, Kurds, Alawis who looked to Syria. In official Turkish doctrine, no massacres took place in 1914; there were no Armenians; Kurds were "mountain Turks"; Alawis were Turkish without ties to the Arab world. Denial of reality was official policy.

"I was raised a Muslim," he said, "but I became a Christian in 1970."

The surprise on my face was difficult to conceal. In all the years I had spent in Muslim countries, I had met only one convert from Islam to Christianity, a professor of philosophy at the American University of Beirut. I had met many converts who had gone the other way, from Christianity to Islam. In Cairo, I knew an American Jew who had become a Muslim. Western Protestant missionaries in 19th-century Syria concluded after many failed attempts that Muslims could not be converted to

Christianity, so they concentrated instead on turning eastern Christians, Catholic and Orthodox, into Protestants. Kavak was the first Turkish Muslim I met who had become a Christian. He was not to be the last.

"In 1914," he recounted, "the grandfather of my father was murdered. It was at the time of the troubles. A Muslim mullah took his son, my grandfather, and raised him as his own son, as a Muslim. Our family were all Muslims. My mother was an Arab Muslim, and we spoke Arabic at home. We read the Koran in Arabic."

"How did you change?"

"One of my family was a candidate in the elections when I was a teenager. His opponents asked people in Merdin, 'How can you vote for an Assyrian Christian?' We did not know what they meant. So, we went to Assyrian villagers, who told us, 'Your family are Assyrian.' They told us we were related. Then I learned that my great-grandfather had been killed because he was an Assyrian, when many Assyrians died along with the Armenians."

"Was that reason enough to become a Christian?"

"When I was at the university, studying law," he said, "I read the Bible and the Koran. Mohammed was a great leader and a clever man, but I did not find him to be a real prophet. I think maybe some Jewish people helped him, because the Koran is very close to the Old and New Testaments."

"Is your wife a Christian?"

"She is Turkish from Istanbul," he said. "I explained my situation to her very clearly before we were married, and she accepted it. She is ready to be baptised, but I want her to study first."

"Is religion important here?"

"Many educated people here are not Christian, but they are not really Muslim. They don't go to the mosque and don't like Islamic life. It is something that exists only on the identity card, Muslim, Christian or Jewish."

"Identity cards still state your religion? I thought this was a secular state."

"The Turkish Republic was founded in 1923," he said. "This is not a long time for a state, especially for a people changing their system from Islamic to secular. But we have come a very long way."

How far had this corner of Turkey come, separated as it was from the world to which it had belonged for millennia? In 1918, when the Turkish army retreated from Syria north into Anatolia, it abandoned the province of Alexandretta, the harbour at Alexandretta town, the city of Antioch on the banks of the Orontes and the fertile fields, mountains and forests in between, its Arab population and its Armenian and Turkish minorities. For the next twenty years, it was divided from the rest of Turkey, ruled by the French as part of their League of Nations Mandate over Syria. In 1938,

France held a referendum on the province's status and created the so-called Republic of Hatay. A year later, the French gave it back to Turkey. Since then, it has been cut off from the rest of Syria. It seemed doomed in this century, as a frontier province of states to either its north or south, to be separated from at least half its historic self.

In the centre of Alexandretta's seafront, near the port, lay a large marble plaza. On it a giant black monument, shaped like a wave about to sweep away the town and all its people, appeared to rise out of the Bay of Alexandretta. On its high summit stood two life-size sculpted figures: a woman holding an olive branch and a soldier standing to attention. Between them a large Turkish flag, secular red with the white crescent and star of Islam, fluttered in the breeze. Behind them the wave was about to crest, and below them, on a level fashioned into a smaller wave, stood four larger figures marching in a V-formation behind a man in the centre. On the left were two women, one a peasant and the other a sturdy housewife; on the right were two men, a worker and an engineer. The man and woman near the apex of the V together raised a laurel over the head of the man at the front. He stood on the lowest platform, but was larger than them all. A cape was draped cavalierly over his left shoulder, and his strong right arm was outstretched, pointing landward, as though he were emerging from the surf to redeem Alexandretta.

The heroic figure was Atatürk himself at the scene of his final triumph. His confident gaze was fixed on the last province he reclaimed from the Allies, the final piece of Turkey reassembled from the débâcle of the First World War, which saw the loss of an empire and the birth of a modern state. Like Moses, Atatürk had led his people through the water to the Promised Land, without reaching it himself. Less than a year before the French "Armée du Levant" withdrew on his terms, the "Father of the Turks" had died.

Near the Atatürk monument was a small outdoor café. I stopped there to drink a coffee. A waiter said something to me in Turkish, and I asked whether he spoke Arabic. He did. When he brought me a demi-tasse of Turkish coffee without sugar, he sat down and told me how difficult his life was. He said he worked long hours for little money. He had six children. "If I do not work," he complained, "there is no bread." Then he shrugged. "I'm an Arab," he said, as if this were sufficient to explain his impoverished condition. To him and his compatriots, the Atatürk monument symbolised their defeat, the loss of their place in the Arab world and the severing of ties to their brothers in Syria. It mattered little that they, and not their "liberated" and divided Syrian cousins to the south, were living as all Syrians had lived for four centuries – under Turkish rule.

The beachless seafront was built over a large landfill, a few hundred yards of Turkey taken from the sea. On the wide pavement, it was the time of the afternoon promenade. Men pedalled past on bicycles with their wives on the back. Some had children perched in front. One man swept slowly along with one child on his handlebars and, on the back, a woman holding another child. All along the corniche, families were strolling, stopping to buy peanuts or hot, fresh popcorn from the many street vendors. The young boys' heads were shaved to stubble. Women walked by in groups, none veiled, though many from the countryside wore brightly coloured scarves.

Turkish sailors, their European navy-style caps emblazoned TCB, joined the march, stealing furtive glances at the girls. Everywhere the sailors meandered, well-armed Military Police followed like vigilant *dueñas*. The MPs, smartly dressed from their white helmets down to the white spats over their black shoes, wore short truncheons on their hips and carried Belgian FN light automatic rifles. I saw no signs of trouble, and I suspected that, while the MPs were on duty, I wasn't likely to. A few of the sailors were accompanied by their mothers and fathers, who had come to port to visit them.

I joined the parade of humanity on the seafront – Arab and Turkish townspeople, Alawis from the villages, Kurds from the mountains, Christians and Muslims. Mingling among the crowd, hardly noticeable until they approached you, were young boys and old men trying to make money on the pavements. They stood, dressed in old or badly fitting clothes, pleading with passers-by to give them money. Some merely begged, hands outstretched, with nothing to offer in return other than a blessing. Others shined shoes. Some sat in front of old scales, next to bits of cardboard with a few coins on top, and asked people to weigh themselves in exchange for a small donation. Most of the crowd ignored them, content to enjoy the evening promenade. Everywhere, in cafés and outdoors, in small groups and large, men sat at small tables and played cards or backgammon, all the while drinking tea or coffee, oblivious to the procession passing them by.

The sun was slow to set. The sea, where it met the breakwater, was quiet and unmoving. Nothing had disturbed Alexandretta for fifty years, an unpredicted moment of dull tranquillity in a bloody history of more than two millennia. The Bay of Alexandretta lay at the undefined point where the Aegean gave way to the Mediterranean. It was the northern frontier of the Levant – the 440 miles of coast between here and Al Arish in Gaza. Every port on this eastern Mediterranean shore, and every inland city each port served, had been invaded, besieged and destroyed dozens of times before and after Alexander the Great briefly united them in his empire. How long would this historic moment last? And when would the rest of the Levantine coast to the south, troubled by war and insurrection, enjoy again a generation of evenings like this one in Alexandretta?

CHAPTER TWO

THE ARMY OF THE LEVANT

For most of its life, Alexandretta managed to avoid playing a role in history. In the Levant, this meant it rarely became a battleground. Yet armies often passed through, whether Asians on their way to conquer Europe or Europeans seeking victories in the East. In 333 BC Alexander the Great defeated one of the largest armies ever assembled in antiquity, that of King Darius and his 400,000 Persians, at Issus, about twenty miles north of Alexandretta. After the battle, on an empty piece of shore, Alexander established a port town to control the northern route to Syria and named it for himself.

After Alexander's death, the heir to his Asian empire, Seleucus, established his capital inland at the other end of a pass through the mountains and named it in honour of his father, Antiochus. Antioch, not Alexandretta, became the centre of Hellenism in Syria and, later, the third greatest city in the Roman Empire. The city declined to a backwater in the Arab and Byzantine Empires, the Crusader Kingdoms and, finally, the Ottoman Empire. Although the Romans had abandoned it even as a port, preferring Seleucia Pieria to the south, it became popular with Venetian and Genoese merchants who established trading houses there for the caravan trade with China, India and Baghdad. The French and British later won concessions from the Ottoman Sultan to do the same. It became a pleasant Mediterranean outpost, only a short sail from Venice, from which to purchase the spices of Asia. The route went from Alexandretta, through the Beilan Pass, to Antioch and Aleppo, where the great caravans across the desert from India had their terminus.

In 1834, Alexandretta missed its chance at greatness. That year, the Duke of Wellington commissioned Colonel F. R. Chesney to establish a route "between the Mediterranean Sea and H.M. possessions in the East Indies by means of steamer communication on the River Euphrates". The route, for which Parliament voted an initial £20,000, might have become another Suez Canal, which was not constructed until fifty years later. The plan called for an expedition to take two paddle steamers in pieces to the mouth of the River Orontes near Alexandretta. There the steamers, the *Tigris* and the *Euphrates*, would be assembled and sail upriver to a point nearest the River Euphrates. They would then be taken apart, carried to the Euphrates and reassembled to sail downstream to Baghdad. Chesney discovered at the beginning that his 20-horsepower engines were not strong enough to sail against the Orontes' four-knot currents. So, he took the boats apart at the Orontes and carried them the 140 miles to the Euphrates. Although a storm sank the *Tigris*, the *Euphrates* steamed into Baghdad just after New Year 1837.

The expedition explored the possibility of cutting a canal between the Euphrates and the sea, but lacked the resources to undertake the digging. It had been difficult enough to hire local labour to carry the ships. Twenty years later, Chesney, by now a Major-General, and a group of business-men in the City of London obtained permission from the Sultan to construct a railway along the banks of the Euphrates from the Mediterranean to the Persian Gulf. When the British government refused to guarantee Chesney's "Euphrates Valley Railway Company", it was disbanded. Had either the canal or the railway been constructed, Alexandretta would have become the first Mediterranean outlet of the swiftest route to the Persian Gulf and Indian Ocean, Britain's lifeline to India. This might have led to a British invasion in the mid-19th century, to protect the route to India, as the British invaded Egypt in 1882 to seize the Suez Canal. Who knows what would have happened in 1956? One thing is certain: France would never have ceded the area to Turkey in 1939, because Britain would not have allowed France to enter in 1920.

When Kaiser Wilhelm II won the concession in 1898 from Sultan Abdul Hamid to build the Berlin–Baghdad Railway, the German engineers planned a branch line to Alexandretta to provide the first rail link between the Mediterranean and the Gulf. Luckily or not for Alexandretta, the branch line was not constructed, and the little town was left to sleep its way into the twentieth century.

Its last flirtation with history came during the First World War, when it almost became the scene of the decisive battle between the Allies and the Ottoman Empire. In 1914, Sherif Hussein of Mecca, whose son Faisal led the Arab Revolt with Lawrence of Arabia, proposed an Allied landing at Alexandretta to cut Turkey from its forces in Iraq and Syria and coincide with an uprising in Syria's larger cities. Hussein's plan had the support of the British strategists on the ground, Lord Kitchener, Sir Charles Monro, Sir John Maxwell and Sir Henry McMahon, but it was nonetheless rejected by the General Staff. The British had a commitment to their French allies, who, with no troops available, would not permit an invasion of Syria without them. The Allies decided instead to invade Turkey itself at a place called Gallipoli, a historic disaster which resulted in more Commonwealth dead than any other battle in the East.

The Alexandretta in which I had begun my tour of the Levant was the site of neither a decisive battle nor of a great trade route between West and East. It was merely the northern limit of what geographers, ever scornful of the changing maps of soldiers and politicians, called Syria. To the British, it was valuable, like the rest of the Levant, only as a passage to India. To the French, the Levant had special resonances, as Edward Said wrote in his book *Orientalism:* "In contrast, the French pilgrim was imbued with a sense of acute loss in the Orient. He came there to a place in which France, unlike Britain, had no sovereign presence. The Mediterranean echoed with the sounds of French defeats, from the Crusades to Napoleon." For an American traveller like myself, the Levant was filled with reminders of broken promises, beginning with President Woodrow Wilson's to the people of the Ottoman Empire that they would enjoy the right of self-determination in the post-war settlement. To the people themselves, from Alexandretta to Aqaba, avoiding all our attentions and staying well out of the movement of history was the most they could hope for.

When I awakened on my second morning in Alexandretta, I decided to move. I would continue my wanderings through the town, but stay on a quiet beach forty minutes to the south, near the end of the coast road in the village of Arsuz. The morning was pleasantly cool. There was no wind and not a cloud in the sky. Ships lay at anchor outside the port like ornaments on a cake, apparently frozen into the blue icing. Shopkeepers pulling up steel awnings and opening their doors were bringing the quiet of Saturday morning to an end. Small cafés were serving Turkish coffee and bread to workers, and old women were inspecting vegetables in the street markets.

Before leaving for Arsuz, I went to every bookshop I could find, coming upon them nestled inconspicuously between ironmongers' and pharmacies. There seemed to be only four or five, and none specialised in books. They sold stationery, postcards, portraits of Atatürk and worry beads, and along one wall in each there were wooden shelves filled with books in no particular order. One shop had books in English, all paperback editions of Dickens, where I bought *A Tale of Two Cities*. There was a wide range of Turkish works: novels, poetry, engineering textbooks, children's stories and biographies of Atatürk. There were Turkish translations of foreign writers, men like Jack London and Ernest Hemingway, and women like Ayn Rand, Rosa Luxemburg and Barbara Cartland. There were however no books in Arabic.

"Do you have anything in Arabic?" I asked an attractive young woman who worked behind the cash register in one bookshop. She did not look Turkish, her features more Semitic than Asian. I was speaking to her in Arabic.

"No, we don't," she answered in Arabic.

"No books? No newspapers?"

"No."

"Why not?"

She shrugged her shoulders.

I asked for ink for my pens, and she wrapped a bottle in coloured paper like a gift. As I was leaving, a man who had heard me speaking Arabic invited me to his shop next door for coffee. While we drank coffee, other merchants drifted in and out; they seemed to spend much of their day socialising in one another's shops. My accent in Arabic, obviously foreign, was basically Lebanese. They found it amusing, just as I found many of their pronunciations and words incomprehensible. Everyone, whether Turkish or Arab, was hospitable – in a way too hospitable. If I had accepted every offer of tea, coffee or lunch at home with a family, I would have had no time for anything else.

In the now crowded streets, many people spoke Arabic among themselves. I could hear mothers speaking it to their children, workers speaking it as they walked together along the cracked pavements. But no road, shop or advertising signs anywhere were written in Arabic. Everything written was in Turkish.

There was something disjointed about life in Alexandretta. Most people seemed to speak one language at home and among friends and another for official purposes. They thought in one language, yet they had to read another. Even the letters of this other language were foreign, since Atatürk had abandoned the "Old Turkish" Arabic script in favour of a modified Latin alphabet. They had one name at home, another on their identity papers and in public. When the names changed to Turkish, the authorities sometimes made arbitrary choices, often based on nicknames or profession. The same thing had happened in America, when new immigrants arriving at Ellis Island were greeted by Irish policemen who could not understand their foreign-sounding names, so simply gave them new, "American" names. When my grandmother arrived as a child from Mount Lebanon in the late 1890s as Nazira Makary, an Irish cop had re-christened her "Vera McCarey", the name she kept until she married. Her stepfather, Semaan Zalloua, became "Joe Simon". Under Turkish rule in Alexandretta, Hannoud Alexander was now Hind Koba. I discovered later that Mehmet Udimir had been born Mohamed Haj.

The Ottomans had not tampered with people in this way, leaving Arabs, Armenians, Circassians and countless other subject peoples free to speak and read their own languages, free to use their own names. Yet Turkey had become a "modern" nation, adopting Western nationalist ideology that forbade the old diversity of empire. No one complained in public. A few people, who had steadfastly defended the idea that Turkey was a democracy, begged me not to quote them by name on the subject of language and their sympathy with Syria for fear of arrest or reprisal.

I went back to the Hatayli Oteli to collect my bags. Ahmet the porter called for a taxi, several of which were parked across the road in the shade, to take me to Arsuz. Ahmet asked the driver the fare in Turkish. He then etched the figure 7,000 into the dust on top of the car. I said this was too high. The driver cursed in Arabic, so I began haggling with him in Arabic, dispensing with Ahmet as interpreter. We agreed on 5,000 Turkish Lira for a return journey, to include the wait in Arsuz while I checked in and left my bags. I wanted to be back in Alexandretta for an appointment at the old Church of the Annunciation with the Italian Franciscan priest, Padre Giovanni.

We drove along the coast road out of Alexandretta into green hills with the sea, except for a brief inland stretch, always at our right. The driver said his name was Mehrez, or Mehré in Turkish. When he asked me if I wanted to listen to Turkish music on his cassette player, I asked if he had anything in Arabic.

"Who do you like?"

"Feyrouz," I said, the name of Lebanon's most famous chanteuse.

"I don't have Feyrouz, but I have Samira!" He popped in a tape of songs by Samira Tewfic, a popular Arabic singer who sang, like most Arabic singers, about love. With the music blasting in the old American taxi, we drove at speed along the deserted coast where green hills rolled gently into the blue sea.

Mehrez was curious about me. What was my nationality? Where had I learned Arabic? Where did I live? How many children did I have? What kind of work did I do?

"*Sahafi*," I said, the Arabic word for journalist.

He had no idea what the word meant. I tried and failed to explain, but when I fell back on "*kutub*", writer, he understood. It turned out we both had five children, two boys and three girls. When I said we lived in London, he seemed puzzled. I explained that my wife was English. He was silent. Minutes passed, and the hills which had until then hugged the coastline gave way to a fertile plain just north of Arsuz. He asked me again about London. "London is near where?"

Did he mean which part of London?

"No."

Did he know London?

"No."

"What do you mean?"

"Where is London?"

27

"*Fi Ingilterra*," I said. "In England."

"*Fi Ingilterra*," he repeated, knowingly. "*Helou.*" *Helou* means "sweet", but has the connotation "pretty". Then he said London was "*helou*".

I admitted that London and England were "*helou*," and after a few minutes we both agreed that Alexandretta too was "*helou.*"

Mehrez pointed out the sights along the Arsuz road, the onion fields, olive groves and grazing pastures where in summer people from Alexandretta and the villages went for picnics. He offered to stop at several villages where we could drink home-made arak. He seemed disappointed that I had neither the time nor, at eleven in the morning, the desire for a glass of the strong distilled grape with aniseed and asked, "Would you rather have beer?"

We reached the northern outskirts of Arsuz, hideous with new buildings in creative forms of ugliness, as though the houses had been modelled on the Lego designs of a particularly troublesome child. Most of the two-storey structures had just been built or were nearing completion. Trees had yet to be planted, so there was no shade. Concrete dust was everywhere, a side-effect of the Westernising of housebuilding in a land rich with stone and forests which had for centuries until our own provided the materials for beautiful villas, temples and theatres. It was a relief to cross the little bridge at the mouth of the River Arsuz into old Arsuz, with its small cluster of eucalyptus-shaded stone houses. Wooden fishing boats bobbed up and down beneath the bridge, beyond which, almost hidden by pines and eucalyptus, was the Hotel Arsuz.

"Rosuz is the Hellenistik name of this charming little town," I read in Mehmet Udimir's tourist brochure. "Coming to Antakya, Selevkos Nicador set foot to shore here. There are some mozaics and the remnants of stone pillars are to be seen in Arsuz, from the middle ages."

Mehrez drove into the hotel courtyard, where young men were playing soccer. One of them stopped playing and took me inside one of the hotel's two buildings. He was enormously fat, with a gentle, friendly face, and spoke English well. He told me his father owned the hotel, which had opened in 1965, and that his name was Sedat Mistikoglu. He gave me a room in the newer building, a simple bedroom with windows on two sides, one facing the sea and a sandy beach and the other with a balcony over the courtyard. In the bathroom, there was a shower. I left my bags and went downstairs, where Sedat and his younger brother Suat asked me if everything was all right. They were proud of the hotel's modern conveniences, the telephones in each room and the new plumbing. "We have just installed solar heating," Sedat said, beaming.

"What happens when the sun doesn't shine?" I asked, dreading cold morning showers.

28

"The sun always shines here," Sedat assured me.

Back in Alexandretta, I asked Mehrez to take me to the Catholic church. He interpreted this to mean a general tour of Christian churches. He drove to several small churches with tin roofs, first a Greek Orthodox, then an Armenian Orthodox, then a church whose denomination was not indicated. I said I was late for an appointment, that the church I wanted, the "Franciscan" church, was "old and large". He took me to another Orthodox church, which was tiny with a miniature basilica on top. Finally, despite my limited knowledge of Alexandretta's roads, I managed to direct him to the Church of the Annunciation. As we approached it, he made a gesture of recognition, as if to ask, "Why didn't you say *this* church?"

In search of Padre Giovanni, I went into the rectory, along a corridor hung with old French morality prints. One contrasted the death of the sinner, being subsumed into hell, with that of a faithful man ascending to heaven, all in faded pastel shades. Another showed Adam and Eve in the garden, accepting the apple from the serpent. These were the visions of my own pre-Vatican II childhood, the simple messages of an older church. I heard voices coming from a room which turned out to be a large kitchen. Padre Giovanni was sitting with several other people at a long table eating lunch, but got up and walked with me to the courtyard in front of the church. The church was entirely surrounded by a high wall, leaving large gardens front and back. Both were overgrown and the façades of the church and rectory needed paint, at least, and probably repair. With only about 350 Catholics in all of Alexandretta, the cost of repairs would have been difficult to bear.

We sat on a bench, which the young priest wiped clean with his handkerchief, in the shade of a small pine tree. He stretched out his long legs, and his beard with its few flecks of grey lay over his chest down to his stomach. The beard made him look more Greek Orthodox than Catholic. He was tall and thin, with an austere face. He wore the traditional Franciscan footwear, sandals, but otherwise dressed in civilian clothes – a plaid shirt without Roman collar, a cardigan and a beige jacket. The hair on his head was the same colour as his beard, brown with a little grey, cut short.

I asked Father Giovanni why I had met Franciscans in every Muslim country, with the exception of Saudi Arabia, I had visited. For years in west Beirut, the Muslim half of Lebanon's divided capital, Franciscans said mass in their chapel whatever the battlefield conditions outside. They turned up in such unlikely places as Libya, serving Polish, Filipino and other *Gastarbeiter*. They offered the sacraments to visitors like myself in the wilds of Somalia and on the banks of the Nile in Cairo.

"In St Francis's time," he said, in English with a strong Italian accent, "he thought there should be cooperation between Christians and Muslims. For all Muslim people, he became the possibility of living in peace between these two peoples."

"It's too bad he's dead," I said, thinking of Christian – Muslim bloodshed in Lebanon and Egypt.

He told me that there were 4,000 Christians in Alexandretta, the largest community being the Greek Orthodox with 3,000. As well as the 350 Roman Catholics, there were a few Armenians, Assyrians and Protestants.

"In the Orthodox Church," he said, "according to tradition, they say the Mass in Arabic. The Orthodox youth who want to pray in Turkish, they come to our church." Other communicants from outside his congregation were the many foreign seamen, mainly Filipino and Italian, whose ships berthed at Alexandretta harbour.

How were relations between the Christians and the overwhelming Muslim majority?

"Relations are normal," he said. "Unfortunately, I see that between Christian and Muslim people there is no theological understanding. Generally, there is indifference. I heard it said, they are Muslims, we are Christians. Unfortunately, I say, because I am interested in how Muslims live their own faith. I was lucky myself to become friends, because God gave me the occasion, with an Imam. He is young. He came to our church, so we started to become friends. I pay a visit to him. He pays visits to me, and so on. I'm proud of this friendship, because I take it as a gift from God."

"What kind of Muslim is he?"

"I know he is a special confession of Muslim, but I don't know which. Not an Alawi."

"Is there any intermarriage between Christians and Muslims?"

"There are ten or fifteen couples I am aware of, but I know they have some difficulties. Generally, Christians and Muslims don't marry each other. That is a problem, of course. The Orthodox Church believes differently from the Catholic on marriage between faiths."

"How?"

"The Orthodox requires that the partner who is not a Christian must be baptised. As Catholics, we do not ask this. The Catholic Church blesses the marriage, even when the other person is not baptised. If someone, man or woman, accepts to be baptised in order to be with his beloved, what kind of conscience has he about the sacrament of baptism? It is a problem I face with my Orthodox colleagues."

The Orthodox may have been closer to the Muslim outlook. An old friend, who had converted to Islam for what he felt might have been base motives at the time, later became devout. "We believe," my friend explained, "that motive in accepting God as God and Mohammed as his Prophet does not matter. It is important to become a Muslim, to submit to God, whether to get married or to avoid tax on non-believers or whatever. In time, God will act on you, and you become a true Muslim."

I asked Padre Giovanni whether the Christians tended to be richer, as in Lebanon, or poorer than the Muslims.

"The Catholics," he said, "generally come from families who were originally European. They are mostly Latin Catholic. They work in trade and are rich. If we speak of Christians here though, we have to discuss the Orthodox Church, which is much larger. As a minority, Christians face difficulties. For instance, it is not easy to find important jobs in this society. The better jobs go to Muslims. Here in this country, the Christians are second-class people."

"Do the younger Christians want to leave the country?"

"It's not a problem of young people, but of families. That is, there are a lot of families who leave to go to Germany, France, Italy, New York. Of course, it's a problem especially for young people who don't easily find work. This is worse in eastern Turkey, where the Christians are much poorer . . ."

"Do the Muslims you know face the same problems?"

"Among the Muslims, there is the problem of secularisation. Many people do not go to the mosque, don't have a religious feeling. Materialism and secularism are problems for both Islam and Christianity."

The garden was quiet, but for the chirping of small birds, and cool despite the sunshine. Padre Giovanni stood to lead me on a tour of his church, where he said I could come to Mass the next day. We were on the steps of his church when an old woman walked up to him and told him in Italian with a strong southern accent to come inside and finish his lunch.

"This is my mother," he said. "She and my father are visiting from Italy." He promised to return to lunch in a few minutes. She walked back to the rectory, clearly disappointed.

"They built this church in 1888," he said as we walked in, "when Alexandretta had large Italian, French, English and local Catholic communities."

I imagined what it must have been like on a bright Sunday in those last years before nationalism and modernisation crept into the Ottoman Empire. The priest would have said Mass in Latin at the high altar, while several hundred Catholics who spoke different languages in their daily lives worshipped together. Despite changes in the world outside, the interior of the Church of the Annunciation looked unchanged, except that a new altar now faced the twelve rows of pews and the priest would say Mass in

Turkish. The marble floor, in large slabs of alternating black and white, was freshly washed, looking as it must have a century earlier. The Mediterranean sun still shone through the rounded windows above the columns that lined the church, near which old women made the Stations of the Cross. Above the old altar, which symbolically faced God rather than the people, were six large baroque golden candelabra. The tabernacle was gold. There were two side altars, neither recessed, the one on the right with a large plaster statue of St Theresa, the one on the left with a similar coloured effigy of St Francis of Assisi holding the child Jesus in one hand. On the right-hand wall of the church at the back was a large frieze of St George, patron not only of England but of most eastern Christians. Above the caption, *"Sancte George Ora Pro Nobis,"* the saint astride his white charger held a real spear, red tipped with blood, poised to strike the already wounded green dragon, whose teeth were exposed menacingly, like a monster's in an old horror film, sneering at the horse's hooves and the spear at his head. This was the religion of my youth, the religion that was born in the Levant, in which St George vanquished the dragon with his spear and the Archangel Michael conquered Lucifer by the sword. Yet it was the followers of the pacific St Francis of Assisi who kept Christendom alive here. The heroes of the Crusades, the marauding Knights Templar and Hospitaller, had fled long ago.

Padre Giovanni excused himself to discuss something with the women who were cleaning the church for Palm Sunday mass the next day. I thanked him for his time and left.

Walking out of the church courtyard into the road facing Mehmet Udimir's library, I saw a small cinema, the profane neatly adjoining the sacred. A torn poster stapled onto a board in front advertised an Italian soft-porn film starring the Eritrean actress Zeudi Araya. I went in to take a look, but found the cashier fast asleep in a chair. I decided not to wake him. A doorway covered with a blanket led into a bare room with iron and plastic folding chairs set haphazardly on the cement floor. A flat wooden ceiling above and an arched window along one wall gave the room the feel of an abandoned Spanish mission. A white sheet stretched across one wall served as the screen.

Twenty-five men and boys sat in a room that could comfortably seat 200. There seemed to be no minimum age to watch this film of a bad Italian actor fondling the breasts of, first, a bad Italian actress, and then of Zeudi Araya, a lithe African, who herself soon fondled the breasts of the Italian actress, who reciprocated by fondling Zeudi's breasts. I feared for the young boys, some aged eight or nine, not because they were exposed to the sight of bare breasts, which I took to be harmless, but that they might grow up to believe the sole object of sex was breast-fondling. The sounds of the lovers' heavy breathing could hardly compete with the creaking of the old projector. What little dialogue there was, mainly expletives of one and two words, had been dubbed into Turkish. The film itself was grainy, obviously the last print of an extremely cheap production.

Every so often, some of the men got up to leave, no doubt bored. A few more pre-adolescent boys drifted in, without disturbing the somnolent cashier, and sat down to watch the Italian couple find the meaning of life on a tropical island inhabited by a naked black girl. On the wrinkled sheet, an appropriate medium for projecting this particular film, Zeudi Araya sadly waved good-bye to her Italian lovers. They were sailing back to Italy and out of her life forever, which I took as my cue to depart. I did not disturb the cashier. I was certain he preferred his dreams to the twenty pence I would have paid him for my ten-minute excursion into Turkey's world of soft porn next to the "very old" church.

I returned to the church on Palm Sunday. The old altar and pulpit stood as empty reminders of the old Latin Mass, while microphones on the new altar and lectern carried the voice of Padre Giovanni in Turkish to the eighty people, mostly well-dressed women and children, of the congregation. When the priest reached the Pater Noster, he sang it in Latin. Perhaps he did that so that his mother and father, seated at the front, would understand at least part of the ceremony. They sat like two humble Italian peasants, the mother with a black mantilla on her white hair, and the father dressed in a shirt without tie buttoned at the collar. They were indistinguishable from their fellow Mediterraneans in the church and could easily have been Turkish, Greek, Syrian, or any other race of the civilisation at the "middle of the earth". Behind them, children dressed in white held leafy twigs, though I wondered why they did not have palm leaves from the trees outside. The Mass ended, and outside other young boys were drifting into the cinema next door for a glimpse of Zeudi Araya's breasts.

That evening, I strolled about the town. Alexandretta was pleasant, but run-down, with unrepaired roads and crumbling buildings. There was the smell of sea-air, mixed with that of diesel fuel, and the smoke of meat grilling on coals in the popular restaurants. Most of the streets were dark, only half lit by old street lights.

My exploration of Alexandretta's limited night life was brief. On one street near Mehmet Udimir's library, two night clubs stood side by side. One was the Kazablanca, and the other was the Tanca Bar. Their exteriors were lit with coloured lights, blinking in the darkness like Christmas trees, lights that were identical in border towns and ports from Tijuana, Mexico, to Trabzon. They beckoned the stranger into a forbidden world which, at its best, would be merely disappointing. There were men standing outside in cheap light suits, bright ties and pencil moustaches – the uniform of cabaret doormen throughout the world. Two of them were beckoning unwary pedestrians into the Kazablanca, so I walked into the Tanca, which at that moment had no one at the door.

As soon as I was inside, I knew I had made a mistake. It was so dark I could not see. I felt my way along a short, low corridor to a doorway which opened onto a long, only slightly less dark room. When my eyes adjusted, I saw that the ceilings were vaulted, strangely covered in a knitted pattern of wood slats. The twining wood all round gave the cavern a sylvan feel, in the worst and most forbidding sense, recalling fairy stories in which the child is warned not to go into the woods alone at night. I waited for the wolf.

The head waiter, dressed like the doormen of the Kazablanca, motioned me to an empty table. Men, alone or in groups, sat at other tables in rows along either long wall between the door and the bar. In the central file between the men's tables were those of "the girls," who sat together impassively, more than a dozen of them. None was sitting with any of the men. In ill-fitting dresses, with costume jewellery and dyed hair, they appeared to be either plain bar girls, there to encourage men to buy more drinks, or prostitutes. They were unusually ugly and unforthcoming for either. On the wooden dance floor, in front of which a three-man band was laconically playing "Oriental" music, there were no dancers, strippers, or even magicians.

I sat quietly for a minute trying to discern the sights in the room. Suddenly out of the darkness a waiter was standing in front of me. He had dark, greasy hair, and a moustache out of a 1930s film. He spoke to me in Turkish, which I could neither hear because of the music nor understand. I asked for "*bira*," beer in Turkish and Arabic. He returned a moment later with a bottle of Tuborg, an empty glass on a metal tray and a tin dish with a few pistachios in it. He put the tray down on my small round table, and, with a flourish worthy of the uncorking of a bottle of vintage champagne, pulled the cap off the beer bottle. As delicately as any sommelier at Simpson's with a choice claret, he poured the beer into the glass. Then he smiled and asked me to pay.

I did not understand. He repeated the price. I thought he said "bes" something. I recalled from the Farsi name for backgammon, "Shesh-Besh," that "besh" was five. Perhaps he was saying "five something," maybe 500. The band was still playing its loud, discordant music, so it was impossible to be sure. Was it 500 Turkish lira? I handed him a 500 lira note, a little less than one American dollar, but he shook his head. He wrote down a figure: 8,000.

"Eight *thousand*?" I asked, incredulous.

He nodded.

34

I did some quick figuring in my head. "That's over ten dollars!"

He raised his eyebrows, then waved his hand to indicate the beer *and* the nuts. So, that explained it. With pistachios, a fifty cent bottle of beer cost ten dollars. Perhaps I had to take into consideration the cost of the entertainment and the presence of the girls at their private tables.

"That's too much," I said and stood to leave.

The waiter was clearly displeased, but he did not follow me or argue. The band continued playing its awful tune, and the girls sat as placidly as before. I walked into the blackness of the corridor and outside to the cool night. I knew that if I had been somewhere else, say Beirut, the waiter would have tried to force me to pay. He would have chased me and summoned assistance in the form of a security guard with ham fists and a .38 revolver. (In fact, that is exactly what *had* happened to me on my first night in Beirut in 1972.) The people here were mercifully more relaxed. I decided not to sample the delights of the Kazablanca, although a more serious investigator of the joys of Alexandretta's night clubs would have persisted.

I walked along the same street to a normal, non-cabaret bar. It was open to the road with large windows and the inside was as lively as the Tanca Bar had been dead. Scores of mostly young men were talking and drinking beer, seated at stools along the curved, marble top bar or at the wooden casks which served as tables. There were no women – no bar girls, no wives or girlfriends, no young Alexandrettan ladies out on their own.

I ordered a pint of draught lager, which was served with a bowl of nuts by a smiling barman and cost 300 lira. The bar was not exactly clean or well lighted, but it was friendly and relaxed, and cleaner and better lit than the Tanca. There were two television sets, one in each of the two rooms separated from each other by the bar. They were playing the video of a Turkish thriller. In every scene, men were either punching or shooting at each other. In one segment, a group of men chased another group of men in cars. When nearly everyone was dead, the video ended and the barman turned it off and put on a cassette of Turkish pop music. But for the language spoken and the absence of women, it could have been a college beer bar anywhere in the Western world – young men in jeans, glasses of lager, music, a kitchen serving hot sandwiches. One man kindly offered me a beer and tried to welcome me into his conversation, but we discovered we had no common language. I tried English, French, Arabic and a few words of Spanish and Italian. He tried Turkish and what might have been Kurdish. He settled for a clink of glasses and a hearty pat on my back. What more could anyone ask?

At breakfast in the Arsuz Hotel, the old waiter in a uniform of black trousers, white shirt and tie, walked slowly across the terrace carrying breakfast on a tray. He tilted his thin body towards the table as he laid out the small breakfast dishes of olives, bread and white cheese. He poured tea from a tin pot into a cup and asked in Arabic if I wanted anything else.

"No," I said. "Thank you."

The waiter, whose name was Iskandar, Arabic and Turkish for Alexander, had somehow adopted me in my few days at the Arsuz Hotel. From the time we struck up a conversation in Arabic when I arrived, he would not let the Turkish waiters serve me. He was moody and would run his hand through his thinning grey hair and shake his head disapprovingly if I asked one of them for anything. He would always try to give me something extra, sometimes new green olives alongside the black, sometimes fried eggs, which I could see were not being served to the other guests. Despite his moodiness, he was a gentleman who moved and spoke with great dignity. He was proud that he came, not from this village, but from the ancient city of Antioch. He sympathised when I told him my shower that morning had been cold. Apparently, I was up too early for the sun to have had time to heat the water. I suspected he was solicitous because he enjoyed having a guest in the hotel who spoke his language, however badly and with however strong a Lebanese accent.

When I asked Iskandar where I could find a taxi to take me into Alexandretta, he advised me to save money by using the "dolmüs," a taxi which picked people up and dropped them off anywhere on a fixed route.

"Why do you want a taxi?" he asked reproachfully. "Taxis cost 5,000 lira. The dolmüs is only 250." In Turkey, the dolmüs was usually a micro-bus. Like the service in Syria, Lebanon, Jordan and Israel, the dolmüs was the normal transport for the poor. They called it "dolmüs", here because it was "stuffed" with passengers, the way they called courgettes or vine leaves "stuffed" with rice and meat "dolma".

When I reached the Ford micro-bus parked in the main square, it was already filled with fifteen people in twelve seats. We waited a few more minutes to stuff in another passenger before the bus began its journey north. The driver, his dashboard decorated with a turquoise stone to ward off the evil eye, stopped every so often on the way to let someone off or on, often leaving the road altogether to seek out passengers in the villages.

There were more women than men on the bus, and all of them, even the babies, wore gold earrings. The peasant women wore scarves with polka-dots or other designs in lurid colours over their hair. Women were not expected to have to sit next to men. We were about halfway to Alexandretta when a fat old peasant woman with a gold tooth pulled herself with both hands up the step into the bus. She examined us carefully and saw that the only empty seat was next to an inoffensive-looking young man. She hesitated, but finally sat next to him. When another old woman with hennaed hair noticed this unfortunate state of affairs, she picked up the small child next to her and sat him on her lap. She then invited the other old woman to sit where the child had been, an offer immediately accepted. Several people looked with disapproval at the young man, who had done nothing throughout this little drama.

In Alexandretta, Hind Koba took me to meet her elusive brother-in-law, Abdallah Tanzi, who lived in a flat a floor below her apartment near the sea. The building was a representative 1950s study in concrete with small balconies studded along its sides, and in her sister's flat the reception rooms were typically Oriental, with heavy wooden dressers and tables, dark stuffed chairs and dark walls. Abdallah Tanzi was a friendly man in his late 60s, short, stout and bald. A friend of a similar age, taller and thinner, but just as bald, was visiting from Beirut.

Hind's sister asked the maid to bring us cups of tea, and Tanzi showed me his letters of recommendation from American companies he had represented, as well as photographs of his son's graduation from Illinois State University. This son lived in Chicago; his daughter lived in Istanbul, where she worked as an economist; only one child, a son who worked as an engineer, lived in Alexandretta. His English, like Hind's and her sister's, was fluent. The maid carried in the tea, which, unusually, was served in china cups. Tanzi talked about Alexandretta, where he had been born under the French Mandate. "For a married couple," he said, "life is pleasant. For a single person, it depends on whether he has friends. There's nothing special here."

I asked him about 1939, the year Alexandretta ceased to be a part of Syria. "Maybe twenty-five per cent of the people living in Iskenderun at that time left," he said. "They were the minorities, if you'd like to say, the Christians."

"You're Christian. Why did you stay?"

"Because we didn't feel anything. It was everything regular. Nothing special."

"Did you speak Turkish then?"

"Yes, but not as good as now. The mother tongue is Arabic."

"How does life here compare with life in Syria?"

"We hear that life is more pleasant here. There is a big shortage of consumer goods there. The administration is much more democratic here."

"Can you travel to Syria easily?"

"I think it's difficult to get a Syrian visa. Previously, we used to get it at the border. Now, we have to go to Ankara."

"Do any Arabs want this to be part of Syria?"

"Even if there are feelings," he said, "no one here would express them."

"Syria claims Alexandretta. Does that mean anything?"

Tanzi began to answer, but was interrupted by his guest, Georges Sayyegh, who had until then been playing chess with Hind and now insisted on playing chess with me. I explained I had come not to play chess, but to talk. Another man arrived to play bridge. Hind asked me whether I would like to see a videotape of her MBE investiture at the British Embassy in Ankara. She put on the video, which showed her in a crowded reception in the grand surroundings of the Embassy. She looked happy and shy, like a little bird escaped from her cage in Alexandretta excited to find her way to the flocks in Istanbul. The ambassador delivered a speech in which he complimented "Hannoud Alexander" on her years of service to British subjects in trouble. When the tape ended, she showed me the MBE. "Why did he call you Hannoud Alexander?" I asked.

"That was my name," she explained, "before we had to change."

"You had to change your name? Why?"

"When this area was ceded to Turkey, everyone had to take a Turkish name."

The maid came back into the room, carrying a sweet cake which she put in front of me. I thanked her in Arabic, and she went back to the kitchen embarrassed. Sayyegh then insisted we have a game of chess. We played in silence for nearly an hour until I conceded. Sayyegh, having destroyed any chance I had of conversation with this older generation of Alexandrettans, stood up without a word and walked into the next room. There, the three old men were preparing the cards for a game of bridge and called me to play with them. I admitted I did not know how.

Another afternoon, I went to Hind's apartment to visit her and her two sisters. They had just eaten lunch, but she told me to sit down at her dining table while she prepared something. She brought me salad, cheese, bread and *kibbé*, a traditional Syrian mixture of minced lamb and cracked wheat. It was perfect lunch, exactly the food my grandmother would give me when I was young and would drop in on her unexpectedly. Hind and her sisters had lived in the apartment with their mother, who had died a year earlier, when they were girls. All three still dressed in black. Hind was the only spinster, one sister was married to Tanzi and the other to a Lebanese. She was staying with Hind while she recovered from a broken hip. She and her husband lived in a flat on the fifth floor of an apartment building in Sin el Fil, part of Christian east Beirut. With all the electricity cuts, which put the lift out of action, she had become a prisoner.

The sister recalled that the Sin el Fil area had suffered until 1976 from attacks by the Palestinians in the nearby refugee camp at Tel el Zaatar.

"I remember Tel el Zaatar." I said. "I covered the massacre there."

"You remember the massacre, but you don't know that the Palestinians killed every young Christian man they found. When the camp was taken, they found Christians crucified in the cellars."

"I went into the camp the morning it fell," I told her. "All I saw were the bodies of Palestinians trampled underfoot by Christians looting the houses. If there had been crucified Christians, I'm sure the Christian militiamen would have shown them to us."

"We lived with them," she said sadly. "Until 1973, when the first fighting began between the Palestinians and the army, we lived on the Corniche." The Corniche runs along the seafront in Muslim west Beirut between the American University of Beirut and Raouche, a Marseilles-like quarter of flashy apartment buildings, restaurants and night clubs.

"Are relations between Christians and Muslims better here?" I asked.

Hind said nothing, but her other sister answered, "To them, we are all *giaour*." *Giaour*, pronounced g'war, was a word I had not heard before outside literature. Byron used it as the title of a poem in 1814. It was the pejorative Turkish name for "unbeliever." "To them," she repeated, "we are all *giaour*, Christians, Jews, everybody. We were having dinner at some Muslim friends' the other night. Our host was talking about people who had done something awful, and he said they were 'just like the giaour'. When he realised what he'd said, he excused himself, saying, 'I didn't mean you.'"

She said that Turks in Alexandretta had accused the local Christians of treason during the 1974 Turkish invasion of Cyprus. "They said we were secretly supporting the Greeks," she complained. She opened her purse and handed me a photograph of a handsome young man in uniform. "I had to listen to this, and all the while my son was an officer fighting for them in Cyprus. For twenty-one days, we did not know whether he was dead or alive."

We talked about the referendum of 1938, when, according to the Arabs, trainloads of Turks had come from eastern Anatolia with false papers giving their residence as Alexandretta. When France handed the area to Turkey a year later, most of the Christians had left, some to French-ruled Syria, others to Lebanon. In Alexandretta, many Christian Arabs still wanted to be part of Syria. In Lebanon, Christians fought and died to stay out of Syria. In a few cases, they were the same people – wanting Syria to come when they were in Alexandretta, wanting it to leave when they were in Beirut. (I had seen the same kind of thing in Ireland with a Protestant friend, who had fled the violence of Belfast for a peaceful life in the Republic. When I asked whether he would like to see Ireland united under the same government which treated him well in Dublin, his answer was, "Never!")

All three sisters felt things had changed, not least in subtle ways that had nothing to do with politics. In the past, local people had taken their summer holidays in the mountains, away from the heat of the coastal plain, particularly in the village of Sogukoluk. Recently, they had been taking European-style beach holidays at Arsuz and Samandag, burning their skins on the beach and sweating as much as if they had stayed home. "We have a house in Sogukoluk," Hind said. "but we don't use it any more." The mountain resort had lost some of its charm when a convent there closed and later became a house of prostitution. "This forced all the family hotels to become brothels," they lamented. "There were stories of young girls kidnapped in Istanbul and forced to work in Sogukoluk. Finally, the government stepped in, arrested some people and closed all the hotels. Now there are no hotels there at all." Back in Arsuz, I went for a walk on the beach. Next door to the hotel was a single-storey stone house with red tile roof. It was the family home of Georges Sayyegh, the old man from Beirut I had met at Abdallah Tanzi's. I saw him exercising on the sand. He walked up to the fence which separated the hotel beach from his, and we talked through the wire. At the Tanzis' I had found him to be distracted, playing chess or bridge to avoid conversation. He tended to look away when other people talked to him. I had thought his manner strange and unsettling until Hind Koba told me his only son had been killed in Beirut, not by the war, but in a car accident. She said he had not been the same since. Standing there on the beach in his swimming trunks, he told me that he swam every day in Beirut at the beach of the Hotel St Georges. He was looking forward to his return there. I wondered how many people whose behaviour seemed awkward or offensive had lurking within them some tragedy, the death of a son, a daughter, a wife. Sayyegh invited me to visit him when I reached Beirut. "We can play chess." he said.

At twilight, I took a walk through the leafy streets of old Arsuz. The first place I went was the post office, from which I hoped to make a call to my children in London. It was a tiny stucco shed at a bend in the road. A man sat at a vintage telephone switchboard behind a low counter. He spoke only Turkish, but understood a few words of English. He told me to use a callbox outside and sold me several 250 TL tokens. I tried both telephones outside. Neither worked. I walked back in. The operator, unsurprised, gave me a refund for the tokens. He wrote down my number and called the central operator in Istanbul to book the call. He hung up and said it would come in forty minutes. I went to the hotel to bring a book to read.

When I returned to the post office, there were two other men with the operator. One was a middle-aged worker and the other an old man wearing black *sharwal*, the billowing Turkish trousers still worn by old peasants,

Turkish, Greek and Arab, throughout what had been the Ottoman Empire. The old man, who was born when the province was part of Syria under the Sultan Abdul Hamid, and spoke a few words of Arabic, invited me to his house for coffee, but I explained that I had to wait there for my call home.

So much and so little had changed since the old man was born. He dressed as his forebears did in the last century, and he had the hands of a man who worked the land just as they had. It mattered little that there was now a telephone link to London via Istanbul, because he had no need to call either city. There was no longer a Sultan, and the French army had interrupted Turkish rule for twenty years, the blink of an eye, before he went back to living with the *polis* who had kept a kind of order since 1845. Yet there were now a modern hotel, European tourists and a Turkish nation-state, all of which might pass away, leaving old men in *sharwals* whose sons would work the land as they and their fathers had. Or would the land and the sea which had always provided the peasants' and fishermen's bounty be turned over forever to package holidays for the fair-skinned Goths and Gauls who, in centuries past, had been unable to hold them by force of arms?

The sun was nearly setting when I reached the fields outside Arsuz. I had walked along the coast road and then up footpaths through the meadows, some of wheat, others of grass where sheep and goats were grazing. The foothills seemed to hold back a few clouds, leaving the sky near the sea an undisturbed mingling of red and blue, slowly giving way to blackness. Cut into the hillsides were level plots of earth upon which stood small houses, which from a distance looked adobe, the colour of the exposed earth around them. As the sun receded on the horizon, peasants slowly made their way from the fields, carrying their tools. The men wore black *sharwals* or khaki trousers, and the women's long dresses trailed in the dust. Covered in sweat and dirt from a day's labour, they seemed almost the colour of the earth, the colour of the houses they were entering, the colour of the hard ground neither they nor their ancestors had ever escaped. And they were as silent as the crops under their feet.

It was dark when I returned to the hotel. Wedding guests were arriving. The men wore new suits, many with lapels too wide or trimmed in black or brown, and the women wore dresses of chiffon or imitation lace. Shoes were shined, hair combed back and hands scrubbed. Alawis had come from Arsuz and nearby villages for what would be three days of celebrations. Some were the farmers I had watched make their way home at sunset. In the dining-room, transformed for the night like the guests, more than a hundred people danced, clapped in time to the music or sat exhausted after twirling around the floor. They were doing village dances, like the *dabke* in Lebanon or *bouzouki* in Greece, with each dancer holding high the hand of another to form a large circle as everyone's feet kicked in unison to the music. Although the band was Western, with a drummer and synthesiser, its music was modern Oriental pop.

Outside, small children were playing on the beach and in the courtyard, chasing one another through the darkness. Some older children, boys and girls, stood by the windows and stared inside. As the evening wore on, more people retired to the chairs at the edge of the room, some of the oldest dozing contentedly. In the middle of the circle of dancers were the bride and groom, each with dark, curly hair and a little overweight, swaying to the rhythm. She was still in her white bridal dress, and he wore an ill-fitting white suit. Men took turns in approaching the bride and showering her with money while she danced seductively alone. Little boys would dart up to her feet to pick up the 100 TL notes, which they would present to the newlyweds at the evening's end.

This was traditional village revelry, but the modern world was encroaching. A man was recording the evening on a video camera; the band had amplifiers and speakers, superfluous in a room so small; the men wore Western suits, the women shop dresses, costume jewellery and fur coats. A grocer's son had married the daughter of the village sheikh. Arsuz's richest Alawi family was now one with its most respected. These were signs of a new age, of growing wealth. Perhaps there were no more villagers, none of the peasants I had imagined at sunset, only the aspirant *petit bourgeoisie*.

The celebrations ended at midnight, when the band packed its drums and guitars, the video cameraman took down his lights, the waiters dismantled the tables and folded the chairs, and the families made their way home. Before dawn, most of them would be back in the fields.

In Alexandretta I had a lunch of grilled shrimps and a bottle of Efes near the port and then went to a photocopying shop. I had decided to photocopy all my notes and send them home in case something happened while I was travelling. The photocopying shop was on a corner, with picture windows on two sides and old calendars hanging on the walls. Inside, a man was photocopying documents and pages from books for the people queuing up. One of the five or six young men ahead of me in the queue turned and asked me in French whether I spoke French. He then asked where I was from, why I had come to Iskenderun and where I was going. It was not unusual, I had discovered, for strangers to ask the most personal questions. He said he was a French teacher from Istanbul. He asked me if I had read the Bible. He had read both the Bible and the Koran and had translated the Bible into Turkish. "From French?" I asked.

"Yes," he said. "It is a beautiful book."

I said nothing, assuming that he as a Muslim was complimenting a Christian on his faith's holy book.

He turned his back to the other young men in the queue and whispered, *"Je crois en Jésus."* (I believe in Jesus.)

I was startled and looked into his eyes. He was completely sincere. I had once met a so-called "Jew for Jesus" in Jerusalem and found him completely mad. The Jew for Jesus had followed me to my hotel, proselytising on the way, insisting the Temple in Jerusalem be rebuilt. When I asked why, he said matter-of-factly, "Because that will cause the end of the world." Had I now encountered a Muslim for Jesus? *"Vous êtes musulman, n'est-ce pas?"*

"Oui, je suis né musulman."

"Et vous croyez en Jésus comme prophète?"

"Non," he insisted. *"Je crois en Jésus."*

"Et Mohammed était un bon prophète," I said, helpfully.

"Non, Mohammed n'était pas prophète."

We talked a while longer, until each of us had completed his photocopying. He was on his way to Istanbul and I to Antioch, so we could not continue the conversation. He was the second Muslim convert to Christianity I had met in five days. In Antioch, I would learn of others, but I had no idea whether I had by chance met every Muslim turned Christian in Turkey or by an equal chance uncovered a trend. I decided to leave it to the anthropologists and missionaries, but I remembered Sir Steven Runciman's words to me before I left on my journey: "I think the Seljuk Turks might easily have become Christian. They had converted to Islam, but they were very easygoing. It seems surprising, but quite a lot of Seljuk Turks did become Christian from being Muslim. There was a certain amount of inter-marriage. If they had become Christian, you'd have had a new Byzantium." That was at the time of the Crusades. In the unlikely event of enough Turks becoming Christian now, the capital of the new united Europe might be Constantinople.

I found Mehmet Udimir in his library office, where the same ancient Mongol brought us tea. I tried to tell him that I'd had an interesting time in his tourism district and that I'd found people who spoke English and Arabic. *"Arabi?"* he said, his face lighting. *"Takellem Arabi?"* Do you speak Arabic?

Suddenly, we began a conversation. It was then he told me his name had been Mohammed Haj, that he had three sons and that he was an Alawi. He sounded pleased I was going on to Syria, where the president, a fellow Alawi, was "a very strong man." Next time I came to Alexandretta, he said, we would go to his house and drink *arak*.

It was Hind Koba's cousin, an interesting man who had studied at the American University of Beirut in the 1950s, who suggested that I see the French military cemetery before I left Alexandretta. Mr Philippi, or Philipioglu in Turkish, asked me, "If you are writing a book about the Levant, don't you want to see what is left of the only Army of the Levant?"

The taxi driver who was taking me to Antioch that evening did not know how to find the cemetery, but Mr Philippi had written directions in Turkish, which said it was near the *Belediye Ekmek Fabricase*, the Municipal Bread Factory. We drove to a large bakery on the outskirts of town, east of the main highway, and then a hundred yards along the side of a high wall to a monumental gate. A lintel above the gate, supported by three arches, was inscribed, *Cimetière Militaire Français*.

"I never knew this was here," the driver said as he stopped his old Ford.

The arch in the gate's centre was higher than those on the sides, which had their own, smaller inscriptions. On the left were the words, *Aux Morts de Syrie Cilicie*, and on the right, *1ère et 4ème Divisions de l'Armée du Levant*. We had reached the final resting place of the Army of the Levant, a small piece of a foreign field that would be forever France. It was as dismal and tragic as France's Levant adventure itself, an enterprise begun in the Crusades, rekindled when Leibniz urged his plan for an invasion of the Ottoman Empire on Louis XIV, dashed for a century after Napoleon's defeats in Palestine and Egypt, revived in the post-First World War occupation and flickering even then with a token force of paratroopers in Lebanon.

Within the high walls row upon row of stone crosses stood guard over marble slabs. As I walked slowly past each grave, reading the names of the officers and men, or the inscription to each *soldat inconnu*, a young man walked up behind me. Without disturbing the peace of the dead, he quietly told me in French he was the caretaker. His name was Salim, and he was twenty-one. His father had been caretaker for forty years before him. "*C'est territoire français,*" he said of the ground on which we stood. He told me there were 561 graves in all. He left me to pace the ranks, and, as I read the names and dates, I noticed something strange. All of them had died between 1919 and 1922, yet the First World War had ended between Turkey and the Allies in 1918. Enri Bonari, a corporal, had died on 17 February 1921. Auguste Boyer, also a corporal, had been killed on 21 July 1922. There was something even stranger, a spectre that kept cropping up: graves of members of the *Légion Arménienne* and the *Bataillon Assyro-Chaldéen*. Joseph Romechaud of the Armenian Legion died on 1 August 1919, and Gabriel Josim of the Assyro-Chaldean Battalion was killed on 29 March 1921. The Levant Army was a collection of local minorities, hired by the French to fight the Turks, when, after the war, the Allies, having taken Turkey's Arab provinces, launched a campaign to conquer Turkey itself. It was little wonder that, when the Army of the Levant left in 1939, most of the Armenians and Assyrian Christians fled with it.

Salim motioned to me to follow him to the south-east corner of the graveyard, where crescents rather than crosses stood above four tomb-stones. "*Musulmans*," he said. Two of them were simply *soldats français inconnus*, the third plaque had been painted over and was illegible, and the fourth, grave number 238, was marked, "Domani." He may have been a cook or camp-follower, a Gunga Din in the service of the invaders remembered only by the nickname his French masters had given him. He had died with the army he served, but there was no indication of when.

In the centre of the far wall, nearest the sea, was a large cupola supported on four sides by Islamic arches, a structure blending the Western neo-classical with the Oriental. Carved into the stonework was the memorial: A LA MEMOIRE DES MORTS POUR LA FRANCE EN SYRIE-CILICIE. On either side were monuments to the *Tirailleurs Algériéns, Tirailleurs Sénégalais, Zouaves de 3ème RM et 83 soldats inconnus*, who had come from all over the French Empire to give their lives for nothing. The dome was like a temple, hovering protectively above a long slab of stone on the ground. Decorated with nothing more than a simple cross, the slab had no inscription, nothing to reveal who lay beneath it. Salim whispered, "*Le Général.*"

The general and 561 of the men under his command stayed behind while the survivors, Christian and Muslim, French and native, retreated to other corners of the dying empire. The last detachment in Turkey of the *Armée du Levant* remained, buried, numbered and for the most part named and dated, on the only remnant of French territory in the eastern Mediterranean. They had fought and died near here, but there was nothing about their battles worth remembering. Their army had passed through, like so many before it, and left its dead beside a port town which took little notice of history's struggles. As we left them to begin our ascent of the Amanus Mountains, the sun was setting into the sea, extending a finger of dying red light through the darkness into the open tomb of the last commander of the Army of the Levant.

CHAPTER THREE

THE LAST OTTOMAN

"Everybody is Turk," the general said. He was speaking in English with a strong Turkish accent.

"Everybody?"

"Everybody," he repeated impatiently, "is Turk."

General Sami Oytun was the Turkish governor, or *vali*, of the last Arab province ruled, as almost all Arab provinces had been for four centuries, by Turks. He did not resemble the man in the large portrait behind his desk, the sophisticated and handsome, even dashing, man with blue eyes, dressed in white tie and tails, the familiar Moustafa Kemal Atatürk. Atatürk stared, as he did in one costume or another from walls in every government office in Turkey, over the shoulder of his vicar in the region he had forfeited but not forgotten for twenty years, Turkey's southernmost province of Hatay.

General Oytun was short, wore gold-framed spectacles and had hair, cut close where it grew at all, nearly the colour of his brown striped jacket and trousers. The civilian suit was the new uniform of Turkey's military rulers, and in it he might easily have been a small businessman or a brewer. A century earlier, his predecessor would have worn a red tarboosh, or fez, on his head and sported an imposing black moustache. He would have worn the uniform of an officer and ruled the province only long enough to make himself a rich man, before returning to a villa on the Bosphorus.

General Oytun was one of many retired military men rewarded since Turkey's latest *coup d'état* with sinecures in the provinces. Fifty years old, speaking softly but forcefully, General Oytun governed more than one million people in nine districts covering 5,000 square kilometres. His seat was an 18th-century Ottoman palace in the centre of Antioch. "Except for the court," a Turk explained, "he is responsible for everything."

"Syria claims this province –"

"This is not our problem," the governor interrupted.

"Does Syria do anything here about its claim?"

"You have seen that Syria puts Hatay on its tourist maps?"

"Yes."

"That is all it does."

On either side of the large door to his assistant's office hung large maps of Hatay, the map on the left plastic and multi-coloured, the one on the right in relief and painted green and brown. The relief map gave the better impression of the Amanus Mountains towering over the shore and the depression through them to Antioch. In all maps published in Syria, the border was drawn further north to include General Oytun's province, just as all Syrian maps called Israel Palestine.

"What are the percentages of Muslims, Christians and Jews?"

'Ninety-five per cent are Muslim."

"Sunni Muslim?"

"Of course," he said. When he pressed a buzzer under the top of his large oak desk, I feared the floor beneath my chair might open. It didn't.

"And the other five per cent?"

"They are Jews and Christian Orthodox." In response to the buzzer, an assistant came into the office, and the general asked him to bring us tea.

"Any Shiah Muslims?"

"No."

"Any Alawis?"

"No."

I looked across the governor's imposing desk and into his eyes. He was not a man to be contradicted.

"Everybody is Turk."

The assistant returned carrying the tea, two small, clear glasses on a silver tray. I took a sip. With an inch of sugar at the bottom, it was as sweet as treacle. The governor, who had apologised for his English, offered me one of his Turkish cigarettes and lit one himself. He told me to enjoy the tea and wait for an interpreter before we continued.

I had arrived the night before, driving through the dark over the Gates of Syria, the Bailan Pass. The sun had set behind us, and where the mountain road took a sharp turn to begin its descent, we saw the moon. It was a sudden, spectacular vision, the full moon larger than I had ever seen it, its light reflected in the flowing waters of the wide Orontes and shining on the fertile plain below. The moon cast shadows from the high mountains which protected both sides of the vast plateau extending south through Syria and Lebanon, where it was called the Bekaa, to the Red Sea, and then on to the Great Rift Valley in east Africa. Ours was the northern pass east to Aleppo, but there were others which, like steps holding a ladder together, had since antiquity joined vibrant seaports with inland trading cities – Latakia with Hama, Tripoli with Homs, Beirut with Damascus and Jaffa with Jerusalem. The passages had always been open for caravans, invaders and refugees travelling in either direction. The larger, more powerful inland cities had always dominated the coast, a fact of history ignored at their peril by the Crusaders in the Middle Ages and by the United States of America when it stationed US Marines in Beirut in defiance of Damascus in 1983.

We continued along Alexander's invasion route, guided by the moonlight. In the middle of the vast plain, straddling the overgrown riverbanks, lay the silent, ancient city of Antioch.

In the last century, the gates of the city were locked at night. Each quarter inside the walls had its own iron grilles locked shut by watchmen to keep marauders out. If I had arrived after dark in any century before this, I would have camped outside the walls. No one, whether native or foreign, would have travelled alone, and I could have had as many as fifty armed escorts for protection. In the morning, we would have requested permission to enter.

Luckier than an earlier generation of travellers or the first wave of Crusaders who laid siege to Antioch for months before massacring the Greeks, Armenians and Arabs inside I roamed undisturbed for hours on foot through the narrow, curving walkways that made up the streets of the old quarter. The ancient *Zenginler Mahalesi*, or Rich Quarter, had become the poor section long before my arrival. The place was deserted, and I wandered through an enchanting labyrinth of streets sometimes so narrow I could touch both sides at once, streets whose shade would keep the quarter cool on summer days and whose closeness would hold the heat of coal fires on winter nights.

The houses were arranged in winding terraces along narrow alleys. Overlooking the alleys were a few lighted windows, through which I could see huge armoires and large steel-frame beds. On the walls, painted in drab shades of green or grey, hung cheap calendars and posters, sometimes of Atatürk, more often of Sylvester Stallone. Most of the houses presented only a stone wall and closed door to the street, their windows opening onto central courtyards, with fountains and trees, flowers growing in rusted tin cans, tables and chairs for dining in warm weather, some with laundry strung on a line or children's toys scattered on the tiles. The doors of the various rooms of each house led, not to other rooms or to a hallway, but onto the courtyards. The enclosed garden was the heart of family life, open to the sky above, but closed to the world outside. Some of the houses had been divided into two or more dwellings, with makeshift walls across their once lovely gardens.

At one turning out of the Rich Quarter was the Hamman, or Turkish Bath, still open for late-night bathing. Beyond was a wider shopping street, where cars were parked in front of shabby restaurants and shops which in the morning would sell everything from meat to newspapers. At another turn was a wide avenue built during the French Mandate years and at its end a large plaza. There, behind an ornate wall, stood a two-storey stone structure with a grand arcade and beautiful arched windows, the imposing Ottoman palace of the Governorate of Hatay. The palace, like the houses and the courtyards, was dark, and only the dawn would reveal the life within.

Antioch was the most "oriental" city I had ever seen in the Levant, on this or any other journey. Poverty had no doubt spared it the attentions of property developers, who had wreaked such havoc on Beirut and Damascus. I went back to my hotel, the shabby Atahan Oteli, looking forward to the morning's exploring, and lay down to read the copy of A *Tale of Two Cities* I had bought in Alexandretta. "A solemn consideration," Dickens had written, "when I enter a great city by night, is that every one of those darkly clustered houses encloses its own secret; that every room in every one of them encloses its own secret; that every beating heart in the hundreds of thousands of breasts there, is, in some of its imaginings, a secret to the heart nearest it!

"Something of the awfulness, even of Death itself, is referable to this."

The governor's interpreter turned out to be a plump, dark-haired teacher named Ayfer Ozmen, who had a high-pitched voice and an unusual approach to translating between Turkish and English. Before she sat down on a couch, she coyly told me Ayfer meant "Moonlight". Two men in green military uniforms came in a moment after her. She explained they had an appointment with the governor, but would wait until we had finished. "The governor told me before you came that Hatay was easy to govern," I said. "Why is this?"

She spoke to him in Turkish, and he answered through her, "We don't have any terrorism in this area as it is in Europe. We have economic power, and the people of Hatay are hard-working."

"In the governor's experience, has he ever seen any conflict among the religious sects?"

"I don't understand what you are asking," she said.

"Any problems?"

She and the general exchanged some Turkish. "Thanks God, nothing happened. These two gentlemen," she said, indicating the two officers, "are in charge of security, and they agree too." The two men nodded without smiling.

"I understand the Catholics have been denied permission to say Mass at St Peter's Church."

"I don't understand."

I explained that in the ancient church, hewn into the rock outside Antioch, where St Peter the Apostle reputedly held services for the early Christians, the governor had forbidden the saying of Mass.

She translated, "He would like to explain that St Pierre Church is not a church. It is a museum now. At the regular churches, there are services now."

The general talked about Turkey's application to join the European Community. "There is an Atatürk's order," she said, "that says every time you will have contact with Western countries, it's nice." The general smiled at this, as she did. The security officers did not.

I asked about security problems. "Accidents are the main problems," she said, apparently translating the governor's reply. "They get the girls in an unlawful way, to get married. I mean, families don't agree, to let them take the girls to get married."

"Is that illegal?"

"Of course," she said, without reference to the governor, "it is illegal. This is done sometimes because the gentlemen who want to get married to the girls are not rich, they are poor. And we have the traditions, of course. The families want certain things from the bridegrooms. Since they cannot afford to buy them, they do this in this way."

"Do they go to prison?"

"If they struggle, if they fight, of course."

"Do you have sister killing, as in Lebanon, if a girl loses her virginity and her brother discovers it?"

"No," Miss Ozmen answered immediately. General Oytun, who understood the question, corrected her in Turkish. "He says, 'It's not so common, but we do have the problem.'"

For centuries, Levantine travellers have had to rely on translators, or dragomen as they were known from the Arabic word for translator, *turjuman*. Only those who had taken the trouble to learn Turkish were able to avoid my difficulties or the kind of scene described in his book *Eothen* by the English traveller Alexander Kinglake, who toured the Ottoman Empire in 1835. This is Kinglake's account of a typical meeting between the pasha, or local ruler, and the visiting *feringee*, or foreigner:

PASHA.– The Englishman is welcome; most blessed among hours is this, the hour of his coming.

DRAGOMAN (to the Traveller).– The Pasha pays you his compliments.

TRAVELLER.– Give him my best compliments in return, and say I'm delighted to have the honour of seeing him.

DRAGOMAN (to the Pasha).– His Lordship, this Englishman,

Lord of London, Scorner of Ireland, Suppressor of France, has quitted his governments, and left his enemies to breathe for a moment, and has crossed the broad waters in strict disguise, with a small but eternally faithful retinue of followers, in order that he might look upon the bright countenance of the Pasha among Pashas – the Pasha of the everlasting Pashalik of Karagholookoldour.

TRAVELLER (to his Dragoman). – What on earth have you been saying about London? The Pasha will be taking me for a mere Cockney. I wish to heaven that if you do say anything about me, you'd tell the simple truth!

DRAGOMAN. – [is silent].

PASHA. – What says the friendly Lord of London? is there aught that I can grant him within the Pashalik of Karagholookoldour?

DRAGOMAN (growing sulky and literal). – This friendly Englishman – this branch of Mudcombe, this head purveyor of Boughton-Soldborough – this possible policeman of Bedfordshire – is recounting his achievements and the number of his titles.

PASHA. – The end of his honours is more distant than the ends of the earth, and the catalogue of his glorious deeds is brighter than the firmament of heaven!

DRAGOMAN (to the traveller). – The Pasha congratulates your Excellency.

TRAVELLER. – The deuce he does! – but I want to get at his views in relation to the present state of the Ottoman empire. Tell him the Houses of Parliament have met, and that there has been a speech from the Throne pledging England to maintain the integrity of the Sultan's dominions.

DRAGOMAN (to the Pasha). – This branch of Mudcombe, this possible policeman of Bedfordshire, informs your Highness that in England the talking houses have met, and that the integrity of the Sultan's dominions has been assured for ever and ever by a speech from the velvet chair.

PASHA. – Wonderful chair! Wonderful houses! whirr! whirr! all by wheels; whiz! whiz! all by steam! – wonderful chair! wonderful houses! wonderful people! – whirr! whirr! all by wheels! – whizz! whizz! all by steam!

TRAVELLER (to the Dragoman). – What does the Pasha mean by that whizzing? he does not mean to say, does he, that our Government will ever abandon their pledges to the Sultan?

DRAGOMAN. – No, your excellency, but he says the English talk by wheels and steam.

TRAVELLER. – That's an exaggeration; but say that the English really have carried machinery to great perfection. Tell the Pasha (he'll be struck with that) that whenever we have any disturbances to put down, even at two or three hundred miles from London, we can send troops by the thousand to the scene of the action in a few hours.

DRAGOMAN (recovering his temper and freedom of speech).—His Excellency, this Lord of Mudcombe, observes to your Highness, that whenever the Irish, or the French, or the Indians rebel against the English, whole armies of soldiers and brigades of artillery are dropped into a mighty chasm called Euston Square, and, in the biting of a cartridge, they rise up again in Manchester, or Dublin, or Paris, or Delhi, and utterly exterminate the enemies of England from the face of the earth.

I asked general Oytun through Miss Ozmen whether he faced any problems with drugs. Apparently translating the governor's Turkish, she stated flatly, "We, as Turks, don't use them, as a nation."

"I meant, is there much smuggling of drugs through this area?"

She and the governor talked back and forth for a minute in Turkish. Then she said, "The main source of drugs is Lebanon. He would like to emphasise that. Syria supports it, because Syria makes money from it. The drugs are discovered especially from the sea, because they are passing by the sea on our coasts. In the last two years, four tons of drugs were discovered. A great many smugglers were arrested on their way to Italy and Germany."

"What were they smuggling?"

"I don't understand."

"Were they smuggling hashish or heroin?"

She asked the governor. "Heroin."

"Four tons of heroin?"

The security officers interrupted her, and a discussion began among the four of them. After a few minutes, she said, "It was the hashish . . ."

As I began to write down her answer, she added, ". . . which is made into heroin."

"Hashish is made into heroin?"

"Of course."

"I thought opium was the raw material of heroin."

She conferred again with the governor and his security chiefs. Finally, she answered, though I was not certain on whose behalf, "A special acid is used to convert the hashish into heroin."

The governor was smiling. He stood to escort Miss Ozmen and me out of his office through the main door opposite his desk. As we left, I saw him disappear with his security chiefs through a padded door next to the portrait of Atatürk.

DRAGOMAN.– The Pasha wishes your Excellency a pleasant journey.
So ends the visit.

CHAPTER FOUR

MINARETS AND BELFRIES

Ayfer Ozmen confessed she was not a professional interpreter, merely one of those called in by the governor's office for the rare English-speaking visitor. She had been a tourist guide and knew most of the sights in and around Antioch, so she compensated by kindly driving me to see St Peter's Church on Mount Silpius. We drove through Sanay, the industrial outskirts of Antioch, to the cultivated fields of the river plain and up the slopes of the mountain.

Scores of farmers in small trucks were blocking the road, unloading tobacco to sell at the government tobacco depot. The brown leaves had been cured, pressed and wrapped in burlap, ready at the roadside for government inspectors to value. Some of the farmers sat on top of their bundles, as expectant as actors waiting for applause at the conclusion of a performance. The fresh tobacco filled the air with a delicious, savoury aroma, and it was not unpleasant to enjoy the smell while we waited for the tobacco trucks to clear the road. When we finally passed the tobacco market, "Moonlight" Ozmen drove up the hill and turned into the small drive of St Peter's Church/Museum.

We walked up a steep flight of steps to a terrace. The gatekeeper waived the entry fee for Miss Ozmen, who was a sort of unofficial guide. I paid, and we stepped into the paved garden in front of St Peter's. Successive generations of Christians had added carved doors and a grand façade, like that of a Romanesque cathedral, to the little cave where St Peter had waited with his flock outside the pagan city of Antioch. It was a lovely sight, and "Moonlight" and I were alone enjoying it. We went inside to find a huge natural grotto. On the wall, the English version of a framed notice in several languages read:

St. Peter's Grotto

In the 29 to 40 AD period, after the death of Christ, when his Apostles went all over the world to teach his word, St Peter came to Antakya. The first meeting took place in this cave where you are standing. At that meeting, this group who then had no definite

name received the name of "Christian", meaning belonging to the
faith of Christ. Since the first meeting was in this place, it is said to be
the first Christian church. In the 12 or 13th century, with certain
additions to the front part of the place, the cave was made into a
church.

Water dripping from above had long ago destroyed the mosaics and
frescoes that once decorated the church. There were ten old benches
scattered about the grotto, which was nearly bare of ornament. An altar
stood near one wall, something which had surely not been there in St
Peter's time. Nearby, however, was a feature which had. "You see," Miss
Ozmen said, "there was a stone here over the entrance of this place, and
this was the tunnel. Since they were not powerful enough to fight the other
people, they were prepared to escape this way." I tried to climb up the
tunnel, bending low and crawling up steps cut by hand into the rock, but
the passage soon narrowed so that not even a child could have gone further.
When I backed outside, Miss Ozmen was waiting. "The tunnel was
destroyed," she said. "We have a lot of earthquakes."

Another framed notice, now superseded by the governor's order,
announced that the Roman Catholics said Mass there on the first Sunday
of every month at three o'clock. The governor had since reduced this
monthly dispensation to once a year. I supposed Antioch's Christians were
not powerful enough to resume weekly services any more than the
Emperor Julian, with the might of his legions, was able in the fourth
century to restore the old Roman gods to an Antioch which was the capital
of Syria and the third greatest city in his empire. By Julian the Apostate's
time, Christianity had taken too strong a hold. By ours, Islam was firmly
entrenched. If the Turkish state ever succeeded in supplanting Islam with
its national secularism, the mosques might well follow St Peter's in
becoming museums.

Stepping outside to admire the view of Antioch and the plain, I asked
Miss Ozmen the name of the district just below us.

"This part is called Habib an-Najjar, because the mountain is called
Mount Habib an-Najjar. We have a church, excuse me, a mosque that is
called Habib an-Najjar too. It is the name of one of the persons who is
regarded as a holy one, according to Muslims. It is a mythological story.
They killed Habib an-Najjar on this mountain. The body stayed here, and
the head rolled down the mountain."

"Where to? Can I see it from here?"

"No. It is impossible."

"Why?"

"It is eight kilometres far."

55

If eight kilometres seemed a long way for a head to roll, it was no less fantastic than the account of the Muslim chronicler Dimashki in which Habib an-Najjar walked for three days through Antioch with his head in his right hand proclaiming his love of God. Miss Ozmen took me down to the mosque of Habib an-Najjar in a crowded part of the old city. It was a lovely building of light polished stone, above a crypt which she said held the remains, head and all, of Habib an-Najjar. Outside in the courtyard, she asked a caretaker if we could see the crypt.

The caretaker pointed to his head and said something to Miss Ozmen. "Oh," she said. "I cannot go. I am a woman, and I have nothing to cover my head. You go."

The old man led me down stone steps which curved round and round a central column, like the stairs in a tower, until we neared the bottom. There he motioned me to stop. The basement was a foot deep in water. We had to stand on a plank above the water to look at the tomb. It was a small room, without inscriptions or symbols, only the plain stone sarcophagus. There was really nothing to see, but disappointment may well be the only consistent feature of sight-seeing.

When we arrived back upstairs, Miss Ozmen was talking to two old blind men. She introduced me to one of them, a man with a wispy beard and blank eyes. "Here is the muezzin," she said. "We call him muezzin, because he announces the prayer five times a day, according to the Muslims."

Recalling that some of Beirut's mosques played old records or cassettes of the muezzin's call, I asked, "Does he do all the singing himself or does he play a recording?"

"He does it very well. He doesn't live here. He has got a family, and he gets his salary from the government."

"From the government?" I asked, surprised that Atatürk's secular state subsidised the mosque.

"Of course."

"What time is the first prayer?"

Without asking the old man, she answered, "Ten minutes to five in the morning."

I asked, again hoping to start a conversation with the muezzin, who stood silently at her side, "He comes here that early every day?"

"No," she said, ignoring the old man. "He climbs the minaret five times a day. And we can watch from our windows to make sure he is doing his job."

I could not help but sympathise with the muezzin, standing here idly wondering what we were talking about, and climbing to the top of the minaret five times a day while Miss Ozmen watched from her window.

The muezzin said I could look inside the mosque. I took off my shoes and stepped inside, walking over the thick Persian carpets, trying not to disturb the men inside who prayed silent and prostrate facing the *mithrab*, a small niche in one wall indicating the direction for correct devotion. The *minbar*, a platform raised above the mosque like a pulpit from which the Friday sermon was delivered, was empty. In a far corner, near a long window, a small group of men sat talking quietly. The mosque had been not only a place of prayer, but of religious teaching and discussion, from Islam's earliest days. The only decorations, in keeping with the Prophet's prohibitions against representation of the human form, were the geometric patterns and calligraphy carved into the stonework.

"Do you come to the mosque?" I asked Miss Ozmen, when I had put my shoes back on in the courtyard.

"Usually, only the gentlemen come to the mosque. Ladies stay at home. On special occasions, we come to the mosque, but we pray in special places, specially behind gentlemen." The other, older blind man began to speak to her in Turkish. He was stooped over a long walking stick and wore the traditional *sharwal* and white skull cap of the religious man. "He is asking if you would like to see the tomb of Yahya," she explained.

"Yahya?"

"Yes," she said. "A follower of Issa, of Jesus."

The blind man led us to a small room. "I cannot go in without a headscarf," she said. "You can go in."

The bare room was only a few feet square, and I could see all of it from the courtyard outside. "This is a tomb of a follower of Jesus?" I asked.

"Of course."

While she was driving me to my hotel, Miss Ozmen lamented the decline of the tourist trade. "I used to guide many Americans here," she said, "but they are not coming any more."

"Why not?"

"Because of the Middle East situation."

"But Turkey is not affected by the Arab–Israeli war."

"They don't just come to see Turkey," she went on. "I used to receive tourists every day. In the seventies, we had seven cars together, sometimes ten cars, sometimes twenty-five cars, filled with tourists."

"I suppose," I said, "you might attract more tourists if you had a good hotel."

"Yes, Atahan Hotel is the best here."

"The Atahan is not very good."

She turned and looked at me. I feared a car accident or worse. "Not good, Atahan? Why don't you like it?" she asked, bitterness creeping into her high-pitched voice.

"I don't mind it, but it's just not a very good hotel."

"You've been to better hotels?"

The Greek Orthodox Church of Sts Peter and Paul lay at the end of a covered archway in the heart of the impoverished Rich Quarter. If a small piazza in front of the church had not set it apart, it would have been impossible to see its lovely columns and basilica, to know that in the midst of all the houses, winding alleys and courtyards, there was such a beautiful old church. The piazza was already empty; the people had gone home without the long chats common in other cities. Only two old men in dark suits remained on the porch, saying farewell in Arabic. One of them put on his hat and walked away, and the other went back into the church. I followed him inside.

In Arabic, he asked me, "Where are you from?"

"From America."

"From America!" he said, delighted. "Where did you learn Arabic?"

"I studied in Beirut."

"American? In Beirut?" he asked. Grabbing my ear and pulling hard, he added, "They will take you away. All the Americans in Beirut are taken away."

"It's a problem."

I said I had been to the church-turned-mosque and seen the tomb of Yahya.

"What Yahya?" he asked. "That is St John."

We walked around the church looking at the ikons. He said some were three or four hundred years old. All of them had the beauty of an older, simpler faith. "Many ikons are stolen," he said, holding up a large key. "I lock the church every day." He limped as he walked from ikon to ikon, and he realised I was looking at his left leg, which was badly twisted.

"Korea," he said. "I was shot in both legs."

I said, "*Haram*," the universal Arabic statement of sympathy, which literally means "forbidden," but implied pity.

"No," he laughed. "It was war."

"But it is *haram* that you went all the way from Antioch to a war in Korea with the Turkish army."

"It was for America," he explained, strangely proud. "Turkey was with America."

It seemed odd that a Syrian Christian would go from the far west to the far east of Asia to an American war, but his life was of a piece with that of his forefathers. Turkey had for centuries fought alongside other countries, invariably Christian, using non-Turkish levies. She had fought with the British in the Crimea in 1856 against the Russian Empire and, at the cost of her own empire, with the Germans against the British in 1917.

The Roman Catholic chapel of Saints Paul and Peter, though a short walk away, was nothing like the grand Orthodox Church of Saints Peter and Paul. The Orthodox worshipped in a vestige of Byzantium, when Christians ruled the city. The Catholics made do with a room reminiscent of the days when the Christian community was underground, as Saints Peter and Paul might have known it. I came to it, like a knight errant in quest of a myth, having heard from Christians in Alexandretta of its Italian pastor and a "holy woman" named Sister Barbara.

I walked there in the shade of the narrow alleys, uphill and past turquoise talismans, protection against the evil eye, hanging over closed doors. Women, heads covered in scarves, opened their doors to sweep house-dust out into the street or to call their children inside. Waifs, some barely dressed, ran up and down the steep streets shouting and playing, while men in old woollen trousers and heavy jackets trudged solemnly by. Near the top of the hill, the Rich Quarter gave way to a wide, shabby avenue. There I found the old house of the Azar family, prominent Christians who, when the Rich Quarter became poor, sold their house to the Catholic Church and moved to the suburbs.

The front door led through a short, dark vault to an open stone courtyard, surrounded on three sides by the house itself and on the fourth by the stone wall of the adjoining house. Each room opened onto the enclosure, which was shaded by fruit trees and had a gurgling fountain in its centre. At the far end was a kitchen, and on the sides the sleeping rooms and a bathroom. The chapel with home-made altar and several rows of pews was in what had been a modest sitting-room. This was the parish church and rectory of Father Roberto Ferrari, the only Catholic priest in Antioch.

"We had a real church in another area of Antioch," Father Ferrari said. His English was fluent, spoken with a delightful Italian accent. "Many years ago, a French Franciscan decided to use the Melkite church." The Melkites were the Greek rite of the Roman Catholic Church, one of many eastern rites in communion with Rome, like the Maronite, Assyrian, Armenian and Coptic Catholics. Each had its own liturgy, and most permitted married men to become priests. In Jerusalem, each sect guarded its territory and independence. In remote outposts like Antioch, where there were too few Catholics to matter, Latins and Melkites worshipped together.

"After we had been in the Melkite church for twenty-four years," Father Ferrari complained, "the Turkish governor here said, 'This church is not for the Latins. Please leave this area. If not, we will put your things in the street.' I delayed for ten years, but the Papal Nuncio in Ankara asked me not to make trouble."

Father Ferrari, who came from Perugia, belonged to the Capuchin order, a strict branch of the Franciscans. Sixty years old, he had been in Turkey since 1955, serving first at Trabzon on the Black Sea, and in 1973 came to Antioch. His whole body and face were thin, no spare flesh anywhere, a man whose life of denial had left a good nature and a sense of humour as its only extravagances. His thick white hair stuck straight up out of his head. He wore a V-neck jersey over a plaid wool shirt, old trousers, St Francis's sandals and thick spectacles. "There are one hundred Catholics here," he said. "No. I just baptised three babies, so there are 103." He laughed and invited me to have a cup of tea. He went to the kitchen to make the tea himself. I could see why.

While we were talking, I had noticed that a white-haired old woman in a black widow's dress with a brown cardigan was walking in and out of the various rooms, cleaning and carrying laundry. This was Nasra, whose name in Arabic meant "Nazarene." She looked disapprovingly at everything and everyone. For a few minutes, she fiddled with the curtains in one of the bedrooms, opening and closing them several times, looking unhappy whether they were drawn or not. She finally left them half-open and walked back into the courtyard. She swept insouciantly, casting occasional glances in our direction as if to say, why are those two sitting there? I would not have dared to ask her to make tea either.

When he sat down and poured me a glass of tea, I asked him, "Do you have many problems with the governor?"

"Sometimes," he said, smiling as though at a private joke. "Every time, questions, questions. One month ago, though, he gave us permission to say Mass at St Peter's on Christmas Day."

"The governor told me St Peter's was a museum."

"For almost two thousand years, it has been a church," he said. "It was a church until twenty-five years ago when the Turkish police took it." He sipped his tea and said, "Museum," shaking his head at the thought.

He told me Antioch had no Catholic school, so he taught catechism on Saturdays. Remembering Yalçin Kavak and the young man in the photocopy shop in Alexandretta, I asked him, "Do you have any converts?"

"Here it's a little difficult, because it is prohibited. We don't try to convert anyone. In Alexandretta, there are three young people who want to become Christians, but this is a problem for their families."

"Are there others?"

"Some years ago, a major in the army converted in secret."

"Why in secret?"

"He would have lost his job. There would have been problems with his family, and he would have lost his red, official passport."

He did not know of any Catholics in his parish who had become Muslims, though centuries ago most of them had.

A tall young woman with long brown hair walked into the courtyard. She was not pretty in a conventional sense, and the long sweater she wore did not conceal the fact she was overweight, like a jolly friar. There was however something distracted in her manner, an inner peace to her warm, German face, which made you want to be near her. Before the door from the alley slammed shut behind her, two small children ran in squealing and laughing. They tugged at her sweater, and she bent down to speak to them in Turkish. They nodded as she spoke, and one of them kissed her cheek. Then they walked meekly out of the door, like young lions tamed by Daniel.

At the age of eighteen, this young woman, Barbara Kallasch, had travelled by bicycle from her home in Wiesbaden to Israel, where she worked in a hospital and contracted hepatitis. She went to Jordan on what she had intended as a trip by land to India. Failing to obtain an Iraqi visa there, she went north to Syria and then to Antioch, where she planned to remain a year. She took a job in the Melkite church, helping by her presence there to keep it open and assisting pilgrims on their way south. She was now thirty-one years old and was organising local women to weave carpets. "Do you," I asked her, "have a vocation?"

"Yes, yes," Father Ferrari answered for her. "Like Mother Theresa."

"The Franciscans adopted me," she said. "I'm in the third order of St Francis."

"They call her Sister Barbara," Father Ferrari said.

"But you are not a nun?"

"The first time I came here for St Peter's Feast, a man took my picture and wrote in the newspaper that a nun from Germany was visiting. Since then, they have called me Sister Barbara."

"You have been here eleven years. Are you going to stay?"

"I always thought that if someone were here to take my place, I would leave. If you get to know the people here, they are very nice. It is also for the church I stay. My family want me back in Germany. My sisters came to visit. So has my parish priest."

"How do you spend your time?"

"Translations," she said. She spoke five languages, German, English, French, Italian and Turkish. "Also weaving. Helping people. Helping the church."

"What about the future? Would you like to get married?"

"You don't think about marriage when you work like this."

A Greek Orthodox priest walked into the courtyard. Dressed in black, with his black hat and beard, the Abuna Boulos, Arabic for "Father Paul," had come to offer his Holy Thursday greetings to Father Ferrari. As the two clerics shook hands and sat down for a cup of tea, I reflected that eight centuries had passed since the Great Schism between Rome and Orthodoxy. During that time, the Greek and Latin Churches had persecuted each other's adherents over obscure differences of doctrine and liturgy. The Catholic and Orthodox Patriarchs of Antioch had fled south to Syria and Lebanon, taking only their ancient title, "Patriarch of Antioch and the East," with them. They had left behind barely a thousand Christians with only two priests who could at last afford to practise ecumenical fraternity on the Feast of the Last Supper.

Just over the bridge in the new city was the repository of artefacts of the vibrant religion which predated both Christianity and Islam in Antioch. The Hatay Museum, built by the French in their final year of occupation, housed perhaps the best collection of Roman mosaics in the world. In spare, modern rooms and in a garden overlooking the River Orontes were hundreds of beautiful mosaics and statues. The colourful stone, whether carved into statues or broken into pieces for the mosaics, depicted a joyous, rapturous existence of gods, goddesses, heroes and nymphs in a lush, fertile land, the religion of the Hellenes taken over by the Roman conquerors. On wall after wall were depictions of Dionysus, in a chariot drawn triumphantly by two lions, drunkenly supporting himself on the shoulder of a handsome boy, even more drunkenly asleep or at the height of his powers chasing the luscious Ariadne. There were pictures of Zeus threatening with his axe in one hand and his lightning-bolts in the other, Zeus the eagle carrying off the beautiful Ganymede as his mother and father watched helplessly, Zeus the father of all. Perseus was freeing Andromeda, Echo was in love with Narcissus, who preferred his own reflection, and Apollo was seeking the ingenuous wood-nymph Daphne. Most of the mosaics came from the woodland retreat named for Daphne at Harbiye, a few miles outside Antioch. It was in Harbiye that Daphne was metamorphosed into a laurel tree while on her flight from Apollo's attentions. The mosaics had come to the museum, but the laurels grew there still.

In one room of the museum, where Agamemnon was sacrificing his daughter Iphigenia to Artemis and satyrs were struggling with hermaphrodites, a class of ten-year-old children listened attentively to their teacher, taking notes as she spoke in Turkish. The children wore black smocks, the boys' down to their waists and the girls' to the knees, over tattered jeans and cords. They were quiet when the teacher lectured, but, when she left them to inspect the works of art on their own, they frolicked playfully among the statuary of Greek heroes and the mosaics of forgotten deities.

Outside the museum, I heard the strains of a marching band similar to the triumphal music which had been playing outside the hotel on my first morning in Alexandretta. When I went out to look, the steps of the museum were crowded with people, as were the other corners of the square in front of the post office, the cinema and the grand Ottoman municipality building. The whole square was "stuffed" with people, as though it were one great outdoor *dolma*. Of Antioch's total population of 100,000, less than its number in antiquity, at least ten per cent were there in the heat of the afternoon sun, talking, laughing or humming along with the music. At a command, everyone in the crowd suddenly stopped and stood to attention. After a few seconds' quiet, the orchestra began to play the national anthem. It was a solemn moment, thousands of people standing motionless and silent. The anthem ended, and they began talking and relaxing again.

In the centre of the square, next to the large statue of Atatürk astride a horse, its forelegs high in the air as the father of the nation galloped into their lives, a platform had been erected. Both platform and statue were decorated with wreaths and flags. A nine-year-old boy ascended the dais and, to the applause of the crowd, recited a poem. He was followed by another young boy, who delivered a fiery speech. The only words I could understand in his soliloquy, which sounded at least as portentous as Mark Antony's funeral oration for Julius Caesar, were place names – Türkiye, Antakya, Alanya. It was stirring stuff, and from the appreciation of the crowd it was clear that rhetoric had not died in the city where rival sophists of the fourth century had perfected the art of argument. The boy's seemed to be the words which made men march to war.

Pressed against the door of the museum by the crowd, I asked a woman what was happening. She looked at me dismissively and said, *"Turizm Bayram."* So, Tourism Week had begun. How were the thousands of Turks gathered at the feet of Atatürk to know I was the only tourist in their midst? Did it matter?

AD MEMORIAM "II" BASILII NOVARIENSIS ORD. MINOR CAP. MISSIONARII APOSTOLICI/*Ob Zelum Dilatande Fidei* ANTIOCHIAE *Missionem Fundavit* ANNO MDCCCXLVI/*Ideoque Ibidem In Odium Fidei Catholicae Maridie Cultura Jugulutus est Anno Dni* MDCCLI–IV *Idus Maii AEtatis suae* XLVII/*Prope ha Sanctuarium exuviae ejus sepultae sunt.*

The marble tombstone lay for nearly a century over the grave of Father Basilio Novariensio, until the Christian cemetery had been destroyed. It had been moved from church to church, and its latest resting place was the wall in Father Ferrari's kitchen. In the small vaulted room, with its old stove and chopping-block, Father Ferrari was preparing dinner. I leaned against a counter-top, hoping to be invited to eat, and read the inscription on the tombstone. I asked the priest what had happened to his 19th-century predecessor.

"Padre Novariensio received some Orthodox young men into the Catholic Church," he said, chopping celery and onions as he spoke. "One night, some Turks came to the old church and found the sister in the kitchen. They asked her if they could see the church building. She found Padre Novariensio, who took them into the church."

"And then?"

Father Ferrari began slicing tomatoes. "Then, when he was standing with his back to them, they took a knife and slit his throat." He passed the knife across his own throat as he said it, then put the knife down next to the sliced tomatoes. "They left the knife on a window-ledge, and Padre Novariensio bled to death. When the nun found him, he was already dead."

"Who killed him?"

"No one was ever caught," he said. "It was believed at that time and now that the Orthodox families paid the murderers. *Povero Padre Novariensio.*"

Father Ferrari boiled water and began pouring the vegetables into the pot. "You like *zuppa*?" he asked.

Without my having noticed, Sister Barbara had come in and set an extra place at the table for me. Neither of them said anything about it. There was no sign of the old woman.

"Where is Nasra?" I asked.

"She has gone to the Orthodox church," Father Ferrari said, smiling mischievously.

"Is that funny?" I asked him.

"She's a Catholic. All the Catholics who think our church is too poor for them go to the Orthodox church. The new Christianity."

"Do any of the more humble Orthodox come to you?"

"Some of the younger ones," Barbara said. "The Orthodox say the Mass in Arabic, and many of the youngsters come here because they know only Turkish."

Earlier in the evening I had attended Mass, which Father Ferrari said in Turkish for a tiny congregation. The words of his sermon were Turkish, but his gestures were unmistakably Italian.

He poured us glasses of red wine and took slices of prosciutto from the refrigerator. "Presents from Italy," he explained. He laid the slices out on a plate, then prepared a salad and grilled pieces of chicken, all the while talking as though he were doing nothing at all. He clearly enjoyed cooking.

"Do you always cook?" I asked.

"No," he said. "I'm not always here. My parish is very large, all over Hatay."

"Usually, Nasra and I are alone," Barbara said.

"Nasra is out tonight, and I like cooking. So, I cook."

As we sat down to eat, the lights went out. The kitchen was suddenly dark, save for a hint of moonlight through the garden window. "Oh," Barbara said, "the electricity has gone again."

"Your electricity?"

"Antioch's electricity," she said. "It usually goes for only a few hours."

She and Father Ferrari began searching for candles. "Good thing we're in a church," I said, when they returned with nearly a dozen long wax candles which they placed in different corners of the kitchen and at the centre of the table. When all the candles were lit, the room seemed almost magical. The faces of the old priest and the young novice were transformed, deep shadows emphasising every feature, their hairlines, their eye-sockets, their mouths and noses all in contrasting shadows and the rich oranges of the candle light. Father Ferrari allowed me the honour of saying grace.

"Bless us, O Lord," I recited, "and these Thy gifts, which we are about to receive, from Thy bounty through Christ our Lord. Amen."

"I brought some of the candles," Barbara said, "from the front of the statues in the church. The little children in this quarter are afraid of the statues."

"Why?"

"Because their mothers tell them that if they are not good, the statues will come out of the church and get them."

We ate the prosciutto, and Father Ferrari ladled out his *zuppa* of pasta and assorted vegetables, which was delicious. We had begun eating the grilled chicken when Nasra returned from Mass. She sat down to eat, and Father Ferrari began to tease her in Turkish. Barbara gave me an instant translation.

"So, how was the Orthodox Mass?"

"It was fine," the old woman whispered, dipping into her soup.

"More people than at our Mass, I suppose?"

She nodded.

"It must have been wonderful for you," he said, a grin coming to his pixie's face in the candle light. "I suppose that all that power you had in the Orthodox church must have put our electricity out here."

Nasra ignored him, broke some bread and finished her *zuppa* in silence. Father Ferrari could not resist continuing. "Nice music, eh, in the Orthodox church?"

She poured herself a glass of water, sniffed at me as I listened to Barbara's translation and drank.

"Lots of candles, incense and ikons?"

She turned to him and stared. That ended the conversation.

After dinner, Father Ferrari gave us some oranges and made espresso. When he sat down to drink his coffee, he asked me, "I don't understand how you Americans can drink American coffee."

"You get used to it."

"I remember during the war, when the GIs brought their coffee to Italy. I couldn't believe it. They gave me some, light brown and watery in a big cup, and I just stared at it. 'Is this coffee,' I said, 'or *acqua spoca?*' "

I was pleased to be spending the feast of the Last Supper in good company with a meal cooked at home by an Italian priest. It was preferable to eating alone in a restaurant, the usual fate of the modern traveller.

In an earlier age, when hospitality was a normal part of life, most of my meals in the Levant would have been in rectories, monasteries or private houses. When hotels were rare or non-existent, the roads were perilous and travellers had yet to become tourists, hospitality was not a luxury. It was a necessity to be reciprocated. When the English traveller Robert Curzon toured the Levant in the 1833 and 1834, later producing a classic work of travel, *Visits to Monasteries in the Levant,* he often stayed in monasteries or at the houses of English consuls. Other foreign visitors stayed with local dignitaries or the nomadic tribes of the desert. It was over a breach of hospitality, when Paris stole the wife of his host Menelaus, that the Trojan War had been fought just north of here.

I walked home in the dark, through the narrow alleyways, down to my hotel. Through a gap in the rooftops, I caught sight of the moon. The electricity had just returned, but the pretty houses of the poor population of the Rich Quarter were dark. It was late, and I imagined all the little children afraid in their beds that the church statues would find them if they misbehaved. I reached the bottom of the Quarter at the Turkish bath and the closed butcher's shop, and turned into the dimly lit main street, where a few places were open selling grilled meat or coffee, and found my shabby hotel.

So much had happened between the time of the worship of Zeus, Hera and Dionysus, as preserved in the Hatay Museum, and the national secularism of *Pölis Bayram* and *Turizm Bayram* – the rise of Christianity and Islam, the rule of Byzantium, of Arabs, of Crusaders, of Mongols and of Ottomans; and the recurring nightmares of religion put to the use of the new conqueror, of religion dividing society and of religion as *casus belli*. The temples had become churches, the churches had become mosques or museums. Little islands of ancient hospitality, of true Christianity and of devout Islam remained, like strong trees after a storm, to shelter the weary traveller. So much had happened. Nothing had changed.

CHAPTER FIVE

NO-MAN'S-LAND

The old man had a long memory. "The French were bad colonialists," he said. "In the Ottoman Empire, all peoples – Turks and Arabs, Jews, Muslims and Christians – lived in peace. When France came, it wanted to make a quarrel between them. They made minorities into enemies. They brought a lot of Armenians from Syria. They made them into soldiers and gendarmes. When they left, they took all the Armenians to Lebanon. Twenty-five thousand Armenians emigrated. They divided Syria – Hatay, Alawis in Latakia, Christians in Lebanon, Druze in the south. However many communities there were, they divided."

He drew an imaginary map of the Levant with his index finger on the coffee-table, then pressed his finger down in the centre, near Beirut. "The quarrel in Lebanon is the result of French colonialism. Syria's problems too come from the seed of French colonialism. For four hundred years in the times of the Ottomans, there had been no problems with the Alawis. France gave them the idea of having their own state. In Syria, the Alawis are ten per cent. The French gave them the military and other key positions, to use the minority against the majority. All Syrians were merchants and farmers, but the Alawis had the key military posts. Now they rule Syria with their ten per cent."

Kemal Sehoglu was sixty-seven years old, a Turkish gentleman of the old school. A small, clean shaven, thin man with greying hair, he dressed comfortably in a turtle-neck sweater and tweed jacket. We were at his modern house on the banks of the Orontes in Antioch. He spoke softly in English, but was more comfortable in Turkish, French and Arabic. He suddenly switched to French.

"In the time of my youth, at the *lycée*, all the young men were opposed to the French occupation. It was our ideal to force them out. For all of us – Arab, Turk, Alawi, Sunni – passive resistance against French occupation went on for twenty years. All the people here wanted to annex to Turkey. There was the Arab minority which wanted to annex to Syria, but Syria had yet to become an independent state."

Like all Turks, he believed Hatay had always had a Turkish majority.

Arabs insisted they had been and remained in the majority. In Lebanon, Christians and Muslims made the same claims for their own communities. In the age of "majority rule", demography was one key to power. Under the Ottomans, there had been only the rulers and the ruled.

For a year after the 1938 referendum, Kemal Sehoglu explained, Turkey and France maintained a joint administration over the "Republic of Hatay." "Atatürk made Hatay *un pétit état idéal pour tout le Moyen Orient*. Because the state was a little artificial, they wanted to annex it to Turkey."

Kemal Sehoglu was a farmer, who employed Arab and Turkish workers on his lands in the Amiq Plain. We met on my first day in Antioch. His sons had recently returned from universities in North America. Abdallah, whose nickname was Aboush, was twenty- seven and had graduated in 1983 from McGill University in Montreal. Mehmet, whose name was Turkish for Mohammed, was twenty-four and had finished business studies at the University of Denver in 1986. Mehmet looked and sounded like an American, and he was finding it difficult to readjust to life in provincial Antioch. When I asked him how a young man like himself met young women, he answered, "You don't." Then he laughed and added, "You forget about it. If you do start seeing someone, you express your intentions."

"Have you expressed yours?"

"Not yet."

Both Sehoglu brothers wore blue jeans, Aboush with a corduroy jacket and Mehmet with a pullover. They had picked me up at my hotel, just after I had endured breakfast, and driven me along the river to their house. Built in the 1960s, it was modernist and square, like many houses built at that time on the coast of California. Inside, the ceilings were low and the main rooms adjoined in an open plan, with exposed steps leading upstairs and walls without skirting or cornice. Glass doors at the back faced the garden and the river. They offered me a drink, but I settled for coffee.

Aboush was the heavier, more determined and more conventional brother. He was engaged to be married, had chosen to stay in Antioch to learn the family business and to succeed his father when Kemal Sehoglu retired. Mehmet was uneasy. Younger, thinner, he had enjoyed America too much to be content in Antioch. He – not unlike myself at his age and since – had no idea where he wanted to go or what he wanted to do. His brother clearly hoped Mehmet would settle down and stay at home.

"We have a summer place in Arsuz," Aboush said. "A lot of people, let's say the rich, of this area go there. It's more comfortable. I mean, you can meet a lot of people, see girls in bikinis, everything. It's easier there. In town here, it's more difficult."

"Do most young people who go away to be educated find they want to leave Antioch?" I asked.

"Most of them don't come back at all," Aboush said, glancing at his younger brother. "People who go to college in Istanbul, especially girls, usually get married there and settle. If they can marry here, they stay."

"What is there to do at night here?"

"Nothing," Mehmet answered.

"Usually," Aboush said, "we get together with a few friends. We have a lot of business talks with my father. That's it. It's mostly business."

"No movies?"

"In the last five or six years, going to the cinema is almost nothing, because of the video business. Some ten years ago, Antioch was more interesting. We had a lot more concerts. In the early eighties we had some terrorism, and people were afraid to go out to public places. Also, in the last four or five years, they're not making good money in agriculture."

"Are you going to stay?"

"Yes," Aboush said firmly.

Mehmet said, "I don't know yet. After I graduated, I came back here for seven months. Then I went to the States for a few weeks, but didn't come back for nine months."

I asked them about their education in Turkey. They had gone to an American secondary boarding school in Tarsus. "The school textbooks here do not mention the Armenians," Aboush said. "There is nothing on the break-up of the Ottoman Empire. They go straight from the Ottoman Empire to Atatürk. They talk about Westernisation, but they don't teach Western ideas." He then told me what it was like to try to run a modern agricultural business in Hatay. "I went to a neighbouring province to discuss buying wheat from a farmer there. We had to sit outside on the ground. All the time we talked, the farmer had a rifle lying across his lap."

When their father came in, the differences between the generations in Antioch became apparent. Although the father and his sons were close and respected one another, the boys had no interest in or recollection of the Ottoman period. Kemal Sehoglu had spent time in Alawi villages, where he had learned Arabic. He had studied under the French Mandate and spoke good French. His sons spoke Turkish and English. The things he mentioned – the Armenians, the resistance to the French, the mixed communities of Turks and Arabs, the changes wrought by Atatürk – meant nothing to his sons. In the same way, Mehmet's anxieties about finding girls for casual relationships, discovering what he wanted to do with his life and deciding where to live, were alien to the father.

That night the Sehoglus took me to dinner at Antioch's City Club, whose members were landowners and businessmen, in a spartan 1960s building trimmed in Oriental gilt. The dining-room was full when we arrived, nearly a hundred men at different tables, all in suits and ties, eating European-style food and drinking wine. Almost all the men were middle-aged or older and wore moustaches. There was only one woman, who sat at a table for two with her husband.

Mehmet talked again and again about his life in the United States and his worry about the future. He didn't know whether to make films, work in journalism or television or go into business. All but the last meant leaving Antioch. Aboush talked about his fiancée, about settling down and, if the family business did well, moving it to Istanbul. A friend of theirs, who had joined us for dinner, had just completed his national service. When I mentioned a radio report that Turkey was blaming Syria for Kurdish attacks on military posts near the border, the friend said, "Don't believe it. Those Kurds come from Turkey, not from Syria or Iraq. The government here won't admit it, because they don't admit there are any Kurds here."

Whether or not the schools taught the young generation history, they would never escape its hold.

The grocer weighed each bag of vegetables in turn. He wrote the price of every item with a pencil on a crumpled bit of paper, the corn, beans, spinach, courgettes, aubergines, the flour, noodles and rice. He then added the figures on a pocket calculator. Not satisfied, he added them again by hand. This took even longer than that first calculation by machine. When his own arithmetic confirmed that of his calculator, he wrote the total. He could not have found a more time-consuming method, but on the barren stretch of road between Antioch and the Syrian border, he did not keep many customers waiting.

The driver loaded the bags of groceries into the back of his car, next to other provisions we had bought in town – razor-blades, soap, toothpaste, paper plates, a chess board and backgammon set. Sister Barbara and I sat in front next to the driver, a young man who lived near the chapel and hired out his battered old Mercedes from time to time. He turned the ignition key, pumped the accelerator, pulled the choke, swore under his breath and, after a short resistance, the car started. He put it into gear and drove onto the tarmac road, leaving the ramshackle grocery behind in a cloud of black smoke.

"I promised the children I would bring them news from their parents," Barbara said, "but they have no word yet."

The "children" were two Iranian refugees, boys aged eighteen and seventeen. They were living in the five-kilometre stretch of empty land between the Turkish and Syrian frontiers. Turkey used this border area to dump the people it did not want. Its other border posts, on the uncontested frontiers with Iraq, Iran, the Soviet Union, Bulgaria and Greece, lacked sufficiently large "no-man's-lands" into which to deport people. If those other states would not accept the deportees, they would have to return to Turkey. At Cilvegözü, the Turkish authorities could leave people indefinitely in a no-man's-land where the Syrians could not touch them, international aid agencies would not bother about them, and the world's press was unlikely to see them.

"Are you a journalist?" an English-speaking border official asked me suspiciously.

"No," I answered – truthfully in that I was not there in my capacity as a journalist, but as a travel writer.

Barbara negotiated with him in Turkish to permit us into the no-man's-land to see "the children". Our driver followed him in his official car through the border post, past the soldiers who guarded the gates that marked the end of Turkey. A dozen yards further on, at the left-hand side of the road, there was a small camp with a makeshift tepee of poles and plastic sheets, a wooden lean-to behind the tent, an abandoned rusting car with Syrian number plates and an open fire on which several men were boiling water in an old bucket. There were no trees and little other vegetation in the limestone hills. The place was, legally at least, nowhere.

When we stepped out of the car, I saw why Barbara had referred to the boys as "children". The two brothers ran up to her like expectant puppies, excited to see her and running around both of us, ignoring the provisions we had brought, grateful we were there at all. When Barbara showed them the groceries, they lifted them out of the car and led us to their camp.

Ernest and Antonio Panusi had been living there for fifty-six days. A year earlier, they had fled Iran for what they said was religious persecution against Christians and to avoid military service in the war against Iraq. They had walked over the mountains into Turkey, which at first permitted them to remain without passports in Istanbul pending a British visa. Because they had twice visited England and had a sponsor there, they felt they had a strong case for entry. The British Consul in Istanbul denied the visa, so the boys were sent to this no-man's-land. Their father and mother had gone to Ankara to find a country to accept their sons. "Now we are waiting," Ernest said.

Two weeks earlier, three young women from Dominica had been living in the camp. Although the border guard said the women were prostitutes, it seemed the most the "children" did with them was play frisbee. The women had been there three months before they finally left.

It seemed the population of no-man's-land was always in flux. When

Barbara had visited a few days before, there were Ernest, Antonio and a third young man from Iran, an Armenian. Now the three Iranians shared the camp with two Egyptians, a Bangladeshi and a Gambian. They were as ragged a group of men as I had ever seen, lost in international limbo until they could contrive a way out. While there, they begged food from people crossing the border, accepted bread from villagers and hoped people like Sister Barbara would come to their aid. I asked the border guard if there were always people living there.

"Usually always," he said.

"How do they usually get out?"

"If you don't have a passport, we can send you out of Turkey. The illegal people . . ."

"But, if you are here and you have no passport . . ."

"Yes."

"You don't stay here forever. You leave somehow. How do they usually go? Do they go to Syria?"

"Yes. They go over the mountain to Syria, because Syria doesn't have military people on the border. We have military people on the border. They cannot come back to Turkey, because we shoot them."

"How long do people usually stay here?"

"Usually one month, or fifteen days or whatever. If they know this area, they go easily. But if they don't know the area, and they have no passport, they wait until they get a passport. This is international land, not Turkey, not Syria."

Barbara explained that Christians like Ernest and Antonio sought the help of the Church. Others, she said, paid money to shepherds and smugglers to sneak them into Syria. Once inside Syria, they had to avoid the police until they could find their way to some other country.

"Do the Syrians dump people here too?' I asked the border guard.

"No," he answered.

"One day," Ernest told us, "the Syrian police came here, and they wrote down the names of all the people. But me and my brother, we didn't give our names. There was one Iraqi boy. I told him, 'Don't give your name.' But he gave his name to them. The next evening, the Syrians came back and took all the people whose names they had. They came again to take me and my brother by force, but we ran away. We don't want never to go to Syria."

"What happened to them?" I asked.

The border guard answered, "They took the three girls from Dominica to Syria. I think they went to Greece and then to their country. They were call-girls. The Syrians beat the Iraqi boy, because, you know, the Syrians don't like the Iraqis."

72

"The girls had passports?"

"Yes, but their visas expired," the guard said. "Are you sure you are not a journalist?"

"I came here with the Church."

The two Egyptians had been in prison near Izmir for twelve years. When they were released, the authorities gave them expired Egyptian passports. Because their passports were invalid, the authorities dropped them in the no-man's-land. "Why were you in prison?" I asked one of them, a wiry man in his middle age, who answered in fluent English with an American accent. "For hash, man. I was taking it from Lebanon to Italy." Then he whispered in my ear, so the border guard would not hear, "Can you believe it? For hash? These people are uncivilised." He said their families had expected them home a few days earlier. "They just took us from prison to here. They didn't give us a chance."

Turning to the Gambian, a short, thin man, I asked, "Why are you here?"

"I lost my passport at the bus station in Istanbul, and I reported it to the police." He showed me a receipt from the Istanbul police. "They took me to Ankara, and from Ankara they brought me here."

The Bangladeshi gave his details to Barbara, telling her his name was Mohammed Abdul Mosabbir. When I looked at his Bangladeshi passport, it said his name was Shirez Jul Islam. His only problem was that he needed $100, because the Syrian customs officials required all non-Arab visitors to change $100 in foreign currency before they could enter the country. Mohammed, or Shirez, had left Turkey legally, discovered he could not enter Syria without $100 and could not return to Turkey.

The Armenian from Iran was a thirty-five-year-old electrical engineer. He spoke no English, so Ernest translated from Farsi. "He says he is here because Iranians coming into Turkey do not need visas. The Iranians can stay three months. His three months finished three months ago. The police caught him and threw him here. He can go to Syria, but he needs $100."

"Does he want to return to Iran?"

"No. He says he wants to live as a free Christian. He wants to go to America or Europe. His sister and brother are in America."

"Are they American citizens?"

"No, but his sister has a green card. She lives in Los Angeles, but he does not have an address or phone number. Also, he says they would not let him bring his baggage here, which he left in Alexandretta."

"Where?"

"In a hotel."

"Which hotel?"

After conferring for a minute, Ernest answered, "An Iranian home."

"Where?"

"He does not know the address."

"Does he have the telephone number?"

"No."

Barbara and I took details of all the deportees, as well as letters from some to their families and embassies. We promised to contact their consuls, to bring them food and to let them know what we had been able to do. We believed that, when we returned, some of them would be gone. They would however be replaced by other victims of the absurd borders in a region which had done without them for centuries until the British and the French drew them across the map. As we walked to our car with their letters in hand, one of them shouted, "You are our only hope."

The many travellers who had preceded me in the Levant over the ages, from Ibn Jubayr in the twelfth century to Lawrence of Arabia in our own, had not had to contend with borders. They were free to go all the way from Alexandretta to Aqaba without a border formality, customs search or visa. In the post-colonial era, I would have to cross frontiers to go into Syria, into Lebanon, back into Syria, into Jordan, into Israel and back into Jordan, just to traverse a Levant that was less than six hundred miles long. And at each border, there were those who could not make it, because their papers were not in order, because they did not have enough money or because, unbeknownst to them, their governments had offended the regime in one of the countries they wished to enter.

A friend of mine who was crossing into Lebanon from Syria met an Armenian who found himself caught years before without the proper papers, unable to enter either country. By the time my friend met him, he had resigned himself to his fate, opening a small shop between the two countries selling coffee and sandwiches to travellers during their long waits for permission to cross. The absurdity of this has not been lost on the inhabitants of the region, whose grandparents remembered fondly the Ottoman days when they could go from Beirut to Jerusalem and up to Damascus without seeing a single border guard. The Syrian film maker, Doureid Lahham, made a movie entitled *Al-Haddoud*, "The Borders." Lahham, Syria's Woody Allen, wrote and directed the comedy, and starred in it as a taxi driver who plied his trade carrying passengers across the frontiers. The driver, who believed official doctrine about Pan-Arab unity, did not recognise the borders. He endured ludicrous confrontations with officialdom each time he crossed. His yellow taxi was painted with black lines like a net across it, representing the artificial divisions of a land which had been united until 1919. It was a funny film, which sadly was all too true.

When Sister Barbara and I returned to Antioch, we telephoned the embassies and consulates of the men in no-man's-land, none of which sounded surprised at the men's plight. We sent their letters to their families, and I notified the Red Cross and Amnesty International. I had a feeling though that, if they were ever to escape, they would have to rely on bribery or cunning.

On the morning I was to leave Antioch, the Sehoglu family invited me to their house for breakfast. It was early, and Mrs Sehoglu was sleeping in. Kemal Sehoglu, Aboush, Mehmet and I sat around the family dining table for an early morning feast of tea, eggs, goat cheese, fresh yohurt, olives, hot Turkish bread and orange juice, served by a young Arab girl who wore a tight, dark dress and a thick, gold necklace. Kemal Sehoglu and I discussed the reasons why there were no Arabic schools, books or newspapers in Hatay.

"You must remember," he advised me, "they do not teach Turkish in Syria or Bulgaria, where many Turks live. Perhaps ten per cent of Syrians are of Turkish origin, but they cannot study Turkish." He asked the girl in Arabic to give me more tea, telling me, "I learned Arabic in the villages, but I forget." He proceeded to speak to me in Arabic, slowly so I could understand much of it, for fifteen minutes.

The Sehoglus found a driver, who assured them he spoke Arabic, to take me to Samandag, near the Roman port of Seleucia Pieria. According to Aboush, Samandag was a disappointing attempt to create a tourist resort. Its beaches were covered in tar, and the only hotel had become a barracks. The main reason it failed, he said, was the opposition of local smugglers who thought tourism would inhibit their business activities. "There are also sharks," he added. I thanked the Sehoglus for their kindness to a stranger and gave Aboush a copy I had borrowed of *A History of Antioch in Syria from Seleucus to the Arab Conquest*. The book said that Mark Antony and Cleopatra came to Antioch in 37 BC and that Antony's gift to his Egyptian lover was all of Syria and Palestine, land that would be given to and taken from many people in the centuries that followed. Cleopatra lost it after six years. A map in the book showed an unbroken Roman road along the coast from Alexandretta into Palestine. In our time, the coast road ended in the brush just south of Arsuz. It began again at Samandag, and there were many borders between there and Sinai, at least one of them impassable.

As we drove out of Antioch, dark clouds crept over the mountains and rain began to pour. A few miles outside the city, the road to Samandag became a gravel path which wound through small farming villages and fields of barley. After nearly twenty miles of slow driving, during which I discovered the driver knew only a few words of Arabic, we approached the coast. There we found "Samandag, Pop. 27,300." Samandag was as ugly as the countryside was beautiful. The main road through the city, which we followed in the direction of signs pointing to the *Plaj*, was lined with petrol stations, garages, timber-mills and car parts shops separated at intervals by small orange groves and a bridge over a stream.

In the centre of Samandag, there stood another statue of Atatürk, this time in tails and cape. Larger than life, he was doffing his top hat with his right hand like a magician ready to produce a rabbit. Past the main square towards the beach were scores of new, single-storey houses, square and unornamented. The closer we came to the sea, the older the houses became, most of them red or white stucco cottages, a few with second storeys and small vine-covered terraces.

We reached the shabby seafront to find it much as Aboush had described. We could see neither the smugglers nor the sharks, but there were a few fishermen using dynamite, tar-covered sands and an abandoned, rusting motel. Waves washed the deserted beach, where a few small boats waited empty for fishermen to take them out. In the great campaign to resist the rising tide of tourism, Samandag was winning.

The Roman ruins of Seleucia Pieria were a few miles to the north at Cevlik, where the ancient foundations of stone piers stretched from the shore and disappeared in the surf. Here the Orontes flowed into the sea, its deposits over the centuries filling the ancient harbour so that, by the time the Arabs arrived in the seventh century, it was barely usable. Modern Cevlik was a dull seafront village with a few commercial buildings, a post-office shack and a camp ground near a new, little-used marina. I walked through a long passageway cut through the rock which the guide books said was a Roman aqueduct built by the Emperor Vespasian. Without water, it seemed more like a coastal defence which allowed soldiers to move without being seen from the sea.

Disappointed with Samandag, with Cevlik and with the ruins, I asked the driver to take me to the border. Rain was still coming down when we made our way back through Samandag. Suddenly, just beyond the town, a police car drove in front of us and ordered the driver to stop. When he got out to talk to the two uniformed policemen, I remained in the front seat of the car reading a book. I was still reading when one of the policemen tapped on my window.

He spoke to me in Turkish, but the only word I could understand was "passport." I handed him my passport, and he took it to his colleague in the police car who appeared to read my passport details over the radio. The driver and the two policemen resumed talking, and I went back to reading. About ten minutes later, another police car arrived. The officers inside were dressed somewhat differently from the first two. Perhaps they were more senior. They spoke for a little while to the other policemen, and one of them walked over to me. He spoke to me in Turkish, but I said nothing. He called the driver, who made a pretence of translating my Arabic into Turkish.

They went back to the two police cars, spoke on the radios and conferred among themselves. All of them looked solemn. I went back to reading. Another ten minutes or so passed, and I slowly became afraid that, for reasons I might never understand, I would be arrested in this lonely southeast corner of Turkey. The longer I waited, the more difficult it became to read. I stared at the pages, hoping the police inquiry would end quickly. A few more minutes and one of the policemen marched to my window. Would he arrest me for treading through Vespasian's aqueduct or venturing through the failed tourist resort of Samandag?

He tapped again on the window and reached into his pocket. I looked into his face, wondering what he meant to do. He stared back at me. Then he handed me my passport without saying a word. As we left Samandag, I relaxed.

I learned much later that after my departure the police in Antioch had interrogated some of the people who met me there. The same thing would happen in Syria.

It was early afternoon when we reached the riverside village of Cilvegözü, which gave its name to the border post. Cilvegözü was little more than a hamlet of small farmers, who derived additional income from the smuggling which began as soon as the border was laid next to it in 1939. In the late 1970s, most of the smuggling was of consumer goods from Syria into Turkey. With Syria's chronic shortages in the 1980s of foreign exchange and simple consumer items like cooking oil and washing powder, the traffic in household goods was going the other way.

The flow of drugs had also reversed itself. Before the opium eradication programme in Turkey and the outbreak of the Lebanese civil war in 1975, the drugs had gone from Turkey, often by truck, hidden in bags of cement, through Syria to Lebanon. In Lebanon, the opium was processed and exported by air, sea or land. The opium was now grown in Lebanon and sent through Syria and Turkey on its way to growing markets in Europe and America. Perhaps the destruction wreaked by the heroin repaid the West in some small part for the harm done by all the weapons it had poured into the Levant. Evil for evil. At night, for a price, a shepherd or farmer from Cilvegözü and other villages on both sides of the frontier would guide a smuggler over the mountains across a border which for them was little more than a source of profit.

For the traveller, the border crossing at Cilvegözü, like all the other border crossings in the Levant, was a nuisance designed to cause him maximum inconvenience. Cars were not allowed to carry passengers to the customs and immigration buildings, so young boys were waiting near the car park outside the border post to carry luggage. One of them wrested my two bags from me and carried them the hundred yards to the modern immigration post. Inside the tidy office, there was an orderly queue of only three men waiting to present their passports to the border policeman seated behind the counter. The policeman wrote down the details of each passport in a large ledger. He asked questions, wrote down answers and asked for other documentation, while each man in turn searched his pockets for the right bit of paper. Processing each traveller took fifteen minutes, and I waited patiently while other border policemen strolled nonchalantly behind the counter, apparently with nothing to do.

When my turn came, the policeman took my passport, looked at it and stood without saying a word. He walked to a telephone in another part of the room, spoke for several minutes, apparently making references in Turkish to my passport, and then returned to his desk. He noted all my passport details in his book and handed me the passport. This had taken twenty minutes. I walked out of the building wondering where to go next. My young porter tugged my sleeve, and I followed him to a tiny office nearby. He handed me several cards to fill in and led me to several more offices, in one of which my bags were searched. Several officials later, a policeman told me I was free to go. Go where? Without a car, it was nearly a five-mile walk through the no-man's-land to the Syrian border post at Bab al-Hawa. The boy picked up my bags and walked me to a small, blue Volkswagen van with most of the seats torn out. He threw the bags into the back, and I tipped him. Without his help, I have little doubt I would still be there.

While waiting for the van to fill with passengers, I took a radio out of my bag and heard on the BBC World Service a report on Turkey's application to join the European Community. "Turkish standards are ready for EEC standards," a Turkish official was saying. "Community membership will be a guarantee for democracy, as in Greece, Spain and Portugal." Mark Sykes would have agreed. Although his 1916 understanding with the Russians and the French, the Sykes–Picot Agreement, created the borders which still plagued the Levant, he believed the Turks would make good Europeans. He thought this more natural than any union of Turks and Arabs. In his account of a trek with dragoman, cook and six other servants through the then-borderless Ottoman Empire in 1902–3, *Dar-Ul-Islam: A Record of a Journey Through Ten of the Asiatic Provinces of Turkey*, the spokesman of the British Empire wrote:

In speech the Turks are expressionless, quiet and laconic, using few gestures or similes [*sic*]; but with Arabs it is almost possible to follow an argument while not comprehending a word of the language. I have heard a person, who could speak with authority, state there could never be an amalgamation between Turks and Arabs, and I think there is no doubt this is true. A Turk will understand an Englishman's character much sooner than he will an Arab's; the latter is so subtle in his reasoning, so quick-witted, so argumentative and so great a master of language that he leaves the stolid Osmanli amazed and dazed, comprehending nothing. The Turk is not, truth to tell, very brilliant as a rule, though very apt in assuming Western cultivation. This may sound extraordinary but is nevertheless true so far as my experience carries me. Every Turk I have met who has dwelt for a considerable period in any European country, although never losing his patriotism and deep love for his land, has become in manners, thoughts and habits an Englishman, a German or Frenchman. This leads one almost to suppose that Turks might be Europeanised by an educational process without any prejudicial result, for at present they have every quality of a ruling race except initiative, which is an essentially European quality.

Twelve years after he wrote these words, Mark Sykes and fellow servants of two other European empires, France and Czarist Russia, drew the modern boundaries of the Ottoman Empire without consulting a single Arab or Turk. This became known as the Sykes–Picot Agreement. Two years later, having heard from the leaders of the Arab Revolt, Sykes regretted what he had done. In October 1918, he wrote that Britain should "foster and revive Arab civilisation and promote Arab unity with a view of preparing them for ultimate independence." He was too late. Sykes died a few months later in Paris as the peace conference that would divide Syria began.

After half an hour's wait at Cilvegözü, two Syrian families on their way home managed to fill the van, and we paid the driver for what I had assumed would be a lift to the Syrian side. We passed a mosque on the left and, on the right, a statue of Atatürk bidding us farewell. The driver went all of a hundred yards, then stopped his van at the gate which marked the end of modern Turkish territory. There three soldiers in starched uniforms were standing at attention.

The driver told us to get out of the van and wait for a second vehicle to come from the Syrian side. I walked towards the refugee encampment, where the "children" and their friends were sitting around the fire. One of the soldiers refused to let me go any further, so they came over to me. I told Ernest and Antonio that Sister Barbara and Father Ferrari had spoken to their parents, who were staying at the Franciscan rectory in Ankara and were trying to find an embassy to give them a visa. The two brothers were still hopeful, telling me not to worry about them. Antonio said, "We'll see you in England."

I told the Egyptian we had mailed his letters and that the Egyptian Embassy said it would try to issue him a new passport. He complained that if he remained there much longer, he would ask to return to prison, where, "At least, I had a roof over my head." I told the Gambian that Hind Koba in Alexandretta, who as British Consul represented Gambian interests in Turkey, had promised me she would help him. He showed no reaction.

The English-speaking border guard who had been with us before suddenly walked up to me. "Did you do anything for them?" he asked, with what sounded like genuine concern for the deported men.

"Not enough," I said. "If their embassies don't help them, what will happen if they escape into Syria some night?"

"I don't know what will happen to them then."

I rejoined the two Syrian families, with their small children and their bundles of groceries which they hoped to smuggle home, and we boarded an old, rusting Syrian bus. I waved out of the window to the lost souls of No-Man's-Land, who waved back and shuffled through the dust to their camp. The driver collected our fares and started the five-mile journey through the stony foothills to the Syrian side. The last thing I saw before we rounded the bend was a large sign, which warned,

Yavu Yavu
Slowly Slowly
EXPLOSIONS

PART TWO

CHAPTER SIX

SIX-STAR BRANDY

At Bab al-Hawa, the Gate of Winds, all was confusion. The Syrian side of the border was dirtier and more run-down than the Turkish border post, and much more relaxed. It resembled nothing so much as a desert petrol station, where north- and south-bound cars stopped under an open concrete cover for a kind of servicing. All arriving foreigners had to change money, $100, at the official rate at the government exchange office to the right of the carport. Inside, German tourists grappled with exchange rates, wondering how many German marks they would need to buy $100 worth of Syrian pounds. The clerks filling out forms and changing money on the other side of a long table in the dark grey room were little help. I handed them $100, and they gave me, after much writing in triplicate, 975 Syrian Pounds (SL) and a form to prove I had changed the money at the official rate of 9.75 SL to the dollar, rather than the "tourist" rate of 22 SL from the banks inside Syria or the 40 SL available on the black market. I walked across the carport to the police post for an entry stamp. Ancient electric lamps hanging from the ceiling did not work, and the windows were too small to brighten the grey, concrete walls. More than a dozen people, Syrians, Turks and foreigners, stood in the filthy room awaiting entry and exit stamps, but no officials appeared behind the open counter.

The only decoration on the wall above the empty desks was a portrait I would see as often as I had seen Atatürk's in Turkey. The smiling, benign countenance of a man with parted dark hair and trimmed moustache turned up on desks, walls and windows in offices, hotels, restaurants and shops. It was pinned to sandbags at guard posts. It was imprinted on flags, drawn by hand on buildings and spray-painted through stencils on bridges and fences. In schools, children would draw the face in crayon and paste it up in their classrooms. The same face, though in profile, had appeared for a time on Syrian one-pound coins, withdrawn from circulation when devout Muslims complained that Islam forbade reproducing the human form. The same face sat on the shoulders of a hundred statues throughout the land, in town squares, at the side of the highways, in front of government buildings and army depots. In some pictures, the man wore a dark business suit, and his head was bare. In others, he had on a military uniform, his chest ablaze with medals and an air force general's cap on his head. The picture in the border post had been taken many years earlier in black and white, but in other pictures, in more important offices, the man aged through generations of likenesses, the quality of the photography and painting improved, the pictures grew in size, acquired electric backlighting and lavish gold frames. The face would appear as well every morning in the newspapers and every evening on the television news. In the Syrian Arab Republic, only the blind did not know the features of the air force general who had made himself president in 1970, Hafez al-Assad.

Waiting as I so often would for Syrian government officials to come to work or keep appointments, I studied Assad's picture. He seemed more like a trusted uncle than Big Brother. The thin, smiling face did not convey the ruthlessness he had shown his enemies on the occasions when his rule had been threatened. He had held power longer than any Syrian leader since the French army sailed home in 1946. From the time of its first military *coup d'état* in 1949, Syria had had eleven heads of state until Assad ended a terrible period of turmoil that saw thousands of people killed and taken into prisons. Yet not even he, who had ruled so long and maintained an army that spent most of his government's budget, could make border officials appear at their posts.

There was nowhere to sit on the public side of the counter, and those who wanted to leave or enter Syria stood patiently waiting for the border police, for the immigration cards, for the stamps in their passports that would let them in or out. After about fifteen minutes, two men in border police uniforms came in and sat at their desks. One picked up a telephone, and the other said to the crowd, *"Na'am,"* Yes. Several people began to shout in Arabic, asking for immigration cards to fill in. He threw a stack of cards on the counter, and we all grabbed at them, trying to fill them in as quickly as possible to be first in for a visa.

Two Americans trying to leave the country handed the policeman their passports and immigration cards. He handed the documents back and told them to see someone upstairs. Meanwhile, he laboriously wrote the passport details of each person in a large ledger, having some difficulty with the passports not in Arabic. After ten minutes, the two Americans returned, saying there was no one upstairs. I began translating for them. The policeman said they would have to wait. "For what?" I asked. "They just want to leave."

"Okay, okay," he said, putting the other passports to one side and processing their papers on the spot.

When my turn came, I was surprised to discover that the Ministry of Information's telex authorising my visa, a formality required for all writers and journalists, had actually arrived. In years past, entering Syria at Jdaideh from Lebanon and at Deraa from Jordan, I had had to wait hours, even overnight, sending messages to the Ministry by taxi, bribing officials for the use of a telephone to track down an official at home, all for a telex that had been promised before my departure. That the Ministry's message had reached Bab al-Hawa, a border post farther from Damascus than either Jdaideh or Deraa, was nothing short of miraculous. I thought, rather naïvely, that this boded well for the rest of the journey. More forms, more details taken down, payment of 24 SL for the visa, and I was stamped in.

I left to show my suitcases to the Customs officer, who spoke English. I showed him my American passport, and he asked what I had in my bags. I told him clothes, books and a typewriter. He said, fine. Unusually, he did not bother to open the bags and waved a cordial good-bye.

I walked about a hundred yards across a barren wasteland, near a row of freight company sheds, to the exit gate. A few taxis, painted yellow as all taxis in Syria had been by government decree a few years earlier, were parked beyond the barrier. I asked the driver of an old Mercedes to take me to Latakia. We discussed the fare, and he asked a policeman to raise the barrier so he could pick up my bags from Customs. Unlike in Turkey, the Syrian police had no objection. With the bags safely in the back seat, we started our drive south. A few miles down the road, the driver explained that Latakia was a long way, and he wanted to be back in his village near Bab al-Hawa before dark. I asked whether he would prefer to take me to Aleppo. We discussed this for some time, deciding to go to the Baron's Hotel in Aleppo. I believed the Baron's would be full for the Easter weekend, but I could have a cup of tea and a wash there, before taking another taxi to Latakia.

The driver took me through miles of open countryside, over treeless hills, past villages whose mud houses were shaped like beehives, past other villages made of cinder blocks, past fields now green in spring, past women in long, black dresses cutting grass by hand to feed their animals. Along the roadside, there were occasional *ad hoc* customs checks, armed, plain-clothes men in Land Rovers parked at intervals, stopping cars at random to make quick searches. Anyone with contraband cooking oil, soap powder or fruit that he had managed to smuggle in from Turkey was liable to a summary beating and to have his goods confiscated.

In less than an hour, we reached the outskirts of Aleppo, Syria's second largest city that had grown well beyond its historic boundaries over the previous thirty years. Tall stone apartment blocks surrounded the old city. Deforming a skyline of minarets and domes was a large, new, empty cube of a hotel. It had been rushed to completion for the Mediterranean Games due to take place there that September. According to the driver, it was the new Méridien, an opinion contradicted later by Aleppins who told me it was the new InterContinental. When it finally opened, it was neither a Méridien nor an InterContinental, but a Pullman.

We drove through the suburbs from the east towards the city centre, to an area called Bab al-Farraj, where a large statue of President Hafez al-Assad stood in the middle of a large plaza under construction. From the plaza, we turned right up Rue Baron to the Baron's Hotel. When it was built in 1909, the Baron's was on the outskirts of the city facing open countryside. Now, it was miles inside Aleppo, and the only trees nearby were in its own grounds. The Baron's was a pleasant change from the Atahan in Antioch. The Atahan, built in the 1950s, was part of a dull structure of shops and offices along a narrow shopping street. The Baron's had been built in the last, perhaps only, great age of Levantine hotels. When it opened, it had only one floor, with reception rooms at the front and bedrooms at the back. In 1911, a second floor was added, and some time later, a third. Made of large, finely cut stones, with Oriental designs carved into the stonework, it had gracefully arched windows and a wide terrace all around. The Baron's remained an old-fashioned hotel, with sitting-rooms for people to entertain guests, a dark lobby which was little more than an entryway to the bar, salons, dining-room and the large stone staircase up to the rooms. It was rather like a men's club, but for the occasional presence of women. "Everybody seems to have stayed at the Baron's," James Morris joked in his *Market of Seleucia* about his stay there in 1956, "from T. E. Lawrence to the Queen of Sheba, and it has some of the subdued self-assurance of one of the really great hotels."

Because of the Easter holiday, the hotel was fuller and livelier than I had ever seen it. The receptionist, an Armenian named Alishan, told me, much to my surprise, there was a room. "Only one room," he said. "Everyone is here from Damascus for the holiday."

Ahmed, the Baron's tall and amusing major-domo, carried my bags to a room at the back on the first floor. In the corner, the bedroom had windows on two sides, affording a fine view of two of the seediest night clubs in Aleppo, if not the world. "You stay long time, Mr Charles?" Ahmed asked.

"I don't know."

"You'll find some girls," he laughed, "then you stay."

Downstairs, I sat in the salon to the right of the front door. The room, last decorated forty or more years before, belonged to an earlier era. I would not have been surprised to see Noël Coward sitting at the upright piano against the wall. Thick curtains surrounded the high windows over the front terrace. Inside the wall opposite the windows, a glass case displayed mementos of the Baron's early days: photographs of the new hotel in 1911 with a horse and carriage in front, a copy of the bill for an English archaeologist named T. E. Lawrence, and a book of Lawrence's letters turned to a page with his return address as "Hotel Baron, Aleppo." On each wall hung a large French print in a flowery gold frame. Beneath the prints were captions like, *"Gentil Bernard Lisant Son Poème: L'Art d'Aimer"* and *"Cresset Composant Son Poème: Ververt."* Each print portrayed an idealised scene of French men and women frozen in time, their clothes, posture and composition speaking of another age, just as the well-dressed Syrians on sofas below the pictures belonged to an earlier era. If I had drawn a picture of the salon itself, I would have given it the caption, *"Des Familles Chrétiennes Chez Eux: L'Hôtel Baron."*

Two Christian families, apparently from Damascus, were receiving their Aleppo relations on sofas and chairs at opposite ends of the salon. Adults and children alike were speaking French. I sat reading *A Tale of Two Cities*, surreptitiously listening to one family say how lovely Jerusalem was when the older people had last seen it in 1966. That was before its conquest by Israel and its consequent inaccessibility to them. In the other family, one man was talking about Camille Chamoun, who had been president of Lebanon from 1952 to 1958, and how well he looked for his age. The adults drank tea and the children orange juice. Only the peeling paint, itself a symbol of faded grandeur, and a television, mercifully turned off, revealed the age in which we lived. The Baron's *belle époque* was over, locked inside the glass case in the wall.

When the families left, apparently to make their Good Friday visit to church, I put away my book and went outside for a walk. Arriving in Aleppo from Antioch on a Friday, the only official day off in Syria, was like entering another world. Antioch's streets were nearly empty, while Aleppo's on Fridays were so filled with humanity, mostly but not all male, that it was impossible to take a step without bumping into someone. Old mountain peasants in *sharwals*, peasants from the plain in *abaya*, poor workers in dirty, stained trousers, clerical workers in suits or wool trousers and sweaters, a few old city men wearing red tarbooshes on their heads and leaning heavily on their walking sticks. People made their way slowly, not through, but with, the crowd – pushing and bumping into one another without apology or offence as they went. Everywhere there were barrows with street vendors selling small items: sweets, lighters, matches, key-chains, worry beads, postcards, mostly useless but colourful bric à brac. The quiet dullness of Antioch gave way in Aleppo to the busy and bustling chaos of metropolitan life. Unlike Antioch, Aleppo had soldiers every-where – off duty, in uniform, milling among the crowd, many of the conscript country boys looking for excitement in the city, going into the cinemas playing Italian Westerns, Indian adventure films and Egyptian melodramas. Each cinema pasted scores of photographs from its weekly offering on billboards outside, each exposing as much womanly flesh as possible.

I walked past a large, open square with an Ottoman clock tower at its bottom, and up a road to the left. When I turned right into a cul-de-sac of Armenian gold shops on both sides, I found thousands of Christians making visits to the three churches – Armenian Orthodox, Maronite Catholic and Greek Catholic – at the end. The Maronite church was in the middle. To its right were the cloisters and courtyard of the Melkite, or Greek, church. The Armenian church lay down a covered passageway to the left. It was the custom in Aleppo on Good Friday for Christians to visit churches of all sects, an ecumenical gesture unknown in Jerusalem, where the competing claimants to Christ's sceptre were openly hostile to one another. This was one of the rare years on which the Catholic and Orthodox Easters fell on the same Sunday. I found myself caught in a mass of young and old men in suits and girls in frilly, Sunday dresses. All I could do was surrender myself to one of the currents in the stream of humanity, which, as it happened, was moving slowly towards the Maronite church. Around me, people of all ages were talking in Arabic or Armenian. The procession went through a door and up the right-hand aisle. We walked along the route of the Stations of the Cross, past pews filled with worshippers of all ages, under the bright lights of electric chandeliers overhead and hundreds of candles all around.

As we approached the main altar, I saw women behind the rail pick up pieces of cotton wool, dip them in warm oil and hand one to each person coming past. Most people handed the women a Syrian pound coin in return. Old women who received the cotton ball made a sign of the cross with it, rubbing the oil from the cotton into their foreheads. Some people would stop at a picture or statue of our Lord, or our Lady, or some saint, to say a short prayer. Many talked to friends they passed in the pews. We turned down the central aisle towards the main door, in front of which was a large table with priests and laymen who must have been elders of Aleppo's Maronite community. On the table was a small fortune in Syrian pounds, donations collected that day from the passing faithful. The men counted the notes before putting them in neat stacks. I recognised one of them as Anthony Akras, the bespectacled British consul. He introduced me to his teenage son and invited me to tea later at his house.

I eased my way back out into the crowd, into another current moving through the centre of the square towards the Melkite church. We walked into a lovely, almost Norman courtyard, whose spring flowers were in bloom. Through stone vaults and arches, columns and trees, the procession took me into its bosom and across the threshold of a church even more ornate than the Maronite. The scene was similar, thousands of people slowly winding their way past the Stations of the Cross and up to the altar. Here young and old women were again dipping cotton into the oil, but they wrapped each ball in a fresh green leaf before exchanging it for a pound coin from the faithful. As in the Maronite church, women blessed themselves with the sacramental cotton. In the Melkite church, priests were hearing confession in open boxes along the aisles. Contrite Greek Catholics knelt in supplication, seeking penance and forgiveness, while the priest sat inside, in full view of us all, behind the iron bars of the confessional door, looking strangely like an automatic fortune-teller in a cage at a penny arcade.

Outside, another current in the great river of Christianity took me along tiny cobbled streets, first in the open air, then under arches between the buildings on either side, and into cavern-like tunnels. The crowd was all around in the darkness. I was trapped, but there was nothing to fear. Some of the women never stopped talking, and I could see over the heads of most of the people so that, unlike the children half my height, I knew where we were headed. The route took us to the end of the tunnel into the heart of this Christian quarter with its sturdy, stone buildings and its closed Armenian shops. We entered the Armenian church. Again, there was the same close, crowded feel as in the other two churches, the same bright lights and candles, the same women at the altar dipping and handing out bits of holy cotton wool, the same priests and elders at the table collecting money. Like all Orthodox churches, this one was filled with ikons. People would touch them as though reaching for grace. An old woman in black stroked a portrait of St Theresa. She slowly pulled her hand back from the wood and kissed her fingertips where they had touched the portrait. Other old women were lighting candles and making the Orthodox sign of the Cross, right shoulder to left, and kneeling to pray.

The ritual visits to the different churches, enacted every Good Friday in Aleppo, were as much social as religious. Outside in the courtyard of the Maronite church, young men and women stood in clusters, slyly eyeing one another. Their parents were laughing and talking about the decorations, the flowers, the candles and the other people in the churches. Some of them agreed to meet on Easter Sunday. Above us on balconies on both sides of the street, over the jewellers' shops, young and old Armenian women gazed at the crowd below.

This was not the solemn Good Friday I was accustomed to in the West, or that I had seen in years past in Lebanon and Jerusalem. There was no formal church service after the visiting began at three o'clock. Nearly a quarter of Aleppo's million inhabitants were Christian, and most of them were Armenian. The large Christian minority gave Aleppo a cosmopolitan character lacking in other Syrian cities, even Damascus, with its larger population, its diplomatic corps and international business community. Because of their long history and minority status, the Christians of Aleppo tended to ignore sectarian differences, the only significant division among them being more national than religious, between the Armenians and the Arab Christians. That division was more social than political, based on the fact that most Armenians were twentieth-century refugees from Turkey, people whose Arabic was at best a second, and often a third or fourth, language. On Good Friday, even this distinction dissolved, as Catholic and Orthodox Arabs and Armenians went to one another's holy places to remember the Crucifixion, their Lord's sacrifice for them all.

Back at the Baron's Hotel, the manager, Armen Mazloumian, invited me to come on Easter Sunday for lunch with his family. Armen was the son of the hotel's owner, Krikor Mazloumian, and had spent his life working there. He survived by complaining, about the staff, about the clientele, about the handicaps the government imposed on hoteliers, about bureaucratic inefficiency, about the traffic, and about just about everything that came his way. Half-Armenian, half-English, he spoke both languages, and Arabic, perfectly. He was in his mid-thirties, had a brush moustache and usually wore woollen trousers and an open shirt, often with a bandanna tied around his neck. Besides the hotel, he had one passion in life: exploring the hundreds of Roman and Byzantine towns, the so-called Dead Cities, in the open country around Aleppo, the ancient Syrian civilisation that had flourished in the Orontes River Valley from Roman times until the Arab conquest.

That evening, Armen and I had dinner together in the empty hotel dining-room under an old photograph of President Assad, while a young Kurdish waiter named Jemal carried each course silently from the kitchen. "I thought the hotel was full," I said. "Where is everyone?"

"They all go out to dinner, with their families or to restaurants," Armen complained. "They don't spend their money here." Later, he said he would take me to see the Dead Cities, whenever I had time. "When are you going?" I asked him.

"I'm always going, at least three days a week."

After a meatless Good Friday dinner, Armen invited me to enjoy the first of many glasses of "Ararat, 6-Star Armenian Brandy". It went well with the Turkish coffee, and I would eventually come to agree with his father's pronouncement, "This is the finest brandy in the world."

In the morning, as I was going into the dining-room for breakfast, Alishan called me from the reception desk. "Do you need any other books to read?" he asked me. He opened a drawer in his desk and pulled out a dozen old paperbacks in English and French. I looked through them and took a worn copy of Jane Austen's *Pride and Prejudice*. He would not take any money, so I gave him *A Tale of Two Cities*, which I had just finished. He did accept money, however, for the old postcards of Aleppo he kept in another desk drawer.

In the dining-room, a European diplomat who was visiting from Turkey invited me to join him for breakfast. I asked him if he knew about the people living in the "No-Man's-Land." "They are the lucky ones," he said. "In the last six months, Turkey has sent at least five hundred Iranian refugees back to Iran. Some of them had already been guaranteed refugee status in Canada and Sweden. The Turks just sent back two Iranian pilots and the plane they escaped in two months ago. Now, the pilots will surely be executed and probably the others as well."

"What can you do about it?"

"I sent a report to my government. And I tell journalists like you."

"In other words, nothing."

"Nothing," he said. "That's the worst part. *Your* country gives money and arms to the Turks. Maybe America should do something. *You* should do something."

A tall building of the same stone as the hotel, the Mazloumian family's three-storey house lay just behind the hotel's rear terrace. The ground floor was nearly empty, a few old prints hanging on the walls and unused, covered furniture on the floor. On the first floor, Armen showed me what his father called the "antiquities room," its walls nearly hidden by the large photographs Armen had taken of the Dead Cities, wonderful pictures of the old churches, the tombs, the villas and summer houses of the last Romans to dwell in Syria. Over the years, he had created what was probably the largest photographic collection on earth of the ruins, of the same churches from different angles, dozens of villages at different times of the day, monasteries in all seasons.

We walked up to his parents' apartment on the second floor. He unlocked the front door, and suddenly I was back in England. We went through the foyer into the drawing-room of an English country house that might have belonged to a soldier or a diplomat, retired from a life's service in the East. Below a carved wood mantelpiece at the far end of the room, flames were devouring dry wood in the fireplace. Above the mantel hung an oil painting of a black spaniel. The wall to the left was a bookcase, containing hundreds of old volumes, many on the Levant, including early editions of Russell's 1756 *The Natural History of Aleppo*; an 1810 edition of Henry Maundrell's *A Journey from Aleppo to Jerusalem at Easter, 1697*; Richard Hakluyt's *The Principal Navigations, Voyages, Traffiques and Discoveries of the English Nation*; and *The Travels of Ibn Jubayr*. There were also the six volumes of Blackwell's edition of Churchill's memoirs, *Burke's Landed Gentry 1952* and bound editions of *Punch* from the 1930s. Facing the shelves was a large, upholstered couch, and stuffed chairs circled the fire. On tables and walls were family photographs of prosperous Armenian burghers in early twentieth-century Aleppo. There was one of the young Krikor Mazloumian and his English wife, Sally, a nurse at the Altounyan Hospital in Aleppo when they met in 1947. A pretty blonde, she looked like an actress playing a nurse in a World War Two movie. I saw how easily Armen's father must have fallen in love. There were pictures of their three daughters, who had married and left Syria, and of Armen as a boy. The long wall behind the couch had a large picture window, carved in dark wood as in an Elizabethan manor. Once it had presented a fine view of gardens, trees and the old city. All it revealed now was an ugly urban landscape of unfinished, bare concrete at the rear of new office blocks.

Armen led me past a baby grand piano, on which there were more family photographs, asked me to sit by the fire, and went to tell his mother and father we were there. Comfortably settled, listening to the crackle of the burning wood, I looked out of the window and tried to imagine the view before the new buildings had been erected. Again and again, while in Aleppo, I tended to see the city not as it was while I was there, but as it must have been before I was born, as Krikor Mazloumian and the other aged citizens of the city remembered it and painted it for me. I took *The Travels of Ibn Jubayr* from the shelf and looked up Aleppo in the index. On June 14, 1184, the Muslim year 580 AH, the Arab traveller wrote:

Aleppo is a town of eminent consequence, and in all ages its fame has flown high. The kings who have sought its hand in marriage are many, and its place in our souls is dear. How many battles has it provoked, and how many white blades have been drawn against it? Its fortress is renowned for its impregnability and, from far distance seen for its great height, is without like or match among castles. Because of its great strength, an assailant who wills it or feels he can seize it must turn aside. It is a massy pile, like a round table rising from the ground, with sides of hewn stone and erected with true and symmetrical proportions. Glory to Him who planned its design and arrangement, and conceived its shape and outline.

The town is as old as eternity, yet new although it has never ceased to be. Its days and years have been long, and the leaders and the commons have said their last farewell. These are the homes and abodes; but where are their ancient dwellers and those that came to them? Those are the palaces and courts, but where are the Hamdanid princes and their poets? All have passed away, but the time of this city is not yet. Oh city of wonder! It stays, but its kings depart; they perish, but its ruin is not yet decreed.

But for the intrusion of the new office blocks, I could have seen the citadel on the hill. The fortress was the most impressive in the Levant, one of few the Crusaders neither built nor conquered.

Ibn Jubayr believed in the legendary origins of the city's name, from a story of the Biblical prophet Abraham's stay there: "We say that amongst the honours of this castle is that, as we were told, it was in early days a hill whither Abraham the Friend (of God) – may God's blessings and protection enfold him and our Prophet – was wont to repair with some flocks he had, and there milk them and dispense the milk as alms. The place was therefore called Halab." The translator explained that the Arabic word *halab* meant "milk" and that Aleppo was a Europeanised version of Halab. Aleppo, like its southern rival Damascus, claimed the title of the "oldest continuously inhabited city in the world."

An aged, bald man walked slowly into the room. Wearing a green twill suit, leather waistcoat, checked shirt and striped tie, he looked like the lord of a Somerset manor on a Sunday stroll. "Looking at Ibn Jubayr, eh?" he asked. "What will you drink? Brandy?"

Krikor Mazloumian was in his eighties and had gone blind in one eye. The other eye, Armen had told me, was under severe inter-ocular pressure, causing him constant pain. His voice was as rich and deep as any younger, healthier man's. In English, he sounded British; Austrian friends told me his German was so fluent they took him for a Bavarian, and he was equally at home in French, Armenian, Arabic and Turkish. He poured tumblers full of Armenian brandy for both of us and sat down in the large chair that was obviously reserved for him. Although his style, the furnishings of his house and his manner of speech were English, his real passion was Armenia. "You Americans," he said, dismissively, "are so blind about ideology that you won't understand Armenia. All we want is a place for our culture and our national life to breathe."

"Is it breathing in the Soviet Union?" I asked him. (This was before the riots in Nagorno-Karabakh and the Armenian earthquake.)

"As never before. It is thriving. The churches are full. The music and language are flourishing."

Sally Mazloumian came into the room with Armen. A robust woman in late middle age, younger than her husband, she had developed along the lines set in that photograph from the 1940s: her bobbed blonde hair was greying and longer; her fresh, healthy face had grown warm and friendly, the ingenuousness had become maternal with the years. She introduced herself and asked me to call her Sally, which I did, and her husband Koko, which I could not. She put some pistachios, called *fistu halabi* or "Aleppo nuts" in Arabic, on a table for us and told us to sit down. When her husband was talking, she would occasionally, without a word, put some drops in his eye. She was still, forty years on, the devoted nurse Krikor Mazloumian had married the year after the French army left Syria.

The Mazloumian family were comparatively recent arrivals in Syria, though they preceded most of Aleppo's other Armenians. "My grandfather came to Aleppo in 1882, to settle here. Before that, he had been through Aleppo on his way to Jerusalem on pilgrimage. Because of persecutions in our own village in Turkish Armenia, he decided to move to this . . . developing metropolis of the Ottoman Empire. Trade was very good, because Aleppo supplied the whole of south-eastern Anatolia with goods. So my grandfather decided to come and settle in Aleppo."

"What was his business?"

"He opened the very first hotel in Aleppo. He called it the Hotel Ararat. It was in the bazaars. Until then, travellers had been lodged in bare rooms in the upper floor of the *khans* – caravanserais – where they threw their own mattresses onto the floor, slept and cooked in the same room, and washed around the well in the courtyard. In my grandfather's hotel, there was a proper bed, an iron bedstead, and a bedside table, candlestick, washbasin, all the sort of elementary 'mod cons' of those days, and a restaurant, which was also patronised by rich merchants of the town. My father and my uncle grew up in that very cosmopolitan atmosphere, because all the guests in my grandfather's hotel were foreigners. When they reached maturity, each one with the help of their father opened hotels with rather pompous names in the modern quarters of the town. One was called the Azizieh Palace Hotel. The other was the Aleppo Palace Hotel. They had about a dozen or so rooms each and a restaurant. They did well. They charged one gold sovereign a day. Everything was so cheap. They then decided to get together and build a very modern hotel for those days, on the outskirts of the town."

"Why did they call it Baron's?" I had met Krikor Mazloumian on previous trips to Aleppo, but this was the first chance I had ever had to ask him about his family and the hotel they had run for eighty years.

"Because they had been addressed by the Armenian staff of the hotel as *Baron*," he said, pronouncing "Baron" in the French manner, the accent on the second syllable, "which in Armenian means Sir or Mister. My father's guests were intrigued, and they started calling my father and my uncle, Mr *Baron* or plain *Baron*. When the two brothers decided to build this hotel, they called it Baron's Hotel in the possessive, because by that time the name Baron had sort of stuck. It was quite a success from the very day of opening. The hotel flourished from 1911 to 1914."

From then, the hotel's story was linked to the fate of Syria and the Mazloumian family. "When the war was declared in 1914, the hotel was populated by either German generals, heads of German military missions like Leiman von Sanders, or commanders-in-chief like Jemal Pasha of Turkey. For all intents and purposes, it became part of the Turkish Army, although it was run along the lines of a hotel. We were exiled for a year and a half. And shortly after our return, the war ended. Our last guest in the hotel, for the last three months, was Moustafa Kemal Pasha, later known as Atatürk. He was the last man to leave the hotel when the Turks were retreating and the British were advancing. After the occupation of Aleppo, we had the visit of General Allenby for a day or two. I think the British occupation lasted six months or so. It was followed by King Feisal of Syria, whose tenure didn't even last that long. Very shortly afterwards, he was ousted by the French. The French army which occupied Syria kept it until 1946.

"In the 1930s, we had a period of calm and a period when tourism really flourished. We had famous guests in the hotel in the thirties, a lot of airmen, record-breakers, and what-have-you. Almost daily, we had private aeroplanes flying through Aleppo, eastbound, westbound. It was a period which in the history of the hotel is something you can look back upon with nostalgia. During the Second World War, we had the British occupation. Quite a number of very famous soldiers stayed with us: Auchinleck was one, Général Catroux. De Gaulle did not stay with us, but he had several meals in the hotel and addressed the crowds from our terrace. After that we had Syrian independence. Our last illustrious guest was our president, Hafez al-Assad." With that, history seemed to end, leaving only memory and the attempt to survive.

"The Baron's used to be on the Grand Tour. Everyone wrote about it. When did what you might call fashionable travellers stop coming to Syria?" I asked.

"It all stopped with World War Two. After the war, we had very few of those glamorous personalities – Gene Tunney, or the Lindberghs, or the Roosevelts, or royalty, quite a few royal families, the Swedish, the Danish, the British. Now the fashion has turned into mass tourism. It's groups coming in in hordes, and going out in hordes. It's no longer interesting from an innkeeper's point of view. It has none of the charm and attraction."

"Were there any interesting regulars?"

"We had one famous German archaeologist, Baron Max von Oppenheim. He spoke beautiful Parisian French. He was short and stocky. In the old days, it was the hallmark of archaeology to wear the sun-helmet. He'd been digging even before the First World War. In the thirties, old Baron Max used to come here in the middle of winter, even when it was snowing, and he wore his sun-helmet. He had a massive stick, which he moved around in the air to emphasise what he was saying. It was quite a menace if you happened to be in the way. Last time he was here, he was ninety-two. He got ill, and we went to see him in the Armenian hospital. When he came back, I heard the nurses complaining that every time they went near his bed, he pinched their bottoms. Oh, we also had a very courtly Armenian gentleman who used to come to our night club, when we had one. He had perfect manners, always impeccably dressed. He once admitted to me he was so polite that when he was about to make love to a young lady, he would ask, '*Madamemoiselle, permittez que je vous monte?*' " At this, he laughed.

"Did I hear the British used the hotel as their headquarters after the war?"

"After the First World War, yes."

"And they never paid their bill?"

He whispered his answer, as though he were embarrassed, "No, they did not. Anyway . . ."

"How was it during the Second World War?"

"Everything was hush-hush. There was a poster behind the bar of a large ear. In the middle of the ear was a swastika. Everyone was supposed to be careful. I remember we had a young woman staying with a man she said was her brother. She gave her name as Christine Granville, but she was Polish. He was an officer in Prince Victor's Own Regiment, whose motto was, 'From Kabul to Kandahar.' This was the regiment that dethroned his great-grandfather, the King of Afghanistan. He had a ring from Queen Victoria which said, 'From enemy to enemy, from friend to friend.' We used to go shooting great bustards, what you'd call wild turkeys, on the Raqqa road. Some time later, I had a letter from her asking me to send a Red Cross parcel to Hissam, this great grandson of the King of Afghanistan. He'd been made a prisoner of war in Italy. By the time I sent the Red Cross parcel, he'd already escaped. But he was recaptured."

"What happened to Christine Granville?"

"Years later, I read in *The Times* she'd been murdered by an Irishman. Then the story came out. She had run away from Poland to Hungary. She was to all intents and purposes a British agent in Hungary. She spent some time here, she went down to Palestine, she came back here, she went to Algeria. She was dropped in France, where she did great things, saving quite a few lives. Incidentally, she saved Xan Fielding's life." Xan Fielding, a legendary British irregular in the Second World War, had also stayed at the Baron's. "She refused jobs, like Lawrence of Arabia before, offered on the basis of her wartime work. Her last job was as stewardess on a cruise liner. She befriended an Irishman on board. He fell in love with her.

She was not in love with him. He shot her dead in a hotel in London."

Krikor Mazloumian turned the logs with a metal poker, reviving the fire. "I remember another night when a British officer here received an order to pick up a general from the Turkish border, put him up in the hotel for the night and take him down to Jerusalem. The officer met the general, who was in civilian clothes in accord with Turkish neutrality laws during the war, and brought him to the hotel. As he turned to leave, the officer told the general, 'The car will be ready at 8 tomorrow morning.' The general asked him,

'You mean, you're going to leave me alone tonight?'

'Any reason why I shouldn't?'

'Do you customarily leave *Wehrmacht* generals who are defecting to your side unguarded?' The officer then posted two sergeants outside his room until morning. That was what made the work interesting."

"Does it still have some moments?"

"No," Mazloumian said. He looked miserable. Reliving those happier years was the only relief from the pain in his eyes and the decay of the hotel.

As I left him, sitting by the fireplace, Sally was putting the drops into his eyes. As they dripped down his strong, weathered face, they looked almost like tears.

Although Krikor Mazloumian regretted the passing of his hotel's golden age, the Baron's still attracted its share of unusual characters. One evening, a man I met in the hotel bar told me proudly he was an Aleppo Jew, and said he often came to the hotel for a drink. He asked me, as so many Syrians did, that if I should mention him in my book, not to use his name. He thought there were less than a thousand Jews left in Aleppo, about five hundred fewer than the Jewish medieval traveller Rabbi Benjamin of Tudela had counted in 1165 AD, and a far smaller community than had lived in Aleppo before Israel came into being in 1948. "There are many more Jews in Damascus than here," I said.

"Yes, but we are much better."

"Is it difficult for Jews here, with the restrictions?"

"There are hardly any restrictions any more, but we Jews can't win, you know," he said. "The US Embassy gives us multiple-entry visas for America, easily, just because we're Jews. That sounds pretty good, doesn't it?"

"Better than being a Lebanese Shiite applying for an American visa," I said.

"But then, I get to JFK in New York. You know what the immigration officer said? He said I had to go back. He wouldn't let me in, because Syrians were undesirable."

At 10 a.m. on Easter Sunday, I returned to the cul-de-sac of the three churches. The square was nearly empty, much quieter than on Good Friday. At the Melkite Mass, a white marble chancel screen divided the altar from the small congregation. Cherubs' heads, flowers and religious symbols carved into the marble cast their shadows, outlining them sharply against the white. Above the altar partition, along its length from one wall to the other, was a row of ikons. Above each ikon was a white dove, and hanging from the beak of each dove was a white stone ball, like an egg, symbol this and every Easter of rebirth. Hanging from each ball was a brass sanctuary lamp, lit again now that Christ had left his tomb. Many of the ikons in the church represented St George, a favourite with Greek Catholics. Through an opening in the middle of the screen, the altar was visible, canopied and elaborate. The priest, as in the old Latin mass, faced the altar, his back to the people, singing the Mass, with old men near the altar singing the responses. They sang the liturgy like Latin Gregorian chants, *a capella*, and it was beautiful. When Mass ended, the bearded priest turned to bless us, and we filed out quietly.

At 11 a.m., the Maronite Mass nextdoor was a stark contrast: the building was much darker and larger. It had none of the painted columns and blue ornate mouldings of the more rococo Greeks. The congregation was larger, and no partition separated them from the altar. There was a canopy over the altar, but simpler than the Melkite, without the Greek's ornaments, in dark yellow stone like the church building itself. There were similarities as well: the priest faced the altar, and he sang without music. Most of the people received communion, kneeling at the altar rails as Catholics in the West used to. Everyone departed quietly, stopping to speak in low voices on the church steps outside.

The day's major liturgical event had been the 7 a.m. Mass at the Greek Orthodox cathedral. I had missed it, beginning as it did before my breakfast. One Catholic who went said the ceremony took three hours and was attended by hundreds of Orthodox and a few Catholics.

After the Maronite Mass, I went to the Mazloumians' house for an Easter Sunday drink. Just after I sat down with a small Armenian brandy in my hand, the real Easter Sunday visiting began. An old man who sold pianos was the first to arrive. Sally spoke to him in Armenian, offered him a chair and gave him a glass of brandy. She then left the room and returned with more visitors, a couple and their three beautiful daughters. The middle girl, a strikingly beautiful, dark haired child, was named Sevan after a lake in Armenia. The seven-year-old was nicknamed Mauke, Armenian for mouse, and she was surprisingly mouselike. Her response to every question was to put her hand over her mouth, giggle and hide behind one of her sisters. The girls' parents and the Mazloumians talked about their many trips to Armenia, friends they had in the capital, Erevan, and changes they had noticed there over the years.

Sally could not have been kinder to any of us, pouring brandy, bringing more nuts from the kitchen, speaking English to me, Armenian to her other guests, and making certain her husband had his eyedrops. Somehow, though, she seemed aloof and somewhat lonely. All the foreigners who were her friends in 1947 had left Aleppo, as had her daughters. It seemed that most of the other Englishwomen in Aleppo were married to Syrian Muslims, and they did not socialise outside their own houses and families.

Armen said the Armenians were the craftsmen of Aleppo. "There is an old saying in Aleppo," he said. "The Armenian makes, and the Muslim sells." He said an Aleppo Jew once told him, "God created the Jew with a head, the Armenian with hands and the Muslim with a prick." To Aleppo's Jews, he insisted, *goy* referred to Muslims, while Christians were *Ar-ririm*, "uncircumcised Gentiles." The Jews of Aleppo had another saying, "Don't trust the *goy*, even if he's in his grave." Armen considered himself an authority on all Aleppo's communities, the Jews, Christians, Armenians, Kurds, Arab Sunnis, Alawis, and he probably was. He met them all every day in his hotel.

As the afternoon wore on, the other guests left, and Krikor poured the three of us more brandy. He put a record of an Armenian Gregorian Mass on his phonograph, sat down and closed his aching eyes for a moment to listen. We talked about Aleppo, the Armenians who lived there and some of those who left. Krikor mentioned the book *In Aleppo Once*, by a mutual friend in London named Taqui Altounyan, about her illustrious family. Her grandfather was a physician who owned the hospital where Sally had come to work as a nurse after the Second World War. There had been terrible divisions in this talented family, because, as they said, the grandfather had left the grandmother for a younger woman. Ernest Altounyan, the son, who was also a doctor, never spoke to his father again. Ernest had served in the British army and had been a close friend of T. E. Lawrence. The Altounyans' hospital had closed by the 1950s, and no Altounyans remained in Aleppo.

Sally showed me the wedding gift the Altounyans had given her forty years before. It was a book, bound and painted by hand, with flowers drawn on many of the pages. In it were the names of forty years of guests of the family, rather than the hotel, for which there was another book. She asked me to sign, and I put my name there after pages on which I saw Patrick Leigh Fermor, Xan Fielding, David and Ruth Holden, Freya Stark and my old friend, Michael Adams. Almost every signature I mentioned, leafing through the book, brought a story from Krikor or Sally: the marriage at the British Consulate in Aleppo of Robert Stephens and Taqui Altounyan, the second marriage and scandal of the old Dr Altounyan, the murder of David Holden in Cairo.

"Who do you think did it, Charles?" Sally asked me. David Holden was the *Sunday Times* Middle East correspondent, who was murdered after taking a taxi from Cairo airport in 1977. The *Sunday Times*, when Lord Thomson owned it and Harold Evans was the editor, devoted its then considerable journalistic resources to an investigation, but the murder had yet to be solved. "We were told the journalists were ordered to stop their research, just as they were getting near the truth."

Two other prominent Levant hoteliers, Horatio and Valerie Vester of the American Colony Hotel in East Jerusalem, had also signed. "We haven't been able to visit them since 1967," Sally said. Israel conquered East Jerusalem in 1967, and since then no Syrian could legally go there.

"How is Michael Adams?" Krikor asked.

"He's fine. He lives in Devon and teaches at Exeter University," I said. "His sons have become journalists."

"I remember the night he showed up here from Beirut. He was the *Manchester Guardian*'s man there. It must have been twenty years ago, no, more. He was with two other journalists. They came up here. We had some brandy, and they were up all night."

Aleppo was a city of memories, where past and present mingled in the air like cigarette and pipe smoke over Armenian brandy in the fading afternoon light. It was never an imperial capital, and it suffered no sudden changes. It had decayed slowly and become like a beautiful actress, wearing her old jewels and hiding her wrinkles with make-up. Youth had gone, but the grandeur and dignity were unmistakable and indestructible.

Sally asked me to accompany her to the Anglican Easter service that evening. I said I had already been to Mass twice. "Oh, please," she said. "It will be very nice. It is about the only chance all the English wives here have to see one another."

"I'm a Catholic," I told her. "I've never been to a Protestant Easter service. I doubt they'd have me."

"It's beautiful," she said. "You would be very welcome. Anyway, it's in a Catholic chapel. It belongs to the Jesuits. I promise you'll like it." There was no Protestant church in Aleppo, but the Jesuits lent theirs to the Anglicans at Christmas and Easter when their vicar came up from Damascus.

In the evening, Armen drove his mother, his fiancée, whose name was Rubina, and me in his white 1958 Chevy Nomad station-wagon, more a tank than a car, to the Jesuit chapel for the Anglican service. Armen grunted when, as he dropped us off, I asked him whether he was coming in. "I'll pick you up when it's over," he said. Sally raised an eyebrow at her son and said to me, "Armen doesn't go to church." Armen drove off in the Aleppo traffic, and Sally led Rubina and me up the steps.

Inside the tiny modern chapel were about twenty women, most of them formidable English matrons, made more English and more formidable by long years in the East. The room was quiet, and the mood seemed solemn, though some of the women had come only for this rare occasion when they were able to see one another.

We sat in the back. I did not know what to expect. Behind me I saw Anthony Akras, a Catholic like myself, but here in his capacity as British Consul. He handed everyone a hymnal. The hymns would play an important part in the service to come.

The priest walked up to the altar. He was not the sort of Anglican vicar I had seen in England, with starched collar and National Health spectacles. He looked more like one of the "with-it" Catholic priests I had known in California twenty years earlier: bearded, thin, dressed in a long white designer cassock wrapped tightly at the waist. When he spoke, his words came out less as sermon than as a breathless rendition of "Listen with Mother."

"Today," he said, in an excited whisper, "we are going to sing these hymns. So, listen carefully. This is a very *special* day, as I'm sure you all know."

The matrons had no idea how special it was and were exchanging worried glances. The vicar began the service, which had some of the same formulae as the new Catholic vernacular Mass. He would interrupt the proceedings every few minutes to explain to the ladies what he was doing. Perhaps he assumed they had not been to church before. The service proceeded up to the Gospel, which he read from the *Good News Bible* with great enthusiasm, as though he were reading a children's story, a magical tale about a stone and a sepulchre that we had never heard before. The sermon or homily that followed was better still. He talked about birth, rebirth, love, life, children and lions. He went on about C. S. Lewis. Suddenly, he asked his wife, a thin young woman, to stand and read from *The Lion, the Witch and the Wardrobe*. This took about fifteen minutes, and the matrons were stunned. When his wife sat down again, the vicar beamed benevolently at her, like the host of a television talk show. When he pointed his open hand at her, I was afraid for a moment we would have to applaud. He then repeated the story in outline and slowly explained its message. I thought perhaps the repetition of the story of Aslan the lion was for the benefit of a four-year-old girl across the aisle from us, but she was falling asleep. The vicar's intonation never lost its sense of anticipation, as though he were perpetually on the verge of cutting a birthday cake.

"Now," he surprised us, "we are going to have a *special* treat. This is a precious gift which our community in Damascus has come to know and love *very* much." He paused. What could it be? Sally Mazloumian closed her eyes, as though she were trying to imagine herself somewhere else, probably at home by her warm fire. "We have," the vicar continued, "two young men from our Damascus community here with us tonight, and they are going to sing for us." He paused again. The women froze in panic. This was not the sort of Easter to which they had been accustomed in Scotland, Yorkshire or even the Home Counties.

Two well-dressed black men in their early twenties, who had earlier acted as ushers, walked from the back pew to the altar. "These two," the vicar, who may have missed his calling as a television impresario, "are James and Kwachie." The matrons around me increased the pace of their eyebrow-raising as the vicar, or "president," as the new prayer book called him, presented James and Kwachie. "They are from Africa, from *Zambia*. Isn't that right, James?" The young man on the right nodded. "And they are going to sing a special song they learned in their native land, at their church in *Africa*." His emphasis on the word implied that it was a strange and exotic fairyland inhabited only by monsters, princesses and vicars. "And this is a *special* song for Easter."

Without organ music, or music of any other kind, James and Kwachie began to swoon and sing on the altar step. The chorus of the song was, "There is a certain man, and Jesus is his name." The song was pleasant, and James and Kwachie swayed to the tune. On the second singing of the chorus, the two men clapped their hands with the rhythm. The vicar stepped into the aisle and called out, "Let's all clap." He began clapping his hands and stamping his feet, motioning to the matrons to do the same. The four-year-old girl woke up and buried her head in her mother's lap. Most of the women sat absolutely still. Too embarrassed to do anything else, a few women gently tapped their hands together.

When the service was over, and a bemused Anthony Akras had collected the hymn books, Sally whispered to me, "I promise I'll never force you to a Protestant service again."

A Lebanese "businessman" was staying in the hotel to rest from his work in Beirut. One evening on the terrace, he told me he owned a few illegal gambling shops in Hamra, a fashionable quarter of the Muslim, western half of Beirut. "I was a concert pianist," he told me, "but I could not make any money. So I opened a little place with pinball machines. When the war started, I added slot machines."

"Don't you have problems with the militias demanding extortion?" All the militias in west Beirut demanded "protection money" from businesses, particularly from bars and casinos.

"We pay. We pay Amal. We pay Hizballah. We pay the Druze, so no one bothers us much."

"I hear things are a bit quieter now that the Syrian army is back in west Beirut."

"It's much better now. Last year it was terrible. You couldn't do anything. Even the gangsters were afraid to go out at night. I know: I'm a gangster."

Early one evening, I returned to the hotel from a bookshop. Among the books I had bought was *The Golden Reign: The Story of my Friendship with Lawrence of Arabia* by Clare Sydney Smith, a woman who had known Lawrence when he was serving under her husband in the RAF. I went into Mr Mazloumian's tiny office, under the stairs and behind the switchboard, and sat down. I showed him the book.

"I've known most of his friends," Mr Mazloumian said. "I saw him here when I was a little boy. He was just a young archaeologist pacing on the terrace. His friends were Stirling, Ernest Altounyan . . . Now everyone claims to have known him. Do you know William Saroyan?"

"I know his books. I come from California."

"William Saroyan used to stay here when he visited Aleppo. He told me I should write my memoirs."

"Why didn't you?"

"I can't be bothered. Saroyan was a marvellous man. He loved Aleppo, and he stayed here a long time. Later, he came by ship to Latakieh. He met an Armenian there, who invited him home. Saroyan left a few hours later, and the Armenian then wrote a book about their friendship."

"You think it was like that for Lawrence."

"Obviously," he said. "Everyone wrote books about Lawrence. How many of them really knew him?"

"Did you know anything about him?"

"From all his real friends, it seems he was completely above board. He was an ascetic. He was an idealist. He was a bloody fool." Mazloumian was emphatic on the last point.

"Why a bloody fool?"

"He refused all honours, all awards," he said. "The more important thing was, he refused to play any role here after the war, because he was afraid the Arabs would think he had gone into the revolt for personal motives."

I wondered whether it would have made any difference, whether

Lawrence could have used the prestige of his war exploits to plead for justice in Syria. The French and British had ignored both their promises to their Arab allies and the wishes of the American President Woodrow Wilson in their post-war haste to carve Syria between themselves. They could afford to ignore a young officer who had gone native.

Mr Mazloumian invited me back to the house for a drink. We sat by the fire, sipping Armenian brandy and recalling the spirits of Aleppo. Armen came in with a Swedish television crew, who had an appointment to interview his father for a film on Aleppo. I offered to leave, knowing how little most journalists and film-makers liked having their colleagues around while they conducted interviews. The Swedes kindly asked me to stay, so I moved out of their way and listened. I had already heard most of the stories Mr Mazloumian was telling the Swedes, but they managed to elicit one I had missed. It was about his childhood in the First World War.

"Our family fled to Zahle, a beautiful village in the Bekaa Valley, rather than be taken to Mosul. At that time, Mosul meant certain death for all the Armenians moved there by the Turks. In Zahle, I became very ill with typhus. I had a high fever. The one who stayed by my bedside was my grandmother. I remember hearing her pray to God for the life of this little boy. She offered her own life if I lived. And that is exactly what happened."

CHAPTER SEVEN

WHERE ARMIES FAILED

At a desolate crossroads about five miles north of Aleppo, Armen
Mazloumian and I visited a stone monument known as *Qabr Inglizieh*, the
English Tomb. Armen had put me in the Chevy Nomad, fought the
Aleppo traffic, damned everyone who got in his way, and taken me to the
site of the final battle in the Levant of the First World War. The encounter
between British and Ottoman imperial troops was more of a skirmish, but
Britain had left there a three-sided pillar, twelve feet high, to commemorate the event. There was no mention of this battle in Lawrence's
Seven Pillars of Wisdom, nor in the memoirs of other British officers who
fought in the Syrian campaign. It was not clear who, if anyone, won.
Atatürk's retreat, with his forces intact for the defence of Turkey,
succeeded. The British army conquered Syria. In that sense, both sides
won. The only losers were the Syrians, from Alexandretta to Aqaba, who
passed from the subjugation of one empire to two.

"Well, this is it," Armen said. "You wanted to see it." I paced around the
memorial, looking at each of its three faces in turn. One surface was bare
stone, but the other two had English inscriptions.

"ON THIS SITE WAS FOUGHT on October 26th 1918 between
15th Imperial Service Cavalry Brigade 5th Cavalry Division, Egyptian
Expeditionary Forces and THE TURKISH FORCES the last engagement in the Middle East of THE GREAT WAR 1914–1918."

From top to bottom on the other face were the words: "ROLL OF
THOSE WHO FELL IN THIS ENGAGEMENT OR THOSE
WHO DIED OF WOUNDS RECEIVED IN IT."

There followed the names of four British officers and seventeen Indian
soldiers, both Hindu and Muslim, of the Jodhpur and Kashmir Lancers.
Around the monument, a low fence of barbed wire had twisted and fallen
into decay. Within the wire, the English Tomb rose straight from the dust.
There was no marble plaza to accommodate the visitors who never came.
There were no flowers to commemorate the dead, and no one maintained
the site. Weeds grew all around, and trucks drove past without slowing. A
steady wind blew the sand into our faces, a wind that over centuries would

wear the stone away, until first the words become illegible and then the stone itself eroded to formless rock to be taken to a museum and preserved under glass as a "monumental ornament, c. 1800–2000 AD." Yet the stone marked the location where the war which promised Syria its freedom came to an end. It marked the last spot where Mustafa Kemal, who would soon be called Atatürk, covered the retreat of his forces into what would become the Republic of Turkey. This was the site of the battle that sealed Syria's fate, placed borders across its hills, separated families one from the other and resulted in the wars, dispersals of peoples and tyrannies which have marked its twentieth-century history. This was where an empire, an empire four centuries old, had made its final stand. It was not an empire for which Armen, an Armenian whose kin had been murdered in the death-rattle of that empire, was likely to shed a tear.

One afternoon, we got into Armen's Chevy Nomad, which was always parked in a garage under the terrace in back of the hotel. He reversed, as he always did, down the drive and through the stone gateway that led to the busy street in front of the hotel, Rue Baron. There could not have been more than a millimetre of space between the car and the pillars on either side, but Armen never bothered to look and never scratched the car. As we backed into the traffic on the one-way street, a man who looked like a beggar approached Armen's side of the car. He put a grimy hand through the window, but Armen ignored him and continued to pull away. The man stayed with the car as Armen shifted into drive and moved forward with the traffic. We stopped at a red light with the other cars, and the man was still with us. Armen turned his head, regarded the man carefully and uttered a sound that was something between a bark and a growl. "Urrrghhaaaa," he roared at the man, who backed away, startled. The light changed, and we drove off. "That guy's always bothering me," Armen explained. "I keep throwing him out of the hotel, and he keeps coming back."

Armen took me around the low hills on Aleppo's edge, hills which had become suburbs. All the building was in stone, taken from nearby quarries. The stone architecture made Aleppo one of the prettiest cities in the Levant and one of the few whose twentieth-century houses and offices did not offend the eye. They blended with the older buildings, developing themes which had always been used by Muslim designers, the dome, the arch and the tower. Many had graceful terraces and balconies, and even the larger, fanciful houses under construction had charm.

"This is Aleppo University," Armen said, pointing out a rare complex of square, mostly glass structures. "It's not as good as Damascus University."

"Is Damascus University pretty good?"

"It's pretty bad."

Around the university were new stone villas in the Shahba and Omran Quarters, more of the gradual growth of Aleppo. We went on to Aleppo College, which was until 1967 an American high school. After the Arab–Israeli War in June of that year, and Syria's breaking of diplomatic relations with the United States, the school closed. The local Protestant community reopened it. We saw boys playing soccer on the football field, their parents watching from the sidelines as we parked nearby. All the former staff cottages were empty and derelict. "I've been in all these houses," Armen said. "I know all the teachers and missionaries who lived in them. It would break their hearts if they could see them now." As we walked past each bungalow, Armen named its former occupants. "This is where the Millers lived," he said. "Mr Miller was the last American head teacher." Armen seemed melancholy at the sight of the school falling into disrepair. In a way, it was symbolic of the old Aleppo into which he had been born, always declining, always decaying. The new additions, the quality of the new buildings, did not seem to compensate for the loss of the old way of life.

We drove to the modern Chahba Oasis Hotel, nothing more than a collection of mobile homes, each caravan white with orange trim. Even the so-called reception was a small, prefabricated hut. "This," said Armen, who was dissatisfied with the three-star rating the Tourism Ministry had awarded the grand old Baron's Hotel, "is the four-star hotel." The fourth star meant the Chahba could charge more, and the three stars kept the Baron's just poor enough to deprive it of money to reinvest in improvements. We drove past what looked like a large apartment building. "In the sixties," Armen said "that was the Montana Cabaret."

"What is it now?"

"A mosque."

Saad Qawakbi's family had prospered under the Ottomans, and fought on both sides during the First World War. Qawakbi, now in his early sixties, had served as President of Syria's Court of Appeals. As he drove me back to the hotel one evening after tea with his family, I mentioned how much lovelier Aleppo seemed to be than Damascus, because all its houses were of stone. "In Damascus, there is no stone. In Aleppo, we build with it, because it is available, not because people thought it was beautiful."

Further on, he pointed out his law offices in an imposing building near the public gardens. I asked him, "You use the French legal system here?"

"It's like France, but we don't have trial by jury."

"Why not?"

"It's not good. In Europe, the majority is against the jury system. It all began with the case of the *chevalier français*. He was killed by his wife. The jury set her free. The majority of the jury were women. There are many such stories. If you amass a jury, one soldier, one farmer, they don't know the law."

Law had played an important part in the life of Syria from the earliest times, when the Mesopotamians brought the Code of Hammurabi, the Romans later imposed the Lex Romana and the Arabs introduced the Shariah Law of Islam. Different schools of legal philosophy inhabited different quarters of the great Muslim cities, and legal debates took place in the mosques. A teacher of Islamic philosophy had once told me a story, that he said was true, of a Muslim judge or *qadi* presiding at a trial. After hearing all the evidence, the *qadi* was considering his verdict. He noticed the defendant was laughing. "Why are *you* laughing" the *qadi* asked him, "when it is *my* soul that hangs in the balance?"

A lawyer I met later in Damascus told me the government had begun dismissing high court judges who decided against it. There were no juries. Who could trust a soldier or a farmer to deliver a fair decision when souls hung in the balance and lawyers appointed by politicians were so much more reliable? And when even the judges appointed by the president himself to the highest court failed to bring in the required verdict, what was a government to do?

That evening Armen took me to a little sandwich shop near the hotel. It looked like an empty pharmacy, but Armen assured me it had the best sandwiches in Aleppo. Armen had ordered the sandwiches in advance by telephone, telling me the man took a long time preparing his food. When we arrived a half hour after the call, the sandwiches were just being toasted. The man wrapped the sandwiches, small French loaves with meat and spices inside, in paper and handed several to us. "Do you want a Maria or a Toschka?" Armen asked me.

"What do you mean?"

"Here," he said, "try the Toschka. There is a story that goes with these sandwiches." Without waiting to hear whether or not I wanted to hear the story, Armen told it. "There were two girls here who fled from Hungary during the 1956 revolution. One was named Toschka, and the other was Maria. They got jobs as dancers in the cabarets, you know, exotic dancers." His voice dropped an octave as he said the word "exotic." "Every night, after their show, they would go to Waness's restaurant for a snack. Toschka missed Hungary and told Waness that she wished she could have something to eat to remind her of Hungary. He promised her, 'Tomorrow, I'll have something special for you.' Okay, so, Toschka and Maria finished their cabaret act the next night and went to Waness for their snack. Waness gave her a sandwich of *sojok*, melted cheese and spices."

Sojok was a dark, hot Turkish sausage, which some Armenians said was Armenian. I was eating the Toschka as he spoke, and it was delicious.

"Toschka said the sandwich wasn't really like in Hungary, but she liked it. She asked him what he called it. Waness thought for a second and said, 'Toschka, for you.' Maria said she wanted a sandwich too, the same as Toschka's, but without cheese. This explains why, in every sandwich shop in Aleppo, you can order a Toschka and a Maria."

Armen bit into his Maria, chewing on the bread and *sojok*. "Not many people," he said, "know the true story. And if you write about it, don't get it wrong, like your friend from the *Chicago Tribune*."

Armen insisted he had told the same story to a correspondent from the *Chicago Tribune*. He assumed all journalists knew one another, so I was held at least partly responsible for the fact that readers in Chicago were under the mistaken impression that a Maria had cheese and a Toschka didn't.

Aleppo has the best and most extensive souqs in the Levant. They run for miles along cobbled walks, under the domes of stone roofs. Their only natural light comes from grilles overhead. They look like tunnels that had been excavated, not the man-made structure that had expanded west over the centuries from the Citadel to the Antioch Gate of the old city walls. Too narrow for cars, they seem to have remained unchanged, except for their roofs, from the time Ibn Jubayr saw them in the twelfth century:

> As for the town, it is massively built and wonderfully disposed, and
> of rare beauty, with large markets arranged in long adjacent rows so
> that you pass from one row of shops of one craft into that of
> another until you have gone through all the urban industries.
> These markets are all roofed with wood, so that their occupants
> enjoy an ample shade, and all hold the gaze from their beauty,
> and halt in wonder those who who are hurrying by.

When Ibn Batuta came to Aleppo from his native Morocco in the fourteenth century, he found the bazaar "unique for its beauty and grandeur." Six centuries on, the Aleppo souq had far more peasants, gypsies and bedouin, more Kurds, Turks and Armenians, a greater variety of peoples, than the bazaars I knew in Damascus, Jerusalem or Beirut. It remained more Ottoman, more a piece of a vast empire of diverse peoples, languages and religions, than a piece of a nation-state, limited officially to one people, one language, one faith. It breathed variety, heterodoxy, life.

Each of the thousands of shops inside the souq specialised in making or selling something, and similar shops were usually grouped in the same quarter: there would be a row of ropemakers along one corridor, goldsmiths in another, silversmiths, spice sellers, rug-merchants, carpenters, butchers, candlemakers. Each turn in the winding alleys brought with it new sights, new smells. Spices were on display in large, open burlap sacks: hundreds of pounds of fresh thyme, sesame, mint, crushed pepper, cardamom and cumin, ready to be scooped up with small shovels and weighed in brown paper bags. Carpenters made chairs, tables, desks and cabinets to order, and their souq was a constant whir of lathes and electric saws, the floors all around covered in sawdust. Some shops specialised in soap, often made of olive oil, shaped like bricks and sliced like bread, some varieties scented with lemon or thyme. Children crowded into the sweet shops, where fresh chocolates, sugar-coated nuts and coloured bonbons lay on open trays. The patisseries specialised in a variety of Arabic pastries, made of honey, flour and pistachios, some in layers, others wrapped in strings of dough as fine as vermicelli.

In the gold souqs, windows were ablaze with row upon row of bracelets, necklaces and rings, many in a finely woven mesh known as Aleppo gold. In the mornings, bedouin families would flock to the gold shops to buy jewellery for the women and girls. They would sit on stools in the shops, men, women and children, examining each piece carefully, trying gold rings on babies' fingers, putting necklaces on the wives. As secure wealth, gold had been better to the bedouin than the always devaluing Syrian pound. In the early evenings, I would see old bedouin women, perhaps widowed, coming to sell the necklaces, rings and earrings that their fathers or husbands had given them years before.

In one corner of the souq, not far from the Citadel, an old man sat in front of his shop. On his head he wore a red tarboosh, or fez, the traditional hat of Syria's urban middle and upper class. A tarboosh maker, he seemed to do just enough business to keep alive. He said he was the last of a trade that used to employ hundreds of people. He made all his tarbooshes to order, measuring each customer's head and fashioning a wood or metal mould to exactly the right size. With his mould stored in the shop, as he would leave his suit measurements with a tailor, the customer could order as many tarbooshes as he liked as they wore out over the years. Unlike suits, which might expand with age, a man's tarboosh never changed.

Traditionally, the tarboosh had permitted the urban male of the Ottoman Empire to cover his head, but remain free to press his forehead to the floor in prayer. Its disappearance began in Turkey, where Atatürk banned it as part of his campaign to turn Turks into Europeans. Sir Steven Runciman had told me when I went to his house in Scotland before my journey to Syria, "I first arrived in Constantinople in 1924, but at that time women still wore veils. You still saw tarbooshes on every head, and camels crossing the bridge over the Gold Horn. I went back next in 1928. The veils had gone. The men were all wearing cloth caps instead of tarbooshes. And the camels were forbidden."

An amusing, irreverent American travel writer, Harry A. Franck, also noted in 1928, "The red tarboosh has as completely disappeared from Turkey as the dinosaur." Franck noticed that the Turks found it impossible to go bareheaded and difficult to wear European caps. "Even today, after two years of practice, something like six Turks out of ten, at least on the Asiatic and less sophisticated side of the Bosphorus, will be found with the vizor of the cap on the side of the head, or protecting the nape of the neck. Not entirely from ignorance, either: when a man has worn a fez for many generations, an awning over hitherto unshaded eyes may be annoying." He went on, "It is easy to imagine what the thousands of fez-makers in Turkey thought of the Head-dress by Decree. Most of them have gone to Syria, Palestine, Egypt, for few were adaptable enough to change their trade . . ." With the demise of the tarboosh south of Turkey, the fez-makers had nowhere to go – except possibly to America to work for the Shriners. The tarboosh and its craftsmen were going the way of the camel caravan, dying with the last generation born under the Ottomans.

Along most of the passageways of the Aleppo souqs, there were khans. These old caravanserais, or inns, were places for commercial travellers of centuries gone by to put up for the night with their escorts and their animals, where they would do their own cooking and sleep in their own blankets on the stone floor. In the hotel age, the khans had become warehouses and workshops. Near most of them were mosques, where I saw men washing before prayer.

Ritual washing was an important part of Islam, and keeping the body clean was a Syrian tradition predating the Romans. Before private plumbing put most of them out of business, Aleppo had hundreds of public baths. Only a few remained. One was the Hammam Yughul opposite the Citadel, an elaborate octagonal building in finely cut yellow stone where tourists were welcome, but where I found it impossible to enjoy a Turkish bath. It was afternoon, and the bath-keepers had turned off the steam. They let me undress and told me to wait in the bath for the water to heat up. I waited for about half an hour and gave up. I walked down to the Hammam Nahaseen, just opposite the old Venetian consulate in the Khan Nahaseen. The Hammam Nahaseen did not have the Tourism Ministry seal of approval that the Yughul proudly exhibited, but it had the advantage of working. From the souq above, I walked through an open door down stone steps to the large foyer. Around the green walls were divans, for resting after the baths, and in the centre of the room was a fountain with the soothing sound of running water. I left my clothes on a divan, and an old attendant led me into the baths. He turned a valve, and steam hissed out of pipes near the floor. Stone basins against the walls had taps for cold water. The main steam room was surrounded by small alcoves, like cloisters in a monastery. In one alcove, an old man with a short beard, and one closed eyelid where his eye used to be, waited to wash me. He told me to lie down, then scrubbed my skin raw with a glove that would take the grease off a frying pan. Then he washed the newly exposed layer of skin with a soft, hairy cloth. I went back into the steam room, sitting on a stone bench and sweating out all the Armenian brandy the Mazloumians had given me since I came to Aleppo. The masseur was away that day, they told me, so I could not have a massage. I rinsed myself with cold water from one of the basins, scooping it up with a tin bowl and pouring it over myself. I had been there nearly an hour, sweating and washing, before another old man wrapped me in towels and led me back to the divan in the foyer. He took the towels off me, and wrapped me again in fresh cloths.

I lay on the divan, resting, and a boy brought me tea. From the divan, I could see the feet of people treading the cobbles of the souqs above. When the muezzin called from a mosque nearby, several of the bath attendants set out their prayer rugs and prayed. I dressed, paid 55 SL and, feeling cleaner and far better than I had before, resumed my exploration of the souqs.

I went back through the covered souqs and out again to the fresh air at the western end of the markets. There I found the souq of the tomb-makers. In one yard, an old man and a young boy were working with hammers and chisels, carving names, epitaphs and verses from the Koran into marble and stone. Each one sat, quiet and intent, pounding rhythmically, tapping the words, letter by letter, by which we would know the dead. This was where the life of the souq ended, at its western edge, near the gate in the city walls that had long since come down.

Walking around the souqs to the wide road on the east side, facing the Citadel, I found a café and sat at one of several tables outside. A minute later, a young man sat down at another table. He was a study in white, white Wrangler jeans, white open shirt, white zip jacket, white tennis shoes; but from the neck up, he was dark: dark glasses, black hair slicked back and a dark stubble. When he turned to call a waiter, his jacket lifted a little to reveal a 9mm. pistol tucked into his belt. I took out my notebook and began to write about the souq. I included something about the man in white, who undoubtedly worked for one of Syria's many security bureaux. If he was following me, he would not be the last man in Syria to do so.

I looked for the waiter to order coffee when I noticed someone else and wrote in my notebook, "Strange, as I sit here writing, I turn around to look for the waiter to order coffee. What do I see at a table behind me? Another Western, middle-aged man writing. Perhaps he is writing the great Levantine travel book of the twentieth century. Who knows?" I wondered whether he saw the parade in front of the Citadel and jotted, as I did, "Four women, one very old. All with faces covered, three holding parcels wrapped in cloth on their heads. A man with his son perched on a bicycle. Yellow taxis rushing round the Citadel like traffic around L'Etoile in Paris. Men in suits or sweaters walking. Two teenage girls coming home from school: one with a white headscarf, the other with a dress over her school uniform and her face covered. Students wear military-style uniforms at school. Tiny children in brown smocks on their way home from school."

The ancient stone battlements of the Citadel, so well reinforced by the Ayyoubid prince Nur Ed-Din in the twelfth century, were giving way to earth and weeds. The moat was dry. The fortress that was Aleppo's refuge and defence for centuries had become a tourist attraction, closed on Tuesdays, where the Tourism Ministry was reconstructing what it called an "authentic Turkish bath." If I had been a medieval invader, I could not have taken it with ten thousand men. Its walls were too high to scale and too thick to penetrate with catapults. No wonder Ibn Jubayr had written at the height of its glory that "an assailant who wills it or feels he can seize it must turn aside." Like Aleppo herself, the Citadel had not adapted well to modern times. Aleppo had lost much of its purpose with the demise of the caravan, and the Citadel had become a mere decoration in the age of modern warfare.

On its parapet in electric lights, most of them broken, were the Arabic words, "Unity, Progress, Socialism." The Baath Party slogan rang hollow in Syrian ears that had heard them too often. Below the battlements, I watched a flock of goats, sure-footed on the stones, as they wandered up the great walls eating weeds. Where a hundred armies had failed, goats were succeeding.

CHAPTER EIGHT

A CONSULAR CITY

And say besides, that in Aleppo once,
Where a malignant and a turban'd Turk
Beat a Venetian and traduc'd the state,
I took him by the throat the uncircumcised dog,
And smote him thus. [The Moor stabs himself.]

Othello, Act V. Scene ii

Aleppo was the world's first consular city, in the modern sense of the word consul. Until the Ottoman Empire permitted Venice, and later France and England, to station diplomats in Aleppo in the sixteenth century, ambassadors represented their sovereigns only in the capital, at court. Aleppo, the first provincial city with diplomats who looked after their own resident and visiting nationals' interests, retained a certain pride in its consuls. Several Aleppo families carefully guarded their rights to act as honorary consuls for a variety of foreign countries, and the title "consul" still accorded some status to its holder.

The old Venetian consulate lay down one of the twisted alleyways of the souq, past the ropemakers and spice-vendors. I walked inside, through fortified wooden gates, as though into a castle, leaving behind me the darkness of the covered souqs for sunlight shining on an open courtyard. This was the Khan Nahaseen, or Nahas's Caravanserai, large stone vaults on three sides which had become, in the years since the death of the camel caravan, a workshop and warehouses. The consulate was above the caravanserai.

Christian Poche, nephew of the consulate's owner and last resident, Adolphe Poche, met me at the door. He looked like a retired teacher from France. He was thin, with just the impression of middle-age fat showing below the chin and above the belt, and had a full head of hair just going grey, a light moustache and no rings on his musician's hands. He had arrived recently in Aleppo, the city of his birth, from Paris, where he worked as a musicologist. He had returned because of the grave illness of his uncle, Adolphe. Adolphe Poche's only child was a daughter, and Christian had no sons. He was the last Poche in a long line of traders and consuls.

"When," I asked him, "was the house built?"

"I'll show you," he said. He led me along the hallway, which looked like the passage to a dungeon in a Spanish castle, and showed me the date carved into the wall. "1599." The date stone had been covered in glass. "The house is in two parts and has twenty-one rooms," he said, sounding like a bored tour guide who had said all this before. "In Aleppo, they spoke at that time three European languages: Catalan, Venetian and Genoan. This house was built as the consulate of Venice, the Serenissima Republic. After that, it became a Capuchin monastery, but not for long."

"How long was that?"

"Maybe one hundred years," he answered. "We have some papers from the Capuchins. After that, it again became the Venetian consulate. My great-grandfather came here from Austria. He settled in Aleppo, and he married the daughter of the last Venetian consul. I think that was in 1807."

The doorbell rang, and Christian Poche left me standing in the long corridor, with paintings and statues along both walls, a long Persian carpet on the floor and a low, vaulted ceiling. I was looking at an 18th-century portrait of a beautiful woman when Christian returned with two men.

"She was the last woman from the Serenissima Republic," he said. "With her are her professor of music and a Turkish servant. So, you have an idea what it was like here."

I already had some idea of the grand life in Aleppo of the old European consuls, whose families had over generations become Levantine, creatures half-Oriental, half-Occidental, hybrids of the eastern Mediterranean world. I had heard about it from Adolphe Poche, the last consul of the Austro-Hungarian Empire, on a previous visit to Aleppo. Now Poche was ill, dying, the last of the old, courtly school of Levantine diplomacy.

Christian Poche had with him M. Farid Jiha, a man whom I had met earlier at the Baron's and who offered to show me around Aleppo, and a French diplomat. The diplomat, a young man who spoke only French, was introduced to me as M. Berti. Jiha and Berti followed us around the house, and I felt that they had imposed on my private tour. It was only much later that I would learn the reason for their visit, which was more purposeful, if less tactful, than mine. Christian showed us his uncle's study on one side of the corridor and the family chapel on the other.

"The grandfather of my father, who was Austrian," Christian Poche said, "is the reason why you have here the portrait of the last emperor of Austria, Franz Joseph. They kept contact with Austria, because Vienna was for us and for Aleppo the nearest important city in the West. It was difficult to travel by ship. From the land, Vienna was important for Syria and especially for Aleppo. This is why so many Austrian influences stayed in my family." He spoke as he walked slowly through the grand house, a little palace on the first floor above the khan. "You see here," he said, indicating some vases, "Chinese porcelain, because Aleppo was on the Silk Route. The caravans, when they left east Asia, they came to Aleppo and sold this kind of porcelain. Aleppo is one of the few towns in the Middle East where you see it. Now it is very, very rare. Most are 19th century. In Damascus, you can't find these, because Damascus was a religious town. Foreigners could come to Aleppo, not Damascus." He showed me an oil portrait of a European in Oriental dress. "My great-grandfather. When he came from Austria after Napoleon's war in Egypt, he settled in Damascus. It was forbidden for a foreigner to wear European clothes there, so he was obliged to wear Ottoman dress. He left Damascus, because it was impossible to stay, and came to Aleppo."

The Poches had amassed an eclectic collection of art and furniture, with something from every era in Syria's and Aleppo's relations with the outside world – bas reliefs, busts and stone statues from Palmyra, Hittite statuary, Roman mosaics from the Euphrates, 18th-century paintings from Austria and France, dark wooden tables from Spain, tapestries and ceramics from China, carpets from Persia and Kurdistan, and drawings and photographs of the Poche family over the ages.

M. Jiha and M. Berti were carefully examining everything they saw, occasionally picking up a vase or picture for close inspection. They whispered between themselves, lingering behind in some of the rooms after Christian Poche and I had moved on.

Christian showed me some 11th-century ceramics. "These are from Raqqa on the Euphrates. In the 11th century, Raqqa had many large porcelain factories. Then the Mongols destroyed them all." It seemed sometimes that everything the Syrians built over the ages had been destroyed by one conqueror or another. I wondered why they didn't rebuild, but assumed they feared the next round of destruction.

M. Jiha and M. Berti handled the Raqqa porcelain, holding the pieces in their hands as though weighing them. They seemed to agree it was quality stuff.

M. Berti asked Christian some questions, and I went to the window. Below was a small garden with so many trees it looked like a miniature forest. Beyond was a wall which separated it from a side street in the souq. Although we were only about ten yards from the street, which was too narrow for cars, I could not hear any of the noise of people walking and talking. The peace, the tranquillity of the house and the garden, surrounded by similar houses above khans and streets without cars, made it seem like Venice, another place on earth which owes its wonderful silence to an absence of cars and trucks. To think the whole world was like that only a century ago.

Christian Poche came to the window and looked out, and smiled at me as we shared the view of the garden. "My uncle is very ill," he said. "I think he has only a few days, and he will die."

"How many Poches are left?"

"I am the last one. I am the son of Rudolphe, Adolphe's brother." Christian had a sister, and Adolphe a daughter. He had no children.

"What will happen to the house?"

Looking around at M. Jiha and M. Berti, who were poring over the books, Christian said, "I'm not sure."

He led me through a kitchen and up to the roof, which the family had used as a terrace. It joined the other flat roofs of the old city, roofs that stretched for miles all around. Small domes bubbled from some of the flat, cement rooftops. It was early evening, and I could hear the sound of muezzins calling the faithful to prayer from several minarets. Dominating the city, in its centre and high above it, was the Citadel, built of huge stones on the highest hill for miles around. As long as there has been an Aleppo, people sought refuge there whenever the invader came. The Arabs conquered it from the Byzantines only after sending a secret emissary inside to open the gates, and the Mongols succeeded in massacring the entire population when the Aleppins agreed to open the gates in exchange for Mongol assurances not to do any harm.

Laundry hung drying on some of the roofs, and the sight of Aleppo near the Citadel had not changed since the first Poche had set foot there almost two centuries earlier.

The rooftops, like the streets and souqs below, had a life all their own. Families could go from house to house, visiting cousins and uncles, without ever setting foot in the road. "This is what we call a *belvedere*," he said, "in the Italian-Spanish style. It was my cousins'. They lived on the other side. It was above another khan. Every night, we used to go over the roof to see one another, to visit." I looked at the other roofs. "The school, the house there, the other houses – they all belonged to your family?"

"Yes," he said, "but not that one. It was a Venetian house, but it became offices. And that is the Turkish bath. You can go there and have a nice bath." Domes on the roof of the Hammam Nahaseen had small pieces of coloured glass embedded in them to filter sunlight to the bathers sweating below. "Before, when I was a child, there was a café on the roof of the baths. Every night, there was what we call in Aleppo a *hakawati*. That means a man who comes and tells stories. I remember it well from when I was a child. Now, the *hakawati* has completely disappeared. No one can do it anymore."

The hammam roof was bare, and the storyteller was gone, perhaps forever. The reason for his departure had less to do with politics than with the television antennae that sprouted from most of the houses like obstinate weeds.

"When did the café close?"

"In 1956 or so," he said. "After the War of the Suez. With the beginning of the Baath, everyone left, in 1960. Everything was disappearing."

"You uncle once told me he saw Lawrence of Arabia disguised as an Arab in the khan down there."

"Yes, that's true. It was during the First World War. He wore Arab clothes, and he never spoke with my family. He spent two nights here, because it was the khan. You come with your horse or your camel, and you sleep here. I think Lawrence was alone."

"And your uncle recognised him?"

"Yes," Christian said, "but he did not give him away to the Turks."

Lawrence had preferred to travel alone, even to his cost. The most famous instance was his trip to Deraa, a Syrian village on what became the Syrian-Jordanian border. The Turks captured and beat him, but let him go, believing him to be a Circassian. Even before the war, when he would visit Aleppo from the archaeological digs at Carchemish, he took risks in moving alone through wild countryside. In a letter he wrote to Sir John Rhys from the Baron's Hotel on 24 September, 1909, he mentioned briefly, "I was robbed & rather smashed up." This referred to an attack by Kurdish raiders who had stolen his money and left him for dead. He was then the young British archaeologist that Krikor Mazloumian remembered from his early childhood, pacing the terrace in front of his father's hotel. Those were the final years of the empire, of united Syria, an era Lawrence would be instrumental in bringing to an end and, perhaps unintentionally, hastening the decline of Aleppo. Perhaps Adolphe Poche should have turned him in to the Turks.

The year before, Adolphe Poche had told me the story of Aleppo's long decline. "It began in the sixteenth century," he said, "when the Spaniards and Portuguese opened the sea route around the Cape of Good Hope. This reduced, but did not eliminate, the importance of the caravans between China, as well as Persia and Baghdad, and the Mediterranean."

I did not know it then, but Poche's own decline had begun. Although ninety-two years old, he seemed sprightly and composed in his three-piece, brown stripe suit. He was mostly bald, with a band of white hair above the ears, and his eyes were so sharp he wore no glasses. He spoke in English, but would invariably wander into his preferred language, French. "The second blow to hit Aleppo," he went on, "was the opening of the Suez

Canal in 1869, when it lost much of its importance as a trading centre. And the final disaster was the ceding of Aleppo's port, Alexandretta, to Turkey in 1939."

I asked him about the family's history in Aleppo, and he answered, "My grandfather left the Austro-Hungarian Empire and came here. Later, my father and his brothers started a *maison de commerce* in Aleppo. At one time or another, our family were consuls of the Austro-Hungarians, the United States of America, Belgium and Holland."

Adolphe Poche himself had been to Jerusalem during the First World War as an interpreter between the Turkish and Austro-Hungarian officers. "I came back from Palestine," Poche said, "but with General Allenby."

After the First War, he was consul of Austria, without Hungary. Then came the *Anschluss*. "When Hitler offered to keep me on as consul of Germany and Austria," he said, "I refused." He remained consul of Belgium, until German troops invaded it too. When that war ended, he resumed his duties as Belgian consul, a post he later handed on to his daughter's husband.

Our meeting was brief, because he was tired. I promised him then when I came back the following year to write my book, we would have more time together. He seemed so well at the time, with the vitality and charm that everyone recalled from his younger days, that I was certain we would meet.

I had no way of knowing that, when I did return to Aleppo, he would lie dying, and that, when he finally died, I would be in a place where the news could not reach me.

Adolphe Poche was buried with full honours, and his nephew returned to Paris. The doors of the Venetian Consulate reopened, and it was only then that the purpose of the visit of Messieurs Jiha and Berti became clear. A brass sign next to the door read, *Consulat de la France.*

Only two countries based their own diplomats, rather than employ Syrians, as full consuls. Both were the heirs of empires with historic interests in Syria – Turkey and Russia. The Turks governed Aleppo for four hundred years. If the Russians had defeated the Turks in wars the two fought in the eighteenth and nineteenth centuries, they might have ruled the city as well. Once each month, the Turkish and Russian consuls in Aleppo held a meeting. There was a time when such encounters would have produced rumours, prompted tales of political intrigue and led to murmurings in the souqs. That time had long since passed, but it could always return.

The senior consul was the Turk, a debonair career diplomat named Aykut Berk. His residence and offices were in a large house in the new Mohafaza Quarter, so called because the Ottoman "Mohafaza" or

Governor's headquarters were there until the Turks retreated in 1918. When I approached the walled, suburban villa, I saw nearly a hundred Syrians in peasant *abayas*, *keiffiyehs* wrapped tightly round their heads, queuing with young men in open shirts and blue jeans. Some leaned against the wall, smoking cigarettes. Others sat on the pavement in the shade of spring leaves newly grown on the trees. In Damascus, I would see similar queues at embassies, men waiting patiently for documents to enable them to go to Turkey, America, France, Germany, Russia, Austria or Greece.

"Why do so many men want visas to go to Turkey?" I asked Aykut Berk.

"Smuggling," he said in a matter-of-fact tone. "They buy things they cannot find here, bring them back to Syria and sell them." At the border, I had seen men slip the border guards packs of coffee beans and plastic bags whose contents I could only guess. On the Turkish side of the border, as we passed the men in the "No-Man's-Land," I had watched a border guard run out of a shed, hand our bus driver a bag of some kind of jingling metal, possibly silverware, and go back into this office. The drivers seemed always to be stuffing things under their seats or giving cigarettes to the Syrian border officials, with the apparent intention of being allowed to smuggle more contraband cigarettes.

"We issued fifty thousand visas last year," Berk told me. "Right now, we are issuing one hundred and fifty a day. This will go up to three hundred and fifty a day in the summer, and this is for Aleppo alone."

"Doesn't Turkey care about the smuggling?"

"Look," he said, "the smuggling is a function of shortages. Ten years ago, it was the reverse. The Turks were coming here and smuggling things back into Turkey." I liked him and the fact he knew the wheel was always turning. In ten more years, no doubt, the smuggling would reverse itself again. It was no cause for alarm.

"How do you like Aleppo?"

"Aleppo is like any of the cities of southeastern Turkey," he said. "I also spent four years in Cairo. When I was invited to a dinner party and they heard I was Turkish, they would immediately say, my grandmother or grandfather or some ancestor was Turkish. It's the same here."

"Do you go to many dinner parties here?" I asked.

"There are lots of invitations. The people of Aleppo are nice, both Christians and Muslims. An Armenian family has invited me twice. For an Armenian to show hospitality to a Turk is something. There is one Armenian here with whom I'm friendly. From time to time, I go to his shop to have coffee. I say, 'This is an Armenian neighbourhood. If having me here disturbs your neighbours, I won't come.' He says, 'No. You are always welcome here.' "

"Do you notice any differences between the Christian and Muslim families?"

"Immediately," he answered. "You can tell just from the way the house is furnished. Take me to any house in Aleppo, and I'll tell you immediately. All the antiques are in the Christian houses. Tastes differ. The way they entertain is different. For example, I've just been invited to a Christian house for a dinner and a dance and told to come 'in the sixties style.' Even the type of food is different. In a Christian house, whether for a buffet or a sit-down dinner, I have not seen hommous on the table. In a Muslim house, I always do. In some Muslim families, the wife covers her head with a scarf at least. A month ago, a Syrian Muslim friend called and said, 'I'm expecting you for dinner.' I always take along two bottles of wine. I walked in and gave two bottles of very good Villa Doluccia, a Turkish red, to my host. Then I realised I had done something wrong. We had no wine with dinner. He served Pepsi Cola. Later, the man came to my office and explained, 'My wife is very strict and does not allow alcohol in the house.' " Berk laughed and added, "But he didn't give me my wine back."

Georges Antaki sat at his desk in a darkened room, surrounded by leather-bound volumes, receiving visitors. His short black hair was parted sharply on the left, and he wore what looked like an old school tie with blue stripes, a blue pinstripe shirt and a tweed jacket. Clean-shaven, without glasses, he had the look of a slightly overweight boy, despite the fact he was in his early forties. Millionaire, friend of royalty and consul of both Italy and Portugal, Georges Antaki was used to receiving compliments, and he took in his stride the many visitors who were coming that day. Several men and women arrived to pay their respects, as Sicilian peasants might to a powerful clan leader, on the occasion of St George's Day. *"Bonne fête, Georges,"* one woman was saying, as the secretary led me into the office.

Georges Antaki stood and extended his hand like a cardinal. I feared for a moment he expected me to kiss his ring, although we had made an appointment that had nothing to do with St George's Day. We shook hands, and he introduced me to his guests. He began speaking in French. "I am so busy today," he said, exasperated. "So many things to do at once. And today is my saint's day, and there are visitors." He nodded at the other people in the room. "But don't worry. I am happy to help you with your book. Have you seen M. Adolphe Poche?"

"I met him last year, but his daughter says he is very ill now."

"Oh, yes, of course. You should speak to M. Mazloumian too. He knows all the history of Aleppo."

"I'm staying at the Baron's. The Mazloumians have already been helpful."

"And you want to use my library?"

"Very much." Georges Antaki had the finest library in Syria of antiquarian books on the Levant. He had engaged a French librarian to catalogue his thousands of works of history, philosophy, law, literature and travel, dating back to the 17th century. It was a priceless collection, to which he had added the archives of the consulates of Venice, Italy and Portugal. He had inherited the Venetian and some of the French archives a few years previously from Mme Marcopoli, an aged widow whose husband was said to have been the last descendant in Aleppo of history's greatest travelling salesman, Marco Polo. The documents included love letters written by François Picquet, Louis XIV's consul in Aleppo, to his mistress.

"You are welcome to use the library when the consulate is open, every day except Sunday, but it closes at one."

I came the next Monday morning and every morning of the week, poring over the books in the consulate library. It was an ideal room for study, a rectangle of books on the long walls and a door at one end opposite a window at the other. In the middle stood a mahogany table, like a dining table, with a small reading lamp. In front and behind me were rows of first editions by my predecessors in Levantine travel, from Thévenot in 1665 to Brézol in 1911. Most were French, but some were English, and there were French and English translations of the early Arab travellers Ibn Jubayr and Ibn Batuta. My only companion, except when Georges Antaki was taking visitors through the library on a tour of the consulate, was the Emperor Joseph II, two of whose portraits in oil hung above the door.

The consulate had no photocopier, so I spent hours like an ancient scribe copying passages from the different texts into my notebooks. Although Aleppo's late-twentieth-century citizens often lament the passing of the city's golden age, William Eton described a far more pitiful Aleppo as he found it in his book A *Survey of the Turkish Empire*, published in London in 1798:

Aleppo (Haleb) is the best built city in the Turkish dominions, and the people are reputed the most polite. The late Dr Russell (in his *Natural History of Aleppo*) calculated the number of inhabitants in his time, at about 230,000; at present there are not above 40 or 50,000. This depopulation has chiefly taken place since 1770. As this city is built of a kind of marble, and the houses are vaulted, they are not subject to decay and fall in ruins, though they remain uninhabited; they stand a monument of the destruction of the human race: whose streets are uninhabited and bazars abandoned. Fifty or sixty years ago were counted forty large villages in the neighbourhood, all built of stone; their ruins remain, but not a single peasant dwells in them. The plague visits Aleppo every ten or twelve years. About four years ago there was at Aleppo one of the most dreadful famines ever known anywhere.

By comparison, Aleppo in the late 1980s, overcrowded and growing into new suburbs along the hilltops, was thriving. There may have been electricity shortages, a lack of foreign exchange to buy needed equipment and a mismanaged economy, but plague and famine were unknown.

From time to time, I would walk down the hall to Georges Antaki's office to ask him about something I had read in one or other of his books. He revealed himself to be an Aleppo patriot, although his family name, Antaki, meant his ancestors had come from Antioch. "Aleppo," he said one day, "is the cultural capital of Syria. Lamartine believed that Aleppo was to Asia what Athens was to Europe."

The consular tradition in Aleppo, and the world, began in 1517, when the Ottoman Sultan Selim I granted Venice, and then England and France, the right to maintain diplomats in Aleppo. On the Silk Route between China and the Mediterranean, Aleppo had resident merchants from all over the world. John Eldred, an English trader, wrote in 1583, "This is the greatest place of traffique for a dry towne that is in all these parts: for hither resort Jewes, Tartarians, Persians, Armenians, Egyptians, Indians, and many sorts of Christians, and injoy freedome of their consciences and bring hither many kinds of rich merchandises." The Ottomans had to face the task of ruling many foreigners, with their different languages and customs, within the context of their loosely governed empire. Their solution was to govern the foreigners as they did the natives – leaving each community in charge of its own affairs. At first, the consuls supervised the activities of their own traders, who resided in the European quarters of the walled city. The English consul was employed directly by the Levant Company, which had a Royal Charter to conduct trade with the Orient. When a consul died, a new one was elected from among his peers. Each foreign community was called a "factory" or a "nation."

"After Constantinople and Cairo," Georges explained, "Aleppo was the most important city in the Ottoman Empire. The Venetians had a school in Aleppo in the 17th and 18th centuries to train dragomen." The dragoman, a corruption of the Arabic *turjuman*, translator, translated Arabic, Turkish and other local languages for the European consuls. The post became institutionalised, but later a dragoman was any native who accompanied Europeans through the Levant. Some dragomen rose to become consuls themselves, and by the twentieth century, most of Aleppo's consuls were Syrians who in the seventeenth century would have been dragomen.

When the Count Constantin François de Volney published his three-volume *Voyage en Syrie et en Egypte Pendant Les Années 1783, 1784 et 1785* in Paris, he mentioned the consuls of France, England, Venice, Livorno, Holland, the new consul of Russia and a Jewish merchant appointed by the Emperor in Vienna who "shaved his beard to be able to wear the uniform and epaulettes."

"The dragomen had greater privileges then," Georges said, "than the consuls have now, because of the Capitulations." The Capitulations were privileges the Ottomans granted to each European consul to govern the affairs of his own community. Throughout the Ottoman Empire, Europeans could be tried in European courts, marry in European consulates and make contracts under European jurisdiction. The Capitulations would later be seen as the vanguard of European imperialism, infringing Turkish sovereignty. The Ottoman Empire, however, granted the privileges when it was stronger than the Europeans, and the policy merely extended to foreign "nations" the responsibility for their own affairs exercised by the empire's indigenous communities.

In *The Principal Navigations, Voyages, Traffiques and Discoveries of the English Nation*, Richard Hakluyt reproduced "The Charter of Privileges granted to the English" by Sultan Murad, whom Hakluyt called "the great Turke," in June 1580. The charter said the subjects of "Elizabeth Queene of England, France and Ireland, the most honourable Queene of Christendom . . . may buy and sell without any hindrance, and observe the customes and orders of their owne countrey." The twenty-two specific rights granted to Englishmen within Ottoman lands included:

> *Item*, if any Englishman . . . die intestate, hee to whom the
> Consull or governour of the societie shall say the goods of the dead
> are to bee given, he shall have the same . . .
> *Item*, if any variance or controversie shall arise among the
> Englishmen, and thereupon they shall appeale to their Consuls or
> governours, let no man molest them but let them freely doe so,
> that the controversie begunne may be finished according to their
> customes.

Sultan Murad noted that "even as wee have given and granted articles and privileges to the French, Venetians, and other Kings and princes our confederates, so also wee have given the like to the English: and contrary to this our divine lawe and privilege, let no man presume to doe any thing."

The relative status enjoyed by Georges Antaki and the other consuls in Aleppo owed more to Sultan Murad than to the foreign countries they represented. By the end of the empire, the prestige and power of the consuls had grown to extraordinary proportions. Not only did many

Ottoman subjects, usually Christians, appeal to European consuls for protection against their own government, but the consuls themselves demanded and received public honours. Edward Barker, the English Consul in the early nineteenth century, wrote that

the Pacha of Aleppo used to furnish on the occasion of a public entry of a Consul a guard of horse (five led horses), accompanied by certain officers of the State, who walk in the procession of a personage of the same rank as Pacha. A salute would be fired from the Castle, and the Pacha would make presents to the Consul, which in general were a horse, a sword, a pelisse or fur mantle. The Consul, on the other hand, paid a certain sum to the Pacha's retainers on leaving the Palace, through the Dragoman. These presents were always of the most inferior quality that could be given.

The consuls no longer received lavish treatment, nor did they dare to show disrespect to government officials. A consulship was however good for business, no small advantage in a Levantine trading post, and it conferred local prestige.

George's Antaki's library was filled with references to forgotten consuls, to Aleppo and to the other Levantine cities and towns on my itinerary. I spent some of my happiest hours there, reading about Greater Syria over the last few millennia. Inside George's library, I found myself, however briefly and dimly, making some sense of the Levantine world outside.

The life of the poor, traveller and resident alike, revolved around the four sides of an old stone clocktower in the city's central square. Taxis – scores of old yellow cars with lights on their roofs – rattled past the cheap hotels, popular cafés and restaurants selling grilled meats. Along the kerbside were barrows, old wooden trays mounted on bicycle wheels. One barrow had two shelves, one above the other. On top, there were cakes for sale. Tucked into the shelf below, a small boy was sleeping. There were barrows with umbrellas for cover, barrows lit with their own electric lights, barrows selling fruit, barrows laden with garlic and onions, barrows with raw meat hanging from horizontal bars and small braziers to grill the meat and offal. One of these shops on wheels had a makeshift stove and a pot of sheeps' heads on the boil.

On the pavements, men sold shoes and small toys, all spread out on newspapers. One young salesman, a teenage boy in *keffiyeh* and dark robe, held a hooded falcon on his sleeve, but no one seemed interested in buying the expensive luxury. Most of the people walking by at night were men, dressed in flowing *abayas* and the red and white *keffiyeh* of the animal herder, of the landless rural poor. If they were not dressed in peasant clothes, they wore army uniforms – still peasants, but in red and green camouflage, or khaki, or olive drab, depending on their brigade. All were off-duty, unarmed and wandering aimlessly. The cheap hotels, many with large rooms holding a dozen or more beds each, enticed the visitor from Turkey or the Syrian countryside with strings of red, green and yellow lights over their doors and windows. The tawdry restaurants were stark cells with blank walls, plastic tables and aluminium chairs on the floors and unshaded light bulbs hanging from the ceilings. Some displayed raw meat, like trophies of war, in their windows. Many had signs in Turkish assuring pilgrims on their way by land to Mecca that "Alcohol is not served here." Young men pushed their barrows of fruit and vegetables from the old clock tower to the top of the square towards Armenian and Christian districts called Jdaideh and Salibi. Open shops selling fresh fruit juice – orange, lemon, apple, carrot, banana – had colour televisions on their counters to entice those walking past to stop, to watch a soap opera from Damascus and perhaps to buy a glass of juice. Despite the complaints about shortages, there was fruit – orange, grapefruit, lemon, apple – in abundance at the juice shops, in the grocers and on the barrows.

The slow parade of yellow taxis, most of them empty, endlessly circled the clock tower. Not one of the four clocks, one on each face, told the same time. The hands of each dial, unlike the moving, flowing, shouting, running confusion below, was frozen. Each clock had died at a different moment. The time would always be, depending from which side of the square one saw the tower, 6:01, 6:55, 4:26 or 7:25, a.m. or p.m.

Even in the days when the clocks told the time, they did not agree. "The square-squatting clock-tower of Aleppo," Harry Franck wrote in 1928,

shows 'l'heure turque' on two sides and 'l'heure française' on the others, which is symbolic, for Aleppo, once an important city of Turkey, is more Turkish than Syrian. That is, it is about six o'clock on the north and south sides of the tower when it is somewhere around noon or midnight on the east and west. But the clock always struck in Turkish, and even the 'French hour' differed so much on its two sides that almost any one could find one face of the tower agreeing with his own version of the time.

Up from the clocks were the popular coffee houses, where men – only men – sipped sugared tea or Turkish coffee under high ceilings supported by square pillars. Some smoked *narguiles*. A few played backgammon. Some talked, others sat silently, looking almost drugged, their eyes unfocused as they passed the night, often with nowhere to sleep. As they stared into the darkness from their bright cafés, other men walked past. Occasionally, a woman, always with her husband, always with her hair covered by a scarf, appeared in the crowd. One woman pushed a sleeping baby in a home-made pram, her husband beside, but ignoring, her.

At the Cairo Cinema there were posters advertising films of mock violence, karate and sex. At another cinema, a poster advertised a film, " 'Stupid Inspector' An Amusing Contamination of the Hitchcock thriller and the Italian comedy, with Marcello Mastriani and Zeudi Araya." Zeudi Araya, the Eritrean actress, seemed to be as popular in Aleppo as she was in Alexandretta. At the *service* taxi depot, drivers called out destinations south, "Hama, Homs, Latakieh, Damascus." A few men sat in the back seats, waiting for them to fill with the requisite five passengers before the drivers carried them into the night, perhaps to homes in villages on the way, perhaps to cheap hotels in provincial towns between Aleppo and Damascus.

Along one side of the square a high concrete wall enclosed empty ground, nothing more than a pit of rubble. An old man was leaning against the wall. In trousers, he seemed to be an Aleppo native rather than a visitor from the countryside. "Excuse me, sheikh," I said. "What's in there?"

"Nothing."

"What *was* there?"

The man, recognising me for a foreigner, spoke in English. "It was a part of the souq, but the governor didn't like it."

"Why not?"

"He came from Tadmor, and he hated Aleppo. He said Tadmor had no souq like that, so he closed all the shops and sent bulldozers."

"What are they going to do with it?"

"He said they were going to build new offices, but who has money to build offices?"

"I suppose the governor isn't very popular here."

"He was dismissed."

We were in the heart of Aleppo, beating at night when the souqs were closed and the middle classes had gone home. The square around the Ottoman clock tower was the haunt of Aleppo's poor, and most people in Syria were poor, and of its Muslims, and most Syrians were Sunni Muslims. What did they care about Levantine traders, honorary consuls, the Baron's Hotel, the Armenians in their midst, the Christian families who that night would be entertaining one another to dinner and drinking wine forbidden to faithful Muslims? The consuls, the traders, the Armenians and Christians, the memories, made Aleppo unique for me, a Western traveller, because they provided the spice to this Arab, Muslim stew. In cities like Paris or Vienna, from which consuls and traders had come over the centuries, the grand hotels, the jazz clubs, merchants and diplomats were merely boring. In Aleppo, they were enchanted, because they were out of place and time. The Muslim month of fasting, Ramadan, had begun. Before the sun, the people in the square would rise. They would eat in the pre-dawn darkness, the better able to endure the hot day ahead without food, drink and tobacco. When the sun set, and the cannon fired to announce the end of the day, they would return to the square to break their fast with grilled lamb, offal and perhaps the head of a sheep.

CHAPTER NINE

THE SURVIVORS AND THE DEAD

Armen Mazloumian and I took a walk around the Armenian Quarter, Jdaideh, past open shops selling women's dresses, shoes, antiques and televisions. We made our way along stone corridors of bare walls and wooden gates. We passed a door marked Giligian, or Cicilian, School. "This used to be the Dallal House," Armen said. "The Dallals were a big Sunni family. Now it's an Armenian school. Do you want to see it?"

Without waiting for a reply, he opened the large door and stepped into a beautiful garden. The school, like all Syrian urban houses built before the French came, looked like Father Ferrari's rectory in Antioch, only larger, more formal, befitting the status of its former owners. On one side of the square court was a large *liwan*, or open arch under which people could sit in the shade. Twenty feet above the *liwan*'s marble floor was a carved wooden ceiling. On the divan along the *liwan*'s three walls, the head of the Dallal family would have received guests in warm weather, as servants brought tea and glasses of mulberry juice or flower water from the kitchen. In the centre of the courtyard, water sprayed from a pipe in the traditional fountain on a raised stone platform.

Except for some old women washing the courtyard, there was no one in the school. "Where are the children?" I asked Armen.

"It must be a holiday."

"What holiday?"

"How should I know?"

As an unpaid tour guide, Armen had his limitations.

Near the Armenian church, an old man stopped us and spoke excitedly to Armen. Armen listened for a minute and nodded, responding with a few words, and the man left. "What did he say?"

"Nothing."

"He said *something*. What was it?"

"He said the Armenian archbishop was arrested this morning."

"Who arrested him? How?"

"He said some plainclothes agents stopped Archbishop Kataroyan near a bookshop and took him away."

"What are you going to do about it?"

"Nothing." Armen hated the clergy.

Armen Mazloumian carried many prejudices in his Armenian-English-Syrian heart, not least against fellow Armenians, Britons and Syrians. He criticised Aleppo's Armenians because of their insularity, their decision not to assimilate and the inability of many of them to speak Arabic properly. Their poor Arabic, in a few cases worse than mine, was notorious in Syria. One day we were in the countryside with an Armenian driver Armen used when he did not want to drive the Nomad. The driver became lost. Three village girls were standing in front of a house painted with Islamic symbols to indicate its owner had made the pilgrimage to Mecca. Above the door, he had written, "Welcome to whoever visits my grave." The Armenian driver asked the girls for directions. They made him repeat his question several times, and they burst out laughing at his Arabic. I ended up asking for directions, and Armen blushed with shame.

It seemed to me he was hard on his own people, a strong community who had maintained their integrity, language and traditions, all the while surviving in the much larger Arab society. The Abbé Mariti, who toured the Levant in the eighteenth century and whose travels were translated into English in 1791, observed, "The Armenians are a people who possess excellent hearts, and whose manners are mild and civil. They are deep politicians, and acquire great riches by commerce." Nothing had changed in two hundred years, except that the Armenians had endured intolerable suffering and lost a large part of their homeland, and their people, in Turkey.

An Armenian family from Paris was staying at the Baron's Hotel. The couple, a doctor and his wife, had two sons aged ten and twelve, who became the favourites of the hotel staff. Armen was showing the hotel's *Livre d'Or*, its register of famous guests from the previous eight decades, to the family one evening when I walked into the bar. The father had a camera and took a picture of the Golden Book, but Armen was blasé. Showing the book was just another chore, like making sure the waiters had set the tables for breakfast.

The boys asked to see Agatha Christie's autograph. She had stayed in the hotel, where she wrote *Murder on the Orient Express*, in the mid-1930s with her husband, an archaeologist exploring ruins near Aleppo. Armen found the great crime writer's name, "Agatha Christie Mallowan," just below that of her husband, "M. Mallowan." One of the boys took a picture of the page.

"Is there any other signature you'd like to see?" Armen asked the boys.

"Who else is there?"

Armen made some suggestions. "Isadora Duncan."

"No," the boys said, unimpressed.

"Nadia Gamal, the Egyptian belly dancer?"

"No."

"The head of the Syrian Air Force? The Prime Minister of Syria? Cardinal Spellman?"

The boys weren't interested. Agatha Christie was about the only person they had heard of, and that was due to television. Disgusted, Armen closed the book and walked out of the bar.

When the family left, I moved from my table to the bar and ordered a drink from Garabet, the ageing Armenian barman and waiter. He poured a whisky and looked in the refrigerator for ice. Not finding any, Garabet, who rarely spoke, raised a hand to indicate I should be patient. Taking no notice of my insistence that I did not need ice, he shuffled slowly, so slowly that I wondered whether he would ever return, to find some ice in the kitchen.

I leafed through the visitors' book. Although the boys had not been impressed, I was old enough to recognise the names of many who had signed: Mr and Mrs Charles Lindbergh; Eugénia, Princesse de Grèce in 1947, and Michael of Greece in 1966; Prince Bertil and Princess Louise of Sweden; Sir Ahmed Al-Jabir Al-Sabah, who became ruler of Kuwait, in 1935; Theodore Roosevelt, former American Governor of the Philippines; the Earl of Athlone, Governor-General of South Africa, and Princess Alice of Athlone; Lady Louis Mountbatten; the British Orientalist H. A. R. Gibb; and Lebanon's president in 1934, Charles Debbas. Many writers had preceded me: Freya Stark, Jonathan Raban, Eric Newby, Patrick and Joan Leigh-Fermor and my friend William Shawcross. The Lebanese Druze leader, Walid Jumblatt, signed in 1985. A few people wrote sentimental notes:

I join the illustrious alumni of guests at the Famous Barone Hotel of Onnik and Armenak Mazloumian of Aleppo, sustained by Armenak's son Krikor. *William Saroyan, Saturday June 17, 1972.*

In this uncertain world we live in, it is a great pleasure to come back to a hotel like the Baron thirty-four years after my first visit during World War II to find the same courteous and capable management and the same charm. May this quality continue for many years to come! *David Rockefeller, March 8, 1977.*

I did not notice that Armen had come back to the bar until I heard him say, "Go on."

"Go on, what?"

"Go on and sign it."

"Thanks." I took out my fountain pen and put my signature at the end of the book, sadly, in the more mundane 1980s rather than on the pages with the Lindberghs and Agatha Christie.

Garabet, walking as slowly as humanly possible, returned with the ice. "What are you doing?" Armen asked him.

He started to speak, dropping ice cubes in the glass and pointing it at me to show I had ordered it.

"No. Go and get some Armenian brandy from my office, and be quick about it."

Garabet turned and walked away again, barely lifting his old feet from the hotel's worn carpets.

Armen closed the book on my drying signature and grumbled, "It's impossible to get good staff these days."

We drove through hills up to the mountains near the Turkish border and the sea. On the road, we passed cherry trees in blossom and children having picnics in their shade. "The cherry season is June," Armen said. "You can come back and pick some." We saw the plain below us looking like a vast plaid of greens and dark browns. We were on our way to Kassab, an Armenian mountain village known in Syria for its apples. On the ascent to the village, hundreds of apple trees blossomed on either side of the highway.

Reluctantly, Armen agreed to stop at a farm before the village, so that I could meet a farmer. Most Armenians in Syria lived in the cities and were artisans or businessmen. An Armenian farmer, so familiar a figure in Turkish Armenia until the massacres of the late nineteenth and early twentieth centuries, would make a change. We drove into an apple orchard just off the road and met a sixty-year-old Armenian smallholder named Zavon Nazarian. He was about 5' 5" tall, with brown eyes, white hair and enormous ears sticking out from a grey knitted ski cap. He wore a grey wool jacket, nearly the colour of his cap, over an old brown pullover. On his feet were black sandals and dark socks.

He led us to a large yard next to his farm house, where apple boxes were stacked and chickens and grandchildren were running under the trees. Zevon Nazarian spoke Armenian, and Armen translated. When I asked where he came from, the answer was, "My father and grandfather were born here."

"Where in Armenia did your family come from?"

"I don't know. Possibly Cilicia, but we have lived here for four or five hundred years."

He went on, "We're a very large family. We're spread all over the place –

some in America, some in Soviet Armenia. I have three daughters and one son. All of them, except one girl, are married. Everyone in this area is a farmer."

"Do you like it here?"

"I like it, because the bread is from here. Why shouldn't I like it? But it can't be as nice as the homeland. This is the second homeland."

He said that his neighbours in the second homeland were Turcomans in the village of Badrousieh and Alawis in Faki Hassan. In other villages, there were Ismailis and Druze. Syria in its Christian days was home to scores of fractious sects, and under Islam had tolerated every kind of Muslim, even those considered heretics by the majority Sunnis. In the twelfth century, Ibn Jubayr derided "those dissident sects and corrupt beliefs that are found in most of this country."

"Yes, they are all our neighbours," Nazarian said, "the Turcomans and Alawis. We are friends. The people in Kassab are mostly Armenian, but there is now an influx of Alawis and Turcomans. They're gradually moving in, but in 1947, it was all Armenian. Many of the Armenians have gone."

At my request, Armen asked him, "Where did they go?"

"Armenia."

"Why?"

"To save Armenia from disintegrating," he said. "You're Armenian. Don't you know that?"

Zavon Nazarian had been born in the last year of Ottoman rule in Syria, at the time of some of the Turkish massacres of Armenians. How, I wondered, had his family survived?

"Many people were deported from Kassab," the old man said. "We were lucky, because we went to southern Syria for a time. Those who were deported from here to Deir ez-Zour were of course massacred. Some of those who had goats and cows took them to Hama, and then on to southern Syria. Many came back four or five years later."

Syrians referred to that period in their history, the last years of the war and of Ottoman rule, by the term *Safar Barlik*, literally, "travelling across the land." Thousands of families fled their homes, moving on foot with only the possessions and infants they could carry, and sought refuge where they could. The Turks were impressing every man from the age of fifteen to sixty into the army. They were deporting Armenians, whom they suspected of conspiring with their enemies to destroy the empire. Armenian children roamed the hills, hiding from the Turks. "They massacred, they robbed and they burned down houses," Zavon Nazarian said, no doubt relying on his own parents' account of his infant years. "Some people fled to the coast, where French ships picked them up."

"Where did your family go?"

"We went all the way to Amman and Jerusalem. When the Turkish government withdrew, we returned to Kassab. This region stayed without any government for a year or so, until the French came."

"When did you come back?"

"1918."

"Have there been serious problems since then?"

"No. From 1940 to 1942, there was not enough food, because of the world war. We have not been persecuted since the Turks left."

"Did many Armenians come here when the French ceded Alexandretta to Turkey in 1939?"

"They came, thousands of them, for a few months, but most of them went to Anjar." Anjar was a village in the Bekaa Valley in Lebanon, where the Syrian army had placed its intelligence and interrogation headquarters after it crossed the border in 1976. Anjar had a lovely Armenian Orthodox church and an excellent restaurant. Armenian relief groups, like the Armenian Benevolent Union, helped to resettle the early refugees. Wealthy Armenians gave them money to build houses in Anjar.

In Nazarian's house, the calendars on the wall were turned to April, the month Armenians commemorated the deportations and murders of their people. One calendar had a picture of the long march of Armenians across Turkey or Syria to their deaths, a hateful period commemorated every April lest the survivors and descendants forget.

We went up to Kassab, the largest Armenian town in the mountains, and found the Armenian Catholic Church of St Mary the Virgin. There we met Father Aram Kulunjian. Twenty-seven years old, living in a spartan rectory, he told us he had learned English in Venice from a Welshman. "I studied at St Lazaro, a little Armenian island in Venice," he said.

That day, he had said a Mass for the Armenian martyrs. "I don't know exactly the history," he said, "because we don't have any written records here in Kassab about that time."

Folk memories were nonetheless strong, and no Armenian in Kassab would forget the killings. Armen and I went across the road to the Armenian Protestant Church. It was in every way a Protestant, rather than eastern Christian, building. There were no ikons, no statues, no altar. Two pulpits and several chairs stood on a dais. Below a plain cross on the wall behind was a large, childlike painting on paper. It showed Jesus Christ, the good shepherd, holding in his arms the body of a slain boy, the boy's head and arms dangling like Christ's own in Michelangelo's Pietà. Behind Him were the mountains of Armenia, and at His feet were a mound of skulls and bones with the date "1915" written on them. The caption was in Armenian, which Armen translated: "So much blood. Let our grandchildren forgive you. May a living world read the history of the Armenians."

The Armenians, by one means and another, had survived the attempts to exterminate them. They had established a state within the Soviet Union, and they prospered in Syria, Lebanon, Europe and America. Another people in Syria had not been so lucky. Armen showed me their remains in the hills around Aleppo. We went first to Qatoura, part living village, part ancient catacombs and tombs in limestone. Cattle grazed amid ruins just off a gravel track. There were Roman carvings in the rock. Some of the ruins had been used as quarries by peasants to build their houses. Nearby, the guidebook said, was the tomb of a Roman nobleman, Emilius Regius, who died in 195 AD. I asked an old woman the best way to find it. She said "the gallows" were down another path. When we reached it, it did look like a gallows: two tall Doric columns supporting a lintel. In the ground below was a vaulted, empty catacomb with a Greek epitaph. Emilius Regius, master of all he surveyed seventeen hundred years ago, was gone.

The Romans and Byzantines who had left the monuments at Qatoura, and the remains of seven hundred other towns and villages across the Orontes Valley of northern Syria, simply disappeared. Their Latin and Greek inscriptions, their churches, their marketplaces, their monasteries and houses lay scattered across northern Syria just as they had left them in the seventh and eighth centuries of the Christian era. Most were empty, eerie remnants of a vital civilisation that had ceased to exist. Many had become the dwellings of Syrian peasants, who had moved into the magnificent stone and marble towns, like a few hundred African bushmen inheriting a deserted New York City.

In the village of Qatoura, there were a dozen mud hovels, whose owners had put Roman monuments and building stones to good use. Old commemorative marbles covered the wells. Broken pillars became the foundations of earth houses, and Roman basins were used for washing clothes. On a line between her mud house and a Byzantine column, an old woman with a tattoo on her wrist was hanging out a machine-made rug.

As soon as we asked a peasant farmer about the ruins, he became suspicious. An old leather belt held up his baggy, black *sharwal*. On his feet, he wore open sandals, and on his head, a black and white *keffiyeh* pulled behind his ears. Something in his ruddy, unshaven face said he was not about to tell us much.

I wasn't there to collect taxes, but he did not know that. I made the mistake of asking him about the stones in the foundation of his house.

"We buy the stones," he insisted, "and we build the houses ourselves."

"They look like they come from the ruins."

"Never," he said, Greek inscriptions notwithstanding. "There are guards from the Antiquities Department. They protect the ruins."

"I see." Armen was translating, and he did not believe the man either.

"Sometimes," the farmer conceded, "thunderstorms break the stones, and we pick them up."

I asked him about his fields, and he said he and the villagers owned the land and grew wheat, barley, figs and olives. "We have the deeds," he said, just in case I needed proof.

"Are you all Muslims?"

"Yes. Thank God."

I asked him whether he had any children.

"Only one."

"Boy or girl?"

"I have one child," he said. "Oh, I also have four daughters."

In the days that followed, Armen tried to show me as many ruins as he could. He preferred not to waste time talking to the people who lived in and near them. The ancient culture of the Orontes Valley, the Roman and Byzantine cities with their grand cathedrals, magnificent markets, theatres and villas fascinated him. The peasants did not. He spent a few days each week, rain or shine, walking through the Dead Cities, taking pictures and coming to know the civilisation that had lived and died there. Although many of the seven hundred Dead Cities were mere farming villages, they were all built of stone and marble, all had large churches and centres for public entertainment, beautiful tombs and villas. They had all been abandoned intact in the seventh and eighth centuries after Christ. To Armen, the daily life of modern Syria was less interesting than the era when those cities flourished under Christian emperors in Constantinople, when a great Christian civilisation dominated Syria, and Armenia was an independent, Christian kingdom to the north.

One day, Armen parked the Nomad at the end of the road near the ruins of what had been a pretty Roman agricultural village. We walked down a hill along a dirt path to a Kurdish hamlet, Fafirtin, built on either side of the path. Unlike many villagers in other dead cities, these Kurds lived beside, not in, the ruins. Many of the Kurdish houses had been built of limestone, and several men with long chisels were squaring the rocks to make the walls of a small house. I stopped to speak to the stonemasons. Although Kurdish was the language they used among themselves, they spoke to us in Arabic. One of the men was particularly outspoken when I asked him about the ancient Roman church in Fafirtin. It had been built in 372 AD, only fifty-nine years after the Edict of Milan had legalised Christianity in Roman lands. "Church? Ruins?" he asked. "We need electricity, a road and water."

"Don't you have water here?"

"We need a road first. Trucks bring the water, and they charge 100 SL for 3,500 litres."

About two hundred people lived there, surviving on sheep herding and dairy cows. As well as electricity and a road, the man, to the agreement of the others, said he wanted a school for the village.

"Isn't there a school?"

He pointed to a one-room, stone building. "The government gives money, but it is private."

"What else do you want here?"

"I want you to resettle us somewhere else."

"He wants you," Armen said in English, "to resettle him. He thinks you're from the government." By now, a crowd had gathered around us. Armen grimaced, but he continued to translate. When I asked why they lived in Fafirtin, a young boy stepped forward, saying proudly, "Our great-grandfathers came here."

An old man, who said he was sixty-five, asked, "Where shall we go? There is no money. We cannot sell the land. It belongs to the state."

A younger man added, "How shall we go? We have no cars. We have no money. We have no tractors to work the land, here or anywhere."

"Don't many people come to look at the ruins?" I asked. The church was probably the oldest in northern Syria.

"Many people come," they all agreed.

"Why don't you make some money selling them postcards or cups of tea?"

The little boy spoke up again, "We will *give* them tea. Then they will respect us." The men nodded their agreement. They would not, no matter how poor, debase themselves. They would give them tea, as they gave it to us. Their hospitality was not for sale.

The Kurds were known as brave warriors throughout the Middle Ages of Islam. Kurdish soldiers under their great leader, Salah ed-Din, known as Saladin in the West, had liberated Jerusalem from the Crusaders and conquered Egypt and Syria. They were fighters and farmers. When the Allies carved up the Ottoman Empire after the First World War, they gave a state to the Arab Christians, Lebanon; a state that would go to European Jews, Israel; several states to the Arabs, Iraq, Syria, Jordan. They gave nothing to the Kurds, dividing their homeland among Turkey, Syria, Iran, the Soviet Union and Iraq. The Kurds struggled to survive as disenfranchised aliens in all those states, but in Iraq they were being massacred by Arabs, as they themselves had helped in the Turkish massacre of Armenians seventy-five years earlier.

*

When we arrived at Deir Semaan, the great cathedral and monastery of St Simeon Stylites, I asked Armen to let me first see the village within the ruins. Reluctantly, Armen walked with me, pointing out archaeological features and translating for me. The churches in Deir Semaan were small, like chapels, and their roofs had long since disappeared. One of them served as a stable for the domestic animals, a donkey, some goats. Built into the corner of one church was a mud house, where a man in a brown *abaya* walked out of the only door. To Armen's annoyance, I stopped him to ask about Deir Samaan.

"Excuse me," I said, "do you know anything about this church?"

"No," the man answered.

"How many people live here?"

"I don't know."

"Why not?"

"I don't live here. I arrived today to see my brother."

"Well," I persisted, "how many children does your brother have?"

He looked back at the house and shrugged. "About ten."

A thirteen-year-old boy came out of the house. He said his name was Jihad, and he was more forthcoming than his visiting uncle. He invited us into his house for tea. It was a bare room, with mattresses neatly tucked into a corner and covered with a cloth. The family would lay them on the floor at night for sleeping and put them back each morning. We sat on the floor, and a teenage girl came in with glasses of tea. Armen whispered to me that my notebook, into which I was writing what people were saying and descriptions of the village, made them suspicious. "These peasants will think you're a policeman," he said.

"That's impossible. My Arabic is awful, and I speak to you in English."

"That just makes them think you're from the secret police."

If young Jihad had any suspicions, he did not show them. Through Armen, I asked him, "Did you find the house here, or did you build it?"

"The church was already here," he said, innocently. "My father built the house."

He offered to take us for a walk. Behind the church, a man was ploughing behind a donkey and horse yoked together. "Is that your father?" I asked Jihad.

The uncle interrupted, "No. His father is too lazy to do that."

Beside another mud house in the shadow of a Byzantine villa, three women were moulding cowpats into frisbee-size cakes. We asked them what they were doing. All three were friendly and smiling. Their scarves hid only part of their hair. "We make these to heat our water and to cook on our *tannour*." The *tannour* was a Syrian clay oven for making flat Arab bread. Crouched over the cow dung they were carefully turning into fuel, the women looked at me in my Western trousers and shirt, taking notes. "We are hard workers," one of them said. Her voice, the smile on her face and her manner were as innocent as any child's. "This is the way we live. Is your way better?"

The Dead Cities scattered on the hillsides and plains around Aleppo were in various stages of preservation or disrepair, some wholly deserted, others with families dwelling in them as though the ruins were part of their natural environment, with Roman columns as trees and Byzantine tombs mere caves for storing tools. The cathedrals, monasteries, hospices, summer villas of the rich Antiochan Romans and farmers' houses still stood, cut of rough limestone and assembled without mortar. Some had been hamlets, others large towns. The government had mercifully left them alone, not bothering to build roads to them, rebuild them, rope them off and charge admission to Byzantine "theme parks." Only the hill of Deir Samaan had become the preserve of the Department of Antiquities, and that was probably the fault of the fifth-century monk who spent the years 422 to 459 living there at the top of a column sixty feet above the ground.

The door to the government shack selling entrance tickets and guide books to Qalaat Semaan, the Fortress of Simeon, was locked. Armen knocked loudly, and an unarmed policeman opened. "Where," Armen asked him, walking inside, "is Abu Abdo?"

The policeman went out of another door, leading to the ruins, and returned a moment later with another man in khaki trousers and a white shirt. "Armen!" the man, who was in his fifties and a little fat, shouted. "Abu Abdo," Armen said. He and Armen kissed on both cheeks, the customary greeting, and followed this with inquiries about each other's health, families and work. Armen told him we wanted to take the tour. "But it's very hot today," Abu Abdo said.

Armen looked at him severely, and the man relented. "Moment," he said to me in English. He went into another room and returned wearing his blue, state-issue jacket and a military-style cap with visor. If he had to give us the tour, he was going to make it official. Abu Abdo said Armen could come without paying, but I had to buy a ticket.

Abu Abdo spoke a kind of English and had a clever trick of reflecting sunlight from a pocket mirror to indicate interesting architectural features. He pointed the mirror at a small Roman cross atop a Corinthian capital. "You see that cross?" he asked. "It is Roman." We were inside the roofless cathedral of St Simeon Stylites, built after the saint's death around his column. Abu Abdo pointed the mirror at a succession of crosses. "We have here in the church," he said, the splash of sunlight from his mirror briefly alighting, like Tinkerbell, at several points on the wall, "five crosses: Greek

Orthodox, Byzantine, Roman, Latin, the Syrian sun cross and . . . you know that one?"

Luckily I did. "Maltese?"

"Maltese. So, you know? You know this, like Armen, eh?"

I could not tell him my knowledge was based on a few days' stay in Malta, where the Cross was everywhere.

"Is very, very clever," Abu Abdo explained, "is old architecture. All the stones, they put the keystones. After, they come the earthquake in the sixth, ninth and thirteenth century. After come from Antioch, the Byzantine soldiers. They put fortress. They put twelve towers." By the eleventh century, the Byzantine soldiers abandoned their fortress, from which they had protected the road to Antioch. The site had been deserted ever since.

We walked on a floor of marble that Abu Abdo said had come from Italy. He said the church formed a cross, the long sides north-south, and the arms west-east. "You see eight arches around the column, and four apses," he said, shining the mirror on each. "Now we look to holes in wall. The wall was marble." On the baptismal font was a Syrian symbol I had seen in many of the ruins, four stalks of wheat in a circle as though spun on a Catherine wheel. "That is called *Dawrat al-Hayat*, Cycle of Life," Abu Abdo said. "*Dawra* mean, we go up and we come back. Same the moon. Same the sun." This symbol, in a stylised form, had been adopted in Syria and Lebanon by the modern Syrian Socialist National Party, a group that believed in the political unity of what it called Syria, everything from Cyprus to Kuwait. In Germany, it had become, in an even more stylised, rigid form, the swastika.

"This," our guide said, pointing to the remnant of a Roman pillar about as high as my knee, "is St Simeon column." He gave us the short version of the great ascetic's life. "He come here from Kilikia when he was sixteen. He was monk, but he go to live alone. Forty-two years he live in Deir Semaan and Telanissos. He died in 459, July, aged seventy-three." We were at the centre of the church, where the two arms of the cross met. The sun was directly overhead, and it was hot, particularly for Abu Abdo in his blue wool jacket. Although Armen and I were the only visitors, Abu Abdo complained that 6,000 people had come the previous Friday. When Simeon lived, thousands would flock to his column every day to watch him pray, hear him preach and venerate him. In fact, he conceived the idea of the column to escape the crowds who came from all over the Christian world to touch him when he was merely living on the ground chained to a rock.

I asked Abu Abdo how many Dead Cities there were. The guidebook said seven hundred. "Maybe," he said, "four to five hundred Roman village. From all around, you see, there are Roman cities. I go on foot to all the Dead Cities. I know them. I know people in them. Now come all the archaeologists. What they know?"

What neither Abu Abdo nor the archaeologists had adequately explained was why the people disappeared in the seventh and eighth centuries. The Muslim conquest began in the seventh century, but the Arabs did not expel the Christians. In fact, Islam demanded official toleration of Christianity and Judaism. Looking at the stony hills, I saw that the soil had eroded over centuries, that the fertile fields on which the cities had depended for their wealth no longer sustained much life. Many writers said the Byzantine inhabitants had left when the soil began to erode, but they could, like Abu Abdo, have planted trees to save the soil. The erosion might just as easily have taken place after the inhabitants left, when there was no one to till the fields, maintain the aqueducts, repair the walls, tend the trees. The people had survived the Persian invasions under Chosroes I in the sixth century, when he ravaged Antioch and Aleppo, and under Chosroes II, who captured Damascus and Jerusalem. They had survived internal squabbling, that often led to violence, between rival Christian sects, Monophysites and Chalcedonians, Arians and Nestorians. So, why, in the century after the Arabs came, did they leave? Where did they go? How could villages that fifteen hundred years earlier supported tens of thousands of people today barely provide sustenance for a few hundred? I wondered whether, in centuries hence, a traveller might find, in cities and towns like Aleppo and Antioch that I had seen filled with people, only deserted streets and empty tombs.

Armen was driving the old Nomad at seventy miles an hour through fields of red anemones near the Turkish border. A long stripe of daisies and dandelions turned one meadow into a natural flag. It was spring in northern Syria. Lambs ran after flocks of sheep, and shepherds sat on bare limestone hunched over walking sticks.

"You'll like Qalb Lozé," Armen said. "The people who live there now are Druze, and the women are said to be the most beautiful in Syria." When we drove into the village, blue-eyed women were pulling a bucket of water from a well near a fifth-century church. The church was in the middle of the village. The government had erected a fence around it, and a Baath Party flag flew from what was left of its basilica. The Druze women told us the church was closed that day. Disappointed, we got back into the Nomad. Armen drove to the hills nearby to show me ancient Roman summer villas, where the patricians of Antioch had once sat under vine-covered pergolas drinking Syrian wine.

In another Dead City, Basofan, we saw the ruined Church of St Phocas.

Horses grazed where the altar had been. A cow stood in the apse, and hens sat motionless against the foundations. Where the walls had fallen down, the modern villagers had made a rough barrier of rock and cow dung to keep their animals in the church. Armen ignored the livestock and showed me the old crosses and Syriac inscriptions in the stone. It was a hot day, and the village was dusty. When I saw a man wearing a dark purple *sharwal* and red sweater, I asked Armen whether we could talk to him. He might offer us tea. Armen was not interested. Luckily, the man spoke a little English.

He asked us who we were, then invited us into the shade of his house for tea. The small house and the church shared a wall that tilted precariously in the direction of the house. He set out two plastic stools, taking a shorter, wooden stool for himself. He gave Armen a Syrian cigarette, although he did not smoke. He had a light moustache, fair skin and blue eyes. His hands were the only rough things about him. He spoke softly, and he smiled often. He introduced himself, but he asked me not to use his name in my book.

He was the first Devil Worshipper I had met. I knew it was impolite to ask people their religion, but there were usually signs, like a crucifix on the wall, or a Koran on the shelf. His was a traditional, single-room house with a low ceiling, with another house next door for cooking, and a wall around both to keep animals and children within. In one corner, the sleeping cushions were neatly stacked, and dishes were piled on shelves along a wall. There were no talismans, no brass necklaces with "Allah" in Arabic. The only decoration was a photograph of President Assad. The village itself had no mosque, and the only church had celebrated its last Mass thirteen centuries earlier. "We are not Muslims," he said.

"Christian? Druze?"

"No. We are Yazidis."

"What do Yazidis believe?" I asked him.

Open on most subjects and polite to a fault, he would not be drawn on the subject of his religion. "I don't want to talk about it," he said. He spoke freely about himself and his family, telling us he had been born in 1958, that he had left school ten years ago, that he and his wife had three sons and a daughter. They worked in the fields every day except Friday from seven until 1:30, growing wheat, lentils and olives. He thought more than a thousand people, all Yazidis, lived in the village.

His wife brought us tea, and a little girl sat on his lap. He held her, but she did not speak. "My daughter is deaf and dumb," he said. "I took her to the doctors in Aleppo. They said I had to get her medicine from Lebanon. I got it, but it did nothing."

Unlike the people in Fafirtin, he had no complaints. When I asked if Basofan had running water, he answered hopefully, "It will come." As we spoke, the whole family gathered silently around us, listening. "The important thing," he said, turning at last to the philosophy of the Yazidis, "is so long as you are a human being, we are all human beings. We are all the same."

"All?"

"You know," he said, "the Christians and we are one religion."

"I don't see any church or mosque. Where do Yazidis pray?"

"We can pray any time at home. We don't need a church."

He asked whether we would like to hear any Kurdish music, and he put a tape into his cassette player. It was the rhythmic sound of the *aoud*, the Middle East lute.

"You are Kurds?"

"Yes, we are Kurds. We speak Kurdish. We are the original Kurdish religion."

There was a great deal of ignorance about the Yazidis, and everyone I spoke to in Syria was convinced that they worshipped the devil. In fact, the Yazidis believed in God and worshipped an angel, Malak Ta'us, whom God the Creator had left in control of the world. They did not believe in hell. They did not marry outside their faith. Like the Druze, the Yazidis did not accept converts. Like Christians, they baptised their children. If most Syrians were ignorant of Yazidis, the Yazidis too had strange notions about other religions. "I heard," our host said, "that the Druze worship the cow."

He went out and came back inside with some flowers. He gave a bunch to each of us. A little while later, his mother gave us each a pink rose and said something to her son before going outside. "Where is she going?" I asked.

"She's looking for some *arak* for you to drink."

"So, you drink here? In Islam, drink is *haram*." *Haram* meant forbidden.

"The world without drink," he said, "is *haram*."

When we left, with our flowers and a bottle of local *arak*, Armen asked me, "Did you like those people?"

"I think we both did."

"Yeah. I guess he was a nice guy." That was Armen's only admission that there was more to the ruins than ruins.

CHAPTER TEN

THE VILLAGE OF A PASHA

Every few days, I would see a young woman at the Baron's antique switchboard. Tall and wearing long, billowy trousers, she would be learning over a counter, asking Ahmed or one of the Armenian girls to place a long-distance call for her. I rarely saw her face. On the few occasions when she turned around, she looked Scandinavian, with blue eyes and blonde hair tied back with a scarf. The telephones from Aleppo were unreliable, and she would sometimes be there in the morning when I left to go to Georges Antaki's library and still there when I returned for lunch, waiting for her call. I had no idea where she was calling until one day I too placed an overseas call. I was asking Ahmed to put me through to my children in London, and I was reminding him to place her call to Australia. We began to talk, and I mentioned I had read in Georges Antaki's library that the pigeon post from Aleppo to Alexandretta in the year 1600 took only four hours. I said pointedly, so that Ahmed would hear, that Aleppo's communications system had deteriorated since then. Ahmed called the central operator and brought us Turkish coffee.

The young woman's name was Fiona Hill, and she was an archaeologist from Australia. She lived on the River Euphrates, near some digs she had worked the summer before, with the family of the *mukhtar* in a small village called Yusuf Basha – the *mukhtar* was a village head, akin to a mayor. She was studying the similarities between the ruins and the living village, to understand ancient tools and building techniques in terms of their uses in the village. When I said it sounded interesting, she asked, "Would you like to come? I'm going back there tomorrow."

The next morning, I returned to George Antaki's library to consult Ibn Jubayr's *Travels*. In June 1184, he crossed the Euphrates from the north. "When you cross the Euphrates," he wrote, "you come within the confines of Syria and travel within the dominion of Saladin of Damascus. The Euphrates is the boundary between the regions of Syria and those of Rabi'ah and Bakr." Modern Syria had not lost, but gained, territory in that area. The border of the Syrian Arab Republic extended east and north of the Euphrates, all the way to the River Tigris, an area ruled in earlier centuries from Ctesiphon, Mosul and Baghdad. If Alexandretta, Lebanon, Palestine and Jordan were Syria, then everything beyond the Euphrates was Iraq. Syrian propagandists, who claimed all the lands Syria had lost in 1919 and 1939, never offered to relinquish what it had gained.

Ibn Jubayr took little notice of the River Euphrates or of the tiny villages along its banks, but the first town he came to, Menbij, sent him into raptures:

> Manbij. May God protect it. It is a town of wide extent, and healthy of air. It is encompassed by ancient walls of great length. Its skies are bright, its aspect handsome, its breezes fragrant and perfumed, and while its day gives generous shade, its night is all enchantment. East and west, gardens thick with trees and divers fruits enfold the town. Water flows freely through it and enters its parts; and God has favoured it with wells within that are sweeter than honey and delicious to taste. Each house has a well, or even two, and the earth is generous, throwing forth springs of water everywhere. Its markets and streets are broad and spacious, and its shops and booths are like khans and warehouses in size and grandness. The highest of its markets are roofed, and indeed the markets of most of the cities of these regions are of this style. But a lengthy time is on the heels of this town, and ruin has seized it. It had been one of the ancient cities of the Rum [Byzantines], and the remains of their buildings there attest to their great attention to it.

Menbij's people impressed him no less than the city itself. "The population of Manbij is virtuous and worthy," he wrote, "and they are Sunnis of the Shafi'ite rite, so that through them the town is undefiled by those dissident sects and corrupt beliefs that are found in most of this country." Menbij was to be our first stop on the way to the Euphrates.

Fiona Hill and I met at the Baron's Hotel. She had changed out of her trousers and into a long white linen dress, with sleeves down to her wrists. The scarf she had used to tie back her long blonde hair now covered her head. "My village gear," she said. We walked to the clock tower square to find a *service*. There were scores of them double-parked at the bottom of the square, their drivers calling to potential passengers in loud voices, "Homs, Hama, Damascus . . ." or "Latakia, Tartous . . ." The taxis were mostly old Mercedes, but there were also Chevrolets, Pontiacs, Citroëns, all waiting for five passengers before they would leave Aleppo. Most Levantine cities had *services*, although I never knew when or how they originated. Perhaps they went back to the camel caravan, when people would wait until there was a large enough group with camels and guards to deter attacks by bedouin and Kurds before crossing desert and mountain. The camel caravan, still in evidence in the 1930s, had entirely disappeared, but the *service* was everywhere. I had seen *services* in the centre of town in Beirut, Jerusalem, Amman and Damascus, their drivers calling out their destinations like bookmakers shouting the odds at an Irish race meeting. Some of the old drivers in Beirut had told me that, before 1948 and the birth of Israel, they could drive the route from Beirut south to Jerusalem, over the bridge to Amman, north to Damascus and back to Beirut in a day. In the modern Levant, this was inconceivable.

Fiona and I found a car, probably the oldest, most rusted and filthiest taxi in the square. "Menbij?" I asked the driver. "Menbij," he said. He told us to sit in front. In the torn back seat, there were already three people, an old man and two women with tattoos on their faces. I suspected the man had come to Aleppo with his two wives on a shopping spree, because he had bags of flour, tins of cooking ghee and boxes of soap powder. He and the two women smiled at Fiona and asked us where we were going. "Menbij," she said. They were going to Menbij as well.

The driver stood outside the car staring at the square. I wondered when he would get in. "What are you waiting for, teacher?" I asked him in Arabic. "Teacher" was the Arabic term usually addressed to waiters and drivers.

"Two more."

"Two more?"

"Yeah. Be patient."

Confusion rather than impatience goaded me. There were the three old people in the back. With the driver, we would be three in front, the car and boot were packed with luggage. Where was he going to put two more people? He stood, waiting. Unlike most of the other drivers, he was not calling out his destination. Passengers had to seek him out. Fiona was chatting happily in Arabic to the people in the back, and I sat reading. When Fiona said the bus from Menbij to Yusuf Basha left at 1:00 pm, I feared we would miss it if we waited much longer in Aleppo. I offered to pay the two extra fares if the driver left at once. Although this cost only a few dollars more, the family in the back looked at me as though I were an oil millionaire.

Ibn Jubayr did not mention the tedium of the desert between Aleppo and Menbij, and it took him many days longer than it did us to traverse the distance. Nothing he wrote about Menbij itself had prepared me for it. If every town on earth were vying for the name "Nowhere," a mere two or three could hope to compete with Menbij. It was as ugly and as desolate a market town as ever I had come cross in Africa or elsewhere in western Asia. Nowhere did I see the running water and the gardens described by the great medieval traveller. The only things that resembled trees were the television aerials on rooftops and telephone poles stretching into the desert. I did see hundreds of concrete houses, a few concrete municipal and Baath Party buildings, a concrete police station and paved roads between dusty back streets. The buildings not made of concrete blocks had been daubed in mud the colour of the desert. It was a dull, lifeless place. Either it had lost its glory, or Ibn Jubayr, like many travellers before and since, had exaggerated: Menbij was, simply, a dump.

The driver dropped us in what might have been the town square, an opening in the maze of streets and houses where people gathered outdoors to sell fruits and vegetables, where buses collected and deposited passengers, where shepherds marched their flocks, where old men sat on the ground, backs to concrete walls, talking and smoking hand-rolled cigarettes. We had a few minutes before the bus was scheduled to leave, and Fiona suggested we find Abu Afif, a driver who would take me back to Menbij whenever I wanted to leave Yusuf Basha. There were no telephones in Yusuf Basha, so we had to find the only driver in Menbij who made the trip. We found the house, a single-storey concrete building, its low wall partly surrounding a yard devoid of grass and flowers, on a street not far from the square. We went into the garden and knocked on the door. Some children, who had been watching television, saw us from the window and became excited. I could hear them telling their father that foreigners were coming. A short, well-tanned man opened the door, and behind him in the salon the children were scrambling to put little tea-tables in front of the sofa and to hide their toys out of sight.

Fiona introduced me to Abu Afif, a man in his early fifties, who wore trousers and an open-neck shirt. He was usually either smiling or laughing. Fiona said he was a local character of high standing in the desert, who loved to tell jokes and deliver gossip from village to village. He sat us down and offered tea. I doubted we had time, but Fiona accepted, whispering to me that it would be rude to refuse. Fiona asked him about life in Menbij, and he said things were going well. It had not rained in a long time, but otherwise, God willing, people were surviving. He asked her about Yusuf Basha, the *mukhtar* and his family, about a recent divorce there. Time seemed to pass interminably, as it always did when people met in the desert and exchanged pleasantries. If it seemed there was always time, it was because there always was. Fiona explained, after accepting the tea and discussing the social life of Yusuf Basha, that I would need Abu Afif to pick me up in Yusuf Basha and bring me to Menbij. I would be leaving on a day the bus did not run, which seemed to be most days, and from Menbij I could take a *service* back to Aleppo. Abu Afif said he would be honoured to take me, and I said I would be honoured to ride with him. Neither of us mentioned the fare, and it would have been impolite to ask. We were honouring each other, nothing more, by sharing his car between Yusuf Basha and Menbij. He asked whether I would like to see his car. In English, Fiona said to me, "You've got to see the car."

We walked out of the front door and around the back of the house. There, in all its splendour, in shining black and gleaming chrome, its hubcaps sparkling, its red rear lights rising like Roman candles, was a 1954 Chevy sedan. It had four doors, seats covered in clear vinyl, and the original radio. I expected to see a plastic Jesus on the dashboard, and large foam dice hanging from the rear-view mirror. In Muslim Menbij, only a turquoise amulet to ward off the Evil Eye hung from the mirror and various family pictures and Arabic inscriptions graced the dash. They used to say in Lebanon that you could tell a Christian cab-driver from a Muslim by his car interior: the Christian's looked like an altar, and the Muslim's like a whorehouse. The Muslim's, though in fact more respectable than any brothel, was certainly the more colourful. Abu Afif was proud of his car and the condition in which he kept it. He and I shook hands, and Fiona led me back to the square.

We ran to the bus, arriving just in time for the 1:00 pm scheduled departure to Yusuf Basha and the other Euphrates villages. The old, brightly painted bus was nearly filled with passengers, bags of flour, bags of green beans, open bags of lettuce, sacks of clothing and assorted luggage, some piled on the roof and some on the floor where, in an earlier generation, seats would have been. Sitting inside, there were about fifteen men, some on the few remaining seats, others on the bags. They were mostly old, all dressed in the peasant *abaya* and *keffiyeh*. Their hands were calloused and gnarled, the fingers swollen and knotted like cucumbers. These were men who tilled fields, built houses, had two or three wives and many children, men whose lives did not differ from those of their fathers and grandfathers. There were a few old women, dressed in black, but not the drab, lifeless black of the city *chador*, as in Iran, but loose, flowing black robes, with bodices hand-embroidered in red, gold, green and yellow geometric, floral or bird-like patterns. The needlework was as cheerful as the women themselves, who made way for Fiona at the back of the bus. She sat next to an old woman whose pattern of tattoos circled her lips and dripped down her chin. The woman's coloured scarf was falling to her neck. When she turned to talk to Fiona, another crone lifted the scarf from her own head and gestured to me as if to ask, "Why doesn't she cover her hair with the scarf?" Woman's disapproval of the dress habits and modesty of other women was apparently universal and could never be escaped, even in the Syrian desert. I took an empty seat at the front near an old man with a walking stick.

We sat until 1:30, when the driver boarded without a word. A few minutes later, we left. By now, Fiona was on first-name terms with most of the people in the back, some of whom knew her family in Yusuf Basha. No one showed the slightest surprise that a tall, blonde Australian should choose to live in a remote Syrian village. The driver stopped at hamlets on the long, dusty road to the river. He would drop an old man somewhere on the highway, where a dirt track led into the low hills. He would stop to pick up sacks of vegetables and groups of boys in school uniforms, dropping some of each at different spots on the way. It took about an hour to reach the Euphrates and the village of Yusuf Basha.

The term village, *di'ayah* in Arabic, can mean almost anything. It could describe Zgharta, a village in Mount Lebanon with 50,000 people, modern apartment buildings, electricity, international telephone lines, cinemas, restaurants and discotheques. It is also used to described Yusuf Basha, a settlement of about one hundred adobe houses with no running water, no electricity, no shops, no community centre, no cars, no paved roads and only one small and primitive government primary school. Perched on a stony hill, Yusuf Basha made Menbij seem like a metropolis, yet it had a charm Menbij lacked. Concrete had not arrived. The village looked down on the fertile Euphrates River valley that supplied all its people's needs: mud for building houses, poplars for the poles that supported the ceilings, fish to eat, water to irrigate their crops, water for the bushes that supplied their firewood for cooking, water for themselves and their animals to drink, water for the boys to swim in in summer. It was a lovely place, untouched by the vagaries of the twentieth and probably the nineteenth centuries, where the only contact with the changing regimes in Constantinople, Paris or Damascus was military conscription for the young men and, since the 1950s, school. The village took its name from the Turkish pasha who had owned the land in Ottoman times.

The bus dropped us at the bottom of a hill, where the path to Yusuf Basha began. We carried our bags to the village, past a group of young women around a well pulling up a bucket of water. We walked among mud houses set in enclosed complexes, each family having a house for living, another for cooking and washing, a small hut for a waterless toilet, sometimes another house for extra children or married sons, and a shed for the animals, with a mud wall between or around the buildings to keep the animals in. The houses had one door and one small window each, facing the river. Fiona, who had been on a dig at Abu Girgir with an Australian archaeological survey, said, "These houses have been built in exactly the same way for three thousand years."

Fiona opened the door to one of the enclosures. The women and boys inside welcomed the prodigal daughter as though she had returned from a year in Australia rather than a few days in Aleppo. After they had all kissed her, and she had told them about her trip back, she introduced me to the family of Issa Al-Sultan, Mukhtar of Yusuf Basha. None of the family spoke English, so Fiona felt free to give me a brief biography of each. "This is Shemseh, the *mukhtar's* wife," she said, indicating a sprightly woman in her forties, whose hennaed hair peeked out of her scarf. When she smiled, she exposed a few gold teeth. "The *mukhtar* is away for a couple of weeks, but it's probably just as well. He doesn't seem to care for her much anymore. He dismisses her all the time and wants to get another wife."

"What are you saying?" Shemseh asked her.

"I'm telling him about the family," Fiona said. To me, she continued, "Under that dress, Shemseh is beautifully adorned with tattoos. I've seen her when she washes. She is also very explicit in her talk, so watch out."

She introduced a young man in his late teens. "This is Najad." We shook hands, while Fiona said, "He's in his final year at school. He wants to study medicine." Then in Arabic, to Najad, she said, "And you want to study in Australia, don't you?" He laughed.

"This is Samir, the little brother. He doesn't like to study."

Next came the girls, all of whom wore long dresses and scarves like their mother. "This is Najla. She is married, but I'll tell you about her later." A girl in her early twenties with a serious expression and freckles forthrightly shook my hand. In Arabic, she asked me, "Who are you?"

"This is Sabah," Fiona said. "She's a gem. She's fantastic. Very pious. She taught me to pray."

Sabah and I shook hands. Then the next youngest girl stepped forward. Slender, tall and with natural beauty I had rarely seen, she bowed her head slightly. "This is Fadhaila," Fiona said. "As you can see, she is very, very pretty. What you can't see is, she loves to act and to dance. She's also a good mimic. She can do a very good Aleppo accent, in fact, any accent she hears on the radio." Fadhaila had the kind of sensuous, gypsy-like beauty that inspired tribal wars and desert poetry. Her loose shift was embroidered along its hems, and the fringe of her scarf had a row of small coins. The scarf covered only part of her hair. The rest, dark and thick, curled over her forehead and rolled down her back.

The smallest girl was standing behind me when Fiona introduced her. When I turned to see her, she darted behind her mother and laughed. "That, if you could see her, is Aziza," Fiona said, as the twelve-year-old peered around her mother. "She's very smart. And she speaks some English. She prays five times a day, don't you, Aziza? She says she loves fasting during Ramadan."

"Hello, Aziza," I said in Arabic.

"Go on," her brothers urged her. "Say hello."

"She's very pious, not shy," Fiona said. "If we take photographs, she always makes sure her hair is covered and that she has no embellishments. The other girls put on their best dresses and gold."

We took off our shoes and went inside the main hut, where the family slept at night, received visitors in the day and took their meals. Like most traditional houses, this one had no furniture. There was straw matting on the floor, and small cushions along the walls to lean on. Shemseh offered us tea. "Not if you are fasting," I said.

"We fast, but you are Christian," she said. "You are in our house. We must give you tea."

She and Aziza went out and returned with tea for Fiona and me. They asked me about myself, why I had come to Yusuf Basha, whether I had a family. I showed them three photographs of my wife and children. One picture showed all of us on the steps of a church, the girls in long dresses and the boys in suits.

Looking at my wife's long dress, covering her arms and buttoned tightly at the neck, Shemseh said, "She looks nice, your wife." Turning to Fiona, she asked, "Is she Muslim?" She showed the picture approvingly to her daughters.

Then she counted the children. "Five children?" Shemseh said. "Why only five?"

I didn't have the heart to tell her that only three were mine, and the other two were my stepdaughters, so I said, "I want to have more. There is time."

The second picture was of my youngest daughter, Julia, who was sitting with a rabbit in its hutch on the grass. "Is she in a cage?" Shemseh asked me, surprised. "No," I said. "She's playing with the rabbit. It doesn't lock."

The third photograph shocked her. When she looked at the picture of me kissing my wife on our wedding day, she said, "*Haram*," and hid it from her daughters' view. The girls quickly looked at it, giggling.

"Don't they ever kiss in public?" I asked Fiona.

"I don't think they kiss even in private."

It seemed strange that the women in Yusuf Basha should pray and fast, yet leave their faces, some of their hair and their arms exposed. "Covering the face is a city thing," Fiona said. "A devout woman, with her face covered in black, came here once from Aleppo. She was outraged with the women here for not covering their faces and for showing their hair. But they do it because it is prettier than not having any hair. And there is nothing in the Koran saying they have to cover their faces. She criticised them for wearing gold, for tattooing their faces and hands, but that's beautiful. She was outraged that they should be immodest."

"What did they say to her?"

Fiona asked Shemseh what she had said to the lady from Aleppo. She answered, "Nothing." She still had her tattoos, and some of her hair was showing.

Fiona and I walked through the fields of wheat and green beans down to the river bank, where several men were repairing a water pump. The one who seemed most intent on replacing damaged parts was in his twenties, but had grey hair. He was thin, with a thick moustache. He stood with his shirt off, sweating over the ancient machine. He told the others to hold the pump while he turned a wrench, tightening a nut around a large bolt. A young boy, about eight years old, ran up to us and said, "The pump is broken, but Hussein is fixing it." Hussein leaned his whole body over the wrench, pushing with all his strength. The others held the old pump steady. The wrench moved, and Hussein pressed it further, tightening it round and round. He stopped, took some diesel fuel and primed the carburettor. Then he wound a rope around the starter and pulled it free. The motor sputtered and stopped. He rewound the rope tighter, then pulled it with both hands. The motor coughed again, and Hussein turned the fuel tap. The pump jarred into life, smoking and belching. A long, fat hose sucked water from the river through the pump, into a thin pipe that showered water over the fields. The boy cheered, "Water. Look at the water. Ya, Hussein." The boy, named Hassan, not surprisingly turned out to be Hussein's brother.

Hussein seemed strangely silent, packing his tools and setting the water pipes. Fiona told me he was on leave from the army. He had been feeling lost, she said, since his separation from his wife. She introduced Hussein Al-Sultan, cousin of the *mukhtar*, and told him I was writing a book about Syria. We shook hands, but we found it difficult to speak to each other. He spoke no English, and my Arabic, learned in Beirut, was neither fluent nor capable of understanding many of the words in his Euphrates dialect. I liked him. He commanded respect, perhaps because he knew what he was doing, looked older than he was and wore the traces of suffering in his tanned face.

A police patrol boat chugged up the river, and one of the uniformed men on board waved to us. "What are they doing?" I asked. Young Hassan answered, "They are looking for fishermen who should not be fishing at this time of year."

"What happens if they catch them?"

Fiona translated the boy's slang answer. "The cops? They just take some of the fish or some money, and they go away again."

Hassan played a game with Fiona, one they had obviously played before. He would tell her a word in English and ask her what it meant in Arabic. When she guessed, he said, "No, not that," and laughed. "What is it then?" she asked him. He would not tell her and laughed again. "He learns these words in school," she explained. "Half the time, he gets them wrong. The English teachers don't speak English themselves."

Hussein took a drink of water. "Isn't he fasting during Ramadan?" I asked Fiona. "No. Most people here pray. Everyone knows who fasts and who does not, but there is no pressure."

"That is very tolerant."

"Islam preaches tolerance," she said. "Some people want to forget that. Quite a few people have come to me and said, 'Are you Fiona? Are you studying Islam? Well, you are not going to find it in Yusuf Basha.' I say, 'There is Islam here. The people pray, and there is a mosque. They're aware of the law, although they don't follow it too strictly. There is Islam in Yusuf Basha.'"

"What laws don't they follow?"

"They shouldn't be fishing at the moment. Apart from being forbidden by local law, it is *haram*, according to the Koran, to fish or hunt in certain months. When a family here was going through a divorce, a little boy asked me, 'How can they pray five times a day and cause so much upset to each other?' He said it didn't make sense. And young men don't pray until they get married. When I asked them about this, they said, 'How can we pray and then go out looking at all the girls, talking and thinking about girls all the time? It would be hypocritical. So we don't pray until we are married and have more sense.'"

Fiona laughed, as I did, at the thought of marriage giving people sense. Islam in the villages along the Euphrates reminded me of Catholicism in remote parts of Mexico. It may not have pleased the purists and the fanatics, but it was true faith in God.

Fiona began to point out where the different crops were grown, in the slice of green between the river and the desert: the rows of oranges, pomegranates, figs, walnuts, cucumber and cotton. She said the similar villages above the opposite bank were also carefully built just beyond the fertile soil near the river. From the hills behind us came a dust storm, spreading a layer of sand over us and the fields. It was hard to see as we trudged back up the hill to find shelter in the single room of the *mukhtar's* house.

That night, eight of us sat on the floor for dinner. We squatted around a large tin dish on which there were smaller tin bowls of rice, grilled river fish and pickled lettuce. Lying about the large plate were loaves of rough, thick Arabic bread and raw spring onions. It was dark outside, and the only light in the house was a kerosene lamp on the floor. No one spoke. As we ate, I felt we were like wolves in a pack, pulling food from the common prey. Watching the children and their mother, I saw their eyes glowing with the reflected light of the lamp. With their round gold earrings, each girl looked as if she had four eyes, or four magnificent jewels. The eyes and earrings blazed up and down as the girls ate, shining directly at me when they stopped to look. Their motions seemed frenzied, like a gypsy dance. I looked back, particularly at Fadhaila, the prettiest. She could not have been more innocent, but in that moment, in that light, smiling at me between bites of food, she might have been Delilah in Gaza or Salome at Herod's court. I would gladly have offered her my hair – even my head – to prolong the glances she gave me. There was a passion in the air, with the glowing eyes and jewels, her seductive smiles, her wild, curling hair dropping to her shoulders. It was slightly intoxicating, and I knew the passion was fantasy, born of my imagination. Still, I felt strangely primitive, eating as people had eaten there for thousands of years. The more the girls ate, the more I ate. The more they looked at me, the more I looked at them. And I saw something in their eyes, especially in Fadhaila's eyes. Eyes like hers were the inspiration for Arabic romantic poetry, for the exciting tales of Abla and Antar – the desert lovers who, before Islam, were the Paris and Helen of the Arabs. Romance was all in the eyes, often the only part of a girl's face a man might see. In Arabic poetry, to see the eyes was to see all. More perhaps than any other word, *ayoun*, eyes, cropped up in Arabic love poems. The modern Palestinian poet, Mahmoud Darwish, wrote of the power of a woman's eyes in "Lover from Palestine":

> Your eyes
> A thorn in my heart
> Painful yet adorable
> I shield it from the wind
> And stab it deep through the night
> Through pain,
> Its wound illuminates the darkness
> Transforms my present into future
> Dearer than my soul
> And I shall never forget as our eyes meet
> That once we were together behind the gate.

When we had finished eating, one of the girls carried the dinner tray outside. The youngest, Aziza, brought a jug of water for us to wash our hands. Fadhaila brought fruit, and Shemseh poured tea from a brass pot into clear glasses. When I asked to have mine without sugar, this caused a good deal of giggling among the girls and mild surprise from the mother. It was a little like asking for a bottle of ketchup at the Connaught Grill. "No sugar?" Shemseh asked. "Are you ill?"

We then did what the Al-Sultans and every other family did each evening in Yusuf Basha. We sat on the floor talking by the light of the kerosene lamp. We sipped tea and received male visitors, nearly all of whom were somehow related to the Al-Sultan family. They talked, as they did every day, of the most intimate details of their lives with no more self-consciousness than if they had been discussing the weather. They told of marital difficulties, sought advice on how to treat their wives and husbands, contemplated divorce and considered their children's futures. There was, I realised, no privacy in the village. No privacy of thought, of being, of action. There were no secrets. There was nowhere to hide. Life was much as it had been in medieval Europe, when families dwelled in a single room and even the king received petitioners in his bedchamber.

Hussein and his brother, Hassan, came and sat. For a while they did not speak, and there was nothing strange about this. Long periods of silence were not considered awkward. Hussein began to discuss his children and what he should do about them. Because so few families could afford to pay a dowry of 100,000 SL to the bride's family, many arranged an exchange by which the son and daughter of one family married the daughter and son of another. That way, all debts were cancelled. However, if one marriage failed, there remained the problem of how to make good the dowry, so, inevitably, the other marriage would fail as well.

It seemed that five years earlier Hussein had married a girl, whose brother married his sister – both marriages arranged by the fathers. Hussein's wife complained of not having her own house, although it was customary for a new wife to live with her husband's family. She felt she had to work too hard looking after Hussein's nine sisters and his younger brother, Hassan. Hussein did not want to move to a new house, because his sisters were his responsibility until they married. His wife's father decided to take his daughter back. It was not clear whether this was to save his daughter the drudgery of looking after Hussein's family or because he needed her to work in his own house. This wounded Hussein deeply, not least his pride. In the meantime, Hussein's father responded to the insult by demanding the return of his daughter, Hussein's sister, Maria. All children stayed with their fathers, according to custom. Hussein, who had to return to the army, was wondering what to do with his two daughters.

"Both sides are very unhappy," Fiona explained. "If you see them walking around the village, they look fairly gloomy. Just lately, they've decided it's a stalemate, so they will have a divorce, which means going to the authorities to have it marked in the book. A red cross – they cross out the name of the wife. Then it's all official. It's quite simple."

Hussein was coming to accept the end of his marriage, but Maria and her husband were despondent. "The children can visit the mother," Fiona said. "I mean, the children run wild in the village. When I saw Maria, she looked very red-eyed. She'd obviously been crying a lot, because her husband is very nice, and she loved him very much. But she had to come back, because Hussein's marriage didn't work out. She'd been crying a lot, but her daughter was with her then, just visiting."

Hussein's younger daughter, born after the separation, was six months old. His sisters had been trying to care for her, but she had not been weaned. One woman in the village offered to take care of the baby. Eventually, she gave her to the real mother, who would wean her and return her to Hussein.

"What should I do?" Hussein asked. He wanted his wife to breastfeed their daughter, but customary practice was to keep all children in the father's house.

Aziza said she would take care of Hussein's children, but Shemseh shouted, "You'll have to show them you have milk first." Grabbing her own breast, she squeezed it playfully and laughed. The pious ladies of Aleppo would not have liked that.

Disconsolate, Hussein said to Fiona, "Perhaps I should become a Christian. Christians don't have to lose their wives when their fathers say so."

Hassan said, "Okay. Let's bring a priest and go to the river. You'll go under the water Muslim and come back up a Christian." At this, everyone laughed.

Najla, who was more serious than the other girls, said, "Our way of marriage is bad. Everyone gets divorced, because there is no love. We cannot marry the one we love, but our father chooses the one who pays."

Najla spoke from bitter personal experience. It was strange that she should be there, in her father's house, and not with her husband. Later, Fiona told me, "She was to marry a young man who was the darling of the village, but her father forbade her. He likes to marry his children to relations, close relations. I'm told there were beatings involved, and lots of tears, and she was eventually dragged to the wedding with her cousin. She married him, and there were no offspring. It was a good excuse to leave him, and she returned to the family. He took another wife and has three children by her. He came back, and he's taken Najla again. She's just resigned herself. She's had some good offers from quite a few other men. She's just not interested. I think her heart is fairly dead."

"Do divorced women usually marry again?" I asked her.

"They can, but they won't get an offer from a man in the same village. If they accept an offer from someone outside the village, it means they have to go to his village. If Hussein's sister Maria gets an offer of marriage, it won't be from anyone in this village. No man here would take her and then see her first husband. It is not *haram*, but it is indiscreet."

As the night grew late, Hussein left and other visitors arrived. I heard stories of marriage and divorce, of birth and death, of lovers trapped in a net of tradition. I would never again be able to use the term "simple" peasant or "simple" villager, as though machinery and electricity gave modern life its complexity. Their lives were as complex, and as compelling, as any I had known. Fiona told me another story, while Shemseh sympathised with her next visitor.

"A girl here was suspected of being pregnant last year. I told them, 'No, it couldn't possibly be,' because there is no such thing as privacy in the village. I don't see how a couple could get off together and do it. Sure enough, she was pregnant. She gave birth to twins. I'm told they were killed at birth, strangled."

"By whom."

"By the girl's mother. The girl was not damaged in any way, but her brother, who was working in Saudi Arabia at the time, returned to the village. He packed up all his goods, his wife and children, and moved them to town. He won't speak to his sister ever again. He says he will never look at her. Their father is dead, and the mother and daughter still live here on their own. Her cousin had made her pregnant. She was actually engaged to another man, who was doing his military service. He was heartbroken, because he loved her. Now he can never marry her." The story was so sad, I could hardly bear to listen to it: murdered twins, an abandoned girl, a disgraced mother, the shame of a brother and the lost love of a boy away at war. As in the *Iliad*, everyone was a victim, except the gods.

While her elders talked, Aziza played, repeating English words to Fiona and occasionally pinching her sisters and brothers. Finally, Shemseh smacked her gently. The girl laughed, and, as the hour grew late, she put her head on her mother's lap and fell asleep.

Gradually, one child or another would fall asleep, and the visitors drifted away. Shemseh and the older girls put sleeping mats down and laid coloured sheets over the children. Nearly everyone slept in that room, but I would sleep in the hut nextdoor, with Fiona and the boys. Fiona often slept in there alone, but, while I was there, the boys seemed to be chaperones of a sort for their adopted sister. When I went into our room, there were four mats on the floor with sheets. Najad was already in bed, studying by the light of a kerosene lamp. He said that, if I liked, he would awaken me to go fishing before dawn. The boat would be ready. Accepting his offer, I put my bag in a corner and went outside to wash.

The yard surrounded on three sides by the family sleeping-houses and the kitchen seemed to be the model for the old Arab houses of Aleppo, with their enclosed courtyards open to the sky, but these yards had no fountains. Looking for water, I went outside the gate and looked down from the village to the Euphrates. The only light on earth came from the sky above, the reflection of the moon and stars twinkling on the waves in the current. The river carried its water and its seasonally illegal fish south past Babylon and Ctesiphon and Baghdad, past the ashes of a dozen empires, to a Persian Gulf where even that night, Persians and Arabs battled as they had a thousand years before. Mud villages stood silent and still on both banks. Only the river moved, however slowly, past a way of life that moved with the seasons, with the phases of the moon, not forward or backward, but in cycles, "*Dawrat al-Hayat*, the Cycle of Life. We go up and we come back. Same the moon. Same the sun."

In the sky, I saw more stars than I had ever seen. On earth, I saw palms silhouetted against the night sky and the moonlight in the river. I saw where civilisations had been born and died, where self-proclaimed deities and mighty armies had raised their banners in glory and been annihilated, where man had learned to cultivate fields and starved to death, where centuries of innovation, reform and successive cultures had not altered the way a house was built. I saw a land with darkened villages that did not, between them, have a single electric light to blot out the stars. I saw a river, a land and a sky that told me I was infinitely small and insignificant.

CHAPTER ELEVEN

THE ROAD

When morning came, the boys were already gone. They had gone fishing during the night without me, not wishing to disturb my sound sleep. Fiona was in the cooking hut, helping Shemseh to make breakfast. The family had eaten before dawn, enabling them to fast during the daylight hours. I put on my trousers and shirt, folded my sheets and went from the cool mud hut into the heat of the sun. A few chickens were pecking the ground. I opened the kitchen door and saw Shemseh rolling a sheep's belly back and forth on the floor. "What are you doing?" I asked her.

"Making yogurt." My appetite for breakfast evaporated, and I asked where I should brush my teeth. She gave me a clay jug of water and a pan and told me to brush outside. Shemseh came out with a tray of thick Arabic bread, yogurt, cucumbers and tea, and invited me into the house for breakfast.

Aziza was sitting in the room talking to her older sisters when I went in. I sat on the floor, and the rest of the family came in to sit with me while I ate. Fiona said she had already had her breakfast. I ate as much as I could, the yogurt tasting not quite right to me. All the while, Shemseh was reprimanding me for not eating enough. I sipped tea for a while, and the morning visiting began. Neighbours dropped in, talking about nothing in particular, passing the time when there was no work to do. The magic of the night had passed, and the talk now seemed tedious. I was trying to think of an excuse to get myself outside. What could I say? That I had an appointment? No one had appointments in Yusuf Basha. That I was meeting a friend for lunch? That I had to catch a train? None of the usual methods of polite social escape applied. I asked Fiona what I should tell them so I could leave. "We're going for a walk," she announced, standing and leading me through the door. They continued their conversation as though we had never been there. So much for the polite way out.

We did what people seemed to do most of the time in the seasons between planting and harvest; we visited other people. Fiona led me to another enclosure. A thin woman in a blue shift was cleaning the house, and she came out to kiss Fiona. "This is Khadija," Fiona said. Khadija invited us into her house. We removed our shoes, went in and sat on the floor, leaning against the wall. Khadija went to make tea, and one of her daughters came in with a small baby. She breastfed the infant, while she and Fiona talked.

"Khadija is the *mukhtar*'s cousin," Fiona told me. Everyone who was not the *mukhtar*'s wife or child or brother seemed to be his cousin. "She has a lovely way of telling stories. If she gets a gathering of people in the house with the lamplight flickering, she'll tell them a story that usually begins, 'A long time ago, there was a king, and he had a son. The son fell in love with a peasant girl, and . . .' The story goes on like that for hours. People in the room will start interjecting or arguing or gasping, really living the whole story, even if they've heard it before. She never hesitates for a moment."

Khadija came back with tea for us, but not for herself and her daughter, who were fasting. "Khadija," I said, "is a pretty name. It was the wife of the Prophet Mohammed."

"That's right," Khadija said. "God's blessings be on him."

"Fiona said you were a *hakawati*," a storyteller, I said in my poor Arabic. "I wish I spoke enough Arabic to understand your stories."

"You can learn."

"I wish."

"Stay in Yusuf Basha. We will teach you."

"Story telling," Fiona said, "is very popular here. So is making up songs and poems. Sometimes, if you go to a house for the first time, a young man will sing a song of welcome. They will splash you with perfume, and they'll make up a little rhyme with your name in it."

I had seen the Turks offer one another perfume in Alexandretta on special occasions, like Police Day. And in Beirut, I remembered that the Sunni Muslims at public gatherings used to chant poems with people's names in them. I went to a match of the Beirut Sunni football team, *Ansar*, and listened to the crowd chant dozens of spontaneous, risqué rhymes using the name of the club's sponsor, my friend Salim Diab. Perhaps these were ancient Sunni Muslim traditions going back to village life. I had not heard the Shiah, the Druze or the Christians do anything of the kind.

Fiona and I strolled through the fields, down to the river and along a path leading to more fields along the bank. We passed many people from the village out for similar strolls. Hassan, Hussein's little brother, followed us part of the way. We saw some of the girls from the house. We passed the cemetery in which most of the former inhabitants of Yusuf Basha had been buried. There was no grass, only the sand that began at the end of the fertile soil near the river and extended further than the eye could see. There were no carved stones with the names of the dead, only piles of rock, the oldest of them fading out of existence. For these mostly devout

Sunni Muslims, life, both this one and the next, was important. What happened to the corpse, to the empty shell we left behind, was of little consequence.

"Have you been to any funerals here?" I asked Fiona.

As so often happened when I asked her a question, she, like the villagers, told me a story. "There was a girl from a village nearby," she began. "She was going down to the river on a donkey, as you see girls doing here. The donkey slipped at the river and fell on her leg and broke it. She was very sick. She was a young girl, a bit younger than me. They said she was very beautiful, and she was this and that, very virtuous. She didn't recover and died the very day of the *Eid*. We were celebrating the *Eid al-Fitr*, the end of Ramadan, giving sweets to the children, kissing one another and going to the mosque. They brought her here, her family, by tractor, to this cemetery, because she has relatives here. The men dug a grave that day, and we all gathered. The men stood close to the grave, and the women were a fair way back, crying loudly, all wearing black. Closer relatives and the official wailers walked around screaming."

"What is an official wailer?"

"A woman, usually an older woman, whose duty it is to cry and to wail. It's like getting rid of the bad spirits from the dead. They tend to set the mood of the funeral. The men in the meantime gather close to the grave. The girl is washed and dressed in white. She has no adornments, no gold. They put her on a mattress into the grave, and they throw the dirt directly onto her. Then the grave is built up with stones. A sheikh comes and reads the Koran, and the men join in. Then the women come closer once all that's done. They discuss what's gone on. Afterwards, they asked me, 'Did you cry, Fiona?' I said, no, that I didn't really know her. And besides, I was happy that she, who they had told me was so young and beautiful and virtuous, must have gone straight to heaven. I was happy for her. They said, 'Ah, no, no. She might not have. You should have cried. You should have. You should have prayed for her.' "

Just outside the village, we found the remains of a Roman tomb embedded in the rock. The body and sarcophagus had long since vanished, only the empty cave and its impressive doorway remained.

"Do you think you'll die here too, like a Roman far from home?"

"I don't know," she said. "I have to decide whether to stay here or go back to Australia."

"What would you do here?"

"Continue my studies. Do research on the ancient Euphrates villages and the Euphrates today."

"Is it that interesting?"

"It's fascinating. The excavation team will often dig up a room or be

161

puzzling over a doorway, wondering why it's the way it is. I can take one look and say, 'It's the same now in the village.' The archaeologists who work on this site are ethnocentric, and, although they live in villages like this, they never speak to the villagers. They have nothing to do with them and don't notice the environment of the village. I find it shocking, quite amazing. There are so many similarities that it's as if the village we're in now, if you came back in two thousand years, would be the same as the village we're digging up at the moment, exactly the same. Of course, there are implements they didn't have, like the oil drums, the gas stoves or whatever. But everything else is the same. The mud houses are the same, the wooden ceilings were made in the same way. The basalt grinding stones are the same. The doors open the same way. It's not our way of designing doors at all. The design of the town is the same now as it was then. It's haphazard, putting up mud huts wherever there's room. The streets are of packed earth. You'll find it when you're digging. You wonder why. It's obviously been walked across a lot, watered a lot and walked across again. You find new layers of soil when you're digging, and we see the same in this village. It's not a new layer of habitation. It just means they were reinforcing their walls again. If you just look around the living village, you don't have to look far to see the same thing in the ruins. You can see yourself how Biblical it is."

"But could you settle here? Could you get married here?"

"I don't know. I've had offers," she laughed. "But I love these people. And I love my Mum and Dad at home. It's just that people here are so much more genuine. There is no hypocrisy. They don't hide anything."

"What will you do?"

"I wish I knew."

Shemseh invited me into the house. She was alone and bade me to sit on the floor. "I want you to have this scarf for your wife," she said, almost conspiratorally. She had pulled a machine-made black scarf with printed roses on it out of a clear plastic bag. It was far from the folkloric, hand-woven product I would have expected from a small village. It was the sort of thing anyone could buy at Woolworth's, and it was far from pretty. I thought it rude to refuse such a kind offering, so I thanked her. She then pulled more scarves out of the bag, as well as some handkerchiefs, *keffiyehs*, table cloths and bed spreads. None was a local product. She said, "That is for your wife, God bless her. Now, you must take these for your children."

"No, my lady," I told her, using the Arabic honorific for an older woman, *Sitti*. "I can't. You must keep these. I can buy things just like this in the souq."

"I'm like the souq," she said. At last, she had tipped her hand. These were not the heartfelt gifts of a kind hostess, but a bit of Syrian mercantilism. I had to admire her guile. I bought two scarves for 150 SL, but I had no idea what I would do with them. As Fiona opened the door, removing her shoes before she came in, Shemseh quickly hid the plastic bag of dry goods beneath a cushion.

"Did she sell you something?" Fiona asked me.

I realised I was not Shemseh's first customer. Shemseh was an incorrigible capitalist. I had to admire her for her *chutzpah*, even if that was not the word she would have used. Shemseh looked at me, wondering what Fiona had asked me in English. I couldn't betray the old lady.

Hussein, his omnipresent brother Hassan, Fiona and I were sitting in a field, looking down at the river. They had just told me the government was going to build a dam downstream. Water would drown their valley, their houses and their village.

"Where will you go?"

"I don't know," Hussein said.

"How long has the village been here?"

"A long time."

Fiona added, "Most of the old people here know they have been in this particular village for about a hundred years. Before that, nobody knows. Somebody in the Euphrates region must know. They told me the village started as three houses." She repeated this in Arabic to Hussein, who said, "I think we came from the bedouin, a long time ago. We have cousins who are bedouin."

Hassan said, "In the new village, we will have running water, electricity and television." Television would no doubt put an end to Khadija's story-telling, just as it had for the *hakawati* on the roof of the Hammam Nahaseen in Aleppo.

"They'll have all the mod cons," Fiona said, sadly. "They are looking forward to it. But I think that, as the day draws closer, they will mind. There is a village near here that was flooded. The people moved to modern houses. When the flood subsided, they moved back to their original village and rebuilt their houses exactly as before."

"This flood won't subside," I said.

On the afternoon I was to leave Yusuf Basha, Abu Afif's 1954 Chevy came trundling in on time. I was surprised to see him, because people here rarely kept appointments. He compensated for his promptness by coming into the house for several cups of tea. Although a Muslim, he was not fasting. No one in the family seemed to mind, and the women happily brought him tea and sugar and begged him for the gossip of Menbij. He told them someone had had a son. *"Hamdal'ilah,"* they all said, "Thank God." He told them a certain young man from Menbij had gone into the army. To this, there were unanimous sighs of, *"Haram,"* meaning, "Pity."

Before I left, Hussein came to say goodbye. I had grown to like and respect him, and I told him I hoped everything would work out. "I'm going back to the army next week," he said. Perhaps things would resolve themselves in his absence.

I did not know whether he would be sent to Lebanon, where Syria stationed more than 30,000 of its troops. Syrian soldiers were unpopular there, and different Lebanese factions occasionally planted car bombs near Syrian positions. Knowing Hussein, I found it harder to see the Syrian soldier the way the Lebanese did, as a stupid and rapacious occupier. Hussein, like most of his comrades, was just a young man forced into army service, hoping to survive it and come home to family problems. Who could feel bitterness against him? I supposed this had been the way with most occupying armies, ordinary men thrust into the villains' role. For most Lebanese, and they were probably right, the only way to force out the occupying armies of Syria and Israel was to kill their soldiers.

"Don't go to Beirut," I warned him.

"Don't you go to Beirut," he said. "You are always welcome here. This is your home, and we are your family."

Fiona came to the car to wish me a safe journey. We parted friends, and I said I hoped she would make the right decision, choose the right family. I saw the attraction of these warm, decent people. But, somehow, I did not think she would live out her days in Yusuf Basha. It was a place a person had to be born in. Its people affected her, making their concerns her own, and she found it hard to let go. Perhaps she had, for a moment, touched some of them as well. That was the most any outsider could hope.

When Abu Afif dropped me at the square in Menbij, I decided not to wait for five people to fill a *service*, so I splashed out the ten dollars or so for a taxi to myself. The car I found, an old Mercedes with a feather above the radiator and "Allah" inscribed on the dashboard, lacked the panache of Abu Afif's Chevy, but it was going to Aleppo. The driver was unusually silent for a Syrian, but I had no desire to talk either. I gazed out of the window at more and more miles of desert passing between me and the Euphrates. Occasionally, I would see another car, or a flock of sheep and goats, or a village. Then, I had a shock.

Aleppo loomed in the near distance like a foreign planet. Once, it had seemed so provincial, so Oriental, with its domes, minarets and Citadel. Coming from Yusuf Basha, I saw it for the first time through the eyes of a Syrian peasant. In the poorer suburbs of the east, a long carpet of cracked wheat was spread across the pavements. Country people who had recently moved to Aleppo were drying the wheat in the sun as they would in their village. This seemed perfectly natural. Before, I had seen the city of Aleppo growing along the hilltops, as the suburbs ate into the countryside. Now, I realised that the village had come to the city, planting itself outside and growing in. The poor farmers were bringing their customs, their ways, to cosmopolitan Aleppo, as they were to Damascus and Beirut. They were turning their apartments into compact versions of their mud houses – the families sleeping together in one room, cooking in another, washing in another, each room like one of the little huts around their yards. It was not poverty, but tradition, that put a whole family into one room. This was the only security they had in a city that was at once unwelcoming and alien.

I found myself smiling at men in *abayas*, people from whom I had once kept my distance, believing them taciturn and unfriendly. They returned my smiles and my waves with the same kindness I had seen in the village. Before, the peasants had looked strange in Aleppo, walking in sandals next to their tattooed wives. Now, the city-dwellers in trousers or short skirts seemed foreign.

A little further on, I saw the city itself in all its vulgarity and madness. Men in business suits and hard shoes walked the streets. The buildings were higher than the hill on which Yusuf Basha had been built. There were shops with windows and doors open, shops selling goods unheard of in Yusuf Basha – refrigerators, televisions, leather shoes, suits, furniture. People seemed to be too busy selling things to one another to sit and talk. Cinemas displayed posters that before I had found quaintly coy, but that now seemed lewd and provocative. Some women covered their faces in an unnatural way, while others exposed more flesh than would have been proper in Yusuf Basha.

For the first time in all my years in the Levant, I saw how corrupting the peasant and the bedouin found the city. Arab tradition said that every other generation brought a wave of reformers, religious zealots, from the desert to purify the city. It had happened in Saudi Arabia many times, lasting until the luxury of city life corrupted that generation's sons. I wondered whether it would happen in Syria.

The next day, I took a bus to Hama. My only plan was to reach Aqaba by July for the seventieth anniversary of the fall of its Turkish fortress to Feisal, Lawrence and the tribesmen of the Arab revolt. That left me three more months to see the rest of Syria, Lebanon, Israel and Jordan. In between lay borders, demilitarised zones and battle lines that would not have been there had the Turks held out at Aqaba as they did at Gallipoli.

The first city on the road south was Hama, a pretty town with domed and arched houses lying on both banks of the River Orontes. "Hama is," Mark Sykes wrote in 1904, "excepting Damascus, by far the most picturesque city in Syria . . ." Its giant Roman water wheels, *nouras*, still turned, but the water cascaded from broken aqueducts pointlessly back into the river. The slow revolutions of the wheels, in time with the water's flow, acted like a metronome in setting the pace of life in Hama. On the east bank of the Orontes, there were public gardens laid out in neat flowerbeds, well tended and clean. Old men sat on benches, reading newspapers. Children gambolled lazily on the paths. Women and girls walked slowly, with grace and dignity, in the shade of the trees. Most were draped in black from head to toe, but the less modest covered only their hair and left their faces exposed.

Near the middle of the park, there were three wooden cages side by side. In one was a peacock, in the second a vulture and in the third several great bustards. At the far end were two more cages, a strange miniature zoo, one on top of the other: above was an eagle, below a badger. In the quiet gardens, the creaking of the water wheels was the only sound.

Near the main bridge over the river, fifty teenage girls in military-style uniforms were on their way to school. Of the fifty, only two had their heads uncovered. Most wore white scarves to hide their hair, but a few had the caps that went with the uniform.

I walked north along the riverside, passing more of the great water wheels that were once part of an irrigation system that made Syria the breadbasket of the Roman Empire. Both banks of the river were green with grass and plants. On the west bank, I saw some old mosques covered in creepers and shaded by eucalyptus. I walked across an old footbridge towards the mosques, along a deserted cobbled alley with empty Ottoman stone buildings on both sides. On some of the doors to what were once pretty, traditional Arab houses with courtyards and fountains, were signs in Arabic saying, "Entry forbidden." Around one turn in the alley, I saw two men outside a house playing cards. They invited me to sit with them.

"What is this place?" I asked them.

"Down there," one of them said, "is the Turkish bath."

"Is it open?"

"Not any more."

"And the house there, the big house?"

"I don't know," he said. "No one lives there now."

For such a large town, Hama's streets seemed strangely deserted. The grand old palaces of the Keylani and Azzem families, prominent pashas under the Ottomans, were closed. There was not so much as a dog on the path where the men were playing cards. I asked the way to the souq, where I thought I would find some people, and walked up a hill to the main street.

The old marketplace was just behind. In the souqs, people worked in the shops and many more were shopping. The souqs were not crowded, like those of Aleppo. They were in the open air and, with trees planted at short intervals, well shaded and pleasant. Yet, apart from a row of gold merchants in one corner, the only things for sale in any of the shops were cheap imported crockery, kitchenware, badly made shoes and rubber sandals, vegetables and meat. There was no work going on, as in Aleppo. These shops were merely for selling goods from elsewhere. I did see a barber, with a tarboosh on his head, repairing another tarboosh, while a little boy watched him at work. Most of the men shopping wore *abayas*, there from their villages to shop in the city. Most of the Hama men wore trousers.

I saw one girl with her head uncovered, wearing a crucifix, obviously one of Hama's Christian minority. Nearly all the women had their faces covered, but women were fewer in number compared to men. Only men worked in the souq, fathers, sons, brothers of all ages working in family businesses that passed from one generation to the next. To my surprise, there was only one shop selling what were called "Hama print" cloths. Manufactured in Hama, they were pretty white cotton linens used for tablecloths, bedspreads, curtains and furniture coverings. The people who made them would press wooden moulds dipped in black dye onto the cotton in the form of doves, roosters, flowers and geometric forms.

When I asked the shopkeeper why there was so little Hama print in the souq, he seemed reluctant to discuss it. "I've seen far more in Damascus," I said.

"Before," he answered me.

"Before what?"

"Before 1982."

"What do you mean?"

"Before 1982, there were five families who made the Hama cloth. You used to see them, drying the cloths by the river. Now, only one family is left."

One part of the souq backed onto an old mosque. Near the mosque, where there were no shops, merchants sold their wares from a dozen makeshift wooden stalls, like those used in Beirut by men who had lost their businesses in the war. Behind the mosque, I saw where their shops had been. It was a wide, empty field. Tons of rubble had been pushed by bulldozer to the extremities, where portions of buildings stood, their open floors battered and exposed, steel spikes sticking out of the concrete like the rib-cage of half-eaten prey. The open area, which had been a busy souq, with offices and houses, was more than a quarter mile square. The large and small holes in the paved ground had not been filled. Looking as far as I could see beyond the plaza, I saw destruction, shell-holes, bullet-holes, shrapnel-holes, corners of houses fallen and left unrepaired.

The empty hole in the middle of Hama had been, in the spring of 1982, a battlefield. The decisive encounter was the legacy of a long struggle between, depending on one's view of history, rich and poor, landlord and peasant, Sunni and Alawi, Muslim fundamentalist and secular modernist. The struggle, whose roots were buried deep in Syria's once fertile soil, did not end in 1982.

The hills of northern Syria had been the scene of factional religious disputes from the time the first evangelising monotheists, the Christians, divided and subdivided themselves into dozens of rival sects, each referring to the other by the epithet "heretic." Christian feuding outlived the arrival of Islam and four hundred years of Turkish rule. As late as the last century, Syrian Christians continued to persecute one another. John Lewis Burckhardt, a meticulous Swiss traveller employed by English traders to gather intelligence on the Arab world, recorded in 1810, in his posthumously published *Travels in Syria and the Holy Land*:

> It need hardly be mentioned here, that many of those sects which tore Europe to pieces in the earlier ages of Christianity, still exist in these countries: Greeks, Catholics, Maronites, Syriacs, Chaldeans, and Jacobites, all have their respective parishes and churches. Unable to effect any thing against the religion of their haughty rulers the Turks, they turn the only weapons they possess, scandal and intrigue, with fury against each other, and each sect is mad enough to believe that its church would flourish on the ruins of those their heretic brethren. The principal hatred subsists between the Catholics and the Greeks; of the latter, many thousands have been converted to Catholicism, so that in the northern parts of Syria all Catholics, the Maronites excepted, were formerly of the Greek church . . . In those parts where no Greeks live, as in the mountains of Libanus, the different sects of Catholics turn their hatred against each other, and the Maronites fight with the converted Greek Catholics, or the Latins, as they do with the followers of the Greek church. This system of intolerance, at which the Turkish governors smile, because they are constantly gainers by it, is carried so far that, in many places, the passing Catholic is obliged to practise the Greek rites, in order to escape the effects of the fanaticism of the inhabitants . . .

When the Muslims conquered Syria, and established their first dynasty, the Omayyad, in Damascus, it was as much a case of Islam becoming Syrian as of Syria becoming Muslim. The Muslims immediately quarrelled and divided into Sunni and Shiah. The Shiah formed many different sects based on conflicting interpretations of the Koran and of who was and who would be the messenger of God. The Sunnis ruled, and Syria's Shiites, unlike those of Persia, submitted. In Syria, the larger dissident Shiite sects were the Alawis, the Druze and the Ismailis. Alawis often disguised themselves as Sunnis to travel in the Sunni cities of Damascus and Hama. They, like the Druze and Ismailis, learned to keep their religious beliefs secret, lest they be persecuted. Burckhardt noted that the Turkish, Sunni governor of Damascus, Yusuf Pasha, plundered the Alawi districts and stole one of their sacred books in 1808. He also observed that the rival Shiite dissidents could act more cruelly against one another than they dared against the majority Sunnis, as when Alawis fought Sunnis in 1807:

The Anzeyrys [Alawis] and Ismaylys have always been at enmity, the consequence, perhaps, of some religious differences. In 1807, a tribe of the former having quarrelled with their chief, quitted their abode in their mountains, and applied to the Emir of Maszyad for an asylum. The latter, glad of an opportunity to divide the strength of his enemies, readily granted the request, and about three hundred, with their Sheikh Mahmoud, settled at Maszyad, the Emir carrying his hospitality so far as to order several families to quit the place, for the purpose of affording room for the new settlers. For several months all was tranquil, till one day, when the greater part of the people were at work in the fields, the Anzeyrys, at a given signal, killed the Emir and his son in the castle, and then fell upon the Ismaylys who had remained in their houses, sparing no one they could find, and plundering at the same time the whole town.

For as long as Muslims have dwelled in Hama, near the abandoned Hellenic city of Apamaea, its Sunni patricians have regarded themselves as the most devout. Their orthodoxy stood in sharp contrast to the sectarian and obscurantist beliefs of the peasants in the hills. When the Rev. J. L. Porter, a religious fundamentalist in his own faith, visited Hama for his 1896 travel book, *The Giant Cities of Bashan and Syria's Other Holy Places*, he wrote:

Hamah has still thirty thousand residents. It has for centuries been the residence of a remnant of the old Mohammedan aristocracy – a race now distinguished for poverty, pride and fanaticism. They are the determined enemies of all change alike in religion, literature, art, and social life. The age of Mohammed is their golden age; and the literature of the Koran the only literature worthy of the name . . .

I once met a distinguished member of this proud race at the house of a learned and liberal Moslem friend in Damascus. The conversation turned on the progress of art and science in Western Europe. Railways, steam-engines, printing-presses, the electric telegraph, and many other triumphs of modern discovery were spoken of. He listened with perfect calmness and indifference; and as he haughtily stroked his beard he now and again muttered a few words, among which I could detect the not very complimentary *kâferîn* ("infidels"). A beautiful copy of the Koran, a gem of the Leipzig press, was put into his hand. He opened it. "It is printed," he exclaimed, throwing it from him and wiping his fingers as if the very touch was pollution.

The landlords of Hama employed minority workers from the hills, mainly Alawi peasants who, as believers in Mohammed's son-in-law Ali and not Mohammed himself as the true messenger of God, were regarded as non-believers by the strict Sunnis. Enjoying few if any rights, the Alawi serfs found their only advancement came during the French Mandate. For a time, the French gave them their own state along the northern coast in the Jebel Alawi, as they had given one to the Druze in the south. Nationalist sentiment led both minorities to reject Balkanisation, and they quickly united with Damascus. More importantly, the French recruited the Alawis, as they had other minorities, into the army.

The eventual Alawi domination of the Army and Hama's tradition of orthodoxy were a dangerous mixture. The final, explosive ingredient was Hama's long history of revolt, particularly against outside interference in its prerogatives. In 1408, the people of Hama rose against their governor, rioted and attacked government officials, because he had taken sixty Hama men into custody in an attempt to find a murderer. Ninety years later, they laid siege to another governor for burning some of their houses. "The Sultan sent reinforcements from all over Syria to rescue him," Ira Lapidus wrote in his interesting history, *Muslim Cities in the Later Middle Ages*, "and permitted the troops to plunder the town."

In modern, independent Syria, Hama was no less strident in its resistance to central authority. A month after the Baath Party, with its secular doctrine, took power in Syria in March 1963, Hama rebelled. The muezzins rallied the faithful from the mosque with the words, "Islam or the Baath!" The new government sent troops, who shelled the city and launched a campaign to eliminate all members of the underground Islamic movement behind the riots, the Muslim Brotherhood.

The Baath Party in theory stood for all the ideals the devout Muslims of

Hama most feared: rights for women, co-education, equality among religious sects and land reform. In 1970, a Baathist who was also a despised Alawi became president. For the Sunni landowners of Hama, Hafez al-Assad epitomised their worst fears: the rise of the poorer classes, the domination of the Alawis and an end to their hope of establishing a theocracy. It was as if white southern plantation owners in the United States had been confronted in the 1950s with a black socialist in the White House.

The Muslim Brotherhood responded with a guerrilla war against the regime, taking occasional control of parts of different Syrian towns, assassinating Alawi military officers and cadets and conspiring with Syria's external enemies. For a time, the Brotherhood took control of Sunni quarters in Aleppo. Armen Mazloumian recalled that the Brothers attacked Baathists and Alawis. "But," he said, "they did not harm a single Christian."

When the Muslim Brotherhood seized the city of Hama in 1982, the stage was set for an all-out battle in which one side or the other would emerge the victor. In one night, the Brothers captured Hama's Great Mosque, its municipality building and Baath Party offices. They murdered the Baath Party officials they found, and they called for a Muslim rising throughout Syria. The army surrounded the city, shelled it for days and finally, as its predecessors had in the fifteenth century, devastated the town. Old devils were revived: hatred between Sunni and Alawi, revenge of the downtrodden peasants in Alawi army units against their former masters. Both sides fought for survival, and, for the time being, one side had won. The Muslim Brothers went back underground and no longer threatened the government in Damascus. There were no reliable figures for the numbers of dead, but Hama lost anywhere between ten and thirty thousand of its people.

After hours of walking through Hama's souqs, its wide boulevards of shops and offices, after visiting libraries and sitting in cafés, I realised that there was something unusual about the place, beyond the fact it had been the scene of a horrible confrontation. I had seen war-ravaged cities before. They had the scars of physical destruction, the blank looks on people's faces, the fear that the battle might one day resume. But something was missing. I was sitting in a café by the river, listening to the slow creaking of the water wheels, when I suddenly realised what it was. One thing was absent that I had seen everywhere else in Syria. In all of Hama's shops, offices, squares and souqs, indoors or out, there was not a single photograph, painting or statue of President Hafez al-Assad.

From the outdoor café by the river, where the men of Hama sat drinking Turkish coffee and playing backgammon, I walked to a government library in what was called the Arab Cultural Centre. A helpful librarian showed me hundreds of volumes on science and Arabic cultural life. Above the stacks of books, on a long stretch of bare wall between the shelves and the ceiling, was the only portrait of Hafez al-Assad I would see in Hama. The oil painting, like most of the others of him in Syria, captured the serene, confident countenance of a man who had held power longer than all his predecessors combined. But, in Hama, the artist had placed in the president's hands a set of worry beads.

PART THREE

CHAPTER TWELVE

THE OLD CITY

Shortly after my arrival in Damascus, a friend asked me to accompany him on a carpet-buying expedition to the old city. Although I never liked shopping, the old city within its ancient stone walls had always been my favourite part of Damascus, and bargaining for carpets seemed an appropriate reintroduction to the world's oldest mercantile city. We took a taxi to the grand entrance of Souq Hamidieh, the long covered market named for the Ottoman Sultan Abdel Hamid under whose reign it had been reconstructed a century before. It was the time, near the end of the working day, when the traffic in cars and people jostled along the perimeter of the city walls, and workers on their way home were stopping to drink coffee or buy hot pistachios for their wives and children.

We walked through the long paved souq, where some of the shopkeepers were pulling down their steel shutters for the night and others were still sitting on stools in front of their shops. As merchants had done for centuries, they beckoned passers-by to come inside and inspect their wares. It was little changed from a description published in 1736 of another Damascus street by a French Jesuit: "On both Sides of it there are Shops, where all the rich Merchandizes are sold, that are brought every Year by Carawâns from Europe, Armenia, Africa, Persia and the Indies. The artful Manner in which they are ranged, tempts people to buy."

My friend took me to a shop, where the carpets were artfully displayed to tempt him, on a small street at the right of Souq Hamidieh. We sat on a carpet-draped divan and drank tea with the shop's proprietor, while his assistants unfolded dozens of colourful carpets from Turkey, Kurdistan and Iran – rich red Bokharas, red and blue Shirazes, thin Kelims and Kashkais. A West European ambassador came in with his wife. He said his tour in Damascus was coming to an end, and he wanted to take some rugs home. We chatted and watched the carpet-sellers wave their goods at us like capes before bulls.

The shopkeeper invited us to admire the workmanship, the patterns and colours, but my friend insisted on pointing out each flaw in every carpet that interested him. "The weave on this one is a bit loose," he said, pressing his thumb between the threads of a Shiraz. "And this one, this one has been badly repaired. Who did this work? A butcher?" The shopkeeper defended the quality of each carpet my friend denigrated. All this took place before discussion of price, part of the Levantine bargaining process implicitly accepted by both parties. Neither buyer nor seller would have been satisfied with a simple transaction at a fixed price.

I asked the shopkeeper whether there was a lavatory nearby, and he pointed the way to a public toilet around the corner and across the covered souq. I walked to a short, dark passage and found a door to a filthy "Turkish" or "Oriental" commode – a bare hole in the concrete, with a little hose next to it for washing oneself and the floor.

When I returned to the carpet shop, my friend and the ambassador had reached the point of discussing prices. Suddenly, I heard noises from the souq outside, like small firecrackers or doors slamming. Still talking, the others paid no attention. After a minute, I walked outside and found a group of men standing near the lavatory I had just used. I walked through the crowd to see what they were looking at. On the ground in front of the lavatory door was a red footprint and little circles of blood.

"What happened?" I asked one of the onlookers.

"A man was just shot," he said.

"Where is he?"

"The police took him."

"What happened?"

"Two money-changers," he said. "One lent the other some money this morning. When he would not pay the money back, his friend followed him all afternoon and shot him." Private money-changing was illegal in Syria, and dealers risked serving time in prison. I had not realised that another risk was being shot.

"Is he dead?"

"Yes."

"And the other man?"

"They will catch him."

I stepped back into the covered road of the grand Souq Hamidieh, where most shops were by now closing for the night and shoppers and shopkeepers were on their way home. The streets of the souq were nearly empty, and in an earlier century each quarter within the old city would be locking iron grilles to keep intruders out. The Christian Quarter, the Jewish Quarter and the many Muslim Quarters within the walls would be inaccessible to one another until dawn. Gatekeepers would close the gates of the city, so that no one could enter or leave Damascus by night. It was to avoid that restriction that Richard Burton, when he served as British Consul to

Damascus in 1869, chose to live with his wife Isabel outside the walls in the Kurdish hillside quarter of Salhiyeh.

In the twentieth century, the gates remained open, and each tiny quarter of shops and houses retained its old iron grilles only for decoration. The street lights were coming on, reflected in the film of water the street-cleaners used to wash away the day's dust. My friend bought his carpet, and the ambassador returned to his embassy. The old city was still and quiet, and a money-changer was dead. It was as though nothing had happened.

For certain notable travellers over the centuries, the road to Damascus was far more important than the city itself. St Paul, interrupted on his way to the capital of Roman Syria to persecute the early Christians, was only one of many for whom the journey rather than Damascus provided the crucial element in their lives and, occasionally, in history. "And as he journeyed, he came near Damascus," it is recorded of Saul of Tarsus in the Acts of the Apostles, "and suddenly there shone round about him a light from heaven; And he fell to the earth, and heard a voice say unto him, Saul, Saul, why persecutest thou me?" The "light from heaven" took many forms, each traveller finding his own conversion, his own triumph or defeat in the wilds before he or she reached the city walls.

Damascus was the goal of the great Arab Revolt of 1917. The Arab campaign in the desert, the destruction of the Hejaz Railway between Damascus and Mecca, the attacks on Turkish forts and troop-carriers and the rallying of the desert tribes under Emir Feisal and the young British officer, T. E. Lawrence, all pointed to the triumphal procession into Damascus. Yet Damascus marked the end of the great adventure of their lives and of the most romantic moment in Arab modern history, a squalid betrayal rather than the realisation of a dream. In *Seven Pillars of Wisdom*, Lawrence described his first encounter with Feisal, during which their shared recognition of Damascus as the prize of the newly-born Arab Revolt became the first of many bonds between the two men. When Emir Feisal asked the young British officer at his desert encampment near Jeddah, "And how do you like our place here in Wadi Safra?" Lawrence answered:

"Well; but it is a long way from Damascus."

The word had fallen like a sword in their midst. There was a quiver. Then everybody present stiffened where he sat, and held his breath for a silent minute. Some, perhaps, were dreaming of far-off success: others may have thought it a reflection on their late defeat. Feisal at length lifted his eyes, smiling at me, and said, "Praise be to God, there are Turks nearer us than that."

The campaign against the Turks was the story of the struggle, in which the British Expeditionary Force from Egypt played the major role, to reach Damascus. Nothing else mattered, and Lawrence withdrew once the objective had been achieved. For a moment though, he feared the prize would elude him. When he approached the city with Feisal's cavalry in 1918, he heard explosions. "I turned to Stirling," Lawrence wrote, "and muttered, 'Damascus is burning,' sick to think of the great town in ashes as the price of freedom." Damascus was not burning. The sound Lawrence heard was the destruction of their ammunition stores by Turkey's German allies. The city had been spared, and for the moment it was in Arab hands. "When Damascus fell," Lawrence wrote in the epilogue of *Seven Pillars*, "the Eastern war – probably the whole war – drew to an end."

More than a war, more than the Lawrence of Arabia legend, and more than a tribal uprising were coming to an end. The Ottoman Empire, which since its conquest of the Byzantines at Constantinople in May 1453 had maintained unity and a kind of order in most of western Asia, perished with the liberation of Damascus. Once Damascus had been lost, the most the Turkish army could hope for was an orderly retreat north into Anatolia. Their four centuries of imperium in the Arab world at an ignominious end, the Turks left behind them a few memorable buildings, a system of administration which relied on a class of local notables to act as buffers between the people and government, the division of society into "milyets" or religious communities, some Turkish blood in the veins of the ruling classes of the larger Syrian cities, and little else. Those who suffered under Ottoman rule condemned it, just as its beneficiaries praised its success in holding the peoples of the Levant together. Foreign observers were as divided as the Ottoman subjects on the efficacy of Turkish rule in Syria. Sir Richard Burton called it "despotism tempered by assassination." A somewhat later British visitor to Syria, Mark Sykes, took a more charitable view:

One has heard so much of the devastating influence of the Turk, greedy Pashas and incompetent officials, from a host of interested and prejudiced persons, that it is worth while comparing facts of fact with facts of the counsel for the prosecution.

The population of Syria is so inharmonious a gathering of widely differing races in blood, in creed, and in custom, that government is both difficult and dangerous. Twenty years ago the state of Syria from Aleppo to Aqaba was roughly one of mild anarchy tempered with revolutions and massacres, while between Aleppo and Damascus the Bedawin wandered as overlords of the desert, plundering caravans within sight of the very towns and ever encroaching upon the cultivated lands to gain the coveted pastures.

Sykes went on in this passage to detail the chaos in the Hauran plain, the Druse mountain, the Jordan valley and the deserts twenty years before his visit of 1903.

> The Petra district was once entirely closed to travellers for seven years; now, indeed, matters are changed in a great degree. From Aleppo to Damascus the land is almost entirely free from Bedawin attack, and agriculture is pursued by the Fellaheen far into the country; the Nomads act as shepherds for the townsfolk, and the plundering of a caravan is unheard of; railways extend from Damascus to Beyrut, Rayak to Hama, and Damascus to Ma'an. The Bedawin of Kerak are almost abject before the government, and in the town there is a garrison sufficient to punish any outrage . . . The Druses of the mountain have been subdued, at any rate for some time to come, and appear at length to be convinced that peace is better than hopeless war, while their conquerors appreciate their good sense and leave them alone as much as possible.
>   And the Turks have accomplished all this in spite of an impoverished exchequer, in spite of a steady demand for tax-money from Stambul, in spite of officials being months in arrears of salary, in spite of the army being unpaid, and in spite of the fact that *Murray's Guide Book* says that they are hated by every race and creed, and have not the physical force to govern the land.

In the pages of his travel narrative, *Dar Ul Islam*, Sykes emerged as a Turkish sympathiser, someone who believed Syria was better off united and under strong rule to hold together its "inharmonious gathering of widely differing races." Despite his understanding of Syria and its people, Sykes became an architect of the dismemberment of Syria during the First World War. His secret accord with the French, the Sykes–Picot Agreement, divided Syria into areas to be ruled by France and Britain after the Turks retreated. The division was perhaps inevitable, as Ardern Hulme-Beaman, "Late of the Levant Consulate Service," wrote in 1898 in his book, *Twenty Years in the Near East*: "In its heart of hearts each Power expects and waits for the dismemberment, eagerly watching for the first signs so as to grab something for itself." Britain grabbed Palestine, Jordan and Iraq, while France grabbed Syria and Lebanon.

The half-century of European and indigenous misrule that succeeded the Ottoman Empire would make some Syrians who had never known

Ottoman domination lament the departure of the Turks and the intervention, however sympathetic, of Lawrence of Arabia and Mark Sykes.

In the first months after the Turkish withdrawal from Damascus, Emir Feisal became monarch of the united Arab state which, as far as his supporters were concerned, included all of geographic Syria: places that became Lebanon, Jordan, Israel, the little Syria of modern times and the Turkish province of Alexandretta. Feisal appointed governors for his various provinces and established an army. His flag – the green, white, red and black banner of the Arab Revolt he had led – flew over Damascus. Sixty years later, the same flag would fly as the official emblem of Syria's ruling Baath Party. It would also become the flag of Palestine, the banner Palestinian Arab youths would wave illegally in the Israeli-occupied West Bank and Gaza, the official flag of the Palestine Liberation Organisation.

The flag flew until the French arrived to enforce their wartime agreement with the British. For France, control of Damascus was not only vital to its ambitions in the Levant, it was the reversal of the historic injustice that saw the expulsion of French Crusaders many centuries earlier. When the French entered Damascus in July 1920, their commander, Général Gouraud, went immediately to the tomb of the Muslim hero Saladin. Saleh ed-Din, as he was called in Arabic, had expelled the Crusaders from Jerusalem in the twelfth century. The general entered the simple stone chamber, the appropriate resting place of the pious Kurdish warrior who had died without riches, and announced, "Nous revoilà, Saladin."

The French had returned to Syria. Général Gouraud became the first Christian to govern Damascus since the withdrawal of the Byzantines in the seventh century. The Arabs would come to remember with bitterness the defeat of King Feisal's Arab cavalry under Yusuf al-Azmeh, who had gone to the Meysaloun Pass on the road from Beirut in a heroic but futile Charge of the Light Brigade to defend Damascus. France's troubled second sojourn as occupier would last only twenty-six years, far less than the two centuries the French Crusaders had spent in the Holy Land. Damascus, the prize which eluded their Crusader ancestors, was the jewel of the desert commanding both hinterland and coast. It was the only base from which to control all of Syria, but the post-war division of Ottoman lands saw to it that no city, not even Damascus, would be the single capital of a united Syria.

Like Lawrence and Feisal, the French did little with Damascus once they had it. Forty years after their departure, it seemed the French had never come at all. Their legacy was far less notable than the Ottomans'. They left no colony of French nationals behind, as they had in places like Ivory Coast, and their language had not penetrated Damascene society to the degree it had in Beirut or Algiers. The only remnants of French rule were a military dominated by a religious minority, the Alawis, and the ubiquity in Damascene restaurants of frogs' legs cooked to perfection in butter and garlic. Old men in Damascus had told me how in their youth they used to hear the loud nightly croaking of frogs from the watery fields outside the city gates. The frogs vanished during the years of French rule, and the Damascenes, who had acquired the taste, now had to import them from France.

The French, however, did leave scars on the memories of the first generation of Syrians who survived their rule. When Harry Franck came to Damascus in 1927, the city had yet to recover from French suppression of the first of several revolts against the Mandate. Franck wrote in *The Fringe of the Moslem World*:

> Great sections of the mud-and-stone buildings are now in ruins. Many of them should be destroyed, it is true, yet . . . In their quarrel with the "rebels" the French razed square after square of the best old Arab houses, especially about the Street Called Straight and out in the Meidan residential section, where a stroll or a ride discloses more ruins than houses . . . Algerian soldiers, in the flattish red fez and woollen khaki, sleep in rows in mosques, stand guard one by one in minarets overlooking the heart of the city, rifles with sharp French bayonets, and open boxes of hand-grenades within easy reach. Formerly the French not only mounted machine-guns in minarets but sacrilegiously occupied mosques with West Africans, Annamese, and other non-Moslems from among the French colonial troops . . . Bullet holes are everywhere, even through iron trolley poles, through the sheet-iron shutters – there are a few dozen ones left now – that open in the morning and shut at sunset with great noise unknown in the Damascus of a generation ago . . . A long stretch of the rounded sheet-iron roof of the famous old street [called Straight] is gone entirely, and the rest is so riddled with bullets from airplane machine-guns that the sun casts on the hard mud paving hundreds of golden coins the size of oranges. Automobiles, now and then a mounted machine-gun, even an occasional tank roar their way through it . . .
>
> The dragging of bodies of dead "rebels" through the streets of Damascus and draping them about the central monument was only one of many incredible savageries . . .

The shops of old Damascus kept their iron shutters, a legacy of French rule, in case of another rebellion, another suppression. Although the

French used warplanes over Damascus against a civilian population, they were not the first in history to do so. That honour went to Britain, which a few years earlier bombarded another people who had not accepted the Sykes–Picot settlement, the Kurds of Iraq.

Whether strangers came to Damascus as conquerors, like Lawrence or Gouraud, or prospective persecutors, like St Paul, or explorers, like Burckhardt or Doughty, they came with the belief that Damascus was a reward at the conclusion of a long journey. Some visitors battled armies, others the desert and bedouin raiders, to reach the city gates, but all of them were aware of coming to something precious, something special. "When I was a child," a Lebanese friend of mine told me, referring to the late 1940s, "we used to have to hold our heads high in Damascus. Beirut was just a village, but Damascus was the proudest city of the Arab world." With the chronic *coups d'état* and instability of the 1950s and 1960s, Damascus fell into decline. Beirut, which had been little more than a port for Damascus, became the jewel of the Levant. In 1975, the wheel of history turned: Lebanon began its civil war, and Damascus prospered again. In the space of a few years, Damascus had watched another rival perish. "To Damascus years are only moments, decades are only flitting trifles of time," Mark Twain wrote in *Innocents Abroad*, after his visit there in 1867:

> She measures time not by days and months and years, but by the empires she has seen rise and prosper and crumble to ruin. She is a type of immortality. She saw the foundations of Baalbek and Thebes and Ephesus laid; she saw these villages grow into mighty cities and amaze the world with their grandeur – and she has lived to see them desolate, deserted, and given over to the owls and the bats. She saw the Israelitish empire exalted, and she saw it annihilated. She saw Greece rise and flourish two thousand years and die. In her old age she saw Rome built; she saw it overshadow the world with its power; she saw it perish. The few hundreds of years of Genoese and Venetian might and splendour were, to grave old Damascus, only a trifling scintillation hardly worth remembering. Damascus has seen all that has ever occurred on earth, and still she lives. She has looked upon the dry bones of a thousand empires, and will see the tombs of a thousand more before she dies.

When Mark Twain approached the city from the west with his party of American Protestant pilgrims, with whom he was touring Europe, Russia and the Ottoman Empire, he stopped on a hill, probably Mount Kassioun, and recalled an earlier visitor who came to the same hilltop and gazed at the oasis below:

As the glare of day mellowed into twilight we looked down upon a picture which is celebrated all over the world. I think I have read about four hundred times that when Mohammed was a simple camel driver he reached this point and looked down upon Damascus for the first time, and then made a certain renowned remark. He said man could enter only one paradise; he preferred to go to the one above. So he sat down there and feasted his eyes upon the earthly paradise of Damascus and then went away without entering its gates. They have erected a tower on the hill to mark the spot where he stood.

Unlike the Prophet Mohammed, Mark Twain went down the hill and entered the city. He regretted it. "If I were to go to Damascus again," he concluded, "I would camp on Muhammad's hill about a week and then go away. There is no need to go inside the walls. The prophet was wise without knowing it when he decided not to go down into the paradise of Damascus." The city he saw was filthy, with narrow streets and an unwelcoming population that seemed to him to hate even the sight of Christians. It was only seven years earlier that angry mobs, following Christian–Druze fighting in Mount Lebanon, massacred thousands of Damascene Christians. Twain thought, wrongly, that the massacres had been carried out by the Turks, whom he hoped to see vanquished by the Russians. "How they hate a Christian in Damascus! – and pretty much all over Turkeydom as well," he wrote. "And how they will pay for it when Russia turns her guns upon them again!" He neglected to mention that a respected and brave Muslim who had fought against the French in Algeria, Abdel Qader al-Jezairi, tried to stop the mob and offered refuge to hundreds of Christians in his home.

Twain's reaction to Damascus, despite enjoying its abundant water and a good hotel, may have been influenced by a bout of cholera, which he accepted with his usual good cheer. "Syrian travel has its interesting features, like travel in any other part of the world, and yet to break your leg or have the cholera adds a welcome variety to it."

In the early eighteenth century, a French Jesuit noted, "This famous city is nothing but a heap of Houses and Walls half ruined. They call what remains of it a *Sahia*, or *the Village*. The rest scarce deserves that Name." A century later, its fortunes had revived. Wilfrid Scawen Blunt, who came to Damascus in 1881 and returned in 1904, found a fascinating city that was both vibrant and defiantly Oriental. "I find very little change in the town since I was here last," he wrote in his diary for 23 March 1904,

except on the north-western side, where the railroad has caused some building, and a big barracks has been put up. The rest of the city is much what I remember it in 1880, not at all Europeanised. The bazaars which were burnt down in Midhat Pasha's time have been rebuilt and are as busy as ever. There are no modern shops or Frank innovations, or by-laws, or other Christian tomfooleries; things are made too uncomfortable for Europeans for there to be any resident foreign merchants. Newspapers of all kinds are forbidden, the post is unsafe and irregular, and at the Central telegraph office there are no printed forms.

Blunt and his wife, Lady Anne, the granddaughter of Lord Byron, visited the city to study its political intrigues and to buy Arab horses. Unlike Mark Twain, Blunt loved the souqs. His diary entry for 27 March read:

We spent the whole day in the bazaars, which are the best and cheapest in the world. It is a pleasure buying in them because the sellers are so amiable and do not worry travellers to buy. Everything is astonishingly cheap and one might live comfortably with one's family in Damascus on £100 a year.

Not every Western traveller shared Blunt's fondness for Damascus. When the English travel writer H. V. Morton visited the city in 1936, he wrote, in In The Steps of St Paul, "I wish I could like Damascus. It seems to me that this city is living on a reputation gained a hundred years ago, before there were electric trams, gramophones or motor cars; when our great-grandparents rode painfully to it on horseback . . ."

Damascus was the city praised in the Bible for its clear waters from the Rivers Banyas and Barada, the ancient Rivers Abana and Pharphar – rivers Twain called "mere creeks." Damascus was the city from which the Muslims created an empire extending from Spain to Persia, the city attacked but never taken by the Crusaders, the city ravaged in 1400 by Tamerlane, who kidnapped its finest artisans – its famed swordsmiths, jewellers and brass-workers – and sent them to Samarkand. Damascus was the city conquered by the Ottomans in 1516 and held for four centuries, the city the Arab forces under Feisal and Lawrence of Arabia entered triumphantly in 1918 and the city to which Général Gouraud came uninvited in 1920.

The first time I visited Damascus was in the spring of 1973. I was hitchhiking from Beirut to Aqaba, and I found Damascus hot, its streets dirty, the noise from the traffic unbearable and the population dour compared to Beirut's. I came again as a journalist the following October when Syria and Israel were at war in the Golan Heights. In 1974, I contracted paratyphoid in Damascus, and illness coloured my view of the city no less than it had Mark Twain's. However, Damascus came in time to enchant me. The more I visited, the more interesting Damascus became. Its old streets hid beautiful houses, whose gardens gave off the wonderful aroma of jasmine, honeysuckle and coffee. The souqs smelled of thyme and cardamom, sesame and olive oil. The people were hospitable. By the early 1980s, the municipality had cleaned the streets and done away with most of the traffic noise by banning the unnecessary use of the car horn.

I watched the city grow over the years, the acceleration of a process begun in the last century. Houses, hotels, the great Hejaz Railway terminal and several suburbs had already sprung up outside the old city walls before the Turks left. When I first came, from the west along the route Général Gouraud's troops took, only barren land lay between the western edge of the city and the Lebanese border. Fourteen years later, suburbs had grown miles into the desert to the west and into the Ghouta, Damascus's fertile orchards, dwarfing the original city.

Unlike Aleppo's, the city walls were still standing. Within the walls, the old city itself was changing, its character slowly eroded by waves of "modernisation." Old shops and houses, which had stood for centuries, were coming down to give better access to and unobstructed views of the old walls, the citadel and the Omayyad Mosque. Critics of modernisation believed the souqs had been cleared to enable President Hafez al-Assad to visit the mosque and make a quick escape, if necessary, rather than find his convoy trapped in the narrow streets of the ancient town.

One morning, I returned to Souq Hamidieh, the main western opening in the city walls under a larger-than-life portrait of President Hafez al-Assad. On both sides of the long road between the souq entrance and the Omayyad Mosque were shops selling ice-cream, which had been invented in Damascus, Arab sweets, carpets, "traditional" bedouin clothes and jewellery, flintlock rifles from the Turkish years, old Damascene furniture of dark wood inlaid with mother of pearl, cheap trinkets and embroidered tablecloths. This part of the old city had changed little from its renovation under the Sultan Abdel Hamid a century earlier, except that it tended to cater to tourists more than other parts of the old city. The French traveller Alphonse de Lamartine described his tour of the souqs in April 1833 and wrote in his *Voyage en Orient*:

> Explored the bazaars of Damascus. The Grand Bazaar is about half a league in length. The bazaars are long streets, covered with very high canopies, and lined with booths, shops, stores: these shops are narrow and shallow: the shopkeeper sits on his heels in front of the shop, a pipe in his mouth, or the *narguilé* by his side. The shops are filled with goods of every kind, especially with cloths from India, which flow into Damascus by caravan from Baghdad.

Barbers invite passers-by to have their hair cut. Their shops are always full. A crowd as numerous as that in the galleries of the Palais-Royal throngs the bazaar all day long.

Ten years later, the English traveller Eliot Warburton described the Damascus souqs in his *The Crescent and the Cross*:

> . . . here comes a donkey laden with cucumbers, apparently a favourite refreshment, for almost everyone stops him; here a string of tall, awkward camels fills the narrow street; there, seated on his shopboard, is an old man drowsily nodding among the silks of India and Syria; and there are two pale boys playing dominoes in an armourer's shop, from the roof of which daggers hang like the sword of Damocles, and quantities of ivory-handled knives, that make the niche look like a cave of stalactites.

The modern souqs I saw were much the same as Lamartine's and Warburton's. Although the camels had disappeared during the French Mandate, the donkeys still carried cucumbers and the boys still played dominoes. The physical change in the old city became obvious only at the end of Souq Hamadieh, beyond a Roman colonnade, where a new plaza gaped like an open wound before the Omayyad Mosque. The shops which since antiquity had been built near the safety of the original Byzantine church, then of the mosque, had recently been removed. The Antiquities Department despised what its officials called "parasitic" structures, which blocked tourists' and pilgrims' view of the mosque. Shopkeepers who had lost their businesses in the old souqs had been offered places in modern shopping centres outside the old city gates. The outlines of the stone arches of their vanished shops were still visible in the buildings which remained along the perimeter, though the destruction had taken place three years earlier. Of these "parasites" Ibn Jubayr wrote on his visit to Damascus in July 1184, "There is no more beautiful-looking row of shops than this, nor bigger both in length and breadth. Behind it and close by is the cavalry barrack of [the Caliph] Mu'awiyah, which today is tenanted, and in which the cloth-fullers have a place."

Of the mosque itself, Ibn Jubayr noted, "For beauty, perfection of construction, marvellous and sumptuous embellishment and decoration, it is one of the most celebrated mosques of the world. Its general fame in this regard renders valueless a deep description. One of the strangest things concerning it is that the spider never spins its web therein, nor do swallows ever enter it or alight thereon." An abundance of pigeons in the mosque's great courtyard more than compensated for the lack of swallows. The great Jewish medieval traveller, Rabbi Benjamin of Tudela, visited Damascus a few years before Ibn Jubayr, and he too was astounded by what he called "the Synagogue of Damascus," of which he wrote, "There is no building like it on earth . . . One sees there a high glass wall constructed by magic."

The mosque was originally the Cathedral of St John the Baptist, and in the centre of the modern mosque a stone tomb with an open side for viewing held the saint's head. All around it in a room larger than a football field, thick Persian carpets were spread across the floors, and shafts of light from high stained-glass windows shone on the worshippers below. When James Morris visited the mosque in 1956, he wrote of its "great forest of pillars" and continued, "Outside in the bazaars you may meet suspicion and unfriendliness: here in the Great Mosque nobody will question the presence of a Christian, and if you like you may open your air-mail *Times* and see who is engaged without incurring the displeasure of these passers-by." Morris's experience was a dramatic shift from that of Warburton, a century earlier: "The Turks here are more fanatical than in any part of the East, except Mecca; and it is nearly impossible to visit the mosques. The risk incurred in doing so is of that unpleasant kind that had nothing redeeming or tempting in its exploit." By the time of my journeys to Damascus, the Great Mosque was easily accessible to non-Muslim visitors, who were expected to remove their shoes on entering and to show sufficient respect to refrain from reading the *Times*.

Immediately after the Muslim conquest of the city in 635 AD, according to a legend still believed in Damascus though dismissed by many historians, the original church was divided into two. Ibn Jubayr wrote:

> For it had been in two parts, the eastern belonging to the Muslims and the western to the Christians. This was because Abu Ubaydah ibn al-Jarrah – may God hold him in his favour – had entered the town from the west and arrived at the centre of the church after he had already made peace with the Christians. But Khalid ibn al-Walid – may God hold him in his favour – had entered by assault from the east side of town, and had arrived to take the eastern half of the church. So the Muslims took possession of this eastern half and made of it a mosque, while the half which came under the treaty of capitulation, that is the western half, remained a church in the hands of the Christians, until [the Caliph] asked them for it in return for compensation. They refused, whereupon he took it by force, and himself began its destruction.

Although the Christians in the western half of the city were said to have capitulated, it was the eastern side which became the Christian Quarter, just north of the Jewish Quarter, next to the Eastern Gate.

Ibn Batuta visited Damascus a century and a half later, in 1326, and the city impressed him as much as it had Ibn Jubayr: "Damascus surpasses all other cities in beauty, and no description, however full, can do justice to its charms." Like Ibn Jubayr, Ibn Batuta called the Omayyad Mosque the "Cathedral Mosque," because of its Byzantine origins. The North African observed that "all the lanes in Damascus have pavements on either side, on which the foot passengers walk, while those who ride use the roadway in the centre."

Beyond the mosque were scores of open-air markets, on both sides of cobbled lanes, where artisans made and sold their wares in tiny, arched workshops: the carpenters' souq, the gold souq, the brass souq, the ironmongers' souq, the weavers' souq, the tailors' souq. Around corners in the narrow streets were souqs for spices, vegetables, fruits and meat. The souqs, where they were covered at all, had roofs of tin or wood above the walkways. Interspersed among the lively commercial establishments were tombs, mosques, monuments and houses. In Damascus, only the monumental and religious buildings were made of stone, which had been pulled or carried miles, by slaves of the Greeks, Romans and Arabs. Aleppo's ubiquitous building stone came from nearby quarries, but the old houses of Damascus were constructed of mud and poplars from the riverbanks. "The Houses of the City are built of Wood," wrote an unnamed French Jesuit, in *A Journey from Aleppo to Damascus*, published in 1736, "their fronts are backward, faceing inward Courts. Towards the street nothing is to be seen but Great Walls without Windows. But, as ordinary an Appearance as they make outwardly, they are, within, adorned with every rich Paintings and Gildings, Furniture and China, ranged artfully upon little Tables set round the Chambers." The plain façades of the mud houses, many daubed in cement binding and graffiti, still hid beautiful rooms and lavish courtyards, much as Eliot Warburton described them in 1845:

A little lake of crystal lay enclosed by marble banks, and overshadowed by beautiful weeping willows. Little fountains leaped and sparkled in all directions, and shook their loosened silver in the sun . . . At one end of this court, or garden, was a lofty alcove, with a ceiling richly carved in gold and crimson fretwork . . . and a wide divan ran around three sides of the apartment which opened on the garden and its fountains. Next to this alcove was a beautiful drawing-room, with marble floor and arabesque roof, carved niches and softened lighting falling on delicately painted walls.

Seventy-five such houses in Zokak al-Hamrawi, an alley along one side of the Omayyad Mosque, had been declared state property in 1975, when their owners became government tenants. The houses were scheduled for demolition in 1984, but complaints and articles in the foreign press led to a reprieve. I had spent a day with one of the residents just before the reprieve was granted. He and his neighbours felt powerless to save their houses, and they dreaded moving into modern apartment blocks, with neither privacy nor gardens, at the dusty edge of Damascus. When I walked past the houses this time, I was reassured to see them still standing, or leaning, sturdily in the little alley between the Omayyad Mosque and the tomb of Saladin. But for how long?

"Modern Arab architecture is passing through a very critical stage of its history in almost all Arab countries," the Egyptian architect Hassan Fathy wrote in *The Arab House in the Urban Setting* in 1970. "Indeed, we may ask if modern Arab architecture exists at all. Nowadays we can speak only of the Western houses in Arab countries." Damascus had some of the most beautiful Arab houses, their comfort and artistry testified to by generations of travellers and residents, but they were fast disappearing. The old city behind the walls, now only a fraction of a modern concrete capital, was enduring renovation and modernisation. "In house design," Fathy wrote of the Western-influenced architecture of this age, "the introverted plan looking into the courtyard was changed to the plan looking out upon the street. The cool, clean air, the serenity and reverence of the courtyard, were shed into the street with its heat, its dust and its noise." The Arab architect, supported by governments which never asked their people what kind of houses they wanted to live in, what kind of towns they wanted planned, even what kind of government they preferred, "created a large vacuum in his culture." The vacuum had yet to be filled, except by that aching sense of loss which suffused the culture at every level – the loss of unity, of independence, of freedom, of dignity, of hope, of Palestine – all of which began, so far as this century was concerned, in 1918, when the Ottoman army marched north on the road out of Damascas.

When I had come down that road from Aleppo, I had made detours to see Qardaha, the Alawi village where President Hafez al-Assad had been born, and the great Crusader castle of Krak des Chevaliers. If Assad was showing favoritism to fellow Alawis, it was not obvious in Qardaha. It remained one of the poorest villages in Syria, although it had electricity and running water. Its mostly peasant population were in the fields working when I came, and a dog running along a side road was the sole living thing in view. The only house of substance belonged to Assad's family, where the president's mother was said to live, but it was poorer than any presidential house I had seen in the Mddle East, far smaller and simpler than the house Anwar Sadat once maintained in his home village in Egypt's Nile Delta.

The people of the Alawi mountain were so poor that some farmers sold their daughters into indentured servitude to rich Sunni and Christian families in Damascus, there to work long hours, cooking, cleaning and caring for children little younger than themselves. I had seen such girls in Damascus, waiting at tables at smart dinner parties, when they should have been sleeping or studying for the schools they did not attend. When they reached their late teens or twenties, they returned to their villages to enter the servitude of marriage.

Krak des Chevaliers was magnificent, a Gothic masterpiece of military architecture. On a lonely hilltop above a small Christian village, its inner and outer walls were intact, and its cloisters, courtyards and chapel needed little work to become home again to the Knights Hospitaller. From its ramparts, the Hospitallers controlled the passes between the inland cities of the plain and Tripoli on the sea. The castle withstood an attack by Saladin, who had conquered Jerusalem. When Krak des Chevaliers finally capitulated to the Mameluke leader of Egypt, Sultan Baibars, in 1270, two centuries of Crusader rule in the Levant were drawing to an end.

The Crusader knights left strings of castles along the coast and atop the mountain range between coast and desert, some of which Muslim rulers used to good effect in the following centuries. Two of the castles, Raymond of Saint-Gilles' Citadel in Tripoli and Chateau Beaufort in south Lebanon, were still in use by different armies, still the scenes of battles.

"The Crusades were launched to save Eastern Christendom from the Moslems," Sir Steven Runciman wrote in A *History of the Crusades*. "When they ended the whole of Eastern Christendom was under Moslem rule." Sir Steven, who had warned me not to rely on T. E. Lawrence's drawings of the Crusader castles because of their inaccuracies, concluded his three-volume history,

> There was so much courage and so little honour, so much
> devotion and so little understanding. High ideals were besmirched
> by cruelty and greed, enterprise and endurance by a blind and
> narrow self-righteousness; and the Holy War itself was nothing
> more than a long act of intolerance in the name of God, which is
> the sin against the Holy Ghost.

I stood on a parapet and looked down at the valleys leading to Tripoli in the west, Antioch in the north, the Bekaa Valley in the south and Homs in the east. From here, a small force could and did dominate the north of Syria. Yet the domination did not last, and the knights were gone. Like so many Western adventures in the Levant, from the Middle Ages to the recent US Marine landing in Beirut, the Crusades were a futile disaster. When would we learn?

Whenever I had nothing to do or needed advice in Damascus, I would seek refuge at the ABC News office in the Sheraton Hotel. I was staying at the cheaper and older "New" Omayyad Hotel, but I often took a taxi to the garish, much newer Sheraton, owned by the government and managed under contract by the Sheraton chain. Both hotels stood to the west of the old city, which had no hotels within its walls. At the Sheraton, I would see ABC's bureau manager, Tony Touma. A man I liked very much, he spoke English, French and German fluently, as well as classical and colloquial Arabic. His father was one of the few people I met who spoke Syriac, the ancient *lingua franca* of all Syria from before the time of Christ until the Arab conquest. Tony's work for ABC was incidental to his interest in antiques, his knowledge of history and his understanding of how to survive in his country. He was equally conversant with the Mamelukes, who ruled most of Syria and Egypt from 1250 to 1517 AD, and the changes in bureaucracy at Syrian television. Tony was short, always well dressed in suit and tie, with a trim moustache and glasses. Born in Damascus in 1943 and educated by the Catholic Marist Brothers, he served in the Syrian air defence during the October War. He and his half-German wife, Rania, had two children. A Syriac Catholic, who knew I was a Latin Catholic, he was always reminding me to go to Mass.

"Now, listen to me, Charlie, you cannot leave this out of your book," Tony Touma warned me one afternoon. "The Syrians discovered the 'zero,' which made the use of negative numbers possible."

Tony was sitting behind his desk in the ABC News office at the Sheraton, court of his kingdom of news, television and antique dealing. He had made the office a mandatory meeting place for all visiting journalists, ambassadors, Syrian officials, PLO functionaries and entertainers in the Sheraton's cabaret. At any time, you were as likely to meet a belly-dancer as the Austrian ambassador. In fact, I'd met both on the same day, seated around Tony's desk sipping Turkish coffee and heeding his advice.

"What do you call the numbers you use?" Tony asked me.

"Arabic numerals."

"Exactly. These numerals were developed by the Arabs in Syria. With the Roman numerals, there was no zero. Higher mathematics was impossible. Look here," Tony said, taking a pen and paper. "The Arabic numbers are all very logical. Each numeral is made up of angles, and the number of angles defines the numeral."

He then drew the numerals from one to nine at sharp angles:

1 2 3 4 5 6 7 8 9

"You see, nine has nine angles. The next number, the zero, has no angles. In Arabic, 'zero' is *siffr*. From *siffr*, you get the French word *chiffre*, which means 'numeral,' but also means 'code.' And the German word *entziffern* means 'decode' or 'explain.' And in English, you have 'cipher.' You owe all this, and your numbers, to us."

"That's all well and good, Tony," I said. "But why on earth do the Arabs themselves use Indian numerals, which look very different from the Arabic numerals?"

"After the Muslims conquered India," he said, a tone of regret in his voice, "they were so impressed with Indian culture that they adopted the Indian numerals. So now, almost the whole world uses Arabic numbers – except the Arabs."

For Tony, this was merely another of hundreds of historic ironies in all of which the Arabs, the Syrians, and more particularly the Syrian Christians and the Damascenes, were the losers. History played cruel jokes on Syria, and Tony knew every one. Luckily for him, he had a sense of humour. Working for an American news company in Damascus, he needed it.

I went to see a woman who, almost alone, was trying to prevent the destruction of the old city. As the widow of a respected soldier who had been killed by the Israelis, Sehem Turjuman had a reputation which seemed to protect her from prosecution for her outspoken criticism of government policy. She worked at the Ministry of Defence, but in her free time was trying against all odds to save the old city from the destruction of urban renewal. She and a small committee, the Friends of Old Damascus, stood, like Horatius at the bridge, against the combined might of the Department of Antiquities, the municipality and the government.

The experts in the Antiquities Department saw the old houses as "parasitical" structures which made appreciation of old mosques and ancient monuments impossible. The municipality wanted above all to modernise the city. The government saw in its new, modern capital the proof of its success in bringing progress to an ancient land. The best proof of this was the huge new palace, looking like an American convention centre, for President Hafez al-Assad, which stood unfinished and years behind schedule under a large construction crane on top of a hill dominating the old and modern cities.

I went to see Sehem Turjuman at her apartment on the seventh floor of a new building in the Mezze area, near the hideous Dar al-Baath which housed the Ministry of Information. Her modern apartment was one of thousands standing in the west on what, only a dozen years earlier, had been empty land.

Sehem Turjuman, though born in 1933, felt, thought and behaved like a young girl, perhaps because she grew up in a Damascus which had yet to discover the wonders of concrete and the glories of revolution. Everything about her seemed to be a denial both of the world outside and of her own ageing. She dressed like an ingénue and seemed coquettish in the company of men. When I came to call, she answered the door wearing a lavender floral print dress trimmed in purple. In her red shoes, she looked like a little girl ready to go to a party.

She seated me in a drawing-room, where everything was covered in cloth or otherwise adorned, like the properly modest Victorian rooms in which not even the legs of a piano were left exposed. Linen or Damascene brocade cloths covered all the tables. The fitted carpets were thick, velvet curtains were everywhere. The walls of the small reception rooms were blue, with new white cornices. A Pierrot, looking appropriately sad, hung over the mantel of a false chimney. The telephone was a late-Victorian design in pink, surrounded by assorted women's bric à brac, including a silver *kum-kum*, a long silver decanter of flower water with a little sprinkler at the top. I sat looking at the *art nouveau* chandelier, the cushions, flowers, ivy growing up the wall of the enclosed balcony and a 1975 oil portrait of Sehem herself, her golden locks dangling over the shoulder of her blue dress in a 1950s style. On the table lay the book A *Lost Lady*, "a romance by Willa Cather."

Sehem carried in a tea-tray from the kitchen and handed me a copy of her new book, *Ahya Ana*. "This is my book on love," she said, slightly embarrassed.

"What does *Ahya Ana* mean?"

"It's the name of a rose. Literally, it means something like, 'Oh, dear me,' but it is the name of a kind of rose planted in the old Arab houses."

Sehem poured the tea into china cups, a change from the usual small glasses, and offered me milk, sugar or lemon. "It's strange in these days," she said. "I'm a romantic. People nowadays care only for money, for cement, for cars. I care for love, for velvet, for soft things, for a cat, for a nice human being."

I had come to talk to her about the old city. The change in living pattern – from the old Arab house, with its open courtyard and central fountain, its space and sense of communion with the adjoining houses, to the modern, high-rise flat, like the one in which we sat, with its feeling of isolation – may have been the greatest disruption wrought on urban Syria in this century. It seemed more fundamental than either the imposition of unwelcome borders or the establishment of Israel.

"What does the old Arab house mean to you?"

"It means a culture," she said. "It is the identity card of the Arabic people, of Arab life. It is not only the Arabic house from inside. It's a whole city, a whole picture of the Arabic city: the houses, the souqs, the narrow streets and the way of building. It's not beautiful from outside, but the walls, so close, the windows, so close, the doors in front of each other. When you go inside through a narrow path, rather dark, then suddenly you go to the yard, open to the sky, and it's like paradise inside: full of trees, plants and roses, lilacs, jasmine, lemon and oranges, palm trees and this small pool of water in the yard and even inside the rooms."

She became animated, her high-pitched voice rising higher in recalling the beauty of the old city house. "The Arab house has been built in an intellectual way," she explained. "In wintertime, you can have the sun inside your rooms to feel warm. And in summertime, you are against the sun. At the same time, you have this nice air coming to you."

For women especially, the old houses represented a secure life. "Every house I used to see when I was a child," Sehem said, "had a small river passing through. The River Barada was channelled inside every house, rich and poor. The ladies could speak from kitchen to kitchen, because of the river. And they could pass to each other. It meant safety. It meant beauty. It meant inside freedom. The lady in the Arab cities – the Arab lady, Christian, Muslim or Jewish – lived in this house to protect her from eyes outside, to have freedom, to move, to have her little children play inside this big house, safe from the traffic. You can see in old Damascus the houses are very close to the souqs, but the noise of the souq is very far from the house. So we feel we live in peace, no noise except the sounds of the birds on the trees and the water in the fountains. We protect the woman, not to be shown to the outside. She is free inside, and nobody can look at her. Now the new houses are open to the street, so if you go to the bedroom, everyone can see you. It means you are not free. Even the narrow streets have been made narrow, because when wars came to Damascus, like in the Tamerlane or Hulagu period, the invaders went inside for the women. So they protect their families with narrow streets and big gates and doors. I remember each *hay*, each small quarter, had a gate. No one could enter at night, no horse, no soldier."

When the French made the first clearance of the old city in the 1920s, they said they wanted streets wide enough to fire cannon down. The wide, modern boulevards were fine for cannon and car, but they provided no shade in summer and they lost heat in winter.

Mores were changing with the changes of residence. Courtship and weddings had changed with the loss of the old houses. "In the old days," she said, "the bridegroom was the only man who could enter the wedding. In the big courtyard of the Arab house, all the women were without veils, wearing beautiful clothes. The bridegroom comes and takes the woman for his wife. He takes her and goes to the upper room, over the courtyard."

"What about the honeymoon?"

"No honeymoon. Honeymoon up," she laughed. "In the courtyard below, the women danced until morning. All night, there would be singing, playing and eating. Everyone was happy. Hundreds of women would come, sometimes five hundred or a thousand. And all with their children. It was a full life."

"Where were the men?"

"No men," she said approvingly, as if she had just banished them from all weddings. "The men sleep with their relations till the end of this night. So, after the seventh day, the women come again to say hello to the bride, and to the mother of the groom and his sisters, because the bride lives with them."

She hinted that there was a political, even a tribal, motive behind the demolition of the old city. "It is something against the people of Damascus, something against the Omayyad period," she said. "This Damascus has been built during the Omayyad time. So, now you know." She would not say any more on the subject. Others did, however, when I agreed not to publish their names. There was a belief in some Sunni Muslim circles that the Alawi regime of President Assad wanted to erase the city's Omayyad, Sunni past. The Alawis, on this view, were trying to redress the historic balance in favour of Shiism, of which they were one, albeit dissident, branch. The steady stream of tourists from Iran to Shiite shrines in Damascus, and the neglect of the tomb of Mu'awiya, the first Omayyad caliph who vanquished Ali and the Shiites shortly after Prophet Mohammed's death, were ostensibly part of a pattern of the destruction of Sunni traditions, Sunni culture, Sunni power. The old city itself was a haven for the Sunni merchant class, whose shops and houses within the walls were not as easy for police agents to observe and control as the tower blocks and shopping centres in the modern town.

Even in 1833, Lamartine noted the potential for rebellion within the close quarters of the old city. He watched the agas, or notables, of the city,

> dressed in long capes of crushed silk, trimmed with ermine, with sabres and daggers encrusted with diamonds hanging at the belt. They are followed by five or six courtesans, servants or slaves, who walk behind them carrying their pipes and their *narguilés*. At one point in the day they go to sit on divans outside the cafés built beside the streams that run across the city; beautiful plane trees keep the divans in the shade. There they smoke and gossip with their friends, and this, apart from the mosque, is the only mode of

communication for the inhabitants of Damascus. It is there that they prepare, almost in silence, the frequent revolutions which erupt at the moment they are least expected.

While the agas, or notables, may no longer have walked the streets with their slaves and courtesans, there was always the fear of revolution. It had happened in the bazaars of the Shah's Iran, and it happened under the Ottomans and the French in Damascus. When a new faction took power, Lamartine observed, *"Les vaincus sont mis à mort, ou s'enfuient dans les déserts de Balbek et de Palmyre, où les tribus indépendents leur donnent asile."* This was why, to keep power for any length of time in Damascus, rulers had to control Baalbek and Palmyra as well.

Was the transformation of the old city really a part of an age-old conflict between Sunni and Shia for dominance? Some people could not understand the demolition in any other terms. If it was not the Alawis getting their own back, what could it possibly be?

Sehem said that her own family's house in the old city was being demolished, and there was nothing she could do to stop it. Inevitably, Sehem, like most Syrians, turned to the other area where she felt powerless and defeated, Israel. She told me about the night her husband, a captain in the army, had died, as he was delivering a speech. On 8 January 1973, at nine o'clock at night, two Israeli Phantoms bombed three Syrian villages, a military headquarters, a school and the club where her husband was speaking. They had been married only 18 months, and she was pregnant. "I wrote a letter," she said, "to the Israeli pilot who killed my husband. I said, 'I don't know you. I don't know your wife. I don't know if you have children or not. Let me tell you about me. You might have an order from your officers to go and bomb Syria and come back . . .'" The telephone rang, but she quietly disconnected the line without answering. "'If you are still alive, you might go back to your house and have Champagne, because of the victory, with your wife. Let me tell you my story. I was in love with my husband. I was waiting for him. I was cooking for him a very nice dish, with *laban* (yogurt). I was preparing parsley with my hand. I prepared the table and was preparing myself, like my mother, with a rose on the table and a rose in my hair. But he didn't come. I am not your enemy. This is not a war. My husband was not coming to kill you. He was giving a lecture. Why do you come and bomb us? You tell Europe, "The Arab people want to come and put me in the sea. They are killing me." And Europe and America, they don't know *you* are killing *us*. Every house in Syria has a lost man, a brother, a husband, a son, and nobody knows about us.'"

She started to cry, and I realised that her life had stopped at 9 o'clock on that evening of 8 January 1973. She would always be the young bride, with a pale rose in her hair, dreaming of weddings in the old courtyards of ancient Damascus.

CHAPTER THIRTEEN

MELEAGER'S WORLD

If I am a Syrian,
Why do you wonder, stranger?
We live in one country,
Which is the world.

- Meleager of Gadara (140–70 BC)

The loveliest approach to Damascus has always been from the west along the plain of the River Barada. The original city, now a small quarter within ancient walls at the edge of a huge metropolis, lay to the east along a fertile plain, in which the traveller from the west could refresh himself by the river in lush fruit orchards. Traditionally, outdoor coffee-houses on the river's banks welcomed those who had come from the seaport at Beirut, over the Mount Lebanon range, across the green Bekaa plain and through the Syrian desert. Two Dutch travellers, Van Egmont and John Heyman, wrote of the coffee-houses they saw in their 1759 *Travels through Part of Europe, Asia Minor, The Islands of the Archipelago, Syria, Palestine, Mount Sinai & c.*:

> In the same suburbs we entered a sightly coffee-house, and so large, that a thousand persons might conveniently fit in it. There are, indeed, two rooms adapted to the seasons of the year: that for the winter is supported by wooden pillars beautifully painted, and in it three or four basons with water conveyed thither by pipes underground. The summer apartment was in a little island, and the water by its continual motion and noise, together with the verdure and stateliness of the trees, renders this place extremely delightful; the roof was of rush matting, and every side of it open to the wind.
> Every part of the floor was covered with handsome mats for sitting on, according to the Turkish manner; and, I must own, I no

where met with such a pleasant coffee-house; for the water and the shady verdure of the country conveys a pleasure far exceeding all the glitter of the European structures of this kind.

By the time of 19th-century lithographs by the English illustrator W. H. Bartlett and others, tables and chairs had been introduced to the coffee-houses. The cafés still appeared to be places of timeless peace where men contemplated a slowly flowing river in what was possibly the oldest urban concentration on earth. One lovely Bartlett drawing showed cafés at the water's edge, with lanterns providing light in groves of poplars and banyans for the men seated around their tables. In the text that accompanied Bartlett's lithographs in the 1836 edition of *Syria, the Holy Land, Asia Minor & c.*, John Carne wrote of the Damascene cafés:

> . . . a flight of steps conducts to them from the sultry street, and it is delightful to pass in a few moments from the noisy, shadeless thoroughfare, where you see only mean gateways and the gable ends of edifices, to a cool, graceful, calm place of rest and refreshment, where you can muse and meditate in ease and luxury, and feel at every moment the rich breeze from the river . . . Innumerable small seats cover the floor, and you take one of these, and place it in the position you like best. Perhaps you wish to sit apart from the crowd, just under the shadow of the tree, or in some favourite corner, where you can smoke, and contemplate the motley guests, formed into calm and solemn groups, who wish to hold no communion with the Giaour. There is ample food here for the observer of character, costume, and pretension: the tradesman, the mechanic, the soldier, the gentleman, the dandy, the grave old man, looking wise on the past and dimly into the future: the hadjé, in his green turban, vain of his journey to Mecca, and drawing a long bow in his tales and adventures: the long straight pipe, the hookah with its soft curling tube and glass vase, are in request: but the poorer argillé is most commonly used.

No doubt the patrons of the riverside cafés watched in wonder in 1868 when a Scottosh sportsman named John MacGregor paddled his canoe, the *Rob Roy*, along the Barada from its source in the Anti-Lebanon Mountains into Damascus. The fourteen-foot cedarwood canoe, a Union Jack fluttering atop the mast, sparked the interest of most of the city, and the local pasha paid MacGregor the unusual compliment of a visit to his hotel. In those days, the river used to meander into the old city from the west along a wide, shallow plain. As late as 1936, H. V. Morton could write, "In the late afternoon I approached Damascus through miles of apricot trees. It was the hour when the Damascene goes at the end of a hot day to drink coffee in pile-dwellings built out over the river Barada." The River Barada had long since been channelled into a narrow, concrete shell running along the south side of the Beirut road. Once the lifeblood of Damascus, the Barada in recent years came to resemble an open sewer. John MacGregor's canoe would not have easily negotiated the rubbish blocking the shallow stream while I was there.

Just north of the Beirut road, at the top of rolling grass verges, some of the old coffee-houses were still standing. The river, sunk in its concrete trench over the road, could no longer be seen. Yet the view across the road and the river, apart from the cars and crowded buses locked in traffic, was much as it had been in Ottoman times – of the Sinanieh, the complex of mosques, religious schools, domed hostels and hospices built in the 16th century by the Empire's greatest architect, Sinan, whose work in Damascus so impressed Suleiman the Magnificent that the Sultan commissioned him to recreate it on a grander scale in Istanbul.

I walked slowly past a row of three or four outdoor cafés, crowded with men in conversation and filled with the sounds of Arabic music from cassette players, on my way to a relatively new indoor coffee-house at the end of the street. The Café Havana, built in the 1940s by a Syrian emigré who had returned home from a lucrative sojourn in Cuba, was at the bottom of the street of coffee-houses.

A waiter led me to the one empty table by the window, where I sat to wait for the man who had invited me. It was a sunny morning, but the Havana was in cool shade. The waiter slid the window near me open for more air. I had a clear view to the east of thousands of men and women walking along the wide asphalt boulevard, crossing the road on an overhead pedestrian walkway, going in and out of the many shops. Yellow taxis, military vehicles and private cars, mostly old, filled the boulevard. To the north, the cobbled side road with a row of shops led uphill, back towards the outdoor cafés.

Older men in business suits, younger men in jeans and a few young boys with things to sell walked past the Café Havana. I saw two women, covered in black from head to toe, possibly Iranian pilgrims, come out of a clothing store. A small group of Syrian peasant women in floral print dresses with white scarves over their hair were happily window-shopping – something they could not do in their villages, which had no shops and no windows. An old man with his head swathed in a keffieh walked slowly past with his old, bent wife, taking no notice of her or the café.

Whatever the weather outside, the Café Havana was cool and bright. Light grey marble dominated the room. On the floors, the marble lay separated into squares by embedded brass strips. The same marble was on the table tops that lined the windows and the rim of the main room at a level half above the kitchen. Built directly over the kitchen, overlooking the main café itself, was a gallery, empty in the morning, with wooden-arm stuffed chairs placed around low coffee tables, like a 1950s living-room. The ceiling was decorated with replicas of old Damascene painted wood panels, the Islamic geometric patterns in green, red and gold. If Ernest Hemingway had come to Damascus, he would have liked this "clean, well lighted place", and not only for its name.

This was the writers' and artists' café in Damascus, Syria's Café de la Paix on the left bank of the River Barada. Like all such places in the world, it had been invaded by the businessmen whose patronage, unwelcome as it was, kept it going. It was not a café for everyone. For many Syrians, it was too clean, too quiet. A cup of coffee cost 14 SL, nearly $1.50 at the official rate of exchange, more than double the price in the "popular" cafés up the hill. Like the popular cafés, though, the Havana served no alcohol and did not attract women.

I was waiting for Hani al Raheb, a writer and academic who had recently lost his teaching post at Damascus University because of his political views. Either he was late or I was early, but I had time to watch the world of the intellectuals inside and of the "masses" outside the windows. Although all the men at the tables were talking, there was only a soft, not unpleasant din – a contrast to the loud noises, the shouting waiters and the blaring radios of the popular cafés. Most of the patrons were middle-aged or older, wearing suits, some reading newspapers, others talking intently. I was not close enough to hear, but their expressions said the subject was politics.

The waiter brought me coffee in a white demi-tasse and a glass of water. He put a ticket down which said, in English: "Havana Café, 10:57, Total 14.00. Thank you." The sign outside over the front door read: "Café Havana" in Arabic. All the shop, café and restaurant signs in Syria had been in Arabic only for the previous twelve years, when most of the Latin script and names came down. Gradually, however, many businesses had begun restoring the Latin script, under or next to their signs in Arabic.

I sipped the coffee and turned to look out the window again, having read the morning's *Syria Times* in a couple of minutes. Across the cobbled street, I saw an unarmed army commando, wearing camouflage fatigues and a rust-coloured beret, drinking fresh orange juice at the juice shop, where net bags of fresh oranges hung over the front door. Scores of people were walking on the pavement next to the café, and I was watching to see how many of them bothered to look inside. Some stared without embarrassment. Others stole side glances, perhaps attempting to catch sight of a local celebrity. Others, who looked like the men inside, appeared to search for a friend and an excuse to come in. Some of them did. The poorer young men looked slyly in, out of the sides of their eyes, as they passed. It seemed as though they did not want to be seen looking . . . at what? Did they want one day to come in, join the class with money and time to sit and talk here? Or did they look inside to see men they simply didn't like, men they distrusted, men who one way or another appeared to cooperate with or benefit from a system which kept them poor and uneducated? An old peasant, tall and thin, wearing a brown *abaya* and the black and white *keffiyeh* of the farm worker, walked slowly past the window. He did not bother to look in.

Hani al-Raheb, looking like a professor in tweed jacket and wool tie and carrying a large bag, arrived about half an hour late. He greeted several of the men at other tables as he walked in to join me. Out of his bag, he pulled a copy of his book, which had arrived from London in English translation. *The Zionist Character in the English Novel* had been published by Zed Press two years earlier; he had only just received it. He seemed more pleased with the other prizes in his bag, powdered milk, matches and cooking ghee, all unobtainable on the local market. He had bought them that morning at the Writers' Union Cooperative. Forty-eight years old, with dark hair and goatee going grey, he could not have been happier if he'd been a child. "You have no idea how hard it is to find things like this here," he said.

We had met a few nights earlier at the Writers' Union, after which we had gone with several other writers, Syrian and Palestinian, to an apartment to talk and drink tea. They complained how, among other things, the shortages of coffee and the high cost of transportation, tea and accommodation in the city were making communication among dissident writers nearly impossible. When I suggested to Hani al-Raheb that we meet later, he said we should go to the Havana. "It's the only place to talk."

He was right. We talked for the rest of the morning and early afternoon. I enjoyed the Havana with its strong smells of coffee and tobacco, the impression it gave that ideas had not died in Damascus and that somewhere here, there was reason to hope.

In August 1985, Hani al-Raheb had delivered a controversial speech to the Writers' Union. Not long after, the university dismissed him. What on earth had he said?

"There were three main points," he answered. "The first was a direct reference to the terribly widening gap between rich and poor in this country. The rich are those who belong to the National Progressive Front, which has been in power for the last twenty years. And the poor are people like myself, who shouldn't be. A university professor shouldn't be poor. The second point was the list of candidates for the Executive Committee of the Writers' Union. I referred to some of them as 'report writers'."

"Report writers?"

"You know what this means? It means, if I say something against the government, from whatever aspect, they write a report about it to the intelligence services. The third thing was, and I think this was the most infuriating, I demanded freedom of the press."

Even journalists who worked for the Syrian press admitted it was dull, uninteresting and false. Each of the three daily newspapers in Damascus represented one of three points of view: that of the presidential palace, that of the government and that of the ruling party. "Who," a Syrian friend of mine asked jocularly, "could ask for more diversity than that?"

"Six or seven of the pro-government writers attacked me personally, insulted me at the meeting, accused me of being rich, of owning a car," he said. "Then I thought it was finished."

It wasn't. A week later, as he was about to board a flight to Yemen, the secret police arrested him. "My wife and two children were left on the tarmac," he recalled. "My wife collapsed out of fear that I might be taken to prison from there, because if a person is taken to prison from the airport, he simply vanishes. It may be three, four, five years before anybody hears of him."

The police released him unharmed, but they kept his passport. Five days later, the university told him he could no longer teach English literature. Hani al-Raheb was lucky. The head of the Syrian Arab News Agency (SANA) when I first came to Damascus, Marwan Hamwai, had been in prison for more than ten years without trial, because he was suspected of not informing the government of a coup attempt he may have heard about. At least, that was the story SANA officials told me after my repeated attempts to discover what had happened to the man who had been so helpful to the foreign press in 1973. Whenever I asked government officials about him, I was told, "Don't ask."

"Why do you think your punishment has been relatively lenient?"

"The party discussed whether the punishment should be imprisonment or dismissal from the university. They thought they would lose more by imprisoning me, because my name is well known in the literary field."

Hani al-Raheb wrote his first book, a romantic novel, when he was twenty-one. It won the prize for best Arabic novel in 1961. He wrote it in a month.

"Then," he said, "for fear of being disillusioned by the sudden success, it took me seven years to write my second novel, but it was nothing more than an exercise in novel-writing. The third was the real thing. That was *The*

Thousand and Two Nights, about the defeat of 1967. Published in 1977, it looked at the reasons for our defeat. What were the inherent elements of defeat, in the Arab psychology, the Arab character, which had been there for a thousand years, which enabled the Israelis to defeat us? Publishing that book took a year of negotiations with the party and the Writers' Union."

His fourth novel, set in Syria, was called *The Epidemic*. It won the Writers' Union award for the best novel of 1982. "This is the novel for which I should have been punished," he confided, "but those people do not read, you see."

"What was it about?"

"The rise to power of the Baath Party and its moral, social and economic collapse."

"What's the plot?"

"It's a four-section novel. The first takes the roots, the environment, the mostly rural origins of those who are now in power. Historically, it starts with the year 1917, when there was an epidemic here, taking lives by the thousand. When the Turks, with their innate dirt and the destruction they created, were pushed back from Syria, they spread many diseases, such as typhus . . ."

"Deliberately?"

"Not deliberately, no. Just like that, because of the destruction, robbery and killing. Corpses were left in the street to rot, and these became a source of disease. I remember one of my brothers was simply left in the open in the countryside."

I looked at him, surprised.

"Yes, because my mother carried one child. My father carried another. And there was a third for whom there was no one to carry. They simply left him. So, the opening of the novel is real disease, and the end of it is the disease that is spread by the children of those who suffered the first disease. It is a political and moral disease. Between these two, the novel traces certain examples of unruly spirits within a single family who by destroying themselves gave the gospel of something, gave the . . . tidings of the future. By the 1950s, the country was all optimism. They wanted progress, they wanted socialism, Arab unity, redistribution of the land, the liberation of Palestine and so on. The second section takes one example, the woman who raised herself from illiteracy, from absolute dependence on her husband, from solid fear of any individualism – am I talking too much?"

"Not at all."

". . . to personal and economic freedom by becoming – how do you say? – a dressmaker, by getting a divorce, which was something terrible in this society. But she insisted on it. Her rise symbolises in a way the rise of the middle class. I had to use this single female character to avoid the political aspects of the rise of the middle class. In the third section, we meet this class when it is in power. It is now a regime. In the third section, the main struggle is between two brothers. One is a government official, a brigadier-general in the army. The other is a worker. In Arab society, this is important, because family bonds are sacred. Now to reach this point of hopeless struggle between two brothers means a lot in an Arab society, especially if brother is imprisoned by brother. Then suddenly the third brother, who has been away for years, comes home and he too is imprisoned. The struggle goes on until the worker brother is killed at the hands of the secret police, who work for his brother the brigadier. The killing and the final collapse come in the fourth section, the title of which is taken from that period in 1917, *safar berlik*, 'travelling across the land.' The name indicates the confusion, the deaths, the destruction, in Syria from 1916 to 1919. The novel ends in 1977."

"How could this novel be published in Syria? Why did you have no problems as a result?"

He smiled. "It was smuggled into publication by the president of the Writers' Union. I don't think I should tell you what he said, because if this is published . . ."

"Please don't say anything you don't want published."

"We relied on the fact that the leadership does not read. We relied also on the cowardly fear of the critics, most of whom didn't write a word about it. This was only the second book in the history of the Writers' Union to go into a second edition."

"How many copies did it sell?"

He laughed and answered, "The highest sale in Syria, three thousand for the first edition, two thousand for the second."

"I'm told that in Syria the author has to help pay the cost of publishing and that no one can make a living writing."

"This gives you some idea how difficult it is. Our bestseller, Hanna Mina, is the official writer of the Communist Party, and the Communists support him. But even he has to work in the Ministry of Culture to survive."

"What is going on here?" I asked. "A writer like yourself and other critical writers are not in prison, not having too many difficulties being published. And if you can't be published here, you can publish outside. Doesn't that show some liberalism on the part of the regime compared to, say, somewhere like Iraq?" Whenever Syrians bemoaned the lack of freedom in their country, they had only to look across their borders at Iraq, where there was even less freedom, and at Lebanon, where there was too much.

"This is true. But the Syrians are not accustomed to violence up to the level of the Iraqis or Iranians. So, the amount of pressure Syrians face, compared with the amount of meekness in their lives, could be much higher than in Iraq and Iran."

"If you sell a few thousand copies, they are presumably read by people like yourself and never reach a wider audience."

"Yes, *The Epidemic* reached the greatest reading public possible in Syria. Officers in the army read it and were happy to present it as a gift, say, when somebody received a secondary degree."

"How is this possible?"

"The regime is confident that inside each one of us, there is that necessary policeman who works for the government and censors himself without government interference. We have been terrorised into growing this policeman within ourselves."

"Do you have this policeman within yourself?"

"My latest novel was written with a great deal of fear, which sabotaged its message. The point is not clear. So, with the best will in the world, only two out of ten people can get what I want all ten to. Because of this, it was almost a failure."

"What is the book?"

"*One Country which is the World.* The title comes from a poem by Meleager. It is about the position and role of the middle class in the world conflict between imperial forces and non-cultivated masses."

I must have looked somewhat puzzled as I put down my coffee.

"You are not perhaps accustomed to highly accentuated political phrases?" he asked. "We here are so fond of these. The book takes a common experience of many Arab countries, the rise of the middle class, especially after the Second World War. If there is no middle class, such as in Saudi Arabia, one is pushed forward. It is given a chance, so there won't be a gap, or a vacuum, between the regime and the people. The middle class can stand between these two and stop any clash between them. We believe the imperial forces favour developing this class so that no revolution, in a positive sense, would be possible for the betterment of life, for the progress of the people, et cetera."

We ordered more Turkish coffee. At other tables, men like ourselves, well-dressed, polite and animated, were drinking coffee, smoking cigarettes and having similar political discussions, but in Arabic. Outside, the stream of "uncultivated masses" continued its procession from shop to shop, in and out of offices and government ministries, up and down the wide avenues and cobbled side streets.

"Is there anything," I asked Raheb, "in the press here which is at all critical?"

"The regime has its own critics," he said. "This is a clever policy, because it releases now and then the mounting tension. Otherwise, the people might resort to violence, or to passive resistance, or whatever. The regime has ways of releasing this tension, so that people will accept humiliation in matters of freedom, of human rights, without saying, 'No.' The tension is never allowed to reach the point where it might explode."

"Is that how you explain a film like *At-Taqrir?*" *At-Taqrir*, "The Report," was the latest film by Doureid Lahham, the Syrian director-actor who made *The Borders*. Just as he lampooned the existence of artificial divisions across his native land in the earlier comedy, he castigated corruption in Arab society in this film.

"Yes, because *At-Taqrir* is addressed to the higher officials, to the president, and that suggests to the audience that the president doesn't know, or doesn't agree with, this corruption. Whereas, in actual fact, the whole thing is engineered by the president."

"Even *At-Taqrir* has a pessimistic ending. The hero is killed."

"This idea is enough: that the president will do something later."

"But the ending was not the president coming to do something. It was the honest man being killed."

"This is the first time Lahham has used this ending," he said. "As I told you, since *At-Taqrir* is addressed to the president, the criminals who killed the man carrying the *taqrir*, the report, are not the higher leadership – not the president, but those bloody criminals just below. The separation between the highest and those just below is what a regime looks for. If the accusation reaches the top, it becomes serious. This is never allowed."

"Not in any books or articles?"

"Never. One of our best poets, Fayez Khoddour, was drunk one day in a café. He was accused – it was never proved – was accused of saying something about the president. He was taken from the café to a cell."

At that moment, a thin man with an impressive moustache arrived to say hello to Hani al-Raheb. They exchanged a few words. Raheb told me, when the man went to sit at another table, "That was Naji Aloush, a Palestinian writer. He was the president of the Palestinian Union for Writers and Journalists for eight years. Then he had a clash with Yasser Arafat." It went without saying he had lost his job.

"What happened to Fayez Khoddour?"

"He went to prison for thirty months. Now, he works in the Writers' Union as a sub-editor."

"I suppose if you left Syria to write, you could not come home."

"That I wouldn't risk," he said, packing up his bag with his book and provisions. "I cannot develop a relationship with a new homeland, a new society. I am forty-eight. It's too late. This is the human bondage."

(Months later, Hani al-Raheb moved to Kuwait.)

"What will your next book be about?"

"*The Hills?* It's about how far and how near we in the twentieth century are to savagery."

"A continuation of the theme in *The Epidemic?*"

"Yes," he said. "I am accused here of constantly reproducing my vision. My answer is, Dostoevsky did that. I am no better."

I had dinner that night with a friend from Damascus University, a professor who walked the fine line between criticism and prison. "I just cannot understand," I told him, "how people can freely publish books condemning the entire system one day, and the next day a man can be pulled drunk out of a café for saying something critical of the president."

"There are only three subjects which are beyond criticism: the president himself, the army and the party. Otherwise, you are free to say what you like about anything."

"That doesn't leave much scope for free expression."

"You forget that this is a small society, and the political class is even smaller. If you are arrested, there are usually people who can try to help, even informally. When a friend of ours was taken to prison, we spoke to cousins and friends in the government, and we made certain he was not abused. We knew where he was within a day, and he was released not long after. It eases things a little."

I supposed the occasional arrests were the regime's way of awakening that "policeman" that Hani al-Raheb said lived in every Syrian. If all the policemen in all the men who gathered each morning at the Café Havana should one day fall asleep, Syria would have either an overcrowded prison or a revolution. Either way, the café would quickly fill up again.

The person who introduced me to the most people, particularly writers and politicians, in Damascus was not a Syrian. He was an African and my oldest friend in Syria. Omar Alim and I were both in our twenties when we first met during the October 1973 Arab–Israeli War, in a Damascus under blackout in fear of Israeli air raids. I was a 22-year-old freelance journalist, and he was the spokesman of the Eritrean Liberation Front. He had moved there a few years before, following Syria's decision to provide military equipment and training to the Eritreans, who were fighting for their independence from Ethiopia. In 1973, the ELF was socialist, committed to ending the rule of their country by an American-backed emperor. Now, the ELF had disintegrated. Other Eritrean independence movements, primarily the Marxist Eritrean People's Liberation Front, fought on against a Soviet-supported Marxist military dictatorship in Addis Ababa that was struggling to keep the old empire together.

Omar's father, a newspaper editor, had been assassinated by the Ethiopian intelligence services when Omar was a child. Omar had a large black and white photograph of his father hanging on a wall of his apartment, a handsome young man in a suit who looked almost identical to the son who followed him into both journalism and the movement for Eritrean independence. In the early 1960s, before the ELF recruited Omar as its spokesman because of his fluency in languages (Arabic, Italian, German, French and English, in addition to his own Tigrinya and Tigréan), Omar had worked for Reuter in Khartoum covering the Sudanese civil war. After fifteen years in Syria, during which he had watched the ELF become a squabbling band of self-interested politicians, Omar nursed a desire to return to journalism. He kept his hand in by steering his foreign journalist friends through the maze of Arab and African politics. His wife, Aida, was Palestinian, and they lived with their son and baby daughter in a modest flat away from the centre of Damascus.

The ELF kept an office in the "liberation" building near the Omayyad Hotel, along with other groups of exiles, who, like Scottish Highland chieftains in Bourbon Paris, endlessly awaited their chance to return home and seize power. Syria gave small subsidies and office space to "revolutionary" groups from Egypt, Jordan, Palestine, Iraq and various parts of Africa. The revolutionaries liked to believe they were using Syria, but when they strayed from Syria's orders, they would find their telephones cut, their salaries unpaid, their office cars confiscated. They either moved on to new benefactors or rediscovered their loyalty to Damascus.

I had planned to drift around Damascus, talking to shopkeepers, taxi drivers and people in coffee shops, but Omar Alim warned me against wasting time. He insisted on introducing me to the Damascene intellectuals, especially the writers. As head of the Arab Journalists' Federation, he knew most of them. He took me early one morning to see the president of the Syrian Writers' Union, Dr Ali Akla Orsan. Far from the obedient servant one would expect to head the "official" writers' union, Orsan was a closet dissident. It was Orsan who had helped to smuggle Hani al-Raheb's novels past the censors. His office in the Writers' Union building was the first I'd seen in Syria which had neither a large cut-glass chandelier nor, more significantly, a portrait of President Hafez al-Assad on the wall. I had learned to judge the degree of sycophancy of government officials by the size, vulgarity and positioning of their Assad portraits. Anyone with the old black-and-white photograph of Assad taken a decade earlier, placed unobtrusively on a side wall, was practically a rebel. In the last year, a government department had begun issuing full colour portraits with electric backlighting that made the president look radioactive. These were much sought after and usually seen in the offices of cabinet ministers and favoured senior bureaucrats, but the effect of the dramatic backlighting diminished during the frequent power cuts.

When Omar and I entered his large office, Orsan was sitting at his desk in a stuffed chair, facing the wall behind him and listening to a cassette recording of Beethoven's Ninth Symphony. We had to walk through a conference room, with a long table and many chairs, which opened onto his wood-panelled office. He turned and stood up to greet us, moving his silver worry beads to his left hand to shake our hands. He appeared to be a few years short of retirement, the years betrayed by grey hair, but he had brown eyes that looked somehow young and alive to the world they watched carefully. He wore a grey suit with a blue striped tie, and he had not shaved that morning.

He gave us cups of coffee. We explained that I was writing a book whose objectives I had only vaguely defined – just poke around the Levant, or Greater Syria, and write about what I saw. He seemed to like the idea. He and Omar together briefed me on his career. He was a poet who had become a playwright. Most of his eight plays – *Strangers*, which had been produced in Cairo and Kuwait, *The Visitors of the Night* and *The Sheikh and the Night* – were political. His only novel, *The Rock of the Golan*, had been translated into Russian and Bulgarian. His book of poetry, *The Foreign Shore*, was sold throughout the Arab world. He was active in the theatre, directing twenty-one plays, before he became president of the union. "Now," he said with a sigh, "I'm wasting a lot of my time in office work."

Gazing from a bookshelf behind Dr Orsan, and sometimes I imagined listening with approval, was the only decoration in the office, a small silver statue of the early eleventh-century Muslim philosopher Ibn Sina. Known to his European contemporaries as Avicenna, Ibn Sina was the leading Aristotelian of his time. The silver likeness was a Muslim version, book in hand, of Aristotle himself. Europeans often forgot that Greek philosophy was lost to their ancestors until the works of Plato and Aristotle were translated into Latin from Arabic; and many pious Muslims, who looked with pride on a history which included the philosopher, mathematician and encyclopaedist Ibn Sina, chose to forget that the revered master's two great extracurricular passions were women and wine.

I asked Dr Orsan about the state of the Arab theatre, the best of which I had seen over the years in Beirut and in the Israeli-occupied West Bank. "Mostly the Arab theatre is moving backwards," he said. "It's way behind the 1970s, when Arab plays were very advanced."

"Why," I asked, "is it worse now than in the 1970s?"

"I would put that question to the Americans," he answered. I feared a diatribe against the United States. Was he ready to blame even the state of the Arab theatre on American foreign policy? "Between 1967 and 1973, there was a shake-up in the area – political, economic and cultural. After 1973, American aid to Israel was annually above three billion dollars."

"So, you're saying American support for Israel was stifling Arab culture?"

"Not directly. What the Arab regimes were doing to Arab individuals – the absence of democracy, the violations of human rights – was all being done under the slogan that they had to confront Israel. After 1973, the Arab individuals, their values and the unity of their society were destroyed, especially in Syria, but also elsewhere in the Arab world."

Did anyone, writer or other, dare to speak to power in the Arab world? The Syrian poet Nizar Qabbani once wrote

> Sire, and my Master:
> twice you have lost the war,
> because half of our people's minds are suppressed
> and live in close confinement with ants and rats;
> indeed, Sire, can a people survive without expression?
>
> If – free from the henchman's cruelty –
> I could meet the Sultan,
> I would say to him, Sire:
> twice you have lost the war
> because you are ignorant of human rights . . .

"How," I asked, "did the rulers destroy people's values?"

"By corruption – corrupting the individual, corrupting relations among citizens and corrupting the civil service and the administration. They drew them to material relations by imposing consumer values. Also, there was a real cultural invasion that destroyed the indigenous values of the Arab human being. He was told that if he held to his old values, he would fail again, that these values were the cause of his defeat, his failure, his backwardness. There is another, general phenomenon which concerns all Third World countries. This has been planned mainly by Europeans and Americans, to convert people of the area into mouths and hands only – hands to work," he held out his hands, "and mouths to be fed – by them."

He continued his analysis of what had happened to the Arab world since the 1973 October War, a period many other Arabs regarded as a time of progress and hope. "After 1973, we see that regard for knowledge has been converted. For example, second-class labour is now receiving more money than a university professor. This has transformed the whole nation into a second-class society. People pay attention not to knowledge, but to money. If some genius arrives, he is quickly taken up by the Americans or Europeans. There is a severe brain drain. This does not mean that we too are not responsible. We are responsible, especially our rulers, for what is going on."

He offered us more coffee and turned the conversation back to my first question. "All this has affected our lives, especially our cultural life and the theatre. But theatre itself has its own objective reasons. These concern freedom of expression. A second reason is that certain political parties and powers have tried to convert the theatre into an information and propaganda instrument."

I looked up at Ibn Sina, reflecting that he would have shared Dr Orsan's distaste for this application of Plato's doctrine of subordinating the arts to state interests, and asked, "Is there any freedom of expression?"

"Lack of freedom of expression is not a partial thing. It is not the fault of the writer only. This is related to public liberties and the rights of the human being. The writer is part of this. It is related to the fundamental practice of democracy. This atmosphere is dominant in Third-World countries, the Arab countries and, in certain ways, in Europe. We in Syria are part of this world. We in the Arab world are suffering from questions related to freedom of expression. We are also suffering from the credibility of commitment to citizenship and patriotism – the geopolitics, history and cultural personality of a certain nation."

Dr Orsan fingered his worry beads and leaned towards us over his desk. "Aristotle said, 'It is better for people to be governed by good laws than good men.' This is still true. We are suffering from this, especially in the Arab world. We see that people are owned by the ruler, while the opposite should be true. I wrote this in Syria."

It was surprising to hear a Syrian official, especially the head of a quasi-governmental body like the Writers' Union, make implied criticisms of all the three untouchables – the president, the party and the army. That he could publish such criticisms of the system was shocking. Most officials were not so candid, whatever their personal feelings. I remember asking a friend in one of the ministries about the troubles taking place in Damascus between segments of the army in 1984. "What do you mean?" he asked. I mentioned the troops with weapons drawn at the entrance and on the roof of the building where we were sitting. His response had been, "What soldiers?" Shortly before my arrival in Syria, Amnesty International had reported that eighty-two trade unionists, journalists and others detained the previous year were still in prison and had not been tried. Amnesty said some had been tortured and one, a young soldier, had died in custody.

I asked what penalties writers feared in Syria when they deviated from state ideology.

"You might be surprised," he said, smiling, "if I tell you there is a certain margin of freedom in publishing. The writer here, if he says or writes something different from what the ruling classes want, might be interrogated and, in the Arab world, sometimes imprisoned. With whom is he going to differ and for what? He may sometimes differ with the ruler. He may disagree with the beliefs of his people. The writer here publishes in two fields – culture and information. In culture, the margin is wide. In information, it is less. I don't remember a writer here who was imprisoned for his ideas. Some have been questioned. Those who are in prison are not there because of their ideas, but because of their commitment to a certain political organisation. They were trying to come to power. Those in power didn't want them to, so they've gone to prison."

As Omar and I left, walking the length of the office to the door, Orsan turned on his cassette of Beethoven's Ninth. He sat back in his chair, enfolded in the music under the gaze of Ibn Sina's effigy. It was Ibn Sina who wrote, in his essay "The Secret of Destiny," "Do you not see that if anyone were let loose from both bonds [divine law and reason], the load of wickedness he would commit would be unbearable, and the order of the world's affairs would be upset by the dominance of him who is released from both bonds?" In the Levant, those released from both bonds were already dominant and held the people they ruled with other, more tangible bonds.

"It is better for people to be governed by good laws than good men." How far could Dr Orsan push this idea before he would be ordered to give up his office and presidency of the official union? How many articles and books could he publish in favour of this concept before he was brought in for questioning? Ibn Sina himself wrote philosophy from the palace where he served the ruler of Bokhara and from a prison cell. Dr Orsan seemed careful to stay out of both palace and prison, but each in its way would always beckon.

Tony Touma looked through his desk for an old newspaper. "I can't find it anywhere," he said, "but you would love it. It says everything there is to say about the Syrians."

"What is it, Tony?"

"There was an article in one of the Damascus papers about a CIA report on the Arabs. It was on the psychological attitudes of the Arab agents, on how to hire and recruit them. 'Look,' the paper said, 'see what the imperialists say about us!' "

"What did the imperialists say?"

"Everything," he answered, closing his drawer and abandoning the search. "I wish I could find it. It was ten years ago, and I saved it. You see, Charlie, everything the CIA report said was true. The paper said they sent psychiatrists to live in the Arab world and report back on how to recruit Arabs. It made twenty suggestions on how to get along with Arab agents."

"Can you remember them?"

"I remember the first one was, 'Arabs are very individualistic. You should not tell any Arab you are working with another Arab. If he finds out, he will destroy the other one.' "

"Is that true?"

"Of course. Another was, 'Once an Arab arrives at his place of work, he considers his duty terminated.' "

"What do you mean?"

"Just coming to the office is enough. He doesn't believe he has to do anything once he gets there. Oh, and there was another funny one: 'You should treat the Arab like you do your mistress. You can have him as a friend for ten years, but one slip of the tongue, and he is your enemy.' "

I began to write them down.

"Don't forget this one: 'The Arab needs continuous encouragement. You should touch his shoulder, his hair, give him constant reassurance. Tell him he is great.' Believe me, Charlie. It said this, and it was right."

"Any others?"

" 'Never praise an Arab in front of another Arab. It will make him jealous.' "

"Not a bad memory, ten years later. Five out of twenty."

"No, six. I remember it said, 'If you pretend you are innocently approaching an Arab just offering money, he will pretend he is innocently accepting. Don't elaborate on your objective.' "

"Tony, you're great."

"You don't have to flatter me, Charlie."

"The people are still what they were," the seventy-year-old man said, sitting motionless in his chair. "They want to participate in universal civilisation, in the creation of science. The military regime is so strong the people are afraid. The intellectuals are all afraid. We have a regime that kills people even in prison. Intellectuals and non-intellectuals are in the same position: all are afraid."

Although Hani al-Raheb and Dr Orsan felt free to criticise the system, the old man's frankness surprised me. I wrote down what he said, and then asked, "Are you willing to have me quote you by name in my book with what you are saying now?"

"They are always angry with me," he said. "You will only add to their anger."

The man with whom the regime was always angry was neither the leader of an underground organisation nor an active dissident trying to overthrow President Assad. He lived openly in a pleasant apartment in Damascus, and the Baath Party government left him alone. He was, after all, a founder of the party, who had served the regime as both ambassador and cabinet minister. His name was Dr Hafiz Jemalli.

Two friends, a man and a woman, had taken me to see him at his apartment on a quiet, tree-shaded street in a modern section of western Damascus. Although Dr Jemalli felt in some way invulnerable to prosecution, because of his age and former position in the party, my friends did not. They asked me not to mention that they had taken me to see him, so the names Ali and Leila Shehab are as good as any to conceal their identities. I was grateful to them for the introduction, and I was happy to have them escort me to his house. However, as the conversation with Dr Jemalli unfolded, I began to regret a little that Ali and Leila had come. Poor Dr Jemalli could hardly finish a sentence without one or the other of them interrupting to provide me with additional information, to compliment him on his insight or to ask him a question. There was nothing I could do. No matter how impatient you became in Syria, it was bad manners to show it.

Dr Jemalli was a kindly, bald man with wisps of white hair over the ears. He wore a blue pin-stripe suit. Moving his brown worry beads from right hand to left, he shook our hands when we arrived. He led us into his flat, a large, open-plan area divided into four reception rooms, each with its own brass and cut-glass chandelier hanging from the centre of its square of ceiling, each with an arrangement of chairs and sofa. Against one wall stood a glass case filled with ivory carvings of wild animals. One was a ferocious-looking lion, the Arabic word for which was "al-Assad."

Dr Jemalli exchanged reminiscences with Ali and Leila as he walked slowly towards one group of chairs, sofa and coffee table. When we sat down, I noticed his wristwatch. Unlike most in Damascus, his was not held on with a flashy gold band, but had only a simple black strap. When I asked questions, he leaned forward to listen.

"Before the Baath Party came to power," he said, regretfully, "we thought of some future for our country. Now the party governs the country. What we have now, you know, is only hope in something, that change will come. From what, from whom, we do not know."

"Can you reform the Baath Party?"

"It is too late. Definitely."

"What's wrong?"

"There are many things, not one. There are many wrongs. First, there is a state without principle, without the principles to make the country advance and progress. Second, the regime is military."

"Bravo," Leila interrupted.

"Third, the sentiment of every person here is that he is nothing, that he is lost to a wholly private existence, a thinking existence. There is a big difference between our ideal and the reality."

"That's right," Ali agreed.

Leila added, "I'm telling you, a man like Professor Jemalli, he is a strength when he speaks in a democratic, free way."

Ali and Leila asked him to tell me a little about his life. He recounted, alternating between French and English, that after secondary school in Syria under the French Mandate, he had taken his degree in philosophy at the Sorbonne. Leila interrupted to tell me Dr Jemalli was from Homs.

Jemalli said he returned to Syria to teach in an *école normale* for two years, before going back to Paris to take his PhD in "psycho-pedagogy." He remained a professor of education in Syria until 1963, when the Baath Party seized power promising "unity, progress and socialism," and he became an ambassador, first to Sudan and then to Italy. Eight years later, he returned to Damascus as president of the Writers' Union.

"When?" Leila asked him.

"In 1972."

"He was the second president," she told me.

"Third," he corrected her.

Ali said to me, "I think you have already met the fifth president, Dr Orsan."

After his return to Damascus, Jemalli wrote a regular column in the Syrian magazine *Al-Fursan* (The Knight) until 1976. He wrote another column in the daily *Ath-Thawra* (Revolution) from 1982 to 1986. He said he wrote occasional reviews for French and Tunisian publications.

"I translated books. I have always been a writer, from the beginning, even at the Sorbonne."

"How many books have you published, Professor?" Leila asked. When he had no answer, she asked again, "Many? You can't remember?" Then she asked him again in Arabic.

"I want to mention something," Ali said. "One of the best translations ever done, as if it had been written in Arabic, was his translation of Franz Fanon's *The Wretched of the Earth*. You would think Fanon had written it in Arabic, not in French."

Dr Jemalli continued, "At the Sorbonne, I wrote *The Arab Future, Aggression and Civilisation* and *An Arab Thinks*."

"*Un Arabe qui pense?*" Leila said. "No, it should be *What an Arabic*

Person is Thinking. That's it." Satisfied with her translation, she began fiddling with her key chain.

"I became a founder of the party that is now in power, the Baath," Dr Jemalli went on. "We founded it with Michel Aflaq, Salah Bitar, Jamil Drubi and Dr Jamal Atassi. We have an Arab thinker, Nadim Bitar, who is professor of sociology at the University of Detroit. He said in his book that each party in the world has an ideal to realise in its life, but it then changes direction. It makes many, many errors, not only errors, but deviation."

Ali asked Dr Jemalli to repeat what he had said in Arabic. When he did so, Ali translated, "Most of the political parties, when they come to power, they extremely divert their political line in a way you can say, this party is not the old one which I knew."

"What he said," Leila added, "I believe it as a law."

"The worst thing," Dr Jemalli said of the Baath-military regime in power, "is that we can accept a military regime if it really is a military regime. Because the aim of a military regime must be to make a successful war against Israel. This military regime is only against the population, not against Israel."

Ali and Leila interrupted again, until Dr Jemalli discussed popular fear of the regime. "Everyone is afraid. I accepted to be a minister. Why? Because, if not, they put me in prison. Nobody has the courage to tell our president there is something wrong. Our president believes he is an inspired person, with some special relationship with God. If he is inspired, nothing is wrong. If there is some crisis, it is a plot, of Israel or America, but nothing to do with him, because he is inspired. It is impossible to speak to him in natural, physical words."

"When Dr Jemalli wrote," Leila said, "he proved by numbers – like your way in America – that we are going down."

"For two years," Jemalli went on, turning to the propaganda system, "I told Zuheir M'sharqa [a vice-president] what I think. I told him, 'Our information system is wrong. Nobody believes it. Nobody listens to it. We have Radio Monte Carlo, the BBC, many alternatives. The most important news we need, you do not tell them. For example, the war between Iran and Iraq. The media never discussed it. Second, you release information to make our people seem stupid or spies.' To give him an example, we received the other day the secretary-general of the Arab League and the Algerian Foreign Minister. Our radio said they came to see our president about 'national' affairs. Naturally, I assumed they came to discuss *Chinese* affairs. They made it sound like news."

Dr Jemalli apologised for the fact that there was no one to make coffee. He offered us fresh lemonade, and sat smiling, waiting for my next question. Dr Jemalli was part of the generation Hani al-Raheb wrote about in *The Epidemic*, but he was one of the few who had tasted power without contracting the corrupting disease associated with it.

"At independence in 1946," I asked, "did you imagine things would be like this now?"

"Never," he said, taking a sip of lemon juice. "I find the present of Syria dangerous, and we are afraid of the future. But when I visit Libya or imagine Algeria and Iraq, I think that Syria is paradise."

"Why is there this atmosphere in Syria?"

"Because there is no political democracy. There is a plot against democracy, not by the people, but by the foreign powers. Israel wants to be tranquil, to be calm. It is not possible to be calm with Syria strong. Syria must be a country which cannot make serious war."

The telephone rang, and Dr Jemalli walked slowly across the room to answer. By the time he reached it, the ringing had stopped. He showed no hint of disappointment.

"With Israel there is the alliance of the extraordinary," he said when he sat down. "No people in the world has had the chance to have an ally as strong, as rich as America. We have to suppose that without America, Israel could not exist."

Leila interjected, "I add that if no America and no Israel, there would be no communism in the district."

"Apparently," Dr Jemalli continued, "Assad and America are enemies. The real relation though is that they are doing the same thing: making Israel strong and keeping the Arab people weak. For Syria, it is dangerous to be democratic."

"Why?"

"It is dangerous for all the presidents and all the imperialists. If we are democratic, we will be unified. If we are unified, we will be a danger to Israel. If the big force in the region is Israel, we must be killed. There is no solution to our problem without democracy."

"You cannot blame all your problems on Israel. Surely there are problems within – something in the nature of the state?"

"I cannot know the reasons for all the *coups d'état* in the Arab countries. In Syria, I know very well. The first coup was arranged by France and England under Hosni Za'im, for the oil pipeline. It was obvious."

In 1949, Colonel Hosni Za'im had staged the first of the many military coups that plagued Syria's first twenty years of independence. His Western-supported coup, which preserved for a time British access to the Iraqi Petroleum Company pipeline running through Syria, put an end to the form of parliamentary democracy Syria had inherited from France. The last coup came when the air force commander, General Hafez al-Assad, staged his "corrective movement" in 1970. It came as a surprise to most Syrians that Assad had survived nearly as long as all his military predecessors together.

"It was the same for all the coups that came after. You are right to suppose something is wrong in the nature of the state. The problem is that while all the progressive movements – the Baath, the Arab Nationalist Party, the Socialists, the Communists – wanted to make Syria a modern state, a progressive state, they have not been successful. Even in a small, weak state like Lebanon, parties like the Progressive Socialist Party and the Communists have failed. Nobody has succeeded in doing something serious in Lebanon and Syria."

He paused for a moment, looking down at his hands and the brown worry beads almost as if he were ashamed at the revelation he was about to make. "We must suppose," he said, "there is something wrong in our character. I don't know what it is."

He sat quietly, fingering his worry beads and apparently meditating on what was wrong, like a patient who has been to a succession of doctors to explain his symptoms, but must ultimately look inside himself for both diagnosis and cure. I saved my next question, and drank the rest of my lemon.

"We have had only two hundred years of Arab independence in our entire history," the old man said. "One hundred years of the Omayyads in Damascus, and one hundred years of the Abassids in Baghdad. After that, all the governments we have had here were foreign. We want to be Occidental, except in religion, but religion becomes superficial. Another fact is that our land is very poor. We have in Syria, for example, eighteen million hectares. Only two million are cultivated. Cultivated, how? Only with the hope that rain will come."

He held out his hand and began to count Syria's difficulties finger by finger. "One, we were dominated by others. Two, the land is poor. Three, we have been attacked from east and west, from all the people who existed in history from the time of Alexander. And now America. If *Brazil* becomes a great power, it may attack us. We suffer, and no one discusses the problem seriously."

I asked him whether any of the original Baath Party members were still in power. He answered, "One only," and changed the subject. "When we resisted the French, we had to act as a unified people. Now we are divided. We are Muslim. We are Alawi. We are Druze. We are Christian. How did it happen? Syria in the 1940s was liberated from sectarianism, but now we are divided into sects. The army is now composed of Alawi officers. A majority of our army is a minority of our people. It comes only by chance?" Answering his question in French, he said, *"Ce n'est pas par hasard. C'est très préparé. C'est fait par un peuple très divisé."*

He shook his head slowly, as though the answer to some riddle he had been seeking for a long time eluded him. "We have to progress, not regress," he said, the brown worry beads unmoved in his hands. "Before the revolution, our illiteracy was ninety per cent. Now we have seventy to eighty per cent literacy. Still we are regressing. How? How do we not progress?"

CHAPTER FOURTEEN

THIS BAD CENTURY

The daughter looked as the mother must have looked twenty years earlier, tall, thin, with a light complexion and thick, light brown hair. Only the colour of their eyes differed: the mother's were deep brown, the same as the women's eyes that stare shamelessly at strangers from one end to the other of the Mediterranean; and the daughter's were blue, like the Mediterranean itself. Both were artists, the mother a writer, the daughter a painter whose works had just been exhibited in Damascus.

They invited me to tea one afternoon at the daughter's, Racha Khouja's, flat near the Republican Palace in Abu Rummaneh, the fashionable "diplomatic" quarter of the modern city. The apartment was more comfortable and Western than the more common stark concrete flats decorated with only bric à brac from the souq. There were large stuffed sofas and chairs in the living-room. The wallpaper was light with a subtle pattern, and the cornice was a row of simple squares. On the walls hung Racha's paintings, some oils, some watercolours, of the countryside, of doves and of flowers. "Don't you paint what is left of the old city?" I asked.

"Everyone is painting old Damascus," Racha said. "It's too much. I don't like to paint like everybody else." I complimented her on her pictures, and she asked me what I thought of the work hanging in the dining-room. It was a large, ostentatious paisley pattern made of sequins and bangles. I confessed that it was not as good as the others. "I don't like it either," she laughed. "That was a long time ago."

The mother, Salma Haffar al-Kuzbari, sat down on the couch by the window and asked me to sit next to her. Crossing her legs, she leaned forward and lit a Marlboro. Using her left hand, adorned with only a wedding band and eternity ring, she gestured patiently like a teacher, making sure I understood what she was saying. "At the beginning," she said, "people were not used to reading anything interesting or important signed by a woman. Women writers suffered a lot, but I have been very lucky. When my first book appeared, it was received by writers here with great encouragement."

She put her cigarette into an ashtray when Racha brought us cups of

Turkish coffee. She sipped and spoke of the empathy she felt for May Ziadah, the Lebanese woman writer from an older generation who, like herself, had begun writing in the language of the coloniser. "I started like May to express myself in French," she said. "I improved my Arabic, like May, by reading the Koran. Arabic is my language. I love it. It is a very beautiful language. If we respect ourselves, we have to respect our language."

May Ziadah had become a kind of obsession for Mrs Kuzbari, who wrote her biography and edited the book *Blue Flame: Love Letters from Gibran Kahlil Gibran to May Ziadah.*

She chose the title, because the blue flame was a recurring image in Kahlil Gibran's poetry and paintings. In "My Countrymen," Gibran had written:

> The Spirit is a sacred blue
> Torch, burning and devouring
> The dry plants, and growing
> With the storm and illuminating
> The faces of the goddesses; but
> You, My Countrymen . . . your souls
> Are like ashes which the winds
> Scatter upon the snow, and which
> The tempests disperse forever in
> The valleys.

Mrs Kuzbari asked her daughter to bring copies of some of her books, so she could show me her works, mainly in Arabic, on May Ziadah. "May Ziadah was corresponding with the famous Orientalists," Mrs Kuzbari said, "in Italy, in France, in England. She was a fantastic personality."

Racha returned with a stack of books. Mrs Kuzbari continued, "I want to show you the original. This is the first edition. Here are the letters, indicated and explained. Gibran used to send her postcards, when he went to the museum in Boston. Here, you see the blue flame."

On a full page of the book was reproduced Gibran's William Blake-like drawing of an open hand, a flame rising from its palm, with the editors' caption that the flame "became the symbol of his love for May."

"This," she said, "is the blue flame. It was always in his letters and on the back of postcards. The emblem was his. In the letters, he would tell her about art and say he was dreaming she was a princess with a crown." She turned the page and pointed to a drawing Gibran had made of himself at a succession of ages and with various expressions. "He is the father, the brother, the lover et cetera. This is something amazing, you know. They were deeply in love and they never met. It was something Platonic, but something really *insolite.*" It was no more *insolite,* unusual, than the two Lebanese poets themselves.

Mrs Kuzbari said she had already written biographies of Western women, including Georges Sand, when she came to study the life of May Ziadah.

May had begun writing in Cairo at the time of an Arab literary renaissance, part of a cultural revival which brought with it new forms of Arabic poetry, original Arabic theatre and Arabic novels, as well as Arab demands for independence from Turkey. Under the spell of this rebirth, May began to write in Arabic. It was not considered unusual at the time that she, a Christian, should relearn her language through its most powerful expression, the Koran. She spoke nine languages, wrote twelve books and travelled widely. Her house in Cairo became a literary salon for the luminaries of the Arab literary revival like Taha Hussein, Ahmed Lutfi Sayyed and Khalil Mutran. It was at a ceremony for Mutran at the Cairo Opera House in 1913 that May Ziadah came across Kahlil Gibran, not in person, but in the only way she would ever know him, through his written words. A speech Gibran had sent from America was read to the assembled writers and critics, and May began a correspondence with the troubled Lebanese poet that lasted until his death in 1931. They appeared from their letters to have known and loved each other far more passionately than most couples who reconciled themselves to years of wedded domesticity.

"May was the most brilliant Arabic writer of the century," Mrs Kuzbari said. "In my opinion, she was better than Gibran in Arabic. She was a fantastic personality."

Salma Kuzbari began studying May's life in 1968. She explained how in interviewing May Ziadah's family she found a cousin, a physician, who had kept many of her letters. "I told him I was looking for documents, because the life of his cousin was not complete. He was the one who had come to take her from Cairo to insert her into the clinic of the mad. It was a big process in 1937."

"Had she gone mad?"

"She was a genius, but never mad. Her father and mother died. The cousins living in Lebanon and Cairo went to her house to ask for money. She inherited something from her father, and they wanted to have her money. She was famous. She was very rich, because she had the *Mahrousah,* a well-known newspaper in Cairo. She was very sad, very depressed, after the death of her father and mother." She had already been shaken by Gibran's death in New York six years earlier.

Mrs Kuzbari lit another cigarette, apparently incensed at the mercenary behaviour of May Ziadah's relations. "Her cousins came to her to say, 'You are very, very sick. Come to Lebanon, and we will cure you.' She had dreamed of making a house in Lebanon. They accompanied her to Beirut, this Dr Ziadah who had the letters and his cousins. And they put her in the *Asfourieh.*"

The *Asfourieh.* The name gave me a chill. Literally, it meant "Bird Cage," from *asfour*, "bird." There were many throughout the Arab world. The one I remembered was a huge building in the centre of Beirut, near what became the green line between Christian east and Muslim west. I remembered in the years before the civil war feeling a sense of unease whenever I came near this ugly stone institution, with its forbidding façade and barred windows. The traffic around it, the hawkers out front selling old clothes and used books on the pavement, old men with their trays of worry beads and nail clippers, the boys selling Chicklets, the Shiites shining shoes, all the ostensibly normal life of the Beirut souqs could not hide the *Asfourieh*'s purpose: it was the house of the insane in a country which took little or no care of its poor and its handicapped. People did not like to think or talk about what went on inside. Life was bad enough outside. When the country itself went insane, the doors of the *Asfourieh* were opened and the birds flew. May Ziadah, one of the Arab world's most gifted writers, was in another *asfourieh* until her death in 1941. Forty years later, the *Asfourieh* I knew was an empty shell in the no-man's-land between the two halves of the divided city.

Mrs Kuzbari told me about her other books; her fourth collection of short stories had just appeared. I asked her whether or not she wrote about politics.

"No," she said. "Politics is not my domain. My father was a politician, who became prime minister. I wrote one book when he died, *Amber and Ashes*. It was really to console myself after his death."

"Do politics affect your writing?"

"It depends which angle you take, the human angle. I know I have a duty as a writer, because my only weapon is my pen, to express for the others who don't write, what they feel. And to explain to the new generation what we think about our situation, which is very fragile. I know we are going to suffer more and more. And I am preoccupied with the new generation, but they have to understand they are within their rights to ask for their liberty. Our youth has lost its time. They live in an abnormal ambience, because everyone is worried about what is going to happen to our country – war or no war. Youth is anxious. You have to occupy them." She mentioned that the schools in Syria no longer taught languages other than Arabic, which she considered a loss. She paused to think a moment and went on, "Nothing is immortal. Everything will change, but I have no hope."

"Does this come out in your writing?"

"*Bien sûr.* I cannot lie to myself. What can I do? I cannot take up arms and make a revolution. It is not my job. I am too old."

She was too old, and the young were afraid.

"Charlie," Tony Touma said to me back in his office, where he was fielding calls from London and serving tea to the hotel's cabaret magician. "Charlie, I know you'll explain European heraldry in your book."

"European heraldry? What for?"

"Because it comes from here," he said. "The Mamelukes used various symbols on their shields. The Crusaders brought back some of the Mameluke shields as war trophies. They would hang them up in their castles, and these Mameluke warrior symbols became family emblems in Europe."

"May I have a cup of tea?"

"These emblems became the symbols of Europe's royal families and then of the countries themselves – the Eagle of Germany, the Lion of England."

"What about France?"

"The *Fleur de Lys* was a Fatimid sign," Tony said. "It was brought back by St Louis."

Would England have defeated the Spanish Armada, conquered India and grown into a world empire if Richard Coeur de Lion had captured a trophy emblazoned, not with a lion, but a gerbil?

Omar Alim felt more at home in a news office than in the liberation building and was to be found most afternoons at Reuter's. News bureaux in the Levant, whether in Lebanon, Syria, Jordan or Israel, served as men's clubs for all sorts of people, men and women. Visitors felt free to drop in, drink coffee, smoke cigarettes and catch up on gossip. Hospitality did not interfere with work. It was part of the job, albeit a pleasant part.

Omar and I were sitting in the Reuter office, on the third floor of an old office building in the commercial centre of Damascus, not far from the New Omayyad Hotel. Edmond Khlief, a Palestinian in his sixties who was the Reuter bureau chief, and Malek Husseini, an energetic Syrian who was chief correspondent, were entertaining us with coffee and discussion of local journalism and politics. Edmond was complaining about his last trip to Rome with Omar and a Visnews cameraman named Marwan Makdisi, when the three of them were returning from covering a conference in Algeria. He said their connecting flight from Rome was delayed a day. The Italians allowed Omar, with his Sudanese passport, and Marwan, with a Syrian passport, to enter the country. Edmond had no passport, merely the United Nations *laisser-passer* issued to refugees from Palestine.

"They wouldn't let me in, because I'm Palestinian. They let in Marwan, who is a Syrian, a *Syrian*! And then," he said, looking pointedly at Omar, "they let in this Negro." Omar laughed. "But me, born in Nazareth, the city of Christ, thirty years a journalist with Reuter, me they tell to wait. I didn't want to go into their country anyway."

When Edmond's secretary brought us more Turkish coffee, she had trouble finding space for the cups on a desk cluttered with several weeks' issues of newspapers, dozens of periodicals and books, papers and pens. Apart from a new computer, on which he filed to London, the office looked much as it had when I first saw it in 1974. So did Edmond, except that his glasses had grown thicker after several eye operations and his moustache had turned mostly grey.

One of the perennial questions hovering over Damascus was whether the president's brother, Rifaat al-Assad, would return to Syria from his exile in Europe. If he returned, cables would be flying from every embassy in the city to foreign ministries around the world. If Syria had a stock market, it would crash. And the thrill of uncertainty that reigned in 1984 and 1985, when Rifaat's tanks and troops surrounded Damascus, would most assuredly return.

"I don't think so," Edmond said. "Rifaat cannot come back without his brother's approval."

"There are rumours that their mother is dying, and she wants to see her younger son," I said.

"Rumours," Edmond grunted, dismissing the suggestion with a wave of his hand. "There are always rumours."

"Charlie went to see *At-Taqrir*." Omar said.

"How did you like it?" Edmond asked.

"Very much. But I'm surprised it was shown."

"It lets off steam," Edmond said. "Why don't you interview Doureid Lahham for your book? You'd like him."

Doureid Lahham was the producer, director, writer and star of the film *At-Taqrir*, "The Report", which was playing to capacity audiences, not only in Syria, but throughout the Arab world. Lahham's distinctive, funny face – with its grey moustache and large, dark eyes, rather like the old American comedian Jerry Colonna's – was familiar to all cinema-going Syrians. "The Report" was the film I had discussed with Hani al-Raheb, who said the government permitted its distribution because it criticised lower officials rather than the president.

I had been to see "The Report" one afternoon with a Palestinian friend who interpreted for me the more difficult Arabic, which I could not understand. The house was full, mostly with students, at the cinema in the Sham Palace Hotel. The story concerned an honest government official,

Azmi Bey, played by Lahham. He is a man apart – one of the rare men who refuses to accept bribes and is scrupulous in his dealings with the public. It is never stated which ministry or, more interestingly, which country he works in. Audiences took it to be whichever Arab country it was shown in. Unscrupulous businessmen try to persuade Azmi Bey to approve a plan to build a tourist complex which would displace a farming village. He turns down their application, and they attempt unsuccessfully to bribe him. They then buy the minister, who tries to convince Azmi Bey that it is in his interest to approve the plan. Azmi Bey refuses, insisting the scheme is against the law. The corrupt minister dismisses him.

Azmi Bey is devastated. After a period of despondent inactivity, he decides to prepare a Report on corruption within the society. He will deliver the Report so that changes can be made. The film then takes the viewer on a tour of abuses: the rich boys who are not punished when their new car hits a pedestrian; the businessmen who buy government officials; the government workers who are too lazy to do their jobs; the rich throwing US dollar bills at a belly-dancer in a night club while the poor beg for food outside. All were vignettes from real life, to which the audience nodded in recognition and which Azmi Bey records in his Report.

Finally, with the evidence amassed, Azmi Bey marches off to present the Report. He strides through the city streets, his Report in hand like a lance. Suddenly, he is mounted on a horse. He is a medieval Arab liberator, leading a cavalry column of the simple people who have not been corrupted. Fellini-like in its portrayal of Azmi Bey wielding his weapon – the truth – the film shows our hero for a moment marching proudly past a road sign which reads in Arabic, "To Palestine." At the sight of this, the entire audience cheered.

Azmi Bey walks into the football stadium, where the city's populace are gathered for a soccer match. He stands in the centre of the field and holds up his Report. The crowd ignores him. The game begins. He is trampled to death by the opposing teams, and the wind blows away the loose-leaf pages of The Report.

The message was blunt: our society rejects honesty, progress and even the liberation of Palestine. We profit from corruption and do not listen to the prophets in our midst. In fact, we kill them. Is this what you, the audience, are like?

The audience was stunned and silent as we walked down the steps to the door of the cinema. Outside in the twilit street, they began talking again. "It's true," I heard one young man say. Just then, a friend from the Ministry of Information who had been at the film, walked up to greet me. "You'd better watch out," I told him, half joking. "I think this movie was about you and your friends in the Ministry."

Omar, fearing I would leave Damascus with a few stones unturned, said there was someone else I should meet. Edmond asked, "Who?"

"Your cousin," Omar answered.

"My cousin? Which cousin?"

"Colette."

"Colette Khoury?" Edmond laughed. "You'd better watch our, Charlie."

"Why?" I asked, my curiosity aroused.

"You'll see," said Omar. "You'll see."

I let the telephone ring for several minutes and was about to hang up, when a woman answered.

"I'm a friend of Omar Alim and Edmond Khlief," I said. "I think they have spoken to you about me. I'm writing a book."

"Yes, Charles? Is it Charles? Please, come tonight if you are free."

"I would like to. May I bring Omar?"

"Bring anybody, Charles," she said in a husky, but feminine voice. In the background, I thought I could hear the sounds of music and ice clinking in a glass.

"About eight?"

"Anytime." She gave me directions to her apartment in an older quarter of Damascus. They were complicated, confusing instructions which made me regret, not for the first time, the fact that no one in Syria or Lebanon had an address. There was no such thing as a "52 Maple Avenue." It was always something like, "Do you know the Abu Mohammed Café? No? How about the Mayflower Hotel? The Banque Française? Okay, go to the Banque Française, turn right at the little road where there is a man selling flowers. Don't worry, he stays open late. Walk to the fourth building on the left, and ask someone there. Everyone knows the place." Of course, no one ever knew the place, and finding people was impossible on the first try. The cities in Israel and Jordan were different, having normal addresses with numbers and street names. Perhaps these were the different legacies of British and French colonialism. I had always felt that, if the British rather than the French had colonised Beirut, the city would have had street names and numbers and, come to think of it, cleaner streets.

Omar and I arrived late, having been lost in her neighbourhood for thirty minutes or so. We found the building only by chance when we bumped into someone else who was on his way there and offered to lead us. We followed him up the stone steps to her apartment and knocked.

A tall, voluptuous woman in her fifties opened the door. Her hair, eyes, dress and shoes were dark black, but her skin was fair, nearly as pale as the long strand of pearls around her neck. Like concentric circles within the pearls were two silver necklaces, one of which carried a silver Crescent of Islam, the other a silver Crucifix. She was a dazzling vision of Oriental jewellery – gold earrings, gold bracelets with inlaid pearls, rings on both hands, three on her wedding finger alone, and a huge almond-shaped diamond on her right index finger. She raised her eyebrows, and a black beauty spot on her cheek seemed to rise with them, as she looked at the three men on her doorstep. Then she smiled.

Colette Khoury greeted the other man, who turned out to be her lawyer, in French. Turning to Omar in Arabic, she said, "Welcome, Omar. I haven't seen you since . . ." waving her hand over her back to indicate an infinity of time. Then, to me in English, "You must be Charles. Come in, come in."

I walked into the most comfortable, most nearly Bohemian apartment I'd seen in Damascus. We went through a hallway and into a small, cluttered sitting-room. The raucous sound of Arabic music blared from an old television. There were stuffed chairs and sofas, Damascene wood tables and overflowing ash trays. In one corner was a chimney. Paintings, old photographs, rows of bookshelves with volumes in Arabic and French and framed historic documents dotted the walls. Her grandfather, Faris Khoury, had been prime minister, and her father a pre-Baathist politician.

Colette was a writer, by far Syria's best-selling romantic novelist. Hani al-Raheb had said a high sale for any serious novel was 5,000 copies. Colette Khoury's stories, which in Arabic terms would rival Mills and Boon, Jackie Collins and Judith Krantz, sold 50,000 copies each. For each copy, she received a royalty of 20 SL. "I need to sell forty copies to buy one pack of Marlboro," was how she measured her sales. To pay for the whisky and food that accompanied the cigarettes, she wrote articles in French and Syrian magazines and was a "language consultant" to the Ministry of Defence. Her book publisher was, not surprisingly, Dar al-Tlass – the imprint of the Minister of Defence, General Moustapha al-Tlass.

She offered us drinks, pouring whisky and ice into glasses regardless of what we'd asked for. Another man was already in the adjoining reception room, standing at a desk and speaking softly on the telephone. "This is Tony," she said, and the man nodded in our direction. The lawyer walked over to Tony.

Colette handed us drinks and asked if we wanted cigarettes. I was sitting in a comfortable green armchair near Omar. An old Oriental floral carpet covered the floor, and the room had a warmth, a feeling it was lived in which was rare in Damascus, where often the reception rooms were bare except for the chairs lining the walls for formal visits and the solitary photograph of a male ancestor. Colette sat on a large sofa, stroked her

Yorkshire terrier, and alternately took sips from her glass and puffs from her Marlboro.

"So," she said to me, "you are writing a book?"

"Yes," I hesitated. "About the Levant."

"It was not *my* ambition to be a writer," she said. "My ambition was to be a musician, because I love music. I was used to writing how much I wanted to be a musician or a singer. I wrote and wrote so much about wanting to be a music woman that I became a writer." She smiled, the broad lines between her nose and lips becoming more pronounced as she let out the deep bray that was her laugh. "It was my destiny."

"*Faute de mieux?*"

"*Non. Force des choses,*" she said and laughed again, her breasts moving up and down with the rhythm of her giggling.

"What was your first book?" I asked.

Still giggling, she ignored my question. "There is music in my work. All the critics say that. They say my style is musical, because when the phrase is not musical, I look for a way of making it musical."

"What was your first book?" I tried again.

"I used to write poetry," she said. "I was twenty when I published my book of poetry. Then I decided to write a story. It made a noise in the parliament, in politics, in the Arab countries. It was a nice story, but I was saying what I thought. I asked why a girl cannot make her own way. Why is everyone else above her? Why do others choose her husband for her? She must choose herself. I said what I thought about the condition of women, and it was a revolution."

"When was that?"

"It was in 1957. Thirty years ago? Is it thirty years ago already?" She seemed surprised.

"What was the title?"

"*Days with Him.* It is about a girl who was thinking of her days with a man, a musician." As an aside, she added, "So, I chose a musician too." Then she went on about the book. "This girl wanted to live her own life. I said she had to work to win her life. At that time, girls did not work. It was very bad to work. But a girl must earn her own living. If she is free materially, she will be free inside."

The musician Colette chose was a classical guitarist, a Spanish count named Roderigo de Zayas. "I married him, but I divorced him. Then I remarried him here. Then we went to France and the United States. He was living in France. I was eighteen."

"And the second time?"

"We stayed together, but maybe one month. We used to meet every six months to see each other, thinking maybe it will be better. He's a landlord.

He has money, and he plays the guitar. He's a director of the Academy in Madrid, I think. My daughter is from him."

She got up to refill our glasses with whisky, the Yorkshire terrier falling to the floor aggrieved. She sat down again, and the dog jumped up to be stroked. "I never got married again. When my daughter was young, I felt it was bad to marry a man other than her father. I thought she would be hurt to have a strange man at home. I thought that when she was old enough, I would get married. She went away to school and became a doctor, but I was used to living alone. It was very difficult to have a man to live with. I can live with him one day, two days, but not always . . . An Arab woman will not dare to say that, but I say it."

"There are not many."

"Not many?" she roared. "Not one!"

Omar, a proper Arab gentleman, concealed his embarrassment behind a smile. In an attempt to change the subject, he said, "I think you have written fifteen books. Is it fifteen?"

"Fifteen or sixteen," she said.

"Are they all love stories?" I asked.

"Of course. They are love stories, but in a certain part of society, of Arab society. Every time, there is a man, who is from the party, for example, and a woman, who is from the aristocracy, the bourgeoisie or the left. Even the discussions are about politics. So, if you read my books," she laughed, inviting us to laugh in the way she did it, "you will know what is going on in Damascus."

"Are the books political?"

"No, not much. I prefer humour. I think politics is a big man playing a little game. Man is a big child. I have to put politics in my books, because everywhere people speak about politics in my country. If you love someone, and you tell him, 'I love you,' do you know what happens? Down the street, a bomb goes off. When you want to make love to him, you hear another bomb. So, if you don't put politics in a book, it won't be realistic."

"Are your books realistic?"

"They are funny. I criticise a little bit, with humour. Every time you read me, you will have a smile."

"What do you think is funny about the politics here?"

"Funny? It's not funny at all! But you can criticise and be nervous, or you can criticise and laugh."

"For example?"

"This week, I wrote an article about the restaurants in Damascus. You go, and you hear a girl singing. Her voice is awful. You cannot even eat. I wrote that this comes from politics, because when our people begin a political discourse, they open their mouths and do not shut up. You can't understand a word they are saying."

"Was it always this way?"

"Once in the parliament, when my grandfather was there, a deputy was giving a speech, talking, talking. My grandfather offered him a glass of water, to make him comfortable. The man said, 'But I'm not tired.' My grandfather said, 'Please drink the water, because *we* are tired.'"

"Is there any sex in your novels?"

"No," she insisted. "I have romance. You feel my characters have sex, but without my saying it. It's nice to be shy. You don't have sex like you drink a whisky. There is a taboo in sex. It is sacred. It's like prayer. It's very nice, sex, and I'm all for it. Sex is part of a love story, but I don't like sex alone. I'm not against it, I just don't like it. I feel it's cheap, not for moral, but for artistic reasons."

"Is there any violence?"

"No," she smiled again. "I'm a very nice woman. There is violence in my books in conversation. But I don't like physical violence. I have a woman who works in my house, and she used to tell me, 'I want a man who gives me a slap when he comes home, so I can feel the room turning for twenty-four hours.' I said, 'For what?' And she said, 'Because it shows he is a man.'"

"Does she have a man like that?"

"No, she will never find a man like that. She is very strong, and if she finds a man, she will give *him* a slap."

She laughed again and offered us more whisky; the terrier again dropping to the floor when she stood up. The telephone rang, and Tony, who had been talking with the lawyer, answered it. He was an older, bald, meek-looking man, well dressed and speaking softly. Colette leaned over to me and whispered, "He is the man I like. He is my friend. My cousin Edmond is afraid I'll marry Tony."

"What kind of man do you like?"

"A gentle man. An expressive man," she answered, smiling. "Not a man who talks too much, because I talk too much."

"I don't know how you would ever meet one. Is it easier to live alone?"

"If you get used to it, it is rich. Solitude can give you yourself. You will be strong, and you will be great."

She handed drinks to Omar and me, then sat down. The terrier barked and jumped back on the sofa.

"What's the best thing in life?" A stupid question, I realised as soon as I asked. The answer was better.

"There are only two things," she said, dragging on her cigarette, tilting her head back so her black hair brushed her bare back, and the shoulder of her dress slipped to reveal a black bra strap. "Two things: glory and love. I don't know which is better, but I want both. But now that I'm getting old, after glory and love, there is money." She laughed again.

There was a knock on the door, and Colette got up, discomforting the dog again. She returned with a trim man in a dark suit, whom she introduced as General Marwan Deeb. "He works in topography," she explained. "He makes maps. He studied in France, Germany and England, so he speaks many languages. All these people are here *par hasard*. The general wants to see Tony, not me. My lawyer came because I needed him for some things."

It certainly looked like open house, and Colette was the rare sort of woman who could keep a salon where men could drop in, drink and talk. She was the daughter and granddaughter of politicians, and in Arab politics the house was the centre of activity. Around us on the walls were reminders of her grandfather's era: faded sepia pictures of the "nationalist" notables of Damascus, their collars starched and tarbooshes on their heads, as they posed after pressing the French for independence; a caricature of her grandfather drawn for a Syrian newspaper in the 1940s; an early nationalist flag; and notices in Arabic that proclaimed an independent Arab Syria.

Her grandfather, Faris Khoury, was born in Kfeir Hasbaya, a village near the Syrian–Lebanese border in what became Lebanon. From a prominent Christian family, he took a seat in the year before the First World War in the Ottoman parliament in Constantinople. When Feisal arrived in Damascus and proclaimed his Arab kingdom, Faris Khoury served in the short-lived government which the British had promised the Arabs as their reward for supporting the Allies against the Turks. When the French occupiers of Damascus legalised political parties in 1925, he and other prominent Damascenes formed the People's Party to seek independence and the reunification of Greater Syria. After the French troops withdrew in 1946, he became prime minister. He died in 1962, the year before the Baath Party seized power, when Colette was 25.

"I cannot write a novel now," she said, "because I am writing a biography of my grandfather. My father was also a minister, and they put him in gaol. But my grandfather was respected by the people who took power, because he was a nationalist."

"He was also a Christian, born in Lebanon . . ."

"He was born in Syria," she insisted. "Kfeir Hasbaya was in Syria until 1920, but the Lebanese like to say he was one of them."

"Do you think the Christian–Muslim fighting in Lebanon has an effect in Syria?"

"I don't think so. Syria can never be like Lebanon. It is another system.

In Lebanon, it is anarchy. Everyone has his own militia. In Syria, if something happens, it will end in a day. Lebanon is unique in the world." She paused and began to laugh as she added, "At least, I hope so."

She said she travelled a good deal, mainly to Paris where she wrote for the Arabic magazine *Al-Moustaqbal* (The Future). She could have afforded to live, like so many Arab exiles of her background, in Paris or London. Most of the old ruling class had fled after the land reforms, and many writers felt freer outside, but Colette stayed in Damascus. I wondered why.

"I love Damascus, and I love to live here."

"Is it better or worse than before?"

"If you are intelligent, and if you love your country, you can understand that sometimes things are bad. If every time it's not good, you run away, it's awful. Things are bad everywhere. I don't think in Europe or London or the United States, it's better. It's awful. This century, this *vingtième siècle*, is bad everywhere."

"What do you like about Damascus?"

"I like everything Oriental. I love Damascus because I know it. It's my big home. I don't mean this apartment is home. All Damascus is my home. I have a feeling of belonging. It belongs to me, Damascus. Whatever happens, even if the politics go against me, it belongs to me."

She began talking about her favourite writers, who included the Egyptian Yusuf Idris and, not surprisingly, Lord Byron and D. H. Lawrence. "And I love Agatha Christie," she said. "I don't know why I don't write detective stories."

I was curious about one thing, as I listened to Colette, watched her drinking and smoking, surrounded by her mementoes, her dog and her men. "Are the heroines of your novels," I asked, "like you?"

"Never. I need a thousand heroines to make one like me!"

I knew it. She gave Omar, Tony, the lawyer, the general and me more whisky to face the long night ahead.

CHAPTER FIFTEEN

QUEEN OF THE DESERT

If I had come to Syria fifty years before, social custom would have prevented me from sitting alone with women like Sehem Turjuman and Salma Haffar al-Kuzbari. As for Syrian women like Colette Khoury, they probably did not exist. Most women, particularly Muslims, were segregated from men outside the family. A foreign man might see them in the markets, their faces covered in black veils, but their husbands and fathers would not, even at home, allow men from outside the family to meet them. This was a way of protecting the fair sex, more in cities than in villages and among the bedouin. Some city women felt safe, others confined. "If a stranger enters," Eliot Warburton wrote in *The Crescent and the Cross* of his visits to Damascus houses in the 1840s, "the Moslem women retire to the hareem above, and peep from its latticed windows; but I was acquainted with some Christian families, in which the women remained undisturbed by visitors, and continued their embroidery or other work without interruption, though they seldom joined in conversation."

The rare glimpses of Damascene women produced on the whole a favourable response from travellers. The Dutchmen Egmont and Heyman found in their 1759 book "women more beautiful than in any other part." Nearly a hundred years later, Warburton came to a similar conclusion:

> The women of Damascus are said to be very handsome, and I
> think they deserve this, as well as other less complimentary
> reputations. They affect a deep seclusion, like the Cairenes, and
> are rather more ingenious perhaps in evading its restrictions.

Under the Ottomans women enjoyed few legal rights and no social freedom, beyond what they could demand within their households by sheer force of personality. Changes were made under the French Mandate and in the early years of independence, when public education was opened to women. The progressive ideology of the Baath Party, which came to power in 1963, brought a revolutionary transformation in the lives of most women. Girls went to the same schools as boys, and dressed in the same khaki semi-military uniforms. Women studied with men in universities and technical colleges. They worked with men in offices and factories. Women served in the army, although only as volunteers while the men were conscripted for at least thirty months. Women sat in parliament. A woman, the formidable Najwa al-Bitar, was Minister of Culture. Women and girls who covered their faces were a minority on the streets of Damascus, and sister killing – once the surest method of preserving the family honour – was made punishable by death.

Throughout Syrian history, women – whether from what became Alexandretta, the Syrian Arab Republic, Lebanon, Jordan or Israel – were at least as passionate, interesting and heroic as any of Syria's men: Delilah, Jezebel, Ruth, Esther, Salome, Mary Magdalene and Queen Zenobia of Palmyra. The Levant provided fertile ground as well for adventuresses from abroad, like the Queen of Sheba and Cleopatra, for whom all of Syria was but a lover's gift. Countless exotic or eccentric women made their way to Syria's shores, its deserts and its opulent cities. As late as the 19th and 20th centuries, Syria attracted wandering European women, particularly from England, like Lady Hester Stanhope, Gertrude Bell and Freya Stark.

One sunny afternoon, Tony Touma and I set out to visit the untended grave of the beautiful Jane Digby, a 19th-century Englishwoman whose life was every bit as romantic as Lord Byron's. After amorous adventures in England and on the Continent, Jane settled in Damascus at the age of 46 and married the sheikh of a Syrian desert tribe. Her friend, Sir Richard Burton, said of her, "Lady Jane Digby El Mesrab was a woman whose life's poetry never sank to prose." In the mid-19th century, many European travellers, like the Frenchman Edmond About and the English writer and painter Edward Lear, made it a point to visit her, just as Alexander Kinglake had gone to see Lady Hester Stanhope in Lebanon in 1832. Exotic European women were part of the Grand Tour of the Ottoman Empire, at least for those with introductions.

Taking the long way to Jane Digby's grave in the Protestant Cemetery outside Damascus's Eastern Gate, Tony drove up and down the foothills of Mount Kassioun, along narrow roads and wide boulevards within and without the walls, into old neighbourhoods and through more recently constructed refugee camps. As we drove along a pretty avenue in the Shaghour Quarter, Tony told me the timeworn balconies hanging precariously overhead had once been outdoor display cases for prostitutes. "My father said that in the 1920s these were all whorehouses," Tony said, his eyes intent on avoiding the pedestrians walking in the narrow road. The brothels seem to have been introduced by the French and disappeared with them as well. "The French themselves do not deny that they have sponsored houses of ill fame, for the 'good' of their army," wrote the American Harry Franck.

One of their first High Commissioners made it possible and worth while for a French bounder who had lived for some time in Syria to establish as many *"maisons militaires"* as might be needed. This fellow was at last accounts still director in chief of eighteen official houses, with a personnel of two hundred women; boasted of having taken in 238 "passes" on his initial night, with only ten women. It goes without saying that he now wears a diamond in his cravat, if not indeed a ribbon on his chest.

The women must have beckoned from the windows and balconies above us to the passing trade below, something unthinkable in modern Syria.

"And now?"

"Now," Tony said, "families live in these houses." I thought I detected disappointment in his voice.

The road became wider the further we went from the city walls. Tony took us out of Shaghour, but only a Damascene would have known that we had entered another neighbourhood, with another name, another community, another ethos. Trees lined the road, and there were no pavements to speak of. A few men on bicycles fought for gaps in the growing traffic. Grocers and barbers were doing a brisk business. A few goats nibbled the long grass at the roadside. "This is Tabbali," Tony said. "The people here are Christians from the Hauran." Many Christians and Druze had left the Hauran, a wide plain near the Israeli border, after Israel occupied the Golan Heights in 1967. There had already been a steady migration to Tabbali long before that war – villagers leaving the countryside for work in the metropolis. "These Christians are very tough, Charlie," Tony said. "Every man you see keeps a weapon under his bed."

"The government does nothing about it?"

"The government is not afraid of these people."

"Do they ever use their weapons?"

"Sometimes. Whenever a Christian girl goes walking in a short skirt to Palestine . . ."

"Palestine?"

"Palestine is the refugee camp just ahead. It's for Palestinians from '48. Sometimes the boys in Palestine make improper advances or say something rude to the girls from Tabbali. Then the girls' fathers and brothers come out with their guns. Usually, there is just a beating. Then everyone forgets about it."

Tony said the Palestinians spoke Arabic with a distinct accent despite forty years in Damascus, just as many of the Christians of Tabbali retained their Haurani accents. It sometimes took generations to become a true Damascene, in language, dress and urban outlook.

The same was true for the inhabitants of Mount Kassioun, some of whose ancestors had arrived eight centuries earlier. Damascenes still called the foothills where they lived *Muhajrin*, "immigrants." Settlement began in *Muhajrin*, beyond the safety and confinement of the city walls, in the twelfth century at the death of Salah ed Din. His 20,000 loyal Kurdish troops demanded the right to live and then to be buried near the prince who had led them in the conquest of Egypt and Syria and the liberation of Jerusalem. The mountain became known as *Jebel Salhiyeh*, Mount of the Saints, for its many stone memorials to the pious.

Wilfrid Scawen Blunt wrote in 1881 of the houses then under construction on Jebel Salhiyeh, based "on good Turkish models with overhanging stories made of wooden frames filled in with plaster, cheap, practical, and pretty." Many of those houses were standing a century later, often reinforced with new frames and replastered, mixed with the newer and uglier grey breezeblock and concrete houses belonging to an age which had yet to receive a name. Salhiyeh was famous for its view of Damascus, which Blunt believed was "among the first half-dozen great views of the world," the others being those over Cairo, Rio de Janeiro, Lake Geneva, Constantinople and the Red Sea with Mount Sinai in the background. "All these," Blunt wrote, "will stop one's breath for wonder and bring tears to one's eyes."

"You know, Charlie, there are still descendants of the Crusaders living in Syria," Tony said, while we were stuck in the traffic of Palestine camp.

"I hope you're not going to tell me about the blue eyes I see."

"No, no," he said, "not here. In the north. After Salah ed Din defeated the Crusaders, he allowed them to return to Europe. But some were too old or too poor to make the trip home. They asked Salah ed Din for help, so he gave them some land. They call it *Wadi Nasara*, Valley of the Nazarenes. Those Christians still live there. They are very proud people."

It seemed that every wave of invaders and immigrants had left some trace of itself in Syria, in the form of descendants who themselves would know their ancestral homelands in the forests of northern Europe, the plains of Mongolia, the mountains of Armenia or the deserts of Arabia, if they knew them at all, only through legend and myth. The sagas of pious Kurdish warriors, chivalrous European knights or brave Armenian princes sustained whole communities as separate entities through the changing fortunes of Levantine history. Tony Touma had his roots too, in Syria's Pauline Christian conversions and in the Byzantine Empire of which Syria formed a vital part until Arabs flying the banner of Islam suddenly rode north from Arabia. Those roots intertwined with the Arab in him, and

Arab culture and language were just as much a part of his make-up as his Christian family origins.

We stopped just beyond the old city's Eastern Gate, not far from the window Christians liked to believe was the one from which St Paul was lowered in a basket on his escape from Damascus. Paul's window was at the eastern end of the road which once divided Damascus in two, the Via Recta or Street called Straight. If the street was ever straight, it had long since ceased to be so by the time Mark Twain came to Damascus in 1867:

> The street called Straight is straighter than a corkscrew, but not as straight as a rainbow. St Luke is careful not to commit himself; he does not say it is the street which *is* straight, but the "street which is *called* Straight." It is a fine piece of irony; it is the only facetious remark in the Bible, I believe.

Beyond Paul's window were an old building reputed to be the house of Ananias where St Paul took refuge, the churches and shops of the Christian Quarter and several lavish palaces belonging to prominent Christian families. It was just outside the walls near their ancient neighbourhood that the Christians buried their dead.

"This is where all the Christian cemeteries are," Tony said. "The Orthodox Cemetery is over there, and this one is for the Catholics."

He parked his car near a caretaker's house. When we got out, a man in brown gardener's clothes walked up to us. Tony introduced them and explained, "He looks after both the Catholic and Orthodox graveyards. Of course, he is a Muslim." The man, in his late thirties, was friendly and asked Tony in Arabic if I were the Italian. Tony told him I wasn't.

"Why does he think I'm Italian?"

"He knows I am bringing a designer from Italy to our family tomb. Someday, my father will be buried here," Tony said. "Then it will be my turn."

Tony began discussing the site with the gravekeeper, and I walked alone through the gardens. There was a monument to "Lt Marwan Zachem, air fighter killed by the Israeli enemy in 1970." In the centre of his memorial was a photograph of the young lieutenant, looking like a First World War air ace in his flyer's cap and dark moustache.

I came across a grave with a photograph of a pretty young woman who had long, dark hair. Inscribed in the marble below her picture were the dates "1946–1976." Her name was Marilyn Depasquale. Both the photograph and the name seemed to belong to an Italian, not a Syrian. Tony walked up to me and said, "She was an American girl, who married a Syrian. He really loved her, Charlie. You've never seen anything like it. She was killed in a car accident, and her husband still comes every week to place flowers on her grave." A bouquet of red roses, wrapped tightly in lemon leaves, stood in a vase beneath her picture. I was thinking about them, wondering whether the husband would bring roses to his wife every week if she were alive, when Tony drove me to the Protestant Cemetery. There my question about Marilyn Depasquale and her husband was answered.

Over a high iron gate was a hand-lettered sign that read in English and Arabic, "National Evangelical Cemetery, 1913." We tried to go inside, but the gate was locked. Tony said he did not know who had the key. "You're tall, Charlie. Climb over, and I'll wait."

"Where is Jane Digby's grave?"

"It's over on the left, under a tree. You'll see it."

I pulled myself up the iron bars, got a foothold in the lock and climbed to the top. I looked down upon a grassless field, more like a rubbish dump than a cemetery. No one had tended the lawn, pruned the trees or cleared the debris in years. The ground had turned mostly to dust, and a dozen pines in a row along the outer wall were turning yellow for lack of water. The high outer wall on one side and the crumbling houses of Palestine camp on the other three enclosed a rectangle the size of a football field. Laundry hanging out of the windows of the camp's houses dripped water onto mounds of rusting powdered milk tins, egg cartons and torn newspapers. While Tony waited patiently outside, I dropped down into the desolate, forgotten field which was part cemetery, part rubbish tip, in a land and world far from that into which Jane Digby had been born in the spring of 1807.

Jane was a kind of female Byron, a child of the Regency who never adapted to Victorian priggishness. Her lifelong search for love, passion and adventure took her from London to Paris, to a new husband in Bavaria, another husband and lover in Greece and, finally, to Syria, where she died after twenty-seven years as the contented wife of a bedouin sheikh. Her father, Captain Henry Digby, fought bravely at the battle of Trafalgar, and later became an admiral. Her mother was the daughter of the Earl of Leicester. Jane was born at Holkham Hall in Norfolk, and from her early teens was said to be one of the most beautiful girls in England. Letters and diaries from the period contain rhapsodies to her fair hair, her milky skin and her supple body. Before she was seventeen, her parents arranged her marriage to a man twice her age, Edward Law, Lord Ellenborough, who was Lord Privy Seal in the Duke of Wellington's cabinet. When he took Jane on their honeymoon to Brighton, he allegedly tried to seduce the daughter of a pastrycook. The marriage deteriorated from there.

Dissatisfied with her unhappy life, Jane found romance and what she thought was true love with an Austrian diplomat, Prince Felix Schwarzenberg. After bearing Ellenborough a son and heir, she consorted publicly with Schwarzenberg in a London accustomed to its upper classes engaging in outrageous extra-marital affairs. Schwarzenberg was posted to Paris. Pregnant with his child, Jane followed. The publicity surrounding the affair proved too much for Ellenborough, who sued for divorce. At the time, Parliament, which had to debate the merits of petitions for the dissolution of marriage, granted only one or two divorces each year.

In Paris, Jane survived the storm and the public humiliation of her husband. She and Schwarzenberg lived together as lover and mistress from 1829 to 1831. The unconventional *aristocrate anglaise* fascinated Honoré de Balzac, who based the character of Lady Arabella Dudley on her in his *Le Lys Dans la Vallée*. When Jane and Schwarzenberg parted, with the prince keeping the two children, Jane moved to Bavaria. Aged twenty-four, she became the mistress of King Ludwig I, who was then forty-five. After the affair, Jane married the Bavarian Count von Venningen. She had two more children by Venningen, but she fell in love with a Greek count, Spyridon Theotoky. Her affair with Theotoky reached its climax one night when she fled with him from Schloss Venningen in a carriage. Venningen pursued the pair, challenged Theotoky to a duel and felled him with what appeared to be a fatal shot. Theotoky lay bleeding in Jane's arms, but he did not die. Venningen graciously took him to his castle. Jane and the Greek finally left Bavaria together. Again, Jane left her children behind to follow a lover.

In Greece, she and Theotoky were married. They had a son, whom Jane is said to have loved more than her other children. Sadly, the boy died aged six, falling from the top of a staircase and landing dead at his mother's feet. Jane then began a liaison with Greece's King Otto, the son of King Ludwig. She left Theotoky, and she fell in love again, this time with a rough brigand from the mountains of northern Greece. He was General Christos Hadji-Petros, a hero in Greece's war of independence from Turkey, who plundered travellers for a living. He lived with his people, the *pallikari* or brave ones. For a time, Jane shared the rough mountain life as the consort of the *pallikaris'* aged leader. Jane minded little that Hadji-Petros and his bandits lived off her income from England, but when her maid, Eugénie, revealed that Hadji-Petros had tried to seduce her, she left him.

Jane was forty-six years old when, in April 1853, she and Eugénie sailed from Piraeus harbour to Beirut. In Syria, Jane began to keep a diary, made Arabic the ninth language she could read and write, and visited the ruins in Palmyra. Her escort to Palmyra, Sheikh Medjuel El Mesrab, the younger son of the head of the El Mesrab tribe, fell madly in love with Jane. She, however, already loved a young bedouin name Saleh, whom she had met one day riding near the River Jordan. When Jane returned to Syria from a brief trip to Athens to dispose of her property there, she discovered Saleh had married a pretty eighteen-year-old. Heartbroken, Jane set off to visit Baghdad. On the way, Sheikh Medjuel El Mesrab suddenly appeared with an Arab mare as a gift for her. Although Saleh had found a wife in Jane's absence, Sheikh Medjuel had divorced his wife to await Jane's return. He asked Jane to marry him, and she accepted.

"If I had neither a mirror nor memory," she wrote in her diary, "I would believe myself fifteen years old." She was deeply in love with her husband and admired his people. In a letter to her mother in 1853, she wrote, "My heart warms towards these wild Arabs. They have many qualities we want in civilised life, unbounded hospitality, respect for strangers or guests, good faith and simplicity of feeling among themselves, and a certain high-bred innate politeness, quite unlike the coarse vulgar Fellah [peasant]."

Neither the English nor the El Mesrab people favoured the union. Richard Wood, the English consul in Damascus, opposed Jane's marriage to a native, and Medjuel's tribe resented his foreign, Christian wife. After the couple's Muslim wedding at Homs, Medjuel's kinsmen came to accept Jane and called her affectionately "Umm al-laban," mother of the milk, for her fair skin. She and Medjuel lived half the year travelling in the desert and the other half at their house outside Damascus.

Although Jane was a Christian, the Muslim mobs who looted the Christian Quarter during the massacres of 1860 left her alone. Some of the men on their way to kill the Christians asked Sheikh Medjuel whether his Christian wife needed protection, which she did not. Jane herself went into the Christian Quarter and implored the rioters not to harm the Christians. The great Algerian leader, Abdel Qader al-Jezairi, rushed out of his fortress house to defend the Christians and to offer sanctuary to hundreds of them within the walls of his compound. Abdel Qader, not the mob, acted in the best tradition of Islam.

Medjuel, Jane and Abdel Qader became friends with Sir Richard Burton when he lived in the Damascus foothills of Salhiyeh from 1869 to 1871 as British consul. Burton and his wife, Isabel, often entertained the El Mesrabs and Abdel Qader, and Isabel remembered Jane in her diaries.

> She was a most beautiful woman, though at the time I write she was sixty-one, tall, commanding and queen-like. She was *grande dame au bout des doigts*, as much as if she had just left the salons of London and Paris, refined in manner and voice, nor did she ever utter a word you could wish unsaid. My husband thought she was out and out the cleverest woman he ever met; there was nothing she could not do.

Jane remained passionate to the end of her life. Her biographer, E. M. Oddie, who had access to Jane's diaries before they were lost, recorded these words of Jane's: "Sixty-two years of age, and an impetuous, romantic girl of seventeen cannot exceed me in ardent, passionate feelings." Although she had felt similar passion for at least half a dozen men in her life, its sole object for her last twenty-seven years was Medjuel. They are said to have argued ferociously, but to have fought side by side against other bedouin in inter-tribal battles. Jane was sometimes jealous and raged at her husband, but she was able shortly before her death to write, "It is now a month and twenty days since Medjuel last slept with me! What can be the reason?"

Jane died of dysentery during a cholera epidemic in 1881. Before her death at her husband's side, she had purchased a plot in the Protestant Cemetery where more than a century later I had come in search of her grave.

I saw that there were fewer than a hundred graves, and more than half the cemetery was empty. It was nonetheless difficult to find Jane Digby. Most of the headstones were covered in undergrowth and earth. I walked slowly along each row of the dead, pulling back weeds and brushing off years of dust. None of the epitaphs I could read were earlier than about 1830, and none later than 1946. When Jane died, there could not have been more than a dozen other graves to keep hers company. I realised after a little while that the graves were carefully segregated. The Europeans and Americans, their names neatly carved in Latin, English or German, were in one part of the yard, and the Arabs, their names recorded in beautiful Arabic calligraphy, were in another.

Most of the European graves contained the remains of missionaries from Wales, Scotland and Ireland, the fiery Celtic fringe of Victorian Protestant evangelism. There were also many Americans. I wondered what had brought "Thomas S. Mitchell of Philadelphia, died Jan 16 1855 aged 36 years" to Damascus. Some were not missionaries, but consuls or relations of consuls. Others seemed to fit no category at all.

I looked up and down the rows of graves for Jane Digby, but could find her nowhere. I walked back to the gate and told Tony. "Oh, all right, Charlie," he said. "Let me come and look. I'm not tall like you, so you'll have to help."

Tony took off his jacket and rolled up his sleeves. He hoisted himself up, getting a foothold on the lock. He could not reach the top, so I stood still while he put his feet through the bars to stand on my shoulders. Then he climbed to the top, flung his body over and dropped to the ground. "Come with me," he said.

We walked around the graves, and after five minutes, Tony said, "I thought it was here. Oh, my God! Do you think someone has taken the stone?"

"That would be quite a story. 'Tombstone of 19th-century romantic stolen in Damascus.' The Foreign Office would have to send investigators."

"This is serious, Charlie. I know it was here. Now it's gone."

"Who would steal her tombstone? I don't suppose it would sell for much at Sotheby's."

"I can't believe it."

We set out again. I took one end, and Tony took the other. I inspected the graves of long-forgotten German pastors, American preachers and Celtic vicars, come to the Arab world to find converts from the world of Islam to Christendom and, failing that, from Eastern Christianity to Protestantism. The Ottomans had tolerated their presence as they had so many other forms of interference in their domains. The majority of the missionaries, their noble task for the most part unperformed, abandoned Syria for more fertile fields in Africa and the South Pacific. These alone had remained to the bitter end, leaving their bones, and those of their wives and children, as final testaments to their holy enterprise.

"Charlie, come here," Tony said, pulling back the low branches of a China tree. "Here it is. I told you it was here."

Tony brushed the shrubbery and earth from the dark stone to reveal a long, tapered sarcophagus lying flat like the tomb of a Crusader in a Norman church. A raised cross ran the length of the smooth top surface, and around the sides etched in Gothic script were the words: "Jane Elizabeth daughter of Admiral Sir Henry Digby, G.C.B., Born April 3rd, 1807 Died August 11, 1881 My trust is in the tender mercy of God for ever and ever. Ps. LII.8."

At the foot of the long slab, carved to fit just over the base, was a block of Syrian mazoni rock, rough-hewn where the tomb stone was polished, light where the tomb was dark. It seemed to have been an afterthought.

"Her husband put this here," Tony said. "He ran away from her funeral. He was a devout Muslim, and it was the first time he went to a Christian service. He had never been inside a carriage before, and he just ran away as it approached the cemetery. He came back at the end on a horse and just watched. Later, he and his people brought the stone. He carved her name in it with his own hand."

Etched like childlike, phonetic Arabic on the hard Syrian rock were the words, *"Madame Digby El Mezrab."*

"When he finished," Tony said, "he disappeared into the desert."

Medjuel's love survived both the long years of marriage and the death of its object. Jane Digby, Marilyn Depasquale and thousands of other women, in Ottoman times and our own, found in love like Medjuel's the only constant in a changing world. Stones and flowers were merely temporal tributes to an eternal idea.

When I walked into Tony Touma's office one evening, it looked like a theatrical booking agency. Seated on the divan and in chairs were an old man in a three-piece suit, a young man in a yellow and black stage costume, a young woman in a sequinned bathing suit, another young woman whose eyes were ringed in mascara, and assorted other visitors. "Sorry, Tony," I said. "I didn't realise you were busy. I'll come back later."

"I'm not busy," he said. "I want you to meet my uncle, Dr Solomon."

The old man in the three-piece suit stood and shook my hand. "*Enchanté*," he said, reaching his left hand towards my ear and producing an ace of spades.

"My uncle is a magician," Tony explained. "He is eighty-six years old."

"Eighty-six?"

"Yes, and he believes he knows the secrets of long life."

"What are they?"

"Never drink, never smoke and drink lots of water. Isn't that right, uncle?"

Dr Solomon smiled and nodded. He understood English, but preferred to speak Arabic, French or Italian. It turned out the couple dressed for the stage were an Italian magician and his wife. The young woman with the eyes was a belly-dancer. All three worked in the hotel cabaret. Drivers and camera crews from the other news offices in the hotel were drifting in and out of Tony's open door.

"You know the story about the journalist who went to see the oldest man in the world?" Tony asked me. Without waiting for a reply, he began to joke. "He finds the old man in his house high in the Himalayas. 'Oh, old man, how can I achieve long life?' he asks. The old man says, 'Write this down. First, never smoke. Second, never drink. Third, never have sex. Fourth . . .' All of a sudden, there was a terrible commotion upstairs, all sorts of banging and shouting. 'What's that?' the journalist asks. 'That?' the old man says. 'Nothing. Just my older brother and his girlfriends, drunk again.'"

Dr Solomon laughed, then offered to show us his magic. He first asked the ABC driver, a young man named Bachar Hazam, for a handkerchief. Bachar handed him one, and the old man cut it into shreds with a pair of scissors. He then stuffed the pieces into the top of his clenched fist, pulled the handkerchief out undamaged and handed it back. He made coins disappear and reappear, and he and the young Italian traded magician's secrets.

"My uncle learned magic from an Italian who came to Damascus in the 1890s," Tony told me. "But Dr Solomon's real skill is mind-reading."

"Are you psychic, Dr Solomon?" I asked.

"I did not learn clairvoyance," he answered. "It was a gift, a gift I myself do not understand." Mind-reading had been the climax of his stage performances in Europe, Syria, Lebanon and Egypt. He had caused a stir one night in Cairo, when he read the mind of Egypt's King Farouk.

"What was the King thinking?"

"I cannot say now."

From the King's reputation before the army deposed him in 1952, I suspected it must have been how to get someone's wife or other in bed.

The belly-dancer asked Dr Solomon to read her mind. Her stage name was Rulla, and she was a slim, pretty girl from Lebanon. Most belly-dancers were curvaceous, even fat, and not all were pretty. Dr Solomon told her that since his retirement he used his psychic powers only for important reasons. The girl gave him a tender smile, but she was disappointed.

For the better part of an hour, we watched Tony's uncle and the Italian magician doing tricks. When Dr Solomon asked me my plans, I told him about the journey from Alexandretta to Aqaba. I said I hoped to go to Palmyra the next day. Bachar Hazam overheard, and offered to drive me there. Rulla asked if she could accompany us, which was fine with me. Bachar then said he wanted to bring his sister. We would be four. With all the magic, the talk, the drinking and the planning of our trip to the desert, I forgot what I had come to ask Tony.

Palmyra, a city whose glorious hour came when it was ruled by a woman, guarded the eastern approach to Syria from the desert. In ancient times, it was a cosmopolitan oasis for Greeks and Arabs on the caravan route from Babylonia and Persia. Rome made an alliance with Palmyra, annexing it in 250 AD and granting its king, Odenathus, autonomy within the empire. Odenathus had married a beautiful teenage girl named Zenobia. Some chronicles said she was a Greek, who knew the history of her Ptolemaic predecessor, Cleopatra. Others said she was a bedouin. With Zenobia at his side, Odenathus defeated the Persians. When he was ready to seize Syria from his Roman overlords, he died. Queen Zenobia became regent on behalf of their son and set out to complete her husband's work. She was said to be as fierce as the bedouin horsemen she led into battle. Her first campaign drove the Roman armies out of Syria. She next led 70,000 Arabs into Egypt and destroyed its Roman garrisons. Her conquests at the head of fast Arab cavalry, defying the might of Rome in the west and Persia in the east, presaged the more enduring Arab conquests from the Arabian peninsula four centuries later. With Syria and Egypt in her hands, the desert Boadicea turned her attention from conquest to consolidating her empire and transforming Palmyra into the political capital of the East.

Rome counter-attacked, but lost two armies to her Arabs. Then at Emesa, Aurelian defeated Zenobia. Aurelian chased the remnant of her army to Palmyra, laid siege to the city and captured Zenobia as she made her way alone to the Euphrates to seek reinforcements. Aurelian spared the city, after stealing its gold, and left it in the hands of Roman troops. While he marched Zenobia in chains to Rome, the Palmyrenes revolted and killed the Romans in the garrison. Aurelian returned to massacre the population. His troops looted the merchants' lavish homes, overturned the columns and destroyed the temples. Some chronicles reported that Zenobia committed suicide when she learned of the deaths of her subjects: others said Aurelian, who became emperor after his eastern triumphs, brought her to Rome and allowed her to live out her life there in peace. Zenobia's city never recovered from the state of desolation in which Aurelian left it.

Palmyra's history was lost for generations. When Rabbi Benjamin of Tudela passed it in about 1165 AD, he thought he had found a city built by King Solomon. In 1347, Ibn Batuta believed it had been built for King Solomon by genies. In the meantime, bedouin had settled in the ruins, building mud huts alongside fallen marble and stone columns, and the town of Tadmor had sprung up at the ruins' edge. Rabbi Benjamin had found in Tadmor a community of 2,000 Jews, who were "at war with the Idumeans and with the Arab subjects of Nour al-Din, and supplying help to their neighbours the Ismailis." Europeans did not discover Palmyra until English merchants from Aleppo mounted an expedition there in 1678. They went again in 1691, and in 1751 the English historian Robert Wood made drawings which he published two years later in *The Ruins of Palmyra*. Wood believed that Palmyra's civilisation had been more advanced than ancient Egypt's, and he compared the Palmyran empire to Britain's. "The desert was in great measure to Palmyra what the sea is to Great Britain," he wrote, "both their riches and their defence."

Visitors to Zenobia's ruins were rare until the twentieth century, and the routes from Damascus to Palmyra through the Syrian Desert were always long and usually unsafe. European travellers feared bedouin raiders, but in the time of the Crusades Muslims were on their guard against Christians. When the Crusaders departed, the bedouin were the only ones left to raid Syrians, Turks and foreigners who had not paid for safe passage or whose caravans were not protected. The dangers did not prevent a latter-day Zenobia, Lady Hester Stanhope, from making her way there in 1813. "Tomorrow, my dear General," Lady Hester wrote on March 19 to

General Sir Hildebrand Oakes, "I mount my horse with seventy Arabs, and am off to Palmyra at last." Lady Hester Stanhope, a granddaughter of the Earl of Chatham, Pitt the Elder, and niece of William Pitt, had left England in February 1810. She was one of the most charming ingénues of Regency London and hostess to the bachelor prime minister, William Pitt. Her strong opinions on political life were much resented by some, but not all, men in circles of power. Pitt's death in 1807 was followed by the deaths during the Peninsula campaigns against Napoleon in 1808 of her brother, James, and of Sir John Moore, the man she loved. Bereft of the men at the centre of her life, she resolved to leave England. The Continent was unsafe for an English lady, so she went to the Ottoman Empire, stopping first in Greece, where she met Lord Byron, whom she detested. Once in Syria, she announced her intention to visit Palmyra, despite the difficulties. She wrote that a British official in Syria, Sir David Dundas, "insisted upon speaking to the Arab chiefs, and said he would cut off all their heads if they did not bring me back safe."

To Lord Sligo, she wrote, "I cannot enter into the detail of the dreadful stories that were told us of the danger we were running into, but all that did not deter me from my purpose." Undeterred, she set off with, in her words, "two sons of the King of the Desert, forty camels loaded with provisions and water and presents, twenty horsemen, the Doctor, Mr Bruce [Michael, her lover], myself and an Arab dragoman, a second dragoman, and a Mameluke, too [sic] cooks, a Caffagi, four Cairo säyses, the Emire El-Akoar, a stud-groom, Mr B.'s valet, and Madame Fry, two sakas or water-carriers, my slave, two ferráses or tent pitchers, with an escort of Arabs."

Lady Hester had gone to Palmyra in pursuit of a dream, which somehow came true. "Without joking," she wrote to Henry Wynn in June, "I have been crowned Queen of the Desert under the triumphal arch at Palmyra!" Before she left England, a fortune-teller promised her she would be crowned "Queen of the East," Zenobia's title, which Lady Hester bore in her imagination until her death in 1839. As she and her party rode into the ruins, the villages staged a mock battle in her honour. Her physician, Dr Meryon, described her arrival:

> On entering the Valley of the Tombs, Lady Hester's attention
> was absorbed in viewing the wonders around her, and the
> combatants desisted. But another sight, prepared by the
> Palmyrenes, here awaited her. In order to increase the effect which
> ruins cause on those who enter them for the first time, the guides
> led us up through the long colonnade, which extends four
> thousand feet in length from the north-west to south-east, in a line
> with the gate of the temple. The colonnade is terminated in a

triumphal arch. The shaft of each pillar, the right and left, at about the height of six feet from the ground, has a projecting pedestal, called in architecture a console, under several of which is a Greek or Palmyrene inscription; and upon each there once stood a statue, of which at present no vestige remains excepting the marks of cramp-iron for the feet. What was our surprise to see, as we rode up the avenue, and just as the triumphal arch came into sight, that several beautiful girls . . . had been placed on these very pedestals, in the most graceful postures, and with garlands in their hands; their elegant shapes being but slightly concealed by a single loose robe, girded at the waist with a zone, and a white crape veil covering their heads. On each side of the arch other girls, no less lovely, stood by threes, whilst a row of six was ranged across the gate of the arch, with thyrsi in their hands. Whilst Lady Hester advanced, these living statues remained unmovable in their pedestals; but when she had passed they leaped on the ground, and joined in a dance by her side. On reaching the triumphal arch, the whole in groups, together with men and girls intermixed, danced around her. Here some bearded elders chanted verses in her praise, and all the spectators joined in chorus . . .

Lady Hester succumbed to the lure of Syria, and she stayed behind when Michael Bruce insisted on returning to England. In the Mount Lebanon village of Joun, near Sidon, she converted a convent into a grand house for herself and her servants. The "Queen of the Orient" spent the rest of her life interfering in Lebanese affairs, setting a precedent for foreigners in Lebanon which long outlived her.

During the closing years of Ottoman rule, the desert between Damascus and Palmyra remained risky. The last *Baedeker Guide to Syria* published before the First World War warned travellers of an ardous nine-day return journey and advised them to take armed escorts for defence against ambush by bedouin. As late as 1906, the English traveller John Kelman took nearly six days on the road from Damascus to Palmyra, noting, "We were one of five parties which were there in 1906; but during the previous year there had been only two." So exceptional were visitors that, when Kelman's group arrived, local villagers slaughtered a sheep in their honour.

Bachar Hazam drove us to Palmyra in his large American estate car in only two hours. Our "escort" consisted of two women, Bachar's sister Maha and Rulla the belly-dancer, more than enough protection from the dangers we faced. Only Rulla's enchanting voice, singing to Arabic music on the radio, broke the tedium of the desert. If our drive lacked the drama of Lady Hester's journey, our arrival also lacked the splendour and excitement.

No desert sheikhs slaughtered sheep in our honour, nor did bare-breasted nymphs crown us with garlands. When we arrived, all we saw was a coachload of Russian tourists wandering through the ruined city oblivious of our presence.

We parked the car near an old hotel, and got out to walk in the late morning heat. Of all the ruins in Zenobia's ancient city, no building had fallen into such decay and ruin as that hotel. The outside of the Hôtel de la Reine Zénobie resembled an adobe pueblo in the American southwest, abandoned long before our arrival by whichever Navajos or settlers built it.

The lobby was more like a bus stop which, because no one travelled that route anymore, was about to close. Four pink columns, failed replicas of the Greek colonnade outside, divided the lobby in two. Tiles in the same anaemic pink covered the floor. In one wall were huge cracks, several of which had been recently filled with cement and left unpainted. Against another wall, a wooden ladder leaned precariously. The room was dark, save for slim shafts of sunlight filtering through windows at the back.

In the middle of the lobby a diesel stove, its metal chimney contorted to find its way to a far wall and up to the ceiling, waited for winter. The few people inside were there for the shade, the only protection from the sun within sight of Zenobia's stone city, or perhaps for one another's company. The hotel provided modest relief from the heat, if not from the flies. Four old men quietly played cards at a table near a back window, framed by the lobby pillars and silhouetted in the shafts of sunlight as in an Edward Hopper painting. A Syrian man and woman at another table, neither speaking to the other, drank tea in small clear glasses. The old men and the couple were scant evidence that the hotel had yet to die.

Near one wall was a kind of glass counter, which served as the reception desk. It might have been a "curio" shop in an Indian trading post in Arizona. Under the glass were the faded postcards and bedouin beads of a forgotten era. "This hotel," Ibrahim Assad, the manager, told me, "was founded in 1924 by the Nairn Transport Company."

Assad was possibly mistaken. The Nairn brothers had come to Syria from New Zealand to run a coach route from Beirut to Baghdad across the Syrian Desert from the 1920s to the 1950s. They carried passengers and mail in large cars and buses along a more direct path south through the Rutba Wells. I had seen the grave of one of their drivers in the Protestant Cemetery in Damascus. "In 1929, it became a hotel," Assad said, leaning over a small coffee-table littered with empty tea glasses and cigarettes. "The proprietor was a French countess named d'Andurain. From then until 1939, it stayed a hotel. It was nothing from 1939 to 1949, when it passed to a Palestine family named Assad."

"Your family?" I asked.

He smiled, nodded and put his cigarette out in an ashtray. "The countess was a spy," he said, lighting another cigarette. "She used to look down on the lobby from that window there." We looked up at a small panel, no larger than a book, in the wall above the front door. It was closed. There was not much worth spying on any more. "Rooms one and two were hers. During the Second World War, many officers stayed here, French, British, German. She used to sunbathe outside without any clothes on."

"That must have shocked people here."

"That wasn't all. The countess had three husbands. She killed them all. She moved back to France and was smuggling cigarettes with her lover. I think he killed her in Algeria."

I gathered the hotel had seen better days. "Nasser, Sadat, Tito all came here. Indira Gandhi stayed here. Most of Syria's presidents have stayed here. Now, they go over there."

"The Méridien?"

He nodded. An old waiter ambled along the pink tiles, bringing tea. Assad put several spoons of sugar in his and stirred.

I asked whether the hotel had a restaurant. "No," he said. "There is a restaurant outside." Looking around the dingy lobby, I was relieved it didn't have a restaurant – not that the restaurant we found later was any good.

I thanked Assad for the tea and walked outside to find Bachar, his sister and Rulla in the ruins. Zenobia's city spread for miles into the desert, mostly fallen columns and cobbled roads. A group of Russians were posing for photographs on a camel, looking for all the world like American tourists at the Pyramids. One little Russian girl looked beautiful in her red dress, red shoes and grey tights. A red ribbon in a bow round her plaits matched her dress and shoes. She could not have been more than six, but she posed confidently for a photograph with her father in front of a row of standing columns. It seemed odd that Russians should be replacing Americans in taking awkward tourist snaps for the neighbours back home, but I liked to think the little girl would live to show her children and grandchildren photographs of herself and her father in the far-off Syrian desert. Had Czarist troops managed to defeat the Turks in the eighteenth or nineteenth century, the Russians might have had a colonial episode in Syria, as the British and French had, instead of a Friendship Treaty and a few experts on air defence bases.

English travellers, like William Eton, who published his *A Survey of the Turkish Empire* in 1798, believed the Russians were nearly masters of the Levant, just as, seventy years later, Mark Twain hoped they would be. Noting that the Russians had antagonised potential allies in Lebanon on behalf of the sheikh of Acre in Palestine, Eton mentioned what he called "a great mistake the Russians made in their last war but one":

Had they reconciled their [the Lebanese factions'] differences, which they might have done, they would have had for allies all the countries from Egypt to the Curdes, who, probably, would have joined the league, and the army they could have brought into the field would have been more numerous than that of the Sultan; they would have been masters of Damascus, Aleppo, and all that part of the empire.

Masters, as the British and French had been in our century, but for how long? As I watched the Russians, I heard behind me the voice of a guide explaining in English that we were standing in a market street, much like the souqs in Damascus, where ancient merchants sold their wares. "And whenever a caravan arrived," he said, pronouncing "arrived" with three syllables, "all the merchants would gather here in the outdoor *agora*. Do you know what is *agora*?"

The guide, a short-haired Syrian in a grey suit and horn rim glasses, was giving a tour to a man and two women. The man wore white bermuda shorts. He was tall and stout and looked like any American tourist, but he wasn't. Michel Smaha was a Lebanese politician whose fortunes had taken more turns than Zenobia's. When I had first met him in 1983, he tried to convince me that Lebanon's first priority was to resist Syrian occupation. Four years later, he was a Syrian ally, unable to go safely to the Maronite Christian heartland he had once so defiantly represented. His hair was a little greyer, and there was less of it, than when I had last seen him in his flat in Christian east Beirut.

"The *agora*," the guide said, "was the marketplace. All the business, all the debating, it was done here. Now, let's go and see the amphitheatre."

"You see that castle?" Samaha asked me, after we had walked awhile through the ruins. He was pointing to the mountains several miles away, where there was a stone citadel clinging to a summit. It was of much later construction than anything in Palmyra. "That was Fakhreddine's castle."

"Fakhreddine came here?" I asked. The Emir Fakhreddine was a seventeenth-century Lebanese leader, a Machiavellian prince, who had briefly united the tribes of Mount Lebanon, defied the Ottomans and asserted his control over nearby provinces. Some people called him the father of modern Lebanon, a dubious distinction in light of what happened three centuries after his death.

"Yes," Samaha said. "That was the western limit of Lebanon. You see? We Lebanese are expansionists." He laughed.

I thought of seventeenth-century Lebanese soldiers on the hilltops overlooking Palmyra, far from their seacoast in the middle of the desert near the border with Iraq. It made the modern presence of Syrian troops on the mountaintops above Beirut and in Beirut itself seem but a passing phase. In a century or two, who would play the role of occupier and who the occupied?

"Now," the guide said, "we will visit Zenobia's palace and see where she had her bath."

We left them to their tour and went into Tadmor town. Bachar stopped to buy petrol, filling his car from a pump marked in English, "Supper." We passed the public gardens in the centre of town, a green oasis of palms and conifers all leaning away from the wind. Over the entrance were Syrian and Baath Party flags and a sign in English, saying, "Municibalty of Palmyra." Few buildings in Tadmor seemed over two storeys high, but every roof had steel rods sticking out ready for a new floor to be added when a son married. The only building materials used in the last twenty-five years were those which cursed the whole Levant: grey breezeblocks and concrete of numbing uniformity. The old, simple houses of mud or stone were beautiful by comparison, but few remained. Patches of colour thrived in other forms. Public buses, waiting to fill up for the drive to Damascus, were decorated with peacock feathers on their radiator caps and bright paintwork top and bottom. Men had red-and-white or black-and-white *keffiyehs* wrapped around their heads, and women wore black dresses with colourfully embroidered bodices. Some of the women, their hair tied back in patterned scarves, herded little children along the lanes. One mother, her lips outlined in tattoos, breastfed her infant as she waited for the bus in the shade of a small palm. We went to the Museum of Palmyra, rushing through its collections of Hellenistic and Arab artefacts before it closed for lunch.

The sun was burning directly overhead, leaving no shadows in which to seek shelter. Outside the museum, most people had gone home to eat lunch, take a nap and wait for the sun to move along the horizon. Staying out of the sun was a practical necessity, and it was easy to see why shade was a strong image in desert life. I remembered that when Gamal Abdel Nasser, the first and last leader in modern times with a serious claim to leadership of all the Arabs, died in Cairo in 1970, the cry among his followers was, "We have no shade." The leader who had protected them from the full glare of the sun, especially the Western sun, had fallen like a desert palm, leaving them to wander in search of another. They had yet to find one.

We found refuge from the sun under burlap stretched overhead from poles, in a restaurant that was nothing more than an empty patio with a dozen tables and a kitchen in a corner. The restaurant lay on a dusty road between the ruins of Palmyra and the decaying town of Tadmor. We sat there quietly for several minutes under the burlap hoping to see a waiter, but none appeared. Bachar got up and walked to the kitchen, where a few young men were talking. He told one of them to serve us, and a boy in jeans walked reluctantly to our table.

In a thick Syrian desert accent, he asked the Arabic equivalent of, "Whaddaya want?"

Rulla looked him in the eye and asked, "What do you have?"

"Everything."

I looked behind me at the refrigerator in the kitchen. It could not have been larger than the mini-bar in any room at the Méridien.

"Do you have a menu?" I asked.

"What?"

"A menu," Rulla told him. "A card with a list of what you have."

"No," he said, astonished at the suggestion.

She began to ask him for most of the items in an ordinary *mezze*: tabbouleh, beans, minced lamb. To each of these things, the waiter said, "We don't have."

"Beer?"

"Don't have."

"Chicken?"

"Don't have."

"What do you have?"

"Whatever you want."

"Hommous?"

"We have hommous."

We settled on a *mezze* of hommous, laban and salad, with grilled meat to follow. To drink, we ordered *arak*. The lunch turned out to be one of the worst meals I had ever eaten. The hommous was disgusting, thick, lumpy and bitter. The laban, which in Syria is simply fresh yogurt, was warm, had bits of molten lettuce in it and smelled like Heinz salad cream. Worst of all, however, was the salad – an unwashed, chopped head of lettuce soaked in oil and vinegar. Luckily, there was Arabic bread, almost fresh, while we waited for the meat to arrive.

Rulla called the waiter over. "What is this?" she asked him.

"Salad."

"No," she explained. "Bring me some lettuce, garlic, some olive oil – *olive* oil – and lemons. I'll make the salad."

He returned a minute later with the *arak*, plonked a large bottle, half-full, on the table and gave us four large tumblers. "What are you doing?" Rulla demanded.

"*Arak*," he said.

"Where is the ice?"

"No ice."

"Where is the water?"

"No water."

"You have water in the kitchen. Bring it."

Shaking his head, he walked away to find the water. He returned with a jug of water and a head of lettuce in a bowl. It was filthy. Rulla picked it up, shook it like a swagger stick at the waiter and walked to the kitchen to wash it. She made a fairly edible salad, but we were soon to be disappointed again when the waiter brought a plate of grilled bits of meat and liver, all burned dry. He said it was lamb, but we were certain it was goat.

Bachar tasted it. "Goat," he pronounced.

"Goat," Rulla and Bachar's sister repeated. The waiter pretended not to hear.

"We would not eat this filth in Lebanon," Rulla said to the waiter.

"Are you Lebanese?" he asked her.

"Of course."

"So am I."

She looked sceptically at him. "Which village?"

He hesitated, then said, "Sofar."

She titled her head and raised her eyebrows at him. "Sofar? You?"

"Yeah. I just work in Syria."

None of us believed him, but it seemed to allow him to dissociate himself from the food he was serving.

I braced myself for a gulp of warm *arak*, downed it and wished I hadn't. From the kitchen, we heard Arabic music on the radio. Rulla swayed in her seat to the rhythm, moving her arms snake-like over the table, as though she were dancing. Then she began to sing.

We sent most of the food back untouched and asked for coffee.

"No coffee," the waiter said.

"Why not?" Rulla, who had stopped swaying, demanded.

"This is Syria," he said, smiling as though he were among his Lebanese compatriots. "There isn't any in the market."

Bachar got up. "There is coffee in the market," he said to me in English. "This boy is a liar."

Bachar and his sister walked back towards the ruins, leaving Rulla and me at the table. We ordered tea.

I began asking Rulla the questions men stupidly ask exotic dancers, bar hostesses and prostitutes. She told me about her small mountain village in Lebanon, a place I knew. She was a Maronite, and her mother believed she had come to Damascus to visit relations. No one in Syria, she said, knew her real name. After the waiter set down the tea, I looked at her. She was thin with a fair complexion, and she had dark eyes which came to life whenever she was singing or laughing. Her most remarkable feature was beautiful, thick hair that tumbled all the way down her back. Occasionally, she would pull her hair over her shoulder, let it drop to her lap and play with it the way men fiddled with their worry beads. I wondered what could take a Maronite girl from her village to dance seductively in Damascus.

"I need the money."

"Couldn't you earn any money in Lebanon?"

"I worked as a seamstress," she said. "I made about twenty dollars a month."

Each crumpled note the men in the audience at the Sheraton cabaret threw at her when she danced was worth more than twenty dollars.

"It's nothing to be ashamed of," I tried to reassure her. "You dance well."

"My family would be ashamed."

"Do you need the money that badly?"

"I am getting married," she said, throwing her hair back over her shoulder and looking directly at me. "My fiancé is poor. There is no work in Lebanon, except for the *musalaheen*." *Musalaheen* were gunmen.

'Don't you like belly dancing?"

"I don't like some of the men, the way they look at me, but I love dancing. I love music and singing," she said. She began singing to the tune of the Arabic music from the kitchen radio. Like many Arabic love songs, this one had rhymes of words like *lemoun*, *ayoun*, and *zeitoun* – lemon, eyes, and olive – the way sentimental American songwriters used love, dove and above, or moon, June and spoon. Still in her chair, she moved her arms and neck as though she were belly-dancing. Although she smiled seductively and kept her eyes on me, she was all innocence and friendliness. I thought her fiancé was a lucky man.

"Has your fiancé ever seen you dance?"

She stopped singing and turned her face to the side, hiding for a moment behind her hair. "He doesn't know."

"But surely people from Lebanon come to Damascus? Someday he's bound to find out."

"No," she said, sharply turning to face me again. "He will never find out."

"If he loves you, it shouldn't matter."

"He loves me," she said, "but he would leave me." She took a last sip of her tea and told me to pay the bill. "Let's go now," she said, and I followed her to the ruins.

As we left Palmyra later that afternoon, I saw hundreds of goats marching west towards the Valley of the Tombs. A white mongrel chased the car, barking wildly as we gained speed and lost him near a grove of date palms. In the desert, we hit a sandstorm, and the way ahead grew as dark as night. Rulla sang again. There was no music playing on the radio, but she wailed a *capella*, taking no notice of the storm or her fellow passengers. I could not understand the words, but their sadness hit me with more force than the storm outside. Despite the Zenobias, the Lady Hesters, the Jane Digbys and the Colette Khourys, who had escaped convention and found freedom in some part or other of Syria, Rulla was one with the great majority of the Levant's women – Muslim, Christian and Jewish. If they danced and sang, if they dared to find romance, they would take the secret of their joy to the grave.

CHAPTER SIXTEEN

PROVINCIAL LOYALTY

Omar Alim thought I should meet the only Baath Party founder who was neither dead, imprisoned, in exile nor in opposition. His name was Fayez Ismail, and although he too had left the party, he remained a loyal member of the central committee of the so-called National Front, a coalition of the Baath and other "progressive parties" which nominally governed Syria.

I went by taxi to meet Omar at the National Front. On the way, the taxi driver pointed out the government guest palace, a modern stone building in mock Ottoman style. "I was arrested here," the driver told me.

"Why?"

"A bomb went off when I was walking by."

"So?"

"They arrested everyone."

"What happened?"

"The security police took me to an apartment, and they questioned me for a few days. Then they let me go."

Damascus seemed so peaceful, and the streets appeared safe day and night. It was easy to forget that the state held the power to take any citizen away without warning, without informing his family or allowing him to see a lawyer. It was just as easy to forget Syria's enemies in Iraq, Israel, Jordan, Lebanon and the PLO, who had their agents in Damascus itself. Sometimes, a man the police picked up would confess to working for Iraq or Israel, but the validity of the confessions and the methods used to obtain them were similarly suspect.

When the taxi driver dropped me at the National Front headquarters, he sped off, perhaps to avoid the attention of security police guarding the building. Omar Alim, who was waiting for me in the foyer, took me down a corridor, past several rooms in which men were drinking coffee and chatting under portraits of President Assad, to an ante-room. A young man at the desk said Fayez Ismail was waiting for us. We went in. The ground-floor office faced a busy roundabout, and the thick green curtains which covered the window behind the desk did little to muffle the noise.

Fayez Ismail was wearing what looked like a club tie, close in colour to his blue suit. He had dark hair combed back, dark eyes and the look of a man who in his late middle age was putting on weight. Beneath the glass top on his cluttered desk lay a photograph of President Hafez al-Assad. Lest the tiny likeness prove an insufficient mnemonic to anyone who might forget what the president looked like, there were other images of the leader: on one wall hung a large black-and-white framed photograph, and completing the set was an oil portrait of the president in a dark civilian suit. Ismail leaned over the desk, one elbow pressed down on the face of the president, to ask us if we wanted coffee. When Omar and I sat down, Ismail leaned back in his vinyl armchair and asked Omar to interpret his Arabic, because his English was not good.

Fayez Ismail and Hafez Jemalli had been together in the early days of the Baath Party, but their paths had diverged. Perhaps Jemalli could more easily afford to dissent: he was better educated, and he had been born in Homs in the heartland of Syria. Ismail fought for Baathism, spent time in prison, founded his own tiny party and came from outside Syria's contemporary borders.

Ismail began by talking about Alexandretta. Alexandretta was still Syria's northern province when he was born there in 1923. "I opened my eyes to the struggle between the Turks and Arabs when I was in school," he said in Arabic, as Omar translated. "We used to fight Turks with stones and knives. In school we sang nationalist songs." Although Ismail had moved south in 1938, he longed for the return of Alexandretta to Syria. "In history, Alexandretta was always part of Syria. Even during the Ottoman Empire, it was part of the Aleppo *vilayet*. The base of the Arab struggle was Antioch."

He wanted also to see the incorporation into Syria of Cilicia, north of Alexandretta, which France lost in 1923. "I still have stamps from that time saying '*Kilkia*' in Arabic and '*Cilicie*' in French. Most of the big Aleppo families are divided between Aleppo and this area." It went without saying that, in the south, he believed the Golan Heights should also revert to Syria. These were not the only borders Ismail wanted to see banished. "We as geographers believe any country has its geographical borders, embracing the movement of a people through history. We speak of the Taurus Mountains as our border. Herodotus said, 'The Arabic language freezes in the Taurus.' The borders go from the Gulf, the mountains of Zagros, Iraq and the Taurus to the sea. From the Taurus to Suez to Morocco. I'm talking about all the borders now in which Arabic is spoken. When you cross the mountains and deserts, you find non-Arabs. If you go back in history, the movement of the Arab nation was between these borders, with one language, one religion, because we consider Christianity and Islam to be together from this area."

Most of the government offices in Damascus had on their walls, alongside pictures of the president, maps of the Arab world, coloured green, within those borders. The green area stretched from Iraq in the east to Mauretania in the west, and took in Palestine, Somalia and Omar's homeland, Eritrea. The maps proclaimed the dream of unity, but every government in every Arab capital had a vested interest in preserving the borders. The dream, for regimes that could keep power only within fixed boundaries, was permissible so long as it remained a dream. Those who tried to make it a reality languished in prisons all across the green area of the map.

I asked Ismail about his political career. Through Omar, he answered, "I studied law in Baghdad, where we were setting down the basics of Baathism. In 1950, I came back to Syria to begin my work. This was the *coup d'état* period."

"I was imprisoned many times," he said. "We also resisted the coup against unity with Nasser. Because the Baath could not reunite Syria and Egypt, I left the party. In 1961, I founded the Unionist Socialist Party. Many members were martyred or imprisoned, but the Baath maintained a dialogue with us. Then on February 24, 1966, a new branch of the Baath took over. We agreed to join the regime. I became Minister of Municipal and Rural Administration."

Ismail appeared to have liked Gamal Abdel Nasser, a fondness he shared with most of the Syrian people – if not with its leadership, who distrusted the Egyptian until his death in 1970. Ismail discussed with Nasser in 1967 the possibility of restoring the Egyptian–Syrian union, the United Arab Republic, which had lasted only from 1958 to 1961. The talks did not revive it. In 1973, he lost his post in the cabinet. Since then, he had served in the largely ceremonial National Front. He had written four books, all polemics on the Baath or his Unionist Socialist Party.

He turned the conversation back to Alexandretta. "My mother died in January in Antioch," he said. "When I went, we had to inform the Turkish government, and their police followed me. At the giving of condolences, it is the custom for everyone to read a passage from the Koran. I had brought some cassettes of Koran readings. The people said, 'No, this is not right. We all read the Koran. Put your cassettes away.' This proved all of them read Arabic. They are Arabs."

"In 1938," he went on, "only one Arab in Antioch owned a car. Now more Arabs own cars than lived in Antioch then. In the countryside, the aga was a Turk, and all the peasants were Alawis. Now there are no agas in the countryside, and the owners of the land are Arabs. In Antioch, the doctors, the engineers, the lawyers are Arab. The big farms are Arab. Even in Istanbul and Ankara, you will find Arabs from Alexandretta."

I asked Omar to ask him whether this might not indicate that the Arabs were integrated into Turkish society and suffered no discrimination.

"In Istanbul and Ankara, Arab books and historical manuscripts are sold in the souqs. But in Alexandretta, they are forbidden. You will be interrogated if you have Arabic books. No Arab can be appointed to a sensitive position in the state." He went on to tell me that Alexandretta province had a quarter of all Syria's forest land, provided two-thirds of its fish, yielded bounties of fruits, vegetables, grain, tobacco, cotton and olives. There were more than one hundred students from Alexandretta, Turkey's province of Hatay, studying at Damascus University, students who were taught that Syria, not Turkey, was their real home. "Alexandretta might come," Ismail said wistfully, "if there is a change in the international situation. Syria does not recognise its loss. Disraeli once said that the place where Cyprus points its finger will determine the future of the world." The finger pointed straight at Alexandretta, but the province had yet to determine the future of anything.

We all knew Syria was less likely to obtain Alexandretta than the Golan Heights, and the Golan was a distant prospect at best. Although no Syrian official could admit it, Syria was at peace with Turkey and intended to remain that way. It would risk neither war nor closed borders for its lost northern province. In his soul Hafez Ismail must have known that he had as little chance of liberating the province of his birth as his Unionist Socialist Party had of coming to power. Alexandretta would remain a part of Syria only on maps printed and sold in Damascus, the same maps which labelled Israel "Palestine."

Damascus thrived on diplomatic and business receptions. Tony Touma took me to cocktail parties at various embassies and dinners arranged to promote Syrian trade with Europe. One evening, we attended a lavish banquet in honour of Lufthansa airline's regular flights to Frankfurt, complete with a Bavarian band in Lederhosen.

People at these occasions knew one another, because they all had to attend them several times a week. Most of the diplomats were not on particularly good terms with Syrian officials, and the receptions provided some of the gossip they needed for their cables home. They also gave them the opportunity to meet government ministers and military officers with whom they could not obtain appointments in the normal way. They were a chance for women to wear their imported gowns and jewellery. For me, they were one way to hear the latest stories doing the rounds of the international community.

At one dinner, the director of Syrian television told me a joke. Two close friends died at the same time. One went to heaven, and the second went to the other place. The first man missed his friend and asked if he could visit him. The arrangements were made. He went down there and was taken to his friend's room. He opened the door, and there was his friend, sitting in an easy chair, with a woman on his lap. He was smoking a cigarette and reading the newspaper. A television was on. "To think I was worried about you," the man said. "I thought you were in hell." His friend said, "Of course this is hell. The woman is my wife. The cigarettes are *Bafra* (a Syrian brand). The newspaper is *Al-Baath*, and I have to watch Syrian television."

At another occasion, an ambassador recounted the story of the officer and the dog. "A Syrian officer found a dog wandering about in Lebanon near the border," he said. "The dog was skin and bones. It had not eaten in weeks. The officer took it back to Damascus. He built it a dog house. He gave it the best food and fresh water. He exercised it every day. The dog came back to life. It put on weight, and its coat became thick and shiny. After a few months, though, the dog asked the officer to take it back to Lebanon. 'Lebanon is still at war, and you won't have any food there,' the officer said. 'Why do you want to go back?' The dog answered, 'I want to bark.'"

Among the Syrians themselves, the most famous jokes concerned people from Homs. They were Syria's equivalent of Polack jokes in America or Irish jokes in Britain. For some reason, their fellow Syrians unfairly viewed the citizens of Homs as hopelessly stupid. A typical Homsi joke told of the Homsi who saw a goatherd with his goats. The Homsi secretly counted all the goats and then approached the goatherd, asking, "If I can guess how many goats you have, will you give me one?"

"Yes, if you can guess exactly," the goatherd said.

"Okay. One hundred and sixty-two."

"That's amazing," the goatherd said. "Go ahead and choose one."

As the Homsi was leaving, the goatherd asked him, "Are you from Homs?"

"Yes. How did you know?"

"Easy. You chose the dog."

Another Homsi joke was doing the rounds of the diplomatic community. President Hafez al-Assad was paying his first visit to Homs in many years. The military commander of Homs ordered twenty-one of his men onto the parade ground to rehearse the twenty-one gun salute. "When the president steps out of the car," he said, "each of you fires in turn."

"Do we go on firing," one of the Homsi soldiers asked, "if we hit him with the first shot?"

At the government's gaudy Sham Palace Hotel, across the street from the

New Omayyad Hotel, there was a conference of Mayors of Arab Cities. What had been happening to Arab cities, in terms of 20th-century "development", was tragic. The host city itself had fallen prey to the developer's bulldozer, and the other cities represented had little to boast of. I walked across the street one morning to look up an old man I had last seen in 1974. I called him from the Sham's marble and cut-glass, pseudo-Hyatt Regency lobby and went upstairs to meet him in his suite.

"Legally," the old man reminded me, "I am still the mayor of Jerusalem." The legal mayor of Jerusalem, Rawhi al-Khatib, was deported to Jordan by the Israelis on March 7, 1968. He continued to represent Jerusalem at conferences like this, at UNESCO and before the UN Security Council.

As far as he was concerned, Teddy Kollek was mayor only of the western, Israeli half of the city. "Yes, they still come," he told me, when I asked whether Jerusalem residents visited his house in Amman. "Their biggest complaint is the continuance of the occupation. The other complaints are the aggressions against education, against their institutions, against their land."

We sat at a dining-table, like two men doing business. He wanted to talk, not relax. He was in his shirtsleeves, his brown tie loose and his waistcoat unbuttoned, his jacket hanging behind him on the chair. He wanted to tell anyone who would listen of the urgency of saving his city, which he had not seen in twenty years.

We talked about the Revolt of 1936–38, in which as many as 5,000 Palestinian Arabs died, unaware that, as we were speaking, a new revolt against Israeli rule was brewing. Another generation of Palestinians would die confronting, this time, the rule of the settlers whose immigration their parents had opposed fifty years before.

Khatib remained in Jerusalem after the western half fell to Israel and the eastern half to Jordan in 1948, and, the next year, he joined the city council. His fellow councillors appointed him mayor in 1957, a post he held when the Israelis conquered East Jerusalem ten years later. After three weeks of occupation, Israel abolished the council and dismissed the mayor. The United Nations refused to recognise his dismissal, and Mayor Khatib annoyed the Israelis by insisting he was still the mayor. In March 1968, the Israelis expelled him to Jordan.

"The new threat," Mayor Khatib said, "is the 'Greater Jerusalem Plan' for nine cities and sixty-four villages. They have a population of three hundred thousand Arabs and are being threatened with annexation as East Jerusalem was annexed in 1967. The plan was prepared in 1980 and issued in 1982. I received a copy in 1984."

Mayor Khatib got up to bring me a copy of the plan and several

263

photographs of the areas involved. He returned from the adjoining room with a document, written in Hebrew, with translations in Arabic and English. "Only thirteen per cent of the area is designated for Arab dwellings and seventeen per cent to Israelis. Six per cent is for roads, including a new airport. Fifty-nine per cent is for agriculture, for the expansion of Israeli colonisation, but the Israelis have nothing in this area. And they plan to plant more Israeli colonies around our villages."

I explained that my journey was taking me south from Alexandretta through Syria and Lebanon, then to Jordan and Israel, taking in all of what was "Greater Syria". I said that my real interest lay more in history, in the enduring realities of the region, than in specific contemporary plans for Jerusalem or any other city.

The mayor's colleague, Mr Asali, said he too was interested in history. He had written a book on the Maghrebi Quarter of East Jerusalem, a district near the Wailing Wall where the descendants of North African immigrants had lived for centuries. The Israelis destroyed it, bulldozing the houses late into the night, in June 1967 to create a large plaza which gave better access to the Wall. "Almost every month there is a book from the Israeli side," Mr Asali lamented. "There are great scholars on that side, but in the end they always try to prove their case. I try not to exaggerate, not to paint the Jewish side as black."

"Jerusalem has had a sad history," I said, stating the all too obvious.

"Before David came," Mr Asali said, "Jerusalem had a history. The Jews drew a lot from the Canaanites who lived in the city. By the way, Palestinian Arabs are not all ethnic Arabs. Many are descended from the earlier inhabitants."

The earlier inhabitants – the Jebusites, Amonites, Canaanites and the other peoples the Israelites were urged to destroy in the Bible – have left few if any cultural vestiges in the form of language or custom. The Arabs and their language swept them all away, but the people themselves used the name the ancient Israelites gave their ancestors – *Falistini* in Arabic, Palestinian in English.

There was no escaping the Palestinians, their cause and their refugee camps, anywhere in the Levant. When I met Sehem Turjuman, she lectured me, after urging the salvation of the old city of Damascus, on the rights of the Palestinian people. Salma Kuzbari's son-in-law had delivered a speech on the injustices perpetuated against the Palestinians. Syrian government officals, dissidents and apolitical civilians all felt the need to tell the foreigner about the Palestinians. Many Syrians felt that the loss of Palestine was, more than anything else, the loss of a part of Syria itself. The Syrian vice-president had recently been quoted as saying, "Even if the Palestinians compromise over Palestine, we will not."

Driving around Damascus, it was impossible not to notice that 180,000 of them lived there as stateless refugees, many still in camps. The same was true of most of the cities of the Levant – Homs, Hama, Tripoli, Beirut, Sidon, Amman and, of course, Jerusalem. The injustice done to them was felt in one way or another by almost everyone in Greater Syria.

I told Mayor Khatib and Mr Asali that I was going to their homeland and that I would stop to see them in Amman on my way. I had first to visit Lebanon. Perhaps because of the bleeding sores left by the failure of the world to address the Palestine problem, sores which have bled more and longer in Lebanon than anywhere else, I was unable to keep my word to the mayor of Jerusalem. I hope he forgave me.

"Hurry up, Charlie," Tony Touma said to me when I dropped by his office. "You have an appointment with the General."

"Which general?"

"Tlass," Tony said, in a tone of voice which implied the answer was self-evident. "He said he would see you this afternoon."

Tony drove me to the Ministry of Defence. The white ministry building was well protected with barriers, which lifted as if by magic when Tony told the guards he had an appointment with General Moustafa Tlass, the Minister of Defence. We went into the building, where soldiers lounged in the foyer and junior officers walked in and out of the many doors which lined the corridor. Tony spoke to a lieutenant, who said Tlass was expecting us. We sat down for the inevitable wait and the equally inevitable cup of Turkish coffee.

The general was wearing civilian clothes, a neatly tailored blue suit, when we walked into his large office a half-hour later. He was standing beneath a large black-and-white photograph of Yusuf al-Azmeh, who was, in a sense, Syria's first minister of defence. It was al-Azmeh who led the forces of the Arab Kingdom of Damascus in 1920 into the Meysaloun Pass from which neither he nor his men returned. In that glorious Arab "Charge of the Light Brigade", his cavalry attempted to stop the French advance from Lebanon into the Syrian heartland. To the French, al-Azmeh's forces were a minor nuisance on their road to Damascus. When al-Azmeh failed, his king, Feisal of the Arab Revolt, fled. The British gave Feisal Iraq as a consolation, and the Syrians waited twenty more years for their independence, albeit within the Anglo-French borders.

Tlass did not look like the man in the portrait above him. Yusuf al-Azmeh wore an ill-fitting uniform. Around his head was a *keffiyeh*. He looked every inch the rough soldier who had fought the Turks. Tlass was more handsome. He was slender, dressed well, and presented himself as a Renaissance man, interested in rose-growing, photography, poetry and archaeology – on all of which he had published books. Although he was said to be an accomplished rider, it was difficult to imagine him leading a cavalry charge against French mechanised units.

We had come to ask the general for help in getting me across the border and through the many Syrian military checkpoints in Lebanon. A *laisser-passer* from him would save time and questions at both the border and the checkpoints. He agreed to issue an official letter informing the Syrian forces in Lebanon that I was writing a book and telling them to offer me assistance.

He asked Tony and me to sit down, and he sat next to me on a small couch near the window. I noticed on the wall another portrait, one of the full-colour, backlit, larger-than-life transparencies of President Assad, with whom the general had been a cadet at the Homs Military Academy in the early 1950s. Tlass went into an armoured battalion, while Assad chose the air force. They had both joined the Baath Party while still in their teens. In 1970, Tlass supported the "Corrective Movement," the bloodless coup that brought Assad to power. Tlass was a Sunni Muslim, one of many in the cabinet, whose names came up to counter the accusation that the regime was exclusively Alawi. Three years after Assad became president, Syria launched the October War in the Golan Heights, its most successful operation ever against Israel.

I reminded the general that I had first seen him at the end of that war, when he met Henry Kissinger, then American secretary of state, to discuss a Syrian–Israeli troop disengagement. I attended a lunch at which Tlass had flirted shamelessly with the wives of most of the American diplomats, including Nancy Kissinger. Tlass laughed, recalling the incident, and said the *Washington Post* had published an article at the time saying Nancy Kissinger had particularly liked a poem Tlass recited. "At the next invitation," Tlass said in Arabic, through Tony, "she was sent shopping in the souq."

Tlass said he had liked President Richard Nixon. "Nixon was in favour of a settlement. In talks with President Assad, Kissinger said Nixon wanted to offer land for peace. If Israel would not accept that, Kissinger said, the Israelis would have to solve their own problems. Then Nixon was out of the White House."

Tlass did not say so, but many Arabs saw the entire Watergate scandal which forced Nixon's resignation in 1974 as a Zionist plot to undo the first "even-handed" American president since Eisenhower. It was an interesting conspiracy theory, one of many believed passionately by people who could produce no evidence whatsoever in its support.

Tlass was annoyed, like most Arab politicians, with Israeli influence on American policy. "As long as there are no decision-makers on top of the administration, there is no hope," he said. "Why does a US administration which fights terrorism give weapons to the terrorists? Why does Israel spy on the US? Every American feels as nothing in front of an Israeli official. The president of the United States is nothing in front of Israel's prime minister. Any country which wants to be friendly with the US goes first to Israel. Why go to Congress when you can go to Israel?"

I had not come to discuss policy or current events. I wanted only to obtain my *laisser-passer*. If I had wanted to ask questions, they would have been about Tlass's predecessor, Yusuf al-Azmeh, who stared at us from the aged black-and-white photograph. But Tlass wanted to make the point to an American writer, as though I could convince the American people, that Israel was the impediment to peace. "We are forced to go to the Soviet Union," he said, gesticulating as though he were holding worry beads in a left hand which bore only a diamond-studded wedding ring. "The more America gives weapons to Israel, the more we go to the Soviets."

Tlass was angry at Britain, which had severed diplomatic relations because of Syrian involvement in a failed attempt to blow up an Israeli civil airliner bound from London. The culprit, Nezar Hindawi, held a Syrian passport. "The man who killed Abu Hassan," Tlass said of the murderer of a PLO official in Beirut ten years earlier, "carried a British passport. Yet we did not accuse Britain."

When we discussed my interest in the Syrian past, he pushed a button and asked a soldier to bring a copy of his book on Palmyra. When the soldier returned with the book, *Zénobie: Reine de Palmyre,* Tlass inscribed it to me in Arabic. This was the French translation, under the imprint of his publishing house, Dar al-Tlass. Revenues from sales of the book went to Syria's war orphans. Tlass had also written books entitled *Guerrilla War, An Introduction to Zionist Strategy* and *The Fourth Arab–Israeli War.*

None of his books had caused anything like the sensation which greeted his most recent work, *Fitr Sahyoun* or *Matzoh of Zion* in which Tlass repeated as fact the tale of Jewish involvement in the murder of a Gentile in Damascus in the 1840s. The text was grossly anti-Semitic, and the cover drawing portrayed Hassidic-looking Jews in lurid colours slitting the throat of a Gentile whose blood flowed into a cauldron. *Matzoh of Zion* was the bread allegedly made of Gentiles' blood upon which the Jews feasted at Passover. It surprised me anyone could write a book like that, particularly a member of a government whose propaganda emphasised the difference between Judaism and Zionism and claimed not to discriminate against its few remaining Jewish citizens.

Tony had brought a camera along to our meeting, and he took pictures of Tlass and me together. He snapped one of me writing notes as Tlass spoke and another of Tlass handing me *Zénobie.* I later put these photographs, once they had been developed, into the envelope with General Tlass's letter to his forces in Lebanon. That way, Tony assured me, even the soldiers who could not read would know that I had Tlass's blessing. Tony was right, as things turned out, but we had forgotten what any of the multitude of militias opposed to Syria in Lebanon would make of the letter and the incriminating picture of me with the successor of Yusuf al-Azmeh.

CHAPTER SEVENTEEN

ENEMIES OF THE GODDESSES

We were driving north on the coastal highway from Sidon to Beirut. On the left was the clear blue Mediterranean, across which Phoenician sailors had ventured from here to found colonies on the shores of Africa and Spain. To the right were the terraced, fertile foothills of Mount Lebanon. Between the sea and the summit lay the wondrous beauty of Lebanon: the citrus orchards and olive groves, the fields and rivers, the fishermen on the shore and the sheep making their way to summer pastures in the hills. It was a pastoral idyll on a warm summer morning. Then we reached Damour. The beautiful and vibrant seaside village lay in ruins. Palestinian commandos had killed and exiled its Christian inhabitants in 1976, their revenge for a massacre by other Christians of poor Muslims and Palestinians in the east Beirut slums. Not a door or a hinge remained, and some of the places that had housed refugees for a time after 1976 had been bombed from the air by Israel. Everywhere were the charred monuments to Lebanon's glorious freedom fighters: half-standing buildings, mounds of rubble and piles of burning garbage. North of Damour undamaged fishermen's cottages and farm houses stood side by side with the relics of stone villas the war had turned to dust. Large families ate breakfast on vine-covered patios, their children playing among modern ruins as remote to them as if they had been left by the Romans.

I had spent a few days in south Lebanon, a province occupied in part by Israel, in part by Palestinian and Shiite guerrillas, in part by United Nations troops, armed men who wandered the hills that in other centuries had heard the footsteps of soldiers from Greece, Rome, Egypt, Persia and Turkey. I had stayed in the village of Rmailly, near Sidon, at the house of my friend Ali Bayk Osseiran. *Bayk* is the Arabised form of the Ottoman title, bey, now used only in Lebanon. His father, Adil Bayk Osseiran, was Lebanon's Minister of Defence and one of its most respected Shiite Muslim leaders. Ali's driver, a Shiite former policeman named Suleiman Suleiman, was driving Ali and me in Ali's battered white Volvo. Ali sat in front, and I sat behind Suleiman. They were taking me back to Beirut to see Walid Bayk Jumblatt, with whom I planned to stay for two days in his palace in the Druze mountains before going via Syria to Jordan and Israel. I had been in Lebanon almost a month, and, in forty-eight hours, I would be out.

Just before Beirut, we saw the runway of Beirut International Airport, where Syrian soldiers occupied the sandbagged positions held until February of 1984 by the US Marines. The traffic slowed down for a Syrian checkpoint. With Ali, I did not need to show the Syrian soldiers the letter their Minister of Defence had given me in Damascus. Past the roadblock, we approached the outskirts of the unsightly urban mess that Beirut had become. The villages and orchards gave way on both sides of the highway to an unrelenting, hideous complex of two- and three-storey light-industrial workshops, ironmongers, second-hand furniture shops, garages, rundown bakeries, pharmacies and cheap restaurants with apartments above. This was the harsh concrete landscape into which homeless Shiite refugees had been pushed by Israeli bombardment of their villages throughout the 1970s, newer than but similar to the nearby camps of Palestinians forced there in 1948.

Stretched on banners over the roadway and pasted on battered walls were pictures of Iran's Ayatollah Khomeini and the other paper ikons of Shiite Islam: Lebanon's Imam Musa Sadr, who disapeared in Libya in 1978, and the seventh-century Shiite martyrs, Imam Ali and his sons Hassan and Hussein. There were also multi-coloured posters of a modern martyr, Bilal Fahas, a teenage suicide car-bomber who died in an attack on Israeli soldiers. In the middle of the road, above another Syrian army checkpoint, hung a large placard advertising Hizballah, the Iranian-supported Party of God. We had entered not merely another part of Lebanon, but another world.

Somewhere in these slums, I believed, were many of the foreigners kidnapped in Lebanon in the years following the Israeli invasion of 1982. At this time, Hizballah held twenty-three men from America, France, Britain and Italy, as well as an undetermined number of Lebanese. Two of them, the Associated Press correspondent Terry Anderson and the hostage mediator Terry Waite, were friends. Ali and I talked about the hostages. It seemed to me the kidnappers would hold the Americans at least until the US presidential elections in November 1988, perhaps to make them an election issue. Ali said, "Who knows? When will Israel give up the hundreds of Lebanese it is holding?"

Every mile or so, we passed another Syrian army roadblock, where armed soldiers casually waved to cars as they slowed and passed on. We had just gone through one Syrian checkpoint in the Ouzai quarter when, from the left-hand side of the divided highway, a green Mercedes without number plates pulled in front of us. I joked that the Mercedes appeared to have lost its plates, and Ali said many cars were losing them – a reference to the brisk trade in stolen cars. We paid no more attention to the car, whose occupants were hidden behind a curtain drawn across the rear window. Traffic was moving so slowly that we hardly noticed when the Mercedes stopped at a right angle to our white Volvo, cutting us off.

All four doors of the Mercedes flew open at once, and four or five men jumped out, weapons drawn. All of them were young, in their late teens or early twenties, and wore sports shirts with trousers or jeans. Most of them wielded AK-47s or other light automatic rifles and a few had semi-automatic pistols. They ordered Ali and Suleiman out of the car. I stayed alone in the back seat, afraid to move. One young man pointed his Kalashnikov through the right rear window and ordered me out. Two others opened the door and pulled me from the car.

I looked for somewhere to run, but young men with weapons were everywhere. Hundreds of people – men and women coming out of shops on both sides of the highway – could see what was happening, but no one did anything. People in the other cars stuck in the heavy traffic pretended not to see. Twelve years of civil war had taught them that survival could depend on being oblivious to the horror around them.

The two boys who pulled me from the Volvo were dragging me by the arms toward the green Mercedes. I struggled not to get into the car. When it appeared I might break their hold, one bearded man in his late twenties levelled his automatic weapon in my direction and shouted at the top of his voice in accented English, "I will kill you!" The voice frightened me more than the weapon. Another gunman behind me raised his Kalashnikov and hit me on the back of the head with its butt. The blow knocked me to the ground and made me dizzy. They picked me up, and the open door of the Mercedes loomed before me. I hoped that delaying the kidnappers another minute would allow time for someone to call for help from the Syrian soldiers at the next checkpoint, only a few hundred yards ahead. By struggling again, I slowed them down for a few seconds, not long enough. They shoved my legs into the car, and before I realised what had happened, I was sitting in the centre of the back seat.

Into the car jumped two of the youths, one on either side of me, each pressing a magazine-loaded pistol into my stomach. Two more rushed into the front seat, and we drove quickly away. The car moved along the shoulder of the road, skirting the traffic waiting to clear the Syrian checkpoint. Before we reached the Syrians, the driver turned right up a dirt road, scattering pedestrians as he went. We were driving east towards the main airport road, where I knew there would be more Syrian soldiers. I tried to watch where we were going, but they shouted at me Arabic, "*Deer rasak! Deer rasak!*" When I appeared not to understand, one of them said in

English, "Your head down!" I kept my head up, trying both to see and to be seen. The boys on either side of me pushed my head down with their hands. One of them took a wrench from the floor and hit me several times on the back of the head.

The gunman next to the driver got on a two-way radio, saying in Arabic they were bringing in the "fish". I'd been baited and hooked. Now they were taking me home. The boy on my left, who was too young to shave, removed his hand from the back of my head and showed it to me. It was covered with blood, my blood. He paid me a compliment of a sort, calling me *abadai*, "tough guy" or "boss", but he kept his pistol firmly in my stomach.

In a few minutes, we turned left onto the airport road near what had been the headquarters of the Italian contingent of the Multinational Peace-keeping Force from 1982 to 1984. As the driver took the first right, I glimpsed a faint hope of salvation: several Syrian and Lebanese soldiers were strolling through an unused petrol station. I kept my head up so they could see me. They seemed surprised. Immediately the gunmen in our car fired several bursts of automatic weapon fire over their heads. Expecting return fire, I put my head down and covered my ears with my hands. The soldiers did not shoot back, not that my hands would have protected my head if they had. The kidnappers shouted, "Security, security," in Arabic as they fired, pretending they were simply plainclothes security men making a routine Beirut arrest.

As he sped up the road, the driver asked me my nationality, again in Arabic. I replied in Arabic, "My father is Irish, and my mother is Lebanese." This was nearly true, at least in terms of ancestry. He asked for my passport, which was in my suitcase in Ali Osseiran's Volvo. I handed him a small plastic credit-card holder with various press cards in it. He examined the cards, still driving quickly. "You're a fucking liar," he said in English, pointing to one of the cards. "It says here, 'American.'" In Arabic, I said, "I am American, but my father's family came from Ireland, and my mother's family from Lebanon." The driver screamed at me, "You're a fucking American!"

The road gave way to an earth track on either side of which lay the rubble of a dozen years of pointless artillery bombardment. Ours was the only car in sight. Most of the buildings were empty not only of their inhabitants, but of roofs, doors and window-frames. There were shell holes and bullet marks in nearly every wall still standing. A few Shiites who were too poor to live anywhere else had made homes in the ruins. Laundry hung from a balcony that looked as if it would fall under the weight of the clothes alone. A young woman in a floral print shift and headscarf was calling her children and took no notice of our passing.

The dirt road ended at a huge earth barrier, perhaps twelve feet high. It was the western rampart of the Green Line that divided Christian east from Muslim west Beirut. Between the two sides grew a forest of weeds, some higher than the barricade. The Mercedes stopped. Staring sternly down on the desolation from an ageing poster affixed to an arcaded building was the face of Ayatollah Khomeini. Next to him hung what appeared to be an Iranian flag, limp in the windless morning air. Two bearded men stood guard below the flag. Both held Kalashnikovs, and one had a two-way radio. They had been waiting for the fish to arrive.

A few weeks earlier, I had dined in Cyprus, a traditional staging area for assaults on the Levant, with an old friend, David Hirst, the *Guardian*'s Middle East correspondent who had lived in Lebanon for more than twenty years. No foreign journalist knew the Middle East better than he did. One day, gunmen in west Beirut picked him up and threw him into the back of their car. When the car stopped, David quickly threw open the door and jumped out. He ran, and he hid. That had been the year before. Over a pleasant dinner, we drank white wine and recalled the good life in antebellum Beirut. Despite his fondness for Lebanon, David said he would never go back to west Beirut. When I asked him how he had had the courage to run away from his abductors, he answered, "I just couldn't bear the thought of being dropped down that black hole."

Now I had found my way down that black hole, and there was nowhere to run.

PART FOUR

CHAPTER EIGHTEEN

EXCURSIONS

I had not come to Lebanon unprepared. Before my long stay, I had made two forays across the border from Damascus, first to Beirut, then to Zahle in the Bekaa Valley. Everything seemed so peaceful, so seductively welcoming, that fear seemed mere paranoia. No foreigners had been kidnapped in west Beirut since the return of the Syrian army five months before. The Syrians, who withdrew during the Israeli invasion of 1982, came back during a time of heavy fighting and immediately after the last round of abductions, when three Americans, two West Germans, a Frenchman, an Indian and a Briton were taken. The militiamen cleared the streets they had terrorised, and the only armed men out of doors wore Syrian army uniforms. Syria's commander in Lebanon, General Ghazi Kenaan, announced that Syria would guarantee the safety of foreigners in west Beirut. Until Hizballah gunmen grabbed me under the eyes of his soldiers, he had been as good as his word.

My first foray into Lebanon from Damascus began with an invitation from an old and trusted Lebanese friend, Hany Bayk Salaam. It was a Thursday afternoon. I had nothing planned for Friday, the one day in the week when everything in Syria closed except Christian and Jewish shops. Hany said I could spend a day at his place near Beirut, visiting friends and eating better food than anything available in Syria. With Hany and his bodyguards, I would be safe.

Hany was in Damascus as the roving ambassador of Lebanon's president, Amin Gemayel. Although a member of one of Beirut's leading Sunni Muslim families and a successful businessman, he was attempting to mediate between Lebanon's Christians and Syria. The effort was doomed from the start, if only because the Christians wanted the Syrians out of Lebanon and the Syrians had no intention of leaving.

Hany's driver took us west through Mezze, its tower blocks rising out of the sand, home of the new middle classes and military officers who between them controlled Syria's economy and state. Behind the apartment buildings, in the middle of Mezze, was its infamous prison. A site of torture, beatings and long-term sentences, Mezze Prison had, from the time of the French, been synonymous with all Syrians feared most. A Lebanese friend of mine spent 18 months in Mezze. Although he was only twenty-one, all his hair had fallen out by the time he returned home.

Past Mezze and after miles of open, dry country, we reached the border post at Jdaideh. Jdaideh means "new" in Arabic, but there was nothing new about the barren outpost of houses, government buildings and small coffee shops in the bare limestone hills. Hundreds, sometimes thousands, of travellers stopped there for hours of customs, immigration and security checks. It was a dreadful place, and no one was ever certain of getting in or out. Hany, like many other Lebanese and Syrian officials and grandees, did not bother with border formalities. His driver turned down a slip road, exotically called the "military road," where a soldier lifted a barrier and sent us straight through. Our passage from Syria into Lebanon was not recorded, as if we had come through the Meysaloun Pass in the years before 1920 when the French drew the border.

Leaving Jdaideh behind us, we went through a narrow gorge in the Anti-Lebanon Mountains. Years earlier, the Lebanese customs post was on the border next to Jdaideh, but a previous Syrian regime had urged the Lebanese to move it further east to the village of Masnaa. This they did, after someone blew up the old one. Now there was a no-man's-land of several miles. Along the ridge of the gorge passed shepherds, guiding donkeys laden with contraband. A century ago, this would have been the normal trade between the hinterland and the coast. In this century, thanks to the border, the trade was called smuggling. Some smugglers avoided detection by training their animals to walk unaccompanied over the mountain, but most survived by making gifts to border officials.

We reached Masnaa on another slip road to the right. This was ostensibly Lebanon, but another Syrian soldier on the Lebanese "military road" waved us through. Masnaa was larger and livelier than Jdaideh, and dirtier. Scores of shops, most of them constructed of flimsy wood and wire, sold every imaginable consumer commodity to Syrians returning home: dish-washing powder, stereos, oranges, car parts, pocket calculators, watches. Cheap restaurants, money-changers and coffee houses, all built along the roadside like a gold-rush town in the Klondike, served the Syrians and Lebanese who passed daily into each other's countries. Every so often, when the Syrians cracked down on smuggling, the flimsy shacks would disappear or move a bit further from the border, only to creep back when memories of the crackdown faded and officials again began to accept gifts.

We drove along the main Damascus–Beirut highway into the Bekaa Valley. Wedged between the Lebanon and Anti-Lebanon Mountains, the Bekaa was Lebanon's breadbasket – green this time of year with crops irrigated by rivers overflowing with water from the melting snow. Villages littered the plain, whose largest populations were in the Greek Catholic town of Zahle, the Sunni Muslim town of Shtaura and the Shiite Muslim town of Baalbek. The highway cut the Bekaa in two, between its Shiite north and its Sunni and Druze south. Christians lived on both sides, although nearly all of Baalbek's Christians had gone. We drove past shacks and deserted factories, destroyed during one of the forgotten battles between opposing Palestinian factions in 1983.

We stopped at a shop in Shtaura, the largest town on the highway, for a sandwich – *labneh* on thin *mara'ouq* bread, like a crepe, with oil and mint. Shtaura was famous for its dairy products, particularly its *labneh*. Shtaura was also the venue for Sunni honeymoons, at least for those Beirut and Tripoli families who could not afford a honeymoon abroad. "More Sunni hymens have been broken in Shtaura," a Beiruti friend once told me, "than in all the rest of Lebanon combined."

From the foothills at Shtaura, we drove past eucalyptus groves into the Mount Lebanon range. At the summit, we came to Dahr el-Baidar, where Syrian soldiers at their key checkpoint waved us past. The Israelis captured Dahr el-Baidar in 1983. During their years there, it took hours to clear the security checks. Now, the Syrians made it a matter of a nod, taking only a few seconds. From there, the main road to Beirut had been closed since 1976, when it became a new border, between Christians and Muslims in Lebanon. We took the road south through Sofar, once a pine-shaded summer resort, now a barracks for Syrian troops, Palestinian commandos loyal to Syria, and Druze militiamen. Had we turned down the mountain towards the north, we would have entered the Christian zone through a forest called, for some reason, Bois de Boulogne. We drove on through the gutted summer resort town of Aley, devastated in the 1983 Shouf war between the Christian Lebanese Forces and the Druze. Syrian troops had taken up all the military positions and checkpoints which, in my last drive through there the previous November, had been in Druze hands. The Druze were rebuilding their villages, with their limited means, but they had recently destroyed the Christian villages which had been abandoned in late 1983 and early 1984. On Walid Jumblatt's orders, the Druze had blown up or bulldozed Christian houses, schools and churches. There would be no question of the refugees returning, because, as with Palestinian villages in 1948, there were no homes to return to. Jumblatt's justification was that this was the only way to keep out, not Christians, but Shiites. The Shouf was underpopulated, following the exodus of its Christian population, and the Shiites were a fast-growing community. The demolished villages, once so dear to their Maronite inhabitants, would not become the Shiite foot in the Druze door.

The twisting road was the main supply line to Syrian troops in Beirut. It was filled with holes, and its sides were congested with cars, some merely parked for the day, others damaged or destroyed and abandoned. Whenever a truckload of Syrian soldiers approached, we and the other cars had to pull over to the right, finding a place on a non-existent hard shoulder to wait for the convoy to pass. If Syria ever needed the road for a quick deployment of troops to Beirut, a fast retreat or an emergency resupply, their forces were doomed.

We drove down the mountain towards the sea, past the Druze village of Aramoun and onto the coastal plain south of Beirut. To the north, we could see Beirut airport, the slum cities surrounding it and Beirut itself, the peninsula of Ras Beirut dominating the sea. We drove north a few miles along the shore to Doha, a wealthy suburb behind gates, like Palos Verdes Estates in southern California. It was a tranquil island in a sea of chaos: to the south, Palestinians fought Shiites, Israelis fought Shiites and Palestinians, and Syrians dared not set foot below the Awali River above Sidon; to the east, the Druze confronted the lone brigade of Lebanese Army soldiers in the village of Souk al Gharb; to our north, in Beirut itself, a dozen militias vied among themselves for control of the west, the Syrians unconvincingly attempting to provide some kind of order, and a Green Line wasteland between Christians and Muslims awaited only the signal to resume all-out war. In Doha, sitting in the shaded garden near the tennis courts, we did not feel any of that. It was all in the distance, an unbridgeable distance of time and place.

In the evening, I went with Hany's driver Fawzi along the coast road, through Ouzai and the other Shiite suburbs, into west Beirut. I went first to the Backstreet, my favourite bar. Habib the bartender told me his daughter was growing up, three now, and that he managed to make a living despite the awful economic life of the country. It was early evening, and the bar was almost empty, but by midnight it would be full. "You should come back later," Habib said as I left. From the Backstreet, Fawzi drove me to the house of Khalid Salaam, Hany's younger brother. Khalid had a large, detached white stucco house behind walls in a large garden in the Raouche area of west Beirut. Khalid, his wife Hanaify, my friends Salim Diab and Tammam Salaam were all in the living-room, surrounded by Khalid's hunting trophies, having drinks.

"What," Salim Diab asked me, "do you think you are doing here?"

"I came for dinner."

"Charlie?" He always began his advice by using my name in the interrogative. "Charlie? Are you crazy?"

"You know I'm writing a book."

"'You shouldn't be here."

"If I wrote a book about the whole area without coming to west Beirut, you would all accuse me of being anti-Muslim."

Tammam Salam laughed and stood up to shake hands. "He's right, Salim."

Salim Diab was one of my closest friends in Beirut. He was a *bayk*, like the Salaams and Osseirans, a wealthy businessman and a passionate sportsman. He financed west Beirut's Sunni soccer club, *Ansar*, and had once organised a match in east Beirut between his all-Muslim team and a Christian club supported by the Phalangists. It was a brave attempt to blow a hole through the Green Line, but it would take more than a football to break down the barricades. Salim liked to spend time at the football club, helping the "boys," as he called them, to stay out of the militias, to find jobs, to keep up their football and other sports. Although he was only a year older than me, he always treated me like a naïve nephew.

Tammam Salaam was Hany and Khalid's first cousin. His father, Saeb Bayk Salaam, was the nominal head of the clan. Saeb Salaam had served several terms as prime minister of Lebanon and led Muslim forces against the Christian president, Camille Chamoun, in the brief civil war of 1958. He had moved recently to Geneva while he was out of favour with the Syrians. Tammam had taken over from his father, running the Mokassed, the Sunni charitable trust of hospitals, clinics, schools and sports clubs funded mainly by Saudi Arabia. Tammam was about forty, tall and with a shaven head that made him look a little like Daddy Warbucks. He was also the friendliest man in Beirut. Most of his large and extended family were successful, and sometimes it seemed every large Lebanese company had at least one Salaam on its board of directors. A cousin, Salim Salaam, was head of the national airline.

Filipino maids served us a large Lebanese dinner. Ordinarily, I would have sat up late having coffee or a drink and talking, but they all advised me for my own safety to leave early. Salim Diab told me to leave Beirut altogether. When Fawzi drove me back to Doha, it was not late, but the roads were deserted. The only checkpoints belonged to the Syrian army, whose commanders had guaranteed the safety of Lebanese and foreigners alike.

My Friday in Beirut was pleasant and uneventful. Hany Salaam went to London, taking with him my letters to my family, at the end of his latest futile attempt to mediate between the Syrian and Lebanese presidents. He left his driver and bodyguard at my disposal. I saw friends, ate good meals, visited the American University, where I had been a graduate student in philosophy in 1972, and enjoyed the deceptive calm. Everything seemed fine. There was no reason to be afraid. Cooled that night by a sea breeze, I slept peacefully on the hillside at Doha.

A loud explosion awakened me early on Saturday morning. The bomb was nowhere near the house, but its force shook the windows. I went outside and looked down at Beirut. Nothing moved in the early-morning light. A mist was rising from the sea, soon to burn off when the sun came over the mountains. I went inside to shower and dress. Lem-Lem, the Egyptian maid, gave me an early breakfast of fresh orange juice, tea, Arabic bread, olives, *labneh*, jam and a savoury mix of thyme and olive oil to spread on the bread. Then Fawzi drove me in a white Land Rover to Damascus, following the same route through the mountains we had taken two days before.

We turned a corner up to the higher mountains and saw the summit of Mount Lebanon covered in snow. I turned on the radio to listen to the news, and the BBC World Service reported that the explosion we'd heard earlier was a car bomb in west Beirut that had killed at least four people. The sun was bright in the sky, and Beirut's car bombs seemed an eternity away. Not even the Syrian checkpoints on the road, with armed soldiers cavalierly waving cars past, could detract from the calm of the mountains or deprive them of their beauty. We came to the summit at Dahr el Baidar. Behind us sparkled the dark blue Mediterranean, the snows of Mount Lebanon surrounded us, and the vast patchwork of contrasting greens in the Bekaa lay ahead. We sailed through the border posts of Masnaa and Jdaideh using the so-called military roads, while scores of less fortunate travellers waited for permission to pass through this divided land. For us, at least, there were no borders and apparently no dangers.

Emboldened by my first encounter with Lebanon on this journey, I readily accepted an offer from Michel Smaha to go back. I had seen Michel looking like an American tourist in Palmyra, under the castle of the Lebanese expansionist Emir Fakhreddin. When we bumped into each other in Damascus later, he said he was going to Zahle for lunch.

"Why don't you come?" he asked. Lebanon had the best food in the Levant, and Zahle had the best mezze in Lebanon. We would be back in a few hours.

Michel drove, and I sat in front, a Kalashnikov on the floor between us. He too used the military roads, using a pass issued by the Syrians. If I had told him a few years earlier that he would be driving through the Bekaa under a *laisser-passer* from the Syrian army, he would have called me a liar. Like most of the Christians in the Lebanese Forces militia at the time, he was vehemently anti-Syrian. The Lebanese Forces, through their founder Bechir Gemayel, had supported the Israeli invasion of Lebanon in the belief the Israelis would send the Palestinian commandos and the

Syrian army out of Lebanon forever. The Israelis invaded, and then, under fire from Lebanese guerrillas, retreated from most of Lebanon. They left the Christians alone to face the Syrians. Palestinian commandos returned to Sidon, and Syrian troops were nearly everywhere, except in the Maronite Catholic heartland along the coast north of Beirut and south of Tripoli.

"How did it happen?" I asked Michel as we drove towards Zahle.

"We made mistakes," he said. "We did not realise Syria was not going to go away. When we tried to make the best deal we could with Hafez al-Assad, the others saw their chance to take power."

Michel Smaha was a political advisor to the head of the Lebanese Forces, Elie Hobeika, when he signed an accord with the Shiite Amal militia and the Druze forces of Walid Jumblatt, the so-called Tripartite Agreement, under the aegis of Syria. Hobeika discovered quickly, however, as Michael Collins did when he presented the partition of Ireland treaty to his Irish Republican Army supporters, that his rank and file were not prepared to compromise. There was a rebellion, and a young man from Becharré named Samir Geagea took over the organisation. Hobeika and his supporters were exiled to Damascus. He later launched a disastrous putsch from west Beirut that ended in a bloodbath of Christians killing Christians, much as Muslims killed Muslims in west Beirut most weeks of the year. Smaha lived in Paris, but often came to Damascus to see Hobeika.

Elie Hobeika was known in Lebanon for his massacre of Palestinian refugees at the Sabra and Shatila Camps in 1982, under the watchful eyes of his Israeli benefactors. His rival, Samir Geagea, had launched disastrous military campaigns against the Druze in the Shouf and against Muslims and Palestinians near Sidon. In both instances, Geagea's efforts had led to the expulsion of Christian families who had lived peacefully with their neighbours for generations. His critics, particularly among Christian refugees in east Beirut, had a saying, "Where Samir Geagea sets foot, no Christians remain." It was hard to blame Michel Smaha for his disillusion.

It was early spring, and the outdoor restaurants along the Wadi Arayesh, Valley of the Vines, had yet to open. We went to a small restaurant on a hill over the valley. We sat outside and looked down on the plazas built along the river banks, the vines just sprouting the leaves that would soon cast the ravine in shade. In a month or so, the riverside cafés would be filled, and people would flock there from all over the Bekaa, even from Beirut and Damascus, for lunch and dinner. For nearly a mile either side of the Bardouni River, restaurant after restaurant would serve delicious *mezze* and locally made *arak*. In late spring and summer, the ingénues of Zahle would promenade safely and, on moonlit weekend nights, lean against plane trees to wait for young men to ask them to dance.

I had been there hundreds of times, sometimes staying in Zahle's lovely *belle époque* hotel, the Kadri, sometimes going only for lunch. I loved to walk through its shaded avenues and along the lower slopes of Mount Lebanon. My mother's father had been born there in 1889. According to his mother, the first sound the newborn baby heard was the neighing of a horse outside his window. He was taken as an infant to California, where he grew up to train and own thoroughbreds. I had never been able to find his relations there, but there were some farmers in the Wadi Arayesh with the same family name, Sawaya, an Arabised version of Savoy. Their ancestors had come to the Levant from Savoy, like many Genoans and Venetians, as traders. For a time, the Lebanese Forces controlled the town, but the Syrians had been in occupation for the previous year and allowed Hobeika's rebels to keep a base there. Zahle, known as the "Bride of the Bekaa", was mostly Greek Catholic, but it had many Maronites and Shiites.

"We Christians have to understand we are part of this Arab world," Michel said, with our Lebanese Arab food spread before us on the white tablecloth. "And not on sufferance. We have made important contributions. Who built Antioch? Who introduced the first printing press to the Middle East? We still have much to offer, and we can live with the Muslims."

"It's not easy in Lebanon these days," I said.

"We have always lived with the Muslims," he insisted, sipping a small glass of *arak*. "They cannot live together. Do you know that nearly every village in Lebanon had a mixed Christian and Muslim population? There are Christian–Sunni villages, Christian–Shiah villages, Christian–Druze villages, but there are no Sunni–Shiah or Shiah–Druze villages. They cannot live together, but we can live with any of them."

"Tell me something. This has been puzzling me all these months I've been in Syria. In Aleppo and Damascus, Christians and Muslims rarely mix socially. It happens a little in the upper classes, but by and large the communities keep to themselves. There is almost no marriage between Christians and Muslims. They live in separate quarters, and they sometimes have different accents. Their cultures are different."

"So?"

"In Lebanon, the communities mixed freely. I know of dozens of intermarriages, not just in the upper classes. I know Shiite cab drivers with Maronite wives. I have Christian friends with Sunni or Druze wives. Most people were not religious. At dinner parties, there was always a good mix. No one ever mentioned religion. And yet . . ."

"And yet, the Lebanese are killing one another."

"And the Syrians are not."

"It's a good question. Let me know when you find the answer."

Like everything else about Lebanon, it was a question without an answer. Why did the war go on when no one wanted it to? How did Christians and Muslims live peacefully in Zahle, yet kill each other in Beirut? How did some Christians live in Muslim west Beirut and some Muslims in the Christian east? Who was killing whom and why? Whose hand was behind each faction? Why did Iran support the Shiah? Why did Israel support some of the Christians? What had happened in Lebanon to bring troops from America, France, Britain and Italy to try and fail to save it in the 1980s, as France had sent troops, and the Russians, British and Austro-Hungarians their warships, in 1860? What was it about this place that made it compelling, that dared outsiders to take part in its tribal battles, that sent them hurrying out in disgrace? How had the Arab world's most advanced country – with the highest rate of literacy, four excellent universities, legal rights for women, a modern economy that supported both businessmen and poets, regular parliamentary and presidential elections, religious tolerance, a free press, lively theatre and music, modern hospitals, libraries, a bountiful sea and rich farms – become the most primitive? What made the Lebanese poet Kahlil Gibran, who loved the mountains of Lebanon, write these words from exile in America?

Your souls are freezing in the
Clutches of priests and
Sorcerers, and your bodies
Tremble between the paws of the
Despots and the shedders of
Blood, and your country quakes
Under the marching feet of the
Conquering enemy . . .

I hate you, My Countrymen, because
You hate glory and greatness. I
Despise you because you despise
Yourselves. I am your enemy, for
You refuse to realise that you are
The enemies of the goddesses.

Gibran's love turned to hatred, and back to love again in another poem, "Dead are my people." When thousands of Lebanese and Syrians were dying in the last days of the Ottoman Empire, of *safar berlik*, he wrote,

Gone are my people, but I exist yet,
Lamenting them in my solitude . . .

Dead are my friends, and in their
Death my life is naught but great
Disaster . . .

My people died on the cross . . .
They died while their hands
Stretched toward the East and West,
While the remnants of their eyes
Stared at the blackness of the
Firmament . . . They died silently,
For humanity had closed its ears
To their cry. They died because
They did not befriend their enemy.
They died because they loved their
Neighbours. They died because
They placed trust in all humanity.

Still they died, at their own, not the Turks', hands. And still humanity's ears were closed. Nagging and nagging at me was the question, "Why?" Tied and blindfolded, sprawled in the dust of a ruined building on the first day of my captivity, I would ask myself what had happened in Lebanon. Why were its people destroying themselves? What had turned young boys into murderers and kidnappers? And why had I returned? What brought me back? I would have many days to ponder the questions, but there would never be time enough to find the answers.

CHAPTER NINETEEN

A BLOOD FEUD IN THE MOUNTAINS

Let us not be ashamed of the Syrian and Egyptian
blood that flows in our veins.
Let us honor it and boast of it.
                              - C. P. Cavafy, "Return to Greece"

Several armed men in succession stopped our little yellow taxi at the Syrian border post. One of them, not in uniform, asked me, "What is your work here?"

"What is *your* work here?" I asked him back.

"Intelligence," he said. "Give me your passport."

Inside the police post a sign in English read, "Attention! Keep on your entered card from Syria post as it's missing, makes you under responsibility." The Syrian customs officers found some irregularity with the car's papers. They invited my worried driver from Damascus, a kindly man named Abu Munir who worked for Tony Touma, into their offices for a chat. While the customs officers examined his documents and interrogated other travellers in the few *services* going to Lebanon, I walked up to the bridge over the Nahr al-Kabir, the Big River. This creek divided Syria from Lebanon in the north. It was part of General Gouraud's border, a line the French had drawn across rivers and mountains in their portion of the Ottoman Empire's spoils. It was supposedly the river beyond which Syria's Christians would be protected. Nowhere else in the Levant were they as threatened. When travellers drove to the border crossing, Gouraud's line sometimes seemed impenetrable, as officials on both sides demanded documents and searched cars and luggage. I leaned over the wooden gate on the bridge, near a soldier in a kiosk who was waiting to open the barrier for the next car, and looked upriver. About a hundred yards away, from a clearing on the bank, a man was slowly riding his donkey across the river into Lebanon. A few minutes later, a family followed him across on foot. The soldier in his shed at the river's edge didn't seem to mind. Border formalities were for fools like me who didn't have the sense to ford the stream.

About a mile south of the Big River, we came to the Lebanese border post. Eucalyptus grew on both sides of the road among French colonial government buildings. A few policemen relaxed nonchalantly on chairs outdoors. In the customs office, a poster of the Lebanese president, Amin Gemayel, was pasted to a wall. A little beyond the border, we came to the first of many Syrian army checkpoints, whose soldiers had fixed above their sandbag bunker the more familiar face of Hafez al-Assad. In Lebanon, Assad's portrait outnumbered Gemayel's at least ten to one.

The sergeant asked us to give two of his men a lift to another Syrian position a few miles away. Abu Munir was Syrian, but neither he nor any Lebanese driver would have refused. The two soldiers were young villagers, not unlike Hussein Al-Sultan from Yusuf Basha. With their AK-47 assault rifles at their sides in the back seat, they would deter any Hizballah kidnap attempt, unlikely as that was in northwest Lebanon, where only a few Shiites lived.

The sun was slowly dropping into the edge of the Mediterranean as we drove along the coast road towards Tripoli, Lebanon's second city. We passed the Palestinian refugee camps of Nahr al-Bared, the Cold River, and Badawi, both scenes of brutal fighting between different Palestinian factions in 1983. Near the Badawi camp, the flames of excess gas at the Tripoli oil refinery lit up the road, and as we reached Tripoli, the moon glittered on Homer's wine-dark sea.

We drove through Tripoli, looking as devastated as ever. Its rival militias had done some damage. The Palestinians who had besieged one another there in 1983 had done more. The Syrians had dealt the final blow, levelling whole sections of the city with heavy artillery before reoccupying it a year earlier. On the hill above the town stood the Crusader castle of Raymond de Saint-Gilles, *Sanjil* in Arabic, Mount Pilgrim in English. The Syrian flag flew over the parapet, and inside Syrian soldiers were in occupation, as good a position for them to dominate the Sunni Muslim city as it had been for the Crusaders. From the time I had first seen the citadel in 1972, I had met a succession of occupants – the Lebanese police, Tripoli's socialist October Twenty-Fourth Movement, the Palestinians of Yasser Arafat's Al Fateh, the Islamic fundamentalists of the Tawheed militia and, now, the Syrian army. With the citadel changing hands so frequently, I would not have been surprised to see the Crusaders back.

We went into Kobbe, an Alawi neighbourhood on the city's outskirts, where militiamen stopped us at a checkpoint. When they saw the soldiers in the back, they waved us past. One of the soldiers said dismissively, "Ali Eid," the name of the commander of the Alawi militia. The other soldier began complaining about the intelligence services' checkpoints. They were regular army and did not have much time for militiamen and intelligence officers.

From Tripoli, we turned east into the foothills, beginning the slow ascent of Mount Lebanon towards Zgharta. Abu Munir said he had not seen Zgharta in twenty years. A few miles on, the village appeared on the horizon. "This is Zgharta?" Abu Munir shouted. "This is a city."

Zgharta, a picturesque village when my grandmother was born there nearly a century earlier, had become, if not a city, a large town. It had grown, and grown uglier, over the years, sprawling along the main road into concrete and cinderblock suburbs. Still, from the last hill before the centre of the village, the original boundaries without the suburbs looked almost like a walled Tuscan village, its stone houses and convents built up from the foothills and surrounded on all sides by miles of olive groves. In the moonlight, the old form of the village was silhouetted against the sky, the bell-towers of the Maronite Catholic churches silent as we approached. The first time I went to Zgharta was on a sunny late summer's day in 1972, when trees shaded both sides of the little road through the village. Later, someone decided the village needed a highway, and the little road was widened, the old houses cut back, small shops and trees knocked down to make way for four asphalt lanes with electric lamp-posts planted down the middle. The shops became boutiques, and apartment houses went up where the old houses had been. Now fifty thousand people lived there, and it had outdoor cafés, discotheques and restaurants. "This is Zgharta?" I asked myself as I saw young men in expensive cars cruising the main road, while girls in tight French dresses promenaded in the cool evening air. "This is a city." Before my departure, Zgharta would become a village again.

It was time for dinner when I walked into the Qasr Frangieh, the Frangieh Palace, and a butler led me to the dining-room. A dozen people, fewer than usual, sat at the long table. In all the years I had come to the house, I had never seen anyone turned away from a meal. Even when I arrived from covering fighting in Tripoli with my camera crews and drivers, all of us scruffily dressed, the family would insist that we all sit down to lunch or dinner. This was a house of mountain hospitality and mountain traditions. It was the seat of Suleiman Bayk Frangieh, Lebanon's president from 1970 to 1976, now the family and village patriarch. I noticed immediately that President Frangieh's chair at the centre of the table was empty. Mme Frangieh sat in her usual place opposite the chair, and Robert was next to her. Robert's sisters, Lamia and Maya, were there with their husbands. The third and most voluble sister, Sonia Rassi, was in Beirut, where her husband was Minister of the Interior. There were several guests, to whom I was quickly introduced before I sat down. Waiters poured me a tumbler of home-made *arak*. A large *mezze* was already on the table, and they brought platters of *kibbé*, minced lamb with cracked wheat. If Zahle was famous for its *mezze*, Zgharta took pride of place for *kibbé*. Long-suffering village women made it in countless ways – raw, baked, grilled, fried, sometimes with stuffing, in a variety of shapes and sizes. I enjoyed the food, still cooked in Zgharta the way my grandmother had learned it under the Turks.

In the adjoining reception room, about half a dozen men conferred among themselves. One of them was extremely old with a waxed handlebar moustache and a rumpled suit. On his white head, he wore a red tarboosh. Another man with grey hair did most of the talking, while the old man in the tarboosh listened and nodded. They could have been there at any time going back at least two centuries, sitting at the court of the bey or the pasha, just sitting, paying their respects, asking for favours or waiting to perform some task for the *bayk*. The old *bayk* was not there, so his son, Robert Bayk, sat and talked with them after dinner.

I walked through the house down to my room. From the outside, the Qasr Frangieh looked like a Turkish fortress – all of local stone, lying low at the eastern edge of Zgharta, built over an olive grove to the south. Inside, there were two houses, the one a traditional *bayk*'s palace belonging to the father, the other a modern apartment for the son.

Everything in the father's house was grand, from the large Ottoman coloured- and cut-glass chandeliers to the walls dressed in old tapestries, muskets, Greek ikons, ivory and other hunting trophies. It was the preserve of a patriarch who hunted and kept dogs, whose house was a court where politics of village and country were conducted over cups of Turkish coffee, where secrets were whispered into the ear of the *bayk*, where old men arranged matters as though nation-states had never existed, where the rifle was never far away. Although the palace was new, built only after Suleiman Frangieh stepped down as president in 1976, its design and decor were distinctly Ottoman. The walls were bare cut stone, in alternating light and dark horizontal layers, the high vaulted ceilings supported by columns and arches. There were several reception rooms, for gatherings of different sizes. In them, all the chairs were set against the walls, a tradition dating back to villages like Yusuf Basha and the bedouin tent, where men kept their backs to the walls to avoid the dagger from behind.

The son's apartment, on a level lower than the house, looked as new as it was. Ceilings were low, the furniture and chandeliers were art deco, mostly from 1930s France. The walls were papered in a textured beige cloth, and the fitted carpets were another shade of beige. The front wall was open to the garden from floor to ceiling through two arched windows. Books and magazines were scattered on a coffee table between stuffed couches. Behind one couch was a huge pink abstract painting, divided into squares which together composed the body of a nude woman, although this had to be explained to me. Behind the other couch were built-in shelves of books, Chinese porcelain and ivory figurines, an ancient iron bow, an African ivory carved head, some Roman bottles and family photographs. On a table between the two front windows was a framed photograph of Robert and another man staring into the camera, seated in large chairs, the usual Arab political-meeting pose. The other man was the Frangiehs' ally and sometime protector, Hafez al-Assad.

Robert's apartment had two bedrooms, each with its own bathroom. The back windows of the bedrooms opened on a vista of cypresses and acre upon acre of olives. The gnarled trees spread from the house down a valley and rose up to a little village on the opposite ridge.

I unpacked, had a shower and sat down to read at the art deco dining-table, in front of an oil portrait of Robert's grandfather. The old man in red tarboosh and long moustache would not have recognised this apartment, but the house nextdoor, its furnishings and the village politics discussed there would all have been familiar to him.

I went out of the front door to the garden. The flowers, even in the electric light, were an Impressionist's dream of dripping dark pink geraniums, giant red and pink roses, white and yellow hibiscus and jasmine. Above the flower beds, a drive encircled a lawn planted with olive trees, evergreens and roses, spring flowers in red, orange and pink. I smelled the jasmine that crept up the walls of the house, and I listened to the quiet of the night.

Up in the mountains to the east was Zgharta's summer village of Ehden, to which all its inhabitants migrated each July to escape the lowland heat. Before the car, the people of Zgharta would ride and walk up in caravan, firing flintlocks into the air to announce the beginning of summer. Ehden was the older village, where Maronites had lived for centuries before taking the chance of building a village in the foothills where they might more easily be attacked by Turks and Muslims in Tripoli. For some reason though, people said they were from Zgharta, they were Zghartawi, never that they came from the older, prettier, more secure Ehden. Zgharta was the rampart, and Ehden the citadel.

When Robert came down, he seemed tired. He was a reluctant politician, drafted into service when his older brother, Tony, had been murdered by the Phalange Party militia in 1978. Robert was studying at the American University of Beirut when I was a graduate student there in 1972, after which he moved to Paris. We were the same age, and I suspected that, if his brother had lived, Robert would have stayed in Paris, become a businessman and enjoyed his life, paying occasional visits home to the family and its political folklore.

"How is your father?" I asked him.

"He's not well, but he's getting better," Robert said. "Some doctors are coming from Beirut tomorrow. I think he'll be fine. Aren't you having a drink?"

He opened a cabinet and poured me a glass of cognac. "Have you been sitting up there all night with those old men?" I asked. "What do they want?"

"They just come and sit. You can't stop them. They feel they have to come."

"Why do they hang around for hours on end?"

"To ask for something, or in case the *bayk* needs something." He thought a moment and said, "And one other thing."

"What's that?"

"They want to hear what is being said, so they can repeat it."

At lunch the next day, there were the usual number of diners, about a dozen, but the table was set for twenty, in case anyone else dropped by. Four of the guests were physicians from the American University Hospital in Beirut, one of whom complained that fifty of the hospital's doctors had left Lebanon to practise medicine in Boston alone. Robert said the Lebanese Medical Association estimated thirty per cent of Lebanon's doctors had emigrated in the previous year. Lebanon needed its doctors, as it needed so much else. It was losing them, because they found life impossible. Militiamen in Beirut invaded their hospitals and forced them at gunpoint to operate on wounded comrades. Their patients had little money to pay them, and many were tired of being poor in a country where their children could not go safely to school. Added to this was the fact that many physicians in Muslim west Beirut were Christians, who feared being kidnapped.

The doctors had come up from the American University Hospital at Mme Frangieh's request. She was worried about her husband, who was still upstairs in his room. During lunch, Robert went up to see how his father was. Mme Frangieh leaned over to tell me, "These doctors are friends of Tony. You are a friend of the younger. You two are a *bon équipe*. Please do this for me: keep Robert calm. You are of the family now." Iris Frangieh was a Greek Orthodox from Tripoli, but she played the role of matriarch well in Lebanon's most stubbornly Maronite village. She was large and usually jolly, except when she recalled her son who had died. At other lunches, she had spoken to me of Tony. Whenever she thought of him, of the day in June 1978 when Phalangist militiamen came to Ehden and killed Tony, his wife and three-year-old daughter, she could not keep the tears inside. I saw in her eyes, and heard in her voice, the tears and the laments of every mother in Lebanon who had lost a son or a daughter.

Robert returned to the table, visibly agitated. "How is he?" his mother asked.

"Fine."

After lunch, the doctors flew back to Beirut by helicopter. Mme Frangieh went upstairs to her room. Robert stepped into the sitting-room to talk with some older men who had been waiting to see him. Roderigue Dahdah, Lamia's husband, and I sat in one corner of the room to talk while Robert dealt with his visitors. Roderigue knew his country well. He had worked for many years as a journalist for Visnews and could take a detached view. Over coffee, he told me, "When I watched the television yesterday, I had the chance to watch three televisions at once. I saw three Lebanese channels – TV Berri, TV Jumblatt and TV Lebanese Forces." Every militia in Lebanon, including the Frangiehs', had its own flag, its own uniform, its own slogan. Most of them had their own radio and television stations. What Roderigue called TV Berri, for the Shiite leader Nabih Berri, was the Amal-run channel in Beirut. TV Jumblatt was the Druze station broadcasting from the Shouf. The Lebanese Forces' channel, the Lebanese Broadcasting Company, had the best productions, many pirated from France and the United States, and the most sophisticated propaganda. Roderigue went on. "I watched the news on all three. I knew then, finally, the country is finished."

"Why?"

"They are completely incompatible."

"With one another?"

"With reality," he said.

When I laughed, Roderigue explained, "Nabih Berri said, 'Now we must make the guns of Algeria, Morocco, Syria, the Palestinians and the Shiites all one.' If that is so, why is he killing the Palestinians?"

Roderigue and I watched as Robert received his many post-prandial visitors. Under the light of the chandelier, we drank Turkish coffee, smoked cigarettes, received more visitors, drank more coffee, smoked more cigarettes. More men came and went. Occasionally, Robert would whisper something in the ear of one of the men who worked in the house, and he would scurry out on some errand or other. Whenever Robert stood to greet a new arrival, all the men would stand. When he sat, they sat again. More coffee, more conferring in small groups. The hours passed. This was Levantine politics, visiting the *bayk* at his palace, sitting at court. I had seen it before, here in Zghorta with the Frangiehs, in Mukhtara on Sundays when Walid Jumblatt held court for his Druze peasants, in Beirut with

Sunni Muslim notables like Saeb Salaam. Even new politicians like Nabih Berri, a lawyer who had worked his way to the head of Amal and came from a poor family, succumbed to the lure of the flatterers and courtiers who came daily to his apartment in Beirut. Perhaps this kind of politics had its origins in Yusuf Basha, where visiting was the only pastime.

"In England," a small farmer in Zgharta once told me, "if you lose your job, you get money from the government. We don't have that here. You have to go to the leaders and ask for help. If you're with a prominent family, you can draw wages from a factory and a government department and still do no work at all. Who would you blame?" He blamed his own leaders who were not doing as much for him as the Frangiehs were for their people. "You can't say this one's a saint and the other one's a bastard," a visiting Lebanese emigré said of the country's leaders. "They're all bastards."

In the later afternoon, I took a walk down to the riverside. I found a bend in the river, just near an old flour mill, that I had always loved. It was about five in the afternoon, when the heat of day gave way to the cool of the evening. The river was at full flow from the melting snows on the summits, and the branches of tall trees stretched from one bank to the other. This was the River Merdishia, at least in Zgharta. Upriver, other villages called it the Zaraya. It flowed into the Kadisha River, which, at its mouth in Tripoli, Muslims called the Abu Ali. Maps called it the River Rashin. No one seemed to mind what it was called, any more than in the old Lebanon before the war they cared much about religion. The water rushed by, but its flow was not enough to clear the debris – the egg boxes, milk tins and plastic water bottles – that the people of Zgharta had thoughtlessly thrown into the river. No Lebanese, whatever his religion, gave a second thought to throwing rubbish into the cleanest river or the prettiest meadow. The Lebanese were *laisser-faire* to a fault.

Outdoor restaurants on both banks had tables and chairs set along the river's edge, deserted at this time of day. A boy with a shotgun, scanning the sky for birds, walked in a field nearby. Another boy led a cow with a bell round her neck over a stone bridge. That peaceful spot by the river was much as it must have been when my grandmother was born, but the sights on my walk there from the palace would have been as strange to her as her first sight of New York. The new main road bore the scars of its transition from a narrow horse path to a four-lane boulevard, including a tiny church cut in two to make way for progress. The whole route along the new boulevard, which in its previous incarnation was a mixture of small shops, church façades and front terraces of stone houses, had become a modern mall of supermarkets, video shops, pharmacies, bookshops, Yves St Laurent, Christofle silver and Benetton. Here and there, amid the consumer splendour, sprouted souvenirs of war: flags and logos of the

Marada, the village militia, flying overhead or painted on walls; and, on most of the buildings and inside most shop windows, the fading posters of Tony Frangieh, his wife and their daughter, three of Zgharta's many martyrs, dead but not forgotten these last ten years.

Walking from the highway down into the narrow roads of the old village, I came into a part of Zgharta that had not changed: small stone houses, poor apartments with bare rooms, the grocers selling fresh vegetables on tables outdoors, foodstuffs and household wares stacked in dark alcoves of shops without electricity, old men in their knitted wool caps and sweaters, old women in black dresses, widows all.

I walked from the village streets to an old mill, whose great stone wheel, turned by river water channelled into arcades below, ground wheat into flour as it had for at least a century. I jumped over a little stream and found a footpath through the brush. Behind me I saw an old man, about 75, wearing a heavy wool jacket. He jumped over the stream and caught up with me. A moustache crossed his wrinkled face, and he wore the wool cap of the mountain peasant. We walked along together without either of us talking. About twenty yards further on, he spoke up and told me he worked in the mill. Then he offered me a cigarette and lit one for himself.

The path led through a field to a small road. When we found ourselves under an arch where the mill went over the road, he spoke again, in his mountaineer's Arabic. "This," he said, patting the old rough stone of the mill, "has been here eight hundred years."

"Eight hundred years? That's impossible," I said.

"Look at this," he said, pointing to an old cross cut into the stone. "The Crusaders put that cross here."

"The Crusaders?" I asked, incredulous.

He took my astonishment for misunderstanding and proceeded to give me a history lesson. "The Crusaders were Christians who came here from all over the world to fight the Muslims," he explained. "They came from France, from Italy, from England . . ." He paused for breath and went on, "and from America, from Argentina!"

Later, when I was sitting alone at the bend in the river, he walked by. He stopped and handed me some oranges from the bag he was carrying. "Here," he said. "I brought these for you. Zgharta oranges. They make you strong." Perhaps he thought I was an American Crusader.

I was visiting some of my grandmother's cousins early that Saturday evening, when I heard shooting outside, several bursts of automatic weapons fire in the distance. I went to the balcony and saw nothing but undisturbed streets and people sitting out on their terraces.

"What was that?" I asked.

"Probably a wedding," someone said. "You know. They still like to shoot in the air whenever someone gets married."

When I arrived back at the palace, a dozen men sat in an ante-room, and at least twenty more in the drawing-room, far more than usual. It all looked rather boring, and I didn't want to sit around again watching them sip coffee, standing when Robert stood, sitting when he sat. I was sure that if he had knelt, they would all have been on their knees. I went down to Robert's apartment and telephoned my other cousins, Theodore and Lucien Makary.

"Stay where you are," my cousin Lucien ordered me. He was a major in the Lebanese army. "Don't go out of the palace. It's not safe."

"But I was just outside. Everything was fine."

"Are you crazy? Didn't you hear the shooting?"

"The wedding?"

"What wedding? One of the Marada shot a boy from the Douaihy family at the football match. He was the favourite nephew of Father Douaihy." The Marada were ostensibly the village militia, but the Frangiehs' rivals saw it as the Frangiehs' own. Father Semaan Douaihy was an old adversary of the Frangiehs, known among the Beirut press corps as "the pistol-packing priest."

"Is he going to live?"

"He's dead."

"What's going to happen?"

"The Douaihys have already killed two Frangiehs in revenge."

I went back into the main house, realising now why so many men were standing by, the older ones to seek or give advice, the younger ones to fight. The table was set for dinner, fine china and Christofle silver at each place. Mme Frangieh came into the dining-room and invited everyone to eat. The president's chair was empty, and Robert looked tense. It was hard to eat knowing that a war was brewing. At the table were men from four of Zgharta's five main clans, Frangieh, Karam, Moawad and Makary. There were no Douaihys. Assad Bayk Karam sat opposite me at the table. A corpulent man of about my age, he was the new scion of the family with the proudest tradition, dating to his heroic nineteenth-century ancestor, Youssef Bayk Karam. He was a big man, his stomach pressing his white cotton shirt just over the line of his belt. He had a small moustache and rough face, but his manner was friendly. "I knew another journalist whose grandmother came from Zgharta," Assad said. "He was with the *Los Angeles Times*."

"Who was that?"

"I don't remember his name, but he came here in the war of 1975–76. He was worried that if we attacked Tripoli, Zgharta would not be able to protect itself from the Palestinians. He asked about our strategy and our weapons. I remember he had a big black beard."

"Did you take him to the front in Tripoli?"

"Yes"

"That was me. I'm from Los Angeles, but not from the *Times*. I remember that someone took me to the front. It must have been you."

"Do you still think the Palestinians were stronger?"

"Everyone makes mistakes," I admitted.

While we were speaking, a prelate, his cassock trimmed in purple and a monsignor's biretta on his head, came into the room. Robert and a dozen men jumped up to meet him. Without a word, they all began to walk out of the room. Mme Frangieh called after them, *"Arrangez ça très vite, mes enfants."*

"Who was that?" I asked Robert's sister Maya.

"Père Saade. He's a bishop."

"Is this going to grow?"

"It could, It is very serious," she said. Maya seemed on the verge of trembling, until she lit a cigarette.

The bishop and the other men were gone an hour, during which the food had been removed from the table. When they returned, waiters laid fresh place settings and brought back the food and drink. We resumed eating in silence. Robert switched on one of several transistor radios that his father always kept at the table to listen to the news on all of Lebanon's many channels. He tuned to the Voice of Lebanon to hear how the story was playing in Christian east Beirut. Its news broadcast led with a brief account of a shooting in Zgharta and concluded that the situation was under control. Robert was relieved that the Phalangists who ran the Voice of Lebanon were not taking advantage of the feud to stir things up with their Frangieh enemies in Zgharta.

From the radio report and from what I could glean at the table, it seemed the trouble had started at a soccer match between the teams of two nearby villages. When someone began racing his sports car around the stadium, the Marada militiamen responsible for security warned him to stop. Angered and no doubt insulted, the driver came back with the nephew of Father Semaan Douaihy and confronted the militiamen. Shooting started between the young men of both sides, none of whom was older than his early twenties. The driver and Father Douaihy's nephew were dead. A relation of theirs went to the local hospital to find and kill the Frangieh wounded, but he was killed. At least, that was the version I was able to piece together on Saturday night.

I heard later that the Douaihy house had seen the same family gatherings, the same comings and goings of interlocutors. The Douaihys were blaming what they called "the foreigners" for the killings. They did not mean the CIA, the Soviets or even the Syrians. The foreigners were young members of the Marada militia who came, not from Zgharta itself, but from the villages within walking distance. The surrounding area of *Zawieh Zgharta*, Zgharta Corner, took in seven nearby villages. Father Douaihy pinned the blame on these "strangers" and the young man who had ostensibly brought them into the militia, young Suleiman Frangieh. He was the twenty-two-year-old son of Tony Frangieh, who had inherited the loyalty of the fighters in his father's militia. "If they had been killed for the welfare of Zgharta, I would accept it," Father Douaihy told the other family leaders on Saturday night. "But to see them killed for strangers, I do not accept."

Bishop Saade, who was acting as a go-between to stop the killing before it spread, left the Frangieh house to talk to the Douaihys. Someone came from the Douaihy house to tell Robert that the brother of the dead boy had sent all his people home, telling them not to seek revenge. Some of them, though, might well ignore him. At the Frangiehs', more people came and went. There were several settings of dinner at the big table. Mme Frangieh went to bed, and Robert stayed in the drawing room, talking, discussing, trying to calm things. A few tempers flared, but the talks continued. It was two in the morning before Robert went up to his father's room, sleeping there on a small bed to make certain the old man was well and did not get out of bed.

When the sun came up on that Sunday morning, Zgharta, despite its pretensions to metropolitan status, would be a village again. The superhighway, the Yves St Laurent shop, the University of the North, the Iris Franghieh Hospital for the Handicapped, the cinemas and nightclubs would stand idly by while Zgharta's sons observed the mountain's oldest tradition, the blood feud.

I knew about the feuds in Zgharta. My grandmother's father had died in one.

CHAPTER TWENTY

FOUL IS FAIR

Sunday morning in Zhgarta dawned warm and sunny, and the only sounds outside came from birds in the olive groves and bells in the churches. Semaan Boulos Makary, the titular head of my grandmother's family, arrived early for discussions with Robert. In his tailored suit and monogrammed shirt he looked like Don Barzini in *The Godfather*, the man who was playing both sides. The drive was filled with cars, shiny black Mercedes, long Cadillacs, Land Rovers, their drivers standing by for the politicians and militiamen inside. I walked up to the gate, where the guards were drinking their morning coffee, and looked down the main highway towards the centre of the village. Usually clogged with cars, this morning it was empty.

A young doctor was waiting in an ante-room to examine the president, and I asked him whether all the shops were closed. "Only the newsagents are open," he said, "but there are a few others in this part."

"Which part?"

"The Frangieh part."

I had not known until then that the village was divided into family sections, just as I had not known until the war began in 1975 that there were Christian and Muslim halves of Beirut. It was something that meant nothing until there was trouble, and then it could mean survival as everyone scurried to the safety of his family's quarter. My Makary cousins were in the Makary area, and my Zalloua half-cousins, being from a smaller family, were allied to the Karams and lived in the Karam area. I was a guest in the Frangieh quarter. Everyone advised me to stay there.

Several versions of Saturday's shooting were circulating in the village. The only thing they all had in common were the location, the football stadium near the village of Ardé, and the number of dead, three. A man who had spoken to both families tried to give me a balanced account: "It seems a young man who worked for Father Douaihy was at the football match, and he fired his gun into the air. I guess he was excited. The Marada told him to stop. When he refused, they confiscated his car." I wondered for a moment why they hadn't taken his gun instead, but it seemed pointless to ask. "He went to Father Douaihy's nephew, Bahé, for help. He came back with Bahé and Bahé's cousin, Raymond, to get the car. The Douaihys told me that they were unarmed and the Marada shot them dead."

"If they were unarmed, how did they shoot one of the Marada?"

"The Frangiehs say the three young men demanded the car, but the Marada refused. They say a fight started, and both sides fired, killing the two Douaihy nephews and wounding two Marada. Later, the Douaihys sent people to the hospital to find the two boys, not knowing they were dead. That is what the Douaihys told me. The Frangieh version is that they came to find the two Marada wounded and exact revenge. Anyway, there was shooting at the hospital, and another Douaihy was killed and another Marada wounded."

Later that day, someone shot a Frangieh supporter who was driving at the western end of town. He was taken to the hospital with serious wounds.

"What do you expect," the man asked, "when you have all these seventeen-, eighteen-year-old boys with guns and using drugs?"

The killings at the football match had revived the 1957 Frangieh–Douaihy feud, when either 23 or 33 people were killed, depending on which account was the more reliable. At the time, the leader of the Douaihy family was Sheikh Fuad Douaihy. Suleiman Frangieh's older brother, Hamid, led his family and was a member of parliament. Just before the 1957 parliamentary elections, Lebanon's President, Camille Chamoun, used money the CIA had given him to buy votes for candidates who would support his impending bid for a change in the constitution to allow him to run for a second presidential term. Chamoun gave his patronage to Father Semaan Douaihy to take Zgharta's parliamentary seat from the Frangiehs, just as he would use the CIA money to unseat other traditional leaders, like the Jumblatts in the Shouf. Father Douaihy's challenge soured relations between his family and the Frangiehs, who had already disputed water rights on their farms. Unrelated to the conflict, the brother of Maronite Bishop Antoine Abed died in Miziara, one of the villages of Zgharta Corner. The leaders of Zgharta's five clans, except Hamid Frangieh, who was in Beirut, went to the funeral in Miziara. Hamid's younger brother, Suleiman, went in his place. At the time, the Moawad family were allied to the Frangiehs and stood with them in the church.

"It was a hot afternoon, a Sunday, about this time of year," one of the Moawads told me. "It was hot in the church. The moment the funeral started, everyone went inside. Bishop Abed was saying Mass. Outside the church, there was a quarrel that led to the shooting. Those inside heard it, so they started firing. The place where President Frangieh was standing was surrounded by his men. He was standing with his back to a column that protected him. When the shooting started, that column was nearly destroyed. All the Douaihys shot at him. Some of both families went into the confessionals and shot from there. Nobody knew what happened, but one thing: that many people were killed. Some priests were killed. Many of the Douaihy family were killed."

Someone from a smaller family said, "I was nineteen at the time. I was in Zgharta when word came. It was like an earthquake. People were trembling. They put the shutters down on their shops. Cars drove off the road. Everyone went home to his family."

Since 1957, people who had moved into other family quarters in the early peaceful years of Lebanese statehood had been forced back to neighbourhoods where they felt safe. Each family lived within boundaries imperceptible to the outsider, but more tangible than the border between Lebanon and Syria: the Frangiehs in the east, on the road to Ehden; the Moawads and the Douaihys in the centre; the Karams in the north; and the Makarys in the west, blocking the road to Tripoli and the coast. The conflicts reinforced the power of each family leader. After 1975, the same pattern was repeated in all of Lebanon, when mountain feuding became a civil war. "Even if they don't like the fighting," the man said, "they need it. It forces everyone into the safety of his family."

"What happened after the shooting in the church?"

"At that time, Lebanon still had a government and an army. So President Frangieh and his men went to Ehden. It rained heavily. I was at my house in Zgharta. I saw the corpses carried in a truck with their stomachs swollen, their legs spread. They carried them in a *burghul* truck." *Burghul*, cracked wheat, was usually carried behind a tractor on an open trailer. "They put the Douaihy corpses, twelve, I think, in the middle of the green outside Our Lady of Zgharta Church. At that time, Chamoun was very powerful. He began to act against the Frangiehs. Many Frangiehs were put into prison, whether they were guilty or innocent. When Hamid Frangieh heard what happened, he had a stroke. That massacre destroyed him. He was horrified that, for the first time, we had had bloodshed in a church."

It was in October 1957, four months after the Miziara killings, that Hamid Frangieh suffered a cerebral haemorrhage and his brother Suleiman became head of the family.

"President Chamoun sentenced Suleiman *in absentia*. He could not stay in Lebanon. Anyone bearing the name Frangieh or Moawad was prosecuted. This caused the revolution against Chamoun in 1958. This was the thing that drove Suleiman Frangieh into the hands of the Syrians."

In Syria, Frangieh stayed with friends in the Alawi Mountains. Their name was Assad, and he came to know well one of their sons, a young air force officer named Hafez al-Assad. In 1970, Frangieh was elected president of Lebanon and his friend seized power in Syria.

"What do you think is going to happen this time?" I asked.

"I wish I knew."

"Aren't the Frangiehs much stronger in military terms than the Douaihys?"

"They cannot use all their power. Like all those Americans who want to hit Syria with atomic weapons for the sake of American hostages in Beirut, they may want to, but they can't. The fight will not be with positions and battles. Just sometimes, someone from one family will be walking down the street and be shot."

"Can't they stop it?"

"It's quieter now than it would have been before, because no one wants this. The shopkeepers want to be able to sell to people from all families. Businessmen want to work with other businessmen. Workers should be with other workers, regardless of family. But it is hard. It is so hard."

I went through town twice, first in the early afternoon and again at sunset. Usually, there would have been hundreds of people promenading on a Sunday evening. This Sunday, every street was deserted. A few people sat outside their houses, doors open in case they had to run in quickly. Some men sat on chairs in front of their shops, watching for the moment they would have to pull down the shutters. There were no military checkpoints, but armed men stood at the edge of buildings or crouched behind walls at the unmarked divisions between each of the five families' neighbourhoods. The only other cars out had young men inside, and they cruised slowly, like urban American street gangs checking out one another's turf, looking for trouble if there was any going.

At the palace, men were coming and going all day. Politicians, mediators and young warriors strode in, sniffed the air and left again. In the kitchen, the cooks were boiling coffee all day. Just before three o'clock, about a dozen limousines left the palace to go to the Douaihy funerals. Like the Muslims, the Maronites in Lebanon buried their dead quickly. When I asked to go, I was advised not to. "They know you are staying with the Frangiehs," someone explained.

Father Semaan Douaihy said the Requiem Mass. In his sermon, he told the mourners, "As long as we are governed by foreigners, we are not going to be at peace. This collection of militiamen who come as a stick from every 'corner' cannot bring peace to Zgharta. We refuse to be governed by the childish deeds of a child." This was an obvious reference to young Suleiman. "If there is going to be peace in Lebanon, the unity of the

Christians must start from Zgharta. Even if the Patriarch comes, I will not accept reconciliation unless there is understanding and mutual respect. But I give my hand to President Frangieh in order to save Lebanon." Father Douaihy left the church without accepting condolences. "Was that for political reasons?" I asked someone.

"No. He has heart trouble."

A family friend named Ramzi Karam came to visit Robert, and he left his twenty-one-year-old son Bedwi with me. Bedwi was a name I had heard only in Zgharta, an Arabic corruption of Padua, for St Anthony of Padua. A polite young man, he was studying at the east Beirut campus of Beirut University College. I asked him if he had problems being from Zgharta and living in east Beirut, which was controlled by the Lebanese Forces. He said they did not bother him, because he was not involved in politics. But there were many places in Lebanon that people of his generation had never visited. "They say the people who most want to see Lebanon are the Lebanese. I've never been to west Beirut or the south. I've never even seen Zahle."

"Where do you go to enjoy yourself?"

"We usually go into the fields above Ehden and have picnics with our friends." Then he said, "There is a spring there where the water is so cold, it can break a watermelon in two."

I smiled, recalling the same words from my grandmother, who left in 1900. I had been to the spring, and it was cold, but I did not have a watermelon at the time.

We had a subdued dinner that night. President Frangieh's chair was still empty, and Mme Frangieh was staying upstairs with her husband. We were only ten, including Robert and his nephew, Suleiman. Young Slaimie, as they called him, was being blamed for the feud, if not by the Frangiehs themselves, then at least by their critics. "One of our wounded men died after his operation," Slaimie said sadly. That brought the number of dead to four. "He was less seriously wounded. The one who was in worse shape is hanging on for his life tonight." He was young to be a militia commander, although he was about the age Alexander had been when he conquered all of Syria. He sat quietly, his thin young face looking confused, his small eyes watching each of us for signs that we blamed him. I felt sorry for him, and I saw him that night at dinner as I had always seen him: as the innocent twelve-year-old who was told one June day in 1978 that his father, mother and baby sister had been murdered in Ehden. From that day, his grandfather and grandmother had raised him, and it went without saying he would one day command his father's militia. He had neither gone to university nor lived outside Zgharta. He lacked Robert's broader vision as a result, but he was more like the young men he commanded. Next to him was his wife, pregnant with their first child. The burden of his life, of his heritage, was more than most boys could bear. He need not have feared that I would blame him.

"It's all mad," I said. "There is no good reason for the fighting, not just in Zgharta, but in all of Lebanon. It is insane. People are dying for nothing."

"Some of the Lebanese," Robert's sister, Lamia, said, "are trying to hold the country together, to establish a free and democratic country. That is worth struggling for."

Before I could answer, Lamia's daughter Tima broke into the conversation. She was in her early twenties and worked with the handicapped, many of whom had been crippled by the war. "My generation, Mama, doesn't care about the high principles or ideals of your generation. We just want to live together."

"What can we do?" her father, Roderigue, asked. "The Lebanese is like a man walking along the street, and a crane picks him up by the neck. It carries him along just five inches above the ground. If he struggles, he breaks his neck. If he waits, the crane may put him down."

We were waiting for the coffee when Assad Bayk Karam walked into the room. He had come for a reason, and we all went to the living-room to take our coffee. He said he had been back and forth between the two families all day. Neither side wanted a war. "It's quiet now," he said, obviously relieved. "It's like taking a boiling kettle off the fire. We're letting it cool."

Suddenly, an old woman appeared in the reception room. She was dressed in black from her neck to her ankles. Her long grey hair hung in a braid down her back. Around her neck, she wore a medallion with a colour photograph of young Slaimie. Her presence, like the witches' in *Macbeth*, was portentous and eerie. I feared she might annnounce, "Fair is foul, and foul is fair: Hover through the fog and filthy air." She walked up to Robert, bent forward and kissed his hand. He looked surprised and whispered to someone, "What does she want?"

I asked Roderigue who she was. "She walks in the village, everywhere, like that. This is the real Zghortiote. They believe everything. They follow their leader," he covered his eyes with his hands, "*aveuglement*. Absolutely blindly. This is the real peasant Zghortiote."

She told Robert she was praying for him and for the family. Then she disappeared.

Later that night in his apartment, Robert had the last of the day's cups of Turkish coffee. Leaning forward on the couch, he was trying to understand what was happening. "In my press conferences," he said, "I say, 'Your leaders have sealed their fate. Elie Hobeika, the so-called leader of the Christians, committed the massacres of Sabra and Shatila. Samir Geagea, another so-called leader of the Christians, failed in the north, in the Shouf and Sidon. Walid Jumblatt decorates hijackers. Nabih Berri hijacks airplanes. Camille Chamoun and Amin Gemayel just count their money.' Still, people come to me and say, 'We need someone to lead us.'"

I had watched since my arrival in Zgharta the way the Lebanese had courted their leaders, flattered them, waited on them. Some people like to blame all Lebanon's problems on its leaders, but the followers carried some responsibility. What leader could resist their seductive attentions, the implication that he was greater than they were, that they needed him?

"We are trapped," Robert said, "in a cycle of history. A man from the Douaihy family told me tonight, 'We don't mean you. We know you are different.' They associate me with the humanitarian acts – the hospital, the pharmacy, the attempts to bring art and culture here." Robert had used the money the family collected in the form of tax on the large cement factory on the coast, not only to support the militia, but to build a hospital, a centre for rehabilitating the handicapped, a pharmacy that subsidised the sale of prescription medicines, and festivals of music and art. "They say they are against Frangieh hegemony, but they say they don't mean me. They imply they mean Slaimie. They think they can divide the family. It's ridiculous."

My grandmother had been born just after the death of her father, an adventurer named Francis Makary. The Makarys were one of Zgharta's five feudal families, landowners who quarrelled among themselves and to whom all the smaller families of the village had to ally themselves. At one time or another, each family had been dominant in the village. Now, it was the Frangiehs' turn.

My grandmother had saved a picture of her father, taken in Mexico where he was fighting on the side of the revolutionaries. Next to him was a pretty Mexican girl. Some of his relations stayed in Yucatan, but he went back to Zgharta and married. Then he was killed. My grandmother had always said the Turks killed him in one of Zgharta's many rebellions against Ottoman rule. Years later, my cousins would tell me he had died in a feud. They could not however remember which families were feuding at the time. My great-grandmother, Jenny, had her daughter shortly after his death. She married again, to a man from one of the smaller, poorer families, called the Zallouas. She and Semaan Zalloua had two boys in Lebanon, Georges and Sarkis, Sarkis being the Arabised form of Sergius. At the turn of the last century, tens of thousands of Maronites were emigrating to the new world. Jenny and Semaan sailed out of Lebanon with my grandmother, leaving their two boys behind with Semaan's mother. When they had settled in America, they would send for the boys. At least, that was the plan. The time came for the grandmother to send the boys to a strange place called Massachusetts, and she refused.

Semaan and Jenny never saw their two sons again, and they had four more children by the time they moved to California. Sarkis had once come to visit my grandmother, his half-sister, in California, long after his mother and father had died. I remembered a tearful reunion and a poor old man who spoke only Arabic trying to find his way around Los Angeles. No one in the family had ever met Sarkis's brother, Georges, until I first visited Zgharta in 1972. He was a wonderfully kind man, with a thick handlebar moustache, who had lived all his life in the village, a small farmer who also worked as a builder. He had died a few years earlier.

In the early 1970s, I used to visit my Uncle Sarkis in Tripoli, where he lived. I would always find him in a coffee house off Tripoli's central square, playing cards with his friends. He had a butcher's shop there until 1975. Then, Zgharta and Tripoli went to war. Muslim fanatics in Tripoli began hunting Maronites, especially those from Zgharta, to kill in the streets. Farouk Mukaddam, who commanded a secular, but mainly Sunni Muslim, militia in Tripoli, publicly executed some of those responsible for the pogroms. In the meantime, Uncle Sarkis lost his business and his house, and he and his wife hid at a Muslim friend's, like Jews in Europe during the war. When things became quiet, he moved back to Zgharta.

On Monday morning, I did not think there was much risk in going to see my relations on the other side of town. There was not much traffic along the main highway in Zgharta, but most shops had reopened. There were no gunmen or checkpoints. My cousin Hanna Zalloua, Sarkis's nephew who had returned to Lebanon from many years in Australia, took me to see our uncle in the Karam part of the village. Uncle Sarkis was more than eighty years old, but, like many old men in the mountains, he looked healthy and alert. He had a thin face and straight white hair. He looked a little like Father Ferrari in Antioch. He made us sit and drink coffee, and I had to tell him about cousins and aunts I had not seen in years, assuring him that they were all well. It was quiet outside, and the only sound was the deep voice of the old man saying how much he had enjoyed his trip to California twenty years before and how much he missed his half-sister, my grandmother. Visiting relations, a necessary part of my trips to the village, could take hours. I usually sat, drank coffee or tea, muttered a few assurances that everyone was well, and sat quietly wishing I had perfected my Arabic and hoping no one would bring me any Arabic sweets.

From Uncle Sarkis's house, Hanna Zalloua took me to see my cousin Theodore Makary, who lived in a valley just off the Tripoli road in the Makary section. The old family house was a pretty two-storey villa of yellow stone with a red tile roof and a large terrace. Nearby were his olive trees, from which the family made their own oil. He lived there with his wife, children, mother and sisters. His father, who was my grandmother's cousin, had left his wife and children in Zgharta when Theodore was a child and settled in California, where he found a new wife.

Theodore was receiving a lot of visitors himself. He was a colonel in the national police, and some policemen and men from the neighbourhood had come to find out from him what was happening with the feud. His younger brother, Lucien, was visiting from Beirut with his wife, Bahijah, and their children. Lucien's house was in the hills above east Beirut, near his army base.

"Are you crazy?" Lucien asked me when I arrived. The younger and feistier of the brothers, he was a stocky bull with short hair. Reckless himself, he urged caution on me every time we met.

"What have I done now?" I asked him.

"You should stay put in the Frangieh part until this is over."

"Why? Things seem to be getting back to normal."

"That's how they seem to you. What do *you* know?"

Theodore, older, thinner, more thoughtful and less daring than his brother, said, "I think it will get quiet. No one wants to fight any more."

"Is there much resentment against the Marada?" I asked.

"Some," Theodore said. "They're young boys with guns. They make mistakes, and the people here don't like it when boys from other villages carry arms in Zgharta. I think part of the compromise will be that the outsiders cannot go armed in the village."

"Why are people associating young Slaimie with these outsiders?"

"He has some good friends from the other villages, that's all."

"Tell me," I said to Lucien and Theodore. "You two knew Tony Frangieh. Was he corrupt?"

"Were the people who told you that Maronite?" Theodore asked.

"As a matter of fact, they were."

"Never believe what a Maronite tells you about another Maronite." In east Beirut, I had often heard accusations that Tony Frangieh had accumulated wealth by accepting bribes during his father's presidency. Then I met his banker, who told me that when Tony died there was no money in his account. What money he had collected went to his projects in Zgharta. He had been killed because Bechir Gemayel, younger son of the Phalangist Party leader, Pierre Gemayel, was consolidating his power over the Maronites. He killed Tony Frangieh in 1978 and massacred the militiamen of the Chamoun family the next year. By the time Israel invaded Lebanon in 1982, Bechir Gemayel had no serious armed rivals among the Maronites. He was elected president and assassinated a few days later. His death was not a vendetta on the part of the Frangiehs, but no tears were shed for him in Zgharta.

"But," I said, "Tony Frangieh was close to Rifaat Assad, who is more than a little notorious."

"Before the war," Theodore said, "Rifaat saw Lebanon as Monaco, and Tony was the prince."

"All the old Zgharta fighters who were loyal to his father are loyal to young Slaimie," Lucien said.

"Not to Robert?"

"Everyone knows Robert is a civilian. He is not a fighter, but he is good in politics. And he is trying to do something in the north, trying to keep it out of the war and to bring hospitals and schools."

"A kind of benevolent despotism?"

"Benevolent despotism," Theodore said, "is better than any kind of despotism we've ever had here. Do you know the last time the people of this area were asked what they wanted, the last time anyone asked them how they wanted to live?"

"No."

"Nineteen-nineteen, when the King–Crane Commission came from America," he said. "They asked all the people what they wanted. They all wanted a united Syria, democracy, no foreign mandates and no settlers from Europe to take over Palestine."

"No one listened."

"I wish," Theodore said, "they would send another commission. They could ask all of us what we want, and then we could come to a compromise. Why don't they?"

At the end of the First World War, the victors agreed to form an Inter-Allied Commission on Mandates in Turkey. Because Britain and France had already agreed to keep and divide the areas the Turks had left, they did not send any delegates. The United States, which had not been at war with Turkey, sent Charles R. Crane, a Chicago businessman, and Henry C. King, president of Oberlin College, to what was then called Syria to tour the entire area and ask people what post-war settlement they wanted. The King–Crane Commission began its investigations in June 1919. Over the next two months, the Commission visited thirty-six towns, received delegations from 1,520 villages and accepted 1,863 petitions from people living in the region between Alexandretta and Aqaba. More than eighty per cent of the presentations to King–Crane asked for a united Syria, and seventy-four per cent wanted independence rather than a Mandate. Sixty per cent asked for a "democratic, non-centralised, constitutional" monarchy. If Syria had to have a temporary period of foreign tutelage in self-government, the overwhelming majority of its people favoured a single Mandatory Power rather than a division into separate states. Sixty per cent preferred that the Mandatory Power be the United States, with Great

Britain a poor second. Only fourteen per cent, most of them Maronites, wanted France. Just over seventy-two per cent opposed Zionist colonisation and the separation of Palestine from the rest of Syria.

Its investigation completed, the King–Crane Commission recommended to the Paris Peace Conference of 1919 "that the unity of Syria be preserved, in accordance with the earnest petition of the great majority of the people of Syria . . . that Syria be placed under one Mandatory Power . . . that the Emir Feisal be made the head of the new Syrian state . . . [that there be] serious modification of the extreme Zionist Program for Palestine of unlimited immigration of Jews, looking finally to making Palestine distinctly a Jewish state." The commissioners concluded, "Anything else would be a betrayal of the Syrian people."

The people from Alexandretta to Aqaba received nothing they asked for. Instead, their post-Ottoman history has been marred by bloodily suppressed rebellions against the French and British, wars among themselves and against the state the Jewish settlers created, military dictatorships and, in Lebanon, civil war and the preservation of tribal loyalties that made blood feuds inevitable.

"Theodore," I said, "no one listened to King–Crane. Who would listen if they did it again?"

"We have the right to be heard."

I stayed for lunch at Theodore's, the usual minor feast of a dozen different *mezze* dishes, *kibbé*, rice, vegetables and, for me at least, *arak*. "I know you like *arak*, Charlie. I don't usually have it, but I will take a glass to keep you company," Theodore said. "My grandfather liked his *arak* too. He was the brother of your grandmother's father." I was never sure how I was related to most of my cousins, but no matter how distant they all treated me like a son or brother. "The old man, he was in his eighties, came downstairs one day and said, 'I'm going to die today, but don't worry. I am ready.' He sat outside on the terrace, and he asked for *kibbé* and some *arak*. My mother gave him some raw *kibbé* with bread and onion, and she poured out his *arak* with water and ice. He ate his lunch slowly. He kissed everyone goodbye and said he was very happy. Then he went upstairs for a nap. He died in his sleep."

Lucien invited me to stay at his house when I came to Beirut. I said I might stay with friends.

"No," he said, "you'll stay with me. That way, I can protect you."

I had often tried to find out about the Makary family land. Francis Makary had left all his land to his soon-to-be-born child, my grandmother. She had kept a caretaker on to look after the fields until her death. He had died a short time later. As one of her heirs, and the only one with any interest in Lebanon, I had once tried to register my claim. Before the war, I had spent a day in the land registry in Tripoli, looking through Ottoman documents to find what land I might be entitled to. Apparently, some cousins I had never met had taken the land, and they were reluctant to give it back. Records had been altered, and time had passed. I had visited an apple orchard in Ehden that one relation told me was mine, but so many of the documents had disappeared that it was difficult to prove whose land it was.

After lunch, Theodore gave me an old document, the 1830 deed, showing that most of the land between Ehden and Tripoli had once belonged to Francis Makary's father, my great-great-grandfather. My cousin Hanna offered to take me up to Ehden after lunch, and he, my uncle Sarkis and a friend of theirs named Abu Said drove me to Ehden to show me my grandmother's land. They disagreed among themselves as to its exact location, but Abu Said insisted it was just below the village. He pointed out a large, bare plot of earth, and said, "That is yours, there."

It looked pretty sad and neglected. All I had to do was prove it was mine, put up a little house and plant some apple trees. If anyone gave me trouble, I could always start a feud.

While I was having lunch at Theodore's, the Douaihys had gone into the local branch of the Banco do Brasil and ordered its manager, a Frangieh, to close. All the other banks in Zgharta reacted by closing in solidarity with the Banco do Brasil. So, the Douaihys had to let the Banco do Brasil reopen, or no one in Zgharta would have been able to cash a cheque. The village was rife with rumour. Some people blamed the feud on the Lebanese Forces, others on the Syrians. Everyone had his own theory, but no one could deny the potential that existed in the village, just as in all Lebanon, for disruption. How much came from within, and how much from outside, was all a matter of speculation.

"I want you to see my house," Robert said. "I have taken the prettiest house you have ever seen in Batroun. It is the only place I can go to to get away."

We got into his car, bodyguard in the back, and drove southwest through the hills to Batroun. We heard on the local radio that Rashid Karami had resigned as Lebanese prime minister. Karami had been prime minister many times. He was a Sunni Muslim from Tripoli, for the moment a political ally of the Frangiehs and of Syria. He said he was stepping down because his government, composed of rival warlords, had failed to meet in nine months.

I told Robert I had been discussing the feud with various people in Zgharta. Many people were hoping he would talk directly with Father Douaihy. "Don't worry," he said. "I have already decided to call him tonight to express my condolences."

"Someone said the Lebanese Forces might have been involved with the shooting," I said, repeating gossip I had heard. "Apparently, two of the culprits were in touch with the Lebanese Forces."

"I've already heard that too," Robert said. "The Marada had once arrested this employee of the Douaihys who started the shooting. He was wearing a Lebanese Forces uniform at the time, but they let him go."

Batroun lay on the coast just north of the line between the Syrian-held area and the little Marounistan to the south. Robert drove, down lanes barely wide enough for the car, to a small port. He stopped at a fisherman's cottage on the water. It was a typical Mediterranean villa of thick stone walls, vaulted ceilings, arched windows and green shutters under a red roof. He went there when he wanted to be alone, living in the most spartan of conditions. He showed me his sitting-room and kitchen, like any villager's with a few mats, a bare sink and gas stove, nothing like the Frangieh Palace.

We went outside, where about a dozen fishermen had just finished setting their nets out for the night. They all came over to greet Robert, shaking hands and patting him on the back. They were big, hearty people, bare-chested and tanned, the kind of seagoing men who had grilled fish and *arak* for breakfast. They offered us coffee and gave us chairs to sit on. They didn't ask Robert about the feud in the village. In fact, they did not mention politics. They talked about the damage done by floods the previous winter, and they were hoping for good fishing this spring and summer.

Neither they nor we had any way of knowing an Italian ship would dump toxic waste into their waters, poisoning a whole season's catch.

"I think a writer who comes to Lebanon should ask himself why there is so much violence here," said one of my cousins, who was driving me up the Kadisha Valley. "The area is violent. Relations are based on violence. The mountains are rocky. The people are rocky. When we get to Becharré, look at the faces. Look at the violence in the faces. They are not like the faces on the seashore."

"What do you mean?"

"The people of the coast are fat. They are more open. Life is easier. Here the people are thin and tough. They are suspicious."

"All of them?"

"You can meet people in these mountains who have never been as far as Beirut. You can meet people who know Fifth Avenue in Manhattan. They are all the same, fighters, warriors. They came from the Turkish mountains in the eighth century, fleeing religious persecution. They were not farmers. They were mercenaries. They took part in all wars. Everyone in Zgharta and Becharré carries a gun."

Becharré, another Maronite stronghold, was Zgharta's traditional rival. Zgharta was on the Maronite frontier with the Muslims of the coast, and Becharré was the bulwark against the Muslims of the Bekaa plain. I said to someone from Zgharta I had heard the Zghartawi did not like the people of Becharré. "That's not right," he said. "We hate them." Matters had not been made easier by the Phalange Party's choice of a military commander to lead the attack on Ehden, on 12 June, 1978, that had killed Tony Frangieh and his family. He was Samir Geagea, a native of Becharré. His presence at the head of the force gave the political struggle between the Frangiehs and the Phalange an added tribal dimension.

As we drove along, I saw a girl in a red dress walk past a shrine to Our Lady and bless herself. On the other side of the gorge, the village of Hasroun was a chessboard of houses with red roofs and green gardens, lovely stone buildings as yet untouched by concrete. "When you see red roofs in Lebanon," my cousin said, "it means the houses are old and that the aristocrats of the area were living in it."

I was escaping from the feud for a while by going up the Kadisha, the Maronites' Sacred Valley. Most historians agreed the Maronites had settled there in the tenth century. The founder of their sect, St Maroun, lived in the Orontes Valley in the early fifth century. The Kadisha Valley was their first refuge, when the Byzantines began to persecute them for their non-Orthodoxy. Other Maronites found a refuge from Byzantium with the tolerant Muslims of Aleppo. When the Crusaders established the County of Tripoli in the eleventh century, they found the Maronites sometimes reliable, sometimes treacherous local allies. The Maronites saw in the Crusaders, as they would a millennium later in the French, the Syrians, the Israelis and the Americans, outsiders who would help them against the Muslims and against each other. In 1180, the Maronites unified with the Roman Catholic Church, and later an almost mystical relationship was born between the Maronites and "mother France."

The Maronites would slowly migrate south along the ridges of Mount Lebanon, ultimately into areas where other religious minorities, the Shiites and Druze, dwelled. Druze landlords, whose own peasants were too few in number to provide all the silk Europe wanted to buy from Lebanon, invited them. Sometimes, the Maronites would live in peace, sometimes they would displace the earlier arrivals, and sometimes they would be forced to retreat, although never for long. Eventually, they would have the confidence to move to the seacoast, abandoning mountain farming for fishing and trading, living among people of all sects.

Even as their centre of gravity moved south to Kesrouan and Beirut, the Maronites' spiritual home would remain the Kadisha, the Sacred, Valley. More of a gorge than a valley, its steep cliffs ascended from the rapids below to forests of umbrella pines on the summits. Waterfalls dropped down the sheer face of the mountain, apparently lost in an infinite abyss below. From the Cedars to the sea, the thirty miles of narrow valley was not easy territory for an invading army. A few mountaineers could hold off a substantial force, yet parts of it had been sacked by Shiites and Ottomans, at a cost, in the nineteenth century. Wherever it was humanly possible, and in places where it was not, farmers had constructed terraces to plant their orchards, generations of rock walls clinging to the mountain, holding the rich soil that had been the Maronites' only wealth until this century. A string of Maronite villages ran from Zgharta in the west, up the Kadisha Valley, to Ehden, Becharré and the Cedars, where Lebanon's largest grove of the national tree was, like the country itself, dying. At the Cedars, the Maronite homeland ended, and the road dropped down the eastern slope of the mountain to the Bekaa Valley.

In the Kadisha, we drove through tiny Christian villages along the twisting road east into the higher mountains. Most Maronite churches had flat roofs with steeples at the side, simple constructions like the old peasant cottages, but in Arbé there was a surprising construction, shaped exactly like a New England country church, but of stone rather than wood, red tiles rather than black shingles on the V-shaped roof, and a belfry in the centre.

We turned down a side road into the Valley of the Hermits. In the rock-face at certain points, hermits had carved crosses to indicate where they had lived in small caves. Beyond was the Monastery of St Antoine de Qashayya, where monks had lived since medieval times, although the monastery was constructed only in the last century. There, a taciturn young monk agreed to give me a tour. "Monks have been here since 1000 AD, perhaps earlier," the monk said. "There are only five or six monks here now, but more come in the summer." He led me first to a large grotto. It was a church, like St Peter's above Antioch, with a new façade, put there by pious and more prosperous monks in 1865. It had lovely arches made in alternating layers of fine light and dark stone, typical of late Ottoman Christian and Muslim architecture, with three large bells above. Inside, the monks had laid marble on the floors and built arched stonework over the sanctuary at the back. The steps up to the altar were in red marble, and there was an oil portrait of St Maroun behind the altar. Water dripped from the roof of the cave into large pans left discreetly in the right places on the floor.

In the plaza in front of the church, a score of teenage boys and girls ran around a large fountain. Some of them went inside to explore the holy grotto. When an Antonine sister, who seemed to be in charge, rang one of the church bells, they all followed her to a little park outside the monastery walls.

The young monk took me into the cloisters and proudly showed me what he said was the first printing press in Syria. In 1610, this press had produced a book of Psalms, the first of thousands of prayer books distributed to the faithful. The original printed works in the Arab world had been in Syriac script because the Ottomans prohibited the printing of Arabic, the sacred language of the Koran, until the early eighteenth century. The monk demonstrated that the press still worked. He took a plate with wooden handset Syriac, or *Karshuni*, letters, rolled ink over it and set it in the press. Then he turned the handle to imprint the plate on a piece of parchment, raising the plate again to reveal the large black script on the page below. It was part of an 1864 edition of the Letters of St Paul. The ingenious old machine, the marvel of its age, had a metal eagle standing guard on top.

We went on to a room filled with monkish memorabilia: the relics of the recently canonised St Charbel Makhlouf in a monstrance given the monks by Empress Eugénie; another monstrance with a fragment of the True Cross; four-hundred-year-old hand-made vestments, with gold embroidery of Jesus and the angels, a gift from Pope Gregory XVI; a silver censer; the patriarchal caps of Patriarch Salim Rizk and his brother Youssef; and the staff of the Maronite Patriarch of Antioch and the East. "King Louis IX left this staff," the monk said. "He came to Cyprus in 1248 and sent the staff for the monks to offer prayers for the soldiers who died on his Crusade." It was this French king, St Louis, who declared, "We are persuaded that this nation, which we find established here under the name of St Maroun, is a part of the French nation, for its love of France resembles the love which Frenchmen bear one another."

We went into another cave below the monastery, where the anchorite symbol had been etched into the rock. I followed the monk on into another, darker cavern. "This was the grotto of the mad," the monk said. "They used to lock them up and leave them here." The English travel writer E. S. Stevens wrote in *Cedars, Saints and Sinners in Syria* that by the nineteen-twenties and under French Mandate, the monks would release their patients within thirty days if no miracle took place. Before then, they might wait forever for St Anthony to cure them. Near a new altar were sets of old manacles, relics of an age when innocent people could be chained by their hands and feet and forgotten.

The monk went back to his duties, and I walked through the park where the teenage children had gone to have a picnic. They were playing Lebanese folk music, and the girls were dancing the *dabke*, some of them atop the picnic tables, arms linked, kicking their feet in the air. The nun who had brought them up from Beirut seemed glad they could escape the war for a weekend in their ancestors' mountains. Their laughter and music would have pleased the Greeks who had worshipped Adonis in these hills, but the hermits buried here would have seen the children's surrender to worldly pleasures in another light.

A few hermits still dwelt in the valley, but I did not see any. I wanted to visit a locally famous holy man who lived in a little cave nearby, but I was advised not to disturb his solitude. Lebanon needed his prayers.

We went on towards Becharré through the village of Hadshit. "This is a very tough place, like a slum," my cousin said. "They drink lots of *arak* here. On September 4th, the feast of St Romanos, the butcher got so drunk here that he slaughtered a donkey instead of a cow. Many of the men from here work as fighters in Beirut." I remembered my cousin Theodore's words, "Never believe what a Maronite tells you about another Maronite." The houses were rundown and built one touching the other, as though in a city. They could not have been more different from the picture-postcard villages on the other side. In Hadshit, we came to the first Syrian checkpoint, an indication we had left the Syrian-protected principality of Zgharta and entered the area of real Syrian occupation. The soldiers waved us through.

Becharré, despite the Zghartawi antipathy for it, was a beautiful village. There was no superhighway as in Zgharta, and most of the houses were traditional yellow, green and red – yellow stone, red roofs and green slatted shutters. Becharré was smaller than Zgharta, but it had a legacy: the village received all the royalties from sales of the books of its émigré son, Gibran Khalil Gibran, known as Kahlil Gibran in the West.

In 1975, the village opened a Gibran Museum in the abandoned Monastery of St Sergius. Before then, Gibran's personal effects had been on display in his family's house in the middle of the village. The museum's director was a passionate, vigorous man named Wahib Kairouz. Bald in front, with late 1960s long hair at the back, he would swing his arms about and almost sing as he talked about Gibran. He kept the blue flame of Gibran's memory alive, cataloguing his manuscripts, researching his life, writing essays and books about his work and talking gleefully to rare visitors like myself about Becharré's most famous poet and artist. The museum was closed for the time being, but he was pleased to show it to me anyway.

"Gibran was born here in 1883," Kairouz said, as we strolled through the monastery's gardens. "If you want to understand his mysticism, you see it in these hills, in these forests, in the grottoes, in the Roman theatre. Gibran wandered through these hills, and he knew the Phoenician tombs. In his writing and his painting, the grottoes, the hills, they are all symbols from this region. The Dream of Jesus is on this very walk. He spent time in this monastery with the monks."

"Was Gibran really a mystic?" I asked him, thinking how practical most Lebanese were in business and war.

"His mystical side crystallised here. In *The Prophet*, he returns to the Orient. It was an illuminating return. Perhaps he found in the life of the monks here an ideal. He knew a certain monk, Brother Mikhail, who works in The Dream of Jesus cutting a tree. Brother Mikhail, Tanyous in The Dream of Jesus, carved in a rock here, 'I am afraid of temptation. If I work, the Devil cannot come.' This was Gibran's first lesson in mysticism."

"Are you a mystic too?"

"I understand it. I have read the traditions of this monastery. An old Carmelite showed me the secret grottoes and Brother Mikhail's rock. This place began as a hermitage in 1501, when the monks lived in the grottoes. I am a son of the Kadisha. Despite the problems in Lebanon, in Becharré, I have never renounced it. Becharré is the fatherland, the country of my heart."

"Don't you ever think about leaving, especially with the war and your museum closed?"

"As a writer and as a man, I can't live anywhere but under this sky."

We went inside the monastery and up a rock staircase that wound and wound as though up a tower. We reached a small room, like a monk's cell with a tiny window, that was little more than an alcove with a desk and some books. It was Kairouz's office, where he studied and wrote about the art of Kahlil Gibran. We had some coffee, and he let me read through some of Gibran's manuscripts. Gibran had written his first works in Arabic. After the publication of *The Madman* in 1918, all his works were in English. His family had emigrated to Boston in 1895, but sent him back to school in Mount Lebanon in 1897 for five years. Salma Haffar al-Kuzbari had told me in Damascus about Gibran and May Ziadah, and I asked Wahbi Kairouz about their unconsummated love.

"Why do you say 'unconsummated'?"

"They never met."

He said, "There is more than one means of consummation."

During his five years' study in Lebanon, Gibran fell in love with Hoda Dagher, fifteen-year-old daughter of the *bayk* of Becharré. This love too was unconsummated in conventional terms and made the young poet bitter. Gibran's father had been one of the men who sat in the *bayk*'s house, as men sat still in the Frangieh Palace, waiting to do favours and run errands. His job was to count and collect taxes on the goats in Becharré for the *bayk*, who was horrified when the son of his servant professed love for his daughter. One of the Dagher descendants told me Hoda Dagher had loved Gibran, which may have annoyed her father even more, and died a lonely spinster.

Leafing through the Gibran opus, I came across a story, "Khalil the Heretic," that must have been inspired by his hatred of the system that separated him from Hoda:

Sheik Abbas was looked upon as a prince by the people of a solitary village in North Lebanon. His mansion stood in the midst of those poor villagers' huts like a healthy giant amidst sickly dwarfs. He lived amid luxury while they pursued an existence of penury . . . His anger would make them tremble and scatter like autumn leaves before a strong wind. If he were to slap one's face, it would be heresy on the individual's part to move or lift his head or make any attempt to discover why the blow had come. If he smiled at a man, the villagers would consider the person thus honoured as the most fortunate. The people's fear and surrender to Sheik Abbas was not due to weakness; however, their poverty and need of him had brought about this state of continual humiliation. Even the huts they lived in and the fields they cultivated were owned by Sheik Abbas who had inherited them from his ancestors.

"Since the beginning of the creation and up to our present time," Gibran wrote,

certain clans, rich by inheritance, in cooperation with the clergy, had appointed themselves the administrators of the people. It is an old, gaping wound in the heart of society that cannot be removed except by intense removal of ignorance.

Not only did Sheik Abbas die wretched and alone, in this tale, but the hero got the sheikh's daughter and lived happily ever after. In life, Kahlil never saw Hoda again. The sheikhs and *bayks* went on ruling, no matter who their overlords were in Constantinople, Paris, Damascus or Beirut. Gibran returned to live in New York, where his unhappiness and mysticism produced his most successful work, *The Prophet*, and more than twenty other books of poetry and prose. In *The Prophet*, this troubled soul wrote,

Love has no other desire but to fulfil itself.
But if you love and must needs have desires, let these be your desires:
To melt and be like a running brook that sings its melody to the night.
To know the pain of too much tenderness.
To be wounded by your own understanding of love;
And to bleed willingly and joyfully.

Like Hoda Dagher and May Ziadah, Gibran never married. Maronite priests excommunicated him from their church, and he died in New York in 1931. His body was brought to Becharré for burial.

"Here is Gibran's tomb," Wahib Kairouz said, taking me downstairs and leading me to an opening in the rock wall that revealed a lighted chamber. A carved stone sarcophagus wrapped in chains lay on the floor, bound as though to stop Gibran's body from soaring in death as his spirit had in life.

On the other side were Gibran's simple wooden bed, writing-table and easel, all of which I had seen before 1975 in Gibran's house. In an alcove above the bed was a Crucifix. The floor was tiled, but part of the room was still a cave. "This is an Armenian tapestry that Gibran bought," Kairouz said of a large and strange Crucifixion scene hanging on one wall. "It was made by a Father Yaqoub." The eyes of Christ on his cross stared at us. He was surrounded by mourners, among whom were the two thieves, all of whom had Mongolian features. Angels on either side of the Redeemer were catching the blood as it dripped from His hands.

Where the Kadisha River began its tortuous path to the Mediterranean, the snows were melting. Sunlight caught the waterfalls in mid-air, casting small rainbows all along the mountain. Water was everywhere, in thin rivulets on the road, dripping from rocks above, overflowing from ancient aqueducts and falling down the slopes to the river. We reached the Cedars, the ancient grove now an encampment for Syrian soldiers. "I was at first disappointed in the appearance of these forest saints," Eliot Warburton wrote in 1845:

> I had expected to have seen them scattered along the mountain
> that they consecrated, each standing apart like a vegetable
> cathedral: but here was a snug, compact little brotherhood,
> gathered together in the most social group; no other tree was visible
> within several miles.

Warburton counted twelve ancient cedars, but he saw a thousand beginning to grow. He did not know it, but the young trees were dying because goats ate the saplings. When Queen Victoria was told the ancient trees, mentioned so often in the Bible and from which Solomon was said to have built his temple, were in danger of extinction, she financed a stone wall to keep the goats out. The wall still stood, a few stones missing in places, and there were now about four hundred trees, far more than the sixteen Henry Maundrell had counted in his *A Journey from Aleppo to Jerusalem at Easter* 1697. Now the cedars were facing a new danger, one for which a wall was no easy solution – tiny worms called *thaumetopea libanotica* that laid their eggs in the roots and at the fabric of the tree from within. The cedar was an age-old symbol of Lebanon, used on the national flag and so many militias' flags as well. To me, the worms rather than the mighty trees were an appropriate symbol for the militias, eating the fabric of the country until it withered and died.

We drove back towards Zgharta, and I decided to stop on the way and spend a night in Ehden. European travellers of the last few centuries had taken Ehden to be the Eden of Genesis, a fertile mountain garden from which all mankind had been exiled. I arrived out of season, when most of the houses were empty and awaiting the arrival of their owners from Zgharta. Unlike Zgharta, Ehden had not discovered the late twentieth century's preoccupation with concrete. It still looked much as it had in Ottoman times, rows of stone houses, little grocers' and the shops of butchers who slaughtered their sheep on the premises, a central plaza with arcades around it, where in summer people drank coffee and promenaded.

In front of the Church of St George was a statue of Youssef Bayk Karam, whom the Zghartawi revered as a warrior-saint in the Crusader mould, mounted on an Arab stallion. In 1860, this celibate and pious man, rosary in one hand and sword in the other, led his followers out of Zgharta to save the embattled Christians of Zahle from destruction by the Druze. Through the efforts of the French consul and rival Maronite leaders in the Kesrouan, Karam and his mounted column were stopped by Turkish forces before they reached Zahle.

In 1866, Karam's cavalry fought the Ottomans and the new "Lebanese" gendarmes under Daoud Pasha. The Turks attacked Zgharta, but Karam's followers held Ehden and counter-attacked, reaching nearly as far as the outskirts of Tripoli. Despite the early success, Karam found himself opposed by fellow Maronites from Kesrouan, who helped the Turks to crush his revolt. In January 1867, Karam left Lebanon in a French warship for exile in Algiers. He died near Naples in 1889 without ever again seeing his native mountains. His loyal followers brought his body home, and preserved it under glass in a casket in St George's Church.

Ehden had a nice hotel, La Mairie, whose staff told me to see the new discothèque, the Magnum. "People come all the way from Beirut to dance here," they said. I walked across the hotel's car park, through a lavish entryway and into the underground night club. It was a pleasant place, with flashing lights set in the dance floor, a long, well- stocked bar and an expensive sound system. But it was empty. I went back to the lobby and said to the receptionist, "It looks like a good discothèque, but there's no one there."

"It's only ten thirty. Nobody comes before midnight."

This was in a remote village in a "primitive" land in the midst of a war that had begun twelve years earlier. The receptionist sounded like the doorman at Annabel's. "Nobody comes before midnight." I said I would go up to my room to read and return at midnight. "Or wait until one or two, when all the good-looking chicks come," he advised me.

I took out the copy of *Pride and Prejudice* Alishan had given me at the Baron's in Aleppo. "What are men to rocks and mountains?" I read, thoughts Jane Austen had put in the mind of her heroine, Elizabeth Bennet, who was planning a journey she would not be able to make. "Oh! what hours of transport we shall spend! And when we *do* return, it shall not be like other travellers, without being able to give an accurate idea of any thing. We *will* know where we have gone – we *will* recollect what we have seen." I fell asleep reading and missed the opportunity to dance with "the good-looking chicks" in the Magnum, the last of whom I heard leaving when I woke in the morning.

It was dawn when I noticed a little light coming in the shutters. I got out of bed and opened the window, letting in the cool spring air. I saw mountain tops glistening with snow, the sheer cliff faces at the summits giving way on their descent to terraced hillsides. The steep valley below was a tableau of white, pink and red, the blossom of apple, peach and cherry. Two small villages, stone houses huddled around their churches, perched precariously on the hilltops opposite. The sun was coming over the mountains to the east, and the sky was clear blue. The snow was beginning to melt on the higher terraces, as it had in the valley below, and by summer even the summit of Mount Lebanon would be bare. Sheep were grazing in the fields, jumping over the rocky walls that divided one family's smallholding from another's. The flock followed their shepherd from pasture to pasture, like an ancient army blindly foraging its way from conquest to conquest, a dog barking at its flanks like a master-sergeant. This view changed with the seasons, not the years. It must have been the same when Turks ruled and my grandmother first opened her eyes on a world she could not have known was about to die.

The evening I returned to Zgharta, I went to dinner in the Karam part of town, at the house of my cousin Tannous Zalloua. Tannous, a nickname for Antonius, was Hanna's brother. Their sister, Thérèse, was married to a Karam, and another brother and sister lived in Australia. Tannous made his living as a driver, and he was a short, stocky, handsome man with a placid nature. He was a devout Maronite. When he used to drive me in the mountains, he would stop at shrines to the Blessed Virgin and say a prayer. I had always thought of him as a pacific man, one I had never heard raise his voice or lose his temper. While I was waiting for Tannous to pick me up from the Frangieh Palace, one of the Marada asked where I was going.

"Tannous Zalloua is your cousin? Abu B'zoubé?" he asked, surprised.
"Abu B'zoubé was one of the best fighters in the Two Years' War," the man went on. For Zgharta, the civil war began in 1975, against the Palestinians in and around Tripoli, and ended in 1976, when the Syrian army arrived. Many Zghartawi called that time the Two Years' War. "He was very brave, always at the front. You are lucky to have a cousin like that."

Tannous had never mentioned to me that he had fought in the war, let alone bragged about his courage. When we got into his Mercedes, I noticed for the first time a bulge under his jacket where he kept a pistol. As he drove past one of Zgharta's many Maronite churches he made the sign of the Cross.

He had moved out of his old house near the river into a modern flat. The large couches and chandeliers of the bourgeoisie had replaced his simple peasant furnishings, but he still had a calendar in the kitchen with a picture of Youssef Beyk Karam. His wife gave us a delicious dinner, including a light pastry with melted cheese inside, *sheesh barak*, and stuffed vine leaves, *waraq areesh*, prepared in a way made only in Zgharta. The leaves were wrapped very tightly around bits of rice and lamb and cooked in a large pot with small lamb bones. For some reason, the vine leaves made me think of my grandmother, who had cooked them exactly as if she had never left the village. They had several guests to dinner, my cousin Hanna, another cousin I had not met before named Paulette, a shopkeeper and an ophthalmologist. The ophthalmologist wore a suit that, had it been dark, would have glowed.

We spent the evening talking, much as if we had been in Yusuf Basha, about family matters. They knew the names of all their relations in America, relations that they, not to mention I, had never met. They wanted to know whether their relations were in good health, who had married whom, how many children each had, whether anyone had died or, worse, been divorced. They told me about different relations in Lebanon and Australia. No one mentioned the feud, although the Zallouas were cousins of the mother of one of the dead Douaihys.

When I returned to the palace, Robert was upstairs in his parents' house playing *quatorze*, a card game similar to gin, with a friend. He seemed tired. "I called Father Douaihy," he said. "So did Slaimie. We are going to see him next week. My God, I've been trying all this time to defuse the situation and not worry my father. But if someone outside is behind it, we won't be able to contain it here, because they will try to stir it up again."

When the sun rose, Zgharta looked beautiful. It was difficult to imagine anyone would want to disturb the peace of a spring morning like that.

"Spring is beautiful everywhere," Kahlil Gibran had written in *The Broken Wings*, "but it is most beautiful in Lebanon. It is a spirit that roams round the earth but hovers over Lebanon, conversing with kings and prophets, singing with the rivers the songs of Solomon, and repeating with the Holy Cedars of Lebanon the memory of ancient glory." The flowers in the garden and on the hillsides were in the full bloom of spring. I smelled the jasmine growing outside my window, and, from the kitchen, there was the smell of Turkish coffee brewing.

In the dining-room, I had breakfast and heard on the radio that the teachers were on strike; nowhere but in Lebanon could that be a sign of a kind of normality. In Zgharta, there was still tension, but the kettle was cooling. Twenty or thirty years earlier, no one would have been able to subdue the passions that erupted when men of one family killed those of another. In the last century, the Turks had found it difficult to fight the Zghartawi in their mountains: they had found it relatively simple to get them to kill one another. In the past few years, the Syrians, Israelis and others had made the same discovery about the Lebanese as a whole. There had been small outbreaks of Frangieh–Douaihy fighting since 1957, but, with no outside involvement, each conflict had been quickly resolved. The inevitable question on everyone's lips was, was the inspiration from inside or outside? There were so many arms in the village, so many ambitions. The intermediaries themselves were not disinterested spectators. Each had his own motives and intentions. That was one reason why those directly involved had to talk face to face. Everyone feared, but was prepared for, another incident, another round.

At 10:30, Israeli planes above us broke the sound barrier, causing sonic booms. The Israelis, as their spokesmen said, owned the skies of Lebanon. They would overfly often to remind the Lebanese and the Syrians they were there. I assumed they were flying by because of Rashid Karami's resignation as prime minister, rather than because of the feud in Zgharta.

Before lunch, Robert was talking in the sitting-room with the usual collection of retainers and visitors. Two journalists, who worked for a French-language Lebanese magazine, had come up from Beirut. The reporter, a young Lebanese woman, and the French photographer said they had come to Zgharta to cover "the events." They were asking Robert what had happened, and he was trying to play the whole thing down.

"We were not having problems with the Douaihys," he said. "In fact, Father Douaihy was visiting me at about the time the trouble broke out."

One of the household staff walked into the living-room and announced, "The president is here for lunch."

We all got up to greet the old man, who looked tired but healthy. He kissed his children and shook hands with the guests. For the first time since my arrival, Suleiman Bayk Frangieh took his place at the table. Mme Frangieh sat opposite him, and I was between her and Robert. There were also Lamia and Roderigue, Maya and the two journalists. The patriarch in his white cardigan ate slowly, discussed the failure of the last round of Lebanese–Syrian negotiations and occasionally switched on one of the radios in front of him to hear the news.

In the late afternoon, my cousin Theodore and a few friends arrived to play cards with President Frangieh. It seemed the old man was well enough not only for lunch, but for poker. A year later, he would be healthy enough to run again for president. Robert and I went to his dining-room to play gin. We played three games, and he won them all. He played by slightly different, Zgharta, rules. I felt somehow that my grandmother, who had taught me to play, would have been disappointed to see me lose to a Frangieh. The family honour was preserved, however, upstairs, where my cousin Theodore was winning at poker.

We were beginning another game when a young man came in and said, "The Syrians have arrived." A group of Syrian officers, no doubt alerted about the feud, had come to call. President Frangieh's poker game could not be interrupted, so Robert went up to the house to receive them, telling me, "You can play *quatorze* with Joseph."

Joseph was his cousin, a pleasant older man in a grey suit. He shuffled and dealt the cards. Thinking I might do better against Joseph than I had against Robert, I asked him, "Do you play cards much?"

"I was the director of the Casino du Liban."

In the early evening, I sat with President Frangieh in his study. He was in a large chair in front of his green baize poker table. The old man's thick glasses, his pronounced ears and lips, had provided the motif for hundreds of Lebanese editorial cartoons, in which the president was often portrayed as a thundering mountaineer. He had amber worry beads and smoked Lebanese filter cigarettes. The shelves behind him were filled with books in Arabic and French on hunting, guns, dogs, horses and birds. A cocker spaniel slept at his feet. Three televisions and half a dozen radios enabled him not to miss a single news broadcast. His languages were Arabic and French, so we spoke in French as best I could. I asked him where the five families came from.

"The first family known here by the name they use now were the Douaihy," he said. "In the seventeenth century, you find the name Karam. Then the Moawad and Frangieh."

"What about the Makarys?" I asked him, wondering when we entered the scene.

"They have been here just as long, but their involvement in politics is more recent."

"Where do the Frangiehs come from?"

"There is a story, it may be only a legend, or it may be true, I don't know," he said. "There was a brother of Archbishop Sayhuni, who went to France and the court of Louis XIV. He married a Frenchwoman, and when he died, she raised her children in Zgharta. They called her, and her children, the Frank, or the foreigner, which in Arabic is Frangieh." The Douaihy family said their ancestors were also French, from Douai.

"So you're part French."

"Maybe. When we were in Geneva for the Lebanese peace conference, we went over the border to France for lunch. We drove to a little village on the road called Franchi. It was a lovely village of fifty houses, not more, in a very beautiful location. I asked if there were a restaurant there, and the people in the village said there was. We went there, to a small restaurant. There were twelve of us at the table in a room not much larger than this. We looked at the menu. I asked for an omelette for my first course. The proprietress said, 'No. Have the meat.' I assumed she didn't have any eggs. So, she brought meat for everyone. Then she brought everyone an omelette. So, she did have eggs. After we ate, I asked her, 'Madame, why did you insist everyone have meat, then eggs, rather than what we ordered?' She said, 'I am the proprietress here, and you will eat what I give you.' I said to my family in Arabic, 'Now can you doubt that we are from here?'"

He stopped talking to hear the news on one of his radios and resumed, "You know, don't you, that Makary means 'shepherd'?" When the next radio report mentioned the Palestine Liberation Organisation, President Frangieh told me about his last meeting with Yasser Arafat. It took place at the height of the civil war, just before the end of his term as president. My friend Hany Salaam was with the PLO chairman. "I said to Arafat, 'Tell me one thing before you go. Do you believe in death?' He said, 'Why? Don't you?' 'Of course, I do, but I wanted to hear you tell me one honest thing before you leave.'"

Later, he said Arafat was an Israeli agent.

"Why do you say that?"

"He's done more harm to the Palestinians than anyone else," he said. I could see he was sincere in his belief. "Did you see the article in Le Nouvel Observateur on Arafat's work for Israel? Read it."

He may have disliked Arafat, but he hated the Israelis and distrusted the Americans. I remembered that he had told me proudly when I went to Zgharta just after the Israeli invasion that the Lebanese would launch a guerrilla war against Israel. "Lebanon," he had predicted, "will be Israel's graveyard." So it was, until the Israeli army withdrew from most of Lebanon two years later. He insisted the United States wanted the Christians out of Lebanon, saying that at the beginning of the civil war the

American diplomat L. Dean Brown had come to the presidential palace and told him of a US plan to evacuate the Maronites. He accused America of blind loyalty to Israel and insisted it would never help the Lebanese or Palestinians. When I reminded him that President Eisenhower had forced Israel to pull out of the Sinai Peninsula in 1957, he answered, "*Mais Eisenhower était un vrai président, pas un . . . un . . .*" He put down the whisky and water he was drinking that evening in 1982, searching for a word to describe Ronald Reagan. ". . . *pas un valet.*"

"Do you think the feud is over?" I asked him.

"Nearly."

"How could you stop it?"

"It's easier these days than when I was a young man," he said. "Now we can speak directly and quickly on the telephone. We can keep everyone informed. We can contain the passions."

The Frangieh–Douaihy feud had not ended, but the kettle was cool when, reluctantly, I left Zgharta. I said farewell to my relations, to the Frangiehs and to friends who would soon be going up to Ehden, their original home in Lebanon, for the summer. I decided to go home too, to my family in London, for two weeks, before continuing with what I planned to be the second half of my journey.

Because the airport in Muslim west Beirut was unsafe for Americans, I went to the Lebanese Forces' port at Jounieh and took a ship to Cyprus. In London, I heard news of a car bomb in Zgharta. A small bomb exploded in the centre of the village, when President Amin Gemayel came to Zgharta for a meeting with President Frangieh. When people ran to find the dead and rescue the wounded, a second, larger bomb went off, killing several more. I called Zgharta to see if everyone I knew had survived. Theodore told me, "Bahijeh's cousin Yamine was killed." Bahijeh was the wife of my cousin Lucien, and, somehow, in the tangled roots and branches of family and blood in the village, Yamine Moawad was my cousin too.

A few days later, I sailed back to Lebanon.

CHAPTER TWENTY-ONE

THE GHETTO

It was a clear, warm morning when the ship brought me from Cyprus back to Lebanon. The hills above the Bay of Jounieh were dotted green with umbrella pines amid large swathes of freshly cut earth and stone, where new roads connected towns and villages within the enclave known to its inhabitants as Free Lebanon and to its detractors as Marounistan. It was the only place in Lebanon where a kind of order prevailed and nearly the only area not under Syrian or Israeli occupation. It stretched from east Beirut north along the coast, taking in the Bay of Jounieh, the hills of Kesrouan province and the coastal village of Jebail, ending along the ridge of Mount Lebanon in the east and just south of Tripoli in the north. The Syrian army surrounded it on three sides, and its only precarious link to the outside world was across the sea.

The little village of Jounieh had grown well beyond its intended proportions during the war, when it gradually replaced Beirut as the centre of Christian commerce. It had become the unofficial capital of Marounistan, or Free Lebanon. Just above the expanded harbour stood a beautiful old Ottoman house, which many years before had become an indifferent restaurant called *La Crêpèrie*. Most of the other old houses that previously made Jounieh a picturesque fishing port had long since vanished to make way for modern offices, hotels and shopping centres. Jounieh's wartime growth had been inexorable, as Christians left their houses near the front lines in the capital for the relative safety of the central shore. Jounieh had made money out of the war, but at the price of becoming uninhabitable with constant traffic jams and hideous architecture.

The Lebanese Forces militia had constructed a new jetty to accommodate ferries from Cyprus and arms deliveries from around the world. The little jollyboats no longer came out to the cruise ships to collect people and cargo. Passengers on the Cyprus ferry disembarked on land, where scores of taxis and hundreds of relations were waiting for them.

We arrived at seven in the morning, when the dockside erupted into a scene of crying, hugging, kissing, passing of presents back and forth, shouting and thrusting of children into waiting arms like trophies hard-won in athletic competition. The Lebanese found it nearly impossible to conceal emotion, whether they felt it or not. The scene of reunion, as though Odysseus himself had come home, was more cheering than the farewells that would take place later that night, when those departing the self-annihilating land knew they might never return.

A long row of taxis was parked outside the gate of the port. The drivers, impatient as their colleagues at the airport in west Beirut, jostled for custom. Foreigners, few as we must have been, were a better catch than returning Lebanese who knew the fares. Several drivers tried to take my two little black bags and force me into their cars. I settled for a young man who drove me out of the port and along the coast road south towards Beirut. He told me he had come from Iklim al-Kharroub, a largely Christian area in south Lebanon overrun three years before by Muslims and Druze. He had lost his house, his uncle's family had been killed and his own family survived as refugees, technically "displaced persons" within their country, far from home on the Christian coastal strip between Beirut and Tripoli.

He told me he was getting married in fifteen days. His fiancée was a naturalised Australian from Lebanon. He said they would move to Australia. "What will you do there?"

"For work? Barber, taxi driver, carpenter . . ."

It didn't seem to matter. He was not seeking a career, just a way out and the chance to live where his house was unlikely to be destroyed again. He seemed good-natured, a young male who showed the normal Mediterranean interest in young women. On our way, a girl crossing the road stopped him for a chat. In Arabic, he told her, "I'll be back here to see you in an hour."

I assumed that, though engaged, he was exercising the traditional right of the Lebanese male to philander his way through marriage, but I had misjudged him. He drove on, waved farewell to her and then said to me, "I won't be back. I'm getting married, so no more women."

From the northern outskirts of Beirut, he drove me up the hill to Baabda, past the old Serail, the palace from which the Turks had ruled this part of the mountain, and dropped me at the house of my cousin Lucien Makary. Lucien and his wife were out. The maid, an attractive Muslim girl from north Lebanon, gave me some tea and breakfast. I took a long, restless nap after my sleepless night on the ship, and I heard two loud explosions that shook the bedroom windows. Later, my cousin Lucien said in answer to my question that the sounds must have come from a battle between the Christian Lebanese Forces and the Druze Progressive Socialist Party in the mountains behind us. Or maybe it was something else. Not that it mattered.

I awakened in the early afternoon and took a taxi from Baabda down to Ashrafieh in east Beirut. Ashrafieh was the Maronite quarter *par excellence*, near what had become the front line. It had originally been settled in the nineteenth century by Greek Orthodox families who had made enough money in trade to leave their houses on the shore near the Syrian Protestant College, which became the American University of Beirut, for the slightly cooler air of the suburbs. In late nineteenth-century postcards and photographs of Ashrafieh, grand palaces in white or yellow stone dominated the hill over Beirut's harbour. Around the baroque and Ottoman palaces were gardens of rich Greek Orthodox families, like the Bustroses, Sursocks and Tueinis. The Seven Families, as the newly wealthy Beirut Christians were called, were connected by trade, intrigue and marriage with one another and the minor aristocracy and the rising bourgeoisie of the rest of the 19th-century Mediterranean. They prospered under the protection of foreign consuls, including the British, French, Austro-Hungarian, Russian and American, whom they served as dragomen. In the nineteenth century, Beirut was their city, shared with Sunni Muslim traders. The Sultan bestowed on Orthodox and Sunni alike aristocratic titles like bayk, effendi and pasha. In the twentieth century, Maronites moved down from the mountain, surrounding the Greek Orthodox palaces with small houses, then apartment blocks, becoming the majority in the quarter. Later, Ashrafieh became the front-line Christian defence against Muslims, Palestinians and Syrians.

The taxi took me through the old streets to a beautiful Ottoman house called the Tueini Palace. Although the house belonged to the Bustros family, they had inherited it through their paternal grandmother, a Tueini. In the narrow road in front, a man pushed a barrow of vegetables chanting in Arabic, "Cucumbers, tomatoes, onions . . ." The family had since independence rented their own "Bustros Palace" to the government for a small rent as the foreign ministry. The Tueini Palace in which they lived was an impressive house behind iron and stone gates. Built of large, yellow stone, it was a cross between a Roman palazzo and a Turkish caravanserai. Stone lions in a garden of palms guarded the oasis. Marble steps led right and left, around a fountain that had not worked in years, up to the front doors. The house was perfectly symmetrical, built around two long reception rooms, like the apse of an Orthodox church, between the front and back gardens. On either side were corridors leading to dining-rooms, kitchens and bedrooms. The ceilings were about three storeys high, with ornate cornices and chandeliers that could light a football stadium. White marble floors and high arched windows gave the palace a feeling of depth, of empty space to be filled with people. All the rooms were large enough to pace back and forth in without feeling confined. Luckily for the families who resided in the remaining 19th-century palaces, their ancestors had good taste. Those who had been building houses for the last fifty years lost it somewhere along the way, as the foreign architectural traditions, Western and Eastern, from which they borrowed freely and creatively were themselves debased.

The Bustros family in Beirut were three sisters and their mother. Their brother, Fadhi, had sold his share in the house and moved to Cyprus, where he believed his wife and son could live in peace. The four women had recently divided the house among themselves into four self-contained apartments: downstairs, a section each for Naila, with her husband and children, and their mother; upstairs, a section each for Mouna and Gaby. Even with the divisions, the house was beautiful.

I went upstairs to visit Gaby and Mouna, the two divorced sisters whose lives had almost stopped when the war began. Mouna had had to abandon her flat in Muslim west Beirut, because it was on the Green Line. Gaby had returned from New York to be with her friends and family during their time of trial. Both women had worked at various things, mainly in art and design, but neither had made a career or married again.

I knocked on Gaby's door first. Gaby was the youngest girl, and we were the same age. We kissed on both cheeks. Gaby was the most bohemian of the sisters, and she had designed her flat accordingly. She had cut one room horizontally to provide a gallery for her bedroom, with a small kitchen and dining-room below. I sat at the kitchen counter while she brewed the tea and told me everyone in her family was well, despite arguments and the war. Carrying the teapot and cups on a tray, she led me next door to a large living-room with a balcony over the back garden. Banyans shaded the balcony, and the sun cast shadows on the walls. The leaves stirred in the wind like warriors in an Indonesian silhouette theatre.

I noticed an oil portrait of one of her ancestors, a little boy of about nine, in a sailor suit, standing near the outside steps of the palace. The picture was above her fireplace. It had been painted more than a century earlier, but the face – despite the differences in age, gender and generation – was clearly Gaby's own. Gaby, like the boy in the portrait, had large, rounded brown eyes, prominent cheeks with a few freckles, a large, full mouth that went easily into a smile without wrinkling the rest of her face. Like the boy, she had light brown hair. Next to the ancestor were the steps of the palace and a hoop that good Victorian lads rolled along the ground with sticks. Gaby was taller and older than the boy, and she wore jeans rather than a sailor suit. Rather than a rolling hoop, she had on her dining-table cut fabrics for her newest designs – of large pillows. But it was the same face, in the same family and the same house.

"Well," she said, "are you finally writing your book?" She poured the tea and lit a cigarette.

"Yes, I guess I'm about half-way now. I've been through Alexandretta and Syria and north Lebanon. Now I'm doing Beirut and south Lebanon, then Israel and Jordan."

"Who do you want to meet in Beirut?"

"No one in particular. I've lived here long enough. Really, I just want to wander around."

"That's not good enough, man!" she said. Gaby had lived in New York, first with her American husband, whom she divorced, then staying on her own in a SoHo loft. For a few years, she tried to live between New York and Beirut. Finally, she decided to stay full-time in Beirut. Despite the problems, Beirut was cheaper to live in than New York, and it was home. But she had acquired the assertiveness of the modern New Yorker and a command of American slang. She instructed me, "You have to see Bernard Fattal. He is a businessman, an importer. He's a friend of Maurice." Maurice Sehnaoui was Naila's husband. Before he married Naila, he had been married to Mouna. Maurice was an intelligent, witty and urbane banker, who dressed like an Italian, had a deep voice and enjoyed hunting. Although he was apolitical, many of his friends belonged to the Phalange Party or the Lebanese Forces militia.

"Bernard," Gaby told me, pronouncing his name as the French would, "is in love with nature. He has two things in life: his business and personal growth. He always takes regular trips to Syria and Turkey. He loves hunting. Nothing else interests him, only hunting and business. He left two years ago to take an eight month sabbatical at UCLA. He took many courses. This is a forty-year-old man with a wife and three boys. He stayed eight months and worked his ass off. He's come back completely changed. He's brought people over from the States to teach new methods to his employees. He isn't interested in politics. He's been in jail. He's an interesting person." She said she would call him to make an appointment for me. "He has land in the Bekaa and has never stopped going there, despite the Syrians and the Iranians. For him, the future is in Lebanon, but he admits that his children won't finish their lives here."

"Anyone who stays a few months is likely to finish his life here."

"Come on, Charlie," Gaby pleaded. "Don't be difficult, man. Who else do you want to meet? I know. In the Bekaa, there is a Frenchman that my cousin Michel hired to take care of his winery. He speaks Arabic. When the Israelis invaded, they took him to jail in Israel. His family lives in France." It seemed to me inconceivable, with the Hizballah crisscrossing the Bekaa, always ready to kidnap an American or Frenchman, that a French vintner could survive there. He was not in an area protected by Palestinians, Syrians or Christians, but in Kefraya, in the stretch of Bekaa several miles wide between the Syrian lines in the north and the Israeli lines in the south. It lay on the route infiltrators used to attack the Israelis. Surely it was unwise for a Frenchman to be living there? I had to meet him, the last living vestige of a French presence in the Bekaa.

"Who else? Who else?" Gaby asked, pacing and drawing in on another cigarette. "I know, my Uncle Nicolas!"

I had met her uncle many years earlier, a kind old man who functioned as family historian. His son Michel owned the Kefraya winery, had studied winemaking in France and was one of the country's few real gentlemen.

"Nicolas Bustros is wonderful," Gaby said. "He is eighty-eight or ninety. He's the cousin of my father, a character of the last century. He has a prodigious memory. He was in the governments of Camille Chamoun and Fuad Chehab. He's a very colourful, very interesting man."

"How is your other uncle, Moussa de Freige?"

"He died a few months ago."

The old Marquis de Freige, inheritor of a Papal title granted to an ancestor, had farmed his family's lands in the Bekaa. He loved horses, like most of the big Bekaa farmers. He was at the farm in 1976 when the Lebanese leftist–Muslim–Palestinian alliance was in the ascendant and revolution was in the air. The rich, both Christian and Muslim, in the Palestinian-dominated areas were hiding their cars in underground garages, caching their jewels in safe deposit boxes, which, unbeknownst to them, were about to be robbed, and learning the language of the revolutionary proletariat. The revolution spread to the rural areas. Peasants seized the property of the large landowners, one of whom was Moussa de Freige. In the skirmish, one farm worker wounded Moussa in the leg. Then the Syrian army entered Lebanon, and the revolution ended. When I met the old man on his farm a year later, he walked with the aid of a stick. He felt no bitterness about his wound and spent more time discussing thoroughbreds than the war. He had given jobs back to his workers including the one who had shot him, and life in the Bekaa returned to normal for a few years.

Gaby poured more tea and turned the conversation to her own friends, people in their thirties, as were we. "I'm starting to meet interesting people in this country. They are all gay. One is a painter, the other a terrific writer. One lives in Jebail. He took me to meet these friends in Amshit, who are building a house. They don't have much money, but are sensitive, nice to be with, like my friends in New York."

"Unlike your friends in Ashrafieh?"

"Exactly."

Her friends in Ashrafieh were more conventional, mostly *haute bourgeoisie*, traders and dissatisfied wives of traders, men and women who dressed and ate well. The image in Beirut, not wholly accurate, of the bourgeoisie of Ashrafieh was of thick-headed Christians, too rich for their own good, unconcerned with the plight of the country, uncomprehending of any culture beyond that of money, imitating the latest Parisian fads in music, clothing, interior decorating and, for those who read at all, books and ideas. It was an unfair picture, but enough people fitted the stereotype for it to be applied to them all.

Gaby left me to look at her books and sip tea quietly. She returned to work at her sewing-machine on a large dining-table in the drawing-room. She was using pieces of large Damascene tablecloths to make pillows. She was making dozens of them, of her own design. The threads and pipings for the pillows were strewn across the table. Gaby took the threads, pipings and bits of cloth, slowly turning them into something recognisable. It was sad no one could turn the patches and threads of Lebanon into a country, but that lay beyond the skills of the most artful seamstress. Anyway, Gaby had become a designer – a dilettantish woman who has dabbled in most of the arts, always doing well, but not staying with anything long. Materials and labour were cheap in Lebanon. The rapid decline in the value of the Lebanese pound was good for exports, if Lebanon had much to export, which it didn't. Gaby found a buyer in New York at Bergdorf Goodman for her beautiful giant multi-coloured pillows. Somewhere, a *nouveau riche* stockbroker would rest his head on the pillows made by Gaby, daughter of the Lebanese aristocracy from Ottoman times, and feel like a pasha.

I would look up from the book I was reading to see her in her jeans and a loose shirt covered in a pattern like that of a 1950s abstract painting in red, gold, blue and green. Quietly, she sewed as the sunlight, reflected off one of the ugly apartment buildings that surrounded the family palace, began to dim, and the warrior shadows of the leaves faded. Through the high ogive arches of the windows above the back garden, I saw only the trees and the jasmine. The afternoon was unusually quiet. The two great disturbers of contemplation – traffic and war – were far away, leaving Gaby to her work, her sisters to the garden below and me to my reading and the contemplation of Lebanese womanhood.

When we first met, Gaby was in her early twenties, young and vibrant, enthusiastic about life and her crazy American husband. She was slowly becoming Aunt Gaby to her sisters' children, a woman on the threshold of middle age and then of aged spinsterhood, living in the upstairs apartment some day to tell her great nieces and nephews what it was like to live in Beirut during the long war. Everywhere in Lebanon was sadness, even in moments of peace or happiness, because such moments were merely preludes to the reality of decay or the swifter decay of destruction. Why did they stay, the three Bustros sisters? Gaby had a flat in New York, and Mouna owned an apartment in Paris. Naila and her children would have been safer in Europe. "I remember wondering, when I was a child, what it must have been like to live here during those great days, when the Turks were leaving, when people were struggling for independence," Mouna, the eldest, told me that evening in her study. "I am here to live this history. This *is* the time to be here."

The evening concert at the Théâtre de l'Annonciation in Ashrafieh was sold out to polite, well-dressed men and women who sat chatting amiably while they waited for the music to begin. It was a grand, largely Greek Orthodox affair, in a theatre facing the Greek Orthodox Hôpital St Georges. The Russians, historic protectors of their fellow Orthodox in the Levant until 1917, were sponsoring the Lebanese tour of a string quartet called *"Le Quatour à cordes de l'URSS"*. The quartet were appearing in Tripoli, west Beirut, Baalbek and Sidon, in which no sensible American would dare set foot. The United States had brokered the Syrian occupation of 1976, sponsored the Israeli invasion of 1982 and kept its own fleet and troops in Lebanon for nearly two years. The Russians however could move freely almost anywhere in Lebanon, even among the capitalist upper class of Ashrafieh.

Everyone stood for a recording of Lebanon's national anthem. When we sat down again, the four Soviet musicians tuned their instruments and began to play. On either side of the musicians were two studio cameras, with cameramen, from LBC, the Lebanese Broadcasting Company. As the lights dimmed and the first violinist began to play Schubert, I looked at the ticket a friend had given me for the performance. The price was 300 LL, less than three dollars, but a day's wages for an Indian labourer on any of Beirut's construction sites.

In the middle of the second piece, a Mozart quartet, the violinist had difficulty turning the pages of his music. He didn't miss a note. He played with his right hand, the violin tucked tightly in the pincers of his jaw and shoulder, while trying to reach the recalcitrant pages with his left. The pages wouldn't budge. He was on the verge of putting his violin down. In a flash, the Greek Orthodox Archbishop Audi, who was sitting in the front row, jumped to his feet and reached up to the stage and turned the pages. With a wink of thanks from the violinist and the unspoken applause of the audience, the archbishop returned to his seat, saving the Soviet musicians the embarrassment of interrupting their concert.

The Soviets went on to play Shostakovich and Brahms. Two hours after the concert had begun, the lights went up and the audience applauded enthusiastically. More than half of them, no doubt feeling starved of such evenings out since the war began, were standing up, clapping and shouting, "Bravo! Bravo!" The Soviets had played beautifully, and the applause was well deserved. The audience had listened attentively throughout. I looked around at the stylishly dressed women, with their modest jewellery, and the conservatively tailored men, most of them in early to late middle age, and wondered how it was they had earned their reputation for vulgarity. They were better dressed, better behaved and more appreciative of the music, and its significance in time of war, than audiences in London or Paris.

Someone leaned toward me and spoke into my ear, while the clapping continued, "This was possibly the most demanding audience." A woman who overheard added, "And possibly the most receptive." I supposed they were comparing Ashrafieh's Orthodox old moneyed bourgeoisie with the people who would hear the same concert in the Lebanese provinces: the wilds of Shiite Baalbek, the Sunni-Palestinian preserves of Tripoli and Sidon and the mixed bag of west Beirut.

I filed out to the car park with the three Bustros sisters. They talked to many of the older matrons, most of whom seemed to be "Tante" someone or other to Mouna, Gaby and Naila. Mouna, who had helped to arrange the concert, said she was going to a dinner with Archbishop Audi, the Soviet ambassador and the musicians. Gaby and Naila assembled a group of ten people, including me, for dinner at a restaurant and discothèque called Le Retro.

Everyone seemed to have a car there, except for a Maronite in his twenties called Gilbert, a Lebanese "young fogey" in a well-tailored suit. He and I, who had just been introduced as fellow journalists, decided to walk the half mile or so to the restaurant. It was a clear, balmy evening, with the smell of gardenias in the air. The streets were dark where some of the lamps were not working, and we had to walk in single file where cars had parked on the narrow pavements. Gilbert said he wrote about the arts for *Le Reveil*, the east Beirut French-language daily that reflected the views of President Amin Gemayel and the old guard of the Phalange Party. Before becoming a journalist, he had been a teacher. He believed in what was called "Maronitism," the Maronite *raison d'être* for Lebanon's existence, but he was a writer rather than a combatant.

We stopped to look at one of the old baroque palaces of a prominent Greek Orthodox family, each of us commenting on its beauty, and then walked through street upon street of dull apartment blocks. "Look at that ugly house," Gilbert said, pointing to one of them. "So many ugly buildings. The whole thing must be destroyed and built again." He referred to the buildings of modern Beirut, but we both knew he meant the whole country – its institutions, values and myths. It was a belief shared by young men on both sides of the Green Line, albeit with different conceptions of what should replace the old, decayed Lebanon.

At the Retro, with its low ceilings and white tablecloths, six women and two men were waiting for us. I sat opposite a blonde woman named Maria Saad, an Italian-Lebanese who knew some of the Levantine families I had met in Aleppo. Next to me at the long table was Nayla de Freige, who was married to the son of Moussa de Freige, the farmer who had weathered the revolution of 1976 in the Bekaa. Gaby and Naila Bustros quickly introduced me to the others as I looked at the menu and tried to listen to several competing conversations in French, Arabic and English. The waiters had put on the table several bottles of Ksara Red, a disappointment to Naila and Gaby, who preferred Kefraya wine out of loyalty to its proprietor, their cousin Michel. Nayla de Freige and Maria told me they were writing a history of Lebanon for small children.

"Is it true," I asked her, my voice barely audible in the din of conversation all around, "there is no standard history of Lebanon for use in all schools?"

"Yes," Nayla said. "But we want this to be . . ."

"Objective?"

"Yes," she said, then qualified her response. "Acceptable to all sides."

"Is that possible? Any book written on this side probably won't be acceptable in west Beirut."

"We want to be fair, to tell the facts only."

"But are there any facts everyone agrees upon?"

"I think so. We are relying heavily on Kamal Salibi's *Modern History of Lebanon*, which is accepted on all sides."

"How will you treat the 1860 massacres?"

"That will be difficult," Nayla admitted. "We can just report what happened without blaming anyone."

"Does anyone know what *did* happen?"

She laughed.

"What about the origin of the Maronites?"

"St Maroun was a monk from Apamaea whose followers were persecuted by the Byzantines and the established churches along the Orontes Valley. They fled to the Qadisha Valley."

"I've read some extreme Maronite histories which say only the monks

335

came to Qadisha and converted the indigenous population, that the Maronite converts are originally Phoenician."

"There were some conversions, but most of the Maronites came from the Orontes."

"So," I deduced, "they're Syrian, not Phoenician."

"Of course."

"Your book may have more problems on this side."

The *Histoire Illustré du Liban* for children, written by Nayla de Freige and Maria Saad with illustrations by Fadlallah Dagher, was published a few months later by Larousse in Paris. Beginning with "*L'age de pierre*" and ending at the "*Début de la guerre du Liban*", each of the one-page chapters appeared under a large Asterix-like cartoon depicting the era under consideration. It was a fair history primer for children, but all factions could take exception to it. Under Omayyad rule from Damascus in the seventh century, the book tells children, the region "*connait une grande tolérance réligieuse*", despite the staunchly held view in Maronite revanchist circles that all Muslims were intolerant of Christianity. "*Le 30 mai 1860, les druzes attaquent la ville chrétienne de Ba'abda, les combats s'étendent à Jezzine, Hasbayya, Rachayya, Zahle; les Ottomans laissent faire. En moins d'un mois, 11,000 chrétiens sont tués et 100,000 sans abri*," the *Histoire* reported, contradicting the strongly held Druze opinion that the Christians had provoked the killing. The Shiites were barely mentioned, if only because they had played no significant role in Lebanese history until Israel occupied the south in 1982. The Shiites had in a few years made up for lost centuries, and the book ended in 1975 with a statement of Ghassan Tueini's that "*la guerre du Liban n'appartient pas à l'Histoire puisqu'elle continue*."

As the waiters were bringing the first course of our French meal, Gaby turned to our end of the long table and changed the course of the conversation. "There's been a real return to cultural pursuits in the last year and a half," she said, showing the influence of her New York years in spotting trends. "More and more people are starting again in painting, writing, design, music, just forgetting about the political situation and concentrating on what they can do . . ."

"Personally?" I asked.

"In the arts, away from politics," she said. "Some of these are people who had given up their art for years, and now they are going back to it."

A young woman interjected, "I think it's part of the economic problem. The war was not as real for people as the money. They just can't afford anything now."

"Maybe they're just trying to escape, without actually leaving the country," I suggested.

"In a way, the waiting is over," Gaby said. "They are trying to live with what they have." No one was waiting for the war to end any longer before getting on with his or her life. People who had for the previous twelve years delayed their plans, who had postponed the day when they would have to decide what to do with their lives, were either leaving or committing themselves to some form of life in Lebanon. The decision to stay was always provisional, lasting until another round of fighting made survival more difficult and forced them to choose again.

Nayla de Freige told me her husband, Jean, took his mind off the war by going some mornings to the racetrack to see the daily training. The racecourse's position on the Green Line and its closure to the public since its brief reopening in 1983 did not prevent trainers from giving the horses and jockeys a work-out every morning, rain or shine. Punters from both sides of town would come out early to watch, perhaps hoping against hope that peace would reign long enough to allow a meet. Jean de Freige boarded some of his thoroughbreds from the Bekaa at the stables in the racecourse to keep them in training. In Lebanon, as in most places in the world, horse racing attracted two classes of people, the upper and the lower, and all shades of religious belief and disbelief. Several people had told me the track was the best place to see Lebanon's reputedly wealthiest man, nonagenarian Henri Pharoan, whose palace rested on the western edge of the Green Line and who rarely missed a morning work-out.

After dinner, Gilbert agreed to give me a lift from Gaby's, where he had left his car, up to my cousin's house in Baabda. He said he had to stop on the way to deliver an arts review to his office for the next day's paper. We arrived at the *Reveil* building, its neon light on top of the modern structure shining the name of the paper. He went upstairs, and I waited for him in the foyer. An old caretaker sat at a table near the door, and we began to make small talk in Arabic about nothing in particular. When Gilbert came down, he heard us talking and asked me, "Do you speak Lebanese?"

"I speak a bit of Arabic."

"There is no Arabic," he insisted. "We speak Lebanese."

In his car, we began a discussion on language, race and religion. The spoken language, in Gilbert's view, was nothing like the Arabic of the Koran, nothing like the written language of today. The Arabic which came from the Hejaz in the seventh century with the Muslim conquest had adapted to local languages, especially Syriac, and evolved into something else. He said that in Lebanon, it was Lebanese. The argument had nothing to do with linguistics, but everything to do with identity and the importance many Christians attached to being something, almost anything, other than Arab.

Gilbert and I pursued different convoluted arguments to make our points. He believed "Lebanese" was a language in its own right: ergo, the Lebanese people existed in their own right. I thought the Arabic spoken in Lebanon, Iraq and North Africa shared a family resemblance, making it a single language with different dialects: ergo, the Lebanese were, in some way, Arabs. It did not take either of us long to detect the effects of Jesuit education in the other. A dispute between two "jesuited" scholars was like a game of chess. For the previous twelve years along the Green Line, men and women had been dying over variations of just this argument.

The telephone system in Lebanon barely functioned, and making a telephone call overseas via the operator from the house of an ordinary citizen could take days. Some offices, and many politicians, had telephones with international lines that worked some of the time. My best hope of making an international call lay in driving to the *Bureau des Postes. Télégraphes et Téléphones*, the PTT, in Jdaideh, once a village just north of Beirut on the coast highway, lately a suburb within the growing East Beirut–Jounieh metropolis. The PTT in Jdaideh had a *salle de presse* on the top floor of a modern high-rise in which the lift rarely if ever worked. This was the best place to make phone calls, in that a journalist could sit down, read the paper and have a cup of coffee while waiting for his calls. The wait was not usually more than an hour.

The taxi-driver who took me down spoke only Arabic, and was surprised and pleased to be driving an American. Somehow, he turned the conversation towards the subject that obsessed Lebanese: leaving the country. "Have you ever been to America?" I asked him, after he said he loved it.

"*Yareet!*" he shouted, a term which means "if only I could" or "I should be so lucky." He kissed his hand and flicked his fingers forward like birds taking flight. "I wish I could take my family and go."

"Why?"

"It's not good here. Life is very bad." Then he asked me, "What do you think? Should I go or should I stay?"

"I don't know."

"You're American. Of course, you know."

"No."

"Yes."

Many of the poor in Lebanon and elsewhere assumed that the rich sons of imperial powers must have foreknowledge of the Great Powers' plans that affected their lives. Of course I knew. I was American.

"All right," I said. "If you can go, go."

"I really want to go to Germany. I have some family in Frankfurt," he said, becoming serious and confiding, dropping the usual Lebanese flattery. "Germany's better than America."

"How?"

"More work. Better life." He pointed to a bottle of rose water propped on his dashboard. Mixed with boiling water, it turned into something the Lebanese call "white coffee," a warm and harmless alternative to caffeine after lunch or dinner. "This flower water costs 100 LL. In America, it's $100."

"No."

"You can't find it in America," he laughed. "So the Arabs there will pay anything for it."

I asked him where he lived. "I'm from Aley," he said. "The house is finished. The Druze destroyed it."

In the dingy post office, a telephone operator pointed the way to the lift up to the *salle de presse* on the eighth floor. On the doors of both lifts were several pairs of dusty footprints. I wondered why they were there. I pushed the button to call the lifts and waited several minutes. I pushed the button again. And again. More time passed. It was obvious the lift did not work. I kicked the doors in frustration, leaving my own mark next to the others, and walked up eight flights of stairs. At the top, I found a large suite of offices and a press room where I could wait for my calls in more comfort than the post office downstairs, like the business-class lounge in an airport. It had several long tables with telexes and typewriters, the Reuter and Agence France Presse wires, and a bar. It was the fief of Madame Eliane Jabara, Nana to her friends, who in the brief period between the Israeli invasion and the departure of the US Marines in 1984 had run the *salle de presse* in the Ministry of Information in west Beirut. Amal now ran the ministry and its press room, but Mme Jabara had not given up: her office was a rival to the Shiite propaganda coming out of west Beirut.

Mme Jabara was wearing a white summer dress and reading-glasses when I walked into her office, just off the press room. She had brown eyes, brown hair and a dark tan. Unusually for a Lebanese woman of her age and background, she wore no ring or necklace. More commonly, she smoked a cigarette. Twenty years before, she had been a gossip columnist.

"I'm an old Destouri," she said. The Destour, or Constitution Party, had long before ceased to exist, lacking a militia and a strong sectarian base. "My family are all Destouris. All my life I've been close to this idea. Former President Bechara el-Khoury told me something in 1963 that I never forgot. I was just starting at *L'Orient-Le Jour*. He would send me the car, and I would go and sit with him. 'The president of Lebanon should always come from a mixed region,' he said. 'God save Lebanon when the president comes from an exclusively Christian area.' Suleiman Frangieh was the first, and the war followed." Everyone had an explanation for the war, and that was hers.

339

She kindly offered to make appointments for me, and she told the operator to hurry up with my call to London.

In the evening, Gaby and Naila Bustros took me to dinner with two of their friends, Aida and Pete, at the Cellar restaurant. Mouna stayed at home to watch an episode of an ABC television series about a fictional Soviet occupation of the United States, *Amerika*, that was showing over the summer on LBC. At the Cellar, an informal pub and restaurant, Aida told me she lived in Badaro, a neighbourhood near the open crossing between east and west. She said that for the previous few weeks, traders felt confident enough to walk over the line, pushing their fruit-covered barrows. She said she awakened to them every morning singing in their west Beirut Sunni accents the names and prices of the fruits and vegetables. "It's strange, but wonderful to hear that music the first thing in the morning. It's like before the war."

Aida said the Samadi patisserie in west Beirut had begun delivering Arabic sweets – *baklawa* and other sugar and pistachio confections – across the Green Line. "When there is fighting or sniping," she said, "the delivery truck stops and gives a tray of sweets to the west side checkpoint. Then it stops and gives another tray to the east side checkpoint. Both checkpoints have their sweets, and then the truck makes its deliveries."

Home delivery had become a normal part of life. People who were afraid to go out were now ordering pizza, as in New York, and more unusual fare, like rented video-cassettes. "We called up and got *Platoon* the other night."

"*Platoon*," Pete said. "That was a good film."

Naila said. "It was awful. A whole film about a boy who discovers war is senseless? Everyone here knows war is senseless."

Aida had recently returned to Beirut after living eight years in Cyprus. "There are many differences. The Cypriots are just living. The Lebanese are lively." Cyprus and Lebanon had much in common: both had been ruled by the Ottomans, both tiny republics were divided into Christian and Muslim halves and both had communities that looked to outsiders for salvation. There were also differences: Cyprus was at peace. Did Aida prefer the Lebanese? "The Lebanese are creative, active – sometimes too much," she said, laughing.

When I went back to the Bustros's house after dinner, Mouna was reading in her study. "How was dinner?" she asked me.

"Fine. How was *Amerika*?"

"Probably not as good as your dinner. It's just a soap opera, Charlie, about Russians occupying America. We could make a soap opera about the Syrians and Israelis occupying Lebanon, and it would probably be better."

"At least, more realistic."

Mouna was the oldest and, in many ways, the most original of her sisters. She used to visit me in west Beirut, when I had a flat there. We would go to a beach club, and she would say, "Who are all these people? You know, everything has changed. I don't know anyone any more."

"What do you think of it?"

"I don't mind. Every family was *nouveau riche* once, but it takes some getting used to. I know I have to live with these people, but I was only just getting used to the Sehnaouis."

The Sehnaouis were her ex-husband's family, who had made their money in banking and trade only a generation earlier. She and Maurice Sehnaoui had one son, Nicolas, before they divorced and Maurice married her younger sister, Naila. When someone mentioned to Mouna something about her marriage to Maurice, I heard her asking herself, "Were Maurice and I married? Of course. It's so long ago, I just can't remember being married to him." She never showed any bitterness to him or her sister. Mouna was the most self-contained member of the family, and was happiest when she could be alone to read, write or work on projects to help Lebanese artists and artisans to sell their work.

She got up from her chair and pulled an old photograph album from one of the bookshelves. She opened it and showed me a wedding picture. "This was my father at his first marriage in 1929," she said. "He was only twenty-four."

"The bride is pretty. Who was she?"

"The marriage was arranged by the parents. They divorced after two years, because she had epilepsy. Then she married a Frenchman."

"And is this the second wedding?" I asked, looking at a photograph of her father and mother.

"That was in 1943, his second marriage, to Mommy. She was seventeen years younger than he was. The families were against it, but she adored my father."

In the picture, Mouna's father looked like a classic Edwardian playboy, well turned out, with an aquiline profile and hair combed straight back. He was a handsome man, the photograph revealing a hint of the charm I had seen in him when I met him a few years before he died. He used to regale me with stories of his life, an effortless passage from one grand house to another, one royal wedding to another. Between the wars, he toured Europe, travelling from castle to castle, like a prince. When Mouna showed me the photographs of him at Lugano and Capri, posing with forgotten crowned heads of the Balkans, I saw him as something other than the old man I had known. The pictures, sepia treasures of another time, showed a vibrant young man who charmed everyone around him. They brought to life for a moment his and Lebanon's *belle époque*.

Mouna was the keeper of the family flame, protecting the family photographs, the oil portraits, the leather-bound books of Lebanese and Ottoman history. When I was kidnapped a few weeks later, she kept a record for me: she made a videotape of the stories about me on Lebanese television and clipped the stories in the Lebanese newspapers to send to me when I got out.

That evening in her flat, by the light of a small reading lamp, she turned the page of the album to a picture taken during the First World War. It showed the family palace, when it was a hospital for Turkish wounded. Allied artillery shells had set fire to the roof, but the house was standing and would take in British wounded. Seventy years later, Syrian gunners would hit the house, and again the house would survive. Mouna Bustros, who was reading in her sitting-room at the time, would be killed.

One day at noon, I went to IF, a boutique in Ashrafieh run by an attractive young woman named Rosey Abou Rouss. Whenever I had nothing to do in Beirut, I would drop in on shopkeepers I knew and have a cup of coffee. It was a custom in Lebanon to which I easily adapted. At IF, young Lebanese were drifting in and out of the converted atelier near the Université St Joseph. They all spoke fluently and un-selfconsciously in three languages – French, English and Arabic – about clothes and music. One teenage girl went into a changing-room with her mother to try on a dress, and Rosey said business was picking up.

A man walking by the shop poked his head through the door and asked the most frequently heard question in Lebanon, "'*Adaish dollar al-yom?*" "How much is the dollar today?" Anyone could answer – cab drivers, soldiers, shopkeepers. The daily rise and fall of the dollar determined the cost of food, petrol and rent. When I had first come to Lebanon, the Lebanese pound was three to the dollar. The rent on my first house in the mountain village of Broummana was six hundred Lebanese pounds for the year. The pound kept its value for the first ten years of the war, losing only about twenty per cent. Then, suddenly, it had begun a downward slide in the chaos that followed the withdrawal of the Multi-National Peace-keeping Force in February 1984.

Without looking at him, Rosey answered, "One hundred and twenty." My rent for the year in 1972 would have bought three bottles of beer today.

It was 12:27, and I heard a burst of gunfire from the Green Line. Two minutes later, I heard two more. Rosey gave me a cup of Turkish coffee and told me about her main concern: not the war, not the dollar rate, but her stolen car. It had disappeared from a car park near Jounieh, and she had spent weeks trying to track it down. I had heard that most stolen cars found their way to the Christian village of Deir al-Ahmar in the Syrian area of the Bekaa, where they were repainted and sold. Rosey said hers had become the property of one of Elie Hobeika's lieutenants in Zahle, where the rebel faction of the Lebanese Forces kept its headquarters under Syrian protection. I offered to speak to Michel Smaha, the Hobeika adviser with whom I had had lunch in Zahle.

"I've already been to Zahle," she said. "I saw the man, and he said he liked the car. If I want it back, I'll have to pay."

"How much?"

"We're bargaining now." Rosey was a brave woman to go unarmed into the headquarters of a man responsible for the Sabra and Shatila massacres, call his henchman a car-thief, and then begin haggling over the price of her own car. Most of the Lebanese women I knew would have done the same: they were tougher than the men.

The Lebanese Forces, the militia that Bechir Gemayel forged out of all the disparate Christian forces that had existed before 1976, had built its Majlis al-Harbi, War Council, in a concrete bunker on the site of one of its first major massacres. The slums which had been the disgrace of Qarantina, literally the Quarantine of Beirut port where Armenian refugees had settled for a time in the 1920s, had been cleared. Rubble and the bodies of Palestinians and Muslims had been pushed aside and buried with bulldozers, and in their place were the parade grounds, parking lots and bunkers of the Lebanese Forces.

In one of the clean, air-conditioned offices, I met a pleasant and attractive young woman named Naila Hammamji, who worked in the Lebanese Forces' Foreign Affairs Department. After clearing the security guards downstairs, I found my way up to her second floor office unaided. "How did you know the way?" she asked me, when I walked into her office.

"I've been here before."

"Yes?"

"When your other leaders were here."

"Which ones?"

"Well, Bechir Gemayel, then Fadi Frem, then Fuad Abi Nader, then Elie Hobeika," I said, naming the quick succession of leaders of the Lebanese Forces since 1982. "It's rather like Syria in the old days, coup after coup."

"You mean, before Hafez al-Assad?"

"Yes."

"We are looking for our own Assad."

"Haven't you found him?" I asked her, pointing to a photograph on the light brown wall behind her desk of the new leader, Samir Geagea, in a heroic pose. The only other decorations in the office were two pictures of Bechir Gemayel in even more heroic poses.

"We don't know yet."

I began to like Naila Hammamji. She seemed honest and had a sense of humour. Her light brown hair was nearly the colour of her fair, but tanned, skin, and she wore a modest, grey check blouse slightly décolleté. She asked someone to bring us coffee, and I settled in for a friendly chat.

"It's not a military resistance now," she said. "It's political resistance. We have to prove our existence."

"Who does? The Christians? Or do the Lebanese Forces still claim they represent all the Lebanese?"

"No," she admitted, "the Christians. Especially the ones who want to be free, not to live under Arab-Islamic domination. We want to live freely, but the Muslims do not want to share power."

"Some do," I said.

"Those who have power don't want to share it. The silent part are afraid to talk, because of the integrism and the Islamic revolution."

"Surely, their integrism was a reaction to the Christians'."

"We are maturing. We want to create a better nation in Lebanon, not like they made in 1943. That National Covenant was for the short run. We want to create something for the long run, for all the Muslims, Druze, Sunni and Shiite. We are all minorities in Lebanon."

The National Covenant was a gentleman's agreement among the leaders of the different communities to share power among themselves: the president and army commander would be Maronite, the prime minister Sunni Muslim, the speaker of parliament a Shiite Muslim and lesser posts reserved for Druze, Greek Orthodox, Greek Catholics and the smaller sects. Parliament would have a five to four ratio of Christians to Muslims, and Christians would keep a slight advantage in civil-service appointments. All the appointments would unofficially go through the hands of community leaders, reinforcing their positions. Of greater importance than the delicate internal equilibrium was the external balance: the Christians would not seek French protection, and the Muslims would not ally Lebanon too closely with the Arab states. This double rejection of the West and of the Arabs prompted the Lebanese Christian journalist Georges Naccache to write in 1949, "Two negatives do not make a nation."

I was writing down what Naila Hammamji was saying, when the ink began to run in my pen. It spilled down the page, threatening to drip on my trousers. Naila rushed over with some Kleenex. When she bent over to wipe the ink, I could not help but notice an impressive cleavage.

She went back to her desk. Thinking of something else, I said, "History seems always to repeat itself in this part of the world."

"I think we are inheriting the same conflicts because we eat from the same earth," she said. "It's been the same since Abraham's time. We now have the same cries as from the refugees in 1860. *L'histoire se répète*. We are not learning enough from the past. We believe we are stronger than those who went before us."

"But you're not?"

"No. When the French left, the United States and Soviet Union were not strong enough. There was a conflict between France and Great Britain. Great Britain was the winner after France left here. Great Britain was working from the beginning of this century to create Israel. When the French left here, Britain helped Lebanon and Syria to be against the French. Britain was helping the Druze against the Christians. France helped the Christians against the Druze. In the 1930s, the British created a Lebanese Christian movement against the French Mandate. When the French left here, they created a government with the benediction of Churchill. In 1948, when the Palestinians were expelled from Israel, Lebanon was the first country to accept the refugees. Why?"

"Tell me."

"The biggest part came to Lebanon. Four hundred thousand refugees are too many for three million people. This had all been prepared. In Lebanon, if there had been a pro-French government, they would never have accepted the refugees. We accepted. Twenty years later, we accepted the Cairo Accord." The 1969 Cairo Accord between the Lebanese government and the PLO gave the Palestinian commandos the right to carry weapons in south Lebanon, a right they had already taken anyway.

"You're not blaming Britain for that?"

"It was a consequence of the first."

"You say it's not a superpower game here, but indirectly . . ."

"Very indirectly," she said. "They are playing *par personne interposée*. Every three, four or five years, they change the name of the game and some of the players as well. It's like a chess match —"

"In which you cannot have checkmate."

"When all the pieces are out of the game, the black king will shake hands with the white king." She laughed and shook her left hand in her right. "I'm a dreamer. Sometimes dreams come true."

In the Lebanese Forces offices, I met a young man named Gaby. He chain-smoked, and he said he belonged to the National Liberal Party of Camille Chamoun. The party was one of the constituent elements of the united Lebanese Forces. "I like the National Liberal Party," Gaby said.

"They had Druze and Muslim members. They're not fanatics, like some of them."

"I remember them at Tel el-Zaatar," I said, recalling the long siege and massacre in August 1976, mainly by the Tigers' militia of the National Liberal Party.

"In August 1976, I was at Tel el-Zaatar," he said, to my surprise. "We and the Guards of the Cedars were the first in. Then the Phalange came. We fought in Ashrafieh in '78 and Zahle in 1980. I was with the artillery at Aoun es-Semaan. And I was there on 7 July 1981. Well, you know this day."

"Safra Marina?"

"I was swimming in the sea that morning. I saw the trucks come. I watched Bechir Gemayel's soldiers get out. They surrounded the marina and killed all the Chamoun people. I stayed in the water for hours and then had to hide for forty days."

"Then you joined the Lebanese Forces?"

"After the massacre, Dany Chamoun dissolved the Tigers and said we should join the Lebanese Forces." Bechir Gemayel had destroyed his Maronite rivals, killing Tony Frangieh in Ehden, and eliminating Dany Chamoun's militia.

"How old are you?" I asked. Gaby had spoken as the veteran of many battles over the previous twelve years. He had seen more combat than most US Marines.

"How old do you think?"

"I don't know."

"Twenty-six. I was born on 22 September, 1960."

"So, you were fifteen at Tel el-Zaatar?"

"Yes, fifteen. But I left the militia after 1983. Now I need some rest. I want to work on the civilian side."

"How long have you been chain-smoking?"

"Since 1973."

The Lebanese had committed no worse crimes against their stretch of the Mediterranean shore than had the Spanish, the Italians and the French. All of them had built the high-rise hotels, casinos, apartment blocks and amusement centres, beach complexes and concrete marinas. Lebanon, however, had only a small coastline, and the Maronites in their independent principality had even less. Development had accelerated with the war, as the coast of Maronite Lebanon became the only place most Christians felt confident enough to build on. The traffic was dreadful, day and night, and the roads, because they were a public rather than private service, were the only things that had not developed.

I went up the coast to Maamaltein to meet my friend, Emma Maalouf, for a day at the beach. I stopped at the PTT in Jdaideh to make a telephone call. It was a Sunday, and the press room on the eighth floor was closed. I booked my call downstairs in the post office and sat on a bench with Sri Lankan maids and Sikh workers, their beards tied behind their turbans, to wait to speak to London. Without a switchboard, two women behind the counter dialled overseas calls on individual telephones. A third woman sat next to them smoking cigarettes and taking payment for the calls. I read Gavin Young's *Slow Boats to China* for an hour until one of the women shouted, in two loud, rhyming syllables, "Lon-don."

"That's mine," I said, jumping up and running to a booth to talk to my children. Julia, our two-year-old, had chicken pox. Edward, who was seven, told me he had won his bronze medal for swimming, and George, nine years old, asked me when I was coming home. "Soon," I promised.

I went outside and bought a copy of the day's *L'Orient-Le Jour* to read about car bombs, shootings, concerts and other events of the day before. It was late morning, and by the time my taxi reached the coast road, it seemed all east Beirut was driving north to the mountains or beaches. New Cadillacs, Mercedes and BMWs were stuck in long lines in front of and behind old Golfs and Fiats. Young couples glided past on motorcycles, beach-towels slung over their shoulders and without helmets. In one car, two couples were clapping their hands to Arabic music on the radio. We came to two gigantic red-and-white striped power station chimneys just before we went into a long tunnel, then two shorter chimneys off the road as we came out. We crossed the Dog River and its monuments to Lebanon's many conquerors, memorials carved into the rock face by Assyrians, Egyptians, Greeks, Turks, British and French. Then there was the sheer commercial ugliness of the new Bay of Jounieh: the Fiat dealership, the Bally Amusement Centre, the supermarkets, the Hoover dealers, the Loto signs, the new apartments, the Lebanese Broadcasting Company complex with its huge satellite dishes. Here and there stood an old villa, a small palm grove or garden. We turned off towards the sea at the Jounieh Stadium, where I used to watch rugby matches before the war and which had become a helicopter base for the Lebanese army. We reached the little road on the sea that went to Maamaltein, on the northern end of Jounieh Bay. The cars did not move, so I paid the driver and walked the last mile. Relieved, he turned around and headed for Beirut, but not before asking me whether I could help him obtain an American visa.

I walked past a small fish restaurant built on the sand, with a dozen tables under cloth covered frames for shade. Further on was an outdoor bar, then a trailer selling hamburgers. Then I saw a man, sitting on top of his car. He

347

was in a small chair, next to a table, drinking *arak*, treating the roof of his car as a balcony. He laughed and shouted occasional words of endearment to girls walking past in their bathing suits. I thought he would fall off at any minute, but he kept his balance.

I came to the Middle Beach, as it was called, and looked for Emma. There were two signs: one said, "Wimming Pool, Cabins, Beach," and the other just said, "Simming Pool." I tried the Wimming Pool and found Emma on the sand in front of her apartment building, one of the new concrete structures near the water. Emma was an old friend, to whom I had once more or less proposed marriage. Her father had always been kind to me, teaching me how to tie a bow tie, showing me around Cairo and Beirut and making me feel, in my first years away from home, part of his family. Shortly after his wife died, he had told me at dinner that he could not go on living without her. He died a few months later, the only real victim of a broken heart I had ever met. Emma's older sister had been married to Peter Jennings, the correspondent who gave me my first job in journalism at the ABC News office in Beirut in 1973.

Emma was talking on the beach with two friends, Anna and Myrna. Anna was a Greek who had lived in Lebanon most of her adult life, and Myrna was a Lebanese whose husband worked in shipping. Myrna had given me the name of Antoine Makzoumé in Alexandretta.

"Was Makzoumé very helpful?" Myrna asked me.

"Not exactly."

"Did you tell him we sent you?"

I did not have the heart to say he had denied knowing her and her husband, so I said, "I can't remember, but he seemed busy. And he was just leaving for Europe. I had a good time there anyway."

Anna was one of many Christians and foreigners who had been forced during the war to move from west to east Beirut. Still, she had a soft spot for many things and people in the west, including one of its politicians. "I was very sad when Kamal Jumblatt died," she said of Walid Jumblatt's father. "He was something special, a mystic, a good politician, a good man. But when Bechir Gemayel died, it was different. I really cried. He might – I say *might* – have been something."

I took a swim, diving from the small jetty into cold water that seemed surprisingly clean for Lebanon. I swam past the rocks at the entrance of the little marina into the open sea. I took long strokes until I reached the deeper waters where small sailboats, windsurfers and water-skiers made swimming dangerous. I turned back to the shore and had a shower. Then I heard two gunshots, and after a pause a third, from the road. No one on the beach reacted. At the fourth shot, I looked inquiringly at Emma. She said, "That's for the traffic." I should have known.

A young man, about twenty-two, with a beard approached us. He kissed Anna hello. "You remember my son, Charlie?" she asked. Turning to him, she added, "Charlie knew you when you were like that," holding her hand two feet from the ground. He was embarrassed. "You remember when he was so small, Charlie? You remember the beach at Saint Simon? In the good old days?"

"I remember." Saint Simon's beach chalets south of Beirut had become home to Muslim refugees from Qarantina and Maslakh, its sands a communal dumping ground, its restaurant closed.

"And you remember the nights?"

I remembered the music and dancing, the all-night parties, teenage boys and girls sneaking off to kiss by the waves. I remembered a birthday party there for Emma's father, just before the war and his wife's death.

"It's not the same on this side, is it?" she asked.

"It's not the same on either side anymore."

Emma and Anna were Christian refugees from west Beirut, the more open, cosmopolitan west side where they had been at home, despite the war, until Hizballah forced its anti-Christian, xenophobic doctrine on a reluctant and once tolerant population.

"All my friends," Emma said, looking up from the book she was reading, "are people who came from the west side. They held out a long time, ten or eleven years. They still go and visit, but they can't live there anymore. Hizballah was the final straw."

Waiters brought us lunch, a good *mezze*, iced tea and the local Almaza beer. "Charlie," Anna asked me, "will you write about us?"

'I don't know yet."

"It's nice to write."

Emma put baby oil on her skin and lay back to read in the sun. I lay on the sand and read more of Gavin Young's *Slow Boats to China*. Gavin was in Goa, on his world tour, and wrote, "The countryside around Naicavaddo-Calangute was a region of white ornate churches, dotted like pious blocks of sugar icing among the iridescent greenness." It worried me that Gavin's descriptions were more vivid than those I was putting into my notebooks. The sunlight seemed to disappear, and I saw clouds rolling over the mountain, granting us, then depriving us of, moments of clear light. I watched the clouds and wondered why, as an adult, I was barely able to see in the clouds the fantastic monsters, gods and animals I had seen as a child. Where had they gone?

An explosion rocked the ground. The din of voices and waiters serving lunch on the beach came to a stop. Children ran to their parents. People scanned the horizon and the sky for the smoke, for some sign. I looked out to sea for fishermen, who might have been using dynamite. There was a second explosion, louder than the first. Mothers ran with their children down a tunnel under the road to the underground changing-rooms. Then in the sky we saw what had caused the sound: two Israeli jets coming out of the clouds streaked past us.

"Why do they do that?" Anna's son asked.

"Because," Emma said, "they're *mal élevés*."

The planes disappeared, and everyone began eating or swimming again. The mothers returned to the beach with their children. I asked the waiter to bring us coffee.

"I wasn't afraid," Anna said, surprised at her own calm.

"I was," Myrna told us. "You can't help feeling it. It's like feeling cold."

"Now the only thing I'm afraid of," Anna said, "is of being caught on the road. I always crossed from the east side to the west, and I was not afraid of the snipers or the kidnappers. But as I was crossing once, I saw a woman. She was lying on the road. They were just putting newspapers over her. She was dead. I looked at her, and I decided I do not want to die on the road. I don't mind if it's in my own house."

Over the afternoon, other friends of Emma's joined us, and we had more coffee and tea together. When I paid for lunch, I stuck the receipt in my pocket for my accounts. I did not give it another thought, until later, long after my tan had faded, when the receipt, with charges for more than a dozen cups of coffee, became proof that my day at the beach was a secret meeting of CIA agents.

I went up to the British Embassy residence in Rabia one afternoon to contact Janet Hancock, a diplomat who was returning to London and to whom I wanted to give some letters. The mail out of Lebanon was not working. We went up into the hills, through the leafy suburb, the Christians' version of Doha to the south. On the approach to the British Embassy were two barriers. Lebanese paramilitary police manned the first, and private guards hired by the embassy were at the second. I looked at one of the private guards and asked him, "Is that a Sten gun?"

"I don't know," he said. "Sub-machine gun." He handed it to me, and I looked at it. Black with a straight clip on the side, it was a Sten. I would not have slept soundly if I had been the British ambassador, knowing my security staff handed their weapons to any inquirer. I returned the gun, and he let me walk to the house. Just then, a white Range Rover flying the Union Jack pulled up. With her two bodyguards, Janet Hancock waved to me from the window. She was in Beirut temporarily filling in for the ambassador. She was in a hurry and took my letters for family and friends. "I'll mail them from London tomorrow," she promised.

That was my only meeting with a diplomat during my stay in Lebanon, a fact that would be hard to prove later.

Outside the barrier, there was a Sri Lankan woman walking down the hill. About thirty years old and thin, the long braid of her brown hair fell down the back of her green shift.

"Are you going to Beirut?" she asked.

"No," I said, "but I can take you to Antelias, and you can easily find a taxi from there." Antelias was on the coast below Rabia, a short drive into east Beirut.

"I'm lucky," she said. "I have work. Most of my friends here have nothing. Some of them are working on the roads."

"What do you do?"

"I'm the British Embassy maid."

"Is the work all right?"

"The money is no good anymore," she complained. "It's two thousand Lebanese pounds a month. I went before to Sri Lanka to see my family, and the ticket was three thousand pounds."

"That's quite a bit."

"No, it wasn't bad. Now, it's seventy thousand pounds."

I saw she wore a wedding ring and asked, "Does your husband go to Sri Lanka with you?"

"My husband is from Ghana," she said. "I had a husband from Sri Lanka, but I got rid of him."

"Why?"

"He was no good." She had come to Beirut in 1980 to work for a Lebanese family. "It was no good. They paid good money, but they don't know how to treat us. I quit after sixteen months. Then I found the job with the embassy."

"Can you make a living?" I asked, as the driver turned down another bend in the road, past another lavish villa.

"I earn extra money by cleaning the houses of some of the British people."

"I hear you have problems in Sri Lanka too."

"Sometimes I think it's the same all over the world. Christians and Muslims, Sinhalese and Tamil."

"Are you Sinhalese or Tamil?"

"Sinhalese, but it doesn't make any difference." The Lebanese said it made no difference whether they were Christian or Muslim.

When we reached Antelias, there were several taxis parked under an overpass. "Do you speak Arabic?" I asked her. "Or would you like me to ask the taxi how much he'll charge to take you to Beirut?"

"You ask," she said.

I found a driver who was leaning back in his car smoking a cigarette. In my best Lebanese colloquial Arabic, using the pronounciation I had long prided myself upon, I asked how much he would charge the woman to take her to Ashrafieh.

He took the cigarette out of his mouth and said in perfect English, "A hundred and fifty."

"Pounds?"

"Not dollars, mate."

"Thanks."

Mouna Bustros took me to a dinner party given by her cousin, Jean de Freige, and his wife, Nayla. It was a fairly formal evening at a new, modern complex of chalets, swimming pools and restaurants in the hills above the Bay of Jounieh. Mouna and I went up with Jean's sister, Michelle, in a taxi from Ashrafieh. It was just after nine, and we were the first to arrive. We went into the bar, dark and newly decorated, and saw Jean and Nayla waiting for their guests. Jean offered us champagne, while we waited for the other guests to arrive. In small and large groups of well-dressed men and women, they made grand entrances, kissing Jean and Nayla in greeting and looking to see who had arrived before them.

It was not long before there were enough of us to gossip about those who were just coming in. Dany Chamoun greeted Jean and Nayla, and someone said to me, "He's going to run for president." A few minutes later, another friend took me aside and whispered in my ear, "You see that woman? She's President Gemayel's mistress."

"You see the man in the white suit? His name's Samir, and he imports works of art," someone else whispered to me. "The woman next to him is his wife, Sophia. His mistress is here, the one next to Jean." The "mistress" was a flashy woman, much older than his wife, who was a beautiful young blonde. "Sophia learned about it a year and a half after everyone else knew. There was a blow-up, then six months later, she found out he was still seeing her. Then there was another blow-up."

"They're still together," I said.

"Yes, but this is the first time I've seen all three of them out in public together."

Mouna was standing next to me at the bar, unsurprised by all the gossip. I asked her, "Do you think it's the war?"

"Of course not, Charlie," she said. "It was always like this. You're so naïve, so American!" Mouna led me to an empty spot at the end of the bar, away from the rumour-mongering. She was a deliberate woman, who had little time for social convention. "Tell me," she asked à propos of nothing, "how was your time in Aleppo?"

"It was great."

"I remember how, twenty years ago, we used to laugh at the Christians of Aleppo," she said. "They spoke French with the funniest accent."

"They still do," I said. "Some of them sing it."

"We used to go up there in our old clothes, to visit the Dead Cities. We'd take our oldest dresses. They said the Christians of Aleppo had to move around like snakes, keeping down so as not to be noticed."

The barman walked up to us, and Mouna said, "Charlie, order us some drinks." I ordered.

"Now, it's all changed. They live very well. Everyone here was following the party George Antaki gave his parents for their fiftieth wedding anniversary. He did everything. He had interior decorators brought from Paris to redo the house. He had a fifty-carat emerald necklace for his father to give his mother. All seven of her children gave her a necklace with seven emeralds. He gave each of the guests a Verlain pill case from jewellers in Rome. He invited royalty from Europe. Everything was arranged, including a telegram from the Pope." She began giggling like a little girl. "I'm so glad for them. That is exactly what used to happen here!"

"Do the Christians here still look down on the Christians of Aleppo?"

"We wouldn't dare," she laughed. "Anyway, they are older families than we are. A hundred years ago, what were we? A hundred years ago, they were already established in Aleppo. Of course, they are mostly Italians, Austrians, English and Greeks."

By ten-thirty, the forty or so guests were seated at tables on the terrace. I sat with Nayla de Freige, Mouna, Michelle and a pleasant young man named Joseph. "He's very bright," Mouna whispered to me, an observation rather than a criticism, "but he's a social climber." Everyone was drinking and Michelle was telling me about her father, Mouna's uncle Moussa de Freige, the Bekaa farmer who had died recently. She missed the old man.

A dozen waiters served an elaborate, delicious meal, and I learned more about other lovers and mistresses, not that I could keep any of it straight. Some people got up to dance, and Michelle de Freige and I were left on the candle-lit terrace with our coffee and cognac. I watched the dancers and thought they would have more dinner parties, more gossip, more marriages and more love-affairs, just as their parents had. They would ski on Mount Lebanon in winter and sail the Mediterranean in summer, never knowing when the next battles – the all-night artillery barrages that would send them and their children to the cellars – would begin again. They were rich and Christian, and the world would blame them for their own troubles. The world was wrong: they were no more and no less to blame than anyone else in Lebanon's drama. Like the poor and the

Muslims, they were mere actors. Offstage, the playwrights – who may have been the gods on Olympus or politicians in Damascus, Jerusalem and Washington – were writing the next act.

Michelle looked at the empty tables, as though nights like this were not real. The only reality was the war waiting in the darkness beyond our candles. She sipped her coffee and put the cup gently into its saucer. Then she said, sadly, "People who should know say the fighting will start again soon. Each side wants it for its own reasons. There will be more destruction, destruction of houses, destruction of lives, destruction. For what? For nothing."

CHAPTER TWENTY-TWO

MONKS AND MARTYRS

A joke circulating in east Beirut gave some indication of how the Maronites viewed their president. "Amin Gemayel dies and goes to the gates of heaven. St Peter does not recognise him. 'You must know my father, who founded the Phalange Party and protected the Christians of Lebanon,' Amin says. 'Yes, he's here,' St Peter says. 'He is serving at Mass and cannot come down now to vouch for you.'

'Then perhaps my brother. He must be here. He founded the Lebanese Forces, and he protected the Christians.'

'Of course, he's here. But he's also serving Mass, so you'll just have to wait.'

'All right,' Amin says to St Peter. 'But while I'm waiting, would you mind if I went in and took up the collection?'"

A Jesuit was telling me this joke while we sat outside on the campus of the Université de St Joseph in Ashrafieh. We were still talking when we heard the sound of gunfire from the Green Line, about two hundred yards from us. There were three sharp bursts from an automatic weapon. Neither of us took much notice, rather like the first firing I had heard in Zgharta that I thought was a wedding.

"We still get snipers," the priest, an old friend, said. "A fifteen-year-old girl was shot right here just a few days ago. Her father was killed by snipers, and her brother was wounded. The family live on the front line, because they have nowhere else to go. They are refugees from the Shouf."

"Where is the girl now?"

"She's still in intensive care. If she lives, she'll be paralysed from the waist down."

Driving later in the day with a friend, I saw Lebanon through the cynical eyes of a poor, honest Christian. Georges Haddad was one of my few real heroes in Lebanon, a man who lost his job because of his integrity – a poor man who refused to kick back his salary to someone in his office, complained to his employers about corruption and was fired for his troubles. He had drifted since then from one poorly paid job to another.

When he came to pick me up at my cousin's house, he told me he was overseeing the reconstruction of a monastery north of Beirut. We drove up the coast towards Jounieh and then up a new, wide road leading to the top of the mountain.

When we arrived at the Syriac Catholic monastery in Harissa, Georges told me it had been there since 1786. The Syriac Catholics originally rented the land for ten piastres, one tenth of a pound, for two years and later bought it. Many of the monks and students came from Iraq, home of most Syriac Christians, whose communal fortunes had varied over years and regimes. That winter, lightning struck the bell tower and knocked the top off the bell, an occurrence whose possible divine origins were not lost on the monks and their followers. Georges was supervising a restoration project, putting the chapel with its bare stone walls and the monks' cells into living order. Syriacs in, not surprisingly, America provided the funding. We walked in silence through the cloisters, stopping to talk in hushed tones to young seminarians from Iraq who avoided discussion of politics, Lebanese and Iraqi.

Georges said the workers were badly paid: the Lebanese earned 500 LL a day, the many Indian workers made only 300 LL a day. Why the discrimination? "Some of the Indians get 500 LL, but most of them are unskilled. They don't work as well as the Lebanese. The Lebanese we use as skilled workmen make up to 700 LL." Although the rate fluctuated, on that day it was about 125 LL to the dollar, making the Indians' pay $2.40 a day and the Lebanese $4.00. If he spent no money on food, transportation or clothing, the Lebanese labourer could save $1,000 in a year. The Indian would not make his fare back home.

We left the monastery and decided to stop at the great monument of Harissa, the huge white stone statue of Our Lady of Mount Lebanon. Larger than life, she stands at the cliff's edge looking towards the sea which once brought her Crusaders to the ostensible rescue of her flock nearly a millennium ago, that sea that was taking most of her children to foreign lands. Her arms are outspread, like the statue of Christ overlooking Rio de Janeiro in the same Brazil which sent a statue of the Emir Fakhreldine on his charger as a gift to stand guard before Lebanon's Ministry of Defence.

Hundreds of people were gathered at the shrine, scores of them sitting in the shade of the pines in the plaza around the huge monument. Families were going in and out of the souvenir shop to buy plaster statues of Our Lady, Our Lord and the Maronite St Charbel, some of them two feet high, all of them painted in vivid colours. The shop also sold them Timex watches with religious symbols on the faces, multi-coloured rosaries and tiny altars which, when plugged in, lit up. Lebanon had always been a land of shrines and religious symbols, famous in antiquity for its sacred groves to

Adonis and the greater gods, a land where popular religion was the only solace for the poor who believed their fate was in the hands of the rich, the powerful, the stranger and God. Men, women and children were walking up the ramp around the stone base to the bare feet of Our Lady or attending Mass in the chapel beneath: little girls in white dresses, boys running wild under the trees and their parents – they had all come to seek Our Lady's intercession. Georges looked at his co-religionists and said, "Ninety-nine per cent of them don't know why they're here."

Georges and I joined the procession up the ramp to stand at the feet which had come into this world to crush Eve's serpent. We wound our way slowly around, listening to petitions and prayers in colloquial Lebanese mountain Arabic. Several women in bare feet, penitent and near to tears, and other women dressed in black pressed their heads against the stone façade to pray. Mothers were herding their children to the top, where, not surprisingly but somehow sadly, there was a collection box. From below, we could hear the strains of the Maronite liturgy, the beautiful chants only recently translated into the Arabic vernacular from the original Syriac, haunting sounds more like keening than devotion from a people to whom suffering in this vale of tears was first nature.

The view from the top of the ramp was spectacular, one of the finest in the Mediterranean. The coastal plain stretched for miles in either direction, wide only at several peninsulas, including the large headland of Beirut to the south. Ahead in the Bay of Jounieh, I counted twelve marinas and a large port, all of them capable of importing weapons or exporting drugs, all of them peaceful in the afternoon light, all of them products of the war and its new wealth. We returned the way we came, forcing our way past those still making their way up. At various points on the way, women would stop to pray as if making the Stations of the Cross, whispering their troubles into the foundations as if the stones could hear laments.

The chapel below was so crowded that it was impossible to enter. Inscribed above the door were the words: "*Quasi Cedrus Exalta Sum in Libano.*" I could see into the cavern-like interior, lit with candles and smelling of incense, as the Maronite priest was concluding the Mass, kissing the altar and saying to it in a low voice, "Remain in peace, O holy altar, and I shall return to thee in peace . . . I know not whether I shall return, or not, or whether I shall offer, or not, another sacrifice upon thee."

"They are all cowards!" Georges said of his countrymen, who had acquiesced in the destruction of Lebanon by refusing to stand up to the warlords, by participating in the corruption which ate away the fabric of the state and by mouthing the empty slogans of right and left, of East and West, of conquerors and potential allies. "The educated are the worst cowards of all. They should have known better."

Georges was driving me down the mountain in his old, battered car. He used his bad arm, deformed since birth, to change gear, and he turned the wheel with the other. His life had been one of opportunities, not missed, but stolen from him. He should have gone to university, but when his father died he had had to find work so his younger brother could take a university degree. He worked hard, too honest to become rich in a country that produced nothing of value, but in which middlemen, used to bribes, gifts and influence-peddling, flourished.

When a new Mercedes passed us on the highway, Georges asked, "Do you want to buy a Mercedes?"

"Not really."

"Why not? They only cost $3,000."

"Stolen?"

"Of course," he assented. "From some poor guy in Germany."

The trade in stolen Mercedes from Germany, I recalled, predated the war, and would no doubt outlive it.

Georges made a sometimes bitter, sometimes funny, always astute, observation about everything we passed. "You see this beach?" he asked. "This now belongs to Amin Gemayel and his partners. It used to be a public beach." Every Christian believed the president's friends were milking the state for all it was worth, living on patronage in the best traditions of American machine politicians, and the beachside development was a typical example. The Christians wanted to see their enclave between east Beirut and Tripoli as the new Hong Kong or Monte Carlo of the Levant. "East Beirut," Georges explained, looking at the hideous hotels and luxury resorts, "is going to be the brothel of the Mideast. Before the war, it was all Beirut."

Recalling what he'd told me about labourers' wages, he said tomatoes cost 75 LL a kilo, potatoes 6 LL a kilo – relatively cheap in foreign currencies, 100 LL about 20 pence (30 cents) for a pound of tomatoes. He said, "If you want to have an average life for one person, you need at least a thousand Lebanese pounds a day. Most workers make five hundred, some less. You see some people living very luxuriously, and others are living on one meal per day."

"Isn't there aid from outside?"

"The aid from outside, I'm sure, is sold on the market – flour, rice, sugar, dates. When King Fahd sent food from Saudi Arabia as a 'gift to the people of Lebanon', there were dates being sold everywhere on the market." I had seen the sacks of flour marked "From the people of the United States – Not to be sold" on sale in many shops in Beirut. Someone in the Lebanese government had taken it upon himself to "privatise" international aid. It would have been entirely illegal, if there had been any law in Lebanon.

Driving me south towards the urban confusion of Beirut, past the Armenian quarter of Borj Hammoud and what were until 1976 the Muslim slums of Qarantina and Maslakh, Georges told me the story of a Palestinian Christian he knew who had been born in Palestine, was expelled in 1948 and had been trying to assimilate in Lebanese Christendom ever since. He had gone so far over to prove his loyalty to the Lebanese cause that he had joined the Guardians of the Cedars, a method of assimilation analogous to a black man joining the Ku Klux Klan or a Pakistani immigrant signing up for the Brixton National Front chapter. Etienne Saqr, the extremist among extremists who headed the Guardians, claimed credit for such familiar Lebanese catchphrases as, "One Palestinian in the sea, pollution; all Palestinians in the sea, solution."

When the restoration of the monastery was completed, Georges told me as we drove back into Beirut, he didn't know what he would do. He could not go back to his old job in west Beirut, because it wasn't safe for Christians there. Emigration was an option, he confessed, but there were obstacles: obtaining visas, finding work without a university degree, disrupting his children's education, separating the children from his and his wife's parents. He grinned when he talked about it, seeing black humour in his life's overwhelming truth: the poor do not inherit the earth, and little pieces of it are stolen from them every day.

Georges had discovered that the way of Lebanon was also the way of the world. Would it be any better in the West? He had expected his American employers to be different, to stamp out corruption in their Beirut office when he revealed it to them. Americans were not, after all, Lebanese. "I really thought the Americans were different," he told me, recounting the tale of his firing. "But they are just like the Lebanese." Georges had exposed corruption in the forms of theft by local staff of hundreds of thousands of dollars, the use of the office to trade in illegal narcotics, the garnishing of local employees' wages and the supply of prostitutes and kickbacks to visiting American executives, and had sent a report in a confidential letter to the head office in the United States. The American head office had reacted by telling the local office manager to be careful of his disgruntled employee. The office manager had fired Georges.

"Cowards!" Georges yelled. "They are all cowards."

Rudy Paulikovitch sounded like a tout at an American racetrack. "How are you, man?" he asked me, when we met at a dive in Ashrafieh called Broasted Chicken. "Hey, man, long time, no see. How's tricks?"

Rudy was in his forties, a thin, colourful character who smoked at least thirty cigarettes a day and worked for the Chamoun family. His job was undefined, but, for a time, he had been the Chamouns' official spokesman. The last time I had seen him was several years earlier at a hotel in Broummana, when he was a "little short of green, man," and I lent him five hundred Lebanese pounds to pay his bill. At the time, it was $100. By the time of our meeting in Ashrafieh, it was less than two dollars.

"Whereya been, pal? Whaddaya been doin'?" We had coffee, and he told me about his kidnapping.

"You wouldn't believe it. They kept us in the ruins down by the port. They blindfolded us, tied us up, treated us like shit. It was terrible."

"Who were you with?"

"Sniper Georges Sursock."

"Sniper?"

"Yeah. He was a sniper in the early days of the war."

"Well," I said, "it seems to me that a sniper and someone working for Chamoun were a pretty good catch."

"Yeah. But they let us go."

"How?"

"The Chamouns pulled some strings, howdaya think?" he said. "So, whaddaya wanna see Dany about?"

"I'm writing a book, and I wanted to ask him about his father and the family's history, that sort of thing."

"You don't want to write about the election? Dany's running for president."

"I suppose that is a part of it, but I'm not writing about the election. I'm taking a longer view."

"In your book? Hmm. You know, we've written a novel, a friend of mine and me. It's a thriller, you know, the story of that time I got the Israelis to release a Palestinian and the Palestinians to release some Israelis. It was unbelievable, man. Fantastic story."

The bill for the coffee came, and Rudy grabbed it. "I'll get this," he offered. "You remember that five hundred pounds you lent me. Well, I haven't forgotten."

He had not forgotten, but he did not pay it back, even at its devalued rate.

Rudy drove me to the offices of the National Liberal Party in a tall apartment block in east Beirut. The guards in front checked us before we went into the building and up the lift to Dany Chamoun's office. Dany Chamoun was the son of Camille Chamoun, who had been president from 1952 to 1958.

"What did you wear a suit for?" Dany asked me. He had on light blue jeans, grey T-shirt and moccasins without socks.

"When I leave here, I have to see General Aoun." General Michel

360

Aoun was commander of the Lebanese army. "I thought a suit would be appropriate."

"Sit down. Coffee?"

Sometimes, I thought Dany was more American than Lebanese. In English, he sounded American. He looked the all-American sportsman, a big, strong man with broad shoulders and muscular arms and legs. He was a good skier, and, like his father, he loved hunting. He had short, light and curly hair. He was at least fifty, but he looked younger. Many girls had told me they thought he was the sexiest man in Lebanon. He had commanded his militia, the Tigers, at the massacre of Tel el-Zaatar in August 1976.

His secretary came into the office and said, "They're still stuck."

"Oh, God, no," he said to her. Then to me, he explained, "We've got some problems with friends on the boat to the south." It seemed these friends had borrowed his boat to go to the Israeli-occupied zone along the border, to avoid driving through the Muslim areas on the way. A scheduled ferry took civilians to the Israeli enclave. "I told them to wait for the regular boat. Ours hasn't been used in a long time."

He picked up the telephone. "Get down there," he ordered someone. "Get a helicopter down there now!"

He put his hand over the receiver and said, "There could be a massive funeral down there if they don't hurry."

If the Hizballah in south Lebanon saw the Chamoun boat, they would do their best to tow it into harbour at Tyre and kidnap everyone on board.

When he put the telephone down, I asked him, "Who's going to be the next president?"

"There are many hopefuls," he said. "I'm one of them."

"I suspect the Syrians will have the major say in choosing a president. With your Israeli connections, you would be their last choice."

"There could be an explosion in the next year which neither Syria nor Israel wants. This is the normal pattern in the Middle East."

Election years had been tumultuous in Lebanon. In 1976, Syria invaded and imposed its candidate, Elias Sarkis. At the end of Sarkis's term, in 1982, Israel invaded and forced the Lebanese parliament to elect Bechir Gemayel. I understood why Dany thought the next election might bring an explosion, but it needed to be nuclear for Syria to approve of him, with his public connection to Syria's three main enemies, Israel, Iraq and the PLO.

Dany was preoccupied with saving his friends on the boat, and I had an appointment with General Aoun. We agreed to meet for lunch later in the week at his house near the ski resort of Faraya. He said, "Stay and have a coffee, anyway, and one of my boys can drive you up to the Ministry of Defence."

We had coffee, and I looked around the small office. On the wall was a picture of his daughter, who lived in London with her mother. Next to it was a photograph of Dany, with his father and his son, posed with their shotguns. A framed black-and-white picture showed Zalpha Chamoun, then first lady of Lebanon, with her two young sons. A small poster of a torn Lebanese flag had the caption: *"Abandonnez Pas Les Chrétiens du Liban."*

The Ministry of Defence hovered on a hilltop over Beirut like a giant grasshopper, its concrete buttresses the legs of a 1950s horror film monster ready to spring into the air. Artillery fire had long since removed its glass eyes, and it bore the wounds and scars of a hundred attacks. Yet it stood there, Lebanon's Pentagon, headquarters of an army that had split twice. It had watched silently from the hills while the country destroyed itself. Its soldiers had not fired a shot when either of its two neighbours invaded its territory. Words like unity, sovereignty and independence rang hollow as they floated with the wind along the empty corridors and out of the broken windows of the Ministry of Defence.

Guards at a sentry-post told me to walk across the courtyard into the ministry building to the office of the Public Affairs Officer, Major Moawad. I passed a huge concrete mushroom, the bunker that served as a command centre when the ministry came, as it often did, under shellfire. Inside, I found my way upstairs to Major Moawad's empty office and sat down next to his cluttered, government-issue, utilitarian desk. The room was about eight feet wide and twenty feet long, its length stretching between the long open window and a dark central corridor. Five chairs against the wall faced the major's desk, cluttered with his pipe, papers, magazines and a telephone that barely worked. By the windows was an army camp bed. Major Moawad's office was like most of the cells in the Ministry of Defence, where soldiers lived like monks, their solitude interrupted by young soldiers bringing cups of Turkish coffee or telephone calls from senior officers demanding some useless report or other.

On the wall behind the desk hung a stylised colour drawing of a Lebanese soldier, with a cedar emblem on his helmet, his arm stretched high covering his face, a handkerchief in his other hand wiping a large tear from the eye of a woman. In profile, her eye was closed and her hair covered in black. The artist, for whom the woman represented a country whose army did little more than wipe its tears, had signed the poster, "Pierre." In the corner, a towel hung from an otherwise empty hat-rack. The walls were a dirty, military grey, and the floor was small grey tiles. The only feature to challenge the bleakness of the empty office was the view, across the ministry's unkempt plaza to the hills, where a few stone houses stood as reminders of Lebanon before the modern age of ministries of defence.

Major Moawad, whose office I had more than an hour to study as I awaited his return, had only one motto pinned to his wall, *"L'homme politique qui a besoin du secours de la religion pour gouverner n'est qu'un lâche. – Atatürk."* "The politician who needs the help of religion to govern is nothing but a coward." It seemed Lebanon was filled with cowardly politicians, and still awaited its Atatürk.

I passed the time reading the few magazines on his desk. The UNIFIL publication, *Litani*, had an article in its April 1987 issue on IRANBATT, the Iranian battalion in UNIFIL. IRANBATT arrived in south Lebanon on 22 March 1978, when UNIFIL, the United Nations Interim Force in Lebanon, was created as a buffer force after the first Israeli invasion. The Iranians reached battalion strength in mid-June with 514 men. Photographs showed the proud, imperial troops standing to attention, all spit and polish, American-equipped and trained. The new revolutionary regime in Tehran withdrew the battalion on 16 January 1979. In the summer of 1982, ostensibly to defend Lebanon against the Israeli invasion, the Islamic Republic sent other Iranians to Lebanon. With neither spit nor polish, the fifteen hundred unkempt Revolutionary Guards never fought the Israelis, but they had a greater impact on Lebanon than the Shah's IRANBATT ever did.

The magazine had an article on "Observer Group Beirut (OBG)", which had to abandon its patrols along the Green Line in August 1985, but was able to resume them in August 1986. The unarmed observers from New Zealand, Sweden, Ireland and eight other countries observed ceasefire violations and did not take photographs. The article explained that OBG relied only on open sources and did not "do anything that might be suggested to be intelligence work." Unlike Observer Group Lebanon (OGL), OGB was not attached to UNIFIL. The UN created OGB during the Israeli siege of August 1982 and attached it to UNTSO, the force the UN established in 1949. OBG was deployed in September 1982, just when the Israelis violated their agreement with the US not to enter west Beirut. With UNIFIL, UNTSO, the Syrians and Israelis, it seemed Lebanon had far more non-native troops than when the Ottomans had used Circassians and Albanians or the French stationed Senegalese and other colonial troops to keep order. Every army in the country had something to do, except the Lebanese's own, who sat in their barracks awaiting orders.

After several hours of waiting and phoning around the building, I decided the good major would not appear for our appointment. I left the building, walking out of the main lobby with all its large plate glass windows removed and across the plaza, to the little guard post where the sleepy soldiers waved good-bye.

I called Major Moawad later, and he asked me to come back to the ministry to see his commander, General Aoun. He assured me he would keep this appointment, and added that he came from Zgharta and that we were distant cousins. So, at my cousin's request, I returned to the ministry for my appointment with the general. Major Moawad met me in his office, where we had Turkish coffee, and took me down several corridors to meet his commander.

General Michel Aoun wore a blue civilian suit and was sitting behind a large desk in the commander's lavish office. It was from the same post that a previous army commander, General Fuad Shehab, had gone on to become president at the conclusion of the civil war of 1958. Aoun stood to shake my hand, a short man who looked more like a civilian politician or businessman than a military commander with his dark thinning hair, his friendly, round face with a double chin, a white dress shirt doing its best to hide a growing stomach. He sat back at his desk, a Lebanese flag on a staff behind him, and ordered coffee for both of us.

"How many soldiers do you have now in the army?" I asked him.

"Thirty-six to forty thousand. There are twelve combat brigades."

"How much are they paid?"

"Not much. Personally, when I was a colonel, my salary was worth $2,000. Now it's about $200."

"Do you still have American advisers?"

"Yes, but the only real job of the Office of Military Cooperation now is to follow the American arms that arrived before. We send officers to the States, France and Belgium for advanced training."

"But the army hardly exists. Most of the brigades are loyal to the militia commanders of their sect or area."

"It is not the reality. Some of the brigades submit to the influence of their environment. We have to manoeuvre with them to end this period as peacefully as possible. We meet with the officers from different regions and confessions. Those directives are respected by all commanders on their terrain. But they adapt. Some areas are occupied by foreign forces, others by local forces. They come under different influences."

"Different influences? I see Shiite commanders of the Sixth Brigade in Nabih Berri's office taking orders from Amal, or officers in the north taking orders from Suleiman Frangieh. The army doesn't do anything."

"The army is doing everything. It is keeping peace along the demarcation lines. It is keeping the peace in areas where we are stationed. It is helping the administration, because there is a lot of anarchy now in the Lebanese public sector."

"There is no peace in Lebanon, even when there are periods of relative calm. When fighting does break out, the army can't stop it."

"I don't think the country can go on suffering from the bad economy. It is not a question of the army. Lebanon itself will not be able to continue. That is the miracle: that you continue to run a country with this loss. Everything is disintegrating except the army. It is giving a good supper performance. It will be the last institution to disintegrate."

A soldier carried in a tray of Turkish coffee, and the general told me about himself. "I was born in Haret Hureik when it was still Christian," he said. Haret Hureik had become one of the Shiite southern suburbs. "My family originally comes from Jezzine in the south. I studied with the Christian Brothers in Beirut, joined the army in 1955, and became an artillery officer. I studied at Fort Sill, Oklahoma, in 1966, and then at the War College in Paris. For three and a half years, I commanded the Eighth Brigade in Souk al-Gharb."

"I remember when you went up there on an inspection before the Israeli withdrawal."

"So do I. It was 14 July 1983, and I was ambushed in Aley."

"Did the Israelis lead you into a trap?"

He nodded. "Walid Jumblatt said later he preferred an honest adversary to a dishonest ally."

"Are you going to run for president?"

"I cannot think like that. If I think like that, I will fail in my job as commander. If I think of the presidency next year, I would be a big failure for myself, for the army and for the presidency. It will be determined by circumstances, the result of the forces at the time."

The forces at the time would cancel the presidential elections, and the departing president would hand over the administration to General Aoun as acting prime minister. Syria and the Muslims would maintain a rival government in west Beirut, and General Aoun would lead his portion of the army in an attack on Syrian forces in Lebanon that would produce more destruction in Beirut than any previous round of the war. Sitting in his office, sipping coffee, his pot belly pushed up by a tight belt, he did not look as though he had it in him.

At the front gate of the Ministry of Defence, I stopped to look at the large statue of Emir Fakhreddine, astride a stallion and brandishing a sword. An inscription read: "From the Immigrants and Lebanese Descendants in Brazil to Their Country Lebanon. 23–9–81." Fakhreddine was a suitably ambiguous figure to represent modern Lebanon, to stand as the founder of

Lebanon's precarious independence. He never admitted whether he was Maronite, Druze or Muslim, and each community believed he was one of their own. Appropriately, it was a gift from the largest Lebanese community – the emigrants, who in Brazil and elsewhere far outnumbered the survivors left in the homeland and who, like the refugees from Troy, left their imprint far from their country's flexible borders.

"When the Jews came here," my driver said, looking at the statue, "they took all the pictures of themselves they could." No doubt many an Israeli soldier treasured a souvenir of himself posing in 1982 as conqueror, at the foot of the steed carrying the father of modern Lebanon. Within a year, the Israelis had left this part of the mountain. Within two years, they had retreated south of the Awali River. By the time my driver was reminiscing, they were confined to a tiny border strip, miles away, in a part of Lebanon long ago forgotten by the rest of the country. They had become as distant as the last conquerors – but who had they been? Syrians? Egyptians? Byzantines? Romans? Alexander?

That night, I was up late drinking with my cousin Lucien Makary and another officer. We sat on his terrace in the hills and saw Beirut gleaming in the darkness. The electricity was working on both sides of Beirut, and the street lights were on. East and west were bright with lights in windows, on shopfronts and along the roads. The lighthouse in Ras Beirut scanned the horizon with its beam, and a few car headlamps glided gently along the streets in the distance. Between the two sides, like a furrow of tilled earth in the midst of a blossoming field, was a band of total darkness half a mile wide from the sea inland to the foothills below us. "That's the Green Line," Lucien said. "It's been dark for years, and it's growing."

"It looks more like the Black Line," I said.

The three of us were talking about the war, what it had brought out in people, things they had revealed about themselves to others which should have remained secret. Some people had shown themselves to be heroes, risking their lives to save strangers. Others, who in normal times would have lived without any horrible self-knowledge, had become monsters. "I've seen terrible crimes in the army," Lucien told me.

We had drunk several glass of whisky, and Lucien's friend became tense. Suddenly, as he stared into the darkness of the Green Line, he said, "I saw a man put a bayonet through a man's heart." His hand shook the whisky, and ice rang on the glass. He was opening up his own heart of darkness. "He pushed the bayonet tip into the man's chest, past the bone and into the heart, one millimetre by one millimetre, slowly, to make him suffer. He was a Muslim officer, the last one we have on this side. He was doing it to another Muslim. There was nothing I could do to stop it." His hands trembled, and he turned his head away from Beirut's darkness to stare into my eyes.

"Why did he do it?"

"He thought he was doing it for Great Lebanon."

Great Lebanon – 10,452 square kilometres, according to the bumper stickers that had a vogue after the Israeli invasion – was the creation of the French, when they drew the borders of Le Grand Liban in 1920. Before that, Lebanon was the Mount Lebanon range, Le Petit Liban, home of Maronite and Druze peasants. France added the coast, the Bekaa and the south. Was preserving these artificial borders worth the painfully slow murder of a Muslim by a Muslim officer? Was it worth the deaths of 150,000 people? Were Lebanon's borders in any way preserved? The Israelis ignored the southern borders, the Syrians held the frontiers in the east and north in contempt, and the Lebanese themselves lived in fear of crossing those internal, barricaded borders not marked on maps, but etched like bayonet scars into the country's soul.

I went to bed, the sound of shooting between the Christian army and the Druze militia in the hills too distant to keep me awake. All I could see when I fell asleep was a man's heart slowly pierced by the bayonet-point of a fellow believer who killed to save a country that no longer existed.

Soft, consoling voices sang the praise of God. Strains of the Maronite liturgy rose from the church next door, passing our ears on their way to the heavens. Facing me at a table in the upstairs room that served him as office and kitchen was a Maronite priest. He tapped his fingers out of time to the music as he asked me to understand what his country had suffered.

"The real tragedy for us was not the fighting war between Christian and Muslim," he said. "It was the genocide by the world's press, the image of Lebanon and of Lebanese society. The image we have now is terrorism, fundamentalism and fascism. We are the victims of this image."

Father Moannes, in his late forties, wore a monk's black cassock and had a head full of curly salt-and-pepper hair. When he laughed, it was with a slight strain of his tonsils, a boy's laugh that made me smile and moved his glasses up and down his nose. As a monk, Father Moannes had chosen celibacy, although the Maronite church accepted married men as parish priests. He was a professor of anthropology at the Lebanese University and had a reputation as a rational Maronite apologist.

"The values, the challenge of Christianity and Islam to live together, the image of Christian and Muslim, the image in the arts, the joy of living, all of this image is completely destroyed. What we'd like to try to do is to save this challenge between the hills and the sky, between the gods, among Christian, Muslim and Jew."

'What went wrong?"

"What happened in this country? It had on the one side the Jewish society with its own antagonism and on the other the Islamic society with its own antagonism. I can't believe God gave land only to Jews or Muslims. God has chosen humanity, not one people or one land. We can't put ideas in the mind of God. I can't believe God gives holy land for one people. God's message is for all."

"Haven't the Christians made mistakes?" I asked.

"At the social and political level, we have made many mistakes. But we never accepted to say Lebanon is a Christian state. We refuse to have a Christian ghetto. This is the foundation of the state. We refuse to have a mono-society with Christians as the primary group and the others as *dhimmi*." In traditional Islamic society, *dhimmi* were Christians and Jews, who did not enjoy full civic equality with Muslims. "Listen, Charles, maybe in actions, we have made many mistakes. But you put your actions in a moral and political context. It is not the moral system. I, as a Christian, cannot live in a uniquely Christian system, refusing to accept the others. Maybe the Christian groups have made mistakes. We have to ask God's forgiveness. I'm not saying we're a holy society. I'm depending upon 'Christian' values, even when Christians don't live by them." He laughed. "You see, we have been the servants. We came from the second level of society. We were not princes, but the farmers. Our dignity is our work."

"But haven't the Maronite Church and priests held people back, forcing them into a kind of Maronite tribalism?"

"You are completely wrong, Monsieur. I am not a 'Maronite' priest. My priesthood is the church. I am the priest of Jesus Christ. I share my priesthood with what is Maronite, Latin, Orthodox, Anglican. As a liturgical human being, I am a Maronite. My heritage is Maronite. From the Antiochan church. From the Apostles. I am a Mother church. I am not a Latin church or an Anglican church. If Jesus Christ came once more, I am the roots. This church has always been the church of authenticity and change. What really changed in Lebanon was the work of this church – the schools, hospitals, orphans' homes. What is the big revolution of the church? In 1736, the Maronite church held the Council of Lebanon at Louaizé. What did they decide? They demanded freedom and education for women, free education for all, education for old people, to oblige children to go to schools. They insisted on education, freedom and equality for women. You know in France, they decided on full laïcisation two hundred years later. What does this mean – a church of funda-mentalism or of progress?"

"Yet you have to live with fundamentalists, Christian and Muslim."

"Because in Islamic society, God is for the Muslims and land is for the

Muslims. For us, God and the land are for all. Those fundamentalist people have to understand that we can live together. It is an aesthetic problem in the ugly Middle East. Where you kill man, it is ugly. In Syria, man is not free. In Saudi Arabia, man is not free. You remember west Beirut before the war? You knew Rue Hamra? You knew the American University of Beirut? That was diversity. That was freedom."

"I remember Beirut before the war, but its freedom was abused and exploited."

"Freedom in the Middle East is a dream. We have all the evil of dictatorship in political society. The unique freedom was in Lebanon. Really, for us, the big tragedy was preparing the death of God. We believe in the Resurrection. We believe God brings us here to live, not as a concept, but as a human incarnation. We believe in a revolution in human and social relations, to destroy all barriers, social, religious and economic. It is a big challenge for us."

"Haven't you failed to respond to the challenge? I don't mean you personally, but the Maronites."

"A society with one colour is weak. Your dignity is to accept the other when he is different. When you kill another, you destroy yourself. You cannot live alone. God could not live alone, and He made man. My own idea of Lebanon is a land of incarnation, freedom and humanity. It is a marriage of history. We can't speak of this country only with kilometres, only with values. Maybe we are the romantic people in this technological world. You have a mind, but you have a heart. There are seventeen ethnic groups in this country. It means a lot. They came here because it was a land of freedom. If you lose one of those societies, you lose four thousand years of history, of culture, of art. When you are coming from the desert, and you arrive at the mountain of Lebanon, you know you are coming to another world. It is a beautiful country."

"But isn't it part of the larger Arab world?"

"People of the desert go from one oasis to another. They are nomads. There are people of the stones and people of the sands. People of the sands can't build or have a history. They move. People of the mountains plant roots. People of the desert are moving at all levels without identity. Two kinds of mentality. For that you have to safeguard Lebanon. It is a microcosm. Lebanon is not a land. It is the experience of love: are you able to love or not?"

He stopped to make some Turkish coffee at a counter behind him, filling the pot with water, adding the finely ground coffee beans and bringing it to the boil. While he brewed the coffee, I said, "There is an interesting cultural division between east and west Beirut that we haven't mentioned. In east Beirut, the intelligentsia speak French and look to France. In west

Beirut, no doubt because of the American University, they speak English. As I recall, the Protestant missionaries opened the American University in 1866 in west Beirut because of the hostility of the Maronite church to new ideas."

Standing at the stove, stirring the coffee, he said, "English education for us means we are not in the Catholic Church. Catholicity means universality, Latin, French and the Vatican. It was not the mistake of the Maronite church, but of the Protestant American missionaries. It was not their role to convert the Christian confession, but to bring people to Jesus Christ. The real problem was, when they failed to convert the Muslims, they tried to turn the Maronites into Protestants. The priest cannot force you to change sects. I have to respect the Armenian church."

"But isn't there hostility generally on this side to Protestantism, to Britain and to the United States?"

He poured coffee from the brass pot into little cups and brought them to the table. "In the Maronite Church," he said, "the cross is an empty alcove full of light. Our country has been crucified by money, by external power. The new Rome is the United States, and they wash their hands. Since they left, they have supported everything Syria wants to do here. Maybe the Palestinians have been Barabbas to us. To kill us, for what? To receive the Palestinians? Being open-minded?"

"But didn't the United States come here in 1982 to help you, the Christians?"

"Stop being ridiculous. A state is not made without courage, by young people like yours, people without a memory. How did you accept to say to us, 'You have to align your policy with Syrian policy'? How can you push us to be a new slave in the Middle East? We are still here. We shall overcome."

"Are the French any better?"

"They paid here with their lives, their culture, and they did not run away like rabbits."

My eyes wandered out of the window to the new construction near the coastal highway just north of Beirut. "Look at those buildings. When someone is brought up in a hideous environment, he has little reason to save it. Do you think the ugliness all around us plays a role in destroying society?"

"It does for me. Lebanon is an aesthetic problem. I don't agree with this savage urbanism without law. It is a shame for Lebanon to have this kind of construction."

"What can you do about this tasteless development?"

"Change the Lebanese mentality. Have laws to regulate building and planning. You have to change the street to change the mentality of the people. This happened in Paris after the revolution, when they introduced the big boulevards. This kind of construction is a new revolution. We need gardens, we need space, we need taste. As a Lebanese, I can say this. You can't."

"I *can* say, even as a foreigner, that most Lebanese have no focus for their loyalty outside family, tribe and sect. How can they express loyalty to a state that did not serve them, did not protect them?"

"The law must give you and me the boundaries. Until now, we haven't had the real meaning of the state. We haven't had a moral policy. A *res publica*. We haven't had in Lebanon the real meaning of the state."

"Why?"

"It was a young democracy. The real feeling of the homeland was not there at the beginning of our history. It was not a homeland for many of our people, who dreamt of an Islamic land, of an Arab kingdom. For some, it was the store, where they bought and sold. For others, a bus station or a port to wait to go to America. The real feeling of Lebanon was only with the Maronites and the Druze. The Maronites and the Druze are the real identity of the country. The big mistake of the Druze was to destroy the Christians in the mountain."

"The big mistake of the Christians was to make them."

"Yes. Maybe in our country, we have danced the waltz of hell."

I reminded him of a parable recorded by Michel Chiha, a Chaldean Christian whose family originally came from Iraq. A banker and writer, he helped to draft the Lebanese Constitution of 1926. In an article entitled, "Discussions with Patrice," a mythical philosopher named Patrice tells Chiha,

"I read in Ruskin an unforgettable passage. This was the substance: Five men constitute the foundation of the city: they are the priest, the judge, the doctor, the soldier and the merchant. The priest must die rather than contradict his faith; the judge, rather than violate his conscience; the doctor, rather than run from an illness he can ease or cure; the soldier, rather than betray his country. And the merchant? Do you see in what circumstance the merchant must face death? Now, says Ruskin, he who does not know when it is time to expose himself to death is ignorant of how to live. He is incapable of doing something greater when his eyes do not see the eternal law of sacrifice.

"We are a people of merchants," Patrice concluded. "That's why the bones of our fathers are warmer than our lives."

"Is Lebanon just a nation of merchants with loyalty to nothing but making money?" I asked Father Moannes.

"I would like to say, in historical movement, you have the time of the priest, of the judge, of the soldier and of the merchant. Carthage was destroyed when the merchants took over. Rome suffered under its merchant princes. People must be driven with dreams, heroism, dignity, poverty and not with money. The 1950s and 1960s were the time of the commercial state, and we've had this destruction. You cannot serve God and money together. I am not a pessimist. We had a merchant society for half a century. We have now a society of martyrs. This means spring is coming. We've had ten thousand young people killed out of 126,000 total dead in the war. For the United States, this would be the same as 100,000 people killed from the young generation. We sowed the blood of our martyrs. Pure people, lovely people. I believe myself in the power of God to give grace to build a pure society. We baptised our society with the blood of the money-changers in the temple. Now there is a kind of understanding among young people who feel they have to save their country. We have been purified by this Crucifixion. I pray to God for a resurrection for my country."

I finished my coffee and listened for the music of evening vespers from the church outside. Father Moannes leaned towards me, his elbows on the table. "The only law we believe is of love, of charity. The Bible says, my God lives. I can't speak only in a social way. The morning is coming. The full dark gives me full light. Lebanon is not only a crossroads for people, it is a crossroads for gods."

The sun was setting in the sea over the road, and Father Moannes's room was growing dark. Downstairs, someone tuned a ghetto-blaster to rock music on one of Lebanon's FM stations, drowning out the music from the church.

When I awoke the next morning, Beirut was hot and humid. The Voice of Lebanon reported that three bombs had exploded during the night on the west side. The Phalange radio station said this brought to one hundred and forty-three the number of bombs since the Syrian intervention in February. It added that snipers were active on the Green Line and that a rocket from west Beirut had landed at Antelias, near Father Moannes's office, "causing only material damage." All that had taken place before breakfast.

I found a taxi to take me to Dany Chamoun's house in the ski resort of Faqra, near the village of Faraya. We came to heavy traffic on the coast road, saw no sign of damage in Antelias, and reached open road in the limestone hills past Jounieh. At each church we passed, the driver made the sign of the cross. Huge blocks of fissured limestone hung precariously above the road, as did scores of colour posters of Bechir Gemayel, the would-be Atatürk of east Beirut.

When we reached Faqra, a collection of new Alpine ski chalets, Dany Chamoun came out of his house wearing a striped Lacoste shirt, khaki trousers and a khaki fishing hat. Patches of winter snow covered much of the ground, but the mountains were warm and sunny. "At least, you're not wearing a suit," he said. "Hey. There's still enough snow for a little skiing. You want to have a go?"

With him were his two sons, both handsome boys, and their mother, Ingrid. We were standing outside on a long deck in front of the house, above a ravine that led down to the coast. Ingrid was well tanned and healthy, with long hair in light and dark shades of brown. She had graduated from the American University of Beirut in mass communications in 1974, but she had not worked since she and Dany began living together. "You're American?" she asked. "I'm sometimes taken for an American." Her mother was German and her father Lebanese.

Ingrid said she would go and find us some cold drinks, and Dany put out deck chairs for us to sit down. "You know, I was skiing here the other day, and I saw a mountain lion. I couldn't believe it. He ran right by me."

Most of the travellers before this century wrote of the wild animals in the mountains, but, apart from the occasional fox, I had never seen any. I assumed they had been hunted out of existence. Most Lebanese men were avid hunters, and no bird, however small, was safe in the skies over Lebanon when young boys were out with their air rifles.

"It's beautiful here," I said. "But, with the war, do you think it's a good place to raise your sons?"

"I don't know," he admitted, while the boys played in front of the house. "Is New York any better really when you think of the Mafia, of the violence there?"

"I suppose it's easier to get through the day in New York without being hit by artillery or seeing a corpse."

"I know, but what do you do with the people here? You were born here. This is your country. Do you let it rot or do you try? You've had the chance to go and see the rest of the world. You've seen what the world can be like. Do you want to leave these people the way they are?"

"You could have a better life outside." I added, as a joke, "You would have better shooting in England."

"We have the same shoots here. I used to raise partridge and let them loose over there." He pointed to a hill about half a mile away. "I would walk after them with the dog. At least, I would get a bit of exercise. But the fact is this is an important project for me: to try and make a viable and beautiful home for my family, for the rest of the Lebanese. Why should I leave here? I mean, consider these people who live here. You know that every single house probably has a machine-gun or two. Now look at them."

I looked at the houses along the valley, their inhabitants driving peacefully along the roads or rambling in the open fields. "There isn't a policeman for twenty-five or thirty kilometres. And even if there were, he'd probably be drinking coffee or smoking a cigarette. Yet look at the rate of crime here. There isn't any. I'd like to see any part of the world which has this, even Switzerland. Switzerland is the most police-run state you can find. Nobody has what we have here."

"You can't pretend there are no problems."

"Most of the problems here are not engendered by the Lebanese themselves. We have inherited this over centuries of misguided world politics, great power policies. Even today, the whole interaction here is because the world is lame, politically and morally. It's a fact that Lebanon is a founder-member of the United Nations. The main item in the UN Charter is the protection of small states, guaranteeing their security and integrity. Yet there's this whole damn army from a foreign country here that's ruining us, a country that does not believe in any world codes, from the Geneva Convention on. It is an army of occupation. This is an enemy army to the United States. The Syrians shot down your planes. They blew up your embassy. They blew up your marines. The United States allowed an enemy to come into the country that is America's best friend in the Middle East."

"Why then do you stay friendly with the United States?"

"I can hardly go to war with the United States. But I'm friendly with the American people. I mean, there 's a link between our ways of life, our education and our heritage. We shouldn't be quarrelling, but we should be cursing them day and night."

"How did your family get involved in politics? They were not feudal landlords, not *bayks*, like most of the others."

"I guess it started under the Ottomans, when the whole family were taken to a concentration camp in Anatolia. The Turks took my grandfather, my English grandmother, my father and his four brothers until the end of the First World War."

"Why?"

"My grandfather was the tax collector from Deir al-Qamar to Hermel," he said. "Along the route, he helped stir up a lot of anti-Ottoman feeling." The Chamouns came from Deir al-Qamar, the largest and, since 1984, only surviving Maronite village in the Shouf. It had been the scene of the largest massacre of Christians by Druze in 1860.

"Was your grandfather an early Arab nationalist?"

"I guess. The odd thing is that the Arab revival was fuelled by Lebanese Christian literature."

"How did your father start in politics?"

"He was practising law, and in 1934, the year I was born, he ran for parliament. He's been re-elected every time except 1964, when the election results under President Fuad Shehab were a bit rigged. I know. I was involved in that election."

"You mean the way the elections were rigged under your father in 1957?"

He laughed. "Much worse. Anyway, the first time he was in government was when he became Minister of the Interior in 1944. He was already becoming a prominent figure."

"Do you remember when your father was arrested by the French in 1943?" When the Lebanese, supported by the British, were demanding independence from the French, colonial officials had arrested Camille Chamoun and other prominent leaders, including the Shiite Adil Osseiran.

"I have a vivid memory of the night they surrounded the house. I saw a huge Senegalese soldier standing outside both windows. My father couldn't escape. They came at three-thirty in the morning and finally left at eight. They let him dress, and they took him away. They held him at a prison in Rachayya for fifteen days."

"Then the French agreed to grant independence."

"But they did not pull their troops out until three years later. In 1944, my old man was appointed head of the Lebanese–Syrian delegation to the United Nations. He became the Arab spokesman for the Palestine issue."

"A historic irony, considering how he became divorced from the Palestinians."

"He was never divorced from the Palestinians. He became president in 1952 after the riots against President Bechara el-Khoury. He ran against Sulieman Frangieh's brother, Hamid Frangieh. The Muslims gave him a massive vote, because of his work for the Palestinians. Then he tried to initiate several things, a Senate and running the country on a non-sectarian basis. He improved education, and he was successful. Then Gamal Abdel Nasser came along from Egypt. Nasser encouraged the Muslims. After all, my father was a Lebanese, a Lebanese nationalist, and Nasser encouraged the Arab nationalists. That's how the thing went sour."

During his father's six years as president, Dany and his brother, Dory, were at boarding-school in England. Dany went on to study engineering at Loughborough College. "I remember coming back here, and there would be a royal visit from Athens, King Paul, Queen Frederika, Prince Constantine and what's-her-name, Sophie. Those were very pleasant days, very grand. Everybody loved it in Lebanon."

The 1950s and 1960s were the golden age of Lebanon's independence. President Chamoun was the major-domo of a fashionable Mediterranean resort, charming women from around the world with his film-star's good looks and surprising other heads of state with his mastery of political intrigue. Even his enemies, like his neighbours in the Shouf, the Jumblatts, said he was the most charming man they had ever known. I had interviewed him during the civil war, when he was in his seventies and eighties, and he remained an irascible, unscrupulous fox. I wanted to see him on this trip, but Dany had told me he was ill. He had just turned eighty-seven.

In 1957, the CIA provided Chamoun with money to buy votes in the parliamentary elections – defeating candidates who were more pro-Nasser than pro-US, including the Druze leader Kamal Jumblatt. This was the election that led to the Frangieh–Douaihy feud in Zgharta and sent many losing candidates into opposition in the civil war that began the next year. The CIA agent who delivered the funds to buy votes, Wilbur Crane Eveland, later wrote in his memoirs, *Ropes of Sand*,

> Throughout the elections I traveled regularly to the presidential palace with a briefcase full of Lebanese pounds, then returned late at night to the embassy with an empty twin case I'd carried away for [CIA regional monetary director] Harvey Armado's CIA finance-office people to replenish. Soon my gold DeSoto with its stark white top was a common sight outside the palace, and I proposed to Chamoun that he use an intermediary and a more remote spot. When the president insisted that he handle each transaction by himself, I reconciled myself to the probability that anybody in Lebanon who really cared would have no trouble guessing precisely what I was doing.

When the parliament chosen in 1957 was preparing to elect a president in 1958, the first civil war began. "In 1958," Dany went on, "Egypt and Syria formed a union, and they tried to force Lebanon into the union. It was just the first opportunity the Syrians had to do away with Lebanese independence."

Lebanon's golden age, that ended in the early 1970s with the arrival of Palestinian commandos and the Israeli air raids, was marred only for a few months in 1958 when the Muslims believed Chamoun was preparing to amend the constitution to allow him to run for a second term as president. The Sunni Muslim politician, Saeb Bayk Salaam, and other Muslims allied to Nasser took to the streets, and the Lebanese army remained neutral rather than split between Christians and Muslims. Chamoun asked for American help. None came, until the Iraqi army overthrew its pro-Western monarchy, headed by Emir Feisal's grandson, in Baghdad. Fearing a spread of revolution to the other Arab states, the US sent 14,000 troops and Marines to Lebanon, and the British sent a force to support King

Hussein in Jordan. Unlike the disastrous Marine landing twenty-five years later, only one American died in Lebanon in 1958 – an army sergeant shot by a sniper.

"The 102-day operation," Robert Murphy, President Eisenhower's special envoy to Lebanon, wrote in *Diplomat Among Warriors*, "it was estimated later, cost the United States $200,000,000. That financial reckoning reminded me of a call which I had received while in Beirut from Cevdet Dulger, the Turkish Ambassador there. He told me he was delighted with American military initiative, but said jocularly that the United States should have bought off the Lebanese – it would have been much cheaper than sending in the fleet."

When the Marines withdrew, the US gave Lebanon $10 million in aid. The country prospered again, and the army commander, General Fuad Shehab, became president. Shehab ran the country through his powerful military intelligence, tapping the telephones of opponents and arresting dissidents late at night on the South American model. Foreigners who visited Lebanon in those years remembered a country more welcoming and beautiful than Monaco – with the yachts of the rich at anchor in St George's Bay and the casinos filled with high-rolling gamblers.

"Your father went into a political eclipse after 1958," I said to Dany, as Ingrid brought us glasses of fresh lemon juice.

"I wouldn't say it was a political eclipse. He founded the National Liberal Party, and he wrote a book, *The Crisis in the Middle East*. He faced a lot of political persecution, not only against him personally, but against his followers." Dany left his job as an engineer at Beirut airport after the civil war and went into private practice. "My last engineering job was this house in 1985."

"So, when did you go into politics?"

"Completely on my own? In 1975. I was sort of on my own, because the National Liberal Party didn't have a militia. I wasn't even a member of the party, but a small group decided I was the best suited to lead and train their militia. We formed the Lebanese Tigers." The Tigers, *Nimour*, took their name from the plural of Camille Chamoun's nickname, actually his father's first name – *Nimr*, Tiger. "We were about two hundred and seventy strong. We did some of our training up here. Our first camp was down there where that lake is. And then we had another camp on that ridge of rocks. See those rocks down there? It's a beautiful site, you know, for training in clandestine operations."

"You hadn't any military experience?"

"No, but I was always interested in military equipment, military activity, a lot of things like that. I started shooting at the age of five, so I knew quite a bit about weapons. We had ex-military officers who did the training."

"What was the rationale for the militia?"

"Honestly, I was never fully convinced. I always thought, once you create a militia, how do you disband it? Once you issue weapons, how do you collect them? But at the time, my father and the other parties knew they could not rely on the army. You saw what happened to the army in 1958. It did not look as if it was going to perform against the government the Palestinians set up. The Christians were beginning to think, we had better carry some weapons. All those Palestinians were bringing their weapons like crazy from Syria."

"How did you get your weapons?"

"The stupid thing was that we Lebanese had to smuggle in weapons, literally smuggle in weapons to defend ourselves, whereas the Palestinians were getting weapons freely. We had to pay for the weapons ourselves. Palestinians received them freely across the Syrian border without the weapons being apprehended by the army or security forces. The Palestinians were getting free weapons, and all the people of the country had to buy them. And people paid in full. In fact, all the fighting initially was done by people who had bought their own weapons. As I said, I was always worried that, damn it, we're issuing so many weapons, how do you collect them? This is where we are now. We started with rifles, automatic weapons and mortars, then recoilless rifles, and we gradually escalated to heavy field artillery, heavy tanks and heavy rocket-launchers."

"What? No air force?"

"No. I think the aircraft were too expensive," he said, smiling. "We did get free tanks, but no planes."

"Who gave you the tanks?"

"Israel. I received the first two consignments in 1976. They gave us thirteen, but there was a shortage of ammunition for the tanks. We're beginning to develop the manufacture of ammunition now. We already make rocket-launchers here, three-inch rockets, sixty-eight millimetre. We have adapted ground-to-air missiles for ground-to-ground use. We've done a lot of rifle and machine-gun repair."

"When did the Tigers begin fighting?"

"From day one in April '75."

"You lost a lot at first." In the first year of the war, the Christian forces were pushed entirely out of their positions in west Beirut.

"The Tigers won most of their exchanges, but the Phalange lost its hold in west Beirut."

"Then you lost Damour." Damour was a village on the coast between west Beirut and Sidon. It blocked communications between Palestinian forces in the two cities. The Palestinians had an added motive for their attack on the Christian town: revenge for the massacres of Muslims and

378

Palestinians in east Beirut. They destroyed Damour, murdering and expelling its people.

"The Syrians finally threw in five thousand As-Saiqa troops to take Damour." As-Saiqa was a Palestinian group attached to the Syrian army. "We fought for fifteen days. Fatigue set in, and we couldn't take care of our wounded. We had sufficient munitions, but we were seventy-seven people fighting five thousand. We fought for ten days, but we could not hold. I could see the Palestinians at night. They established something like twelve mortar bases, and we had only three mortars and two recoilless rifles."

"Was your father there? He would have been seventy-five then."

"He was there, but I got him to go out by helicopter. I stayed on myself with sixteen fighters at our family's house in Saadiyat, just north of Damour. They lost sixteen in those attacks, and we had four killed. The guy next to me was shooting them with his hand-gun at fifteen paces. They were inside the house. It was really close-quarter combat."

"How did you get out?"

"My father was Minister of Defence, and he called in the air force. They made two strikes. So we made a truce with the Palestinians, then they attacked at three in the morning. That was when we had the close-quarter fighting. I had two thousand people to defend, and we were only sixteen fighters. That night, a little girl was born in the house. She was called Zalpha, after my mother. When the air force came back, we had a second ceasefire, and everybody left. I stayed behind with four other guys, as sort of hostages, until all the other people were out. I finally slipped out at night by sea. My father came and picked me up in the one and only navy coast-guard boat."

"He came himself?"

"Yes. He picked me up at midnight from the house. Then they came and ransacked the place. The irony was that I had to sign a ceasefire agreement with a Palestinian lieutenant who turned out in the Israeli invasion of 1982 to be an Israeli officer."

"After that, you began the attack on Tel el-Zaatar."

The siege of Tel el-Zaatar, led largely by Chaumoun's Tigers, lasted nearly two months. Tel el-Zaatar was a large Palestinian refugee camp in the foothills between east Beirut and the Christian mountain villages. When I was living in Broummana in 1972, I used to pass it every day in my *service* on the way to the American University. The shantytown provided cheap labour for the light industrial factories nearby. In times of tension, the Palestinian commandos there would put a checkpoint on the road. The Palestinians said the roadblocks were for self-defence in a country whose army did nothing to protect them from Israeli attacks. The Christians said they were an infringement of Lebanese sovereignty, and many Lebanese, both Christian and Muslim, resented foreigners who searched their cars and dared to ask them for identification in their own country. When the war was underway, the Christians demolished the smaller refugee camps and Muslim slums on their side of town. Tel el Zaatar was the last and largest. And, as Damour had done for the Palestinians, Tel el Zaatar blocked the Christians' main line of communications.

"It was a forced issue," Dany explained. "I mean, they had cut the road to the mountain, and they had some thirty-seven millimetre anti-aircraft guns. They used to harass the population around them. They were getting ready to encircle Beirut. East Beirut would have been completely isolated."

"So you began the siege?"

"No, we began with an attack. We found Christian Palestinians who had had enough and wanted a guarantee of a new life in an anonymous situation. They removed the mines outside the camp. We were able to infiltrate. Unfortunately, due to a case of vanity in the Christian camp, Amin Gemayel refused to participate with his forces except under his own leadership. So, we gave command to an army officer who is now the commander of the army . . ."

"General Aoun?"

"Aoun carried out the attack too late. He tried to stop the attack at six in the morning. He delayed about two hours. By that time, the first barrage had gone down. At eight o'clock, our guys went in and twelve of them died. It was a major setback."

"Then the siege began?"

"We counter-attacked twenty-four hours later. We started nibbling away at it. In fact, the whole attack turned into a siege. We did not want another massacre, as in Qarantina, people being lined up against a wall and shot. There were many dead, as it turned out. I think in the end two thousand people were killed in the fighting. It went on for fifty-one days. We lost ninety-nine killed on our side."

Phalangist fighters had led me on foot with Doyle McManus of UPI into the camp the morning it fell, and we saw the bodies of men, women and children. Children's heads had been shot away from their bodies. Families had been butchered in their houses. Bulldozers were scooping up corpses and dropping them into pits. Cars belonging to looters drove over the dead, crushing their flesh and bones into the asphalt road. Human blood flowed in the gutters, and my shoes were so drenched with the blood of the dead that I threw them away. My clothes had the stench of death, and the air was mixed with putrid smoke. I had walked through the gates of hell. "I was there," I said to Dany, recalling images that would never leave my memory. "It was still a massacre."

"Yes. But the whole thing was reversed. It was no longer a Lebanese fight. It was a fight against the Palestinians and the extreme left organisations. It was no longer a sectarian battle. The press picked that up, and it changed the whole configuration of the war in Lebanon. We captured the Palestinian command. At the same time, we took Nabaa." Nebaa was a mixed neighbourhood of Palestinians and Shiite Lebanese in east Beirut. "We had our Shiite collaborators, because the PLO had Shiite members. We promised them there would be no eviction of Shiites, only Palestinians. But Amin Gemayel carried out the evictions of the Shiites anyway. At the same time, the Christians made major gains in the north, pushing Palestinians up the northern coast. Our morale was high. We had twice the area we had before we started the battle of Tel el Zaatar. We stabilised the fronts. We opened our roads, set up artillery bases and got ready for winter. This is contrary to what the Syrians say. They say they came to save the Christians."

"As I recall, you were losing when the Syrians came into Lebanon. The Palestinian-leftist coalition was about to impose its terms on the Christians."

"That is not the truth. That is not the truth. The Palestinians were not doing well at all."

"All that time you kept up, and you still keep up, your contacts with the Palestinians."

"It's life. I live here. This is the whole thing about Lebanon. You know, I went across the lines and I met up with Abu Hassan three times during Tel el Zaatar." Abu Hassan, Ali Salameh, the PLO security chief, was later assassinated by Israel. His wife was a Lebanese Christian beauty who had been Miss World. Dany and Abu Hassan were known to be friends, even when their followers were killing one another. "I went into Sabra camp in west Beirut to see him, in the middle of the fighting. But, you know, this is exactly what happens with the Arabs everywhere. They fight, and they meet during the fighting, and they go back to fighting. And one day they decide to live together. It's the history of the people."

Ingrid came out with the boys. "Dany, I think we'd better go to lunch now." Dany drove us all down to an outdoor restaurant near Faraya. Ingrid's mother and father and a friend of Dany's with his young son were waiting at a table in a small grove of trees. At lunch, discussion jumped from one topic to another, the way our hands scooped food from the different plates of *mezze*. Dany told me about the first contacts with Israel and the Israeli commitment in weapons that led to the invasion of 1982. He said the Syrians, even during the short time they supported the Christians, knew about the Israeli connection, although they disapproved of it. He told me how Bechir Gemayel had massacred his Tigers at Safra Marina and became supreme commander of the Christian militias. He had just left the house when Bechir's men attacked, but they went after him later. "What could I say when Pierre Gemayel phoned up?" Pierre Gemayel was the father of Amin and Bechir, head of the Phalange Party, a sometime ally, sometime rival of Camille Chamoun. "What could I say when he tells me he was very sorry about what was happening, that some bandits were responsible? Now, I have to admit I'm relieved to be out of the militia business. I never liked it."

"But you're still in politics. How can you accomplish anything without the Syrians?"

"How can we deal with the Syrians? You have seen how they behave here. You saw what they did in Hama."

"Any military regime would have gone into Hama for its own survival."

"You think they were right?"

"No, but Hafez al-Assad had no choice. The Muslim fundamentalists had taken one of his largest cities and called for a revolution in all of Syria. What did they think he would do?"

"Anyway," he said, "with the involvement of regional powers here, especially Iran, it is going to be difficult to get a unified Lebanese attitude to evicting the Syrians from Lebanon. Really, the Syrians are the one and only detrimental factor in Lebanon.

"You used to say that about the Palestinians."

"The Palestinians are not going to be powerful in Lebanon. There are not many left, maybe four thousand fighters in the whole country. With Christian and Shiite opinion running against them, they won't have a hope. At my last meeting with Yasser Arafat, we made it clear that the Palestinians as a people are welcome to stay here until their problem with Israel is settled."

"You still meet with Arafat?"

"Sure."

"Where?"

"In Iraq."

"And you still meet the Israelis?"

"Of course."

"What a country!"

"We agreed with Arafat in Baghdad that we will never again have Palestinian military bases here, that Lebanon will not be used as a world terrorist base."

During the Israeli invasion, some PLO officials had told me, they bought ammunition from the Chamouns when their stocks were running low. Despite all their battles against the Palestinians, the Christians had a friendly relationship with Yasser Arafat, who was now helping them to obtain arms. Dany Chamoun and Walid Jumblatt remained friends, despite the fighting between Druze and Maronite in the Shouf.

After lunch, after consuming a *mezze*, then grilled chicken with garlic, *arak*, fresh fruit and coffee, I was ready for a nap. I tried to sleep in the car, sitting next to the driver and watching the hills pass. I thought about what Dany had said, "They fight, and they meet during the fighting, and they go back to fighting. And one day they decide to live together. It's the history of the people." It was the unending history of the tribes, and I could not make any sense of it.

The taxi took me from lunch with Dany to Charles Rizk's house above Faraya. Like Dany Chamoun's, his chalet was made of stone, concrete and polished wood. Originally built only for the ski season, the chalets were becoming year-round homes for people avoiding the war in Beirut. I found Charles Rizk and his wife, Naila, with their lunch guests in the garden. I already knew the guests: Mouna Bustros, Naila Bustros and her husband, Maurice Sehnaoui, Mouna and Naila's cousin Michel Bustros and Sara Sallum, who had been my neighbour in west Beirut.

I asked Sara where she was living. "I'm still living in the west," she said proudly.

"She's one of the last Lebanese patriots," Charles Rizk joked. Sara was a Christian, and she stayed on the Muslim side despite the fact that her antiques gallery in west Beirut had been looted and closed.

"I refuse to accept the partition of Beirut, of Lebanon. I go east and west. I come from Faraya just as I go to Sidon." Sara was a determined woman, and she had scolded a young Muslim militiaman at a checkpoint who remarked on her being a Christian. "I am a Lebanese," she told him, "just like you."

"Would you like a drink?" Charles Rizk asked me.

"No, thanks, just a coffee."

"Sure you don't want a drink?"

"I've just come from lunch with Dany Chamoun. I had quite a bit of *arak*. I think I could use a coffee."

"What does Dany think about the situation?" Charles asked me. "Is he pessimistic?"

"No. He's neither optimistic nor pessimistic."

Naila Rizk brought me a Turkish coffee, and I dropped into a stuffed chair to rest. Charles Rizk, a big man with fiery red hair, sat in the chair opposite. Born in 1935, he had taken his doctorate in law from Paris, then taught law and worked in politics most of his life. He had a good political sense and knew Lebanon's history. "We need allies," he said. "Now, the Christians are alone. Israel won't help again, and the United States is not interested."

"Who else is there?"

"I think we have to get Egypt back into the region. It is the only way to counter-balance Syria. This may mean, however, an Islamic revolution in Egypt."

"That might be worse than the revolution in Iran," Mouna said.

"There is no difference," Michel Bustros said, "between a Shiah or a Sunni Islamic revolution."

I put in my own, unfounded opinion. "I think the Sunni fundamentalists would be more reactionary than the Shiah."

"Egypt is the only way," Charles Rizk went on. "But Egypt is lost now with . . . what's his name?"

"Hosni Mubarak."

"You see. We can't even remember his name. He's zero."

The late Lebanese mountain afternoon wore on, all of us sitting contented drinking coffee and talking, much as we had done before the war. Michel Bustros offered us glasses of the new pear liqueur from his Kefraya winery, "Nectar de Kefraya." Served cold, it made a delicious after-coffee drink. Charles and I discussed Lebanon in English, while everyone else was using French. Charles had written a book on Arabism and Islam, and he said he was working on a sequel. The problem that nagged at him was how to find an ally to help Lebanon wean itself from Syria. In the 1840s, Egypt eliminated, however briefly, the Turkish monopoly of power in Mount Lebanon. "It has to be Egypt again," Charles said. "Who else is there?" I suppose I had had too much *arak* at lunch, too much Nectar after. Dany Chamoun had already given me the answer. Two Arab capitals had traditionally vied to control all Syria, including Lebanon. One was Cairo, and the other was Baghdad. Dany had just returned from Baghdad.

Dany Chamoun had laid the groundwork for the Christians' newest alliance, just as he had for the previous, disappointing support from Israel. It would not be long before Lebanon ate the bitter fruit of Iraq's support for the Christian campaign, led by General Michel Aoun, to expel Syrian troops from Lebanon. Like previous meddlers in Lebanese affairs, the Iraqis would provide just enough military aid to sustain the battle, but too little to end it.

"Dany tells me you're rationalising Hama," Rudy Paulikovitch said to me a few nights later in the bar of the Mira Mar Hotel near Jounieh. As a new press centre, the Mira Mar was a poor substitute for the recently gutted Commodore Hotel, itself an inferior successor to the Old St Georges. I did not feel disloyal to the Commodore, so long as its manager, Fuad Saleh, was with us at the bar.

"Rudy, he couldn't have told you that."

"Dany said, 'What's wrong with this guy? How can he rationalise Hama?'"

"Rudy, that's not what I said. Look at it this way: what was Syria's alternative? What did the Muslim Brothers expect? Of course, it was mass murder. I did not say it was right, only that it was inevitable. Anyway, how can you guys rationalise Tel el-Zaatar?"

There were several visiting American, British and French journalists at the bar. Fuad Saleh, his German wife Felix, Patrick Bishop of the *Sunday Telegraph* and a resident British correspondent named Robin Mannock were also having drinks. It was rather like the old days, before Hizballah scared us all out of west Beirut.

Rudy and Patrick Bishop were having dinner in Jounieh, and Fuad Saleh was taking his wife to a family party. Two French journalists, one of them an old friend I prefer to call Pierrot, and I took their driver, Tony, up to Jebail. The ancient Phoenician port with its Crusader sea castle lay a few miles north of Jounieh, past the Casino du Liban. When we arrived, the electricity was off. The moon cast a shadow of the old castle walls over the still waters to the shore where small wooden fishing boats were beached for the night. The only light onshore was from the candles outside on the tables at Pepe Abed's restaurant. Pepe Abed, a Lebanese Mexican emigré who had run restaurants in Lebanon for forty years, gave us a table outside, facing the water.

The decorations at Pepe's, apart from the fishing nets, consisted mainly of pictures of Pepe in his restaurant with celebrities of yesteryear like Anita Ekberg. Other signed photographs showed his heroes like Bechir Gemayel and the member of parliament for Byblos, Raymond Eddé, who was living in exile in Paris. Pepe looked older now, more tired than he had in the pictures with his guests. He still wore his old yachting cap and leather jacket, and he was having eye problems and his glasses were thicker than I remembered.

Pierrot, his friend and I looked at the menu. Pepe sat down and advised us, "The best thing is the grilled shrimps. They are fresh today." Without our saying a word, he told the waiter to bring us a *mezze* and grilled shrimps. Turning to Pierrot, he asked, "*Avec de l'ail?*"

"*Avec beaucoup de l'ail,*" he instructed the waiter. "*Et une bouteille de Kefraya blanc.*"

Pierrot held up two fingers. "Two bottles of Kefraya white," Pepe said to the waiter.

"How are your restaurants in west Beirut and Tyre?" I asked Pepe.

"Finished."

"I went to your place in Tyre last year," I told him. It was a similar restaurant, also on an old Phoenician and Crusader port, but smaller, called the Admiral's Club. "The restaurant was open. It was run by a Christian."

"Yes," Pepe said. "He's a Christian and a cretin." *Il est Chrétien et crétin.* "He doesn't pay any rent."

Two Americans who had retired after years of working in Iran, Warren Kennedy Greedy and Linda Betts, ran the Admiral's Club until 1976. Pierrot and I used to go down there, eating in the restaurant and staying in the small hotel above, covering Israeli raids or just having weekends with friends. Warren, a wiry old man with a thick grey beard, had found a wounded stork on the shore and given it a steady diet of fish and made it the restaurant's mascot. I asked Pepe what had happened to Warren and Linda.

"I don't know. I haven't heard anything since I left."

"And the stork?"

"Gone. I think someone shot him."

"Like Drake's parrot," Pierrot said. Chris Drake, a BBC correspondent, had kept an African grey parrot in the bar of the Commodore Hotel for many years. The parrot used to do a perfect imitation of the whistle of an incoming artillery shell, but it had disappeared when the hotel was looted in the last round of Druze–Amal fighting.

"And my hotel near Bab Idriss," Pepe said, "gone too. And the Acapulco Beach, gone." The hotel near Bab Idriss, the Acapulco Beach Club and the Admiral's Club all lay in the Muslim areas and were lost to Pepe for the foreseeable future.

Pepe took us down to his cellars, where he had a winter bar. "Down here," he told us, "I keep all my antiquities, from every period of history." It was a treasure-trove of Hittite busts, Roman columns and Phoenician anchors in an underground grotto. He had a roll of signatures on one wall, his famous guests. At the top was "Bechir Gemayel, 7 August 1982." A month after he had signed, Bechir was assassinated.

"Bechir used to come here all the time," Pepe said. "He brought Ariel Sharon for dinner before the invasion. Could Sharon eat! He had four bowls of hommous himself. And drink! We did not have a chair big enough for him."

After dinner, Tony the driver took us back along the coast road to the Mira Mar. The other French journalist was tired and went up to bed. "Good," Pierrot said. "He's a boring guy. Now we can enjoy ourselves." Pierrot and I went to the bar, but it was empty, so Pierrot told Tony to drive us to a discotheque, the Mandaloun, in the east Beirut suburb of Dbaye. The Mandaloun was in a cave-like room with large picture windows facing the sea. We took a table near the dance floor, where we caught the full blast of the music and the glare of the flashing lights. The Mandaloun was packed with the *jeunesse dorée* of east Beirut. We ordered drinks and watched the youngsters dance. Pierrot drank whisky and looked bored. The girls were pretty, but most had dates or were in large groups. They were much younger than either of us.

"Let's find Tony and tell him to take us to Tiffany's."

It must have been three in the morning when we got into Tony's car. "A *Tiffany, Antoine*," Pierrot said to him. "Tony," I said, "I hope we're not keeping you up too late. I suppose you want to sleep."

"When Mr Pierrot in town, no sleep!" Tony jammed the Mercedes into fourth gear and sped along the road to another night club.

The next thing I remembered was sitting at the bar with a double whisky, a cigarette, and hookers from Colombia all around. One of the Colombian women was telling me, "I have two children in Bogotà. They have two and four years. Life is very bad in my country."

"It must be pretty bad if you have to come and work in Lebanon."

"Is very, very bad."

"How old are you?"

"Twenty-five. I came here when I was twenty-three."

I had seen generations of hookers come and go in Beirut. They seemed to succeed one another in waves of nationalities. For a time, Swedes were the favoured prostitutes for the rich, and Egyptians for the poor. In the lull between 1977 and 1980, British girls worked the bars on Phoenicia Street in west Beirut. I met one Englishwoman who stayed on, working behind the bar, although she had been raped by Syrian soldiers. Just before Hizballah closed the street in 1984, I remember meeting girls from Peru. Now, the business had moved to the east side, and the girls were Colombian.

"Do you want to come with me?" she asked. "You can take me to a room in your hotel. No problem."

"You're a prostitute?"

"Yes."

The girl on my other side was pretty, but a little fat. "Please buy me a drink," she begged. "How about a bottle of champagne?"

Behind us, the cabaret act of women stripping and dancing to canned music didn't seem worth watching. I got up and walked to a booth where Pierrot was entertaining two Colombian prostitues, telling them jokes. "Ah, Charlot," he said, when I sat down. "Things are not so bad in Lebanon. Not like before, no, not like when we lived here. Still, we come back." He lit a Gauloise. "You know, girls, this guy and I, we used to have some good times during the war!"

We reminisced for awhile, but I was too tired to go on. "I think I'd better get some sleep," I said.

"You don't like it here? Let's go to the casino."

"The casino?"

"I was there last night. I can go and win back the three thousand francs I lost."

Pierrot was one of those friends who seemed always to be there, one of the things that made being a journalist worthwhile, knowing that when out on a story in some dreadful place, Pierrot would take me for a good night out. Although I was younger than he was, I just could not keep up. I heard Pierrot's voice, "Charlot, you're falling asleep. You go. Tony will take you and come back for me later. Anyway, I want you to remember me just like this."

The last thing I saw was my friend Pierrot, far from home in a dangerous land, sitting in a booth, with pretty Colombian women on either arm, champagne in a bucket on the table, a cigarette in one hand, a glass in the other. As I walked out the door, he proposed a toast, "To life." And both Colombians kissed him.

One night, I went back to the port at Jounieh where I had landed. A Lebanese Forces militiaman let me sit on a deckchair near his sandbag outpost to watch the people saying farewell to relations they might never see again. This was how Lebanon's brains and blood were being drained, not by the actual murder of its citizens, but the steady exodus of those with the money or the skill to escape. Many of them were poor, and class differentials were observed as much at the port as in the society at large. People with money and *wasta*, the Arabic equivalent of clout, arrived at the port in limousines. Their chauffeurs drove them right up to the dock, where they did not have to bother with customs formalities. For the rest, the system for departure, as at the borders, was designed to cause as much inconvenience as possible. At the entry to the port, Lebanese Forces guards, one without a left arm, opened suitcases and searched them thoroughly. The Lebanese Forces had learned in Israel to look through a suitcase. Other guards stood around with their M-16s, smoking cigarettes and looking bored.

Once their luggage had been checked, the departing passengers had to go to passport control three-quarters of a mile away. Taxis were standing by to take them, and no one at the concrete building, which looked strangely like a drive-in restaurant, observed the theoretical queue to hand over their passports. Taxis returned them to the dock, where porters piled bags onto hand-carts and passengers waited for the return of their passports. Boys rushed around with airport baggage trolleys, offering to carry the bags the two hundred and fifty yards to the ship. Most people waited under an awning, where men sold food and drink from the open side of a truck. Another man in a white short-sleeve shirt that revealed the stump where his right arm had been was selling wristwatches.

Finally the gangway was opened and a few people began walking towards the ship. Most did not rush to leave. Men in dark trousers and light sports jackets smoked cigarettes and continued talking, trying to ignore the ship that would carry them away from their country. A pretty girl in her twenties lingered with two older women on a bench. In a few minutes, most people were standing. More passports arrived, and the militiamen called out the names of their owners, who collected them and walked up the gangway. When their customers began to leave, the two men who worked selling food from the truck took a break to sit under the awning and play draughts.

Some people, men and women, began to weep. Families were dividing into those who were leaving and those who would stay behind. One woman had to be pulled away from a young man, probably her son, who turned away from her to walk alone to the ship. Some relations would linger on with those who were departing, walking part of the way to the ship, clinging to the exiles until the last possible moment. I could not always tell who was leaving, who was staying, until the last moment before stepping aboard, someone let go of a hand and gave the final wave.

One little boy in shorts and a T-shirt a size too large for him seemed puzzled by everything going on around him, tears streaming from their eyes. Finally, his father took his hand and led him to the gangway. Looking back, he kept saying, "Good-bye, bye-bye," to each of his relations in turn. He said it to his grandmother, his grandfather, his uncle. He could not stop saying good-bye. He said it to everyone he passed, to the militiamen, to the baggage boys. Then, with tears in his own eyes, he searched for someone, anyone else to whom to say a last farewell, and saw me sitting unobserved by the sandbags. His father tugged his hand, and the boy looked at me and whimpered, "Bye bye." Then he, his Lebanese father and European mother walked to the penumbra at dock's end, out of sight of their family, perhaps never to return, like my grandmother a century before.

Tomorrow, someone said, the airport would open, and it would not be necessary to take the ship to Cyprus. For most of them, it would always be necessary, because they would not dare to cross that Green Line. The sea was their only way in or out, as it had been for centuries. It was twilight, and the sky was turning dark red. In the small harbour, fishing boats and small sloops bobbed at anchor in the wake of the great ship as it carried little pieces of Lebanon away forever.

CHAPTER TWENTY-THREE

THE FAMILY AND THE PLAIN

On the labels of the Kefraya wines was a drawing of a large château. It was a stone folly with a tower, built on a hilltop surrounded by pines, just outside the village of Kefraya. The picture showed a field of vines in the foreground. The château behind was the country house of Nicolas de Bustros, Michel's father. It might have been in Provence, but it lay in the Bekaa Valley – in the middle of the no man's land between the Syrian and Israeli armies. The château on the label was a symbol; the winery itself was a modern factory a mile away.

Gaby Bustros had taken me to her uncle's château to meet the Frenchman who produced the wine. We were waiting for him in the château courtyard with the caretakers, a Lebanese couple in their eighties named Wadiaa and Marta Khairallah. Other people were sitting on benches on that warm morning: several farm labourers, an old farmer in a white *keffiyeh* who smoked hand-rolled cigarettes and a dark-skinned man from the winery named Abu Hassan. Abu Hassan said the Frenchman was on his way.

Marta Khairallah, her white hair pulled back and tied with a scarf, had given us some awful coffee and offered to give us breakfast. Without waiting for a reply, she went into the kitchen and returned fifteen minutes later with a tray of tea, olives, Arabic bread and fresh *labneh*. "This *labneh* is delicious," I told her. "Is it from here?"

"I made it," she said, somewhat offended at the suggestion she might have bought it.

Gaby and I ate the breakfast, and Abu Hassan told us that Marta's husband, Wadiaa, had "the gift."

"He can find water. He is a water diviner."

We looked at the old man, who was short and had two fingers missing from one hand. He said nothing.

"Not only can he find water on the land," Abu Hassan went on, "he can locate it with just a map. People bring him a map of their land. He will hold the divining rod over it and show where the water is. He has found seven wells on this property, all of which we are using."

"How can he do it with a map?" I asked him.

"He has the gift. Believe me. Draw a map of your house and property in London. He will tell you where water is."

I sketched an overview of our house and garden and handed it to the old man. He took his forked divining rod and held it over the paper. He closed his eyes, and the point of the stick traced a line from the road into the house and back again.

"This is where the water comes in," he said. "And this is where it goes out."

"That's right. Those are the water mains, and those are the drains."

He closed his eyes again and the divining rod made a small circle inside the house. "And you have water here, under the house. You can have your own well. Good."

What might have been good news in the Bekaa Valley meant only one thing in Notting Hill: rising damp.

Just then a slightly overweight Frenchman with shoulder-length light brown hair and bright green eyes came through the château gate. He had thick lips, from which an unfiltered cigarette dangled, and a nose shaped a bit like a pear. The breast pocket of his short-sleeved cotton shirt bulged with a French passport and a pack of Lebanese Cedar cigarettes. Yves Morard was thirty-four, and for the previous seven years he had worked in Lebanon to make the Kefraya wines as good as any in France.

Abu Hassan drove Yves, Gaby and me through the vineyards. Yves would give Gallic shrugs as he spoke in French, then translate whatever he said into Arabic for Abu Hassan. "It's good you came now," he told us. "It's the quiet time for the wine. From the first of September until March, I work twelve hours a day, minimum. I sleep at the winery. There are three shifts working twenty-four hours a day. Last year, we crushed five hundred tons of grapes. This year, one thousand tons."

"How did you happen to end up in Lebanon?" I asked him.

"I had taken my degree in oenology. I used to work six months here and there in France, and I took a technical diploma. When I was studying for my exams, I had a three-year old son then, I saw an ad for a vintner in Lebanon. I knew nothing about Lebanon. I called. After I passed my exams, they called back. When I met Michel Bustros, he looked at my hair. 'Do you have any prejudice against long hair?' I asked him. No answer. Then he said, ' If you come to Lebanon, you will get twenty years experience in two years.' He was right. I discovered he had two hundred and fifty hectares." He pointed at the endless rows of vines, neatly tied and pruned, tiny grapes beginning to grow. "Two hundred and fifty hectares! Do you know what that means?"

"No."

"In Burgundy, three or four hectares is the average. My father had seven hectares. I signed for three years, and I stayed." He stayed half the year in Lebanon, returning to his wife and children for the rest of the year in Dijon, where he kept a small vineyard of his own.

Abu Hassan drove us to the Mataam Sabaat Ayoun, Restaurant of the Seven Springs, south of Kefraya for lunch. It was a small place in the foothills on the west side of Bekaa, with tables outdoors in the shade of a walnut tree surrounded by a vine-covered pergola. The four of us sat at a cloth-covered table on which the leaves' shadows moved as the wind blew. The sound of the wind mixed with the water rushing along a channel to small reservoirs where the restaurant kept at least a hundred live trout. A waiter gave us a *mezze* of whole stalks of fresh thyme with onion garnish, *labneh* and olive oil, aubergines ground into a paste called *m'tabbel*, the local *shanklish* cheese, cold artichoke with garlic, a fattoush salad, hommous, olives, lettuce, cucumber, green pepper, radishes, carrots, parsley, mint, *arak* and beer.

Abu Hassan was ten years older than Yves. He had deep-set eyes that were always on guard, and his devotion to Yves was obvious. "He is my protection against kidnapping," Yves told me. "He goes everywhere with me."

"Do you feel safe here?"

"We give jobs to many Shiites," he said. "If I disappeared, Michel Bustros would close the winery, and they would have no work. And Abu Hassan guarantees my safety. He is Shiite."

"Are you the only Frenchman left in Bekaa?"

"I think so."

"Fifty years ago, this valley was filled with French officials, French soldiers, French gendarmes, French priests," I said. "Now there is only you."

"If France can help make wine, it's better than having an army."

A young farmer in khaki trousers and shirt, his head wrapped in a red *keffiyeh*, walked by, hoe in hand. He trudged up the hill and cut herbs, collecting a huge bundle. To my right on the hilltop was an old church.

"So," Gaby asked him, "what are your good vintages?"

"I don't like Lebanese wine too old. The Lebanese have their vintages, but four years is old enough. When I drink, I want a good red wine. Not a heavy, old, thick wine. I prefer a girl of twenty-five to an old woman of seventy-five."

He told us about the *recolte*, the harvest, the *cuve*, the vat, and the *caves*, the wine cellars, and the grapes, syrah, mourvèdre, grenache, cabernet sauvignon. He loved his work. "Seven years ago, I asked Michel to plant all these grapes. The grapes will be ready in 1992, the wine in 1995. In seven more years," he promised, "I will have wines as good as Châteauneuf du Pape."

After the *mezze,* a waiter brought us a tray of grilled trout and fried potatoes.

"Are there many differences between making wine here and in France?" I asked.

"Here it is impossible to work as in France. I have to adapt, and they have to adapt. When I came, I said I wanted the wine vats to be just as clean as my bathroom. But I adapt. The thing that shocked me the most in Lebanon – the most tiresome thing – is that we are forbidden to enter one another's *caves.* In France, we visit one another and have a dialogue about the wines. The only exception is the Nakad Winery in J'dita. He lets me in to taste his wine and talk with people about it."

Lebanon's wineries were Kefraya, Ksara, Musar, Nakad and five smaller properties.

"Have you had a good time living here?"

"Interesting. Five years ago today, the Israelis arrested me."

"What happened?"

"In 1982, the Israeli invasion came right through here. I was hiding in the winery, when shelling started. They hit the building. I knew that if the distillery area was hit, it would explode. So I ran to a drainage pipe under the road. A Merkava tank went right over my head, stopped and began firing. Another Merkava drove up, and its cannon was three metres from my head."

"What did you do?"

"I smoked my cigarette." He laughed out loud. "What could I do? That night, they camped near me. At ten o'clock, someone shined a torch in the hole. I put my hands up, and they told me to come out. They threw me against the M-113," an American-made armoured personnel carrier, "and I felt for my passport in all my pockets. Nothing. They tied me up and put me on the ground until morning."

In Arabic, Abu Hassan said to me, "Don't write about this."

"It's okay," Yves said. "Anyway, I said my passport was in the house. They asked me for my telephone number in France. They called to tell them I was alive. They interrogated me three or four times. Someone called my mother. Then she called my wife, who called Michel Bustros in Paris. He called the Quai d'Orsay, who called the French ambassador in Israel. Finally, they let me go."

"You came back?"

"Why not?" he shrugged. He lit a cigarette. "Remember, *la France a perdu une bataille, mais la France n'a pas perdu la guerre.*" He held his finger up as he said it, and he laughed. France has lost a battle, but France has not lost the war.

We went back to Yves' house in a village near Kefraya to have siestas after lunch. I rarely took afternoon naps, but, when I did, my dreams were usually too vivid. In this dream, I was in a car with a driver I did not know. He took me through south Lebanon, stopping at every Hizballah checkpoint. He would get out of his car and chat with the gunmen, while I sat inside the car. At one checkpoint, he started an argument with the bearded Hizballah gunmen. They opened the car and ordered me out. I ran and ran and ran. I woke up. I was sweating in the heat of the late afternoon, and I took a cool shower before we went to the Kefraya Winery.

"Right now," Yves said, holding a glass of red wine up to the light, "we have four reds, three whites, two rosés. We are also making *arak*, brandy and the Nectar pear liqueur. Not bad, *hein?*"

I tasted the red. "Not bad at all." Yves was showing Gaby and me the giant vats in which the wines were stored, the funnels down which the grapes were poured at harvest time, the crushing machines, the storage facilities, the *arak* and brandy distilleries. He led us downstairs to a copper still. The brandy was waiting, still fifty per cent alcohol. "When the first drop is ready," he said of the brandy, "we slaughter a sheep and eat it grilled." He showed us a bottling machine, a red Heath-Robinson contraption about the size of a sports car, from Ets Ducourneau.

We were upstairs having a glass of wine, when a man in a greenish safari suit walked into the winery. About five foot nine and in his mid-forties, he had a moustache and dark hair. Yves called him, "Salim!"

"Yves, how are you?" Salim Nakad, who owned the Nakad winery, said. "I need your advice." Nakad opened a folder from the Krugman printers in Bavaria and showed Yves three wine labels, one each for Nakad's red, white and rosé wines. "What do you think?"

Yves picked up an unlabelled bottle and held the Nakad labels against it. "They're good," he said.

"What's wrong with your old labels?" I asked him.

"I'm starting to export now. The distributors said the wine was good, but that the label looked like a death notice."

"No," Yves said, "this is much better."

I asked Nakad how long he had been growing wine in the Bekaa.

"My father started in 1923," he said. "But you know, they've been growing wine here for ages. Near our cellars, we found a Bronze Age wine press. We also found two Bronze Age coffins of a warrior and his wife. They were in perfect condition."

"I suppose they needed warriors to protect the wines," I said.

"They still do."

"Salim, come and taste my new reds. I want to know what you think," Yves said. He put out several glasses each for Salim, Gaby, himself and me.

We all tasted the Château de Kefraya '85, the Côteaux de Kefraya '83 and the Côteaux de Kefraya '86."

They all seemed good to me. "This," Salim said, holding up the 1985 Châteaux, "will be an excellent wine in two years. This is a good red wine. The others? They are not as good, but I think the '83 will be better than the '86."

"We keep trying. Sometimes good, sometimes bad. *La France a perdu une bataille, mais la France n'a pas perdu la guerre.*" Yves winked and held up a finger. "Anyway, try the Blanc de Blancs. Good? Light and a little fruity. It will be good with Lebanese *mezze.*"

"I thought wine tasters were not supposed to swallow the wine," I said to Yves.

"I like it, for now. But when the harvest starts in a few months, I cannot drink at all."

Salim Nakad said he had begun in a small way to export to the United States. "I went to Seattle for seven months," he said. "My daughter has leukemia and needed treatment. She's better now. But there was a Lebanese restaurant in Los Angeles that has begun ordering my wine."

"I'm from Los Angeles," I said.

"Do you like your California wines?"

"Very much."

"The Californians are very good," Yves said. "The Californians bought vines from Burgundy, some more from Bordeaux. They have the most modern methods. In Burgundy, they break up ice and throw it in the vats with the grapes. It's archaic. It is wine folklore. In California, they set the temperature with computers."

"It's a rare Frenchman who admits the Californian wines are good."

"We have a lot to learn about wine. When some experts came here from France, they said there was not enough acid in my wine. You need acid to prevent the growth of bacteria. But I found that here there was no bacteria. It's dry here. I could reduce the acid content for better wine. It is against all my education, but it's better."

In the evening, we drove south to Lake Karaoun for dinner. We passed a Lebanese army checkpoint south of Khirbet Kanafar. Although the Syrian lines did not come this far south, Syrian intelligence officers usually lurked in the background at the Lebanese roadblocks. We came to another checkpoint, where four Lebanese soldiers from one of the country's many forgotten infantry brigades sat around an open fire cooking their supper. They looked up at us when we slowed, but they did not bother to stand. This was the last checkpoint before the Israeli-occupied zone began south of Lake Karaoun. This was the heart of the no-man's-land, between the Syrian and Israeli forces: no soldiers, no police, only civilians and

395

guerrillas. Nearby in the village of Machgara, just before the Israeli lines, the Syrian Socialist National Party based its fighters for attacks against Israeli forces in the south. They cooperated, and occasionally clashed, with their nominal allies in Hizballah. Machgara was the threshold of the easiest passage to Marjayoun, where the so-called South Lebanon Army, the Israelis' own Lebanese militia, kept its headquarters.

The headlights of Abu Hassan's car shone on the farm walls and trees lining the empty road. Occasionally we passed another car coming in the opposite direction. Whether they were civilians out for dinner, or guerillas returning home from reconnaissance missions in the south, it was too dark to say. A few people were walking among the houses in the larger villages; in the smaller ones the streets were empty and dark.

Abu Hassan turned left down the hill towards the lake. The first restaurant we tried was closed. We went on to the Chalet du Lac, a popular resort before the war. It was a pretty restaurant, with a wide balcony over the lake. It looked alpine, as though we had come to Lake Geneva. The restaurant was empty, and its owner was about to close when we arrived, but he welcomed us gladly. He took us through his restaurant past a dozen empty tables covered in white cloth, around the potted plants and a waiter watching colour television. I noticed a scale model of a tourist develop-ment in the middle of the room. The architect's replica showed a high-rise hotel, bungalows dotted along the shore, swimming pools and a marina *à la* Marbella. "This seems a bit optimistic," I said to the *patron*.

"We'll build it. You'll see."

"When the war is over?"

"*Insh'allah.*" God willing.

From the terrace, a gentle slope rolled down to the lake. Lake Karaoun was man-made, built after the earthquake of 1956 rocked south Lebanon and led to demands for a dam to provide electricity as in other, more developed parts of Lebanon. The Naccache Dam slowed the flow of the Litani River, providing electric lights and a beautiful lake.

"I learned to water-ski on that lake," Gaby said. "I miss this country. I live here, and I miss it."

"Some things are still here."

"What?"

"Things like this restaurant, this lake, these people. They can't destroy everything."

"They're trying."

The owner brought us a light *mezze* and some grilled chicken. He served us Nakad wine. "What? You don't have Kefraya?" I asked.

"Only Nakad."

"It's okay," Yves said. "We like Nakad."

Yves took a sip. "*Alors*," he said. "I've told Salim not to make the white wine so heavy. It should be light and fruity to go with this food."

The full moon over the Anti-Lebanon glowed dark orange, like a dying coal, and etched a stream of glitter across the lake from our terrace to the silent village of Sokmore on the eastern bank. A cool breeze swept over the lake, rustling the branches of the pines below our table and of an old walnut tree on the hill nearest us. The Big Dipper was clear in the sky. On our side of the lake, Mount Lebanon was covered in forests, orchards and green fields. The hills of the Anti-Lebanon opposite were bare.

"Look there," Abu Hassan said, pointing to the Anti-Lebanon. "From all the way north to here, there is not one tree. Not one. They cut them. If they grow, the goats eat the saplings."

"That's the difference between the west and east Bekaa," Gaby said. "It's always been that way."

"It looks very quiet there." I said.

"No one goes out at night," Abu Hassan said.

"Why not?"

"There's nowhere to go. There are no cinemas or night clubs."

"What about visiting?"

"They don't even go out to visit one another."

"Was it that way before the invasion?"

"No," Abu Hassan said. "Before Israel came, they did go out. When the Israelis invaded, all the people welcomed them and threw rice – all of them. Don't listen to what they tell you now. I saw them throwing rice. Then the Israelis brought the Lebanese Forces. The Lebanese Forces worked with the Israelis and abused the people. When the Israelis withdrew in 1985, the collaborators had to leave with them. But they all have family. Everyone is related, so there were reprisals. Ten days ago, someone threw a grenade into a house wounding a woman and her children. Another man, whose brother was in the Lebanese Forces, was assassinated. No one rests easy now. No one."

A taxi took Gaby and me the next morning from the Château Kefraya back through the lines, past checkpoints of the Lebanese army, then of the Syrians. We reached the Beirut–Damascus highway and turned left into the hills. The car took us past Gaby's family's old farmhouse near Chtaura. She looked at it and said, "The refugees are still living in the house. I'm glad someone is using it." Years before, we had visited a large Muslim family who had occupied the house. They had lost theirs in Israeli bombing further south. Gaby checked that everything was working and asked if they had enough to eat. She never asked them whether they planned to leave.

The road went further up the mountain, and I looked down on the wide sweep of the Bekaa plain – the green fields, the plots of freshly planted dark brown earth, the groves of fruit trees and the vineyards. In Arabic, the Bekaa was "*Sahel Bekaa*," the Plain of the Bekaa, rather than the English and French Bekaa Valley. It was more a long plain than a valley between two mountain ranges. The Arabic expression for welcome was "*Ahlan wa Sahlan*," *ahlan* meaning family. "Family and plain," was hardly a sensible welcome, but it was a contraction of a longer phrase that meant, "You have come to your family, and may you have travelled here across a gentle plain." Whenever I looked at the Bekaa from the mountain, I imagined that the Bekaa was the gentle plain the poets meant, and that I had walked across it to my family.

The highway cut the plain in two, and I regretted that I could not go north of the road to Baalbek. I wanted to see again the Roman ruins, the Palmyra Hotel and the springs of Ras al-Ain. I wanted to visit friends who lived there, to interview again Hizballah and Amal people. I wanted to describe Baalbek as it had become, comparing it to the town I had known fifteen years earlier, when it was the scene of one of the world's great music festivals. I wanted to contrast it to the place Mark Twain had described in 1867.

I remembered a hotel, the Palmyra, whose guest book was as filled with prominent signatures as that of the Baron's in Aleppo. Michel Alouf, the Christian grandson of the original proprietor, had once shown me the *livre d'or* in which were the names of General Allenby, who conquered Syria; General Gouraud, who annexed the Bekaa to *Le Grand Liban*; Marie of Roumania; Alfonso of Spain; the Duc d'Orléans; the Empress of Abyssinia; Charles de Gaulle; Jean Cocteau; and Jeanne Moreau. The stately stone building, overgrown with jasmine, faced the best Roman ruins in the eastern Mediterranean, the Temple of the Sun and the ancient city of Heliopolis. After Hizballah established itself in Baalbek, Michel had had to serve me brandy in teacups. Like all the other Christians of the town who had left, Michel finally gave up. He sold the hotel to the Shiite Husseini family, one of whom, Hussein Husseini, was the speaker of Lebanon's parliament. "We begged Michel to stay on," one of the Husseinis told me in Beirut. "We don't want the Christians to leave. But he could not make a life anymore." The only Christians who stayed on were the Greek Catholic archbishop, who had himself been kidnapped for a time, and the priests and nuns who ran the local Catholic school to which Shiites with money still sent their children.

I dared not return to Baalbek. The reasons for my reluctance lay in the realm of international politics, in the hatred that existed between my country and Iran. Why had Iran brought its ideology to Baalbek rather than some other Lebanese town? Why had the Iranian Revolutionary Guards gone to Baalbek in 1982 and made it one of Hizballah's headquarters? Why was the town that had once played host to Kaiser Wilhelm, where Duke Ellington had played jazz under the stars, where Ella Fitzgerald had sung and the Bolshoi Ballet danced, become the most dangerous place in Lebanon for an American or west European? I found an answer in a travel book written in 1906 by an observant and perceptive Englishwoman, Mrs A. C. Inchbold. In *Under the Syrian Sun*, Mrs Inchbold wrote from the then new Palmyra Hotel, "A seat in front of the open window before the hotel balcony afforded entertainment as varied and animated as the shifting scenes of a kaleidoscope." The population of Baalbek at the time was about four thousand Shiites and a thousand Greek Orthodox. From her seat near the balcony window, Mrs Inchbold watched both communities.

Rivalry and rancour flowed to a dangerous extreme for at least two weeks of our stay in Baalbek. The exciting cause was a mere quarrel which took place at a Greek Christian wedding. When the nuptial ceremony was in progress, some mischievous Metawileh [an archaic term for Shiite] youths entered the church uninvited, and created a disturbance by attempting to take their seats in the place reserved only for women. The chief men of the church came to remove the disturbers, who resisted, but were finally evicted with force.

After the church service was over, the procession took its way to the house of the bride, and while on the route the same Metawileh youths, who had evidently been watching their opportunity, insinuated themselves into the strictly feminine portion of the bridal cortège, not only angering but seriously alarming the Greek women.

"What are these strangers doing in our midst?" they screamed out indignantly, and called upon their men for rescue from a danger which the darkness of the hour enhanced.

A scrimmage of a serious nature was only arrested by the earnest intervention of the priest. It takes very little to fire the hot Eastern blood, especially where religious fanaticism is always the dominant chord of the emotions.

Next morning a member of the chief Christian family in the town was walking with a friend near the serai when he was confronted by one of the Metawilehs who had been concerned in the church episode.

"You put me out of the church last night," he shouted. "Take that this morning," and he struck the Christian boy in the face.

Then he took to his heels like the wind. He was promptly caught, however, and clapped into prison.

Immediately the fat was in the fire, burning and spitting finely. For this act of open violence towards a distinguished townsman was at once regarded by the Christians as ominous of bad feeling emanating from high authority in the Metawileh ranks behind the delinquent. They declared that he had been incited to overt defiance and insult of a purpose.

The incident nearly led to open warfare. Three hundred armed Shiites came into Baalbek ready for battle, and Christians from Zahle and Deir al-Ahmar were said to be preparing to march. The outnumbered Christians sent a deputation to the Ottoman governor in Damascus, who despatched troops. The commander of the Damascus garrison came in person to resolve the dispute, and he spent nine days on the terrace of the Palmyra Hotel deciding which community had been at fault. Without the Turkish intervention, the fighting might have spread as it had in 1860. It was unfortunate the Turks had not been in Beirut when the first shot was fired in 1975.

Mrs Inchbold noticed a feature of the Shiites of Baalbek that became evident to many others only after the Iranian revolution in 1979: "Their secret sympathies are all centred in Persia, which they consider the stronghold of their religion and its Shiite doctrines." When Persia was weak or uninterested in Lebanon's Shiites, they too were weak or quiescent. When Persia was strong and active, the Shiite tribes of Lebanon grew bolder.

The Shiites of Lebanon, who as a community had stayed out of the Lebanese civil war, began to assert themselves only after the mullahs had seized power in Iran and looked for fellow-Shiites in the Arab world to carry the banner of their revolution. Like the other Lebanese communities before them, the Shiites finally had an outside benefactor to assist them. Like the other communities, they discovered that outside help had a price: usually, obedience to the paymaster. The Christians found it with Israel, and the Druze made the same discovery with Syria.

The Shiites needed commerce to make money, schools for their children to achieve their aspirations and contact with the outside world, where many of their relations had made their homes. By obeying Iran's dictates to kidnap foreigners, so that Iran would be able to bargain with the hostages to buy arms and win back its frozen assets in France and the United States, they cut themselves off from the Western world. Trade in their parts of Lebanon, apart from the lucrative sale of Bekaa hashish and opium, came nearly to a halt. Lebanon's Shiites, most of whom had nothing to do with Hizballah, found it increasingly difficult to obtain visas to any country where they might be able to make a living. Iran's Lebanese Shiite clients frightened away the teachers and aid workers who had come to Lebanon to help the poor, and the Shiites were the poorest community in the country. Iran would help them so long as they did what they were told, but Iran would not lessen their poverty. Some day, Iran would withdraw its Revolutionary Guards and stop paying Hizballah. If all outsiders did the same with their clients, the Lebanese would have to learn again the art of living together or, at a minimum, prolong their tribal battles without imported weapons. Only then I might be able to return to Baalbek.

CHAPTER TWENTY-FOUR

THE SLUMBER OF THE DEAD

In the autumn of 1982, Beirut had been quiet. The Israeli guns had stopped firing. Palestinian commandos and Syrian soldiers had left the city. I had gone alone to the centre of Beirut, where the barricades between east and west had only just come down, and I wrote:

> Beirut's deserted central square, the Place des Martyrs, is still being cleared of the rubble of two foreign invasions and eight years of civil war. The Lebanese army and the American, French and Italian troops of the Multi-National Peacekeeping Force have removed the land mines, but the people who made it the bustling heart of antebellum Lebanese life have yet to return. Before the war the Place des Martyrs was Beirut's meeting place between east and west, Christian and Muslim. During the war, it was the dividing line. The gunmen – Christians in the east, Muslims and Palestinians in the west – who faced each other for eight years are gone. On either side stand the façades of buildings without roofs or backs, giving it the air of a movie set where filming was completed long ago and everything of value taken away.
>
> Lining the east side are the stone fronts of the old Prefecture of Police, a few cheap hotels, a private bus company and the Gemayel Brothers' Pharmacy, the pre-war livelihood of the ancient Christian leader whose party militia, the *Kitaeb* – Arabic for Phalange – won the war for now and whose sons, Bechir and then Amin, were successively elected to the Lebanese presidency late this summer. Behind the terrace lie the ruins of small shops, apartment buildings and whorehouses. Some of the last, like Chez Marica, were the haunts of French soldiers and bureaucrats under the French Mandate from 1920 to 1943, only to fall on hard times later when their clients were poorly paid Syrian and Palestinian workers. The prostitutes, like the other downtown traders, moved to other quarters after the war began in the spring of 1975.
>
> A hundred yards across the square, on the west side, the Zahra

Cinema is gone. The high-ceilinged coffee houses where old men smoked their narguiles and played backgammon are gutted, as are the gold, silver and vegetable souqs which lay beyond them. Only a few hundred yards from the ruins on either side do the buildings begin to take on normal shapes and signs of life emerge, with laundry hanging out of windows and fruit sellers pushing their barrows up winding streets.

The only surviving structure in the Place des Martyrs is a statue midway between the two sides. It stands over the spot where the last Ottoman military governor, Ahmed Jemal Pasha, erected gallows in 1915 to hang Lebanese, Syrian and Palestinian patriots who opposed the Turkish occupation of their land. The bronze figures of the martyrs are twisted in agony, the horror on their faces like that of Rodin's Burghers of Calais, as though the sculptor knew their deaths presaged the butchery to follow. Next to the monument is the only living person in the square, an old man with a box camera. Ever the optimist, he paces slowly around the martyrs, waiting for tourists to arrive and pay him to take their pictures, as they did before the war. Beirut is reunited, even peaceful, for the first time in eight years. But the war is not over. It has simply moved outside the capital, where under the Syrian and Israeli occupations it continues apace.

Now I had returned to the Place des Martyrs, but I had not imagined how much more damage it could sustain. Within a year of my previous visit, the war would move down from the mountains and back to the capital. Each year that followed brought with it an escalation, more fighters in the streets, heavier weapons fired at hospitals and houses, more bodies in the cemeteries. In February of 1984, while the Shiite and Druze militias were expelling the Lebanese army and the Multi-National Peacekeepers from west Beirut, the Lebanese Forces occupied the west side of the Place des Martyrs, their first territorial gain of the war.

"Why don't you take some pictures?" Elie, one of the two young Lebanese Forces escorts who had taken me to the Place des Martyrs, asked. "You must need some for your memory."

He was wrong. I would not need a camera to remember the sight of the Martyrs' Square. As badly damaged as some of the old buildings had been in 1982, they were worse on this summer morning. All the words that came to mind then, "damaged, destroyed, gutted," seemed inadequate to depict the scene of devastation around me. The authors of Genesis were unable to describe the nothingness that preceded the First Day and so called it "without form, and void" in the King James Version, "waste and void" in the Douai. The Place des Martyrs had become unimaginable waste, terrible void. The sight of it made me certain that if the war left only two Lebanese alive, they would make their way to this square and, with the last strength in their bodies, beat each other to death with stones from the beautiful buildings they had destroyed. As I entered the open plaza from the east side, I could not stop myself from whispering, "Oh, my God."

The façades of most of the buildings that had stood vacant on my earlier visit now had holes in them so large they were barely standing. On the east side, we wandered behind what had been the Prefecture of Police and the Gemayel Brothers' Pharmacy, narrow, welcoming, slightly wicked streets now open to the wind and rain. I found an old building just behind the police station. A few plinths of an old balustrade hung from its balcony, and a sign dangled from a corner. Of the ten letters that had for years welcomed visitors from far and near, only one remained, the "r" in "Chez Marica."

In the square itself, the rubble that had been cleared after the invasion was back. The statue in the middle of the plaza miraculously survived, much as it always had, with only a few more bullet holes, a few more wounds in the figures of the martyrs. The two martyrs who lay writhing on the ground still struggled towards the two standing figures, still reached in vain for a hand to pull them from their agony. The horror in their faces no longer evoked an adequate premonition of the butchery that followed their deaths. One Lebanese flag and two Lebanese Forces flags flew from the sculpture, as though the militia were claiming the square like a dog peeing on the ground to mark his territory. Near the statue, across the square from east to west, the militiamen had built a large earthwork barricade between the east and west sides. The old front line had run north-south, across empty space. When I asked why the earth mound ran across the width of the square, Elie's colleague, Najib, said, "Snipers. The Palestinians and Hizballah are up there." So, I thought, west Beirut had managed to hold on to one corner of the square, for what it was worth.

From the east side of the plaza, Elie, Najib and I ran in a bunch, in case any snipers were awake to our north. If we had run separately, the first runner would have alerted the sniper, who could have picked off the next two. We reached the west side, running into what had once been a shop. Some Lebanese Forces militiamen were relaxing on stools near an open fire with Turkish coffee on the boil. Scattered on the earth floor near the fire were plastic bags and paper plates of left-over hommous and grilled chicken from a take-away restaurant, yesterday's dinner. A fly was crawling up the neck of a brass tea-kettle. On the bare brick walls, they had pasted two pictures of Bechir Gemayel, their martyr. In one, he was framed in cameo, like a saint on a holy card. In the other, he sat astride the shoulders of his men and waved in triumph. The sound of a flute came from the floor above us, as though someone were charming a snake or playing a dirge.

We crouched through a hole in the back wall and walked into the narrow street of what had been the gold souq. It was dark and smelled of musty, burned wood. Elie and Najib took me into one of the shops, that had once had windows full of bracelets, necklaces and rings glowing under neon lights. The back wall was gone, and we ducked to enter the darkness that lay behind. It was another building, and we made our way up the remnants of a stone staircase with wrought-iron railings. Sand everywhere made the stairs into a kind of dune. "I know this place," I said to Najib and Elie. "I used to meet a friend here at her father's office." We were inside an old, arcaded building along Bab Idriss in what was the mercantile centre until 1976. Emma Maalouf's father had run his textile importing business from there, and I would occasionally have coffee with him in his office and wait to take Emma to lunch.

"Get your head down," Elie said. "We're coming to a window."

I kept my head below the window line, out of the sniper's sights, at the landing. We went up to the top floor where sandbags and metal barrels of sand made a kind of bunker for the snipers on our side. They needed the cover. All the walls were gone, and only bare concrete columns supported the roof.

We poked our heads up and surveyed the edge of the new frontier between east and west Beirut. Below, the thriving commercial entrepôt of Bab Idriss was a swamp. Weeds grew twenty feet into the air, and pools of dank water bred thousands of mosquitoes. Only the more famous monuments survived. "Do you see the Omari Mosque?" I asked Elie.

"No. Where is it?"

"There, look to your right. That is the oldest mosque in Beirut."

"Is it?"

"It was here in the Crusaders' time. And look there, that's the French Cathédrale St Louis," I said, pointing north. "And there is the Orthodox Cathedral of St George. And up there was the *Asfourieh.*"

"I guess you know it better than I do," Elie said.

"You never saw it before the war?"

"I don't remember. I'm only twenty-four, and I was eleven when it began."

"I was nine," Najib said.

"You don't know what you missed," I said, remembering the years before the war. "You could take *services* from the square to any part of Lebanon for only a few pounds. You could go anywhere in Beirut for twenty-five piastres. At the north end of the square, you could get the *services* to Ashrafieh and on up the mountain to Broummana. From the south side, to the American University and Hamra. There were buses from here up to Tripoli or down to Tyre. That café there sold the best *shawarma* in Lebanon." For a moment, I saw it as it had been, alive and welcoming, palm trees where the weeds now stood, open markets where mosquitoes buzzed in the swamp. I remembered the Roman columns in the middle of the food market, and the chickens in cages waiting to be killed. I could see the hustle and hear the noise of a thousand shoppers haggling over prices, of old porters with wool caps on their heads carrying crates of fruit and vegetables on their backs. I saw the spot where on my first day in Beirut I had bet twenty-five Lebanese pounds, eight dollars at the time, that a bean was under one of three identical thimbles moved by a deft hand around a table top. I lost. It was the first of many times the Lebanese would outwit me, the first of many lessons I would learn. That Beirut, that Lebanon was dead, and this was its graveyard.

I looked down at the Cathedral of St George, now deformed like a man with leprosy, so numbed with the virus that he could not feel the burns and cuts, stones fallen from its parapet like fingers lost from a hand. The only downtown Elie, Najib and the other children of their generation had ever seen was the wasteland around us. I desperately wanted them to know it had been different, that it might be different again. "You could come down here all day, do your shopping, have lunch, meet your friends for a movie, see thousands of people wandering around and not know or care who was a Christian or a Muslim."

The boys looked bored with my reminiscences, and we wandered into the Byblos and Empire Cinemas. The smell of burned wood and damp theatre seats was stifling. In the Empire, the silver screen had become a giant hole exposing the dead tableau of the Martyrs' Square. We saw, as though the projector had frozen on a single frame of film, electricity poles without wires, broken roads without traffic and animal carcasses dried by the sun. The only sound and motion came from a broken water main pouring water onto the cracked pavement.

We went behind the cinema, and Elie pointed to a hill on the west side. One stone building stood nearly untouched on the summit. Scaffolding, relics of its reconstruction during the optimistic, somewhat quiet time after the Israeli invasion, covered it like a widow's veil. "You know what that is?" he asked.

I nodded.

"Our parliament," he said. Then he added with disdain, "The only democracy in the Arab world."

It was noon when I went from Christian east to Muslim west Beirut. There were several crossing points between the Christian and Muslim sectors, manned on both sides by soldiers and militiamen, but only one was open when I wanted to go. It was called the museum crossing, because the national museum stood at the eastern end of it. There were no cards to fill as at the legal borders. There were no customs checks. Anyone was free to go from east to west, or west to east, any time of the day. The fact that almost no one took the chance was due to snipers, the possibility of kidnapping on either "other" side of town and a mutual belief that the "other" side was alien and not worth a visit.

The sandbag bunker at the army checkpoint on front of the *Musée Nationale* was just out of sight of the road between the two sides, out of the line of sniper fire. The mock Greek columns of the museum's façade were crumbling, but still stood. Stacks of sandbags protected the museum, but every exposed part of the old building had been hit with bullets or shells. It was the repository of Lebanon's national treasures, the artefacts of its Phoenician, Greek, Roman, Arab, Crusader and Turkish heritage. If it ever reopened, there would no doubt be an additional exhibit, of souvenirs of the civil war. Perhaps by then, someone would be able to tell the next generation what it was all for.

The soldiers checked that we had permission to take the car across, and our car was on a list they had. Without that permission, we would have to walk, making good, slow targets, if the snipers were working that day. Someone told me they had not shot anyone in at least a week. We turned the corner at the museum to the long, exposed road between east and west.

We were the only car on the one hundred and fifty yards of road between Christian and Muslim Lebanon. Weeds grew in an island in the middle of the road, and the pavements were empty. We drove quickly and it was not a long road, but the drive seemed to take forever. I supposed the prospect of snipers, the fear of kidnapping when we reached the other side and the memories of that road before and during the war made it seem like a journey of a hundred miles. Over the years, I had seen Palestinian commandos, soldiers from Saudi Arabia in the short-lived Arab Deterrent Force, Israelis, French and a succession of Lebanese militiamen on that empty stretch of road. At almost every step of this hundred and fifty yards, someone had died. A man walking home, a woman taking her child to school, doctors on their way to heal the wounded in hospital, all had fallen on that path to the sniper's bullet. Still people came, out of courage or necessity, risking their lives to say, "My country is not divided. I will not let them separate me from the rest of my land, the rest of my people." Still they came, still they died. If they had placed monuments where each innocent life had been taken, the road would have been one long memorial to senseless slaughter. I remembered one day when civilians on both sides planned a "peace march" to the crossing point, Muslims coming from the west, Christians from the east, all planning to meet in the middle along that road, to greet one another and say to the gunmen they had had enough. A few hours before they were due to commence, militiamen on both sides of the city showered the road with artillery shells.

On our left stood the high walls of the Beirut racecourse, where even then horses trained in the early morning. The track had opened briefly during the lull of 1983, when the prevailing optimism allowed the Lebanese to gamble on peace and horses. It closed a few months later. Overgrowing the walls were bougainvillaea and jacaranda, both purple in early summer bloom. On the right was the *Palais de Justice,* its white porticos relatively untouched. I had been arrested there in 1974 with Peter Jennings, my colleague at ABC News, for the crime of having gone to Israel, where we made a film about life under occupation. Soldiers had led Peter and me handcuffed to each other down that very road, in those days clogged with traffic, from the *Palais de Justice* to the military jail, while shoppers looked on amused at the foreigners under arrest. They put us in a cell with about thirty Palestinians. The Palestinians could not have been nicer to us, offering us their biscuits and cigarettes. After several hours there, we were sorry to leave, though not so sorry that we asked to stay.

We passed the tall apartment block where the military intelligence, the army's notorious Deuxième Bureau, had run its operations to "clean" west Beirut in 1983. Plainclothes agents took Palestinians, Shiites and dissidents to the building, beat them mercilessly and occasionally lost them forever. The interrogators lost not only innocent lives, but the goodwill of the Muslims who wanted to believe that the new Christian president, supported by the United States, would treat them fairly. Military intelligence operatives held me, my camera crew and driver there one day. We saw men, their shirts tied around their faces and blood streaming down their bare chests, led from one interrogation room to the next. It was frightening, although as Americans we were relatively safe from beatings by an army that was being trained by US Army advisers. While we waited for our own interrogation to begin, I managed to sneak down the corridor to an empty office and use the telephone to call the Commodore Hotel. I asked the Commodore's manager, Fuad Saleh, to notify my colleagues to make the appropriate calls to obtain our release.

The Palais de Justice and the Military Intelligence Bureau, despised symbols of the *ancien régime* in the middle of a no-man's-land, had escaped the war relatively unscathed.

Lost in my memories of the road, I was surprised when we reached the first checkpoint on the west side. The Lebanese soldiers, dressed like the troops on the other side, were Shiites. They belonged to the Sixth Brigade, the unit that had gone over to the Shiite Amal militia in February 1984.

They sat in full view of any sniper on the east side, on chairs in the middle of the road, with no protection from shells or the sun. "*Ahlan*," one of the soldiers said. "Welcome." He did not even stand up to look at the car. We went on a few yards to the second checkpoint, belonging to the more formidable power in west Beirut, the Syrian army. The Syrians stopped the car, then let us proceed.

We drove through the city's enormous Pine Forest, the branches cut from the trees by flying shrapnel. Lebanon's Emir Fakhreldin, who had built a castle as far away as Palmyra in the seventeenth century, had planted the forest to stop the tide of sands that threatened to destroy Beirut three centuries before Beirut destroyed itself. The French had built their High Commissioner's residence there during the Mandate, and it was Beirut's largest public park. Kurdish families used to picnic there on the weekends.

At the edge of the pine forest was a cemetery where I had attended many Muslim funerals, sometimes as a reporter, sometimes as a mourner. I had seen individual and mass funerals there, of victims of massacres, of Israeli bombing raids, of shelling. I had seen the funerals in April 1973 of three Palestinians assassinated one night by Israeli commandos, who killed them in their beds and escaped by sea in the night. The Lebanese army had done nothing to stop them. In fact, the only people who resisted the Israelis were some Lebanese drug-smugglers who, when they saw the soldiers boarding their boats, thought they were unwelcome competitors in the hashish trade and fired at them.

Whole phases of Lebanon's history were buried in that cemetery: in one area, the victims of Israeli pre-war bombings; in another, Muslims massacred in east Beirut; in another, the dead of Sabra and Shatila in 1982; and, growing daily, the men, women and children killed by snipers, by random shellfire and by car bombs in the mundane cycle of life and death in modern Lebanon. Both sides of Beirut had cemeteries whose tombstones recorded each moment of the war.

"Oh, friends of my youth who are scattered in the city of Beirut," Kahlil Gibran wrote in *The Broken Wings*, "when you pass by that cemetery near the pine forest, enter it silently and walk slowly so the tramping of your feet will not disturb the slumber of the dead, and stop humbly by Selma's tomb and greet the earth that encloses her corpse and mention my name."

We went through the *Forêt des Pins* to the piled-up earth barricades left behind by the Multi-National Peacekeeping Force near the Palestinian refugee camps they had come to protect against a repetition of the Sabra and Shatila massacres. An old man was carrying a bag of groceries into the breezeblock confines of the camp, and other old men sat on stools in the shade. This was a rare day off. For most of the time, the camps had been besieged, but this was one of the days when the Shiite Amal militia agreed to a ceasefire. People could shop, store food and water and wait for the fighting to begin again.

We drove along the airport road, called in wire-service parlance the "kidnap-plagued airport road" just as Beirut was "the war-ravaged capital." My friend, Juan-Carlos Gumucio, Beirut correspondent of the Madrid daily *Diario* who had worked for many years for the Associated Press, had catalogued the news agency clichés: weapons were "Soviet-made"; militias were "Syrian-backed" or "Israeli-controlled"; Shiites were "poor" or "homeless"; Palestinian refugee camps were "besieged"; Christians were "right-wing"; the president of Lebanon was "beleaguered"; artillery fire was "random" or "savage"; civilians were "terror-stricken"; and the militiamen of Hizballah were, in truth, "Iranian-trained." Lebanon was "war-weary."

A mile down the airport road, we came to a large and isolated concrete mosque with a green dome. It had been there for several years, but always looked incomplete. Steel struts poked out of the cement, and most of it had not been tiled or painted. I had seen Hizballah rallies there in years past. The mosque was quiet but for the slight murmur of an Iranian flag blowing in the wind. At the mosque, we turned right on a wide boulevard leading to the sea. As for almost every other place on the drive, this road had a particular memory for me: on 5 February, 1984, I had been on that road going in the other direction. At the bottom, near the sea, I saw more than a hundred Amal militiamen massing for an assault. At the top of the road was a Lebanese army checkpoint, this on the final day of Lebanese army authority in west Beirut. We were driving up towards the checkpoint. I knew that in a few minutes, the half-dozen soldiers there would either surrender or die. I had to decide whether to warn them or not, whether to play however minor a role in a story I was covering, when a shell fell near the checkpoint and the soldiers went into their bunker. We drove like hell to the airport.

To the right of the road was a huge garbage dump dug out of the sands, where rubbish was burning in high mounds. The burning rubbish in a capital whose public services had collapsed made Beirut seem like a plague city, where fatal disease lurked everywhere and the dead were taken silently away by night. The smell of the fires was awful, carried over the road by a sea breeze to the shanties of the southern suburbs. A little further on was the Beirut Golf Club, where golfers managed to play eighteen holes on quiet days and where gardeners still watered the grass and tended the greens.

At the end of the road, we turned right along the coast highway in Ouzai. Although this was part of the Shiite suburbs, girls in tight jeans were shopping under the nose of heroic martyrs whose faces were pasted on most of the shop fronts, Hizballah and Amal boys who had died fighting either

Israel or each other. This was the row of two- and three-storey shops and apartments I would see in my final moments of freedom a few weeks later, the shabby butchers' with live chickens out front in wood cages, clothes shops and car-repair garages. It was a hot day, and the road was dusty, crowded with people and cars. On the right was the sea, for most Beirutis their only escape from what passed for life in Lebanon. We passed the Miami Beach Restaurant, one of my favourites before and during the war, that served excellent fresh fish and kept live lobsters in a tank by the door. Then we came to Saint Simon Beach, a collection of wood cabanas for the west Beirut bourgeoisie before the war. When Muslim refugees came from east Beirut in 1976, they moved into the cabanas. The private beach became a camp, and it remained a camp. At a petrol station just beyond, I saw a long queue of cars and an attendant with a cigarette in his mouth who was filling the car of a bearded Shiite mullah. A few bearded boys lounged in groups of four or five in cars along the roadside. They did not appear to have any weapons, but they had almost certainly put them away at home when the Syrian army returned to Beirut.

On the left as we drove south were the high earth walls of Beirut airport, its deserted US Marine bunkers weathered by years of rain. Ahead on the left was an empty beach, where the Marines had landed and placed an observation tower and a sign saying, "Green Beach." The tower and the sign were gone, replaced by an Iranian flag. On the road beyond, separated by a concrete wall about waist-high down the middle of the highway, were a few buildings, small shops selling cold drinks, beach shacks with roofs of palm leaves, and miles of open beach, where people lay on the sand or swam in the sea. Nearly all the people on these "popular" beaches were boys or men. A few beach shacks had terraces shaded in palm leaves.

We reached a Syrian checkpoint under a concrete bridge at Khalde, the same place the Israelis had manned their checkpoint on the road to Beirut. It controlled Syria's access to the coast highway south and into the Druze mountains to the east, their lifeline to the Bekaa and Syria itself. While the cars queued for inspection, a man whose body and limbs were badly twisted tried to sell their occupants packs of Chicklets gum. I bought some, although I did not chew gum. I remembered once, a few years earlier, how an old man had tried to sell me a flower near the Commodore Hotel in west Beirut. He had four or five roses, all nearly dead, and he begged me to buy one. "But I don't want any flowers," I said.

"I don't give a shit about flowers," he shouted at me. "I want to eat."

I was so ashamed that I bought flowers, Chicklets, newspapers, shoe shines and pencils from poor old men who had no other way of surviving. "Remember, my brother," Kahlil Gibran had written,

> That the coin which you drop into
> The withered hand stretching toward
> You is the only golden chain that
> Binds your heart to the
> Loving heart of God . . .

A truckload of Syrian soldiers passed the queue and took the road up into the mountains, probably going home on leave. The Syrian soldier who stopped us was polite and let us go on without any difficulty. "They are much more polite this time," the driver said. In their first occupation of Beirut, from 1976 to 1982, the Syrians had antagonised all the Lebanese with their lack of civility at checkpoints. They would say, "Go," rather than, "Please, go," to passing cars. Now, they were saying "please." It made things easier, allowing the Lebanese to keep a small measure of pride, but it did not stop Syrian soldiers from publicly beating men whom they either suspected of some infraction or simply did not like. At another checkpoint, I saw a Lebanese man, his face swollen and his shirt covered in blood, standing dazed in front of the Syrian bunker.

South of Khalde, we passed stone villas on the seaside and new apartments in the foothills. Palms and demolished houses lay on both sides of the road. We passed the Kangaroo Beach Restaurant and the Friendly Beach Restaurant, and we took the turning up to Doha and the house of Hany Salaam, where I would stay for a few days. There I met a young man named Ramzi Husseini, who would be my constant companion driving the streets of west Beirut. He was in his late twenties, had a strong build and curly hair and drove a new black Mercedes. He worked for a friend of Hany Salaam's who was out of the country, and Hany in effect borrowed him for me. Ramzi had been a bodyguard of the Shiite leader, Imam Musa Sadr, who disappeared in Libya in 1978 and to whom all Lebanon's Shiites paid reverence. Ramzi was nearly ten years my junior, but he was a good protector and, as it turned out, something of a teacher.

Before the Israeli invasion of 1982, west Beirut had become a Palestinian colony. Palestinian commandos ruled the streets. The Palestinian flag flew from rooftops, and posters on most Beirut walls displayed colour pictures of Yasser Arafat or his Palestinian rivals, George Habash and Ahmed Jibril. The slogans chanted in west Beirut were Palestinian, "Revolution until victory" and "Down with Imperialism, Zionism and Colonialism." The Palestinian commandos misbehaved in west Beirut from 1975 until 1982, but they achieved an hour of glory in the summer of 1982. Young boys with small weapons, the sons of the peasants who had been expelled from Palestine in 1948, held off the Israeli war machine for nearly three months.

Israel's modern American weapons hit Beirut day and night throughout the summer, but the siege of west Beirut served only to unite its people, however briefly, under the Palestinian banner – the same flag Emir Feisal had flown in his march across Syria in 1918.

The Palestinians agreed to withdraw, according to Yasser Arafat, to save Beirut from destruction. Philip Habib, the American negotiator who arranged the PLO departure, said his motive too was to save Beirut. They should have known better. Beirut was not saved. Too many armies over millennia had withdrawn from Levantine cities with promises of safe conduct. Too many leaders had made sacred agreements with superior forces to abandon the fight and open the city gates, only to see their people massacred. When the Mongols agreed to spare Aleppo if its rulers merely opened the gates of the Citadel, they proceeded to annihilate the population. Richard the Lionheart's conquest of Acre on the coast of Palestine in 1191 was no better. Acre's Muslim garrison surrendered on Richard's promise that he would grant it safe conduct. Richard, in the words of the historian Sir Steven Runciman, "ordered the massacre of the twenty-seven hundred survivors of the garrison at Acre. His soldiers gave themselves eagerly to the task of butchery, thanking God, so Richard's apologists gleefully tell us, for this opportunity to avenge their comrades who had fallen before the city. The prisoners' wives and children were killed at their side . . . When the slaughter was over the English left the spot with its mutilated and decaying corpses." Why was history always repeating itself, especially in its bloodiest episodes? Why did no one, victor or vanquished, see the inevitability? It had happened too often for the people involved to have been unaware of the risks. The Palestinians left with their weapons, and west Beirut had only the written promise of the United States that its people would not be harmed.

Philip Habib convinced Washington that the presence of US Marines would reassure the Israelis to permit the evacuation of Palestinian fighters from Beirut. Arafat and his men departed by sea, hypocritically claiming victory in defeat. Their "mission accomplished," the Marines left too. Someone assassinated Lebanon's president-elect, Bechir Gemayel. Then the Israeli army entered west Beirut, just as most other Levantine armies had entered undefended cities as soon as their opponents had withdrawn. Could it have been any different? Did the history of the region permit any other form of warfare? The Israelis brought their Lebanese Forces allies with them from east Beirut. As these Maronite miltiamen had done in Maslakh, Qarantina, Tel el Zaatar and elsewhere to other unarmed Palestinian civilians, they began killing them in west Beirut's Sabra and Shatila camps. And the killing continued day and night, until it became too embarrassing for the Israelis to allow it any longer. The US had to send the Marines back to Lebanon, because American diplomats and soldiers had guaranteed the lives of those dead Palestinians.

Meanwhile, west Beirut had ceased to be a Palestinian colony, and, like many former colonies, it descended into chaos when competing natives backed by outside powers laid rival claims to it. Palestinian civilians kept to themselves in their camps. They feared arrest by the army during the eighteen months of government rule until 1984, then murder by Amal during the confusion that followed.

Before 1982, it was easy to find Palestinians to talk to. They were everywhere. They provided the intellectual force in west Beirut, discussing politics and art, exploring their history, trying to understand what faults in their own society had made them refugees. I loved argument with them: they were raised in a Socratic intellectual tradition. They were secular. They had abandoned tribalism. They had turned their backs on sectarianism. There was give and take. They admitted to admiring aspects of Israeli society they found missing in the Arab states: democracy, a free press and open debate. They forced me to think, particularly as a young man in my first year out of the United States, to question my own premises. Then the war began in Lebanon, and they became more Levantine. As the battle progressed, they regressed. In the words of one of my favourite Lebanese historians, "The Palestinians became another Lebanese tribe." Their backs against the wall, they had only themselves to rely on. They saw that their enemies were legion: even the Sunni Muslims, whom the Palestinians had supported at least in part as fellow Sunnis, were prepared at the last minute to become Lebanese again and make an accord with the Maronites against them. They knew the Lebanese proverb, "If you are a sheep among wolves, you will be eaten."

Driving with Ramzi through west Beirut, I saw all the old Palestinian offices where I had drunk Turkish coffee and argued politics. They were now closed and empty. The Palestinian Research Centre had long since been bombed, and its respected director, a lawyer and Hebrew scholar named Sabry Jiryis, deported from the country on a trumped-up charge of transporting a bomb in his car. That was just after someone had assassinated his wife. A few Palestinian commandos had returned to the camps, but they were hiding, ready to defend their families when the Amal assault began again.

Shafic al-Hout was about the only Palestinian politician left. Part Lebanese in blood and temperament, he had begun his career as a teacher, become a journalist and ended up in politics. He was born in Jaffa in 1932. In 1948, his brother was killed in a clash with the Israelis, and his family fled to Beirut. There, they rented furnished rooms, believing, like most Palestinians, they would soon be going home. He studied at the American

University of Beirut, became an Arab nationalist and taught English, biology and mathematics in Beirut and Kuwait. He wrote for the weekly magazine *Al-Hawadess* and joined the PLO in 1964. He had edited the Beirut daily newspaper *Al-Moharrer* until a bomb, no doubt planted by the Syrians or their agents, blew it up. I had first heard him speaking in 1974 to a group of American businessmen, captains of industry on a Middle East tour arranged by *Time* magazine for its biggest advertisers. He told them in a private session at the Hotel St Georges in Beirut, "The US is going to have to speak to the PLO sooner or later. Why not do it now and save a lot of lives?"

Since then, a hundred and fifty thousand, perhaps more, people had been killed in Lebanon. Israel had invaded Lebanon twice, first in 1978 and again in 1982, and lost more than six hundred soldiers on Lebanese soil. Syria occupied most of the country, and America had left nearly three hundred of its own dead in Beirut.

Shafic was relaxing in his flat on the Corniche el-Mazraa, once the main thoroughfare through this Sunni Muslim-Greek Orthodox part of west Beirut to Ashrafieh, now blocked at the Green Line. Still in his blue-striped Egyptian *gallabieh*, he poured us Turkish coffee from a red thermos flask on a cluttered coffee-table. Books were stacked on the floor in the hallway, and the day's Arabic newspapers were open in the breakfast room. We sat on a couch in the small sitting-room, near framed photographs of his wife and children on an upright piano. Shafic al-Hout had not changed in years, still with his ruddy complexion and freckles, still ready to talk all day about politics, newspapers and history. Only the hair was different, going grey on his head and his upper lip.

"If you quote me on the Syrians," Shafic said, "please be kind." He did not have much good to say about Syria. The Syrians, after all, had completed Israel's task of expelling the PLO from Lebanon when they forced Yasser Arafat to retreat by sea from Tripoli in December 1983. The Syrians were supporting, probably commanding, Amal in its assault on the Palestinian refugee camps. Shafic was safer if no one quoted his views on the Syrian army that controlled the portion of Beirut in which he lived.

"Look," he said, pouring the coffee, "at the way things are running. They took Alexandretta and gave it to Turkey. The French cut Syria into five statelets for a while, and now Lebanon is turning into cantons. The genius of the West, of colonialism and imperialism, was to stress issues that divided the areas they controlled. The whole world, even Europe, is motivated by sectarian, regional and religious differences. But the Arabs as a people hardly had time to breathe."

"Well," I said, "you've had more than forty years since the French and British pulled out."

415

"Look, we were just coming out of Turkish tutelage, uneducated and poor. We finished in the morning with the Turks, and in the evening we were subject to colonial tyranny by the British and French. The divisions and subdivisions of Sykes–Picot were a permanent job for the British and French. We never had a chance. If you sum up the last fifty years as fifty days, we've had a fight for every single day."

"If you blame the Sykes–Picot borders, can you get rid of them?"

"I was against these boundaries, but now the most patriotic slogan is, 'God save these countries!'"

"Why? Rather than get rid of the old borders, people are erecting new ones. Lebanon has them everywhere."

"There are certain factors. There is something called the Arab person. Maybe he'd like to be defined in a separate state. But we share a common history, of an Islamic movement which Arabised these countries. True, not all Arabs are from the desert. But the language, the culture. It has an Islamic content, maybe."

"But isn't that important?"

"To a great extent, it's psychological. If we are different, it is not more so than a Texan from a New Yorker."

"But you and I saw Arab nationalism die in the streets of Beirut, when Arab slaughtered Arab. The idea is dead, and its secularism is giving way to Islamic fundamentalism."

"I don't think the Western countries fear anything in this area – whether communism or Islamic fundamentalism – as much as they fear Arab nationalism. It unites the people. The others divide them."

I sipped my coffee and thought about Arab nationalism, an idea that had energised the last generation of Arab intellectuals. But it had failed to achieve its stated goals – unity of the Arab world, the liberation of Palestine and progress. Its most charismatic proponent, the Egyptian leader Gamal Abdel Nasser, had died in 1970. "No one," I argued, "has come along to replace Gamal Abdel Nasser, and the idea of Arab nationalism is dying."

"I never saw in my life supporters of anyone like the supporters of Nasser. I remember when he died, there were four million people on the streets of Cairo. The whole Arab world wept. Have these people disappeared? Have they been brainwashed? Who is the substitute? No one has been able to fill the vacuum left by Arab nationalism. Nasser was a great loss. Nasser was the sheikh of the sheikhs of the tribes. He was strong. He did not need an intermediate sheikh to come to him. He was a pope of all the Arabs. The Arabs need a patriarch, a pope, especially in an era when the institutions are not well organised to replace the leader. With Nasser's death, and the deviation of Egypt at Camp David, the Arabs lost not only a leader, but a compass."

"What about Marxism?"

"Communism is out of the question. It can come to America, but not here."

"That leaves," I said, "fundamentalist Islam."

"If Arab nationalism failed in twenty-five years to find a common denominator to unify the people, Islam will also fail. It introduces a new kind of division – which kind of Islam? Sunni or Shiah? Even the Shiah are divided into sects."

"And most Muslims are not Arab anyway. You have non-Arabs –Iranians, Pakistanis, Indonesians. The fundamentalists want to create one state for them all."

"An Arab is an Arab, not an Iranian," Shafic said. "I cannot tolerate Iranians leading me. I cannot, as an Arab, tolerate even to hear the Koran read with an Iranian accent."

"But the Hizballah say there is no difference between Shiah and Sunni Muslims."

"It's a Shiah doctrine they are trying to impose. There is a hell of a difference in practice on the ground. The Shiah believe in an expected imam. The Sunnis believe in a *khalifa*, a chosen ruler. This to me as a Sunni makes me feel free to choose my ruler, not a religious choice of the sheikhs. The Shiah and Sunni for the last thirteen hundred years have not observed one feast together. It is not a mistake that the Shiah celebrate the end of Ramadan the day after the Sunnis. It is a point of difference, to say, 'We are not you.'"

Shafic unscrewed the top of the thermos and poured us more coffee. Swirling it in his cup, he mused, "The war between Iran and Iraq has aroused Arab nationalism. For example, I do not approve of Saddam Hussein in Iraq or of any other anti-democratic leader, but we have to support Iraq. There is tyranny in Iran."

"There may be more tyranny in Iraq."

"No matter. Arab territory is more important. I have to consider the homeland first."

"What about in Lebanon?"

"Every sect in Lebanon always had an outside capital to count on. Here we have so many sects, each counting on a capital to protect its interests. Take Walid Jumblatt – a progressive socialist and a Druze tribal leader. Do you think he doesn't have his Western affiliations – in London, the US, even Moscow? The Maronites are split between America and France. Traditionally, the Druze were courted by the English. The Sunnis were protected by the Turks, later by the Egyptians. For the Shiah, this is their first chance in recent history to have a capital they can count on. So, it's only natural they lean on Tehran."

"But to what end? They are no better off now than they were before the war."

"If history has a lesson, it is that Lebanon stayed on its feet through compromise, not total hegemony for any party."

"How did you Palestinians get it so wrong?"

"The problem was the leadership came here. A movement which should have fought Israel found itself drowning in Lebanese waters. A great deal of our effort went in vain because of our involvement in Lebanon. We were not invited into Lebanon. We came in because it was a garden with a fence. After King Hussein threw us out of Jordan in 1970, we should have gone to Damascus. At that time, during the Vietnam war, Cairo or Damascus was our Hanoi, not Beirut. Cairo was impossible under Sadat, and Damascus rejected us. So we took a left turn and ended up here. We put up our first tents, and we grew. It was never our strategy to make this our headquarters. Those of us who already lived here said, 'This country cannot stand us. It cannot support our dreams.' When the Lebanese government failed to put an end to our expansion, the Maronites took over and began arming themselves."

"Wasn't the reaction inevitable?"

"Yes. It was inevitable. God knows how much we warned our own leadership, how much we tried."

"But, as bad as things were in west Beirut when you were ruling, they are worse now."

"Oh, God," he laughed. "Infinitely. Yasser Arafat's gift is that however he feels about you, he smiles and harps on what is common between you and him. This is why you can hardly find among the leadership any hatred of Arafat. The Syrians are arrogant. Compare the way Arafat treated the Lebanese Muslims and leftists with the way Syria does. He treated them like partners. The Syrians treat them like minor officers in the army."

"I wasn't thinking of the leaders so much as the lives of ordinary people. This anarchy is killing them."

"People who were happy to see Arafat leave in 1982 are praying to God for his return. With him, they had money, security. Now, after all these killings, all these different flags waving, we have ended with a country more backward than it was in 1943, the system they were rebelling against. Now they are much more reactionary."

"How long," I asked, an obvious but unanswerable question, "can it go on?"

"These cantons cannot survive. Just imagine each canton with its own currency or trading by barter. They know it cannot work. They are not that stupid, but they are that tribalist."

"What about you?" I asked him. "How can you go on living here? I remember when they blew up your newspaper offices after the Syrian army came in 1976, and they must dislike you now. They're killing PLO people in the camps."

"I'm settled here in my flat. I stay out of the way. If I go out and have my picture published, people will call and I'll become part of the scene. I don't want that."

We'd emptied the coffee in the thermos, and he walked me to the lift. "Take care," he said. "I won't tell you not to go around, but be careful."

"You be careful," I said. I was certain he was in greater danger than I.

Ramzi drove me back to Doha to celebrate Eid al-Fitr, the breaking of the fast at the end of the month of Ramadan. The Sunnis were observing it that day, and the Shiah would have their feast the next. Hany Salaam was in London, but his mother who lived next door always gave the lunch for the whole family. Fatima Salaam was known to everyone as Umm Hany, Mother of Hany. She was born Fatima Khalidy, a daughter of one of Jerusalem's most prominent Sunni Muslim families, a family of scholars.

"I was married in Tel Habib fifty-three years ago," she said, using the Arabic name of Tel Aviv. Her husband, Mohammed Salaam, came from a Sunni merchant family in Beirut. "My father was a judge, and he sat in court with a Christian and a Jewish judge. My father had to flee Palestine when the son of a Jewish judge came and warned him that he would be killed if he stayed. The son apologised for the behaviour of the others, but my father left." There were still Khalidys in Jerusalem, where they maintained the Khalidy Library of Islamic manuscripts.

Her children and grandchildren were arriving in small groups at her house, while we sat talking. Khaled, her son, came with his wife and their two daughters. He kissed his mother and sat down to tell me about Rashid Karami's resignation as prime minister. "That Karami is a smart bastard," he said. "He resigns, and yet he stays on as caretaker prime minister. Every Sunni is lining up to be the next prime minister. I mean it. Even my driver believes he will be prime minister."

"Soon we'll see every Maronite lining up to be president," I told him. "I saw one of the candidates, Dany Chamoun."

"Dany is very charming, but he has no political sense. He is too obvious about his relations with Israel. They all have secret relations with Israel, but he has his photo taken in Jerusalem."

Other members of the family were arriving. Umm Hany's nephew, Tareef Khalidy, taught history at the American University and wrote books on Arab history. His wife, Amal, was a Shiite from south Lebanon. Umm Hany's daughters Sulafa and Maha arrived with Maha's husband, who was also a cousin. There were guests from outside the family, including

Christians like Dr Munir Chamaa and his wife. Chamaa was a brave physician who stayed on at the American University Hospital despite its intolerable working conditions and the fact that Hizballah had kidnapped him for a time. He continued teaching young doctors, who would take their skills to other lands.

When the time came for lunch, Umm Hani presided at the end of a long table covered in platters of Lebanese food. Hany's Egyptian maid and an Ethiopian woman, who had a cross tattooed on her forehead, served the lunch. Umm Hany put the final touches to each plate. The feast was *kibbé* baked in a flat pan, raw *kibbé*, chicken in cream, stuffed grape leaves, stuffed courgettes, *hommous*, *foul*, a kind of pizza called *laham bajeen*, cheese pastry called *sambousek*, onions and salads. Then there were Arabic sweets and a kind of milk pudding called *mahalabieh* with an apricot sauce. "What's this called?" I asked about another dessert. "It's a Palestinian dish. I don't know what it's called," someone said. We sat and ate and talked at the table. Politics did not come up. The men were in shirts without ties, and the women wore cotton summer dresses. It was a long leisurely lunch, followed by coffee and people falling asleep on chairs in the living-room. It was just like Thanksgiving dinner in California, but in Lebanon we were thankful to have even an afternoon to eat in peace.

Later, I went to see an old friend who had worked as my driver for many years, Qassem Dergham. He was living at the Riviera Hotel on the Corniche. Qassem was a thin and wiry man with a clipped moustache and short hair. He had an intense loyalty to the organisations and people for whom he had worked, and he loved to talk about all the stories he had covered in his years with ABC News. "Do you remember that time the Israelis arrested us in south Lebanon?" was how he usually started the revival of some old memory. "You know that one time when the hijacker shot up my car? Why did you make me drive away? We should have talked to him." Qassem had driven us everywhere in his old Mercedes, and he arranged interviews with Shiite politicians and militiamen. He had worked at times as a cameraman, soundman and television news producer, and his only recreation was golf. He played several times a week, when work was slow. I was sure that in another country, under other conditions, he would have been a professional golfer. He always wore golf shirts and cotton trousers. When ABC News closed its Beirut office, he went to work for the Worldwide Television News (WTN) agency. He had an apartment in the southern suburbs with his wife and seven children, but he was staying in the hotel to be near a telephone for work.

Quassem's mother was a Maronite, and he had no prejudice against any community in Lebanon. The kidnappings that drove his foreign colleagues out of Beirut sometimes made him ashamed to be a Shiite. When John McCarthy, a British journalist with Worldwide Television News, was kidnapped from the car in which Qassem was riding in 1986, he took the abduction as a personal insult. He had spent the next several months, often at the risk of his life, pursuing leads to find John. Nothing I said could convince him the kidnapping had not been his fault. He refused to give up chasing every lead, every rumour that might lead to John's freedom.

When I arrived at the hotel, Qassem invited me up to his room for coffee. "I just came back from Baalbek," he said. "Hussein Musawi, he told me that soon he will give us news of John McCarthy."

"Qassem, you know Musawi is a liar." Hussein Musawi was part of the collective leadership of Hizballah, nominal head in Baalbek of a militia called Islamic Amal. Qassem and I had interviewed him several times at his house near the Iranian Revolutionary Guards' base in Baalbak. On this trip, however, I had no intention of meeting any Hizballah people. In fact, I did not want any of them to know I was in Lebanon.

"No," he insisted. "Hussein Musawi promised he would try to find John."

"Qassem, his people kidnapped John. They don't need to find him. They have him."

"No," Qassem said. "He promised."

No matter how many times the Hizballah leaders lied to him, Qassem would listen and take hope that they would give him some sign that John was alive and well. So far, all he had were promises.

From Qassem's balcony at the Riviera, I looked down on an empty compound that was, legally, the Embassy of the United States of America. It was empty. An American flag flew over the largest building in the complex, guarded by Shiite, Druze and Sunni Muslim young men in olive drab fatigues. Wire mesh covered each building in the compound. The whole area was enclosed in two defences I had seen appear around the US Marine headquarters a few weeks after it was blown up in October 1983: dragons' teeth and razor wire. Dragons' teeth were large blocks of concrete set at short intervals with sandbags or piles of dirt in between. Razor wire was a thick barbed wire, only far more lethal. At the gate, weighted barriers prevented suicide drivers from taking cars through at speed and blowing themselves up, not that any had tried since the embassy had been vacated. Some of the suicide bombers may have been crazy, but I doubted whether any were insane enough to die destroying an empty building. Most would rather save themselves for an embassy full of diplomats or an Israeli convoy.

There had been so many US embassies since the war began in 1976 that it was not always easy to know which building was the real thing. The old embassy in Ain Mraisse near the Spaghetteria Restaurant had been scheduled to be replaced in 1976 by a new, purpose-built concrete monster on the sea just south of Beirut. When someone killed the American ambassador, Francis Molloy, that year and dumped his body near the site of the building, the US abandoned it. The building still stood, unfinished and empty, not far from the new Iranian embassy, some Hizballah offices and a Syrian checkpoint. The US kept the old building in Ain Mraisse, a nondescript apartment house rented from Kuwaiti landlords, until a car bomb destroyed it in April 1983. Then the State Department bought the "Industry Institute" further south along the Corniche and began renovating it. Meanwhile, the US established an embassy "annexe" in the Christian hills east of Beirut. In September 1984, the unexpected happened: a suicide car bomber blew up, not the embassy in west Beirut, but the annexe in the supposed safety of the Christian east. "I told them there was no reason to feel secure in east Beirut," an American officer said to me at the time. "Hell, they killed Bechir Gemayel in east Beirut, blew up the whole goddam building he was in. Neither side of Beirut is safe." The State Department decided to rebuild the annexe as a fortified bunker and not to station any more diplomats in west Beirut.

The new "embassy" below us had closed before it opened, a memorial to the failure of the United States, despite its Marines and battleships, to impose its will in Lebanon. Washington maintained it as a diplomatic fiction to demonstrate American faith in another fiction, the unity of Lebanon. American diplomats worked out of the annexe in east Beirut, vainly trying to gather information about hostages. The official, albeit empty, embassy along the Corniche in west Beirut gave work to a group of young armed men, a corps that Qassem said changed every three hours.

The US mission was at the bottom of a hill. Above it stood the old lighthouse of Ras Beirut and a pretty white villa with ogival arches on its terrace and bougainvillea and pines growing in the garden. From the lighthouse or the villa, even the worst marksman in Lebanon could have hit the embassy. When work began on the embassy's renovation, an American security man who had opposed moving there said, "There we go again, taking the low ground."

It was sunset, and the guards were lowering the flag. "They put it up every morning," Qassem said, "and they take it down every night." They pulled it down without folding it in the traditional manner, but there was no American diplomat or Marine within miles to tell them to show the proper respect. The guards were joking among themselves, one playfully pointing his M-16 at another.

Qassem and I left the Riviera to meet our friends Juan-Carlos Gumucio and Nora Boustay, a young Lebanese woman who wrote for the

Washington Post, for dinner at the Spaghetteria. Juan-Carlos was a big, burly Bolivian, whose black beard made him look like a Shiite militiaman. Ramzi Hasseini, my driver, drove Qassem and me to the Spaghetteria and stayed in the car to watch everyone coming in and out while we had dinner. The restaurant had undergone some changes over the years, with a new clientele of the war's *nouveau riche* – the opportunists who had taken advantage of the disintegration of the state to make fortunes exporting drugs, importing arms or dealing in narcotics.

The waiters and food remained reliable and familiar, the same as I had known them when the old Italian restaurant had been a favourite with the professors at the American University. Fayez, one of the waiters from Rashidieh camp, had aged with the suffering of years, as his people endured more and more and he earned less and less. He wore the same black bow tie and white jacket he had before the war. The original proprietor was a moody Italian whose wife seemed always to be sitting at the cashier's desk counting the money. They had gone back to Italy after the Israeli invasion, but the new owner served the same pastas and grilled fish. Open windows faced the sea, just across a new road that had destroyed the picturesque neighbourhood of Ain Mraisse by putting twenty yards of concrete between its old houses and the beach.

After dinner, Ramzi drove us to a new night club near the American University, called the Blue Note. On the ground floor of an old house, it had high ceilings and a garden at the back. Most of the young boys and girls sitting at its round tables or dancing to the music were enjoying themselves, drinking wine or beer, smoking cigarettes. They were too young to remember a time when their country was not at war. Rock and blues music played on a stereo, and waiters brought drinks to the many tables. Later, Ramzi drove vigilantly behind us as we walked down the road to the Backstreet. The bar was all lit up inside, its red walls gleaming, for the thirty-fifth birthday of the half-French, half-Greek proprietor, Philippe Ducque. It was deceptively like an ordinary evening out in a normal place.

"Not bad," Juan-Carlos said, looking around the Backstreet at the beautiful young women, the dancing, the champagne and Philippe's huge birthday cake. "Not bad for 'war-torn, mostly Muslim' west Beirut."

"Charles," Ali Hamdan, a Shiite dress-shop proprietor and part-time spokesman of the Amal militia, said to me over lunch at an Indian restaurant in west Beirut, "perhaps you can explain something I don't understand. Why is there this lack of trust between the Westerner and the Oriental? I've known many Western journalists in my job. They never want to be friendly. They don't want to have anything to do with us except for the job."

When I had first met Ali Hamdan, he was starting out as a spokesman. He was twenty-three and clean-shaven, a soft-spoken young man eager to convince journalists like myself that the Israeli occupation of south Lebanon was hurting the Lebanese. Born in 1960 in Nabatieh, a large Shiite town in south Lebanon, he must have been fourteen when the Israelis launched a massive air raid on the town and the Palestinian refugee camp just above it that had destroyed hundreds of houses. I was twenty-three then, but I had not forgotten the tears of the women who had buried their children. Was Ali one of the children at the funerals? When Amal called on him nearly ten years later to become its spokesman, Ali was starting to make some money with his dress shop in Hamra.

I did not know, as we ate lunch, that he had gone to school with Imad Mughnieh, a Hizballah functionary closely involved with the kidnappings of foreigners. Nor did I know that Ali had accompanied the French hostage Michel Seurat when he went briefly during his captivity to his apartment in west Beirut to see his Syrian wife and collect some personal things. Marie Seurat's book about her husband's kidnapping and death, *Les Corbeaux d'Alep*, had yet to be published. Now, Ali had grown a beard in the new Shiah style, and he carried a set of worry beads.

"I don't think it's a question of the Westerner and the Oriental, Ali," I said. "Journalists just don't trust spokesmen. We learned that in the States, mainly in Washington, where spokesmen and public relations people are paid to lie. You shouldn't take it personally."

"But I'm not a liar," he said, offended.

"I don't care if you lie to me. It's my job to find out who's lying and who's not. If a journalist is so lazy he believes everything he hears without checking, he's making a mistake."

"But, Charles, I don't lie to you."

"If you had to, if you had to lie to me to protect Amal, you would. I know you would. Sometimes, you have to. But I'm not obliged to believe you."

The Indian Restaurant was on the ground floor of an apartment building near the lighthouse, overlooking the empty American embassy. A dark place, it had once had Indian waiters and cooks, but the Lebanese who had replaced them turned out good curries and tandooris. I asked Ali what he thought about having the Syrians back in Beirut.

"Those last few weeks before they came were something terrible. Druze, Sunnis and Shiites all killing one another."

"What would have happened if the Syrians had not come in?"

"Massacres," he said. "It cannot even be thought about."

I knew he had returned to the American University, so I asked, "What are you studying at AUB?"

"Professor Khalidy is giving me a tutorial in geopolitics, about all this area between the Amanus Mountains in Turkey and the Sinai."

"I should take the course with you to help me with my book."

"Come on," he said. "I wanted to understand why, throughout history, Lebanon has been dominated by whoever is in Damascus."

"What did Prof. Khalidy say?"

"He laughed, like he always does. And he said, 'Yes, you want to study the role of the coastal cities and the inland cities.' And he designed a fascinating course."

Tareef Khalidy wore a blue and white pinstripe *abaya,* and his sandals clicked on the floor as he wandered around his study looking for matches to light his Dunhill cigarette. At that moment, he looked more like a pasha than a professor of history at the American University of Beirut.

"I was sent to Ireland when I was thirteen," Tareef said, sitting down to light his cigarette. Only a few wisps of hair covered his head, but his face was a ball of long, greying fur. "That was at the suggestion of Jerome Farrell, an old retired official of Mandatory Palestine. My father was his deputy. He lived in a village in southern Ireland. They sent me there off and on for five years. He taught me Latin and Greek during my summer holidays. He became a father-figure, and I would go to visit him from Oxford. He died in 1960."

"Have you been back since?"

"I took a sentimental journey to Castle Townsend, County Cork, with Max." Max, whose real name was Mohammed Ali, was Tareef's son. Home from graduate school at Columbia University, he was sitting next to his father.

"How did you like it?" I asked Max.

"It was okay, but he kept stopping at every pub on the way."

"Okay, okay, disapproving youth. I had not been there in almost thirty yers, and I wanted to transmit some of this sentimental lore to my son."

"Thanks," Max said, laughing.

Amal Khalidy came in to say it was time to go to lunch. They were meeting some other AUB teachers, as Tareef did every Saturday, at the Duke of Wellington pub in the Mayflower Hotel. "Go change, you," she said to Tareef.

"Can't I go like this?" he asked her, looking down at his robe.

"No. Go and change."

Through Amal and Tareef, their children were related to most of the large Lebanese and Palestinian families, Shiite and Sunni. Tareef's aunt was Hany Salaam's mother, giving the Khalidy children many Salaam cousins. Tareef's sister had been married to another Salaam, Assem, an architect. Amal was from a Shiite family in south Lebanon named Saidi. Her brother, Ramzi, was married to one of Adil Osseiran's daughters, Afaf. Their net of Sunni and Shiah relations in Lebanon and Palestine could be cast across the Bekaa Valley, Beirut, south Lebanon, all the way to Jerusalem.

Tareef returned wearing an old sports shirt and khaki trousers, wrinkled and badly creased above the knees.

Amal's eyes opened wide in horror. "Where did you get those?"

"In the drawer."

"They must have been there for a year," she said. "You can't wear those."

"I will wear them." Neither was arguing. Each was stating a position.

"And you can't wear those running-shoes," Amal said.

Tareef said nothing. In his wrinkled trousers and running-shoes, he led us triumphantly out of the comfortable old Beirut flat, down the stone staircase to their aged car. Ramzi followed in his black Mercedes as we drove to the Duke of Wellington. We went past the French Embassy, looking, behind its high walls and barbed wire, as embattled, empty and pointless as the American. We passed the American Unversity's medical gate, so-called because it faced the American University Hospital, where guards under a large banyan tree perfunctorily checked students and teachers for weapons and identification.

"We had another nice trip near Oxford," Mohammed Ali was telling me in the car. "We got bicycles and cycled near Oxford for a month and a half. But he wanted to stop at every pub again."

"So?" Tareef said, driving wildly like Mr Toad, waving his arms and wondering why the other cars did not get out of his way.

"I didn't mind," Max said. "They were nice pubs." Max was a thoughtful young man, born, like generations of his family, to be an academic. He had read philosophy at Oxford and gone to America for graduate school. His black moustache did not make him look older than he was, but he had a serious side to him, balanced in large part by the inheritance of his father's eccentric sense of humour.

We found our way to the Rue Jeanne d'Arc, a pretty side street connecting the American University below with "once-fashionable" Rue Hamra above. Along Rue Jeanne d'Arc were several flower shops, their sprays of roses, carnations and daffodils spilling onto the pavements. Whenever I had bought flowers from one of those shops, the Shiite girls who worked there, heads modestly covered, would give me a rose. Near the flower shops was Beirut's best chocolatier, Chantilly. Once owned by a prominent Jewish family, Chantilly made all its rich chocolates and ice creams by hand. Its owners had sold and left, when it became impossible for Jews to survive in west Beirut. Hizballah had kidnapped and murdered so many Jews that almost none remained. Until 1982 both the Christian militias in the east, who were trying to ingratiate themselves with Israel, and the Palestinians, who were proving they distinguished between Judaism and Zionism, offered the Jews protection. Shiite refugees had moved into the old Jewish Quarter, Wadi Abu Jamil, and Jewish businesses like Chantilly had been sold. Every so often, the picture of some innocent Lebanese Jewish hostage would appear in the Beirut newspapers above a caption stating that he had been murdered by Hizballah in revenge for some Israeli action or other in south Lebanon.

Jeanne d'Arc was a street of pubs, not only the Duke of Wellington, but the Pickwick and the Cock & Bull. They all sold draught beer. In some ways, they were nicer than the English pubs they were imitating, usually serving better food and keeping longer hours.

Inside the Duke of Wellington, a portrait of the Iron Duke, the same as on the £10 note, hung over the fireplace. Stag's heads were mounted on either side of him. George the barman looked much as he always had, portly with a tartan waistcoat, more reserved and dignified than many barmen in London. Amal Khalidy's brother, Khaled Saidi, was already at a table near the bar with several AUB professors. One of them was an American, a kindly man who loved Lebanon and refused to leave, despite the kidnappings. "The only American men left living in west Beirut are me and ——" he said. Turning aside to me, he asked, "Did you enter the country legally?" He was referring to an executive order from Washington banning Americans from coming to Lebanon. The State Department issued journalists automatic exemptions, but I had not bothered to apply, any more than most of my colleagues and I had when Americans were banned from travelling to Libya. Our attitude was that we went where the news was, not where the State Department said we could go.

"I'm here legally, as far as the Lebanese are concerned," I said, "but they did not stamp my passport."

"I'm worried about my children," he said. "What can they do? They have been living here with me, but they will have trouble when they try to go to the States. We spoke to the American Civil Liberties Union, who believe the executive order is unconstitutional."

Tareef ordered drinks for everyone, and the subject turned to the real issue of the day, neither American constitutional law nor Lebanese warfare, but university politics.

"We just can't get good PhDs to come and teach here anymore," one of the professors was saying.

"Why don't we use our good MAs," Tareef asked, "and forget about these lousy PhDs?"

"We need at least forty-two PhDs to keep our accreditation with the New York Regents."

Tareef picked up a rubber band and fired it at the wall. "Take that, New York Regents," he said. He fired another one, just missing George behind the bar. "Take that, PhDs."

At lunch later in the Istambouli Restaurant, while Ramzi waited and watched in his car outside, Tareef had recommended that I read the book *An Arab-Syrian Gentleman and Warrior in the Period of the Crusades: Memoirs of Usamah ibn-Mundidh.* Usamah had written his memoirs in the mid-twelfth century, and a Beirut publisher, Khayat's, had reprinted a 1929 English translation by the Lebanese historian, Philip Hitti. I went to Khayat's bookshop on Rue Bliss, the long street running parallel to the upper wall of the American University campus. There, I asked Mr Khayat if he had Hitti's translation. He said he would look, and he returned a few minutes later to say there were no copies left.

"Do you have any in the warehouse?" I asked him.

"There is nothing left in the warehouse."

"Why not?"

"The militias broke into it during the last big round between Amal and the Druze."

"Did they loot the books?"

"I wish they had," the old man said. "They don't read. They just destroyed the books. They tore them up, trampled them, burned them. There is nothing left."

"I cannot believe it," I said to him.

"If there is a plot against this country, it is to destroy the mind. The best libraries have gone, the *Bibliothèque Nationale* in the old parliament building has been destroyed. The St Joseph University collection has been shelled. Now, imported books and periodicals are so expensive that no one can afford them. Soon, reading will be a lost art."

Mr Khayat said he had one copy at home. He would photocopy the book and bind it for me. His family had published and sold books for most of the century, and he kept one flicker of literacy glowing amid the storms of barbarity. I thanked him for the book, but I was really thanking him for tending the flame in Lebanon's dark hour.

A report on the radio one morning spoke of an attack by five hundred Hizballah fighters on an Israeli unit in south Lebanon. This was the first time Hizballah had engaged the Israelis in a battle rather than suicide attacks or hit-and-run guerrilla raids. Recently, Hizballah had staged a parade of five thousand supporters in Baalbek. The Shiite movement,

428

supported with Iranian money and the Iranian Revolutionary Guards' missionary zeal, was growing. Hizballah paid the highest wages of any of the Lebanese militias, and it was attracting more fighters.

Amal, rather than the Christians, had more to fear than anyone else from Hizballah's growth. While Hizballah attacked Israel in the south, Amal besieged the Palestinians in Beirut. "I understand what is happening," Ali Hamdan said to me on the campus of the American University. "Imam Musa Sadr warned us." Imam Musa Sadr had been the leader of Lebanon's Shiites and the founder of Amal. A Gandhi-like figure to Lebanon's Shiites, he had once gone on hunger strike to persuade his followers in the Bekaa Valley not to attack the Christian village of Deir al-Ahmar.

"In 1975," Ali went on, "when the clashes began between the Palestinians and Syria, the Imam started to cry. He said the fighting was shameful. 'The Arabs are going to butcher the Palestinians,' he told us, 'and we are going to be the knife.'"

Ali and I were standing in the shade of old banyan trees, their roots winding down from branches above into the earth. We were near the wall surrounding the nineteenth-century stone house of the absentee American president of the university. It was ten in the morning. John Munro, one of the few Englishmen still teaching there, walked up to us. "Have you heard?" he asked.

"What happened?" I ventured a question that in Lebanon could elicit almost any response – true or false, momentous or trivial, but invariably bad.

"It seems they've shot down Karami's helicopter."

"Who did? Where?"

"Someone just told me the helicopter came down. He didn't know anything except that Karami and Rassi were on board."

Rashid Karami had only recently resigned as prime minister, and I did not understand why anyone would want to kill him. Rassi was Abdallah Rassi, Robert Frangieh's brother-in-law and the minister of the interior. They had taken a Lebanese army helicopter from their homes in the Syrian-controlled north bound for their offices in Syrian-controlled west Beirut to avoid driving through the anti-Syrian Christian centre.

John Munro said he was on his way to have shoes made for about $30 a pair. His expatriate's salary was in dollars, an advantage in the only country in the world where the value of the dollar had been rising that summer. Four years earlier, the dollar was worth four Lebanese pounds. It had reached 122 LL. Within the next two hours, when the banks would close abruptly, it would be 125.50 LL, bringing the price of John's shoes down by about five cents.

Ali and I walked on to the faculty cafeteria to have coffee. The faculty ate upstairs, and the students had their own cafeteria downstairs, a system of segregation accepted in American universities. Although Ali was in fact a student, he took the liberty as Amal spokesman and Ministry of Information official of using the faculty dining facilities. Ali and I took a tray up to the cashier, an unshaven man with little to do, and ordered two coffees. He asked the man if there had been any news on the radio and told him what we had just heard about Rashid Karami. While the man prepared the coffee, he took a small transistor radio out of the drawer and fiddled with the dials. Nothing happened. "The batteries are dead," he said.

"Why don't you buy some?" Ali asked.

"Why? Batteries cost eighty pounds. I would rather spend it on food than hear about Karami."

We went with the coffee to a table near the window from which we watched the students walking back and forth from their classes, particularly the girls in their summer dresses taking advantage of the de-Iranianised atmosphere of the Syrian reign in this part of Beirut. We talked for awhile about Lebanon, the Israeli raids of the previous few days on villages in the south and the sad prospects for the future. When we were leaving, a teacher told us Karami and Rassi had been injured slightly and taken to hospital in Jebail. "Don't worry," Ali reassured me. "They never kill the leaders."

Ramzi drove us towards Ali's office in the Ministry of Information, a modern building on Rue Hamra opposite the offices of Beirut's leading daily, *An Nahar*. At least, the Ministry would have a radio. Thousands of people were out shopping on the sunny Monday morning, everyone and everything relaxed as we drove. Shopkeepers sat on stools outside their shops, drinking coffee or talking to friends. Beggars asked for small sums of money. Maids and poor housewives haggled with vegetable sellers over the prices of the produce on their barrows. *"One hundred pounds* for a kilo of tomatoes?"

In the Ministry of Information's *salle de presse*, once in the hands of Christians and now run by Ali and his friends from Amal, a radio played on the table. A couple of employees, of the kindly type who lurked in almost every office in Lebanon doing nothing in particular but ready to do anything from making coffee to typing out telexes, were listening to the news. "What's happening?" I asked one of them. It was now about eleven o'clock. "Karami is very bad," he said. "But Rassi is okay."

"Who shot them?"

"No shoot. Boom!"

"Where?"

"Boom inside. Under seat."

From the ministry, I went to see a banker friend, but he was not in the bank. I left him a message and returned to the car park, where Ramzi was sitting with the attendant, both of them listening to the radio. In Arabic, very solemnly, Ramzi told me, "Karami is dead."

"*Haram*," I said. Pity.

"*Haram?*" the attendant blurted out. "*Haram Karami? Haram Nehne.*" Pity Karami? Have pity on us. "We are the ones who will suffer," he said, raising his hands towards the sky as though at any moment it would be dark with rockets and artillery shells.

Ramzi drove us out of the car park, just below "once fashionable" Rue Hamra. The scene of a half-hour earlier had suddenly changed. People were walking quickly, shopping for bread and supplies in case of a siege. As we drove past the Beirut house of Walid Jumblatt, men shuffled nervously, hands behind their backs, fingering worry beads or key chains. The beggars had disappeared. Shopkeepers were closing or standing ready to close. People were leaving their offices to drive to the safety of home, and traffic grew worse. We were losing time, and I shared the general impatience to be on my way.

I was going to the house of my friend Assem Salaam, a cousin of all the other Salaams, who lived near the Green Line. Ramzi drove us up a hill from the ruins of the Hotel St Georges on St Georges' Bay. We drove past the old presidential palace, long since abandoned in favour of a hideous 1960s mock-Holiday Inn above the city in the Christian mountains. Laundry hung from lines outside the windows, shell holes went unrepaired and weeds were visible behind a twelve-foot wall in a garden where presidents had entertained royalty and diplomats. Nearby was the unfinished Murr Tower where Syrian soldiers stood ready behind sandbags and sand-filled barrels painted with the Iranian colours of its previous Hizballah occupants. A few shopkeepers stood just inside their arched doorways, ready to pull down the steel shutters if anything happened.

I remembered walking down the same street at the end of June 1975 from an old house on the hill. The newly appointed prime minister, Rashid Karami, had just told a crowded press conference that he had formed a "cabinet of national unity" and that the fighting was over. As I walked down that road towards the Hotel St Georges, I was nearly killed by a sniper. Ever the optimist, Karami would be found by the Syrians nine years and many deaths later, just as he was leaving his house in Tripoli to go fishing, to form another last-chance national unity government.

Ramzi continued up the hill, parallel with the demarcation line between east and west, past the Greek Orthodox patriarchate, past the façades of destroyed houses, to the graceful stone Arab house of Assem Salaam. Assem was in his garden, wearing denim Oshkosh overalls. He asked me into the house, and we sat on a couch next to his terrace. I told him the news we had heard on the radio about Karami's assassination. Assem had known Karami. "Who would want to kill Rashid?" he asked. "He had no militia. He had no personal enemies. The Lebanese Forces wanted him to resign, and he did resign. Why kill him?" There were two variables: who and why. Unfortunately, we knew neither and, as with so many other deaths in Lebanon, we were unlikely to learn. It was possible the man who planted the bomb on the helicopter did not know himself who had paid him.

An architect, Assem was overseeing the restoration of Walid Jumblatt's palace in Mukhtara. It was a beautiful place, damaged a little in war and decayed over the years. "The work is coming along well," he said. "Whenever Walid gets some more money, we do some more restoration."

I mentioned how badly damaged the old Chamoun Palace had been on the coast at Saadiyat, near Doha. "I designed that house," Assem said. "We were working on it while the civil war was on in 1958." The leader of the opposition to Chamoun at the time was Assem's uncle, Saeb Bayk Salaam. "Did your Uncle Saeb mind?" I asked him.

"Of course not," he said, smiling. "This was part of the *entente cordiale* among the rulers."

Assem asked if I had time for a coffee. Before I answered, he advised, "I don't think you should stay on this side. Something might happen. Nothing might happen. You never know, but you should be safer in the east for awhile."

The traffic headed east was heavier than usual. Cars along the wide Corniche el-Mazraa stretched back a mile in three lanes. We moved past the Nasser Mosque, built just before the war by west Beirut's Sunni community in honour of their Egyptian champion, its high minaret overlooking little now but destruction, filth and fear. The highest Sunni official in the land, although from the north of Lebanon, was dead.

As we neared the museum crossing, we were the only car left. Those without permission to drive – those who were not journalists, soldiers, officials or men of influence – were going across on foot. When Ramzi drove quickly to the last west side checkpoint, the Muslim soldiers there could not have been more relaxed if they had been having lunch in a Neapolitan trattoria. They lounged outside on deckchairs near a small shed without sandbags, their weapons lying on the ground nearby. They looked at us, uttered a greeting and waved. For the next one hundred and fifty yards, the road was deserted. At the other end, in front of the museum, the Christian soldiers were equally nonchalant. Inside the Christian sector at twelve-thirty, we heard the first explosion.

It turned out to be a stick of dynamite thrown, like two others that afternoon, from a car at a pile of rubbish in the streets of west Beirut. Either someone was hoping to stir up trouble or it was the first salvo in a new "Keep Beirut Tidy" campaign.

Ramzi dropped me at friends in Ashrafieh where he and his employer had influence to protect him, and said he had to hurry back to west Beirut. "I have to get back to my boys," he said. As he drove off, I wondered who "his boys" were.

On the east side later, I took a taxi. When the radio announced that all schools, banks and government offices were closing for a period of national mourning, the driver demanded, "They close for one *za'im*?" A *za'im* was a strongman. Lebanon was ruled by *za'ims*, leaders of communities who included the *bayks* like Suleiman Frangieh in Zgharta, Walid Jumblatt in the Shouf and Rashid Karami in Tripoli. "They never closed for the twenty thousand who were killed."

"Twenty thousand?" Most estimates of those killed in the war put the number at about one hundred and fifty thousand, perhaps more.

"The young people. The twenty thousand young people martyred."

Later, I took an Armenian driver. When we discussed who might have killed Karami, he said, "Our side blames Syria. They blame Israel. Who knows?"

Over dinner that evening, my Greek Catholic host said, in all sincerity, "In 1976, the American secretary of state sent a letter to the French saying there would be no peace in Lebanon until all the political leaders were killed."

"Are you saying," I asked him, "that the US killed Karami, Kamal Jumblatt, Tony Frangieh and Bechir Gemayel?"

"Why not?"

All we would learn was *how* Karami had been killed. Someone had planted explosives in the back of his seat on the helicopter before he boarded. When the bomb went off over the sea south of Tripoli, the prime minister was blown to pieces. Abdallah Rassi was injured. The helicopter's pilot, Captain Antoine Bustany of the Lebanese Army, was seriously wounded, and his co-pilot, Captain William Mulless, reacted quickly and landed on the highway just inside the Maronite area near Jebail. The bomb might have been placed on board while the helicopter was at its base in the Maronite zone, in which case some Christians probably killed him, or while it was in Tripoli, in which case the Syrians did it. Neither side had an obvious motive.

The next day, I went to Tripoli for the funeral. Ramzi was in west Beirut, and I felt safe enough in the east simply to use taxis. I asked a Christian driver, an elderly man named Khalil Zeinoun, whether he minded going north through the Syrian lines to Tripoli.

"Of course not," he said. "My village is in the north."

"Where are you from?" I asked him.

"Akkar," he said, pointing north.

"Which village?"

"Qobayat."

Qobayat was the home of the Abdallah brothers, one of whom, Georges Ibrahim Abdallah, was serving a long prison term in France for terrorist offences. "Do you know the Abdallahs?" I asked him.

"Of course," he said. "I took a bunch of journalists up there to see the family, when there was all the trouble in France. Georges Ibrahim was with the PFLP. I know his mother and father. They are very nice. We saw two of his brothers. They are nice too."

Khalil Zeinoun told me about his last drive north. "I took a man from Baabda all the way up to his house in Zgharta, where he picked up his money. Then I had to drive him to a sweet shop in Tripoli, you know, Arabic sweets, *baklawa* and those things. Then I took him back to his house, where his wife was waiting on the balcony with her hands trembling for the sweets."

"Why did he have to go to Tripoli for the sweets?"

"We Christians cannot make sweets," he said. "Only the Muslims make good Arabic sweets. In Tripoli, they make the best."

"Well, you can buy some sweets in Tripoli today."

"Not today. Everything is closed."

All of Lebanon had closed to honour the dead prime minister. Flags flew at half mast in both the Muslim and Christian areas, the Muslims showing respect for one of their own and the Christians because he represented in his office national legitimacy.

When we reached Tripoli, Syrian soldiers stopped us at a roadblock and said we would have to walk the rest of the way. The streets were filled with people, and all but official traffic was banned. Khalil Zeinoun was about to park his car, when I handed the Syrian soldier my blue letter from his Minister of Defence, General Moustapha Tlass. The soldier read the letter, folded it neatly back in its envelope with the photograph of the general and myself and saluted me. He told Khalil to drive on. Khalil Zeinoun looked at me with new respect. When we came to the next Syrian checkpoint, he held the letter up and told the Syrian soldiers to get out of his way.

The funeral was impressive, if unmoving. It was too public to be moving, too crowded to be unimpressive. The whole city was out as I had never seen it before, to bury its *effendi*. Not a balcony along the two-mile

434

route of the funeral march was empty or even partly empty. The pavements were full with people, pushed from the road onto the pavements by Syrian and Lebanese soldiers. Men in suits and boys in jeans lined the route, a guard of honour for their fallen leader. Professional women wailers were out in force, setting the tone for the mourning city. Some women ululated, and others tore at their clothes in grief.

Bands marched past, playing funeral dirges. Each political leader in turn marched along the parade route at the head of his delegation of mourners. Walid Jumblatt led several hundred Druze in their black moutain *sharwals* and turbans. Robert Frangieh walked slowly at the head of a hundred Maronites in dark business suits from Zgharta. Adil Osseiran, the Minister of Defence, led a group of Shiite retainers from south Lebanon as his son-in-law helped him to walk in the morning heat. The Mufti of Beirut, Sheikh Hassan Khaled, wore his long robe and turban and marched side by side with several Salaams, including Tammam, at the head of hundreds of Beirut Sunni gentlemen. Each phalanx of followers marched without women behind its leader, arm-in-arm, from Rashid Karami's house to the Grand Mansour Mosque to the cemetery, while the people of Tripoli watched them go past. Some of the leaders there had opposed one another in the civil war of 1958 and in the non-violent political struggles of the years before 1975, but they were all for the moment allied to one another under the Syrian umbrella. The Syrian Socialist National Party had the poor taste to wave its party flag, but none of the other delegations carried a banner.

I walked behind the funeral parade to the mosque. The courtyard of the Grand Mosque was like a fortress with cut stone walls on four sides, *liwans* in two of them as in a traditional Arab garden. The mosque itself was at the end of the yard, opposite the entry gate, which had been shut to keep the crowds outside. Syrian soldiers, Lebanese soldiers and Lebanese police milled around the courtyard among the mourners and the press. Most of the soldiers wore combat fatigues, the Lebanese soldiers in US olive drabs with M-16s, the Syrians in Soviet red camouflage with AK-47s, all of them in high black boots. From inside the mosque came a great commotion, when, in the heat and stifling atmosphere, one of the politicians fainted.

Karami's death was a loss for Tripoli, which had no Sunni politician of stature to replace him in the higher councils of government. Like most Lebanese politicians, he had inherited his position. His father, Abdel Hamid Karami, had been the mufti of Tripoli, the most senior Sunni religious leader in the city. Abdel Hamid Karami had the distinction of serving as the only Arab governor of Tripoli, when King Feisal appointed him to the post during his short-lived Arab Kingdom of Syria in 1920. The elder Karami, like Feisal, lost his job when the French invaded

Damascus. After independence in 1943, he became prime minister in more than one Lebanese cabinet. When he died, the people of Tripoli erected a statue in his honour at the southern entrance to their city. His son Rashid lived to see the statue torn down by pro-Palestinian Lebanese Sunni militiamen in 1975. That was a period of revolutionary ferment in Tripoli, and it would have been easy to see the destruction of the old *effendi*'s statue as an act by democrats destroying the feudal order. But the leader of the militia that destroyed the statue, a well-educated and urbane Sunni named Farouk Mukaddam, was the scion of a feudal family which had been the Karamis' rivals in Tripoli since before the Ottomans. In 1976, Mukaddam reigned supreme in Tripoli with Palestinian help. In 1982, the wheel had turned again, and Mukaddam took refuge in the Maronite heartland.

Both the Karamis and the Mukaddams saw themselves as Arab nationalists, and both had opposed the Islamic fundamentalists who briefly took power in Tripoli after the Israeli invasion of 1982. Yet they had never cooperated politically, their historic antagonism taking precedence over the politics of the moment. Neither Rashid Karami nor Farouk Mukaddam had married and given birth to sons, but brothers and nephews waited to keep the family names, family rivalries, alive for another generation. In the future, no one would remember which family had favoured the Russians, which the Americans, in the long-forgotten and irrelevant Cold War. All that mattered was who had survived.

After the funeral, Khalil Zeinoun and I went up to Zgharta, where most of the politicians had stopped for lunch at the Frangieh Palace before returning to Beirut. The house was crowded with tribal leaders, who were welcomed into the sitting-room by Frangieh women dressed in black. Walid Jumblatt, whose father had been killed the same way as Rashid Karami, walked up to me and asked, "Well, who's next?" I was sure he imagined it would be himself. Walid was tall and skinny, in his late thirties, and he was dressed in a dark suit rather than his usual blue jeans and leather jacket. He had fair skin, a prematurely bald head and dark eyes that bulged out of their sockets. Most of Walid's followers were neither progressive nor socialist, but, officially, he was the head of the Progressive Socialist Party founded by his father, Kamal. His power derived in reality from his inheritance of the feudal leadership of Lebanon's Druze. His father and grandfather had died violent deaths, and his great grandfather, Said Bayk Jumblatt, led the Druze when they massacred and expelled the Christians from the Shouf in 1860. Just after the 1983 fighting in the Shouf, when most of its Maronites had fled or been killed, Walid's mother, May Jumblatt, told me that life in the Shouf had become deadly dull without Christians. Commerce had come to a halt, and most villages lacked electricity. There was no night life. When I sympathised, she responded, "But why are you sorry? The Druze love it like that."

I asked Walid whether I could visit him in Mukhtara. I wanted to see again the place where Said Bayk Jumblatt had presided over the destruction of the Maronites, the same Ottoman stone house where Walid himself directed his campaign against the Maronites more than a century later. "Sure," he said. "Do you want to come to Mukhtara with me now?"

"No, tomorrow."

"Fine. *Ahlan wa sahlan*," he said. Walking out, he added, "Just call Akram Shuhayb at my office in Beirut, to confirm the arrangements."

I called Akram that night, and there was no answer. The next morning, I left messages by telephone and telex. He did not call back.

Only later did I come to the conclusion I should simply, as in years past, have gone by taxi to his house without any warning, rather than take precautions against kidnapping by making plans through his Beirut office. As more than one army had discovered to its cost, this was not a land for making plans.

CHAPTER TWENTY-FIVE

DISRESPECTFUL DANCING

Ramzi took me south from Doha to Naamey, another destroyed Christian village, just north of Damour, where Muslim refugees from east Beirut had settled. Most of the people in Naamey were called Arab al-Maslakh, Arabs from the Maslakh. Maslakh, Arabic for slaughterhouse, was a slum of wood and tin shanty houses along the coast road in the Christian half of Beirut. In late 1975, Christian militiamen laid siege to Maslakh and the neighbouring slum, Qarantina. Don McCullin took some haunting photographs of the slaughter that followed, of triumphant militiamen displaying their booty. Many of the inhabitants escaped to west Beirut, some of them to become the dazed shock troops of the Palestinian commando groups, others to join Walid Jumblatt's Druze militia, most to attempt to survive without becoming involved again in the war. Naamey was run down, many of the houses still covered in the grime and smoke from its conquest by the Palestinians and later by the invading Israelis. Ramzi drove to a petrol station in Naamey, spoke to some men, and then stopped to talk to a family standing in the road. Ramzi introduced me to a young man named Bibi and a family with two little girls who approached the car. Everyone in Naamey seemed to know him.

"What do you think of the girl?" he asked me, as we drove north towards Beirut.

"Which one?"

"The little girl with the red scarf."

"She's pretty," I said, using the feminine of the Arabic word for pretty, *helouie*, which also means sweet.

"She's my girlfriend," he said proudly.

"But she's only thirteen."

"No," he said. "She's sixteen. Her name is Zeina."

We went into Beirut, where he took me from friend to friend, house to house, office to office, guiding me around and protecting me at the same time.

*

That evening, I had planned to meet Juan-Carlos Gumucio for dinner. Ramzi and I would pick him up at his apartment on the Corniche at nine, and we would go to the Tokyo Japanese Restaurant. After that, we would probably have a drink at the Backstreet. I had just finished my shower when Ramzi and a neighbour knocked on my door. The neighbour said, "There is trouble in the area." They both looked winded, and Ramzi was covered in sweat, his dark, curly hair sticking to his forehead. "You may not be able to go to dinner in Beirut tonight."

The way they looked, I thought I might have to pack quickly and flee to the mountains. I imagined hordes of Hizballah militants marching up the hill, chanting, "Death to the American," and surrounding the house. "What is it?" I asked.

"There's been fighting in Naamey," the neighbour said. Ramzi jumped in to explain, "I went down to Naamey to see my girlfriend, but there was trouble when I got there. Everyone was in the streets with guns. There was some shooting, and the Druze are moving tanks in."

"Why?"

"Do you remember the man we spoke to this morning? The one with his wife who stopped to say hello? His name is Bibi."

"Yes."

"He assassinated Imad Naufal, the Druze security chief in Naamey, at seven-thirty tonight," he said, still standing in the doorway. "Then everyone started shooting. Six more people have been killed." It was nine o'clock, and seven people had been killed since seven-thirty in a village only a mile and a half away. I had not heard a sound.

"Why?"

"Bibi is an Arab al-Maslakh, but he belongs to the PSP. It must be some problem in the PSP." The PSP was the Progressive Socialist Party of Walid Jumblatt, in effect, the Druze militia.

"So what is happening now?"

"Jumblatt is out of the country today, but the Druze are sending tanks. There could be something terrible between the Druze and the Arab al-Maslakh Sunnis in the PSP. The Syrians are massing their troops on the road."

"What is going to happen?"

"I don't know, but it is a good thing Amal is not involved. Imad Naufal killed someone in Amal last January, when the Druze and Amal were fighting. If they think Bibi was paid by Amal, there will be real trouble."

I supposed an internal PSP bloodbath would have been slightly milder than an all-out confrontation between the PSP and Amal.

"So you two think I should not go to dinner in Beirut tonight?"

"If you still want to go," Ramzi said, "there is another driver who can take you. I have to go down to Naamey to control my men."

I was not sure what he meant by "my men," but I knew I did not want to drive on the coast road that night.

"We talked to Khaled Salaam on the telephone," the neighbour said, "and he thinks you should not come, because you might not get back."

The neighbour walked home, and Ramzi found the other driver and told him he would not need to take me to Beirut that night. I've never seen a man look as relieved. I walked across the garden to Umm Hany's house, where there was a working telephone. I called Juan-Carlos to tell him why I could not come to dinner. "You're kidding," he said.

"No," I insisted, "the Druze are sending in the tanks."

" 'Soviet-supplied'?" he asked. "Or 'Syrian-backed'?"

"Well, I'm not going down the 'hotly contested' coast highway, through the 'battle-scarred and divided' capital just to meet you at a restaurant in the 'once-fashionable' Hamra area."

"How about a drink in the 'war-ravaged' hotel district?"

Umm Hany sat knitting while I spoke to Juan Carlos. When I hung up, she said, "I think you are wise not to go to Beirut tonight. You don't know what will happen."

Walking in the garden between the two houses, I saw Hany's long-eared cocker spaniel standing on a balcony outside the kitchen door. Above him, on the roof, a black cat was waiting to pounce. The dog turned his head to look at me, and the cat dropped onto his back, digging its claws into the dog's flesh. The spaniel turned to bite the cat and, with the same motion, pushed it off the balcony to the garden a storey below. The cat ran off into the darkness. Even the animals had absorbed the local atmosphere.

Ramzi told me the next morning he had stayed in Naamey until four o'clock. He said the bodies of Imad Naufal, his two body guards and one of his assassins lay in the road all night. No one could retrieve them in the midst of the shooting. The Barbir Hospital in west Beirut had sent blood to the clinics nearby, and Bibi's wife and children had been evacuated to safety. "Where is Bibi?" I asked.

"I don't know, but I think we'll get him out of the country."

Ramzi was going back to Naamey, after stopping at home to see his wife. A young Shiite driver named Majed was taking me to lunch in Beirut. He came from Nabatieh, where some bombs had recently exploded. He blamed Israel for them, but he seemed more worried by the lack of money.

"I take home about six thousand Lebanese pounds a month," he said. "I have four children. One pair of children's shoes cost two thousand LL. If I buy shoes for all four children, I am already two thousand LL over my salary."

"What are you going to do?"

"I'd like to leave the country."

"I suppose the militias pay more."

"I know. Look at my family. I have one brother in Hizballah and one brother in Amal."

"What is the difference between the two?"

"Amal wants Israel to leave the south, peacefully if possible. It will talk to them about it. Hizballah won't talk. Hizballah won't make any agreement."

"Which do you think is better?"

"Isn't it better not to use the gun if you have the choice?" he asked me. "Hizballah has only one goal: for Israel to leave Lebanon. After that, it doesn't care about anything."

"What do you think of the Palestinians?"

"They made a big mistake," he said. "They came to Hamra. They smoked big cigars, drank whisky and had one woman here, one woman there," pointing to each arm in turn. "If they went to the borders only and fought Israel, everyone in Lebanon would be with them. But they did not. If they fought Israel like my brother did, we could say they were *feda'i*, but they were not *feda'i*." *Feda'i*, the Arabic singular of *fedayeen*, meant fighter in a noble cause.

"Was your brother *feda'i*?"

"Yes. He fought Israel. They killed him."

Quiet had returned to Naamey, and Ramzi drove me to the Tokyo Restaurant for my postponed dinner with Juan-Carlos Gumucio. Gaby Bustros, who was visiting from the east side, Nora Boustany and a French stewardess from Lebanon's Middle East Airlines joined us. The dignified old Japanese woman who owned the restaurant served us sashimi and tempura. After dinner, Ramzi drove us on to the Backstreet. We had a few drinks, met old friends and spent an evening like many when I had lived in west Beirut. When it was time to go, Ramzi took the others home and returned for me. "I'll be outside," he said.

"No, I'm ready to go now."

"You don't have a woman?" he asked, shocked.

I had no excuse. When I got into the car, he asked me, "Where to now?"

"Home, to Doha."

"Now? What time it is?"

"I guess about one a.m."

"It's early," he said. "Let's go have some fun."

He sped into the night, through the Syrian checkpoints and past houses of sleeping families on the road south. We were almost to Doha when, instead of taking the overpass left into the hills, he turned right towards the sea. We stopped at a hotel, the Friendly Beach. "You'll like it," he said, "and my girlfriend will be here."

We went from the darkness and silence of the seashore into a room alive with light and noise, as though we were passing from the death of one civilisation to the birth of another. Several hundred men, women and children, most in their best clothes as for a wedding, sat at long family tables grouped around a raised dance floor. On the tables were large *mezzes* of *hommous*, *foul*, *tabboule*, *kibbé*, salads and bread. Most tables had bottles of whisky, several of which looked like jeroboams of Johnny Walker Red Label, next to buckets of ice and bottles of Sohat water. A large band played synthesisers, horns and drums, the blaring sound of modern Arab pop. On the dance floor, people of all ages were doing Western disco dances, then Lebanese folk dances, then combinations of the two. Ramzi kissed a woman hello, then told me, "She owns the place."

The way she kissed him, I thought *he* owned the place. She gave us a big table next to the dance floor and told the waiters to bring us bottles of whisky and ice.

The music stopped, and everyone began shouting, "*Ya, Ali, Ya, Ali,*" and clapping. An impresario then introduced Ali, calling him up to the dance floor. "*Ya, Ali, Ya, Ali.*" A twelve-year-old boy wearing a white dinner jacket and bow tie jumped onto the stage and grabbed the microphone. The band started playing an Arabic love song, and the boy sang, moving about the floor with the speed and energy of Little Richard. As Ali sang about eyes and lemons and love, he beckoned everyone to join him on the dance floor. He sang as they danced around him. He had a beautiful, trained voice that reminded me of boys I had heard singing mournful ballads for pennies on the streets of Galway more than ten years before. He had more self-confidence than some singers twice his age, and his singing made several people positively melancholy.

Ramzi looked around the room for Zeina, his young girlfriend, but he did not see her. He called the owner over and asked if she had seen the girl. "Not yet, my dear," she said, "but it's early." It was two o'clock.

Ramzi poured us both whisky and ice. "What happens," I asked him, "if the Shiites find out about all this drinking and dancing in their area?"

"We're all Shiites," he said. Then he introduced me to men named Ali, Hassan, Hussein, Fawzi, Musa, and women with names like Zeinab, Samira and Miriam. Several sat at our table and had drinks with us. A woman named Leila, who spoke English, asked me to dance. On the dance floor, I found myself next to a ten-year-old girl with long hair and a blue party dress, her hips swaying and her eyes closed as she danced with her older sister to the music and the soulful voice of young Ali.

The music was too loud, the room too crowded, for conversation, but

Leila tried to tell me above the din that she had studied in the United States. "I love New Orleans," she said.

I began to have a kind of hope for Lebanon. These people, in their garish suits and crinoline dresses, were the poor Shiites whom the religious zealots claimed to represent. They were villagers and city workers, poor people who were beginning to make money. Some had been to West Africa, where thousands of Lebanon's Shiites had established businesses and made fortunes. Others had small shops in Beirut. They were breaking away from their traditional, feudal leaders. Gone were the days when the thugs of Lebanese Shiite politicians and landowners like the late Ahmed al-Assaad would beat up a man for abandoning his traditional peasant robes and wearing trousers, "like the *bayk.*" They were making money and turning their backs on the old ways, but they had not rushed into the arms of the Party of God. They, like Lebanese of all sects, wanted to enjoy their lives, to come out at night and forget about the misery and the killing around them. If anything, their night life was more abandoned than the discos of east Beirut or the Backstreet in west Beirut. The mullahs would not have approved, any more than ascetic Christian monks liked to see Maronite children dancing together in the forests, but no mullahs watched in the night club of the Friendly Beach.

When we sat down again, Ramzi was still looking, between drinks and greetings, for Zeina. He leaned across the table and said to me confidentially, "You see that man over there?" He pointed to a man on the dance floor, but I could not tell which one.

"I think so."

"I am going to kill him." He was as matter-of-fact as if he had said, "I think I'll have the lobster tonight."

"Why?"

"I have to."

"Why?"

"I don't like him."

"Don't do it," I said, thinking to myself, "My God, I don't even know which man he means."

"You see how disrespectful he is? His dancing is not respectful."

"That's no reason to kill him."

Ramzi took another drink. He had been a good friend to me in Beirut and was willing to risk his life to save mine. I liked him and would not have been disrespectful to him under any circumstances. I doubted he would kill the man, but I could not be certain. I changed the subject.

"How can this place survive here?'

"They pay protection money."

"How much?"

"Five thousand pounds a month."

"To whom?"

Ramzi poured us both fresh tumblers of whisky and said, after taking a sip, "To me."

Young Ali jumped off the dance floor to the thunder of clapping from everyone in the room. He bowed and picked up money people had thrown him. He strutted back to a table, where he was sitting with his proud mother and father. In a few years, I knew, he would own Las Vegas. The band played wild music, and more people rushed up to the floor to do Arabic dances. Girls tied scarves around their hips to begin innocent but seductive swaying, and men clapped slowly and kicked their feet more or less in time with the beat of the drums.

"Ramzi," I said. "You take protection money?"

"I protect the whole coast," he said. "Everything from Khalde to Jiyye. No one bothers these people. I have two hundred militiamen on my payroll, and they make sure everything is all right."

"From Khalde to Jiyye," I said. "But between Khalde and Jiyye, there are Amal, Hizballah, Druze, not just one militia."

"I know. I have my men in each of the militias, everywhere on the coast."

I excused myself to find the lavatory, and I asked the owner where it was. She pointed to a door at the far end of the room. I negotiated my way around the tables and dancers. Some of the people to whom Ramzi had introduced me patted me on the back, saying, "Welcome, Charlie." When I opened the door to the lavatory, I was glad I had been born a man. The floor was a sea of paper napkins, and the toilet seats were broken. In the villages from which many of these people had come, there was no plumbing.

When I walked back towards the table, the woman who owned the night club asked whether I was enjoying myself. Then I asked her, "Does Ramzi protect this place?"

"Of course," she said. "Ramzi is wonderful. A really wonderful man."

Before we left, the proprietress told Ramzi that Zeina had sent word with a friend that she had to stay at home with her mother that night and would not be coming. He relaxed, and I suspected he had been worried about her in case of another flare-up in Naamey. When he drove me home, as the sun was rising behind the mountain, he had forgotten all about the man he was going to kill. He had a date the next night with Zeina.

Adil Bayk Osseiran was receiving a delegation of six women from south Lebanon. Adil Bayk had been the Shiite minister in the first Lebanese government at independence in 1943. He had been the speaker of the

444

parliament, and he still served his country as Minister of Defence and Agriculture. He was eighty-two years old. The women delegates had come to see him at the house of his son-in-law, Razi Saidi, in west Beirut. The ladies were all properly turned out in long dresses and well-coiffed hair. Four of them sat on a sofa, and two others on chairs in the living-room. Whether the matrons had come to see him in his capacity as one of south Lebanon's largest landlords, as Shiite Muslim clan leader, as member of parliament, as minister of agriculture or as minister of defence was not clear. I doubted whether they had given it any thought. One of the respectable matrons began to ask him a question, addressing the old man as "*Fakhamat ar-ra'is . . .*"

Her companion immediately corrected her, "*Daoulat ar-ra'is.*" "*Ra'is*" meant leader or president, and in Lebanon, there were three presidents –the Maronite "president of the republic," the Sunni "president of the government" or prime minister, and the Shiite "president of the chamber of deputies," or speaker of the house. Each was a president, and each man who had held any of these posts remained "*ra'is*" for the rest of his life. "*Fakhamat ar-ra'is*" was the correct honorific for the "president of the republic," and "*daoulat ar-ra'is*" for the speaker.

"*Daoulat ar-ra'is,*" she asked him, "do you think Israel will occupy us again?"

"Israel," he said, shrugging his shoulders in acceptance, "can do anything it likes."

People from his fief in the south would come to see him at all hours of the day and night, and it did not matter that he was eighty-two years old and had a tremor, the result of a botched surgical procedure, similar to Parkinson's Disease that from time to time made his head shake painfully and violently. He had been arrested, along with Camille Chamoun and the other politicians pressing for independence, by the French in 1943, after which he had been in every Lebanese parliament and nearly every government that followed.

"*Daoulat ar-ra'is,*" another woman asked him, "what will we do if Israel comes back?"

Adil Bayk answered her in Arabic and turned to me. "These ladies are asking me whether Israel will invade again. I told them Israel can come again. And then we will have to fight them again. There is no other way."

"But," a woman on his left said, in English, "it's very hard for us." She told me, "I had to ask the Israelis for permission to go home."

"Where do you live?" I asked her.

"Nabatieh. My father was sick, and I went to visit him from Beirut. The Israeli soldier asked me, 'Where is your permission?' I said, 'This is my country. Where is your permission to be here?' He said I could not go to

Nabatieh, and I had to come back to Beirut." She had tears in her eyes as she recalled the incident. "My father was very sick."

"*Ma'alesh*," Adil Bayk said to her, the Arabic equivalent of, "It's all right. Don't worry."

She told him of other, similar hardships, and he said again, "*Ma'alesh*," implying that other people in south Lebanon had faced much greater hardships.

Adil Bayk sat erect in a stuffed chair, his daughter Afaf at his side. He wore a dark blue suit and tie and black Oxford brogues. His white hair was neatly combed over his leonine head, and his white moustache had been perfectly trimmed. He was invariably friendly, but he had a reputation for toughness. Palestinian seasonal workers accused him of underpaying them on his farms, but he was one of the only Lebanese politicians no one had ever accused of corruption. A businessman I knew had once gone with an Osseiran cousin to ask Adil Bayk in his capacity as minister of agriculture for a waiver to export olive oil. Lebanese law prohibited the export of olive oil to keep the local price down. "Adil Bayk looked at his cousin and said, 'I am not surprised that you would ask for this.' Then he turned to me, 'But you! I thought you were better than that. You know this is against the law. How dare you ask me to break the law?' I tell you, I was ashamed." When I told that story to a Shiite friend from the south, he explained, "Adil Osseiran is not honest just because he likes to be honest. He is honest, because he is too proud to be dishonest."

"Afaf tells me you are writing a book," Adil Bayk said to me. "What is your book about?"

When I told him, he said, "I think maybe your book will help the British and American people to be impartial."

"I doubt it, but I hope so."

A maid brought us fresh orange juice, the most common refreshment among the citrus-rich southern Lebanese. It made a change from coffee and tea.

While Adil Bayk talked in Arabic to one of the women, another leaned forward in her chair to tell me, "We are the ladies of the south. We are the, how do you say, Community of Women for the South. We have projects to help the orphans, the hospitals and the schools. We are also opening an old people's home."

"Where?"

"Near Nabatieh. Now we are on our way to the World Peace Congress in Moscow. We want the world to hear about our suffering."

"I hope the world listens."

"I doubt it," she said.

*

446

"My great-grandfather and grandfather were the consuls of Iran in Sidon," Ali Osseiran, Adil Bayk's son, said over dinner that evening at Ramzi Saidi's. Ramzi was away, and Ali's father had gone home to Rmailly, near Sidon. His sister, Afaf, was saying, "I apologise for this simple meal." Ali had not told her we were coming to dinner, and the simple meal was a chicken curry with rice, several salads, fresh tomatoes and cucumbers, then cheese, fresh fruit and cakes.

"The Shiah have always looked to Iran, the only powerful country with a Shiah government," Ali said. "Every community has its protector. For a long time, under the Shah, we had no one. Now, again, we have Iran."

"Who do the Sunnis have?"

"They had the Turks. Later, they had Egypt. Then they had Saudi Arabia. For them, it's like having no one."

"Everyone seems to expect another round of fighting."

"But there has been no change in the balance of power outside, so why should they fight inside? Also, Amin Gemayel and Camille Chamoun are friendly with Nabih Berri and Amal. The Lebanese Forces are friendly with Walid Jumblatt. So, who's going to fight whom?"

"I've heard it said that the Syrians are angry with Amin Gemayel for not reaching an agreement with them, for not taking any steps towards them."

"Perhaps. Some say Syria would like to open a front against Gemayel and the Lebanese Forces, giving weapons to Frangieh and long-range artillery to Hobeika."

"Turning Maronites against Maronites?"

"Yes, but I doubt it will happen."

Ali had just arrived from England, where he spent part of each year with his wife, Sara, and their children. He returned to Lebanon whenever his father needed him. "I wanted to stay in London for the British elections. I wanted to see Thatcher win again," he said, hoping for a reaction from me.

Ramzi's older son, Ibrahim, came into the room where we were having dinner. When I asked him what he'd been doing, he said, "Reading."

"What are you reading?"

"*The Lord of the Rings*. Have you read it?"

"No."

"If you do, you have to read *The Hobbit* first. Otherwise you won't understand it."

"What else have you been reading?"

"I liked *Catcher in the Rye*. It was very funny."

Ibrahim was thirteen, but had an adult's poise. His English, French and Arabic were fluent, and he thought nothing of arguing politics with men of his father's generation. When he wandered out of the dining-room, I said to his mother, "Your son is very bright."

"Yes," she said, "but he's not tall yet. He still has to grow."

"He doesn't seem short, but the important thing is, he has a brain."

"Oh, yes, this one? But he's not happy. The children are not happy anymore." Afaf and Ramzi had two sons and two daughters. "Those five days at the end of January were awful. The fighting was just from here." She pointed to a roundabout, now manned by Syrian troops, just beyond the window. "We had five-inch shells hitting the dining-room. There was no electricity, no water, no servants."

Ali laughed. "No servants? Come to London."

"It was hard, Ali. You know it was. We finally had to move down to the Summerland Hotel, because my mother-in-law said she did not want the children to stay here. You remember Sunday when the Israelis made the . . . what do you call them?"

"Sonic booms?"

"Two sonic booms. Amr, the little boy, said, 'Let's run down to the shelter.' They were very affected by that fighting. Later, Amr strutted around to show he was not afraid."

After dinner, we went into the study where Afaf showed us family photographs. There were new pictures of her family in the three major centres of Shiite Lebanon, the Bekaa Valley, Tyre and Beirut. "Here is Ramzi at Karaoun Lake," she said. "And this is the Litani River." The countryside in the pictures was pretty, the vineyards, the blossoms in the orchards. "Ramzi took this picture," she said, showing me a shot of the Litani gorge. "Ramzi is interested in everything now. He's taking photographs. He's bought all these watercolours – all by Lebanese artists."

On the walls were portraits, still lifes, abstracts, all Lebanese, but lacking a common theme or style, like Lebanon itself.

Before Ali and I went to south Lebanon on Friday, I took one of my two suitcases, my typewriter and my notebooks to Gaby Bustros's house in east Beirut. I would not need many things for a few days in the south, just what I could fit into the other bag. Later I would lose all the notes I took in south Lebanon and west Beirut over the next five days, just as I would lose the diary that I had kept throughout the trip. Everything else would have to come from unaided memory, a memory that was feeble at best. I remember arriving back at Gaby's and stowing my notebooks and typewriter to await my return. Michel Bustros was arriving as I was leaving, and I thanked him for letting me go to Kefraya to taste his wines and meet Yves Morard. Michel, an elegant, silver-haired gentleman in his late fifties, asked where I was going. When I told him I was planning to stay with the Osseiran family near Sidon, he said, "Be careful."

"Sidon can't be any worse than the Bekaa."

"Much worse," he warned me.

I thought that everyone in Lebanon believed his own area was safe and everyone else's dangerous. Friends in west Beirut would tell me I was fine in their neighbourhoods, but not in a restaurant two hundred yards away. People in the south told me I was safe there, but that I should not go to the Bekaa or the north. Where you lived was safe: everywhere else was not.

I went back over the Green Line at the museum for the last time and drove down to meet Ali Osseiran at his sister Afaf's house. From there, we would go to Rmailly to spend a weekend in the south. Then, I would go to Beirut on Monday and Tuesday to look got Walid Jumblatt and go to Mukhtara, spending the days seeing friends and the nights back in Rmailly with the Osseirans.

Without my notes for those five days and with the passage of time, I cannot remember all that happened, everything people told me, every village and town I saw. Some day, Hizballah or the government of Iran may return to me my notebooks and diary, and I will see how reliable my memory was.

CHAPTER TWENTY-SIX

THE LAST DAY

It was early when I woke on my last morning in a child's room at the Osseirans' house in south Lebanon. A light wind rippled the sea, and small waves beat the stone foundations of the old Crusader sea castle in Sidon. From my window atop a hill just above Sidon, I watched the city coming awake. Men carried hot Arabic bread and *mena'eesh* from the bakery ovens, and *services* began to settle in the city square, ready to take commuters to Tyre in the south or Beirut in the north. The fishermen were already out in their small boats, casting their nets near the shore.

The alluvial plain on both banks of the Awali River was green with banana plantations and citrus orchards. A concrete bridge crossed the Awali near the sea, Syrian soldiers on the north side facing Lebanese Sunni Muslim militiamen on the south. A year before, Shiite militiamen were on the north bank. Three years before that, Israeli tanks were in position on both sides of the bridge. Before the invasion, Palestinian militiamen checked the papers of those entering and leaving south Lebanon. The Syrians I saw would not go south of the bridge, perhaps fearing an Israeli reaction. For the time being, Sidon and its large Palestinian refugee camps were under the control of Yasser Arafat's PLO, as it had been from the early 1970s until 1982, together with the Lebanese Sunnis whose militia Arafat subsidised.

Over the previous weekend, I had gone with Ali Osseiran into Sidon and the villages further south. We had met with Ali's relations, his friends and my friends. Ali's ancestors, originally from Iran, had been consuls in Sidon of Iran at the turn of the last century. "When my father used to come into the Serai in Sidon," Ali's father told me once, showing me the portrait of a striking man in a tarboosh, "all the people used to turn their heads and look. He was *that* handsome." The Osseirans had bought land and become *bayks*. So far as I could tell, they had excellent relations with Sidon's Sunnis and its remaining Christians. After visiting one of Ali's cousins, a friendly and talkative Shiite mullah, we went to see a Catholic priest who ran a local school and the Sunni member of parliament for the city.

One day, I had gone without Ali to the Ain el-Helouie refugee camp to see the mother and father of my oldest friend in Lebanon, Rashid Hamid. Rashid's parents had lost their house, as did everyone else in the camp, during the Israeli invasion of 1982. The houses that were not destroyed in the assault were bulldozed later, and Rashid's parents moved to a rented apartment in Sidon. His father, Ali, rebuilt his little shoe-repair shop in the camp, and he was working there when I surprised him with my visit. We went to see his wife, Souad, in their Sidon flat, and they both remained cheerful. Rashid had long since moved to the United States, married an American and brought his six brothers over. His parents had recently gone to visit Rashid in New York. "He wanted us to stay," his mother said. "But how could we? We don't speak English. We don't know anyone there." So they lived in Sidon, only an hour's drive, if the border had been open to them, from the village they had fled forty years before.

Rashid had been born in the village of Ain Zeitoun near Safad in northern Palestine. He was two when the Israelis occupied the village, and his parents became part of the Palestinian Arab exodus to Lebanon. We met at the American University in 1972, and he took me often to Ain Helouie camp to see his family in their tiny tin-roof house. I went back there many times, as a journalist when the Israelis bombed the camp, as a friend on quieter days. When I tried to find the Hamids immediately after the invasion of 1982, it was nearly impossible. All my points of reference had been destroyed. It took me hours of wandering through the camp's rubble and asking people where Abu Rashid was. I had arrived early one morning and wrote in my notebook:

At Lebanon's largest Palestinian refugee camp, Ain Helouie, women and children begin queueing for food about an hour before the United Nations Relief Works Agency (UNRWA) distribution centre opens at seven a.m. A hundred or so wait in the muddy road to receive their monthly ration: ten kilogrammes of lard, one kilo each of sugar and rice and two tins of corned beef. They also receive flour, a small gas camp stove and canned goods from Haifa, a city where some of the women were born. This obscene ritual, re-enacted every day since 1948 in the camps of Lebanon, Syria, Jordan, Gaza and the West Bank, is all the more tragic at Ain Helouie, because these women have no homes. The IDF [Israeli Defence Forces] bombed and bulldozed them to rubble during the summer invasion. I ask, "Where do you sleep on cold winter nights?" One woman says she and her children stay in a disused garage. Another is too proud to play humble refugee and shouts, "We are not asking you where you sleep, so why do you ask us?" The Israelis, after several reversals of policy over tents and

451

pre-fabricated houses, are allowing them to reconstruct their breeze-block shelters. Work proceeds slowly, because most of the working-age men are in the Israeli military prison near the Lebanese village of Ansar.

When I found the Hamid family, they asked me to call Rashid and let him know they were fine. All they had lost was their house and their possessions, but they had not been hurt. They were worried about two nephews, who had gone missing. I drove to the Israeli prison near Ansar to see if the boys were there. I wrote down what happened next:

Ansar camp straddles the road between Tyre and the large Shiite village of Nabatieh. Watchtowers line its perimeter, and it is surrounded by barbed wire. When I arrive, an Israeli guard tells me to wait ten minutes for his commander to arrive. I pass the time in a squatters' hamlet outside the prison. The people, Palestinians and Lebanese, live in rusting tin shacks and are reluctant to talk. They say they hear occasional shooting from the camp – the IDF admitted that the day before two prisoners had been accidentally shot and killed – and that the camp has grown in size as the Israelis extended the wire outwards. Finally, a sergeant arrives and invites me into the camp. A big, friendly man on reserve duty, he is an agronomist. He says he must radio a general in Nabatieh to ask for permission for me to see prisoners. While we wait, I ask how big the camp is. "I can't tell you how big the camp is," he answers. "All I can tell you is how many children I have."
"How many?"
"Two, girls." Then he asks me, "Have you been long here in Israel [sic]?" He offers me some army coffee, the quality of which he justifiably apologises for, and the general radios back from Nabatieh to say, "Permission denied." I tell the sergeant-agronomist I'll bring him good Turkish coffee from Beirut if he'll get me permission to see the prisoners. He is not optimistic, and I drive on to Tyre to find the International Red Cross tracing bureau opposite the old Rivoli Cinema. Several women are in the office, asking about their husbands and sons at Ansar. A Lebanese woman volunteer asks me the names of the Hamids' nephews and looks them up on a computer print-out. Their names are there, along with 6,000 others, which means they are still alive. When I ask if anything can be done to obtain their release, she says, "Ask the Israelis."

The Israelis departed a few years later, holding onto a little stretch of

Lebanese territory along the border. The people of Ain Helouie rebuilt their houses, and the young men found new attackers: first, the Christians of the Lebanese Forces, whom Israel brought into the area and took with them; and the Shiites of Amal, who attacked and assassinated Palestinians, especially the young men. Amal wanted to be sure it, and not the Palestinians, filled the power vacuum left in the south after the Israeli withdrawal.

I had coffee and cakes with the Hamids that last weekend, and we talked more about families, theirs and mine, than about politics. I went on to see the commander in south Lebanon of Yasser Arafat's Al Fateh, a man I knew from years before as Abu Ossama. I visited the camp hospital to speak to the Palestinian and Indian doctors who cared for the wounded. The doctors were sitting in a makeshift staff room, tired from long days and nights of sewing the wounds from Amal attacks, Israeli raids and internal Palestinian fighting. On the television, they were watching an old John Wayne film, in which I could hear the Duke saying something like, "Sure, I fought all the way to the Elbe and kissed those Russian bastards like everybody else. But I tell ya one thing: I don't like Commies."

My clearest memory was of walking with Ali Osseiran through his family's fields in the brown hills near the sea. We walked up and down rows of newly sown wheat, and Ali explained to me what the different strains of wheat were, what advantages each offered in different soils and climates, what the Lebanese preferred for their bread. He told me about the varieties of oranges and lemons he grew, about the breeds of dairy cows he had kept and later abandoned in the war. We were in the Shiite hills between Sidon and Tyre, a range known as Jebel Aamil, where the Shiites had fought against the Turks, the French, the Palestinians and, only after the 1982 invasion, the Israelis. It was rocky land, not as fertile as the Bekaa, but hard work made the crops grow. Ali crushed some budding stalks of wheat in his hands and pressed the grains into my hand. "You need land somewhere," he said, "to feel alive. I want my children to have this land. This is their place."

"It's not safe now," I said, or something like it.

"It will be."

That last morning, I took a cold shower in Ali's apartment, thanks to a solar heating system that was as inefficient as the hotel's in Arsuz had been at the beginning of my journey. Ali lived in the upstairs flat above his parents in their new apartment house. I shaved and dressed, then found Ali already receiving people in his sitting-room, much as Robert Frangieh had done in Zgharta.

One of the visitors was an old man, his cousin Ali Khalil. Ali Khalil spoke perfect English and told me about his years in the British army during the

453

Second World War. He told me the names of some of the other Arab soldiers and of the British officers under whom he served in the North African campaign. He asked if I knew any of them in London. I wrote all their names in my notebook, agreeing to ask what had become of them when I returned to England. He told me about the war and said, "Really, those were the best days of my life."

In 1947, Ali Khalil said, he joined the Arab Liberation Army of a Lebanese soldier of fortune named Fawzi al-Qaukji. It had been said of Qaukji, who was still alive in Beirut when I first went there, that during and between the two world wars he had spied for and against the British, the French and the Germans. His band of irregulars fought in Palestine, trying to expel the Jewish settlers who were exiling the Palestinians. Ali Khalil crossed the Lebanese border with Qaukji and fought in northern Galilee and Nazareth in what became the Arab world's most humiliating defeat. He said that Qaukji had opposed the Arab order to surrender Nazareth to the Israelis, and he finally retreated back to Lebanon. The old man looked an unlikely soldier, not much more than five feet tall and thin enough for a good wind to blow him off his feet. Yet he had fought in two wars, winning one for the British and losing the other for the Palestinians.

His family would eventually come to blows with the Palestinians for whom he had fought in 1948. Many, but not all, of the Khalil family of Tyre had sided with the Israelis against the Palestinians. When Israel withdrew, most of the Khalils took refuge in east Beirut. Ali Khalil and his cousin, Dr Saadallah Khalil, who ran a free hospital for poor Palestinians and Lebanese in Tyre, stayed on undisturbed. Ali Osseiran's mother was a Khalil, and her brother, Qazim al-Khalil, was one of his father's most bitter political enemies.

I told Ali Khalil that I had wanted to go to Tyre on this trip, but the Osseirans had advised me against it. Although the mostly Shiite port town was under Amal control, too many Hizballah fighters freely roamed its streets and no Syrian soldiers were there to prevent kidnappings. My last trip to Tyre, I told him, had been a year earlier. Juan-Carlos Gumucio and I had gone down to cover an Israeli sweep through the south, following the capture of two Israeli soldiers in a Hizballah ambush.

We had stayed at the worst hotel in Lebanon, the only beach-front hotel in the world without a single window facing the sea. Much of the old *laisser-faire* ambience of Tyre, with its mixed Shiite, Christian and Palestinian population, had faded after it had become a mini-Islamic Republic. Amal, bowing to Hizballah pressure, had banned the sale of alcohol, and only a few restaurants dared to serve whisky – and that in teacups. Amal had also forbidden girls to wear swimsuits on the beach, lest they provoke impure thoughts in the men. The women, whether intentionally or not, had turned the tables on their men: their wet cotton dresses revealed more, sticking to their skin, than their bathing costumes ever had. I would go swimming in the afternoons and see them frolicking in the waves in their transparent clothes, sexy but nonetheless conforming to Tyre's new religious code of modesty. Some months later, in the library of the Travellers' Club in London, I came across a similar instance of the apparently wanton behaviour of the women of Tyre in the Abbé Mariti's 1791 *Travels through Cyprus, Syria, and Palestine*. The Italian abbot, who admitted he was not "insensible to female charms," had arrived at a hill near Tyre with a party of Europeans.

> . . . we perceived at a small distance, a group of Arab women
> on the brink of a rivulet, in which some of them were washing
> their clothes, and others bathing; but they were all perfectly naked.
> This spectacle produced such a sudden effect on one of the French
> gentlemen, as plainly shewed that he was of a very warm
> temperament. He wished immediately to descend the hill, in
> order, as he said, to observe these people a little closer. Knowing
> better than my companion the disposition of the Orientals, I
> pointed out the dangers to which he was going to expose himself,
> either from the women themselves, or the Arabs that he might
> meet: but all my remonstrances were ineffectual: for he was
> determined to gratify his curiosity, even at the hazard of his life.
> . . . Our companion was then no longer able to contain himself;
> he stamped the earth with his foot, cursed his bad fortune that he
> had not at least brought a spy-glass with him, and even reproached
> nature with having placed such a distance between the hill and the
> rivulet.
> . . . In short, he burst from the cottage with so much velocity,
> that he had reached the borders of the rivulet before we well knew
> of his departure.
> I was much surprised to see all the women come forth from the
> water, and, advancing towards him naked as they were, invite him
> to take a place amongst them. Our French friend then redoubled
> his compliments, and employed the most expressive signs to shew
> his gratitude. He was eagerly received, and almost immediately
> surrounded by a circle of these females; but their caresses were
> only a snare to enable them to punish his presumption. Women
> are every where treacherous. These Arabs attacked him all at once,
> some tearing his hair, whilst others mauled him with their fists;
> and I am persuaded that he would have fallen a victim to their
> fury, had not his courage delivered him from their hands. He

afterwards avoided, as well as he could, a shower of stones discharged after him; some of which, notwithstanding his activity, were not without effect.

Reading that passage in the all-male preserve of the Travellers' Club, I was relieved that I had not ventured to swim closer to the women of Tyre, clinging clothes or not. As the good abbot wrote two centuries ago, "The recital of this small adventure is here not at all improper, as it may serve in some measure to shew the character of the women of the Levant, whom it is dangerous to approach when united. They indeed resemble all the women of the earth, who, for the honour of their sex, require a great deal of respect from the men in public; but at a private tête-à-tête they are not always so modest." It may also "serve in some measure to shew" the unchanging character of Frenchmen.

"Shall we go down to breakfast?" Ali Osseiran said to his cousin and me, as his other guests left. We walked downstairs to his parents' dining-room, where a breakfast of fresh fruits, yogurt, Arabic bread and fruit juice had been laid. Adil Bayk Osseiran was at the head of the table, and his wife, Souad, sat next to him. Some Osseiran cousins were already at the table. A servant was shaving Adil Bayk, carefully scraping the razor across his soapy skin. With his tremor, it was safer to let someone else shave him. "What time did you get in last night?" Adil Bayk asked me, looking up from the shave as we walked in. Then he warned, "It is dangerous to stay out late."

"Yes," one of the visiting cousins said, "you never know what the Communists might do."

The Lebanese Communist Party had occupied a Catholic school a few hundred yards from the Osseirans' house, put a checkpoint on the road and erected a radio transmitter for their station, "Voice of the Masses." The Osseirans resented the Communists' presence so close to them, not least because the radio broadcasts wreaked havoc with their telephones. Instead of a dial tone, I would often hear old speeches by the Party chairman, Georges Hawi. So far, the Communists had not kidnapped any foreigners.

"You must take care," Ali's mother insisted. She was not referring to Communists or Hizballah, but to my eating habits. "You must eat more." Every morning, to please her, I ate far more than I normally did at breakfast: tea, bread, eggs, cheese, fruit, olives, yogurt, *labneh* and fresh grapefruit juice. And every morning, she would say, "You don't eat a thing. Are you all right? Did you sleep well?"

Mme Osseiran's sister, a delightful and formidable widow named Umm Hany Saidi, had explained to me one of the reasons Ali's mother and father treated me as a member of their family. She said I resembled their older son, Abdallah, who had been murdered in 1971. Ali's mother and father never discussed this with me, but I always felt like a second, albeit wayward, son when I was in their house.

"You have to eat more," Adil Bayk said, wiping the remainder of the lather from his face. "And you should get to bed earlier."

We went outside, and Ali Khalil went to his car to find a small briefcase. He came back and took out two photographs. "You seem interested in the history," he said. "I'd like you to have these." One picture showed him in 1947 in the uniform of the Arab Liberation Army, a weapon in hand and a *keffiyeh* wrapped around his head. The other was of the Arab garrison in Nazareth, just before its surrender.

"I can't keep these," I said. When he insisted, I promised to have copies made and return the originals. I was planning to go to Nazareth, where I would ask whether anyone remembered Ali Khalil's old unit. I opened my suitcase. I had already packed it with ordinary possessions that would not attract the notice of any customs officer or soldier in the world, but which later aroused the serious suspicions of my captors. Each innocent scrap of paper and clothing would become a piece of "evidence" in the case against me: the daily diary of my journey to date; notebooks of the previous week; receipts, including the bill for my lunch with Emma Maalouf in Maamaltein; instant camera; transistor radio; and a long manuscript about Iran's influence on Lebanon's Shiite militias written by a young Lebanese journalist who had asked me to correct her English grammar; Gavin Young's *Slow Boats to China*; an old Hachette *Guide to the Middle East*; a Roman Catholic prayer book; photographs of my family; and, most damning of all, the envelope containing the photograph of me with the Syrian Minister of Defence, General Moustapha Tlass, and his blue *laisser-passer* authorising Syrian forces in Lebanon to render me assistance. To the rest, I added Ali Khalil's photographs, more damning "proof" of my work as a spy. Then I zipped the bag and put it into the back of Ali Osseiran's battered Volvo.

Adil Bayk and Mme Osseiran came out to say good-bye, and I thanked them for their kindness and hospitality. Adil Bayk would follow later, when his driver took him on his daily trip to the Ministry of Defence. Later, he would wait in vain for his son to arrive for lunch at the American University of Beirut Alumni Club.

It was ten in the morning when Ali Osseiran, Suleiman Suleiman and I set out in Ali's car for the hour's drive to Beirut. A few miles up the road, we reached a Syrian checkpoint. It reminded me of a Syrian soldier at a similar checkpoint who had begged a ride from Suleiman and me the night before. I told Ali about it. Suleiman and I, who were driving down from Beirut, agreed to give him a lift, believing a Syrian soldier in the car would give us added protection. Most of the Syrian soldiers, like Hussein al-Sultan from

Yusuf Basha, were conscripts waiting only for the day when they could return home with enough money to marry and build a house, probably not unlike many Israeli soldiers in Lebanon. Most were friendly and had stories to tell. This boy was no exception. He was about eighteen. His helmet was too large for his head, and he held his AK-47 upright between his legs in the back seat. He smiled as we talked, me in my primitive Arabic, he in a thick village accent. He told me the name of his village in Syria, and he said his mother was Lebanese. "She is from Baalbek," he told us. He said he hated the army and, after a pause, he asked me, "Do you like Arabs?" I answered politely, "Yes." Then he said he wondered what a foreigner could like about them. "I hate Arabs," he insisted. Then we dropped him at a Syrian checkpoint near Sidon.

Ali listened to my story, part of which I had read him from notes I had made the night before. He concluded the soldier suffered from a cultural inferiority complex. "And," Ali said, "he's not the only one."

"But isn't there something terribly wrong with this culture and this society?" I asked Ali. "Something the boy senses." I mentioned the assassination of his older brother, Abdallah, in 1971. "Did they ever find the murderer?"

"Yes. He was a member of the Zein family." The Zeins were another large, landowning Shiite family. "He went to prison, but he went free when the Palestinians 'liberated' the jails."

"Doesn't that kind of thing, even before the war, and all the killing and destruction now, make you think there is something, not just wrong, but evil in the heart of this society?"

"No. Why do you say it is evil? It is a problem of underdevelopment. We are an underdeveloped society."

It was only a short time later that we entered Hizballah territory in south Beirut behind a green Mercedes without plates, and boys who were either underdeveloped or evil stopped our car at gunpoint.

PART FIVE

CHAPTER TWENTY-SEVEN

THE BLACK HOLE

As I sit in a corner of my dim cell lacing the
   seeds of little light stretching them to these
   lines for you
I was struck with the joy of a child:
Beloved,
With all the might of their hatred that tears this
   life apart
They cannot put my mind in jail.

     Fouzi al-Asmar, "To the Beloved Motherland,"
         in *Poems from an Israeli Prison*

When the green Mercedes stopped at the wrecked building on the Green
Line, the boy on my right and another gunman pulled me by the arms out
of the car, ordering me in English and Arabic to close my eyes. The last
thing I saw was Ayatollah Khomeini's face staring down from the poster on
the wall. They led me over a small mound of earth into the building with
the Iranian flag. We turned right into a room with cracked walls, peeling
plaster and a floor half covered in sand.

They led me to a far corner, where they emptied my pockets and told me
to remove my belt. I had been jailed in the Middle East before and recalled
that most jailers took shoelaces as well. These did not. They did, however,
ask for my wedding ring. When I refused, one asked, "What do you want it
for?"

"My wife put it on me, and I've never taken it off," I said.

"We won't steal it," he replied, offended. "We'll give it back."

Reluctantly I took off the plain gold band and handed it to him. They sat
me facing the corner and tied my wrists tight behind my back with cloth.
Someone told me not to move or turn my eyes away from the corner. A boy
with a nasal voice walked over to me, poked me with his pistol and said,
"You CIA."

Sweat dripped slowly down my face, the beads of water falling in no discernible pattern on the concrete floor. After more than an hour of squatting motionless in a corner my legs became numb. My hands lost all feeling. The cloth binding them behind my back was too tight, and my blood stopped circulating. To force blood into my hands, I slowly clenched and unclenched my fists. "Why move hands, Dallas?" the nasal voice, incapable of pronouncing my name, asked. "No move hands, Dallas." I let my hands go limp.

The nasal voice and several others, all belonging to armed teenage boys slumped against the wall behind me, were arguing in Arabic over which of them had been the bravest during the kidnapping. Believing them to be preoccupied, I ventured again to open and close my hands. "No move hands, Dallas," the nasal voice shouted. Its owner stood, walked to me and jabbed a pistol into my back. He then sat down again with the others. For a few minutes, no one spoke. The only sound in the dusty room came from mosquitoes. I stared into the corner and watched two spiders, one near my feet and the other above my head, waiting in their webs to land their prey.

For the next half hour, I said silent prayers. I worried about my wife and children. How would they hear the news? Would a friend tell them or would word come suddenly over the radio? Who would tell my sixty-six-year-old father in California? I remembered that the father and brother of my friend Terry Anderson had both died of cancer after his kidnapping in March 1985. My thoughts turned to Ali and Suleiman. I prayed neither of them had been taken hostage, not only for their sakes, but for my own. If they were free, they could be with the Syrian army even then arranging my rescue.

My hopes vanished when I stole a glance to my left. Seated against the wall, their hands tied, their eyes blindfolded, were Ali and Suleiman. How would their families take the news? Why did their families have to suffer because of their hospitality to me, an American? Ali's mother and father had already suffered the shock of the death of one son. They did not deserve the kidnapping of another. Suleiman was due to be married in three weeks in Nabatieh. What would his fiancée do?'

In all the coming and going in the room, I had not heard them arrive. They had not said a word. They probably did not know I was there either. I decided to let them know. "Excuse me," I said loudly in English. "May I have some water?"

"Why water?" the nasal voice said. "You death."

I let a few minutes pass before asking to speak to my friends.

"What do you want to talk to them about?" another voice asked.

"I just want to know how they are."

"No."

I wondered why Ali and Suleiman were blindfolded and I was not. Did the kidnappers not care whether I saw their faces because they planned to kill me? One of them approached to make sure my hands were still tied tightly. I said to him, "I need to ask you something."

"Is it about your situation?"

"No. I want to go to the toilet."

He and the others debated in Arabic whether to let me go. Finally, he said, "Okay, you can go." Untying my hands, he whispered in my ear, "My English is not good. Stand up and look down at the floor. If you look up or make a noise, I will kill you." He said it not so much as a threat but as sound advice under the circumstances – like warning a child not to step off the kerb.

I could not stand, because my legs were numb. He helped me massage them to get the blood flowing. Then he led me by the hand through the ruined building to the end of a corridor strewn with dirt and garbage. He waited outside with a few other gunmen, while I stared at a wall etched with bomb cracks and childish Arabic graffiti. I then used the floor as my toilet. The fact they agreed to let me perform this basic human function suggested to me they were not going to kill me. It was a relief of sorts, even if a long imprisonment seemed almost as bleak a prospect as death.

Tied up again in the corner, unable to move, my world became one of sound and smell rather than sight. The boys would occasionally check their weapons, the click-click sounding as though they were about to fire. A motorcycle pulled up, then roared off minutes later. Around sunset, I heard the sound of frogs croaking in the swamp along the Green Line. The motorcycle returned again. Someone untied my hands and helped me to stand. Ali and Suleiman were also standing. The person helping me up said, "Close your eyes." He told us all to sit down again, with our hands untied. Someone handed each of us a white paper bag. Inside each bag were two sandwiches of chicken, garlic and pickles on small French loaves. I had no appetite, but I told myself, "If they feed you, they won't kill you." The sandwiches were still hot, so I assumed the sandwich shop was not far away.

"Bebsi?" some asked, meaning "Pepsi." With no *p* in Arabic, the word often became "Bebsi."

"No, thank you," I said.

"What you drink?"

"Water."

"You want beer?" another asked. "It's okay if you want beer. We can get it."

"No, thanks. Just water."

They gave me a plastic bottle of Lebanese Sohat water. As I ate my second sandwich, I felt a sudden but painless sting in my back, then another in my neck. I realised one of the guards was throwing stones at me, a pointless irritation he never explained.

The nasal voice asked Suleiman his name, where he came from and his job. Suleiman answered, "I am a driver for Adil Bayk Osseiran."

"We don't have bayks here," the voice said. For him, the era of the bayk was giving way to the epoch of the mullah.

"I drive for Adil Osseiran," Suleiman demurred.

"That's better."

When we finished eating, they retied Ali's and Suleiman's hands. This time they gave me a blindfold. It was an inconvenience, but also a sign they were treating me like the others. Instead of tying my hands, however, they put them in French-made police handcuffs, a sign they were treating me differently.

When it became dark, they lit candles and placed them on the floor. Looking down through the blindfold, all I could see were their shadows on the floor and their shoes. I began to recognise them by their shoes: brown lace-ups, black moccasins, black boots, brown sandals. One of them, who wore brown lace-up shoes and had earlier offered me a beer, suddenly sat down next to me. Another one handcuffed Brown Shoes to me, untied my blindfold and told me to look at the floor. The bearded boy in brown shoes, who had a trimmed beard, French-designed shirt and stylish trousers, began a bizarre conversation.

"Are you Israeli?" he asked.

"What?"

"Are you working for the Israelis?"

"Don't be ridiculous."

"Please," he said softly, in almost fluent English. "I'm a Christian working for Israel. They've been holding me here for two weeks."

If I had not recognised him by his shoes, I might have believed him. As it was, I assumed he was either insane or part of a singularly inept ruse to pry a confession out of me. We talked for a long time. He pretended to be a Lebanese Christian hostage, and I pretended to believe him. Occasionally, a guard would walk up to him, tell him not to talk and pretend to slap him across the face. I pretended to sympathise with him when he pretended to cry. He did not mind that I looked him in the eyes, although I would be able to recognise him.

I lost track of time, but it must have been around midnight when one of the kidnappers, who called himself Moustafa, entered the room to announce that we were leaving. He led me and the boy handcuffed to me outside into the back seat of a white car, probably Ali's Volvo. He left us alone together for the next twenty minutes. The boy said he wanted to escape.

"Fine," I said. "Let's go."

"But they will kill us."

"Then let's not go."

I toyed with the handcuff on my wrist. "What are you doing? Are you taking it off?"

"No. It's too tight."

"I'm afraid," he said. He pretended to be afraid. I pretended to be confident.

A little while later, he was taken away. Another guard took his place, handcuffing his wrist to mine. I heard the squawk of a two-way radio outside the car, and I looked up. There, leaning his head and arms through the window, stood Moustafa. For a moment, we stared at each other. I could see clearly his brown eyes, his dark curly hair and unkempt beard. Looking me in the eye, he said, "If you lift your head up again, I'll blow it off."

I put my head down. Three more gunmen got into the car, and soon we were speeding along the dirt road back the way we had come. "Keep your eyes closed," one of the gunmen instructed me, as he pressed a pistol into my ribs. I squinted to see where we were going. We took a circuitous route, avoiding Syrian army checkpoints, to an apartment building in a heavily populated area about ten minutes away.

When we arrived, they hustled me quickly out of the car. I deliberately tripped, making a noise I hoped would awaken the neighbours. One of them shouted, "Shut your mouth." I realised they had learned what little English they knew from American movies, probably Westerns and thrillers.

They pushed me into the building with their guns. We went into an elevator, up to what felt like the fourth floor. We moved quickly across the landing and into the open door of an apartment. One of them pushed me up against the wall and blindfolded me. He led me along the hall into a room with two beds and several mattresses on the floor. I lay down on one of the beds, and someone removed my handcuffs.

Ali and Suleiman arrived with the other gunmen about five minutes later. They were untied but blindfolded. Someone told them to lie down. They put Ali on the other bed and Suleiman on the mattress – preserving the class system even during kidnapping.

They asked all three of us various questions, then told Suleiman and me to sleep. After a pause of a few minutes, a soft-spoken, serious guard asked Ali questions about me. I pretended to sleep. He asked Ali if I understood Arabic, and Ali answered, "A little." Then he asked why I had come to Lebanon, why his family had welcomed me as a guest and whether I had a family. All of Ali's answers were truthful, but sympathetic to me. He said I

465

was a journalist, that I had taken time off my work to write a book and that I was midway in a journey from Alexandretta to Aqaba. Ali said all of his family were close friends of mine, adding, "My parents treat him like another son." I felt guilty that I had landed the Osseirans' real son, and someone they treated like a son, in this horror. Ali told them I was married and had five children, three of my own and two older girls by my wife's previous marriage. The questions were neither harsh nor friendly. After a half hour of interrogation, he ordered Ali to go to sleep. Someone turned out the single bare light overhead. Soon, all of us in the room, captors and captives, were asleep.

The next morning, they moved us into an empty room with a window and balcony covered by red shutters. Hanging from the ceiling was a bare light-bulb and next to it a long chain. We sat for an hour or two without talking, until the guards brought two beds and a foam-rubber mattress. They took lengths of chain, the kind used for bicycle locks, and fastened them around the beds. They shackled me to one bed and Ali to the other. They shackled Suleiman to the chain that hung from the ceiling and told him to lie on the mattress, preserving the class system even in kidnapping.

We spent all of our first day in the apartment chained, blindfolded and lying down. Several guards, who had taken part in our kidnapping the day before, stayed with us in the room. They did not permit us to speak to one another or to make any noise. The rattling of our chains might be heard by the neighbours. On that first afternoon, someone knocked on the door and asked whether a certain person was there. The guard who answered the door told him, "No. There is no one here by that name." Before he closed the door, I dropped my chains on the floor as loudly as I could. The guard grabbed me, shouting, "Shut your mouth."

I began to test my limits with our captors by asking for things – a shower, a razor to shave, bottled rather than tap water. I also asked them to return the wedding ring they had taken from me, along with my books and family photographs. "It's in the lab," one of the guards said of the ring. "When it is finished, you can have it back."

In the first few days, they brought us hot sandwiches, usually falafel or chicken, from a shop nearby. After dinner, they gave us apricots. I began using the apricots in my first hopeless effort to communicate with the outside world. When they let me into the bathroom, I would take an apricot with me. With my fingernail, I etched the words, "HELP, HOSTAGE," into the skin of the fruit. I slowly opened the window over the toilet, tore a piece of the screen loose and pushed the apricot out. It was a long shot, at best, that any English-speaking person passing the building would happen to pick up the apricot and see my message. Still, it was better than nothing.

It became crucial for me to protect my mind, which began to wander aimlessly for hours on end. Chained to the bed, blindfolded, unable to talk to anyone or to read, I decided to channel my thoughts along six specific lines and no others: my family, a novel I planned to write someday, prayer and meditation, an autobiography, telepathic communication and escape. Each day I would devote a certain amount of time to each of those subjects. If I found myself daydreaming, I would stop and say to myself, "Pray," or "Work on the novel," or "Talk to the family." The telepathy was fanciful, but I tried to send mental messages to Tony Touma's psychic uncle, Dr Solomon, in Damascus. "Doctor," I would say to him in French each day in my thoughts, "this is Charles Glass. I'm on the fourth floor of a five-storey building with red shutters in the southern suburbs of Beirut. Please tell the Syrian army."

Unable to talk to Ali and Suleiman, I began to talk to my family. Each day I pretended to have one member of my family with me: my wife on Wednesday and Thursday nights, my stepdaughter Beatrix on Friday, my stepdaughter Hester on Saturday, our son George on Sunday, our son Edward on Monday and our two-year-old daughter, Julia, on Tuesday. They would cuddle up with me at night, and I almost always slept peacefully. They would take meals with me and help me through difficult moments. Later, I would date certain events by recalling which member of my family was with me when they took place: my wife was there during my first interrogation, Hester during my last, George when I was moved to my final apartment, and Edward ran down the road with me on the night I escaped.

I would occasionally see the humour in my predicament and laugh to myself. Two thoughts would invariably make me laugh. One was Yves Morard's slogan, *"La France a perdu une bataille, mais la France n'a pas perdu la guerre."* This would usually come to mind whenever I had some setback. The other was a joke my friend Salim Diab had told me, one that I felt before the kidnapping I had no right to laugh at: "How can you spot a Shiite elevator boy in Paris? He's the one who asks you, *'Quel otage?'*" (*Etage* is floor, and *otage* is hostage.)

Although Ali and I were only ten feet apart, the guards refused to let us speak. If I wanted to tell Ali anything, I would speak to the guards in the knowledge Ali could hear me. I would say, "How are you? I'm feeling well today." Occasionally, when the guards were not looking, I would reach over to Suleiman, who was closer, and squeeze his hand to let him know I was all right.

Sunday, the twenty-first of June, was our fifth day in captivity. Nothing had happened. There had been no interrogation session, no punishment, no torture. The guards had not permitted us to shower or shave. Finally,

467

one of them relented and told us we could use a razor in the bathroom. Once in the bathroom, I sat down on the toilet, took the razor and cut the palm of my hand. Then I removed the cardboard roll inside the toilet paper and opened it out. Using a feather from the pillow on the bed, I wrote a message in blood on the cardboard. "Please help me. My name is Charles Glass. I am a hostage on the fourth floor of this building." I hurriedly pushed the note out of the bathroom window. Then I shaved.

The guards ignored my repeated requests for books to read. Instead, on the first Sunday afteroon, they brought in a radio and played rock music on a Beirut FM station. The first song I heard was by Eric Burdon and the Animals, "House of the Rising Sun." *There is a house in New Orleans, they call the Rising Sun. It's been the ruin of many a poor boy, and, God, I know I'm one.* Next came the Bee Gees' singing "Massachusetts." I thought I was in for a nostalgic musical tour of America, and I longed to be in either New Orleans or Massachusetts. Some of the guards sang along.

I had expected the guards to be fanatical and devout, but I never saw them pray. The only person who prayed, prostrate to Mecca, that first week was Suleiman. The guards were all young. They liked Michael Jackson and Madonna. One of them was disappointed when I told him Madonna was American, but he said he liked her anyway. They said they enjoyed drinking whisky and having girlfriends. "Do you have a girlfriend, Glass?" one of them asked me.

"No."

"Why not?"

"I'm married."

"So what? I have three girlfriends."

Five or six guards were always with us in the apartment. They carried pistols with silencers and never left us alone. As time wore on, they began cooking food in the apartment rather than buying sandwiches. Each morning, they gave us tea and bread. When I contracted gastroenteritis, I asked them to give me the standard Lebanese remedy: boiled rice with yogurt. They seemed happy to oblige. When I said I was bored with their cooking, one of them went out and brought me a hamburger.

After five days, they let us take showers. When we finished, they took our clothes and issued us with blue jockey shorts, blue undershirts and blue Adidas tracksuits. They replaced our shoes with rubber sandals. The tracksuits were unbearable in Beirut's summer heat, so we sat on our beds all day in our underwear.

On the evening of the eighth day, the guard who had pretended to be a Christian hostage came running into the room. He sat in a chair next to Ali's bed and began telling awful jokes in Arabic. A Christian friend, who had been held hostage for a week a year earlier, had told me that on the last day of his captivity his guards had become friendly to him. I sensed what was about to happen. After about thirty minutes of telling jokes about people from Homs in northern Syria, some of which I had already heard in Damascus, the guard ordered Ali and Suleiman to stand, unlocking the chains around their ankles.

I jumped up and said, "I'm going with them." One of the guards pushed me down on the bed. The comedian warned Ali not to speak to me. Two guards led Ali and Suleiman out of the room, and I did not see them again. I heard the lift doors open, then the sound of a car starting its engine and driving away until I could hear it no more.

I was alone now with one of the guards. He had a pistol in his right hand pointed at the floor. "Don't worry," he said.

"I am worried."

"You be okay."

"Right now, I need a friend. From now on, you are my friend."

I stood and put my hand on his shoulder.

"Don't worry," he repeated.

I asked him if I could go to the bathroom. He unchained me and led me across the hall a few steps to the bathroom door. I went inside and tried, despite the darkness, to look outside. I wanted to see what might have become of the apricots and notes I had thrown out. For the first time, I had a good glimpse out the window, because a light was shining from a kitchen door on the left. I discovered that all the notes I had thrown had fallen only a few feet to a kitchen balcony. Suddenly, the door opened behind me. I grabbed my blindfold and put it back on. A voice behind me, the familiar nasal voice, asked, "Why look window?"

"I was not looking window."

"You look window." He called the guard who had been briefly sympathetic and told him in Arabic I had looked through the window, something they had expressly forbidden me to do from the first day.

"Glass," the sympathetic guard said in English, "not window. You my friend? You not friend."

They led me back to my bed, relocked the chain around my ankle and turned out the light. Ali and Suleiman were gone, and my notes in blood lay just outside the kitchen door. The only people who were likely to find them were my guards.

Two days later, Friday, one of the guards asked me if I would like to read. When I said yes, he gave me the back number of a Lebanese English-language weekly, *Monday Morning*, that had been in my suitcase. Two of the stories in that issue could not have been more depressing. One told of the second birthday party of Terry Anderson's daughter, born after he had been taken hostage. Father and daughter had never seen each other, and the little girl had blown out her two candles wishing for her father's freedom. The other article was about Marcel Coudari, a French hostage who had been released. He said life had become so bad in captivity that he had asked his guards to kill him. They gave him a pistol so he could commit suicide. When he pulled the trigger, the chamber was empty. His guards laughed.

They wheeled in a television set in the afternoon to watch the highlights of the World Cup. They asked me if I would like to watch. I had no interest in soccer, but I needed any diversion. They unchained me and sat me down in front of the set, with four or five of them behind me. They told me not to turn around, to watch only the television. For the next hour, I saw clips of all the matches of the World Cup, culminating in Argentina's victory over West Germany. When the highlights were over, I sat waiting to see whether they would let me watch the next programme, like a child who had come to play hoping to be asked to stay for dinner. They put my blindfold back on, led me to the bed and put the chain back around my ankle. They then watched an old movie, and I said silently, "Beatrix, you brought me luck today. They let me read and watch television for the first time. Thanks."

I fell asleep. It was late when Moustafa, the bearded gunman with the two-way radio, arrived. He sat on the floor with my guards, asking them how I had behaved. He spoke into the radio a few times. I pretended to be asleep. I felt a hand shake me and heard a voice say, "Get up. Get up."

"What's happening?"

The guard who had previously said he was a Christian hostage announced, "You are going home to see your family now."

My prayers were being answered. Ali and his family, I thought, must have put pressure on their fellow Shiites to let me go. My captors had told me my wife was in Beirut trying to obtain my release, and I imagined I might see her that night.

They took my blindfold off, told me to keep my eyes closed and then led me outside to a waiting car. We drove for about five minutes. But five minutes, I told myself, was not far enough. The usual release points were the Beau Rivage Hotel, where the Syrians had their intelligence offices, and the house of Mohammed Hussein Fadlallah, the mullah who acted as a spiritual guide to Hizballah. Both must have been more than five minutes drive. We got out at a luxury apartment building. Something was wrong. The guards took me up to a second-floor apartment.

This apartment was unlike the previous one. It was properly furnished, and a family lived in it. I heard a baby about six months old crying and saw a three-year-old boy through my partly closed eyes. Someone replaced the blindfold and led me to a bedroom on the right. The room was dark, and they made me lie on a foam rubber mattress against the wall. They chained my wrist and ankle to a central-heating radiator. A man who seemed to be the father of the small boy told me in fluent English, "Just go to sleep."

"I thought I was going home now."

"Who told you that?"

The guard said, "I did."

"Maybe tomorrow."

"Tomorrow morning," the guard said.

"No, tomorrow night," the boy's father corrected him.

I knew now they had no intention of setting me free. When I awakened in the morning, I asked the guard who had told me I was going free why he had said it.

"I say to you what he say to me."

"Who?"

"The chief."

"When am I going home then?"

"Maybe one day. Maybe one month. Maybe one year."

"One *year?*"

"Maybe never."

Late that night, Saturday, they awakened me to move me again. We drove for a few minutes to another apartment building and walked up two flights of stairs. They put me into a dark room, shackled my wrist and told me to lie on a cushion on the floor, locking the door behind them.

The room was still dark when I woke. I could not tell whether it was day or night. I lay without moving on the cushion, my head propped on a hard pillow in the corner, until one of the guards unlocked the door. He told me to put my blindfold on whenever anyone came into the room. He then came in and turned on the light. "Breakfast?" he asked.

"May I have some tea?"

"No tea." He put Arabic bread and something that tasted like rancid cheese on a plate and left the room, locking the door.

I removed the blindfold and looked at the room for the first time in the light. It was about ten feet by twelve, and all four concrete walls were painted grey. The only window in the room was covered completely by a sheet of rusted metal screwed into the wall. The chain around my wrist led through a tiny hole in the wall to another room. On the bare tile floor was a foam-rubber cushion, about two inches thick, on top of a straw mat. Against one wall were two changes of underwear, a box of Kleenex, some plastic plates and utensils and a plastic rubbish bag. There were also two plastic Sohat bottles, one for drinking-water and the other to pee in. The room had been set up to serve as my long-term jail cell.

I was left alone all day. That night, I heard someone unlock the door and

I quickly put on my blindfold. A guard said, "Plate." I handed him one of the plastic plates. He poured stewed tomatoes from a tin onto the plate. When the guard left, I poured my first dinner in the new cell into the rubbish bag. The guard returned to unlock the padlock on my wrist. He led me to the bathroom, explaining it was the place I was to do all my washing – of my body, my clothes, my dishes and my sheets. He closed the door. The bathroom had one window, which opened onto a fan protected by three layers of metal screen. Above the basin, I saw myself in a mirror for the first time since the kidnapping. I'd lost a little weight and had a few days' growth of beard. Otherwise, I was unchanged.

After the guard locked me up for the night, another young man, much more severe than the others, came in and squatted next to my mattress. "If you make any mistake," he said, "I will kill you. And I am prepared to die myself."

He asked what I thought of his English. I said it was good. "But I make mistakes," he said. He told me he was studying for his English exams and asked if I would help him. "If I have time," I said, but he did not see the joke.

The next morning, several people came to the flat. I heard a commotion outside my room and a hurried discussion in Arabic about a meeting with Ali Osseiran at four o'clock. Perhaps Ali knew who these people were. Even I could tell by their accents that most of them came from south Lebanon, and Ali would have picked up far more than that. My hopes were rising, and I prayed some good would come. Four o'clock came and went. It was after ten at night when the young man who was studying English came into my room with a letter. He handed it to me and said, "Read this."

I pulled my blindfold back a little and read a note, written in a childish hand. "Dear Ali," it began, in English, "I am glad to hear you are free and hope your family is well. Do not worry about me. Please tell Ziad Wahibi to forget what we discuss in our meeting we had. I tell you do not hurry to rescue me. I am fine. If you try to rescue me. I will die. Charles Glass."

"You are going to write this for us," the young man said.

He handed me a blue Bic pen, telling me to copy the note in my own handwriting. I did so, leaving the grammatical errors. When I asked him who Ziad Wahibi was, he answered, "We'll tell you tomorrow." I said no one would believe the note, because I had never heard of Ziab Wahibi. I asked him whether I could write a letter to my wife and another to my children. He allowed me to and promised to drop them in at the Associated Press office in west Beirut, a promise that was never kept. When he left with the note and my letters, I kept the pen and hid it inside my mattress. I was suddenly happy. The guards had been telling me all along that Ali and Suleiman were still hostages, but in another location, and this was confirmation they were free. I said a rosary to thank God for their freedom and went peacefully to sleep.

The same young man returned the next morning, now ordering me to read the note into a tape-recorder. I complied, emphasising the grammatical errors and mispronouncing the Arab names. I hoped the tape would tell Ali I was alive, that he would reassure my family and that he would understand the words were not my own. The note puzzled me. I had not discussed a rescue with anyone, and I had no idea who Ziab Wahibi was. The guards would not tell me. It was only later, after my escape, that I learned Ali had received the tape. I also discovered that "Ziad Wahibi," in fact Ziad Wehbeh, was the real name of Abu Ossama, Yasser Arafat's Al Fateh commander whom I had seen in Sidon. It seemed, Palestinians would tell me later, that Abu Ossama felt responsible for my safety in the south and had taken measures to secure my freedom. The tape made it clear that, if he persisted, I would be killed. The tape, plus a direct threat from Hizballah, also stopped the Osseiran family from exerting pressure that might jeopardise my life.

Most of the time, they left me alone with my thoughts. My novel – about an English and an American writer who kept crossing each other's paths, sleeping occasionally with the same woman, but never actually meeting – was making progress. Each man represented in a way an imperial idea: the now less innocent Quiet American, treading in the wake of a departed *Pax Britannica*, both lost and degenerate in a Levant that had not recovered from its own tribalism and centuries of foreign domination. Each day, I would take the story a stage further, often rewriting earlier passages that seemed not to work. Like the prisoners in *Kiss of the Spider Woman*, I was surviving partly in a fantasy world.

I talked to my family, thinking what they would be doing at any given time of day. I prayed, making a rosary out of threads from my blindfold. My understanding of prayer and meditation changed profoundly as the days passed. At the beginning, I prayed quickly, asking God for my freedom and promising to amend my life in return. It was as though I were making a deal with the Almighty. Gradually, my prayer became meditative. I prayed in the later days to make myself known to God, asking less, offering more, praying for others, especially for the other hostages. The rest of the time, I plotted ways to escape.

I used the pen I had kept to write another note, in English and Arabic, offering $10,000 to anyone who could help me. But I had no way to get the note out. When I finally managed to open the bathroom window unseen, the fan was spinning too quickly for me to push anything through it. But one morning when I was saying my rosary, there was a power failure, a common occurrence in Beirut. A guard came into the room and led me to the bathroom, closing the door. I slowly pulled the window open, hoping the guard would not see me through the translucent glass panel in the bathroom door, and I stretched back the screen. With the fan stopped, it was easy to push the note out. I said a prayer to thank God and Mary for their help.

It became vital to do something every day that would lead to my escape. As well as a series of notes I sent through the fan during power failures, I stole a metal spike from the bathroom cistern to use to bore a hole through the wall of my room to the apartment next door. I heard the voices of a couple with children, and I believed if I could just get through the wall and pass them a note, they would help me. It was exhausting work, and I always had the fear the guards would come in while I was digging. But I bored an inch or two every day through the solid concrete, sometimes swallowing the dust rather than let it be found. When the time seemed right, I worked on a plan to bribe one of my captors. I had come to the conclusion that I had a moral duty to my family to escape, no matter what the risk. My compelling fear was that my children might one day ask, "Didn't you do everything possible to get home?"

I began to distinguish between the guards and the interrogators. Only the interrogators spoke good English. The guards were there to give me food, let me wash and make certain I did not escape. One of them told me his salary was four thousand Lebanese pounds, about thirty dollars.

"A day?" I asked.

"A month," he laughed.

Most of the guards were friendly or, at least, correct. A few were sadistic, refusing on occasion to give me water and letting me go more than a day without any food. One guard, whom I called Hikmet, spoke pidgin English and said to me one day, "I'm sorry. You good man. If from me, I let you go."

Late on the night of Monday, 6 July, two senior members of the group came to me and asked, "Do you want to go home?"

"Yes," I said, blindfolded and wondering what they looked like.

"Are you willing to cooperate if it helps you to go home?"

"Yes," I said, without a moment's hesitation.

"Then read this."

One of them gave me a handwritten statement that began, "I Charles Glass. Many of you know me as journalist, but few know the truth. I used the press as cover for my main job with the CIA . . ."

"This is not true," I said.

"That does not matter," one replied. "You are going to read it in front of the camera. Then when you get out, you can deny it."

474

"If I read this, I may never get out."

"If you don't read it, you'll never see your family alive again."

For emphasis, his colleague waved a pistol under my nose. I was then ordered to write the statement out again in my own hand, correcting any mistakes in grammar. They gave me another blue Bic and some paper. They left me alone for half an hour, while I copied out the statement, correcting only two of the many errors.

"You didn't correct any mistakes," the interrogator said when he returned with the guards and a cameraman.

"Yes, I did. I changed the verb strength to strengthen."

"I made two mistakes only?"

"Yes."

"Oh," he said, flattered and pleased. "I thought more mistakes."

"No. Your written English is good." God help me, I thought, if he shows the statement to anyone who speaks English. I asked him if I could have some bottled water before we began recording.

"Why do you always have to drink bottled water?"

"Because the tap water gives me dysentery."

"What?"

"Diarrhoea. I've had diarrhoea for the last twenty days."

"Maybe you get used to the tap water. Try it for a few more days, then we'll see."

They wheeled in a roll-away bed to use as a tripod for the BetaMovie video camera. Opposite the camera, they set up a table and a box for me to sit on. Removing my blindfold and making me put on the blue Adidas jacket, they ordered me to keep my eyes closed and to keep my head down on the table. I was to wait until the cameraman was ready before I looked up and read the statement. I wondered how I could send some sort of message to let my family know I was well and to persuade my colleagues in the American networks not to broadcast this rubbish.

"When I say, 'Go,' look up," said the young man I came to think of as the director. "Wait five seconds, then read. Go!"

I raised my head to a sight so ridiculous I had to suppress a laugh. Three young men stood facing me. To hide their faces, two of them had covered their heads with T-shirts, and the cameraman held a tea towel over his head, like an old woman in a shawl. The boy on the left pointed a pistol at my head, and the one in the middle directed. They looked like a Monty Python version of a Hizballah mobile film unit.

After waiting five seconds, I lifted the two-page statement close to my face, so it would be obvious I was reading a prepared text. I tried to get my crossed fingers into the frame to provide another clue that I did not mean what I was saying. I made my voice tremble, a transparent device to indicate the statement was being read under duress and that it should not be broadcast. I also read in an American Southern accent to indicate I was in Beirut's southern suburbs.

"I Charles Glass. Many of you know me as journalist –"

"Stop," the director shouted. "Head down."

I put my head back on the table.

"Hold the paper away from your face. Let's go again."

The cameraman had trouble rewinding the tape, and the director told him to hurry. "Okay. Go."

I looked up again. I was counting five seconds when the cameraman let the tea-towel fall open around his face. I recognised him, but tried not to show it. He was a Shiite I had known years earlier in Beirut. He quickly pulled the towel back over his face, and I read the statement. I trembled and tried to look as though I were holding back tears. I read a few lines, and the camera stopped rolling. "Stop," the director said. "Head down."

I heard them talking among themselves. The cameraman fiddled with his equipment. "Let's go again. Head up."

When I looked up this time, the boy on the left was waving his pistol, silencer over the muzzle, wildly in the air. I tried to ignore him while I read the statement all the way through.

". . . I used the press as a cover for my main job with the CIA. I worked in different positions to reach my goals. I collect information for the benefit of the CIA. For that I made secret missions they ordered me to do them."

I squinted intentionally at the text, looking down and back at the camera. ". . . And as I am expert on the Middle East, I have been on many secret missions to the area. My share was to tie up relations between the Israelis and the Christian society to Maronite leaders. Many meetings and many visits happened and I have attended some of those meetings. I come back to Lebanon on secret missions from the office of the CIA in London . . ." They had by that time read my diary and some of my notebooks. They knew about my interviews with Dany Chamoun and General Michel Aoun. "I worked with Dany Chamoun to visit the USA and to meet officials and know how their thinking will be going on. I told him that in a meeting between me, him and General Michel Aoun who is also an expected president. We discussed the new Israeli plan in the region . . ." The notebooks contained my observations of south Lebanon and details of my interviews with Palestinians in the Ain el-Helouie camp. ". . . I met with some of the Palestinians top officials and we discussed the last battles in the Palestinian camps with Syrian troops and their allies. Also I discussed with them the problems between them and I told them some American recommendations about that and how they should do in coming actions and I promised to meet them again, but I am now here and I hope to pass this period well."

The director had told me to write a message to my family at the end of the statement. When I read the last line, I dropped the trembling and the Southern accent to say, "I want to send my love to all my family."

We recorded it a few more times. Apparently satisfied at last, they went to the room next door to watch the tape on their VCR. They returned in a state of agitation. We would have to record the statement again. "It's not you," the director said. "There was something wrong with the camera." I knew, even if he did not, that his cameraman did not know the first thing about cameras.

We recorded the statement again and again, and it must have been after midnight when they seemed content. I was exhausted and thirsty. They rechained me by the ankle and marched out of the room without a word. As they closed the door, Hikmet slipped in and handed me a cold bottle of mineral water. "This is from *me*," he said, and he rushed out.

Before I fell asleep, I said a prayer for Hikmet, thanking God that even under the most unlikely circumstances, one human being could not help being human.

The next morning, the team returned to record the statement once again. Something else had gone wrong with the camera. We recorded it twice more, Southern accent and all, and they left in a hurry. I learned later they delivered the tape that day, 7 July, to the Reuter office in west Beirut. What was their motive? None of the other hostages had been required to say publicly they worked for the CIA. But because I was the only foreigner taken hostage since the Syrian return to Beirut, Syria had been pressuring Hizballah to let me go. The kidnappers used the videotape to discredit Syria's efforts on the day the United States ambassador to the United Nations, General Vernon Walters, had gone to Damascus to raise the hostage issue with President Assad. My false confession presented the Syrians as defenders, not of an innocent journalist, but of a CIA agent. Syrian television did not broadcast the tape, but everyone else – in America, Europe and Lebanon – did.

Reuters reported that the "Organisation for the Defence of a Free People" had delivered the videocassette. This was the group, using one of Hizballah's many pseudonyms, that had claimed responsibility for my kidnapping in Sidon on 1 July. With the tape was a typed message that said my confession was the result "of the preliminary investigations of the American spy Charles Glass so that you may know how dangerous such people are . . . The investigations will gradually reveal all the agents linked to him in this mission."

The next day, Wednesday 8 July, the "investigation" began. I misread the signs when the director arrived early that morning with two colleagues and gave me back my wedding ring, my prayer book and the three family photographs that had been in my suitcase: one of my wife, the five children and me on the steps of Brompton Oratory in London; one of my wife and me kissing on our wedding day; and one of our youngest child, Julia. It pained me to look at the photographs, to contemplate the suffering I was causing and to recall what I had lost.

"Why did you come to Lebanon?" the director asked, translating his colleague's Arabic.

"I'm writing a book."

"Is that all?"

"No, not exactly," I admitted. Even with the blindfold, I could sense their expectation. "I'm writing a few articles while I'm here for the *Spectator*."

"What's that?"

"A magazine in London."

Expectation gave way to disappointment. "What else were you doing? You must have had an important reason for coming to Lebanon."

"My book is important. Telling the truth is important."

"No, more important than that. If a man with children takes risks, he must have important reasons."

"I didn't think it was such a risk."

"Don't you think there was a risk of, as you call it, kidnapping? Didn't you think you will be kidnapped?"

"If I had known I would end up here," I said, pointing to the chain and lock on my ankle, "I would not have come."

He translated for his friend, and they both laughed.

The interrogation continued for three days, partly in the form of direct questioning by one or another of two hostile men. They claimed to have evidence I worked for the CIA. "We have the evidence," they said. "Why don't you just admit it?" Occasionally, they would say, "If you don't tell the truth, we may have to kill you." Or they would try another approach. "Don't worry. We won't kill you. We don't believe in torture, which is better than the Israelis do with our people in south Lebanon."

Later, they changed the method of interrogation by telling me to write answers to a long list of questions. The written questions focused on my activities in Lebanon, who I had met, who my friends were in Beirut. They also asked me to identify the publications I had worked for, interestingly, to reveal everything I knew about the hostages and their captors in Lebanon. I was always made to believe I was on trial for spying.

In my responses, as Mark Twain said, I mostly told the truth. I knew my answers could be checked against my notes, my diary and any press accounts with details of my career. On the second day of my interrogation, they returned with follow-up questions, asking me to write down every country I had visited since 1976 and why. They seemed particularly intrigued by my trips to Rhodesia in 1977 and 1979, convinced this was more evidence of my CIA background. They wanted me to write down everything I knew about kidnappers in Lebanon. I supplied only those details I knew had already appeared in the newspapers: that the kidnappers were believed to be part of Hizballah, that they used cover names like Islamic Jihad, and that Iran directed their activities.

When they read this answer, they asked, "Haven't you ever thought we might be Palestinian?"

I said I had not. It made little sense, despite the fact that a Palestinian group had kidnapped the British journalist Alec Collet. I said the Palestinians would have no reason to kill me. "Think about it," they said. They lectured me on the suffering of the Palestinian people. They gave me a copy of a scholarly study based on eye-witness accounts of the Israeli expulsion of Palestinians, *Palestinian Exodus from Galilee, 1948,* by Nafez Nazal, a book I had read years before and which referred to the destruction of Ain Zeitoun, the village Rashid Hamid's family had been driven from. One young interrogator handed me a copy of a PLO propaganda book on the massacre at Tel el-Zaatar in 1976. He asked me, "Have you ever heard of Tel el-Zaatar?"

In some of the sessions, they would confront me with one or other of the papers or photographs they found in my suitcase. "What is this?" an interrogator asked me, holding up the receipt from my lunch with Emma Maalouf at the beach.

"A lunch receipt."

"Lunch? Who did you have lunch with?"

"Friends."

"Wasn't it a CIA meeting? Why did you have so many cups of coffee?"

The old photographs of Ali Khalil in Nazareth puzzled them, and they found the photograph of me with General Moustafa Tlass particularly suspicious. "How do you know General Tlass?" they asked.

"I'm a journalist. I interviewed him."

"You're a liar."

The interrogations were a great strain. One night I lay in bed and thought about hostages like the American University librarian Peter Kilburn, who had been held for more than a year and then murdered, together with two British teachers, Leigh Douglas and Philip Padfield. I prayed to God to take me that night, to let me die of natural causes rather than let me live for a long time and then be killed. If I were alive in the morning, I would regard it as a sign I would not be killed and that I should persevere. On another night, I felt so much stress that I broke down and wept. I averted despair by reading the prayers in the book the interrogators

479

had returned to me. "Bless me, O Lord, and defend me; preserving me from a sudden and unprovided death and from all dangers, and bring me to life everlasting with you."

They left some other books, which helped me to take my mind off myself. Most were in French. Leonardo Sciascia's *Sicile Comme une Métaphore* had some moving passages on the kidnapping and murder of Aldo Moro. The others were *Le Rempart des Besguines*; *La Petite Fadette* by Georges Sand; Anatole France's *La Rôtisserie de la Reine Pedauque*, which allowed me to laugh out loud; and a French translation of *The Forsyte Saga*. The only English books they gave me at first were Harold Robbins' *The Dream Merchants* and the February 1972 issue of *Reader's Digest* from which an article on page 128 on the Islamic pilgrimage to Mecca had been clipped out. This convinced me my captors were from Hizballah and not Palestinian: only a Hizballi would have kept such an article. They would take the books back as I finished and replaced them with Errol Flynn's autobiography, *My Wicked, Wicked Ways*; Leon Uris's *Armageddon*, which had a cover blurb saying, "By the author of Exidus"; a thriller about air aces called *Final Approach*; and a volume of Victor Hugo's poetry. All the books had been read many times before, and I wondered if any had passed through the hands of other hostages. They also gave me a small electric fan, which, when the electricity was working, provided some relief in the unventilated room.

In the days that followed my three-day interrogation, they left me alone. I made a chessboard out of paper. I played imaginary games with my sons, George and Edward – who invariably checkmated me. I marked a calendar in a blank page of my prayer book, making coded notes to remind me what had happened on certain days of my captivity. Never in my life have I been as acutely conscious of time: I was always aware of the date, the day of the week, and the number of days I had been held. I read the books and put them to an added use. I began tearing out pages, on which I wrote notes in Arabic, French and English offering $10,000 to anyone who would tell my friends where I was. With trepidation, I slipped them through the bathroom fan when the electricity was off. Over the weeks, I put out nine notes in all, each more colourful than the last, one a whole book cover upon which I drew a ribbon like a birthday present to attract someone's attention. I continued digging my way through the wall, and, reading an article in *Reader's Digest*, I had another idea. In "Meet the Real Casanova," Ernest Hauser wrote of Casanova's attempt to escape from the prison in the Doge's palace in Venice, "With an iron rod he had picked up during his exercise walk and which he sharpened on a piece of marble, Giacomo [Casanova] worked at night and, after three months' labour, had cut a hole through the floor under his bed." I took the spike I had been using on the wall and tried the floor under my cushion. It took days to loosen a tile under the mattress, but there was no penetrating the steel-reinforced concrete of the floor. I went back to the tiny hole in the wall, extending its length each day.

The routine was deadening, interrupted by short but intense periods of depression or euphoria. Little things sent my spirits soaring or plunged me into confusion and pain, often physical pain. Hikmet cheered me up one night by cooking me a special treat, spaghetti with meat sauce. It was not so much that it was a change from the usual fare of sandwiches made of hommous, fried potatoes or tomatoes. More importantly, it was someone making a gesture of kindness to a stranger. Another guard brought me fresh-squeezed orange juice one morning, which made me happy and grateful. The same guard unlocked my chains and allowed me to exercise in my room for fiteen minutes. He was one of the few guards who prayed every day.

Other guards were less kind. One Saturday, the power was off, the weather was stiflingly hot, and the guard on duty, for some reason, decided to punish me by keeping my door closed, refusing to feed me or replenish my supply of bottled water. I spent the entire day in heat and darkness, trying to ignore my thirst, to think clearly and not allow depression to consume me. I would cheer myself up a little by recalling Yves Morard's words, *"La France a perdu une bataille, mais la France n'a pas perdu la guerre."*

Earlier, one of the senior captors had said to me, in a sympathetic way, "This is not so bad for you. You will learn how prisoners feel. You will understand what our people go through in Israel. You will feel for prisoners everywhere." He was right, but my empathy extended beyond prisoners and hostages to include the blind and the paralysed. They did not have the hope that sustained me: that one day, the blindfold and chains would come off; but I tasted what it was like not to see a human face or be able to walk where I liked. I discovered in myself unknown reserves of patience, and I thought of Herman Hesse's *Siddhartha*, who said, "I can think, I can fast, and I can wait." The words rang again and again through my mind. And I waited.

When one of the guards told me that it was sunny outside and that most of Beirut was flocking to the beach, I asked him if he had seen any sailboats. No doubt he guessed I was trying to discover whether the apartment was close enough to the shore for him to see the boats, but I was also thinking of an old friend, Dr Nureddine Kouche, with whom I used to sail often off the Beirut coast. If there were any wind at all, I knew, Nur would be out in his boat, escaping for a few hours the filth of the city.

*

It was not until the following Thursday, 23 July, that anything happened to give me hope. A young man, whose voice I had not heard before, came into my room late that night. "Hello," he said, his manner warm and friendly. "I've come to talk to you." He asked if I needed more books and promised to bring some. I did not know what to make of him. Although I was lonely and vulnerable, I realised that a sympathetic interrogator might be a trick. He sat on one end of my mattress, and he assured me that he was not part of the "organisation." He said my captors had come to his house and asked him, because his English was better than theirs, to talk to me. He had with him the answers I had written to the interrogators' questions. He said the organisation would not release me until I convinced them I did not work for the CIA.

"Does that mean if I convince them, they will let me go?"

"Not necessarily." He looked at my written answers and said, "You're writing a book. What about?"

I told him.

"Why did you go to the south?"

"I could not tell the story of the area without writing about the place in the greatest turmoil."

We discussed my predicament. I asked, "How do I know they won't just hold me and later, when it suits them, kill me?"

"They not only won't kill you, they can't kill you."

"Why not?"

"They would only kill you if you killed one of them. They have never killed a hostage."

"That's not true. After the US bombing of Libya in April 1986, they killed three hostages – two British teachers, Leigh Douglas and Philip Padfield, and an American librarian, Peter Kilburn."

"They were not killed by these people."

"Who killed them?"

"I should not tell you this, but I will. I know all about this case. They were kidnapped by a man who has a shop. He kidnaps people and sells them, like a shop. It's his business. He sold those three to Muammar Gadhaffi, who is insane."

"What about the CIA man, William Buckley? They killed him. Now they're saying I'm CIA. So, why shouldn't they kill me too?'

"I believe his death was an accident."

I asked if he had any news of my family.

"I believe they are all fine."

"And my father? I'm worried about him. He's sixty-six. Do you know if he's well?"

"I don't know," he answered, in a distracted way. "My own brother just died in a car accident, and I haven't been reading the newspapers."

"I'm sorry. Forgive me. I've become so absorbed in my own problems, I forget about other people."

"It doesn't matter. My voice doesn't usually sound like this, but I've been crying since a few days." He told me about his brother and the death. I believed everything he said, possibly because I wanted to. When he got up to leave, I was sorry he had to go. "Are the guards treating you well?" he asked. "Do you have enough to eat? Do you need anything?"

"All I need are more books."

He returned the next two nights, bringing me a thick bestseller by Howard Fast called *The Immigrants*. "This is a wonderful book,' he said. On both nights, we talked for hours. I grew to like him, but I never saw his face or knew his name.

"I need some information from you," he said, "to convince the organisation you are not a spy."

"What kind of information?"

"In your work as a journalist, you must have heard something about what the CIA is planning."

"I know nothing about the CIA."

"But they talk to journalists. Haven't they said anything about the Marines coming to rescue the hostages?"

"They wouldn't say it to me."

"Are you sure?"

"First of all, this is not the kind of thing diplomats talk to journalists about. Second, you have all my notebooks. You can see that I haven't met a single American diplomat since I came to Lebanon. For my book, I'm talking to historians, teachers, taxi-drivers, anybody but diplomats."

"I believe you, but how can I make *them* believe you?"

"If they read my articles or watched my television reports, they could see that diplomats are not likely to regard me as sympathetic to superpower interests."

He said he would look up my articles in the newspaper library at the American University. On his third visit, which was on Saturday night, he said he had to leave the country for ten days, but would see me on his return.

"I would like to talk to you again," I said. "But I hope I am no longer here in ten days."

"Is there anything you need?'

"If you go to Europe, could you send something to my wife?"

"What?"

"Some nursery rhymes for my children."

"Where are they?"

I took a piece of paper from my prayer book on which I had written five

483

verses, one for each of the children. I handed it to him, and he read them aloud. The first was for Julia:

"Julia Mary, Julia Mary, Julia Mary Rose,
Everybody loves her, everywhere she goes,
Julia Mary, Julia Mary, Julia Mary Rose,
Who's she love? Who's she love? Only Julia knows."

He read the other four, and I thought from the tone of his voice that somehow the children's suffering touched him. He promised to mail them from Europe, but insisted it had to remain our secret. The organisation would consider it a breach of security. There were no secret codes in the rhymes. I just wanted the children to have something from me to let them know I loved them. If my wife did not receive them, it would mean the young man had been lying. She never did.

My main hope of rescue lay in the notes I was pushing through the bathroom fan. Every day, children played outside my window. I prayed that the little boy who went by every morning on a skateboard would find a note and take it to his father, who would claim the $10,000 reward for him. I imagined the money would pay for his education and thus save him from the fate of working for one of the militias. But weeks went by without anything happening. I had to devise another plan.

The notes were landing under the bathroom window, behind the building, which for all I knew was nothing more than a rubbish tip. I had to find a way to get a note out the front, where more people could see it. My guards were in the habit of hanging the wet laundry I had washed in the bathroom basin to dry from the front balcony. One day, I slipped a note into a wet bedsheet. When the guard hung it out to dry, the note, I hoped, would fall to the ground in front of the building.

All that morning, I prayed desperately that none of my captors would find the note, even if it failed to attract the attention of a friendly neighbour. I spent the rest of the day, reading, playing chess and continuing to bore through to the next apartment. I had used nearly the entire length of the spike, about a foot, but I had yet to reach the other side.

That afternoon, two guards came into my room and searched through the books on the floor. Without saying a word, they left. I heard them talking on a two-way radio in the next room. Half an hour later, one of my interrogators rushed into the room. The worst had happened.

"Now," he said in the voice of a scolding teacher, "haven't we been good to you?"

"What do you mean?"

"Is there anything you want? You have enough food, enough water, books. Isn't that right?"

"Yes."

"Then," he shouted, "what is this?" He held two of my notes under my nose, so I could see them below the blindfold. Not only had they discovered the note from the wet sheet, they had also found one I had dropped through the fan. "I'm sorry," I said. "I had to do something to see my wife and children."

"If you do mistakes, you will never see your children. Do you see this?" In his other hand, he held a grenade. "You know what this is? You know we can kill you at any time? If anyone comes for you, we can kill you and we can die. We are not afraid to die."

I did not answer, but I knew that even if he and the more dedicated Hizballahi welcomed martyrdom, the $30-a-month guards standing behind him did not.

"You write Arabic?" he asked.

"A little."

After he had made me explain how I pushed the notes through the bathroom fan, he asked the guards in Arabic, "Then how did this note get to the *front* of the building?" He did not ask me, and I never told him.

"Where did you get the pen?"

"It was the one you gave me."

Realising he had breached his own security, he made me return the pen from inside my mattress. I was hoping he would not find the spike hidden inside the pillow. It was so sharp from boring through the concrete, he would have to assume I was saving it to use as a weapon.

"How many of these notes did you send?"

This was a question I did not want to answer. He had two notes in hand and might have had more. From that apartment, I had dropped nine in all. "Four, I think," I said.

He ordered one of the guards to go downstairs and search for the other notes. "You realise," he said, implying I had abused his hospitality, "if we don't find the other two pieces of paper, you will have to move."

The guard returned without any other notes. "Now we will have to move you," he said, "and we have to take these away." He removed the books I had, leaving only my prayer book.

They walked out of the room and locked the door. I took off my blindfold, feeling depressed. I prayed in desperation. "Why, God? Why did You let them find the notes? All I had asked was that the guards shouldn't find them. Was that too much to ask?" Then I felt guilty, knowing I had no right to doubt the God who had preserved me thus far, and I begged forgiveness. I read one of the prayers in the book: "Your will be done, O Lord. The Lord has given, the Lord has taken away; blessed be the name of the Lord."

The thing I had most dreaded was the best that could have happened. That night, my last there, neither my captors nor I knew that their discovery of my notes and their decision to move me hurriedly to a more secure location would be the first step on my road home. I knew La France had lost a battle, but I had no idea La France was about to win the war.

CHAPTER TWENTY-EIGHT

RECALLED TO LIFE

Dark is the night, and dreadful the noise of the
waves and whirlpool.
Little do they know of our situation, who are
travelling merrily on the shore.

- Hafiz, 14th century Persian Muslim poet

The next day, Sunday, was my last in the apartment that had been home
for just over a month. The sealed room had become familiar to me, and in
a way I had begun to feel secure there. I had grown used to the routine, the
simple meals served morning and evening, the daily trips to the bathroom.
Once or twice a week, they would let me shave. The things around me in
the room had become my valued possessions, a link to the material world:
not only the sheets, dishes and changes of underwear, but the spike I had
hidden away, the hole in the wall the guards did not notice, even a red ant
who used to appear from time to time. During the week for part of my time
there, a woman and child had lodged in another room in the apartment.
No doubt their presence had been part of a cover to convince the
neighbours a family lived there. The sound of the woman cooing to her
baby daughter, "Samira, my heart, sleep now," consoled me. The mother
could not have been more than seventeen herself, and she would
sometimes lose patience with the baby's crying, "Enough, Samira. That's
enough." In the evenings, she sang to the child. They never came into my
room, but I heard them most weekdays and was told they went home on the
weekends.

I had grown used to the regular changes in guards. I would miss the
guard who let me exercise without my chains for fifteen minutes each
morning on his three days a week. I would miss another guard, who risked
talking to me only when the other guards were not there to warn him
against fraternising with the prisoner. He told me to call him Hassan and
said he was nineteen, one of six children of a Lebanese Shiite father and a
Palestinian mother. Hassan had taken his guard's job at a monthly salary of

$30 in a city that offered few if any other forms of employment. He once asked me if I had read *Animal Farm*. "It's a good book," he said. "Very interesting. Do you think Lebanon is like that?"

One morning, Hassan had come into my room to take me on my daily trip down the corridor to the lavatory. He used both hands to unlock the chain around my ankle. I could see down from my blindfold that he had put a 7.62 mm magazine-loaded pistol on the floor within my reach. It made me nervous. Did I dare to pick it up? If I picked it up and Hassan resisted, was I prepared to kill him? Was I prepared to kill the other guard, Hikmet, who was watching television in the next room? I had been praying too much, had become too spiritual and mystical to let myself commit murder. I knew they were all prepared to kill me on orders, but I could not pick up the pistol. The moment passed, and Hassan, pistol in hand, led me to the bathroom.

Most of all, I would miss Hikmet, of whom I had grown fond. He was twenty-four. When I complained to him one day about being chained like an animal, he said, "No, please don't say that. You are not an animal. You are a good man. We are friends, you and I." One evening, when I sat blindfolded on my foam-rubber mattress, I heard Hikmet moving things on wheels into the room. Then I heard the mechanical clicking and whirring of electronic equipment. "Okay, Glass," he said. "Stand up." I stood, and he unlocked the chain around my ankle. Then he told me to sit in the middle of the floor. "Okay, Glass. Take off blindfold, but don't turn around."

When I unwrapped the cloth over my eyes, I saw in front of me a television set attached to a cassette recorder. It played *Heartbreak Ridge* with Clint Eastwood. "Good movie, Glass? You like Clint Eastwood?" Later during my imprisonment there, he said my hair had become too long, especially for Beirut's summer heat. "You want haircut?" He made me promise not to look. I took off the blindfold and kept my eyes closed while he clipped away. "Good haircut, no? Not finished yet. Now, shave." He took out a shaving brush and gave me a barbershop shave. It felt wonderful.

One afternoon when the other guard had gone out to buy food, Hikmet sat on my mattress. He seemed as lonely and bored as I was. "Are girls beautiful in London?"

"Very."

"If I go to London, you think girl marry me?"

"There are a lot of Lebanese girls in London. Do you want to marry a Lebanese?"

"No. I want marry English girl. You think she marry me?"

"Well, what do you look like? Are you handsome?"

"Not handsome, no. Not ugly. Average, like you."

Hikmet was in the rotation only a few days a week, and I used to look forward to his return. He would cook me special treats, pasta, rice with vegetables or chicken with garlic, while the other guards restricted my diet to sandwiches. One of the interrogators reprimanded Hikmet for treating me too well.

On my last day in the room, 2 August, Hikmet sneaked in for a moment to ask, 'Why you leave notes, Glass?"

"I had to get out of here."

"But I told you. I not let them hurt you." He felt I had betrayed him. "Now they take you away, and I not see you anymore."

I knew that, apart from the apparent betrayal, he was worried that they would blame him for having been so lax that I was able to smuggle the notes out.

Each day, I had done push-ups and sit-ups to avoid becoming too weak. The spike I had kept hidden in my pillow had all along been a reserve weapon, its point sharpened from weeks of being filed against the wall, to be used only if I felt they were going to kill me. I practised with the spike a single, whirling motion in which I would quickly reach behind me and bring it down into a guard's temple as he knelt to unchain me. It was my insurance, a last resort to save my life, and I knew I could not take it with me.

By evening, cars were arriving outside. I heard a commotion in the apartment. A large group had come to take me to a new location. I was frightened to leave my familiar surroundings and face the unknown. I tried to calm myself. I told my son George not to worry and suggested we get some sleep. I knew they would wake me when it was time to go. A few hours later, the loud sounds of several boys with weapons coming into the room woke me up. They turned on the light, and I quickly put on my blindfold. "You see this?" one of them said, showing me a pistol wrapped in a T-shirt. "If you do a mistake, you are dead."

Their uncharacteristic nervousness, something they had not displayed since the day of the kidnapping, increased my fear. One of them ordered me to remove my blindfold and keep my eyes closed. "If you open your eyes, I will kill you." He told me to put on the blue Adidas tracksuit. I placed my prayer book, with the cotton rosary and family pictures inside, in my pocket. Everything else I left behind. They pushed me into the elevator, the pistol pressed into my back, and outside into the green Mercedes. Instead of sitting me up in the back seat, as on the previous moves, they shoved me onto the floor. Three boys with weapons sat in the back seat, one of them kicking me several times as we drove. We stopped at another building only five minutes away. They dragged me out of the car and rushed me into a lift, which took us a long way up – five or six storeys. Someone was waiting on the landing when the lift doors opened, and he led us into an apartment.

They tied my blindfold back on and threw me against the wall in the corridor. "Wait here," someone said in Arabic. "Don't move." I stood against the wall for fifteen minutes, listening to them move furniture in the dusty flat. They led me into a dark room, pushed me onto a mattress on the floor and chained my ankle. The mattress, wedged between a wall and something that felt like a large wooden crate, was filthy and had bedbugs. Half a dozen boys scurried like hamsters around the apartment. At least three of them went to bed in the room. One guard put a pistol to my head and warned me not to make a sound. While they talked, I felt in my pocket book for my thread rosary and prayed until I fell asleep.

The next morning, I peeked under the blindfold to see light filtering through the slats of wooden shutters, the closed doors to a balcony. This was the first time in six weeks I had seen natural light. I lay quietly on my back, pretending to be asleep, stealing glimpses of the room under the blindfold. On my left was the wall through which a chain passed from a small hole near the floor. The chain was locked around my left ankle. The wooden "crate" on my right turned out to be a large wardrobe. It was about seven feet high and acted as a partition between me and the sleeping guards. The room was caked with dust, as though the flat had been partly furnished but uninhabited for months. Unlike my previous cell, this one was not equipped with metal over the shutters. Probably because they had had to move me without warning, this location had not been prepared as a prison.

The guards were stirring, talking and joking among themselves, some going into the kitchen and others into the bathroom. One of them unchained me and led me into a room opposite, where he told me to sit quietly in a corner on the floor. He sat next to me, while the others prepared the room I had slept in. I heard them opening and closing the shutters, sweeping the floor and moving the wardrobe. I did not hear them nailing the shutters or screwing sheet metal over them.

After about an hour, they brought me some *mena'eesh*, still hot and covered in thyme and olive oil. It was so hot it must have come from a bakery within walking distance. The neighbourhood sounded busy outside – heavy traffic, children shouting and men hawking vegetables from pushcarts. When I finished the *mena'eesh*, they took me to a bathroom at the far end of the hallway. It was filthy. There was no shower, no hot water and, worst of all, no window or wall fan. They were not going to give me another chance to reach the world outside.

The guards put me back in the room where I had slept, for the first time locking chains around both my ankle *and* my wrist. The guard who shut the padlocks warned me in English, "Do not do any more mistakes." When he left, I removed my blindfold and examined the new prison. It had the same grey concrete walls as the old one, the same tile floors, but instead of a single solid-wood door, there were four French doors panelled in translucent glass leading onto a corridor, and instead of a sealed window, the large wardrobe had been moved to block the balcony shutters. On the floor were a small plastic basket containing some toiletries, two pairs of my own white cotton boxer shorts and a white T-shirt that had been taken from my suitcase, a mattress, a pillow, a plastic plate and spoon and a bottle of tap water.

Through the glass, I could make out the guards' silhouettes. Watching them move past it, I felt like someone in Plato's cave watching the mere shadow of reality. When none of the guards seemed to be watching my silhouette, I carved a calendar into the wall using the corner of the padlock on my wrist. I marked out little lines for each of the forty-seven days I had been a captive, and I wondered how many more I would etch into the wall before I was free.

In the previous location, the guards had rotated regularly, and I ate, exercised and used the bathroom according to the routine or whim of the guards on duty. Everything changed in the new location. There were two guards who never changed. They were disciplined, and they no longer made random gestures of kindness or cruelty. They took me to the bathroom at exactly the same time every morning and evening. They gave me the same food every day at the same times: a *labneh* sandwich and tea for breakfast; beans, rice and bread for lunch; and a cheese and jam sandwich on Arabic bread for dinner. They refilled a litre-and-a-half bottle with dirty tap water whenever it became empty, although on the days they forgot or ignored my requests for more water, I became dehydrated. They spoke to me only in Arabic and always to tell me what to do, never to have a conversation. They never came into my room unarmed.

After a few days, I knew their routine by heart. In the morning, they went to the kitchen for their breakfast. Then they would give me breakfast. An hour later, they unlocked my chains and took me to the bathroom, locking me in while I washed and brushed my teeth. I could not shower, and they did not allow me to shave after the first day. The rest of the morning, they cleaned the apartment, and one of them would usually go shopping. They would have lunch, after which they gave me my lunch, silently placing my food on the floor. In the afternoon, they would invariably watch television in their room, which was opposite my own. For the most part, they watched American sitcoms and Lebanese game shows. When the news came on, they would turn down the sound, lest I have any idea what was happening in the world outside my room, but I managed to hear a few interesting reports. I learned one day that Camille Chamoun, the former president and father of Dany Chamoun, had died at the age of eighty-seven. Another day, I heard the friendly, familiar voice of Walter Rodgers, in an ABC News report from Moscow that the Lebanese Broadcasting Company had stolen, as it usually did, off the satellite. In the evening, the two guards would have dinner, give me a sandwich and watch more television. Every Monday night, they watched the mini-series, *Amerika*. At some time during their television watching, one of them would unchain me and take me to the bathroom. The television transmission ended at about midnight, and they then washed their dishes, went to the bathroom and to bed. The stertorous breathing of one and the snoring of the other always let me know when they had fallen asleep.

I began to believe that at last I might have a chance to escape. By moving the wardrobe, I could open the shutters and reach the balcony. That much would be easy. The hard part would be removing the chains from my wrist and ankle. I pulled a small nail out of the back of the wardrobe and used it to try to pick the locks. After wasting hours on this, I realised I had to think of something else.

On my second morning there, the guards wrapped masking tape around my wrist chain. The chain was making too much noise whenever I moved, and they did not want the neighbours to hear me. They left two links of the chain untaped – the first and the sixth – for the padlock to go through. I moved the tape from the seventh link to the sixth, so that when they took me to the bathroom that evening and relocked my wrist chain, it gave me an extra link. From that night, my wrist chain was always just loose enough for me to slip out of.

The real difficulty was the ankle chain. Its links were smaller, and the guards kept it tight. There were fourteen links around the ankle and about two more feet of chain leading to the hole in the wall. To slip the chain off, I would need at least eighteen links around the ankle. The problem was how to get the extra four links. I had to make it appear to the guards that the chain was tight while loosening it link by link. I tried to twist and turn the links, but to no avail. I approached it as a problem in mathematical logic, capable of solution. Then I hit on the answer. By doubling over alternate links and tying them together with threads from my blindfold, the chain would seem tighter. The link between the two tied links would no longer be part of the circumference of the chain around my ankle, at least until I broke the threads. The apparently tight chain would be long enough to slip off the ankle when I broke the threads. To disguise the thread, I rubbed it with rust from the chain.

On the first morning that I tied two links together, the guard who relocked my chain did not seem to notice. I listened carefully as he put the padlock on and snapped it shut. I prayed he would not see what I had done, because he would certainly have regarded it as a "mistake." When he left the room, I took off my blindfold and looked at the chain. The thread was intact. I counted the number of links around my ankle: fifteen. It worked. If, in the days ahead, I could add three more links to reach eighteen, I would be free.

It took me nearly a week of adding thread between trips to the bathroom to reach eighteen links. It happened one morning after the guards had relocked my chains. I decided to leave that night. I prayed and planned every detail of the escape, going over it step by step in my mind again and again. Once I heard the guards' heavy breathing and snoring, I would wait until they were in deep slumber. I decided to move the wardrobe away from the wall before I took off the chains. In case the guards came in, they would not at that stage discover what I had done with the chains. The wardrobe was bulky, but I was sure I could slide it a few feet from the shutters. Only then would I break the threads and take off my chains. I would quickly put on my tracksuit, leaving everything else except my prayer book, rosary and photos of my family. Then I would open the shutter door and slip out to the balcony. In my mind, all that day, I was already free.

That night, the guard who relocked my chains after taking me to the bathroom inadvertently broke some of the threads. I felt it snap as he wrapped the links around my ankle in the semidarkness. When the guard left, I quickly counted the links: seventeen. I panicked. I began tugging at the chain like a wild beast, trying to pull it off even if it meant taking a part of my heel with it. I tried to pick the lock. I even tried to lubricate my heel with shaving soap. Nothing worked.

Meanwhile, I could hear the guards watching the Walt Disney movie *The Love Bug*. When it ended, they suddenly rushed into my room – a break in their routine. Through the translucent glass, they must have noticed my struggling. They ordered me to stand up, and they searched me. They unlocked my chains and ordered me to stand against a far wall while they searched my bed and the toiletries basket. Then, after relocking my chains, they left the room. I counted the links around my ankle: down to fifteen. I looked for the little nail I had used to try to pick the lock. They had taken it. I looked in my prayer book and found they had removed the rosary as well.

I was near despair, and I uttered a silent cry, "God, don't you ever want me to go home? Do you want me to remain here forever?" As soon as I said the words, I begged for forgiveness. I went to sleep disappointed, not so much with my circumstances as with myself.

The guards had made a call on their two-way radio, and early the next morning one of my interrogators arrived. "I told you never to do any mistakes," he said. "Now you have done a serious mistake."

"What?"

"You know the mistake you have done. Do you want to die? Do you want to make us kill you?" He was screaming, and he grabbed my blindfold, twisting my head to the side. "Do we have to kill you?"

He shoved an open hand under my nose, showing me the little nail and the rosary the guards had taken from me.

"What were you doing with these?"

"That is a rosary."

"What is it?"

"A rosary. It is like your worry beads. Catholics use it for saying prayers."

"And this?"

"It's a nail I found on the floor."

"This is very serious."

"May I have the rosary back?"

"I'll let you know."

It was something out of Kafka. I wondered what they imagined I was going to do with a small nail and a rosary. The interrogator and the guards left the room. Later that afternoon, after the interrogator had gone, one of the guards came into my room to tell me in Arabic, "I don't like you. You are a very bad man."

On a few nights, the guards would be joined by other members of the group for dinner and television. I had gone to sleep one of these evenings, when the sound of artillery fire outside woke me up. The light was on in the corridor, and I saw the figures of several guards moving behind the glass. They had grabbed their Kalashnikovs and were running back and forth in panic. It was obvious they did not know the source of the artillery fire or what to do about it. Outside, other young men of one militia or another were reacting to the sound of shellfire, and they shot their rifles pointlessly into the air. If I were lucky, I thought, one of the shells would hit our apartment. It didn't, and I went back to sleep.

I spent the following days alone, my solitude interrupted only by the silent delivery of food and my accompanied visits to the bathroom. I made another rosary out of brown thread from my bedcover, and I revived the idea of writing notes to smuggle outside. The bathroom was impossible, but I might be able to throw a note from the balcony. All I had to do was move the wardrobe and open the shutter, that is, if I had some paper to write on. I would use the label from a plastic water bottle and a photograph of my daughter, Julia. For ink, I still had my blood and had already cut myself with a piece of hair-thin wire I had found in the dust on the floor. I was going to avoid having my guards find the note by putting it into an empty plastic water bottle and throwing it as far from the building as possible. I was going to decorate the bottle with coloured threads from my bed-cover to arouse someone's interest.

I was working on this scheme one night when my guards burst into the room to make another bed search. I was already anxious, because they had given me no water to drink that day and the thirst was having an effect on my nerves. They pushed me into a corner and searched the room. I hoped in vain they would not find the paper I had hidden. One of the guards rechained me, foot and wrist, making the chain for the first time so short that I could not lie flat or move more than a few inches from the wall. When he snapped the locks shut, he asked the other guard how to say "excuse me" in English. "Excooz me," he said, laughing. They left, and I discovered my paper was gone. To make matters worse, my chains were so short I could not reach the wardrobe or the shutters.

Coming on the defeat of my escape plan, the lost opportunity to send a note shattered me. I lay on my side, unable even to lie flat, and wallowed in self-pity. I took the new rosary out of its hiding-place and said my prayers. As I prayed, my depression began to dissolve. I felt somehow that God was comforting me. I had nothing to fear. If I could not send a note out, something that loved me seemed to be saying, it was because a note would not be necessary.

With no functioning shower or hot water, my skin was developing sores. My weight loss was accelerating, and I was always dehydrated. The guards would not speak to me. Occasionally, I would find a bedbug and be forced to kill it. With the ants and spiders, few as they were, I imitated Saint Francis of Assisi by refusing to harm them. I concentrated on prayer, my family, amending my life, writing a novel, telepathy and escape. Like a hermit in the caves of Mount Lebanon, I was becoming more and more mystical. Unlike a hermit, I was still trying to find my way out.

I returned to work on making the chain tighter, gradually tying the threads from my blindfold around alternate links. The number of links around my ankle varied from sixteen one day to seventeen the next, and back again. One Monday morning, I woke early and marked off my sixty-second day into the wall. My son George was due to leave and Edward to arrive. The guard took me to the bathroom as usual. We returned, and he locked the chains around my wrist and then my ankle. When he left, I counted the links as I did every morning: eighteen.

I refused to permit myself the euphoria I had felt the previous time. There was a danger things could still go wrong. I would not risk being unchained for my evening trip to the bathroom, when the guard might again snap one of the threads. When they brought me lunch and dinner, I told them I was too ill to eat. They said nothing and took the food away. When one returned to unlock the chains for the evening bathroom visit, I said I was still sick and wanted only to sleep. Without a word of sympathy, relieved of a tiresome chore, he closed the door behind him. It was the last time he would ever see his prisoner.

That night's television viewing seemed to take an eternity. While they watched the game shows, I planned. I would wait until at least an hour after I first heard their snoring. I had to be certain they were sound asleep before I moved. I decided to take my prayer book, both because the prayers had sustained me and to keep the notes I had scrawled in code in the margins as a record of what had happened during my captivity. I would also take the rosary, the three pictures of my family – including the picture of Julia with the half-written note in blood on the back. Despite the heat, I decided to wear the blue tracksuit rather than a white T-shirt, because it would be harder to see in the dark. I decided to go barefoot rather than put on the rubber sandals, because I would probably have to do some climbing once I reached the balcony. When I was praying, I had the distinct impression that God was urging me to escape, telling me I had nothing to fear. I also felt the Blessed Virgin Mary was counselling me to wear the sandals. I tried to explain to her patiently that the sandals would only get in the way if I had to do any climbing.

The guards finally turned off the television. Through the glass door, I saw their shadows moving back and forth. One went towards the bathroom, the other to the kitchen. I heard running water, dishes being washed, doors opening and closing. I prayed they would not make another bed search that night and unlock my chains. They went to their room, and it was not long before I heard one guard's strained breathing. A few minutes later, I heard the snoring of the other. I waited. The snoring was unsteady. It would stop and start. God, I said, please let him sleep soundly. The snoring gradually became regular, until it was a reassuring hum.

For an hour, I lay quietly listening to the snores, praying and going over every detail before I went to the balcony and what I might have to do once I got there. "By morning," I told myself, not intending to heighten the drama, "I will be free or dead." Either way, I would be out of that prison.

I slowly pulled the chain over my left wrist, finding it tighter than I thought. Oh, my God, I thought, what if it won't come off? I twisted my left hand, contorting it in every possible way, pulling the chain with my right. It scratched the skin as it moved towards the knuckles. I squeezed my bones together, pulling, pulling on the chain. It would not budge. I tried again. An instant later, it was up to the fingers, sliding off so quickly it almost dropped with a clang on the floor. Then I pulled the links on my ankle chain, breaking each of four threads, one by one. The chain was loose enough to slide easily over the heel and off the foot without a struggle.

I put on the tracksuit and placed the prayer book, rosary and photographs in my pocket. I walked barefoot to the wardrobe. Lifting the base, I moved it a few inches from the wall. The wood squeaked. I stopped and waited to know whether it had woken the guards. The snoring continued. A few more inches. Stop. More snoring. I went back to the wardrobe, moving it slowly, testing whether the angle was wide enough for me to slip behind and reach the shutters. I had to move it a few more inches, so that at one end it was three feet from the wall. I squeezed in and opened the door, slowly turning the handle of the grey wooden shutters. "Here we go, Edward," I said silently to my son. "Don't worry about a thing." I opened the door and stepped out.

I gazed on the world beyond my cell for the first time in sixty-two days. The sky was clear. Below me, apartment buildings and trees reflected light from the streetlamps. The night was warm and still, and a car was passing on a cross-street in the distance. Otherwise, the streets seemed deserted. I took a deep breath of fresh air and closed the shutter door behind me. I searched for a way off the small balcony. There was a straight drop down six or seven storeys, impossible to reach the balcony below. The roof was too high. I climbed on the balcony ledge and crawled to the corner of the building to see whether there was another balcony on that side. There wasn't.

The only way off the balcony was through the shutter door into my room, where I could put my chains back on and go to sleep, or through a door leading into the kitchen. Although I had no idea what I would find in the kitchen, I went that way. I stepped quietly inside, noticing the other end of my chains which came through the hole in the wall and were padlocked to the floor. I went to the door leading from the kitchen into the main corridor and peeked in. I could see the open door of the guards' bedroom, opposite my own, and made out the foot of one of the sleeping guards. He was snoring. I did not dare to breathe.

I walked into the corridor, which was lighted overhead, and turned left towards the front door. Slowly I turned the key to unlock the door. There were two bolts, which I pulled back. I turned the handle and moved the door slowly towards me. I slipped out, taking the key and closing the door. I used the key to lock the door behind me and ran down the stairs.

There were two apartments on every floor. I looked quickly for names on doorbells which might have been written in English, in case a foreign-educated doctor lived there and might be willing to help. This could have been safer than risking the road outside. All the bells were either in Arabic or had no name at all. A few of the doors were pasted with pictures of Ayatollah Khomeini – not apartments whose residents were likely to be helpful.

When I reached the ground floor, I went out of the open entrance to the building. Looking right and left, I decided to go left up the road where there seemed to be a crossroads about two hundred yards ahead. To the right, the road seemed to stretch indefinitely into the Shiite southern suburbs. I ran full speed up that street. Broken glass, small stones and rubbish lay all over the asphalt road. I cut my feet as I ran. I realised I'd done no climbing to leave the building. Mary was right: I should have worn the sandals.

I was running as fast as I could, feeling fresh and healthy despite the fact that I had not walked more than the few paces between my bedroom and the bathroom for sixty-two days. I was feeling the exhilaration of freedom, but I was a long way from home. Whenever I heard a car approach, I quickly hid in the shadows. Sometimes I stood dead upright in the dark corner of a wall, or I would crouch behind a pile of rubbish. I could not afford to be seen: the guards might have awakened and called their masters on the two-way radio. If they found me, they would surely regard this as a "mistake."

There seemed to be a small mosque on the corner, but as I came closer I saw it was an outdoor watermelon stand below a mosque-like dome. Three young men slept peacefully near scores of melons. I considered waking them, but their ages and beards made me decide against it. They were more likely to turn me in than to help me out.

I turned right at the crossroads, and I ran in and out of several apartment buildings, looking for a friendly soul or a telephone. On the first-floor balcony of one building, a man and a woman were drinking coffee. I tried to call up to the woman. I realised I had not spoken above a whisper for more than a month and had not spoken at all in the last week. I could hardly talk. I said in barely audible Arabic, "Excuse me. Please, do you have a telephone?"

"No."

"Thanks."

I saw a light further along the road and walked towards it. It was the yellow neon of an open bakery. When I reached it, no one was there. I went inside, past the counter and cash register, past the ovens into the back where a baker was stirring dough in a large vat.

"Do you have a telephone?" I asked him in Arabic.

"Yes, in front."

"May I use it?"

"Please do."

I walked back to the counter to look for the telephone. Another baker was standing there. He asked me what I wanted. When I said I needed a telephone, he said, "We don't have a telephone."

The first baker came and told him, "Let him use the telephone."

"I told him there is no telephone."

"There is a telephone."

"No, there isn't."

I was losing time. The guards might wake up at any moment, and a patrol could be searching for me. I had to leave the area immediately. The bakers continued their argument, wasting my time, and I walked outside to think of another approach. A car drove up. I was looking for a place to hide when I saw a man, woman and child in the car. They were stopping to buy cakes or bread.

I walked up to the car and asked in Arabic, "Would you please take me to the Summerland Hotel?"

"Are you a foreigner?" the driver asked.

Not only was my Arabic not fluent, but I was a strange sight: a week's growth of beard, barefoot, wearing a blue tracksuit, whispering in an American accent. The bakers stepped outside, and the man asked them, "Do you know him?"

One baker said, "No."

"Who are you?"

"I am Canadian," I lied. "My family is Lebanese. Will you please drive me to the Summerland? It is late, and there are no taxis. This is very important."

"I don't have much petrol."

"Please." I said. "It is very important. I will give you $500."

The offer of money seemed to increase his suspicion. "Why do you want to go to the Summerland?"

"Our baby is very sick. Our doctor friend, also a Lebanese Canadian, is at the hotel. I am going to bring him back here."

"Where do you live?"

"Over there."

"Where?"

"Over there," I said, pointing vaguely in the direction of some apartment buildings. "On the third floor."

The woman said, "Take him to the Summerland, for the baby."

"I will take you," he said. "But I cannot bring you back. I don't have much petrol."

"No matter. The doctor does not know our house, so I am coming back with him in a taxi."

"Get in."

I sat in the back with their son, who appeared to be about nine – the age of my son George. The boy told me he had an aunt in Canada, but he did not know which city. I said I had a son about his age.

We drove down the empty roads at top speed. It had been nearly an hour since my departure from the apartment. In a few minutes, we came to a Syrian army checkpoint. The driver, in accordance with local custom, stopped his car and turned on the inside light. The soldier looked at us without asking any questions. I thought he would ask for identification or want to know where we had come from, but he didn't. He told us to drive on. We came to two more Syrian checkpoints, following the same procedure. About five minutes later, we were at the Summerland Hotel. I thanked the driver, his wife and child. Months later, the Amal leader Nabih Berrie told me in London that the man belonged to his militia, and that he did not know until he read about me in the newspapers that I was a hostage. "If he had brought you to me," Berri joked, "*we* could have claimed the credit for freeing you."

I jumped out of the car in the car park, which overlooks the sea at a level above the hotel. I ran down the drive to the hotel entrance, past the Meccano discothèque, where a group of Beirut's *jeunesse dorée* were leaving after an evening's dancing.

Standing outside the front door were some Syrian officers. "Are you Syrian army?" I asked.

"Of course," one of them said.

"Then come with me."

"Why?"

"Never mind," I said impatiently. I heard one of the officers say, "*Majoun*", "crazy", as I left them to go into the hotel.

The doorman and receptionist were surprised to see me walking into the dark marble and cut glass lobby. "Mr Glass," said the receptionist, "Mr Glass, what are you doing here?"

I knew the hotel staff from the many times I had stayed there or used the hotel's beach. "I've just escaped from Hizballah," I explained. "Hide me."

I was afraid of being recaptured.

"Come quickly," the doorman said. He led me to an office and told me to sit down. I was trembling. I sat next to a tray of hotel food, probably the staff's dinner. "Mr Glass, do you want anything to eat or drink?"

"No, thanks."

The receptionist called the hotel security chief, who had to decide what to do with me. The last thing he wanted was for my captors to try to take me back.

I booked a call to my wife in London and telephoned Dr Nureddine Kouche, who lived across the road from the hotel. I did not use my name on the telephone, for fear Hizballah might have the lines bugged. It was 2:30 a.m., and I awakened him and his wife. I said, "Nur, this is your old sailing friend. I'm at the Summerland. Can you come down?" He said he would be right there. I then called Qassem Dergham, my colleague and driver for many years at ABC News. As soon as he heard my voice, he said,

"Wait there. I'm coming." Both were good friends: Nur and I had sailed frequently together off the Lebanese coast in good times and bad; Qassem and I had worked as collaborators on scores of stories, and I knew he would have been tireless in his efforts to find me after my kidnapping. Like my captors, both of them were Muslim. Nur was the first to arrive. We hugged, and I told him the story of my escape. "Don't you want to examine me, Doctor?" I asked. "You're fine," he said, a diagnosis confirmed later in London with X-rays, urinalysis and blood tests. Qassem came next. When he saw me sitting in the office, twenty pounds lighter and haggard, he began to cry. I nearly cried myself when we kissed on both cheeks.

The hotel security chief told us the only force which could guarantee my safety in that part of Beirut was the Syrian army. He said a Syrian general was holding a big party downstairs in the hotel night club, the Layalina. He went there to inform the Syrians of my presence, returning ten minutes later with a Syrian major who had obviously been enjoying his whisky.

"Come," the major said in Arabic, grabbing my arm and trying to pull me out of the office. Nur calmed him down and asked him where he was taking me. The major said Nur could accompany us to see his commanding officer. Qassem would wait at the hotel for other friends I had called and meet us later at the Syrian headquarters. But the major would not let me wait for the call to my family.

I was regaining my composure, and I believed I would be safe in the hands of the Syrian army, something I would not have believed in 1980 when the Syrians were being blamed for assassinating journalists in Beirut. We went first to see General Ali Deeb, Syrian Special Forces commander in Beirut and the most decorated general in the Syrian army after his assault on the Golan Heights in 1973. General Deeb was just waking up, wearing combat trousers and olive-drab undershirt when he greeted me. He spoke good French, and his English had a French accent. He was short, but muscular with a ruddy complexion and short hair combed forward like Napoleon's. He could not have been friendlier.

He sat down behind a table and offered me a folding chair facing him. Nur and I talked with him for about an hour in the apartment which served as his headquarters. "You have caused us a lot of trouble, you know," he began in a kind, joking way. "Our president ordered us personally to find you."

"I wish you had," I said.

"How did you get out?"

I told him the story of my escape, which he seemed to enjoy.

Young soldiers brought us fresh orange juice, then tea, then Turkish coffee.

"Do you know where you were held?"

"I think so."

"Tell us, because we did not know where you were."

He asked me if my captors had spoken about the other hostages, whether my captors had mistreated me, if they told me who they were. Nur went back to his house to bring me some clothes, saying, "You can't walk around in that tracksuit. It makes you look like a hostage."

General Deeb lent me a razor, and I shaved. Nur returned with a change of clothes and presents from his wife, Najwa: fruit, a bottle of water, shampoo and after-shave.

"Is there anything you need?" General Deeb asked.

"All I want is to go home."

"Good. First you will go to see my *commandement*, and they will take you to Damascus."

"Damascus? I don't want to go to Damascus."

"But you must."

"Why?"

"Syria must have the honour of presenting you in Damascus."

"If it's all the same to you, General, I'd like the honour of presenting myself in London to my wife and children. I don't want to waste a day in Damascus. I'll take the morning flight to London from Beirut."

"It's not up to me," he shrugged. "I'm afraid you must go to Damascus."

"Am I still a hostage?"

"No, of course not. You are a free man."

"As long as I go to Damascus?"

He laughed, as did Nur and I. I went a short time later to see Ali Hammoud, deputy to the Syrian intelligence commander in Lebanon, General Ghazi Kenaan. He too said I would have to go to Damascus, after stopping on the way for a few hours in the Armenian village of Anjar, where the Syrian army kept up its intelligence headquarters in the Bekaa Valley. He said the announcement of my escape would have to be made in Damascus, not in Beirut. An officer whispered in my ear, "The generals don't care if you leave from Beirut or Damascus But if they let you leave from Beirut, *they* will go to prison."

At about five that morning, I sat in the front seat of a Syrian intelligence car with an escort officer, his young son and two security guards at the head of a four-car convoy of Special Forces commandos. I said farewell to Nur and Qassem, and we set out on the drive to Damascus.

As we drove south along the coast highway, I said to the escort officer driving the car, "I think this is the spot where I was kidnapped."

"No," he told me. "It's a little further ahead." About two hundred yards to the south, he indicated a new sandbag bunker in the middle of the highway, where a dozen Syrian soldiers were manning a checkpoint.

"This is where you were kidnapped. We put this checkpoint here because of you."

I thanked God for my deliverance and begged Him not to let me lose the feeling of closeness I felt to Him during my captivity. I prayed and then thought of Dr Manette in *A Tale of Two Cities*. Had I been "recalled to life", as he had been from his tower in the Bastille, in order to save or help someone in a way I could not now imagine, years in the future? I hoped so.

I wanted now to help all the hostages I was leaving behind – no matter who was holding them.

On that same coast highway where I'd been kidnapped with my friends sixty-three days earlier, I looked behind me to the north at what was perhaps going to be my last view of Beirut and the Lebanese shore I had loved since 1972. There were ghosts on that highway, of the foreign armies I'd seen there: the Palestinians, the Israelis, the Americans, the French and now, after a five-year hiatus, the Syrians, all waving their flags and blowing their trumpets, helping the Lebanese slowly to destroy their country.

We turned left up into the foothills of the Shouf, fief of the Druze leader Walid Jumblatt, where rebuilding had begun. Stonemasons were constructing walls along the road as they had a century ago. In the pre-dawn penumbra, Druze peasants wearing their black *sharwals* and white cloth caps were carrying bread in wicker baskets slung over the backs of donkeys. As we approached the summit of Mount Lebanon, I saw the sun rising over the tops of the umbrella pines.

I pulled the windscreen visor down to shield my eyes and told my escort officer this was the first time in sixty-three days I had seen the sun.

He pushed the visor back up. "Then look at it," he told me. "Look at the sun."

That was the end of the journey. If I had been one of the intrepid travellers of previous centuries in whose footsteps I had been wandering, I would have gone on to Israel and Jordan, ending at Aqaba as I had planned. My family would have received a message telling them I had been detained by tribal brigands somewhere in the Levant. Two months later, another letter would have told them I had escaped and that they could expect a longer letter from me when I arrived in Jerusalem. Finally, from Aqaba, I would have sailed home across the seas with time to understand and absorb all that I had seen and heard before I told it to my children.

INDEX